Border Forays and Adventures

From The Manuscripts of
Lyman Copeland Draper
and
The Wisconsin Historical Society

Edited By
Robert Barton Puryear III

© 2006 by Robert Barton Puryear III

All rights reserved, including the right to reproduce this book or any part thereof in any form whether in print, electronic format or any other media. Reviewers may use brief excerpts with the permission of the author and publisher. The Wisconsin Historitcal Society will freely grant permission to self-publish and distribute printed transcriptions taken from the original transcripts within family and other limited circles. However, reasonable payment for larger printings will be required.

First Edition
October 2006

ISBN 1-933912-46-4

Cover: "The Capture of Jane McCrea," by Frederick Coffray Yohn, by permission of the Chapman Historical Museum 348 Glen Street, Glen Falls NY., 32801.

Formating and other prepress work by Westview Book Publishing Co., Inc.

Westview Book Publishing Co., Inc.
P.O. Box 210183
Nashville, TN 37221
www.westviewpublishing.com

This book is dedicated to my mother, born Helen Rodes Tate, on February 11, 1906 in Charleston, South Carolina and died of breast cancer on October 19, 1954 in Nashville, Tennessee

Table of Contents

Chapter I	De Soto's Expedition- Battle of Mauvila	1
Chapter II	Massacre of the French by the Natchez Indians - Destruction of the Natchez	9
Chapter III	First Fight with Indians West of the Blue Ridge	15
Chapter IV	First Exploration of Kentucky	19
Chapter V	Adventures of Robert Stobo and Jacob Van Braam	29
Chapter VI	Captivity and Escape of Mrs. William Ingles	47
Chapter VII	First Military Expedition Against the Western Indians	53
Chapter VIII	Armstrong's Kittanning Expedition	61
Chapter IX	Destruction of Fort Loudoun by the Cherokees	75
Chapter X	Ambuscade of the Devil's Hole	85
Chapter XI	A Perilous Journey up the Maumee	93
Chapter XII	Logan the Mingo Chief	109
Chapter XIII	Indian Eloquence - Speeches of Garangula, Pontiac, Shegenaha, Skenando and Big Elk	131
Chapter XIV	Dunmore's War	139
Chapter XV	Battle of Point Pleasant	155
Chapter XVI	Dunmore and his Field Officers	171
Chapter XVII	Field Officers of Point Pleasant	179
Chapter XVIII	Sketch of Cornstalk	203
Chapter XIX	Tragical Death of Jane McCrea	215
Chapter XX	Battle of Oriskany	223
Chapter XXI	Ambuscade at Fort Henry - Wheeling	231
Chapter XXII	Foreman's Defeat	235
Chapter XXIII	Battle and Massacre of Wyoming	239
Chapter XXIV	Clark's Conquest of the Illinois	247
Chapter XXV	Indian Attack on Boonesborough	259
Chapter XXVI	Captivity of Simon Kenton	279
Chapter XXVII	Bowman's Expedition against Chillicothe	297
Chapter XXVIII	Rogers' Defeat - Remarkable Adventure of Basil Brown and Robert Benham	305

[ed. note: unfinished in Manuscript]

Chapter XXIX	Andrew Poe's Desperate Encounter with two Indians	311
Chapter XXX	Gnadenhütten	317
Chapter XXXI	Crawford's Campaign against Sandusky	353
Chapter XXXII	Capture of Hicketty Fort, and Battle of Cedar Spring, By Shelby, as given in Haywood's History of Tennessee	363
Chapter XXXIII	Josiah Culberson	367
Footnotes		377

Preface

Permission was granted to me by the Wisconsin Historical Society to edit and publish this book in a letter dated December 29, 2003. I had been writing the life history, as well as I could, of one of my fourth great-grandfathers, Samuel Barton, who fought in the great Indian battle on October 10, 1774 at Point Pleasant, Virginia, now West Virginia, also called Lord Dunmore's War That one day battle took place at the confluence of the Ohio and Kanawha Rivers.

The principal adversaries were Col. Andrew Lewis for the white settlers and Cornstalk for the various Indian tribes. For my book, I felt that I had sufficient coverage for Andrew Lewis, but needed more on Cornstalk. At the Tennessee State Library and Archives, I found a reference to him in the Lyman Draper Manuscripts. It turned out to be an entire chapter on a 35 millimeter roll of film. But in getting to that chapter, it was an ever so slow process of barely turning a crank on a film reader, not knowing how much or how little was to be found and reading a little on each page. I did finally discover a wealth of information on Cornstalk, but only after finding much more information about others whom I had written. Not only that, in this slow reading process, I soon became interested in topics of which I knew little or nothing.

After reading about the life of Draper in William B. Hesseltine's book Pioneer's Mission - The Story of Lyman Copeland Draper, 1954, copyrighted by the Wisconsin Historical Society and published by the Greenwood Press of Westport, Conn., it was evident that Draper had a burning desire to publish Border Forays and Adventures. My ever so slow reading of the handwritten pages of text while slowly seeking Cornstalk had whetted my appetite for the remainder. Rather than picking citations from these pages for inclusion in the proposed book on Samuel Barton, after reading about Cornstalk, and Jane McCrea, and Andrew Lewis, and Michael Cresap, and Logan, and Dunmore, I began reading Chapter I of Border Forays, "De Soto's Expedition - Battle of Mauvila, 6 April, 1538 - September 1543." I had always thought I had a basic understanding of pioneer life and the slow westward development of America. But I learned a lot more.

Border Forays depicts scenes and tells the history that should be shown to, and read by, the public. They are not all pretty pictures. It is full of blood and unspeakable horror. It is full of heroism. It has tragical mistakes, such as at Gnadenhütten,, where Christian Indians are killed by the wrong side. Yet from page one to the last word, there ever rings the bell of liberty and the freedom of movement of man to conquer a new nation. It shows clearly that unconquerable spirit. The trials of man, woman, and child are not spared. Both the horror they suffer and the deep unrelenting spirit and tenacity shown by them is clearly depicted in Border Forays and Adventures - all found in a difficult film to read in the Draper Manuscripts.

It is a strange book to read, for it is not one continual theme, but, to a great extent, a series of independent vignettes or stories that rest on their own bases, independent of each other. But, when put together they tell a picture of the struggle for America. For those reasons I wanted to give to the public the book that Lyman Draper wanted so very badly to publish, but was refused. His work is more important than one single man and his life and family. So, Samuel Barton and his many exploits will have to remain in my notes, as they did with Mr. Draper, for he also wrote about Samuel Barton. In his investigation of that early pioneer, Draper wrote of two personal Indian attacks on his life. The first may be found at 32 S 318-319 of the Draper Manuscripts, which reads:

Samuel Barton wounded prior to the Battle of Bluffs which occurred April 2, 1781

Col. Sam'l Barton – Prior to the regular attack in Nashville, or the French Lick Station, Barton went out to search for a cow which he thought had calved - he was fired on a little above where is now the Nolensville turnpike stone bridge, by a party of ambushed Indians – a ball entered his left hand between his thumb and fore finger & ranged up his arm to his elbow; he ran for the fort. The river at that time backed water up the ravine, & the Indians endeavored to cut off his retreat, & drive him east of the back waters, so that he could not gain the fort – just at its head he made a leap some few feet, & as he struck he slipped & fell upon his wounded arm & added to his injury. The firing of the guns that wounded him also alarmed the dogs who came rushing from the fort towards him; & he, all bloody, was fearful lest they should attack him; but they passed on full jump by him as though he was not there & made for the Indians & seeing the dogs pass him, Barton encouraged them on. The Indians, their guns being empty, had to keep off the dogs as well as they could, & retreated. By this time Samuel Martin & others came out of the fort & met Barton. During the subsequent attack, Barton wanted a gun to take part in the defence (sic) – though he was still feeble from his former severe wound.

Draper covers a second attack on Samuel Barton's life, some five years later when he wrote at 1 S 57-58 of his manuscripts:

In July '86 Southerland Mayfield, Maj. Sam Barton, John Campbell & Wm. Stewart of (sic) a Sunday visited Col. Robertson to notify him of Indian sign, --- started to return, & Col. R. cautioned them not to return on the trail — for he wondered that no one had been waylaid on that trail & killed — Barton, Southerland Mayfield & Campbell started & had scarcely forded Richland (Creek) entered a glade skirted by thick cane; were fired on, Barton shot plumb through in at one side & out at the other — Campbell was shot through an arm & through the side — Barton fell after going near 300 yards; Mayfield jumped down, lifted Barton upon his horse, & mounted behind him & escaped — the 3rd horse followed both in due time recovered. Robertson—Robt. Weakley, Stewart & James Donelson hearing the firing, mounted their horses & cautiously pushed through the fields in a circuitous way to avoid the cane — but the Indians had gone, pursued Barton's party to where Barton fell from his horse & was re-mounted — & pursued no further, Gen. R. & friends returned.

This Donelson was killed trapping, at a pond near Clarkesville.

Col. Barton when the Revolution broke out, resided on New River (Virginia), & went to Wmsburg when Dunmore fled to the shipping; was in Capt. Crocket's Company at the taking of Burgoyne.

The reference to Williamsburg would involve the Battle of Gwynn's Island. "At the taking of Burgoyne" involves the Battles of Saratoga where Samuel Barton actually served as a sergeant in Capt. Thomas Posey's Company, both serving under Colonel Daniel Morgan in his ultra famous rifle regiment.

With Lord Dunmore's War, the Battle of Gwynn's Island, the Battles pf Saratoga, his Indian fights in 1781 and 1786 and his political life in the earliest days of Nashville, Tennessee (then North Carolina,) I had plenty of information to continue writing on Samuel Barton's life, but chose to transcribe Border Forays and yield to that great writer and collector of American history, Lyman Copeland Draper and his Manuscripts. I hope that he will be pleased. I use the words "great writer" loosely in speaking of Draper for he actually published only one book on his favorite subject of American history and its early pioneers, that being King's Mountain and Its Heroes, and it is a notable work. But in his work and travels he wrote profusely - all of which is a part of the rich heritage his Manuscripts hold. He could perhaps better be called a great compiler of history of the early pioneer and history of America.

Draper was born September 4, 1815 in New York State and by the time he was in his teens had developed an interest in writing and history. This interest, in one manner or another, would continue until his death on August 27, 1891, a few days short of his seventy-sixth birthday. According to Hesseltine, at page 9, "Lyman never grew more than an inch beyond five feet, and in his most robust manhood he weighed less than a hundred and fifteen pounds." But it does not take a big body to make a big and significant man.

Draper's life long passion was to collect and to write the history of the ever westward movement of man from the Eastern Seaboard into the Ohio Valley and the Trans-Appalachian areas. As such he accumulated over 500 volumes of manuscripts, maps, records, and drafts which are now known as the Draper Manuscripts.The Wisconsin Historical Society held its first annual meeting January 18, 1847. At an early annual meeting of the Wisconsin Historical Society on January 19, 1853 Draper became a member. The Society had been rather inactive, and was reorganized with

Draper being elected corresponding secretary at the following annual meeting held January 18, 1854. He retired at the January meeting 1887. In his will he bequeathed his materials to the Wisconsin Historical Society and it is from the films of those voluminous materials that Border Forays has been transcribed and edited. Much of the materials associated with his will has been microfilmed onto 123 rolls of film covering, with individual rolls on such subjects as the life of Daniel Boone, Samuel Brady, Joseph Brant, George Rogers Clark, William Henry Harrison, Simon Kenton, and Tecumseh. as well as the Illinois, Kentucky, North Carolina, South Carolina, Tennessee, and Virginia Papers to name a few. Some of the above subjects were carried on multiple rolls.

When Draper retired in 1887 the library and archives collections numbered 123,500 volumes of books, pamphlets, documents and newspapers and was one of the largest North American history libraries in the nation. Today it is estimated that Library alone has a collection equal to 711,000 volumes and the archives, which measures its holdings in cubic feet of documents, holds another 99,000 cubic feet of research materials, roughly a 700% increase in size, and still one of the nation's largest history libraries. In addition it has developed other historical programs. Draper would be proud of his successors.

Border Forays, reel number 10 of that collection, involving five of the manuscripts noted above, was actually written by Draper and an assistant, Consul W. Butterfield. It was written during the middle 1870's. While they began as friends, they parted bitter enemies, with Butterfield being excluded from Draper's will for his share of the royalties and even excluded from the Draper Collection itself. I am sure there will be errors made in my transcription from the manuscript film, which included a little over 1,000 handwritten pages. The writers of those papers, in many cases had very difficult handwriting to read - especially the footnotes, which are so very important to me. I have used endnotes at the end of the book instead of footnotes, for the sake of the casual reader. At the same time I wish this to be a reference to those who wish to go even deeper into research. Thus the importance of the accuracy in the sources contained in the footnotes in the manuscripts, and yet even there, because of unreadable writing, I am sure there are mistakes. But what can not be read, can not be read.

In addition, when the handwriting in many instances appeared apparently very plain, the writer's capital "L" and his capital "S" looked exactly the same. For that reason a man's name, or a place, or a reference citation may be in error. I can only assure the reader that I have attempted to try my best to be correct. In some instances, the writers of the manuscripts made spelling errors, a least according to present day grammar. The word "traveled" was forever spelled " travelled." Likewise the Kanawha River, the site of the Battle of Point Pleasant was most of the times misspelled, not only there, but in other chapters, sometimes stricken through and corrected, often not. Where the Indian tribe Shawanese was used,I hope that I have now spelled that Shawnee. I have corrected the spelling, or at least tried. I probably have made some myself. I have only added a footnote, rather than an endnote at certain places which indicate something rather odd, such as, an editor's note or an uncompleted chapter, or of a chapter not numbered on the Border Foray microfilm, for where Hesseltine notes 31 chapters, I end up with two extra writings noticed at the end of the microfilm which I included.

As every writer should thank his help, I must thank mine. They know who they are. I sincerely hope that the reader of our efforts may feel the same way as we do, not as to our personal battles and forays over how this word and that word was spelled, but as to the overall underlying meaning. And that we did. The stories contained in Border Forays clearly show the efforts and hardships with which the earlier pioneers of our great country lived and died to secure my freedom, and your freedom.

I would be remiss if I did not thank two people for helping me to transcribe the many pages. The first is Mr. John H. Castleman, Jr., who types much, much faster than I do with my right index finger. He is a whiz. The second person is my dear wife, Ann, who put up with me while I was transcribing for hours on end. Finally she offered to help me, and even did much in either reading to me, or typing herself, or delving into an unabridged dictionary to try to find a difficult and almost unreadable manuscript word. She literally hates blood and violence. There are in this book things which even I hate to read, much less type and then go back and read again looking for writing errors. And yet Ann became much interested in the stories and offered, not only the help, but spurred me on. For that I will be eternally grateful.

We wish you enjoyable reading. May God Bless America. It is what Border Forays and Adventures is all about.

R.B.P. III

Chapter One

De Sotos' Expedition - Battle of Mauvila
6 April, 1538 —— 10 September, 1543

The interior of the vast country resting upon the Gulf of Mexico on the north, remained, for nearly half a century after the discovery of America, unknown to the civilized world. Ponce de Leon, in pursuit of immortal youth, had, with his three brigantines, plowed, it is true, the turbulent waters of the gulf-streams, _ landing upon the coast of Florida to kindle anew his imagination as to the mystical fountain and no less mysterious river of Eldorado. But, upon a second voyage, without having previously made any progress inland, the return cavalier was mortally wounded by a hostile native and soon after breathed his last in the island of Cuba.

Other adventurers, within a few years, followed up the discoveries of Leon _ all of them, however, meeting with disasters. Notably among these was P´anfilo de N´arvaez, who, after catching glimpses of ulterior regions, perished miserably in the Gulf, not far, it is conjectured, from the mouths of the Mississippi. Thus it was that, while the general out-line of the country along the shores to the southward and eastward, had been seen, yet, beyond this dim boundary was an unexplored territory _ a terra incognita _ for play of the wildest fancy, in that most credulous age of the world's history.

Hernando de Soto, whose exploits in America had previously secured him fortune and fame, was now the willing and ambitious courtier of Charles V. To undertake, at his own cost, the exploration and subjugation of Florida;[1] where, it was fondly believed, gold was as plentiful as had been found in the land of the Incas, and cities as magnificent as had been conquered in the realms of Montezuma's. The renowned cavalier was made Governor of Cuba and President of regions yet to be vanquished.[2]

No sooner was Soto's project announced when many more adventurers came forward than could be received. Several hundred were accepted; _ men, mostly, in the bloom of life _ brave men of Spain and of Portugal as well. On the sixth of April, 1538, his fleet left the port of San Lucas for Cuba, where he was detained over a year. Sailing from Havana the eighteenth of May, 1539,[3] the "armada" anchored near the west coast of Florida, the eighth day out; the commander landing, the last day of the month, at Tampa Bay,[4] about six hundred men and over two hundred horses.[5]

After some weeks of delay, the army having with one voice asked to be led into the land, Soto prepared for his advance to the exploration and conquest of Florida. Most of his ships he sent back to Cuba. A fort had been erected, and a small number of horsemen and foot-soldiers were left to defend it until they should receive orders to join the army. They had charge also of the remaining vessels. An officer with a detachment from the main body had already marched into the wilderness. On the fifteenth of July, the armament began its march for gold and glory.[6] The troops clad in helmets and coats of mail, carried swords, lances, arquebuses and cross-bows. Following them were greyhounds to chase Indians, and bloodhounds to destroy them. Crucibles for refining gold, and chains and collars for captives were in abundance. Instruments of a forge and metals _ particularly iron and steel _ had been provided. Priests and monks swelled the throng carrying robes, and relics, and sacramental bread and wine. Soto's experience in former expeditions in the New World greatly aided him in preparing for this adventure. He struck boldly into an unknown wilderness. There was a grandeur in this, although prompted by a cruel avarice and an insatiable ambition for renown.

Over three months of marching through wild and toilsome waters, across deep rivers and through almost impassible swamps _ first in a northeasterly direction then westerly, still however, evidently within what is now the State of Florida[7] _ brought the weary army finally with some loss from hostile Indians but with many captives, to a point, it is believed, not far from the head of Appalachee Bay. As it was not the intention of Soto to advance so far into the country as to render it impossible to keep up communication with his force upon the coast, and as he had discovered a harbor, which answers to the modern one of St. Marks, whither his vessels could be sent, _ he determined to go into winter quarters at "Apalache."[8]

A small detachment was now sent back to the fort at Tampa Bay with instructions for the brigantines to go forward to St. Marks with the infantry, while the cavalry of the garrison were to make their way by land to the main army. The purposes of Soto were successfully carried out. A harbor, doubtless the present Pensacola, was afterward discovered to the westward; when the vessels were dispatched to Havana with orders to return there in six months with supplies.

Early in March, 1540, the wanderers again turned their faces from the sea _ this time to the northeast _ lured onward by Indian stories of gold, until, marching, it is conjectured, twice across the State of Georgia,[9] they reached, from the east, the far-famed "province of Coca,"[10] in what is now believed to be the northeast part of Alabama. Moving thence in a southerly direction,[11] they came at length to the Indian town of "Mauvila,"[12] situated on a wide and deep river, doubtless the Alabama;[13] the army having, in its seven months' march, met with strange adventures but no gold; it had lost a number of its men, and encountered many obstacles from the hostility of the savages and the wilderness of the country through which it had passed. Soto had not scrupled to seek, continually, new dangers; and, when found, he was never lacking in courage to avail them or in good fortune to overcome them. Indian Towns on the route were, if thought necessary, destroyed; their occupants killed or made captive. Courtesy was sometimes _ but rarely _ extended; _ violence was the rule. This, it will be seen, now brought to the army its bitterest fruits.

It was at nine o'clock, on the morning of the eighteenth of October, 1540, that Soto, with Tuscaloosa,[14] a gigantic chief of the country, by his side, arrived at Mauvila _ the home of the sachem. The town was built on a plain and surrounded by walls of wood and earth. The houses were large _ all fronting a square. An eastern and western gate opened into the town. A space had been cleared for considerable distance outside the walls. No such formidable works of defense had been seen by Soto and his followers any where in the country.

Soto reached Mauvila with only one hundred horse and an equal number of foot; the larger portion of his troops had not arrived. Tuscaloosa, who, at a distance from his capital welcomed the Spaniards, had, meanwhile, sent swift runners through the country assembling his warriors in good number in the town before his arrival. It was the organization of a mighty ambuscade. They lay concealed in the houses, armed with bows and arrows, stones, and their war-clubs.

Soto and Tuscaloosa, with the vanguard, entered Mauvila escorted by a train of warriors, gaudily plumed. As they passed along, they were entertained with songs, music upon Indian flutes, and the graceful dancing of Indian girls. One of the largest houses in the town was assigned to the commander and his principal officers; an adjacent one, to his servants and attendants. Tuscaloosa desired that the residue of the troops should be lodged outside the walls; an arrangement Soto did not at all relish; _ he hesitated. The spirit of the haughty chief, now that he was prepared to let loose his dusky braves by the thousands, upon the unsuspecting Spaniards, rose within him. He declared his independence by refusing to come forth into the presence of the white chief, at his bidding. Just at that moment, the entrapped soldiers, for the first time, caught a glimpse of the situation.

The war-whoop was given. A wild and prolonged yell from the infuriated savages startled the very depth of the surrounding forests. It was an out- burst well calculated to strike terror to the heart of the Spaniards. Torrents of warriors poured forth from their lodges, attacking the troops, who were scattered in all directions, unsuspicious of such a dark whirlwind of fury. Though vastly out-numbered, Soto and his men boldly faced the impetuous flood. Hand to hand, they fought, slowly retreating, until they were fairly without the walls of the village; leaving five men dead upon the field. A farther retreat brought them a considerable distance from the town, when a halt was called, and the commander, undisturbed, seized a moment to comprehend the aspects of affairs. But this respite had only been obtained through the heroic exertions of a few _cavaliers who had mounted their horses, and a small number of other horsemen who had just arrived from the main army. These had joined their forces and were thus enabled to give protection to those fighting on foot.

Upon the first furious onset of the enemy, many of the cavalry who had their horses outside the wall, sprang forward to secure them. Some, the most fleet of foot, were enabled to mount their steeds; others could only cut them loose and drive them before them; while not a few were obliged to abandon theirs _ to be quickly shot down by a cloud of arrows.

A large part of the baggage and effects of the army, which had arrived borne upon the shoulders of many chained captives, was now seized by a portion of the savages and with triumphant yells deposited in their lodges; when its pillage went on amidst the beating of wooden drums and ear-piercing shouts of exultation. The captives, too, were laid hold of, _ their irons knocked off, and weapons placed in their hands. They were then arrayed to fight against the Spaniards.

The savages who were still fighting outside the town, rent the air with their victorious yells. Soto now, for the first time, began to act on the offensive. Heading his cavalry and followed by the infantry, he charged furiously upon the enemy, and, with great slaughter, drove them within their fortifications. They would have followed them into the town, but the Indians rallying upon the walls sent among them such showers of stones and arrows as to compel a retreat. Observing the movement, the savages again sallied forth, some through the gates others letting themselves down from the wall. Again they closed with the Spaniards. Again it became a hand-to-hand fight. For three long hours the terrific conflict went on, first one side gaining ground then the other. Backwards and forwards they fought. The encounter was a desperate one. The Spaniards, who were occasionally reinforced by squads of horsemen arriving for the first time upon the field, kept their front to the enemy. So close and hot was the contest that the sweeping swords and piercing lances of the soldiers were frequently seized by their savage assailants. Finally, the Indians gave way, retreating within the walls of their village, closing the gates and manning the ramparts.

As the whole of his forces had now arrived upon the theater of conflict, Soto determined to attack the fortifications of the enemy, and, if possible, take their village by storm. It was a bold resolve. Dismounting his cavalry who were the best armed of his men, they were formed into four divisions of foot. Taking bucklers for defense and battle-axes to cut open the gates, they made a simultaneous charge. Valiantly they were met by the besieged, with their war missiles. The ramparts, however, were soon forced and the soldiers rushed into the town. The savages fought bravely, but were no match for the assailants. A horrible carnage ensued. The ground was covered with slain Indians _ but the survivors fought on, asking no quarter. And still the battle raged. Still it waxed hotter, if possible, and more sanguinary. The destruction of human life was awful. As the numbers of the natives melted away, their fierceness grew more frantic and terrible; it was the heroism of despair.

To add to the horror of the scene, the town was set on fire by the Spaniards.

The houses being of combustible materials were soon wrapped in flames and smoke. The raging element increasing in volume, made fearful ravages among the Indians. Many perished in their lodges; others, blinded by the smoke were set upon and cut down by the invaders, while attempting to escape from the burning dwellings. The village was doomed; yet the shouts and yells and battle-cries of the combatants still rose over the perturbed waters of the deep-flowing Alabama. Then numbers of the cavalry dashed in at the gate, riding hither and thither, and carrying every where death and destruction to the savages. Not a native surrendered. No one laid down his weapons. Each one fought to the last. All within the walls were slain. Just then the sun went down. The town was in ruin. Heroically had perished her brave defenders.

Such was the sanguinary battle of Mauvila. A more bloody fight between civilized men and Indians has never occurred upon the soil of our country. Not a large number of Spaniards were killed out-right, but many were grievously wounded.[15] The slaughter of the savages was enormous. Soto was wounded but not mortally; the fate of Tuscaloosa is uncertain. But for the superiority of their weapons, the invaders would have been overwhelmed. As it was, the conflict was a very disastrous one to the army. The Spaniards had gained the victory, it is true; but so dearly had the brave warriors of Tuscaloosa sold their lives that a defeat could scarcely have been more calamitous to the adventurers. Besides the loss of a number of horses, all the camp-equipage and baggage had been consumed in the flames of the burning village: supplies of food and medicine, clothes, books, instruments, utensils, pearls, relics and robes of the priests, their flour and wine; _ all were destroyed.

Soto's army passed the night upon the battle field __ amid the ruins of Mauvila. Many wounds demanded immediate attention. Only one surgeon survived; and every thing in his department had been burned. Various expedients were resorted to, for relief of the sufferers. Bandages were made from the shirts of the living and the dead. Fat from the bodies of slain Indians served as ointment. The horses killed were flayed and the flesh used as sustenance for the wounded. Notwithstanding the utmost exertions of their comrades, a number died before any relief could be afforded. Although suffering excruciating pain from his wound, the commander gave his whole attention to alleviating the agonies of his men.

The next morning's sun rose upon a sad scene: Piles of the dead presented a spectacle sickening and revolting in the extreme. Just how many Indians perished could not be known: within the walls, "two thousand and five hundred, little more or less," says an eye witness.[16] Many were slain upon the open ground out-side the ramparts;[17] and, far in the woods, in every direction, lifeless savages were afterward discovered. The battle of Mauvila was well-nigh an extermination of the Indians upon the Alabama who paid allegiance to their renown chief, Tuscaloosa.

Soto again turned his face from the gulf, where, in the Bay of Pensacola, ships had arrived from Cuba with supplies, as he had previously directed. But, lest his followers should desert him, he at once resolved to march away from all danger; so, on the eighteenth of November, 1540, the army began to move northward; still in pursuit of gold _ "the igny_-fatuus of their hopes."[18] Had the world ever before seen such a roving band _ with a leader whose recklessness of time and life could, seemingly, only be reconciled with a desire to terminate in a romantic way a very romantic existence? Their wanderings, now abundantly attested, give to their adventures the semblance of fable.

The route of the army led to the north and west, until, far up in the interior of the present State of Mississippi, in the country, it is conjectured, of the Chickasaws, Soto, just one month after leaving Mauvila, having, in his march thither, encountered many difficulties, from the determined hostility of the natives, went into winter quarters "in the province of Chicaco." Here, afterward, while in fancied security, one dark and windy night, the Spaniards, shrouded in sleep, were suddenly attacked by the savages, who set fire to their encampment. A number of the soldiers were burned to death; others were killed by the Indians. However, after a desperate encounter of several hours, the enemy were repulsed.

During the month of April, 1541, the adventurers proceeded northward, soon coming to a fort,[19] on a narrow and deep stream,[20] where they encountered fierce resistance from the Indians. Fifteen brave cavaliers here met their fate. Seven days hence brought Soto and his men, to a mighty stream _ "Rio Grande" of the Spaniards _ without doubt the Mississippi;[21] so broad, "if a man stood still on the other side, it could not be discerned whether he was a man or no."[22] It was the first time a European had ever, it is believed, looked out upon the magnificent flood of the Father of Waters.[23] One hundred and thirty-two years elapsed before it was again visited[24] save by Soto and his fellow-adventurers; _ previous to which time all knowledge of it had well-nigh faded from the memory of the Old World. It was first seen by the Spaniards nearly two years subsequent to their landing at Tampa Bay. _ Through all these long months, the phantom gold had beckoned them onward with its deceitful allurements. Now, the army rested upon the banks of a river far wider and deeper than any yet seen, or that Spain or Portugal could boast of. No page of American history more readily awakens enthusiastic admiration than the one which recites its discovery. The imagination delights to paint the picture of the brave cavaliers gazing, with mingled wonder and astonishment, out upon the panorama of moving waters. It had been well for Soto had he been satisfied now and retraced his steps. But hopes of soon reaching wealthy and populous regions, like the alluring mirage of the desert still enticed him onward.

The armament crossed the Mississippi,[25] wandered many months in regions beyond it,[26] meeting with hardships and strange adventures _ returning at length, worn and weary, to the "Rio Grande." Here, upon its banks, the commander sickened unto death. On the twenty-first of May, 1542, he fell a victim to a malignant fever; lamented by all his followers. His remains were sunk in the restless flood of the Mississippi.[27] He slept in its sullen embrace. It was a grave worthy his career, hiding away forever a boundless ambition. "He had crossed a large part of the continent in search of gold, and found nothing so remarkable as his burying place."[28] Thus died, in a savage wilderness, surrounded by the tumults of a camp, the indomitable but misguided adventurer, Hernando de Soto.

The residue of the army, under the leadership of Luis de Moscoso, now attempted to reach, by land, the country to the westward which had been conquered by Cortes, where there were Spanish settlements. After many months' wandering,[29] failed in their endeavors, they returned to the Mississippi. In seven rudely constructed brigantines, fleeing "from the Eldorado of their dreams, transformed to a dismal wilderness of misery and death,"[30] they descended the river to its mouth, boldly entering the gulf, determined to perish or reach New Spain.[31] On the tenth of September, 1543, over four years after their landing at Tampa Bay, "three hundred and eleven Christians," blackened, haggard, and shriveled, clad in skins, entered the river now known as Tampico, in Mexico; reaching, soon after, the Spanish town of Parnnco,[32] situated upon its banks. They all straightway went to the church to pray, and to give God thanks who so miraculously had saved them.[33]

Chapter Two

<u>Massacre of the French by the Natchez Indians -
Destruction of the Natchez</u>
1729 - 1731.

Toward the close of the seventeenth century, the country on either side of the Mississippi river, extending eastward and westward somewhat indefinitely, was claimed by France, by virtue of priority of discovery, as a part of her territorial possessions in north America, and given the name of Louisiana.[1] It was afterward made to include the vast region between the Great Lakes and the Gulf, from the Allegheny mountains to "old and new Mexico" and possibly to the Pacific Ocean.[2] The first thirty-years of its history includes the first half of the era of its colonization and settlement.

Iberville, an officer of the French king, at the head of a colony of some three hundred Frenchmen, made settlements in 1699, upon Dauphin Island off the mouth of Mobile Bay and at Biloxi in the present State of Mississippi. In 1713, the population amounted to three hundred and eighty individuals, residing principally upon the site of what is now the city of Mobile and on Dauphin Island. At this time, Crozat, a rich merchant of Paris, came into possession of the country under a Royal charter.

The first settlement upon the banks of the Mississippi south of the Illinois country, was in 1717, where the city of Natchez now stands. This year Crozat surrendered his charter to the king, leaving the colony little improved but considerably increased in population: it now numbered near eight hundred inhabitants. The government then passed into the hands of an association known as the Western Company; Bienville, a brother of Iberville, who had previously been Governor, being reinstated in that office.

Scarcely had five years elapsed, before the establishment at Natchez _ although others had been formed above and below that point in the meantime, particularly New Orleans, in 1718 _ had become the finest and most populous one of the colony. The division of the whole country into nine civil and military districts and three ecclesiastical ones, _ the location of the Capital at New Orleans,

_ the sending of priests and friars among all the native tribes, _ the increase in the agricultural interests generally, _ the introduction of a large number of slaves, _ troubles with the Indians, _ the accession of P'erier to the office of Governor; _ these were the important events transpiring in Louisiana from 1721 to near the close of the year 1729.

As early as 1716, a fort called Rosalie[3] had been built upon the site of the present city of Natchez and occupied by French soldiers. The colonists who soon after settled in its vicinity had continued down to 1729, with two notable interruptions, to enjoy a fair degree of immunity from savage atrocities, partly because of the protection it afforded, but more, it is said, on account of the peaceable proclivities of the natives who lived in the immediate neighborhood. These were the Natchez Indians.[4] They were located upon the east side of the Mississippi,[5] in a few villages,[6] at no great distance from the fort: _ It was a tradition of theirs that they once had a population of over two hundred thousand. In 1722, they could not count two thousand warriors; and, in 1729, their fighting men were, probably, something less than one thousand.[7]

The government of the Natchez Indians was an anomaly; such, indeed, that a near parallel could not be found, probably, among other native tribes of America. It was a complete despotism. A head-chief _ "Brother of the Sun"[8] _ ruled over all, holding, with slight checks, the lives of the whole nation in his keeping. "These people," writes an eye-witness, "blindly obey the least wish of their great chief. They look upon him as absolute master, not only of their property but also of their lives."[9] Under him were petty chiefs _ lesser Suns _ a kind of princes who with the princesses formed a sort of nobility. The government was hereditary; it was not, however, the son of the reigning chief that succeeded his father, but the son of his sister. The old men prescribed the laws for the rest of the people. Below the nobles all were slaves, virtually.

The religion of the Natchez tribe was peculiar; in some respects it was unlike that of any other nation of Indians. They worshiped the sun from which the head chief and privileged class claim to be descended. Before its rising, the great sachem took his stand in front of the door of his high-raised cabin, which opened toward the east, and saluted the luminary with howlings as it appeared above the horizon. Within a temple; where were stored many curious relics, was kept a perpetual fire. Guardians were appointed who were very particular to prevent its ever blazing. So sacred was this fane that but few ever saw the inside. They believed in a future state, where there were rewards consisting principally in feasting; and punishments made up of privations of all enjoyment. They thought those who had been the faithful observers of their laws would be conducted into a region of pleasures, where all kinds of exquisite viands would be furnished them in abundance; while their joyous and tranquil days would flow on in the midst of festivals, dances, and other delights: in short, that they would revel in all imaginable happiness, while the violaters of the laws would be cast upon land entirely covered with water, without any kind of corn, and be exposed to the sharp bites of mosquitoes; that they would ever be warred upon by all nations; and never eat meat, _ nothing but the flesh of crocodiles, and spoiled fish.[10]

The language of the Natchez was peculiar: it had two dialects; one, the vulgar _ spoken by the common people; the other, the noble _ used by the higher dignitaries and women, which last class had an affected and quaint pronunciation.[11] The vocabulary of the nation had no affinity with that of surrounding tribes, showing them to have been a distinct people.[12] It was a tradition of theirs, that they came from the west.[13] Except in their language, religion and government, there was little to distinguish these Indians from other natives, although they have been considered to have advanced in civilization considerably beyond other savages of the south.[14]

Fort Rosalie, in 1729, had for its commanding officer, Chopart,[15] a man represented as totally unfit for the position. He had previously been in the verge of losing his office for misconduct to his own countrymen. He now undertook, for some cause, to possess himself of the ground upon which was located one of the villages of the Natchez. This was resented by the nation. The chiefs sat in council and determined not upon individual punishment but the destruction of the settlement; Nay, further: they resolved to send deputies to surrounding tribes, that, if possible, a simultaneous attack might be made upon the settlers every where, and the French totally extirpated; making the action of Chopart, if not the cause of, at least a pretext for the conspiracy.[16] Such were the deep-laid schemes of these infuriated savages.

The resolutions of the council were kept a profound secret by the chiefs; and messengers were at once dispatched to neighboring tribes to draw them into the plot. With the Choctaws, who had their hunting grounds and villages between the Tombigby and the Mississippi, the deputies were entirely successful.[17] They solemnly promised to join in the conspiracy and to afford every aid in their power for the entire destruction of the French.[18] The day was fixed upon to strike the blow. Meanwhile there was every where a profound tranquility.

The Natchez, as the time approached, perfected, with the utmost concealment, their plans of operation. Nevertheless, through some Indian women, it became known to subalterns of the garrison of Fort Rosalie, that a general massacre was in contemplation, yet the commander of the post turned a deaf ear to the intelligence. So far from giving it the proper attention, he had the informers arrested for attempting to excite suspicions against a friendly tribe.[19] His injustice provoked, or, at least, promoted the deadly plot; and now his obstinacy stood in the way of employing necessary measures for preventing its execution.

The morning of the twenty-eighth of November, 1729, found the wily savages every where in the settlement _ in the fort, in the village, and in the two grants _ prepared to commence, at a concerted signal, their bloody work. It was two days prior to the one agreed upon with the Choctaws. Causes inducing an anticipation of the time were unknown to the latter; but this, although producing, in the end, an estrangement between the two nations, did not prevent the massacre of the

French.[20] The Natchez, to avoid suspicion among the inhabitants which their presence might awaken, invented a plausible pretext for their coming. They had been careful in all places to outnumber their unsuspecting victims. They had taken, also, artful measures to deprive the settlers, at that moment, of their arms and ammunition, to a great extent; which were now in their own hands, to be turned to a deadly account.[21] A discharge of fire-arms _ and the carnage began.

In the fort, in the village, upon the plantations _ the slaughter went on, amid the most terrific yells of the savages. Some were shot, some tomahawked, others beat to death with clubs. The slain were scalped. Only one of the garrison evaded the Indians. A number of the women were cruelly butchered; many others were spared to make slaves. With a single exception, there was no where any resistance. At one of the French houses there were eight men; these fought for their lives _ two only escaped. The owner of the dwelling, who happened to be a short distance away, after killing four Natchez, fell dead, pierced with many wounds. The savages lost twelve of their number, at this point; which was all their treachery cost them. Of the French, two only were suffered to live _ a tailor and a carter; about twenty, however, succeeded in eluding the assailants, though nearly all of them were wounded; the residue of the male population were barbarously murdered. Of the negro and Indian slaves, some were killed, and a few got away, while the remainder were captured and generally well treated.

The Great Sun during the massacre, was quietly seated under a tobacco shed, calmly watching the progress of the slaughter, smoking his pipe in the greatest apparent tranquility. His warriors brought to his feet the heads of the commander and leading Frenchmen, arranging the latter in a row around the former. All the others were piled in heaps. The bodies were left to the dogs and birds of prey. When the rush of death was ended, the plundering began. Houses, magazine, _ all were rifled of their contents. The stores, merchandise and other effects, they divided among themselves. All the French houses, together with the fort, were then burned.

Now that the butchery was ended and their vengeance so fearfully wreaked upon the settlers _ and having captured a considerable quantity of brandy _ they gave themselves up to drinking, singing and dancing.[22] As a sequel to this wilderness tragedy, it may be stated that a small post up the river among the Yazoos was attacked and every Frenchmen killed.

Thus ended the massacre of the French at Natchez. Its recital is the saddest page in the early history of Louisiana. No event ever produced such horror in the minds of the people of that infant colony. It stands forth, in bold relief, as an almost unparalleled Indian atrocity. It shrouded the remaining settlements in sadness and gloom. So deadly a stroke at once arrested the rapid advance of the prosperity of the colonists. It was a long time before they fully recovered from the stunning effects of the blow. For a while it seemed to paralyze the bravest of the country's defenders. The affair in all its details, was so pitiless and cruel, as to call for swift revenge. And the avenging arm of the French proved scarcely less dreadful than the merciless ferocity of the enraged savages.

An account of the frightful carnage reached New Orleans on the second of December. It was brought by one who had escaped the fury of the savages. The Governor P'erier, at once bestirred himself. He caused news of the event to be carried every where _ even to the remote settlements of the Illinois. He dispatched ships up the river, as safeguards and to observe the enemy's movements; and even to France, for reinforcements and supplies. The Capital was immediately placed in a state of defense, and friendly tribes invited to fall upon the Natchez. Forts were ordered to be built in different places; and the most exposed plantations and grants to be fortified. Meanwhile a Frenchman was found willing to trust his life among the Choctaws to engage them if possible in the interest of the colonies. These Indians, now that they had been foiled in their endeavors to take part in the conspiracy, and seeing a good opportunity presenting itself to aid in the extermination of, as it seemed, their old-time enemy _ resolved to assist the French in this emergency. Assured not only of their friendship but help, the Governor moved a small army to the north as far as the home of a friendly tribe, opposite the mouth of Red river, where a fort was erected and the coming of the Choctaws awaited.

The Choctaws marched directly against the Natchez; surprised them on the morning of the twenty-seventh of January, 1730; took sixty scalps and eighteen prisoners in less than three hours; delivering from captivity fifty-seven women and children, with the tailor and carter who had been spared, and about one hundred negroes. They drove the enemy into two forts erected in their Great Village in anticipation of the coming storm; and then quietly awaited the French, who made their appearance on the eighth of February. The combined forces immediately laid siege to the fortifications.

On the twenty-fifth, the Natchez being hard pressed began a parley; which resulted, on the twenty-seventh, in the delivering to the Choctaws all the French women and children, as well as negroes, who were prisoners in their hands. During the night of the twenty-eighth, the whole of the besieged escaped from their forts, some going to the Chickasaws but the larger number crossing the Mississippi. The nation still numbered about five hundred warriors; and, although leaving their ancient seat, were not subjugated. Those remaining east of the great river continued their depredations. The allied army, having first demolished the enemy's rude works and began the erection of a post to secure the navigation of the river, returned to their homes.

The Natchez who abandoned the east side of the great river, sought one of the branches of Red river for a home, where they built a village. Here they erected a fort modeled after one of those they had left to the French. Meanwhile, though they made no attempts to return to their old hunting grounds, they did not discontinue their acts of hostility to the colonists. So, another expedition was set on foot against them by Governor P'erier.

A little army consisting of marines, troops of the Western Company and colonial militia, ascended Red river, went into the Black River, and from that into a stream called Silver River (Washita), thence into a small lake near where the Natchez had made their stand and were now living. A march of a quarter of a league brought the army in sight of the enemy's fort and village; and, with drums beating and flags flying, they advanced to the capture of the fort. The Indians, who had shut themselves within their fortification, held out bravely; but fate was against theirs. A large number, however, contrived to escape. Forty-five men and four hundred and fifty women and children _ afterward sold as slaves in St. Domingo _ were captured. This was on the twenty-fifth of January, 1731. From that day, the Natchez Indians, as a nation, ceased to exist.

There were still three hundred warriors of the Natchez living. These became scattered; _ much the larger number, in two bands, taking refuge among the Chickasaws with those of their tribe already adopted by that nation. There was no abatement in their animosity to the French; and they continued, whenever a favorable opportunity presented itself, to attack them with implacable fury. Bienville, who had succeeded P'erier as Governor of Louisiana, demanded of the Chickasaws that they should be given up; which was refused. This, with their now open hostility in conjunction with the Natchez warriors, determined the Governor to attack them.

The war began in March in 1736, and ended, without advantage to the Colonists, in 1740; _ who could only console themselves with the delivery into their hands by the Chickasaws of but a portion of the hated Natchez. The others finding, in the end, that they were an incumbrance to their generous protectors, retired to the country of the Cherokees, farther to the eastward. Finally, the various remnants of the once proud nation of the Natchez _ once the most important in all the great valley of the Mississippi below the Ohio, if tradition is to be credited, _ found a resting place with the Creeks, who then inhabited the vast extent of country now included in the States of Georgia and Alabama, and became incorporated with them; losing their nationality, but occupying a separate village and preserving their language among themselves; and numbering, when removed beyond the Mississippi river, but three hundred souls.[23]

Chapter Three

First Fight with Indians West of the Blue Ridge
18 December 1742

The surging tide of emigration, not long after the expiration of the first quarter of the eighteenth century, began to flow into the Great Valley of Virginia _a delightful region of country, extending from the Blue Ridge to the Allegheny mountains and southward from the Potomac nearly three hundred miles. This territory, which is a continuation of that table land in Pennsylvania known as the Valley of the Kittatinary, received its first settlers in the northern part.[1] Afterward, a scattered population made its appearance in the middle portion; upon the upper waters of the James river and its tributaries, in what is now Rockbridge county, in the vicinity of that wonderful curiosity, the Natural Bridge.[2]

In 1738, all the territory west of the Blue Ridge to the utmost limits of Virginia, was formed into two counties of Frederick and Augusta; _ the former embracing the northeastern portion of the Great Valley only, while the latter was made to include a country so vast that several States have since been carved out of it.[3] Within the first four years after it was erected, Augusta county received a considerable accretion to its population, confined, however, to the area watered by the James and Shenandoah rivers and their tributaries.[4]

At this period, the country was entirely free of Indians, though inhabited, at an early day, by the Massawomeces, a powerful nation; supposed to have been, in some way related, to the Iroquois.[5] These were followed by Shawnees, who, at a comparatively recent date, were settled in the vicinity of what is now Winchester,[6] but moved afterward to the waters of the Ohio.[7] The eastern section of the Great Valley continued, however, to be visited by savages _ bands of northern and southern nations at war with each other. Nor was this surprising, as it lay directly in the way of the Catawbas of the south,[8] and the Six Nations of the north;[9] which tribes, notwithstanding the Colonies had made earnest endeavors to reconcile them, were, and had been for a long time, at deadly enmity.

About the first of December, 1742, twenty-two Onondagas and seven Oneidas, of the Six Nations,[10] under the captaincy of Jonnhathy, started upon the war-path against the Catawbas. The party set out without the knowledge of the Great

Council of the Confederate tribes, which, just then, was anxious for a reconciliation with their ancient foe, because of the solicitations of the English.[11]

The Indians floated down the Susquehanna in canoes to John Harris' _ now Harrisburg. From that point, they would travel through Pennsylvania and the back parts of Maryland and Virginia to the destination _ the country of Catawburg. John Hogg, one of the magistrates of Lancaster county, gave them a pass for their safe traveling through the inhabited parts of the Province, they were then in, _ at the same time explaining to them that it would be no protection beyond its limits, adding that the Virginians might, perhaps, use them ill if they traveled that way, as there was no good understanding between them. But the warriors determined to go forward despite the suggestions of that officer. They made their way along the Kittannary Valley, meeting with no interruption or ill usage from the inhabitants, and giving no cause for offense. They finally reached the Potomac some distance above which is now Harper's Ferry, and crossed into the Province of Maryland.

The course proposed to be taken from the Potomac lead across to the Shenandoah, thence up that river and along the Valley to the North River, a branch of the James; thence down the latter stream to its confluence with the former; and from that point, still skirting along the west side of the Blue Ridge, to the head waters of the Roanoke. They would yet have many miles of travel to the Catawbas.

The sooner had the party reached the Shenandoah, than their troubles began. They endeavored to find a magistrate to have their pass renewed, but were unsuccessful. There were no deer to be seen, so they were in great want of food. In this emergency, they did not scruple to kill a hog now and then. This fact they were afterward free to acknowledge.[12] As they progressed up the Valley, the settlers became more and more alarmed __ at least, more solicitous for the safety of their stock.[13] The Indians, when met, were roughly treated; but, as yet, there was no serious affray. It was evident to the savages that there was danger ahead; and they sought to avoid a conflict, by marching onward as rapidly as possible. After several occurrences of an exciting nature between some of the Indians and squads of settlers, in which however no blood was shed, the party arrived, the middle of December, at a "big house,"[14] the home of John McDowell,[15] afterward the site of the Red house, on the road from Staunton to Lexington, in Rockbridge county, Virginia.[16]

There was, at this time, a militia organization in Augusta, at the head of which was the Lieutenant of the county, William Beverly, who, under the laws then in force, had general charge of, and supervision over, military affairs, co-extensive with its limits. The force consisted of one regiment of twelve companies, numbering about fifty men each.[17] James Patton was Colonel. The captain of each company had bounds assigned him, for his special watch-care and over-sight. It was a precautionary arrangement to protect the inhabitants, in case of an attack from prowling savages.

The depredations of the band of Indians who had just left the house of Captain John McDowell where they had been well treated, caused complaints to be made by the settlers, to Colonel Patton, against them. He issued orders "for Captain John McDowell and Captain John Buchanan to forth with muster their companies, and follow the Indians until they were clear of Captain George Robinson's bounds," which reached a point about fifty mile southward of the plantation of McDowell. About forty militiamen of the companies were soon assembled under command of the two captains, ready to move in pursuit of the war-party. The first day's march brought them in the vicinity of the mouth of the south branch of the North river, where they encamped. This was on the evening of the seventeenth of December, 1742.

The Indians, after leaving McDowell's, moved off to the left of their proposed course, toward the hills, hunting for two days undisturbed. On the third day, they traveled to the southward until they reached a camping place on the North River, very near the spot where their pursuers soon after bivouacked undiscovered. On the morning of the eighteenth, they had moved some distance down the east side of the stream when they were overtaken by the militia, who were mostly on horseback. The settlers, fearing a collision of arms, notwithstanding their intention was one to escort the band only, and see that no more harm was done to stock _ sent forward a white flag. The whole force was soon well up with the Indians, when, unfortunately and, probably, accidently, a gun by one of the militia was discharged.[18] The nearest Indian instantly gave the war-whoop _ an alarm which put the residue at once upon the defensive.

Quickly following the Indian's "field cry," was the report of many guns. Captain McDowell fell from his horse dead, receiving three bullets _ one in his head, one in his left breast, and a third in the middle of his body. The firing was now pretty general on both sides; but the Indians did the greatest execution. They rushed among the militia with their tomahawks. The engagement had lasted but a short time,[19] when the savages fell back, carrying with them their dead, among whom was a cousin of Shikellamy,[20] and their wounded. They were pursued by a small number of the settlers, but with little effect. In the meantime, the residue of the Virginians became demoralized and fled the field, leaving their dead behind. Captain Buchanan and Lieutenant James McDowell attempted, but in vain, to rally them. The squad who followed the retreating Indians returned and the whole force continued its retrograde movement. Colonel Patton now came up with a few men and endeavored to stop the flight. He earnestly entreated them to turn back, _ to keep the field and take care of their dead. But they were deaf to all persuasions.

The Indians, at no great distance from the battlefield, halted, made a fire, and attended to the wants of their wounded "by giving them such physic as was most suitable." Here they passed the night. In the morning, Jonnhathy sent some of his men to the spot where the engagement took place, where they found the dead white men, whom they stripped. It does not appear, however, that any were scalped. Several horses were found grazing near their dead riders, and a considerable amount of provisions lay scattered about, of which the savages partook bountifully, as they stood in great want of food. After this, upon consultation, ten of their number were dispatched to the Six Nations to give them an account of the affair and to take directions for their future behavior. They were enjoined not to kill or in any way molest any white men on their journey homeward. The rest of the band, having their wounded with them, took to the mountains and reached home in safety, being pursued, as they supposed, by the Virginians all the way to the Potomac.

Scarcely had the Indians left the scene of the engagement, on the morning of the nineteenth, when the militia arrived upon the spot, under command of their officers. Colonel Patton seeing no enemy nor any probability of further trouble, ordered the bodies of the slain to be taken to the house of Captain McDowell, near which they were afterward buried.[21] Thus ended the first deadly conflict between Anglo-Americans and the savages west of the Blue Ridge. The battle was fought "on a flat," on the east side of the North river, between three and four miles above its confluence with the James.

This "unhappy skirmish" caused the most serious alarm in all the frontier settlements of Virginia. The Governor, with the advice of the Council, sent at once, a considerable quantity of arms and ammunition to the back country, for the defense of the inhabitants in case of need, and took immediate measures for averting the hostility _ of the Six Nations, _ being ably seconded by the executives of Pennsylvania and New York, and by the Commissioners of Indian Affairs of the latter Colony. The Confederate Tribes not only listened to these overtures, but consented to hold a treaty _ with the Virginians. Pennsylvania and Maryland were also represented. It was held at Lancaster, in June and July, 1744. It opened the way, by the Six Nations relinquishing their right to all lands in Virginia,[22] for that mighty _ emigration which broke through the barriers of the Alleghenies, and, in the end, swept, in a resistless tide, over "the vast, illimitable changing West !"

Chapter Four

First Exploration of Kentucky
1750

At the commencement of the year 1750, the utmost inhabited parts of the Provinces of Virginia, beyond the Blue Ridge, to the westward, were a few scattered settlements upon the Greenbrier and New river. No hardy settlers had yet fixed their abodes upon any of the waters of he Monongahela. The country of the Great Kanawha and the Big Sandy, Holston, and Clinch rivers had not a vestige of civilization. To the westward of all of these streams and south of the Ohio, lay an unexplored country __ a derelict region, once the home of redmen but, at that period, the hunting ground only of roving bands of savages _ The Dark or Bloody Land, called, by the Indians, Kentucky. But the time had arrived when a portion, at least, of this extensive territory, afterwards so famous in the annals of border life and warfare, was to be explored by civilized man.

By an order of the Virginia Council of the twelfth of June, 1749, leave was granted to a numerous company of adventurers called the Loyal Company, to take up and survey eight-hundred thousand acres of land, in one or more surveys, beginning on the North Carolina line and running westward and northward for quantity. Four years were allowed the Company to survey and purchase rights for this grant, which time was afterward extended another four years, when the land described as "lying on the branches of the Mississippi, in the county of Augusta." The Company proceeded to make surveys. They sold many tracts at the rate of three pounds for each hundred acres, to persons who settled upon them.[1] One of the prominent and most active members of the Loyal Company was Dr. Thomas Walker _ a native Virginian, and a man of more than ordinary energy and talent, a resident of Albermarle county.

Walker was born in King and Queen county in the year 1710, in or near the little hamlet of Walkerton on the Mattapony, where his father, Thomas Walker, then resided. The son received a respectable education and afterward studied medicine with a brother-in-law, Dr. George Gilmer, in Williamsburg, _ becoming one of the most skillful physicians of his day, in the Colony.[2] He was first located in the practice of his profession in Hanover county. The spot selected for his home in Albermarle county, was a beautiful one, at the eastern base of the South

West Mountains, and called by him "Castle Hill."[3] Engaging early and extensively in the purchase and sale of lands, he was finally induced to make an exploring trip beyond the Blue Ridge. In April, 1748, accompanied by James Patton, James Wood, John Buchanan and Charles Campbell, together with a number of hunters and woodsmen, he went on a tour of discovery down the Holston river. It was his first visit to that Valley. But this exploration resulted only in a partial examination of the country watered by that stream.

In the month of March, 1750, Walker, Ambrose Powell, Colby Chew, William Tomlinson, Henry Lawless, and another, again crossed the Blue Ridge; this time to explore the country far west of the settlements,[4] for the purpose of looking out a good country for a land-grant.[5] By the middle of the month, he had reached the Staunton river in the Great Valley of Virginia _ the head waters of the Roanoke. On the sixteenth, he kept up the stream to the home of one William English (Ingles), who had erected a mill on a small creek.[6] Crossing over to New river,[7] the explorers came to a settlement of people who were of the Society of Ephratu (Dunkers),[8] and were "the upper inhabitants "upon that tributary of the Great Kanawha at that date. They, too, had a mill. It was "the furthest back" of any in the Colony. As they lived on the west side of the river, which, at that point, Walker found to be about four hundred yards wide, the party was obliged to swim their horses over. These settlers were found to be very hospitable. "The Dunkers," wrote Walker, "are an odd set of people, who make it a matter of religion not to shave their heads, lie on beds, or eat flesh; though at present, in the last they transgress, being constrained to it, as they say, by the want of a sufficiency of grain and roots; _ they not having long been settled here. I doubt not the plenty, and deliciousness of the venison and turkies have contributed not a little to this."[9]

The party left the Dunker settlement on the twentieth, having purchased of the residents "half a bushel of meal and as much small hominy," before setting out. That night they lodged on a small run between Peak and Reedy (afterwards known as "Reed") creeks.[10] The next day they reached the vicinity of one James McCall, on the latter stream, when they encamped. Walker went to his house, lodged with him that night, and purchased some bacon _ as much as he thought they needed. A large spring about five miles below "Davis's Bottom." on the Middle Fork of Holston river, was reached on the twenty-second. The day following, they kept down that stream about four miles, and camped. Walker and Powell then went in search of Samuel Stalnaker, who was just moved out in that vicinity, intending to remain there permanently. They found his camp and returned to their own, in the evening. On the twenty-fourth, the whole party went over to Stalnacker's to assist him in raising his house. They then camped about a quarter of a mile below him. "In April, 1748," wrote Walker, "I met Stalnaker, between the Reedy creek settlement and Holston's river, on his way to the Cherokee Indians; and I expected him to pilot me as far as he knew, but his affairs would not permit."[11]

The Stalnaker settlement was left by the adventurers on the morning of the twenty-ninth, _ they keeping "nigh west to a large spring on a branch of the North Fork of Holston." It began to snow in the morning of the next day and continued until noon when the tops of the mountains northwest of them were clothed in white. On the twenty-eighth they traveled "to the lower end of the Giant's Ditch on Reedy Creek." On the thirtieth, the party kept down that stream, on the banks of which they lodged that night. During the day, fresh tracks of about twenty Indians were discovered. The savages had passed up the creek the night previous. While in camp, at this point, they caught two young buffaloes; one was killed, the other was marked and turned loose. The next day, the travelers continued down the creek[12] to the Holston, where an elm was measured, which proved to be twenty-five feet round, three feet from the ground. Following down the river to the North Fork, and up that branch about a quarter of a mile, they forded the stream. "In the fork," wrote Walker, "between Holston's and the North river are five Indian houses built with logs and covered with bark. There are, also, an abundance of bones, some whole pots and pans, some broken ones, and many pieces of mats and cloth."[13] On the west side of the "North River," they discovered four more houses, similar in their construction to those in the "fork." They encamped four miles down Holston, "opposite a large Indian fort."

The following day _ April 1st, 1750[14] _ Walker marked his name, the day of the month, and the year, on several beech trees. The day after, they bid farewell to the Holston, traveling through small hills until about noon, when one of their horses being choked by eating seeds too greedily, they stopped for the night, having traveled seven miles. On the third, the journey was renewed, their horse having recovered. This day they reached "the Rocky Ridge" _ now Clinch Mountain. Walker went up to the top to look for a pass, but found it so rocky that he concluded not to attempt it there. "This Ridge," he writes "may be known by sight, at a distance. To the eastward, are many small mountains and a buffalo road runs between them and the Ridge. The growth of trees is prime in the top and the rocks look white."[15] After seven miles travel, the party encamped for the night. On the fourth they kept "under the Rocky Ridge," crossing several small streams, to "the head of Holly creek." They saw this day many small "licks" and plenty of deer. About three o'clock in the afternoon of the fifth, the "Ridge" appearing less stony, the adventurers passed over, and encamped on a small creek about a mile from the top. "My riding horse," wrote Walker, "choked himself this evening; I drenched him with water to wash down the seeds, and it answered the end."[16]

There was no forward movement on the sixth, but the next day the party made eight miles, it snowing most of the time. In the evening, a large bear was encountered by the dogs belonging to the company. Bruin was finally shot, but not until he had so badly wounded one of Walker's dogs that he could not travel; so they carried him on horseback until he recovered. The next day being Sabbath they rested in camp as was their habit. They traveled on the ninth to a river, "which I suppose," says Walker, "to be the one the hunters call Clinch's River, from one Clinch, a hunter who first found it."[17] The stream was crossed with much difficulty; as they could not find a ford shallow enough to carry their baggage over on their horses; so they had to build a raft. They succeeded in landing only a portion of their effects upon the opposite side when their rude craft became waterlogged. The next day they waded the stream and carried over the remainder on their shoulders. They then traveled about five miles and lodged for the night on a small creek.

Moving generally in a westerly direction, the adventurers continued their journey over Powell's Mountain and across Powell's river, passing near the mouth of Wallen's creek,[18] until, finally, they struck the eastern base of a chain of mountains having a trend to the southwest. Following along this elevated range, they soon saw to their right,[19] a remarkable depression . This they entered; and when at the summit of the pass, Walker gave the name of Cumberland to the formations and gap, after the famous Duke of Cumberland.[20] Taking an old Indian trace,[21] which lead to the northward, Walker and his companions soon stood upon the soil of what is now the State of Kentucky _ the first of civilized men, who as explorers, visited, so far as is known, any portion of its territory. White men had previously caught transient views of the Dark Land from along what are now its river boundaries; none, however, seeking its hidden mysteries, had before set foot within its present limits.

The first water-course reached by the party was Yellow creek. Here, upon a "beach tree, which was standing as late as 1779, one of the men cut in large letters, his name and the date of their visit. "Ambrose Powell - 1750."[22] "I saw," writes Daniel Bryant "the initials of the names of Dr. Walker, Ambrose Powell, and party, and a date, cut in the bark of a beech tree, on the bank of Yellow creek, as I passed there in 1777."[23] It was thus, for those who might come after them, these thoughtful adventurers left records of the times when, and the places where their explorations were made. They then continued their journey in what is now Bell county,[24] Kentucky, until they reached a considerable stream, to which Walker gave the name of Cumberland.[25] This was the present river, so called. They saw the Cumberland Ford with its cane and other wild natural scenery. This was called by Walker "Cave Gap." On the afternoon of the nineteenth of April, at a "lick," Powell was bitten in one of his knees by a bear. They were then not far south of the Cumberland, at a point, however, several miles northwest of the Ford, in what is now Knox county. That day, they rode seven miles. The next day, they moved down the creek from where they had encamped, two miles to the Cumberland river. At this point, Walker thought it proper to cross; so, they commenced a bark canoe, for that purpose.

The next day being the Sabbath, the party rested in camp. That morning one of their horses was found unable to walk. Walker then proposed that, with two of the company, he would proceed, and the others should remain there until his return, which was agreed to, and lots were drawn to determine who should go _ all being desirous of it. Ambrose Powell and Colby Chew were the fortunate persons. On the twenty-third, they carried their baggage over the river in the canoe which they had completed. The horses were made to swim the stream. When all were safely across, Walker, Powell, and Chew departed upon their reconnoitering expedition, leaving the others "to provide and salt some bear, build a house, and plant some peach stones and corn." The spot where they parted with their companions was a little over five miles below the present town of Barboursville, on the north bank of the Cumberland, three-fourths of a mile above the Swan Pond, in Knox county, Kentucky.

Walker and his two companions traveled about twelve miles the first day _ twenty-third of April _ and encamped on "Crooked Creek" _ one of the forks of Indian creek which falls into the Cumberland about two miles below the Swan Pond. They found the mountains in the vicinity small, and flat land in abundance. That day, they "got through the cool." The day following, they kept on in a westerly course, eighteen miles, getting clear of the mountains, but finding the land poor, the woods very thick, and laurel and ivy in abundance. Their horses suffered much for want of food. Fresh tracks of seven or eight Indians were discovered, but the savages could not be overtaken. The next day, continuing their course five miles west, the laurels growing worse and the food scarcer, while the land appeared much the same, it was determined to return to the rest of the company. Keeping on their way a mile further, they then turned southerly, _ "reaching the Cumberland river," writes Walker, "at the mouth of a water-course I named Rocky creek."[26] This stream when within a few yards of the river, they found suddenly away an inclosed several acres before it again returned and fell into the Cumberland. The party were at the mouth of what is now known as Mourne's creek, about five miles in a direct course from the present site of Whitley Court House (Williamsburg) in Whitley county.

The three adventurers went up the north side of the Cumberland river eight miles, on the twenty-sixth, and encamped on a small branch, called by Walker "Indian creek," now known as Watts creek. "Here," he writes, "a bear broke one of my dog's fore legs."[27] On the following day, having crossed the stream, they journeyed onward to "Meadow creek," which singularly enough, now bears that name. Down this branch they went to the Cumberland. Here, Walker observed another creek flowing from the south, having its confluence with the river below. This was Big Poplar creek of the present day. A mile further up the Cumberland brought the explorers to the remains of several Indian cabins. Among these, they observed a round hill, then twenty feet high; though not now so elevated, it is still to be seen at that point.[28] They made their camp that night on the bank of the river some distance above. On the twenty-eighth, still keeping up the river, they came to the spot where they had separated from their companions, whom they found all well. But the lame horse was as bad as when they started, and another had been bitten in the nose by a snake. "I rubbed the wounds," writes Walker, "with bear's oil and gave him a drench of the same, and another of decoction of rattle-snake not sometime after."[29]

During Walker's absence, the three men who had remained upon the bank of the Cumberland had been very busily engaged. They had built a house twelve by eight, cleared and broke up some ground, and planted corn and peach-stones; all, of course, in a very primitive style, and on an extremely limited scale. They had found time, also, to kill several bears and cure the meat. The Swan Pond[30] was found to be much frequented by fowl. It was three-fourths of a mile from the house. On the last day of April, Walker "blazed" a path from their cabin to the river. Preparations were then made for departing from their primeval settlement. Their lame horse they concluded to leave in the wilderness; the "bitten one" they took along. The spot then, where, for the first time, within the present limits of Kentucky, civilized man had raised a cabin _ where for the first time, his hands had felled its forest trees or disturbed its virgin soil by planting corn in its rich alluvium, _ was left to its own silence and desolation.[31]

Leaving the Cumberland, the explorers set off north, across several hills and creeks, until, arriving in a valley, they encamped for the night. On the next day's march, they reached a stream to which Walker gave the name of "Powell's river," down which they traveled along an Indian road, much frequented, to the mouth of a creek on the west side, where the party went into camp. Walker observed that the Indian trail followed up this creek; and his conclusions were, that it was the Warrior's Path, which led through "Cave Gap," (Cumberland Ford), on to "Cumberland Gap." Keeping down the river, on the second of May, they saw, at the mouth of a creek on the east side, not less than a hundred buffaloes at a "lick." They lodged that night on the banks of the Powell," which, at that point, was very crooked. They crossed a narrow neck of land the next day, at the river again; when, afterward keeping down its course, they came to an Indian "camp" that had been built the Spring previous. The adventurers there took up their quarters for the night.

On the fourth of May, they crossed another narrow neck of land to the river again, threading their way down the stream until it turned to the westward, when the left it, and went up a tributary, which Walker named "Colby's creek." They reached "Tomlinson's river" _ Middle Fork of the Kentucky _ the next day. This they found about the size of "Powell's river." Walker cut his name on a beech tree which stood on the north bank, where they made their lodge for the night. He observed plenty of coal on the south bank opposite their camp.[32] The following day was Sunday, so the party remained at rest. On Monday, they moved down the river, but very slowly, as their way was embarrassed by trees that had been blown down _ from appearance about two years before. Tuesday, the eighth, they left the Middle Fork passing up a creek on the north side, reaching "Lawless' river" _ the North Fork of the Kentucky _ on the ninth, which they found much like the other two streams. The mountains in the vicinity proved to be very steep _ their tops very rocky. Leaving the "Lawless," they traveled several miles, but were glad to return to it again, as the small creeks and mountains, were found impassable. They stayed on the river, the next day, dressing an elk's skin to make moccasins, _ most of their shoes being quite worn out.

The adventurers left the North Fork of the Kentucky on the twelfth, finding, as they progressed, the mountains very bad. Coming, at length, to a rock which, it was judged, would shelter two hundred men from the rain, they concluded to stop, put their elk-skin in order, and make their shoes. Under the rock they found a soft kind of stone, in taste much resembling alum. Below it, there was a layer of coal, about twelve inches thick; and under that, white clay. A run, near by, was named by Walker, "Alum creek." Monday the fourteenth, their elk-skin being prepared, they set at work making their moccasins. Their awls had all been lost, so they were obliged to improvise others. One was made from the shank of an old fish-hook; two were manufactured out of horse-shoe nails. Their "Indian shoes" being completed, they took up their line of march again, crossing "Hughes' river" _ now Quicksand creek, a large eastern tributary of the North Fork of the Kentucky _ lodging that night on a considerable branch of that stream.

For the next eight days, the explorers encountered many obstacles. The laurel and ivy and fallen timber continually beset their path. Besides, they had many ridges to cross as well as creeks. And, to add to their discomfort, it rained a large share of the time. Walker was seized with a violent pain in his hip. Altogether, it was a discouraging time, and, as a consequence, little progress was made. However, the Licking was finally reached, to which stream Walker gave the name of "Miller's river." This was on Tuesday, May twenty-second. The next day, they began a bark canoe which they finished on the twenty-fourth, and in it crossed the river about noon. They found game very scarce in that vicinity. Leaving the north side of the Licking, on the day following, they journeyed about four miles on a ridge, reaching a camping place for the night on a small "branch."

The party kept down the creek almost to the Licking, on the twenty-sixth, thence up a creek and along a ridge until their dogs aroused a large elk. They followed the animal some distance, but one of Powell's dogs was killed in the chase. "Tumbler" was honored by having his name given to a creek where he fell. The explorers crossed two mountains, on the last day of May, and made their lodge just by a den of wolves. The animals proved very impudent, notwithstanding they were twice shot at; _ they kept up a continual howling about the camp. The next day, four young ones were caught. Crossing a mountain, the travelers soon struck the Paint Lick creek, a tributary of the West Fork of the Big Sandy, in what is now Johnson county, Kentucky. On the second of June, in the forks, at the confluence of Jenny's creek, several of the men inscribed their names on a beech tree, at a salt spring, or "lick," which, more than forty years after, were still legible.[33]

Following the course of Paint Lick, they soon reached, the West Fork of the Big Sandy, which Walker named "Frederick's river."[34] They went up the stream half a mile to a ford, where they crossed, and then proceeded, on the north side, three miles, above, where they found elks very plenty. June fourth, at ten o'clock in the forenoon, they left the river. Reaching "Falling creek," they traveled up it, until five in the afternoon, when a very black cloud appearing, they turned out their horses, and were just stretching a tent, when it began to rain and hail. A violent wind succeeded, blowing down their tent and a great many trees about it _ several large ones very near them. The whole party, scattered in great confusion, running different ways for shelter. However, the storm soon subsided and no one was hurt. Horses, dogs, and baggage were found all safe. The next day, after keeping on a ridge for some distance, they struck the head of a creek down which they continued, the day following, until it became a large "branch." It was found to have a very swift current. They traveled eight miles that day and encamped. The following day _ the seventh of June _ the party journeyed down the creek twelve miles further, to its junction with a larger stream, which Walker named "Louisa river" _ now known as the East or Tug Fork of the Big Sandy.[35]

The explorers were upon what is now the extreme boundary of Kentucky, ready to pass over to the territory of the present State of West Virginia. For over fifty days these adventurers had pursued their desirous way across streams, over ridges, through entangled forests; _ beyond the Cumberland Mountains. They had observed the quality of the soil, the growth of timber, the general direction of the water courses, and the existence of extensive coal measures. No where, however, had they seen redmen _ no where had they come upon their homes; nothing had been met with but tracks of wandering parties, who were on the war-path against equally savage enemies north or south, or hunting in the interminable woods. On the whole the outlook was far from an inviting one. Nothing had been discovered of that marvelously rich region, almost on the confines of which they had concluded to change their course. In ascending the Cumberland mountains and in passing through Cumberland Gap, they had unlocked one of the great gates leading to, but stopped short of, one of the most fertile and magnificent reaches in the Valley of the Mississippi. It was reserved for others to explore the valleys watered by rivers that Walker and his companions were the first to discover; where, ever since their settlement, the richness of the soil, and the exuberance of their products, have continued almost without rival in America.

The party crossed the Tug Fork on the ninth of June, homeward bound. The spot where they passed over this branch of the Big Sandy, and first set foot upon the present State of West Virginia, was a short distance above the mouth of Pigeon creek, in what is now Logan county. Beyond the head of that creek, they encamped for the night. Their course now lay easterly to the junction of the Greenbrier and New river, across the Guyandotte and the heads of Coal River, a branch of the Great Kanawha. The loss of a tomahawk on the eleventh, though a trivial matter, must be mentioned, from the singular circumstances of one having been found ninety-five years after marked "Thomas Walker" _ together with the remains of a powder-horn, an Indian pipe, and a leather shot-pouch __ under a rocky bank of Salt river, in Mercer county, Kentucky.[36] The Guyandotte was reached on the twelfth. The next day, the mountains were found very difficult, the tops of the ridges being so covered with ivy and the sides so steep and stony. They were obliged, frequently, to cut their way through with their tomahawks. On the Clear Fork of the Guyandotte turkeys were plentiful and elk were also seen. In hunting there, three bears were killed. On the eighteenth, having prepared a good stock of meat, they left the Clear Fork, crossing several "branches" and ridges, _ the woods continuing bad, the weather hot, and their horses so far spent, that all were obliged to walk.

In crossing, early on the morning of the nineteenth, one of the head branches of Coal river, they met so impudent a buffalo, that they were obliged to shoot him or he would be soon among them. In attempting, on the twentieth, to cross Cherry Pond Mountain, between Guyandotte and Coal Rivers, they found it so high and difficult that they were obliged to camp on the side of it. The next day Walker's riding-horse was bitten by a snake. Having no bears oil left, he rubbed the wounds with fat meat, which had the desired effect. On the twenty-third, they reached the head of Coal river, deer and bear plenty, so, too, laurel and ivy. For several days past Coal had occasionally been seen. On Piney creek, a branch of the Kanawha, which Walker named "Dismal creek," the banks were the worst, and the laurel the thickest, they had yet seen. On the twenty-eighth, in the afternoon, the explorers reached the Great Kanawha, just below the junction of the Greenbrier and New river. After considerable difficulty, they finally succeeded in crossing the river, when they encamped.

The party began their journey up the Greenbrier the next day, continuing it until the sixth of July without any incident occurring worthy a narration. On that day, they left the river, when they reached a creek called at that time "Anthony's creek," wrote Walker, "which affords a great deal of very good land, and is cheaply bought up." "We kept the creek," continues the journalist, "four miles and encamped. This creek took its name from an Indian called John Anthony, who frequently hunts in these woods." "There are some inhabitants," adds the writer, "on the branches of Greenbrier, but we missed their plantations."[37] On the seventh of July at mid-day, as they were keeping up a creek, they were overtaken by five men, who informed Walker that he was only eight miles from inhabitants living on a stream then known Jackson's river, a branch of James river _ so called at that day. With these men they "exchanged some tallow for meal," and parted. That night, they made their camp on the top of the Allegheny mountains.

On the eighth of July, the party, "having shaved, shifted, and made new shoes," reached, about noon, the home of Walker Johnston. In the afternoon, they moved over to Robert Armstrong's, and there, they staid all night. "The people here," writes Walker, "are very hospitable. They would be better able to support travelers were it not for the great number of Indian warriors, who frequently take from them what they want, much to their prejudice."[38] The party reached the Hot Springs the next day, where they found six invalids. Walker observed that the spring-water was very clear, and warmer than new milk. One of his Company he left here. Having now a path, the five men rode twenty miles on the tenth, and lodged at "Captain Jemyson's below the Panther Gap."

The day following, they rode thirty miles to Augusta Court House, now Staunton, Augusta county, where Walker found Mr. Andrew Johnston, the first acquaint he had seen since the twenty-eighth of March. Mr. Johnston loaned him a fresh horse and sent Walker's "to Mr. David Stewart's, who was so kind as to give them pasturage." At eight o'clock in the forenoon of the twelfth, leaving the rest of his company at this point, Walker "set off" for home, lodging that night at Captain David Lewis', about thirty-four miles from the place of starting in the morning. He reached home the next day _ July thirteenth _ about noon, unrecognized by his family but, quickly known by an old watch-dog. "We killed in the journey," writes Walker, "thirteen buffaloes, eight elks, fifty-three bears, twenty deer, four wild geese, about one hundred and fifty turkeys, beside small game." He adds that they have killed three times as much meat, if they had wanted it.[39]

Chapter Five

Adventures of Robert Stobo and Jacob Van Braam
1754 - 1760

The determination of France, about the middle of the seventeenth century, to confine the colonies of Great Britain to the Allegheny mountains as their western boundary, brought on a Seven Years' War; which was, in the end, a contest for supremacy in North America, between these rival powers. In 1754, the conflict began in earnest. It ended in the total annihilation of French domination upon the Ohio and St. Lawrence. In the opening scene of this bloody drama, George Washington, a very young man, one of the Adjutants-Generals of Virginia, was a conspicuous actor. Sent in 1753, by Dinwiddie, the governor, to the French who had secured a foot-hold upon the Allegheny, to complain, in the name of the King, of their encroachment upon lands "in the western parts" of that colony and to warn them to peaceably depart therefrom, _ he acquitted himself so creditably, as to secure an appointment, early in the ensuing year, to the chief command of two companies of one hundred men each, which were to be raised by Virginia, to march immediately to the Ohio, to build one or two forts, before the French could descend the river, as they had threatened to do, and unite their forces with parties from New Orleans.

The command of one of the companies under Washington was given to William Trent, who, being acquainted with the frontier, was sent forward to enlist his men among the traders and back-settlers, and ordered to commence, as soon as possible, a fort at the Fork of the Ohio, now Pittsburgh. Washington was stationed at Alexandria, Virginia, to render arms and men and superintend the transportation of supplies and cannon intended for the fort. Dinwiddie now endeavored to arouse the other Colonies to a proper sense of their danger. His own legislature voted means sufficient to warrant an increase in the military establishment of four more companies, the whole six being put under the command of Joshua Fry, as Colonel. The Governor was authorized by proper authority, to call to his aid three independent companies, commanded by officers with royal commissions; two from New York and one from South Carolina _ North Carolina voted aid, and sent word that a respectable force would soon be sent to join their neighbors in the common cause. Ten companies had, in the mean time, been collected by Washington at Alexandria where he continued his head-quarters until the beginning of April, 1754.

On the second of the month, Washington, with two companies of about one hundred and fifty men, began his march for the Ohio. It was the commencement of his first campaign and the opening one of the Old French War. He was to be followed by Col. Fry with the remainder of the regiment. He arrived at Wills creek, now Cumberland, Maryland, on the twentieth, having been joined on the way by a detachment under Captain Adam Stephens. Here, Washington found Captain Trent, some of whose men had previously commenced a fort at the junction of the Monongahela and Allegheny, where he had recently left them busily employed upon the stockade. On the twenty-fifth, under the command of an ensign, these men all arrived at Wills creek. They had, on the seventeenth, capitulated to a French force under Contrecoeur, who had dropped down upon them from Venango, but had permitted them all to retire with their working implements. The unfinished fort was enlarged and completed by the French, and given the name of Duquesne.

Notwithstanding the French had secured a lodgement at the Fork of the Ohio, Washington, although Colonel Fry had not reached him, determined to press forward and erect a fortification at Redstone creek, now Brownsville, Fayette county, Pennsylvania. On the twenty-ninth, he set out from Wills creek with one hundred and sixty men. Their progress was very slow; it was marked with every discouragement. Learning finally, that the French were coming out to meet him, he, at a place called Great Meadows, four miles east of the Laurel Hill, on a stream emptying into the Monghiogheny, and ten miles east of the present Remintown, Fayette county, Pennsylvania, cleared away the bushes and threw up an entrenchment. The spot is not many yards south of what is now the National road, a little over fifty-two miles from Cumberland, Maryland.

Washington made every preparation in his power to receive the French, but none came. Scouts were sent out, but no enemy was discovered. The commander afterward received intelligence that a party was at no great distance away. He determined to forestall their hostile designs. Leaving a guard at the Great Meadows with the baggage and ammunition, he set out with a detachment, _ being reinforced, on the way, by some friendly Indians. They came upon the French in their encampment, and a brisk engagement ensued. Washington killed or captured the whole force, except a Canadian, who effected his escape. Among the slain was Jumonville, the leader of the party. The Virginians lost one man killed and three wounded. The prisoners, twenty-one in number, were afterward conducted to the Great Meadows; thence, under guard to Dinwiddie. This event occurred on the twenty-eighth of May, 1754. It was the beginning of a series of deadly conflicts, which culminated on the thirteenth of September, 1759 upon the Heights of Abraham, in the decisive battle between the heroic Wolfe and the brave Montcalm.

Washington, having now the best of reasons for expecting a formidable attack from the French, prepared for the coming storm by strengthening, his entrenchments at the Great Meadows into a palisaded fort, to which he gave the name of Fort Necessity. Colonel Fry having died suddenly at Wills creek, upon the former, as Lieutenant Colonel, now devolved the command of the regiment; while James Innes of North Carolina, who had arrived in Virginia with about three hundred and fifty men, was commissioned by Dinwiddie as Commander-in-Chief of the expedition, which had been reinforced by the two independent companies from New York. Washington's scanty force was augmented to three hundred, by the arrival of the men who had been under Colonel Fry _ increased to four hundred by Mackay's South Carolina Independent company. On the same day _ the tenth of June _ Washington was informed by French deserters that Fort Duquesne was completed. On the eleventh, the laborious march for Redstone was resumed, Captain Mackay's Independent company being left to guard the fort. At the settlement of Christopher Gist, about thirteen miles distant, such intelligence was received as to induce the commander to halt, throw up entrenchments, and send word to Captain Mackay to join him with all speed. The French had received reinforcements, and no doubt a large force would instantly be detached against him. Upon the arrival of the Independent company and the foraging parties, a council of war was held, when it was determined to retreat.

Washington, with his little army, reached the Great Meadows, on his return, the first day of July. He immediately exerted himself to enlarge and strengthen Fort Necessity. Early in the morning of the third, the French under De Villiers, numbering six hundred, with one hundred Indians, drove in his out-posts. Washington formed his men on level ground outside the works, to await the attack. About 11 o'clock, a desultory fire of the enemy began. The commander finally fell back into the trenches, but the French and Indians remained under cover of the woods sixty yards distant, and keeping up, throughout the day, a heavy fire of musketry. Washington, about midnight, signed articles of Capitulation. These recited, in a preamble, that it was the intention of the French not to trouble the peace and good harmony which reigned between the two governments, but only to revenge the assassination of Jumonville and to hinder any establishments on the lands of the French King. Then followed the stipulations. These granted leave to Washington to retire with all his garrison peaceably into his own country; that he should receive no insults from the French; and that the savages should be restrained to the full extent of De Villier's power. The army was permitted to carry away every thing but the cannon, which the French were to keep; and the garrison, as it marched out, was to be allowed the honors of war. The English gave their word of honor "not to work upon any buildings" at the Great Meadows or any part west of the mountains "during the space of one year." As the Virginians had in their power "an officer, two cadets, and most of the prisoners made at the assassination" of Jumonville, they promised to send them back to Fort Duquesne. And, for surety of their performing this, as well as all the other stipulations, two hostages _ Captains _ were to be delivered to the French: Robert Stobo and Jacob Van Braam.

Robert Stobo was born in Glasgow[1] Scotland, in the year 1727.[2] His father, William Stobo, died in 1740, leaving Robert under the guardianship of his nearest friends, who saw that his education was not neglected. His mother dying sometime after, he with his own consent was sent to Virginia to serve in a store of some merchants of his native town, where he performed his engagements with approbation. He resolved, finally, to settle, at least for some years, in Virginia; so, in 1747, he returned to Glasgow to arrange some business matters; after which, he again crossed the ocean, making, however, for the next seven years little progress in the mercantile life; but gaining largely in the esteem of the people and securing the friendship of Governor Dinwiddie, who, when the French began their encroachments upon the Ohio, appointed young Stobo ranking Captain in the regiment of which Washington was Lieutenant Colonel. He was then a resident of Petersburg.[3] He marched with his company, under that officer, to the Great Meadows, planned Fort Necessity,[4] and after the battle of July third, 1754, was delivered into the hands of the French, along with his associate, Van Braam.[5]

Jacob Van Braam was born in Bergen-op-Zum,[6] Holland; and, in 1753, was a resident of Fredericksburg, Virginia, where Washington, on the first day of November, then on his tour of the Ohio, met him and engaged his services as interpreter, he having previously been fencing-master to the young Virginian. Upon their return from the trans-Allegheny country, Van Braam received a commission as Lieutenant in one of the companies
organizing under authority of Dinwiddie, to resist French aggressions upon the western frontiers of Virginia. Washington as Lieutenant Colonel of the regiment, before marching to the westward, had expressed a desire to have his fellow tourist promoted to a Captaincy. He had previously seen service in the British army,[7] and the commander was impressed with his efficiency. "I would by leave," he wrote to the Governor, "to mention Mr. Van Braam for a command who is the oldest Lieutenant and an experienced soldier."[8] And again from the Great Meadows nearly a month before the capitulation: "Captain Van Braam has acted as Captain ever since we left Alexandria. He is an experienced, good officer, and very worthy of the command he has enjoyed."[9] He was soon after commissioned for the office he was so worthily filling.

Van Braam acquitted himself with credit during the battle at the Great Meadows. When the English were called to a parlay the second time by the French, he was sent to confer with them. In this there was no alternative although he understood their language but indifferently and was less acquainted with the English tongue,[10] for Chevalier de Peyrouney, who was a Frenchman, was desperately wounded and, of course, disabled from that service; and there was no other one of the garrison who could speak French at all. Van Braam, by the flickering light of a candle, as the rain fell in torrents, essayed to translate orally the articles of Capitulation to Washington, which were written in French.[11] As understood by the commander, they were deemed satisfactory and signed. But, what is not at all surprising, when they came to be correctly translated, the meaning, in several sentences, was altogether different from what had been honestly been given by the Dutch interpreter. And the misfortune was that some of the passages were derogatory to the honor of Washington and his soldiers. It really seemed to the public _ though nothing was further from the fact _ that Van Braam had been suborned to soften the offensive articles when called upon to translate them. Hence, when the Virginia House of Burgesses, not long after, thanked Washington and his officers for their bravery and gallant defense of their country, soon Van Braam was excepted, under the full belief, doubtless, of his having purposely misinterpreted the articles of capitulation.

On the fourth day of July, 1754, the English army retired with the honors of war from their forlorn fortress, at the Great Meadows, taking up their line of march for the "inhabited parts" of Virginia. Thus were the French left absolute masters of the Valley of the Mississippi. But no sooner had the garrison marched out of Fort Necessity than it became evident, to Stobo that the stipulations agreed upon between the belligerents would not be faithfully carried out on the part of the French. Indians gathered around him loaded with plunder, among which was his own portmanteau containing, besides other articles, a box of valuable jewelry. A short time after his arrival at the Fort Duquesne, he was strengthened in his belief of the faithlessness of the French, by the arrival of Indians with English prisoners taken after the capitulation, some of whom were soldiers of his own company. These transactions, in his view, directly conflicted with the provisions of the articles of capitulation, wherein the English commander had leave "to retire with all his garrison, and to return peaceably into his own country." "I spoke to the commander, several times," he wrote, afterward, "concerning the prisoners, telling him, as we had come to a capitulation, he had no right to hold them." And especially was it, in his judgment, in contravention of the assurance, of the French, that they would restrain, as much as should be in their power, the Indians who were their allies. Therefore it was that Stobo believed he was disengaged from all ties or obligations of an hostage; considering himself only as a prisoner of war who could, if an opportunity offered, rightfully inform his countrymen of passing events around him, and give them whatever knowledge he might acquire of the conditions and plans of the enemy; and that, too, without becoming a spy or a traitor.[12]

The genius of Stobo seems to have been wonderfully awakened by his resolution to turn his captivity to as good an account as possible for his country. He soon sought out methods whereby he could effect his purpose. He found friends upon whom he thought he could rely among some of the Indians who thronged the Fort. Treated leniently by the officers of the garrison, he availed himself of every opportunity to gather information which he imagined would be of service to his friends could he be successful in communicating it to them. He carefully gleaned all the particulars possible of the transactions of the French with the

Indians, the disposition of the various tribes, the number of men in Fort Duquesne, and their expectation of reinforcement. Then with great secrecy, he exercised his talent in drawing a plan of the fortification. Van Braam was kept in entire ignorance of his operation.[13]

On the twenty-eighth of July, 1754, he wrote a letter directed "To the Commanding Officer at Wills creek,"[14] enclosing his draft of Fort Duquesne. In his communication, after giving, in detail, the result of his observations and the knowledge he had obtained in various ways, he says: "When we engaged to serve the country, it was expected we were to do it with our lives. Let them not be disappointed. Consider the good of the expedition without the least regard to us." "For my part," he adds, "I would die ten thousand deaths, to have the pleasure of possessing this fort but one day." After this out-burst of patriotic feeling, he continues: "They are so vain of their success at the Meadows, _ 'tis worse than death to hear them!" He closes with this zealous admonition: "Strike this Fall! As soon as possible, make the Indians ours. Prevent intelligence; get the best; and 'tis done. One hundred trusty Indians might surprise this Fort. They have access all day, and might lodge themselves, so that they could secure the guard with their tomahawks; _ shut the sally-gate, and the fort is ours!" He trusted his long communication to an Indian named "the Song." This letter, giving so much intelligence _ detailing so much information in relative to Fort Duquesne and the ease with which it could be captured; breathing so much zeal and fidelity; and expressing such loyal and generous self-devotion, reached its destination in safety.[15]

On the twenty-ninth of July, Stobo again wrote the Commanding Officer at Wills creek (Col. Innes.) This letter, like its predecessor, was all aglow with the spirit of patriotism. "Let the good of the expedition be considered preferable to our safety," are his words. "Haste to strike!" An Indian _ "Delaware George" _ was the bearer of his second communication. Before sending it off, he found opportunity to add to it, a list of deserters and prisoners in Fort Duquesne. He mentioned one of the former as the cause of all the misfortune at Fort Necessity. "He deserted," wrote Stobo, "the day before the battle. The French got to Gist's at dawn of day, surrounded the place, imagining we were still there; gave a general fire; but when they found we were gone, they were determined to return with all expedition, thinking we had returned to the inhabitants; when, up comes 'Mr. Rascal';[16] told them he deserted the day before, and that the regiment was still at the Meadows, in a starving condition, which caused his deserting; and hearing they were coming, deserted to them. They confined him; told him if true, he should be rewarded; if false, hanged. This I had from the English interpreter,"[17]

The twentieth of September, 1754, found Stobo still in Fort Duquesne; but that day brought with it a change in his quarters. Dinwiddie had steadily refused to give up the French prisoners taken in the skirmish with Jumonville, in fulfillment of the articles of capitulation of the third of July, at the Great Meadows, his plea being, that, since the surrender of Fort Necessity, the enemy had taken several British subjects and sent them prisoners to Canada, which, in his view, though greatly to the disgust and vexation of Washington, was a cause sufficient for the detention of the Frenchmen.[18] However, he finally sent a flag of truce offering to return Drovillon and the two cadets for the hostages.[19]

The offer was rejected. Stobo and Van Braam remained in custody, being ordered on the twentieth _ the very day the flag left Fort Duquesne _ to Canada for greater security.[20] Their journey Allegheny to Verango (mouth of French creek), thence by way of Le Boeuf (Waterford), Presqisle (Erie), and Niagara (mouth of Niagara river), to Montreal. They had large indulgence granted them by Governor Duquesne upon their reaching that city. Not long after this arrival, prisoners captured by the Indians upon the northern frontiers, began to reach the city, being ransomed by the French residents, from the savages, among these were James Johnson, his wife and three children, captured at Charlestown, New Hampshire, on the twenty-ninth of August, 1754. The two hostages were evidently to relieve the wants of the unfortunate captives, to the extent of their ability. "Among the presents I received," afterward wrote Mrs. Johnson, "was one of no small magnitude, from Captains Stobo and Van Braam, two gentlemen who were delivered by Maj. Washington as hostages, when he with the Virginia troops, surrendered to the French and Indians. In compliance with their billet, I waited on them one morning, and, at parting, received a present of one hundred forty-eight livres.[21]

The leniency extended to Stobo and Van Braam was evidently interrupted by the arrival of the new Governor, Vaudreuil, in June 1755. "The two English Captains," wrote that officer from Montreal, "who are here as hostages, have had as much liberty as if they had been invited to learn thoroughly our situation. They have had the run of the villages of our domiciliated Indians with whom they have had conferences, and have even advised their Governors of our forces and plans."[22] This was, in the opinion of Vaudreuil, no longer to be tolerated. Their liberty must be abridged. They were sent to Quebec, and imprisoned on the twenty-fifth of June. The same mishap befell Johnson _ his wife and two youngest children. They arrived from Montreal on the twenty-fourth of July, 1755, and all were conducted directly to jail. The approach of winter found them still deprived of their liberty. Mrs. Johnson in giving a description of their place of confinement says : "Our prison was a horrid defense from the blasts of December; with two chairs and a heap of straw, and two lousy blankets; we may well be supposed to live uncomfortably; but, in addition to this, we had but one poor fire a day; and the iron grates gave fine access to the chills of the inclement sky."

"Our former benevolent friends, Captains Stobo and Van Braam," continues the writer, "had the peculiar misfortune to be cast into prison opposite to us. Suspicion of having corresponded with their country men, was the crime with which they were charged. Their misfortune did not preclude the exertion of generosity; they frequently sent us by the waiting maid, bottles of wine, and articles of provision. But the malice of Frenchmen had now arrived to such a pitch, against all our country, that we must be deprived of these comforts. These good men were forbidden their offices of kindness, and our intercourse was entirely prohibited." "We however found means," she adds, "by a stratagem, to effect in some measure, what could not be done by open dealing. When the servants were carrying in our daily supplies, we slipped into the entry, and deposited our letters in an ash-box, which were taken by our friends, they leaving one at the same time for us."[23] The two generous hostages were finally relieved of their imprisonment, upon confessing the writing of a letter to Dinwiddie:[24] and given the city limits, on their parole.[25]

After the capitulation at the Great Meadows, on the third of July, 1754, Washington and Mackay conducted most of their men in safety to Wills creek, where, on the twelfth of September, Col. Innes commenced the erection of Fort Cumberland. The next year saw the English and French preparing for hostilities on a larger scale. The former determined, if possible, to drive the latter from the valley of the Ohio. This undertaking was intrusted to the unfortunate Braddock, who, after penetrating the wilderness to a point only nine miles from Fort Duquesne, with a large army of regulars and provincials, fell into ambuscade on the ninth of July, 1755, and was totally defeated. All his papers fell into the hands of the French; among which were the original letters of Stobo, with his drawing of the fort.[26] These were transmitted to Canada,[27] and, on the thirtieth of September translated, at Quebec, into the French language.[28] They were then dispatched to France.[29]

Upon the receipt, by Vaudreuil, of Stobo's captured communication from Fort Duquesne and his plan of that fortification, he and Van Braam were committed close prisoners at Quebec _ there to remain until instructions should be received from the French King concerning them. The two, however, managed in course of time to effect their escape; but a large reward offered to any one who should bring them in dead or alive, drew so many in quest of them, that Van Braam gave himself up,[30] and Stobo was soon captured. The latter was now incarcerated in a dungeon _ dark and long unfrequented. Upon entering it, he found neither chair nor stool; nothing but a dismal couch of straw, through the covering of which the white blades of wheat had penetrated and grown full four inches in height above the canvas. Before it, on the floor, was set an earthen pan of water, and over it laid a piece of bread. In this dark and noisome cell he could, at first, scarcely distinguish the closest object; yet his eye-sight soon became so keen, that he could discern small objects at a considerable distance.[31] The treatment of Van Braam was quite as inhuman.[32]

In the Autumn of 1756, the original letters of Stobo, with the plan of Fort Duquesne were returned from France, accompanied by a Commission from the French King for a Council of War, to try the hostages for their lives on a charge of high treason; execution, however, of the judgment was to be suspended until the further pleasure of the French monarch.[33] The prisoners were, thereupon, ordered to Montreal, from Quebec, for trial. They left under an escort on the twenty-eighth of September. "I do not know," wrote the Reverend Claude Godfrey, from the latter place, "what our General proposes to do with them. The English here say, that if a Frenchman had played, in their country, the trick that Stobo has played here, he would have been hanged."[34] Upon their arrival, they were both examined touching the letters written to the commander at Wills creek, while they were in Fort Duquesne, and, also, with regard to the plan of that fortification which accompanied the first letter. Van Braam, under oath, was questioned as to what he knew of Stobo's transactions before their arrival in Canada. His knowledge was meager indeed.[35] But as to himself, he protested he had never violated his obligations of hostage. The court were convinced of the truth of his asseverations. He was acquitted.

Put upon his parole, Van Braam had the city limits for his prison-bounds. He remained in Montreal until its final surrender to the British on the eighth of September 1760, when his imprisonment, of over six years duration, was ended. He soon after made his way to Virginia, arriving in Williamsburg in November.[36] On the nineteenth of September following, he received a Captain's commission in the Sixtieth, or Royal American regiment _ a complete vindication of his faithfulness to his adopted country. He retired upon half-pay, in 1763. He afterward married; _ moving "on a good farm" in Wales, in 1768.[37] In 1770, he made application, through George Mercer, in London, to Washington, for the entry of his portion of military lands under his Majesty's proclamation of October, 1763, to which, for the services rendered and hardships endured he was so justly entitled.[38] As time had completely vindicated his sincerity, reliability and patriotism as a British soldier during the Seven Years' War, the lands were readily granted.

Upon the revolt of the American Colonies, Van Braam was ordered by Amherst to London. Obedience was nearly all he remembered of military discipline. He was made oldest Captain in the third battalion of his regiment _ the Sixtieth. He had been out-spoken against the American war and pleaded hard to be left out of the service, but all to no avail. He must embark for east Florida or lose his half-pay. He sailed in the early part of 1776, determined, however, to sell out of the army whenever an opportunity offered. To this end, he afterward returned to England and purchased a Major's commission.[39] He was promoted the fourteenth of June, 1777.[40] He again returned to America, but a firm resolution to quit the service as soon as possible.[41] This he accomplished on the twenty-second of October, 1779;[42] having, however, been obliged previously to make the campaign of that year and the previous one, in Georgia. He now retired with his family to Devonshire, England; but his sentiments with regard to the proceedings of the British Ministry were so well known as to cause his final retirement to France. In this retreat, in 1783, he was remembered by Washington, with his compliments. It called forth a patriotic response: "Give me leave," he replied, "present the sentiments of my soul in congratulations for your successes in the American contest and in wishing you a long life to enjoy the blessing of a great people whom you have been the chief instrument in freeing from bondage."[43]

Before his inquisitors, in Montreal, on first day on November, 1756, Stobo, was bold and defiant. That he had disregarded the ties and obligations of an hostage was, he affirmed; because he believed the capitulation at the Great Meadows broken as soon as made.[44] He openly acknowledged to the court that the writing of the letters from Fort Duquesne and the drawing of the plan of that fortification.[45] The quality of hostage identical with that of a citizen of the country where detained, he regarded as not applicable to himself in any view of the case; but his judges were of a different opinion. He was convicted of high treason and sentenced to be beheaded. "I suspend the execution of his sentence," wrote Vaudreuil, "agreeable to the King's orders." [46] Stobo was remanded to his dungeon in Quebec. He was subsequently remanded to a cell in the common jail, _ no approval of the sentence against him, having arrived from France. From his new quarters he resolved to escape if possible. He was in hopes that, if he could gain the woods upon the opposite side of the St. Lawrence, he might be able, notwithstanding a six weeks journey southward through the wilderness would have to be made, to reach, finally, the English settlements.[47]

The window of Stobo's cell was barred up and down but not across. He determined, if it could be done, to cut a groove in the stone sill some distance along from one the bars, then to spring it in the furrow sufficiently far to allow him to squeeze through. His only implement for this labor was a knife round at the point used by him to cut his victuals. The hole was carefully filled when he was not at work, with bread chewed for the purpose, covered with sand taken from the orifice. It was a long time before his work was completed. Meanwhile, he had to make preparation for his journey. He contrived to save up from his daily allowance, and secrete from the eagle eye of his jailors, full thirty pounds of provisions, consisting of dried ham and tongue and bread and cheese.

Stobo now only awaited a fit opportunity to attempt his flight. During a violent storm on night, the opportune moment, in his opinion, had arrived. Tying his handkerchief around two bars, one of which was to sprung at its lower end, along the groove in the sill; he inserted in it a stick, which, by turning, acted as a screw. He soon had the iron sufficiently displaced to admit of his egress. Securing his provision to his person, he pushed himself between the bars, then dropped down outside; striking fortunately, into a mire below, which broke his fall. The sentries as Stobo had calculated, owing to severity of the storm, had deserted their post. Once clear of the jail, he made all haste through the rain and hail, into the country where a barn, on a hay-loft, unperceived, he secreted himself as day light appeared.

The sooner was it known that the prisoner had made his escape than the drums beat the alarm. A large reward was offered for the apprehension of the "condemned traitor." The whole city was soon in an uproar. The reward for his capture was tempting. Different parties scoured the country at great distances. Meanwhile, Stobo feeling confident of the search continuing, remained in his snug quarters in the farmer's barn. About midnight of the third day, he stole out from his lurking place watchfully and silently, striking for Charles river, which he forded with budget upon his head as the water reached to his chin. The next day, he remained in a neighboring wood, seeking, at night, along the river's bank, for any stray skiff or canoe with which to cross the St. Lawrence. The next evening, just as he had got below the falls of Montmorenci, he was surprised by some gentlemen who happened to be riding that way, _ seized and dragged, of course reluctantly, back to Quebec. Again the dungeon was his doom.

It seemed to the hapless Stobo that fate has decreed he should pass many more months in the dreary and dismal abode of his loathsome cell. The thought was too much even for one so resolute and determined as he; _ his spirits failed him; his looks grew pale; his long black hair turned gray; his body wasted away. But relief came unexpectedly and strangely. A lady had become interested in him. She was a cousin of Vaudreuil; and, through her intercession, and from the fact that no confirmation of his sentence had been received from France, Stobo was taken from his dungeon and placed in quarters much less unhealthy; where he could walk upon the ramparts of the fortress. He soon recovered his spirits and health, as a consequence of the change. His good conduct and great care never to transgress the rules of the prison brought on, as a natural result, in the course of time, less watchfulness on the part of those in charge of him. He particularly ingratiated himself with the family of his host. Finally, some English officers, prisoners at Quebec, had leave to visit him.[48]   This was in the Spring of 1759, _ nearly two years and a half after his trail and condemnation, and almost five years after the battle of the Great Meadows.

The fortunes of war had brought to Quebec many prisoners. Among these was Simon Stevens, a Lieutenant in Major Robert Rogers' corps of rangers, who was captured in a skirmish a short time before the attack on Ticonderoga, [49] and one by the name of Clark, a Scotchman born at Leith, a ship-carpenter by trade, who had with him a wife and three small children.[50] Stevens was one of the English officers allowed to occasionally to visit Stobo. At their brief interviews, they formed a plan of escape. It was determined to make the attempt by way of the St. Lawrence; in hopes of ultimately reaching Louisburg, on the Island of Cape Breton, the nearest English settlement on any water route from Quebec. From the very nature of the case, it would be a most desperate undertaking, as more than one thousand miles would have to be accomplished before making that friendly port; but they resolved to make the trial at all hazards. Clark and two provincials, Elijah Denbo and Oliver Lakin, likewise prisoners, were let into the secret by Stevens, and readily agreed to join in the adventure. The night appointed for the rendezvous was the thirtieth of April, 1759. They were all to meet at Clark's. The latter lived a little way out of town. By some mishaps, the time of departure was necessarily postponed to the next night.

The whole party consisting of Stobo, Stevens, Lakin, Denbo, Clark, and his wife and three children _ nine souls in all _ with arms, ammunition and stores about ten o'clock in the evening, of May first, 1759, embarked, in a large canoe made of birch bark, upon the river St. Charles. The frail craft was urged rapidly down that stream, into the St. Lawrence; thence to Isle Madame about seven leagues below Quebec; when, meeting the advancing tide _ and, as daylight was fast advancing, _ they moved in shore, landed, and, taking their frail vessel, their provisions, and arms, they sought the shelter of a neighboring thicket.[51]

The escape of Stobo the third time brought out as usual an offer by proclamation of large reward for his apprehension. Again their were busy hunters searching for the fugitive. Again the city and the country for miles around were carefully watched _ but, this time, watched in vain. "An Englishman, named Robert Stobo," wrote Montcalm, from Montreal, "has just made his escape from Quebec; he was a hostage for the capitulation of Fort Necessity, in 1754; had been tried by court martial in November, 1756, but on order from the King and condemned to be beheaded for illicit correspondence with the enemy. The execution of the sentence had been suspended, pursuant to his Majesty's intentions. He took some Englishmen along with him. This is his third escape." "I do not know," continues the writer, "whether we shall be as successful as on the two former occasions in recapturing so well informed a man."[52]

About ten o'clock on the second of May, the party again moved down the river with a good breeze blowing. A little before night they had made about two leagues below the Island Lacroille. The wind now proving contrary, they disembarked to go on shore in the north side of the river; but the gale was so high as to make it impossible. The south shore was sought by the adventurers, but the wind still increasing it was deemed dangerous to land on account of the rocks. The storm coming so suddenly upon them, they came well-nigh perishing. They were obliged to lay in the river all night. However, by morning, they succeeded in reaching the shore, but in a sad plight. Here they spent the day recuperating their wasted energies. About nine o'clock the next morning they were again afloat. During the day they discovered a birch bark canoe with three Indians in it. The savages after following them a short distance, gave up the chase. Before the party could reach the north shore, night came on a very thick fog, which obliged them the second time to lay in the river all night.

On the fifth, they put into a small cove, went on shore, and hauled up their canoe. Clark and Lakin then went out to kill some ducks. They had proceeded but a short distance when they discovered smoke, and immediately returned to give the alarm. Leaving Clark's wife with the canoe and baggage, the men went out to reconnoiter, when two Indians were discovered. Stobo spoke to them in French, informing them that he and his companions were in pursuit of English prisoners who had escaped from Quebec. The Indians it appears, were engaged at that point upon the river, to light signal fires in the event of the appearance of any fleet of the enemy. Upon the attempt of one to escape, both were shot and scalped. In their wigwam, were some fine beaver skins and other articles which were appropriated by the men. This happened on the fifth of May. On the ninth, early in the morning and just as the party had risen they discovered a large ship coming up the river. The men immediately put out their fire and went to repairing their canoe. Soon after, they saw a two-mast boat coming directly to the place where they lay. It was resolved to capture the craft and make prisoners of the crew. Stobo and his companions secreted themselves lying close among the rocks, right ahead of the approaching boat, which ran up into a small creek. Where upon, the party fired two guns, when the crew called for quarter. Down rushed Stobo and his party upon the beach and captured the whole of them, four in number. And old, gentlemanly-looking man who had acted as helmsman desired to know whose prisoner he was. He was informed into whose hands he had fallen, and that he might now, with his men and shallop, speed the English on their way to Louisburg or their lives would pay the forfeit; it was the fortune of war. The boat was the property of the old man, who had been some distance below for a cargo of wheat. As the load was too heavy for expedition, about one half of the grain was thrown overboard. Snugly storing away their effects taken from the bark canoe, they hoisted sail with the departing day; and, doubly manned, they turned the shallop down the river _ much to the delight of some but greatly to the dismay of others on board, as may readily be imagined. The boat was built to be propelled by oars as well as by sails. Sometime in the afternoon, as they turned a headland, a French frigate came suddenly to view standing up the St. Lawrence. It was a dreadful apparition to the Englishmen. The party saw but little chance to escape. They resolved, however, to make a desperate effort. Stobo took the helm, and, threatening his prisoners with instant death should they slacken their labors at the oars, boldly continued his course.

The usual for the shallop to "bring to," was fired by the frigate; but the only answer was, an increased effort at the oars, and the crowding of all sail. A second report brought no response. Then came one with ball and still the little craft hastened on its way. Shot after shot succeeded; but, fortunately, not one of them struck their boat. It was not long before they were out of reach, but they did not relax their efforts. Throughout the night, they continued every exertion. By morning, they were many miles distant from their dangerous enemy. It was a lucky escape. About sunrise, on the tenth, they arrived at the Isle of St. Barnaby _ passing between the Island and a French frigate which lay about two miles away, and which saluted them with several shots; nevertheless the party escaped without accident reaching the Metis river, ten leagues below, very much fatigued. Here the prisoners were set on shore. They were given all the wheat except four bushels, also a gun with some powder and shot. The crews parted, after interchanging compliments, and the adventurous Englishmen again made sail, with moderate weather down the St. Lawrence.

On the morning of the thirteenth they passed Gaspe. But with the morning came fresh dangers. They beheld into the bay of Chaleur where they discovered a sloop lying nigh on shore. This vessel upon consultation, they decided to board; but the attempt proved abortive, arising to rapidity of the tide. On the fifteenth the wind was so very strong that the party was driven upon shore and their boat filled with water, which was finally bailed out. They then ran into a small creek. Upon examination, they found their stores greatly damaged. They had only two days' provisions left. The next day they caught some fish, which raised the spirits of the forlorn voyagers. By the nineteenth their supplies being nearly exhausted, despondence came over all. Just then they discovered a Schooner and a Sloop standing towards them. The party was still in camp on shore, and the two sails proved to be French. They anchored about a league off. The next day, on the eighteenth, they were still on shore _ mainly endeavoring to haul their boat upon the beach, to repair it if possible, it being very much damaged. They moved it but very little, and returned to their tents which they had erected on the shore. The two vessels weighed anchored and were lost to sight; while Stobo and his companions made some little headway in repairing their boat. On the twenty-first, Clark still employed in trying to repair it, to the dismay of all, the schooner and sloop were now seen returning. The party on land thereupon launched their boat, which was seen by the vessels, and they sent a canoe on shore. It contained two men and a boy. The three landed, but had not gone far when all were seized by the Englishmen who had concealed themselves for that purpose. They at once safely bound the captured Frenchmen.

The party soon learned from their prisoners the force and armament of the two vessels. They were told the crew of each left on board was but four in number. Stobo and his companions resolved to capture both Schooner and sloop if possible. By this time, night had set in. The two men were securely tied to trees _ their arms piniond backwards around the trunks, _ and left in care of Mrs. Clark who was given a tomahawk to dispatched them should they attempt to escape. The boy they concluded to take with them. He could be of service in making the proper responses when hailed. They took their own patched-up vessel as it was believed the other one would not carry six persons. The wife of Clark was told to watch the two men until their return. The Englishmen, about one o'clock in the morning, were along side the enemy, rowing silently as they approached one of the vessels. There was a light in the binnacle, but none of the crew were on deck. Stobo was the first to leap on board. An instant more, and one of the Frenchman advancing, up the companion-way. A shot from Stobo's pistol sent him backward, in a trice. The remainder immediately surrendered. They were marched to the hold and safely locked down, _ the master of the craft alone excepted. He was retained on deck to be questioned

The vessel Stobo and his men had captured was the schooner. The Englishmen now weighed anchor and sailed themselves along side the other vessel. The crew of the latter were ordered on board the schooner; whereupon several shots from small arms in the hands of the assailants brought them to terms. They came on board and all except the master were confined in the hold taking from the sloop six small arms, one swivel gun, and some provisions, the vessel was set on fire; when the victorious party, sailed for their camp. The small boat was about on shore and the woman with her three children and two prisoners, brought aboard; then they again set sail upon their adventurous voyage. It is doubtful if the annals of war can show a more daring exploit.

After sailing about five leagues, six of the prisoners were put on shore. They were furnished with three days provisions, one gun and some ammunition. There were retained on board the Schooner, the two masters, with three others of the prisoners. The adventures ordered these to take the vessel to St. John's Island; where they all arrived on the twenty- seventh of May, 1759. The commandant at St. John's treated the party very courteously; and, when they departed, he ordered a Sergeant and twenty privates as a guard on the Schooner. At length, on the sixth day of June _ full six and thirty days from Quebec they made the welcome court of Louisburg. [53]

"Just now," is the language of a letter written on the seventh of June, from Louisburg, "just now an officer reports that he saw a gentleman who had been a prisoner at Quebec for five years, that he, with four others, had made their escape in a canoe."[54] And again two days afterward: "I wrote you about a gentleman who had made his escape from Quebec, after being five years a prisoner. He is a man of a most enterprising genius; his name is Stobo."[55]

A retrospective glance at the more important events transpiring from the date of Braddock's defeat to the landing of Stobo at Louisburg _ including and internal of nearly five years _ discloses an outline of four important campaigns. In 1756, England declared war against France. It was followed by Montcalm's capture of Oswego on the fourteenth of August, and a general desolation of the frontiers by the Indians. The campaign of 1757, was distinguished by the fall of Fort William Henry and the cruel murder of a large number of the garrison by the savages. The unsuccessful attack upon Ticonderoga, the capture of Louisburg, of Fort Frotenac, now Kingston, Canada, and Fort Duquesne, ended the campaign of 1758. Its results were favorable to the English. Three expeditions were planned for 1759; one, against Niagara, one against the French upon Lake Champlain, and third against Quebec. General Wolfe went up the St. Lawrence with eight thousand troops and many battle-ships. But the English fleet passed by Stobo unobserved, while in the gulf.

A detailed account of every material event occurring to Stobo from the time he left Fort Duquesne until his escape from Quebec, was taken down by the officers at Louisburg. The information given was considered of so much importance that an express boat was dispatched with the intelligence to England notwithstanding the English fleet had sailed for the St. Lawrence. It was also believed that a man of so much enterprise and possessed of so much knowledge of the enemy's movements and preparations,[56] and of the country around Quebec, might be of great service to General Wolfe. A vessel was, therefore, immediately ordered to get ready to convey Stobo back to Canada.[57] Before sailing, he gave directions that his share of the proceeds of the sale of the schooner and sundry articles of value captured with the vessel, should be bestowed upon the wife and children of Clark.[58] As for himself, he had nobler gains in view. Only four days after his arrival at Louisburg, and the indomitable Scotchman started upon his return to the scene of his long imprisonment.[59]

Stobo was well received by Wolfe and made a member of his military household. He generally accompanied him in his reconnaissances; and, upon one occasion, at the Falls of Montmorenci, was slightly wounded. His presence becoming known to the Canadians, he was frequently appealed to by them for protection to their property; he thus had it in his power to reciprocate former favors.[60] Stobo pointed out to the British commander a spot where, in his opinion, the army might be landed, whence the heights might be scaled to the very place to put his troops on shore, during the night of the twelfth of September, _ climb the rocks to the Plains of Abraham and gaining, the next day, a victory and a grave. Before this decisive battle, which crumbled to the dust the French domination in America, Stobo was sent with dispatches, to General Amherst, who was operating against the enemy upon Lake Champlain. On his way out, his vessel was captured by a privateer. No sooner, however, had the danger become than his letters were thrown over board. He, with crew, was sent, in a sloop, to Halifax; as the Frenchmen had already more prisoners than they could well secure. Stobo made his way thence to Amherst; and was with that General until he finished the campaign of Lake Champlain _ driving the French into Canada.[61]

The campaign over, Stobo visited Virginia, arriving at Williamsburg, the capital, on the eighteenth of November, 1759,[62] with a letter from General Amherst to the Governor, which was, the next day, laid before the House of Burgesses, then in session; where upon they "resolved that one thousand pounds be paid by the treasurer of this colony, to Captain Robert Stobo, over and above the pay that is due him from the time of his rendering himself a hostage, to this day, as a reward for his zeal to his country, and the recompense for the great hardships he has suffered, during his confinement in the enemy's country." The House also, requested the Governor "to take Captain Stobo into his special care and favor and promote him in the service of the Colony." They then tendered him a vote of thanks for his steady and inviolable attachment to the interest of the country; for his singular bravery and courage exerted on all occasions during the war; and for the magnanimity with which he had supported himself during his confinement in Canada. In conclusion, they resolved that he be congratulated in the name of House on his safe and happy return.[63]

Stobo's answer to the Virginia Assembly spoke the sentiments of a patriot: "The distinguishing tokens of favor and benevolence," he replied, "which you have vouchsafed voluntarily to confer on me, _ and that unanimously and immediately upon my happy return to this country, _ have administered to my heart the greatest consolation of which it was susceptible; gratified every wish it was capable of entertaining; and imprinted upon it the most indelible sense of gratitude with which it could be possibly affected." "To be informed," he continued, "by the voice of the public, that I had discharged my duty to their satisfaction, and merited their thanks for my conduct is the highest glory my ambition could aspire to, and will determine me, upon future occasion, to exert myself with all the vigor and alacrity which the united ardor of gratitude and duty can inspire."[64]

On the first day of February, 1760, Stobo had a furlough granted him under full pay[65] for one year, to visit England. He sailed on the eighteenth. At the entrance of the English Channel, his vessel was overtaken and captured by a French privateer. The passengers and crew had to pay, as the price of their liberty, twenty-five hundred pounds, Stobo's proportion of which was one hundred twenty-five pounds. He reached London on the twenty-second of March, where he was welcomed with distinguished honors. To the Prime Minister he applied for a command in the Regular army. Pitt gave him an open letter to Amherst wherein he wrote; "As I have taken a great share in the general attention that is paid here to this officer's merit, his sufferings, and his zeal for his Majesty's Government, I shall esteem it as a particular favor if you will honor him with a company in the army under your command." With these credentials, he sailed on the twenty-fourth of April for New York, where he arrived after a prosperous voyage, anxious not to lose an hour of the approaching campaign in Canada.[66] He was commissioned Captain in the Fifteenth Regiment of Foot, on the fifth of June, following.[67]

Stobo's regiment was assembled at Montreal immediately after its surrender, in September, 1760; and was one of the corps which occupied that city for several months. The next year it proceeded, by way of Lake Champlain and Albany, to New York, being encamped in June on Staten Island. In October, it sailed for Barbados. Early in 1762, the regiment was employed against the Island of Martinique which surrendered in February. War having been declared against Spain, the regiment was attached to the commandant destined to attack the Havana, which capitulated in August. It remained here eleven months. In the later part of 1763, the regiment arrived in Canada, where it was stationed until the summer of 1768, when it embarked for England, landing at Portsmouth in July. Here it had its quarters at various places in the south and midland counties until the summer of 1770, when it was reviewed at Chatham by King George III.[68] In June of that year Stobo died.[69] He had never married, his company had been sought by the great and the learned of his country. "Surely," wrote Hume, soon after Stobo's arrival on Great Britain, from Canada, with his regiment, "surely he has had the most extraordinary adventures in the world."[70] Such they seemed to England's great historian; and time, surely, has not lessened their character, in the estimation of Americans.

Chapter Six

Captivity and Escape of Mrs. William Ingles
1755

Although Virginia had, for a long time previous, claimed the great Valley of the Ohio as a portion of her chartered possessions, yet few of her citizens at the commencement of 1754, had ventured into the wilderness beyond the Alleghenies. Here and there could have been seen an Anglo-American; _ but the tide of emigration which had just begun to break the barriers of the mountains, was turned back by the approaching storm of war with the French and Indians. An incipient settlement upon one of the eastern branches Monongahela had already been destroyed by the savages;[1] and afterward, when Washington had returned from the Great Meadows, discomfited by the enemy, the settlers upon the Greenbrier, New River, and Holston, trembled for their own safety. And well they might; for, before the close of the year, the savages made their appearance upon the western border; and the frontiermen, for the first time, had an experience of the horrors of Indian warfare. The first who fell victims lived upon the Holston; three were killed and one made prisoner who afterward escaped. This was in the month of October.[2]

The Western Border War, however, was not fully inaugurated until the next year. On the eighteenth of June, 1755, upon the waters of the Holston, in the present county Washington, Virginia, the merciless savages made their appearance. Five of the settlers were killed and two taken prisoners, one of whom, soon after, regained his liberty.[3] On the twenty-third of the same month, a party of "French Indians" fell on the inhabitants of Frederick county, Maryland, killing two men and one woman, and carrying eight persons captives into the wilderness, three of whom afterward made their escape.[4] Soon after the event, nineteen more of the inhabitants of Frederick county, fearing the incursions of the savages, left their habitations, to go for security and protection to Fort Cumberland. On their way, they were ambushed by Indians, three only out of the whole number escaping unhurt. A boy whom the Indians had scalped and left for dead, subsequently got into the Fort.[5] About the same date several parties of French and Indians appeared in the county of Hampshire, Virginia, on Patterson's creek within a few miles of Fort Cumberland and cut off several families.⁶ On the third of July, seven persons were massacred by the savages upon New River in what was then Augusta county. Seven of the settlers who were wounded, made their escape; but eleven were hurried captives into the wilderness.⁷ Such were the opening scenes⁸ in the drama of the Western Border War _ a strife which continued, almost without cessation, for forty years.

Towards the close of July, 1755, Col. James Patton, then lieutenant of Augusta county,⁹ Virginia, a resident of that part now included in the county of Rockbridge, started out with ammunition and other supplies, for the use of the frontier. He stopped on the thirty, at a plantation _ the residence of the widow of George Draper and her son-in-law, William Ingles _ in what is now Montgomery county, adjoining the present village of Blacksburg, to refresh himself, his convoy being about five miles in advance. Here he was beset by a party of sixteen Shawnee Indians _ one account says thirteen _ who killed and stripped him. Casper Barrier, Mrs. George Draper and a child were also massacred. One James Cull was wounded, but escaped. Mrs. William Ingles and her two sons, aged respectively two and four years, together with her sister-in-law, Mrs. John Draper, and Henry Leonard, were made prisoners. The savages, taking the horse of Col. Patton and their captives, also all the "plunder" they could carry, struck for New River, down which they hastened. They were followed by a party of frontiersmen, but succeeded in eluding their pursuers.¹⁰ "I am hardly sorry," wrote the Governor of Virginia, "for the death of Col. Patton. It is a real surprise to one that the few Indians who have been in Augusta should have gone to great lengths in robbing and murdering." "I fancy," he adds,"there has been a general panic over the whole country."¹¹

The Indians hurrying down the Great Kanawha, treated their prisoners roughly, some, very cruelly. Mrs. Ingles, however, seems to have been, from the start, a favorite with her captors. They permitted her to ride one of their horses and carry her two boys _ George and Thomas _ with her. She had frequent opportunities of escaping; but, hoping to keep her children with her, and that all would eventually be liberated, she made no attempt to flee. Keeping down the river, they finally reached a little salt spring not very far from its mouth. Here the Indians camped, and, for two days, made salt. Then they pursued their journey down the Ohio, to the Scioto, where, at the mouth of that river, was their principal town in what is now Scioto county, Ohio, opposite the site of Portsmouth, its county seat. It was then called the Lower Shawnee Town in contradistinction to the Upper Shawnee Town, situated on the south side of the Ohio a short distance above the mouth of the Great Kanawha.¹²

The day after the arrival of the prisoners at the Scioto, they were compelled to run the gauntlet;¹³ Mrs. Ingles being the only one exempted from this punishment. A few days subsequent to this, the captives were divided among the several claimants. Mrs. Ingles and her children were, unfortunately, separated; the later being taken to another town,¹⁴ while the mother remained at the Lower Shawnee village. For the next three weeks, Mrs. Ingles grew in favor with the savages, by making hunting shirts for them, of checks and coarse linen goods, brought thither by French traders from Detroit. When one of these garments was finished, the owner would run through the town, holding it up with a stick, proclaiming its qualities and declaring that the maker was "a very fine squaw."

Mrs. Ingles was the taken to Big Bone Lick, in what is now the county of Boone, Kentucky, to assist in making salt. This famous "lick" for where so many large bones have been found,[15] is about twelve miles a little west of south from Burlington, county seat of Boone county, and one and a half miles, east of Hamilton on the Ohio river. At this point, seeing no hope of having her children again, or rescuing them from the savages, and her own situation being, at best, a very distressing one, Mrs. Ingles resolved to attempt an escape. An old German woman, who was also a prisoner at the "lick," she prevailed upon to accompany her. Getting consent of the Indians to go out and gather grapes, and, previous to starting, providing themselves each with a blanket and tomahawk, they set out upon their perilous journey, passing as they started, three Frenchmen _ traders _ sitting upon one of the big bones cracking walnuts. With one of these three men, Mrs. Ingles exchanged tomahawks.

It being the determination of these brave-hearted women to take the Ohio river as their guide, until they could reach the mouth of the Great Kanawha, they at once made their way to that stream; and then threading along through the interminable woods, but always keeping its waters in view, they walked rapidly onward for their distant homes. Their reliance for food was wholly upon the spontaneous productions of the forest, such as walnuts, grapes, pawpaws, and the like, which furnished them a very scanty and precarious sustenance. When night came on, the absence of the captives was remarked by the savages at the "lick," who, as was afterward learned, began soon to entertain the belief that both were lost; it never occurred to them that they were making endeavors to escape. A thorough search was at one instituted, but all in vain. The conclusion derived at was, that they had been killed by some wild beasts.

Up the Ohio, the determined women pursued their devious course, until the Licking was reached, which they found too deep to ford. This stream they were obliged to ascend a considerable distance before crossing; when they moved down its eastern bank until they came to the Ohio again. After a few days journeying from the "lick," they arrived opposite the Lower Shawnee Town, where, in a deserted cabin, they found some corn. They stayed all night here; and, in the morning, just as they, upon the point of leaving, a horse was discovered in a lot near by. They were not long in concluding to press the animal into their service, as will be readily imagined; so, loading the beast, as best they could, with corn which they had now found in abundance, they started forward with renewed energy. Some Indians out hunting were seen during the day, but the women, by carefully concealing themselves, escaped discovery. Upon reaching the Big Sandy, they found its waters too deep to cross, and were obliged to move up the river until they could find a safe passage. After some days walking along its banks, they finally came to a large drift extending across the stream. In attempting to get their horse over the logs, it became hopelessly entangled and had to be left.

Taking as much corn as they could conveniently carry, the two wanderers descended the eastern side of the Big Sandy until the Ohio was again in view. In that way, they continued their journey _ ascending one side of every large stream until they could cross it, and then going down the other side _ determined to keep, so far as lay in their power, always near the Ohio. In order, occasionally, to shorten distances, where points made into the river, or where the stream made a considerable bend, they would "cut across;" but in so doing, they sometimes had to pull themselves up steep acclivities by shrubs and bushes, so worn down were they by fatigue and starvation, and then literally slide down on the opposite side. Their corn soon was gone, when they had again to resort to such things as the wilderness produced to sustain life; frequently eating roots, the qualities of which were entirely unknown to them. In the extremity, the old German woman became disheartened; blamed Mrs. Ingles for persuading her to leave the savages. She declared they must die in the woods. Her suffering had, doubtless, crazed her to a certain extent. She be came ill-natured and finally attempted to kill Mrs, Ingles, who, being much smaller and weaker than her companion, resorted to every means in her power to conciliate her. At length, they reached the Great Kanawha.

Mrs. Ingles now took fresh courage. She knew that more than half the journey had been performed toward her home. She had an abiding faith that the residue of the distance could be accomplished; at least, it was her determination to press forward _ to never give up, so long as she could move one foot before the other. It seemed incredible that such a determination should have been persevered in against such appalling dangers and obstacles. But who can measure the fortitude of woman, when putting to its severest trial? Under the cruelest sufferings, she rises superior to man.

Up the Great Kanawha, to within fifty miles of the place of Mrs. Ingles captivity, the journey was much the same, as along the Ohio. At this point, the old German woman again relapsed into a melancholy ill-nature. Again she attempted to kill Mrs. Ingles, who escaped her by being more fleet of foot. This happened one evening just before dusk. Upon getting free from her crazed companion,[16] Mrs. Ingles secreted herself under the bank of the river until dark; when, hearing no more from her, she ventured out from her place of concealment. By the dim and flickering moonlight which soon after appeared, she was able to grope her way along the margin of the stream; but she had walked only a short distance, when she espied a canoe at the waters edge; in this, after several trials, she succeeded in crossing the river.

Mr. Ingles was now upon the northern bank of New River, the principal southern branch of the Great Kanawha. She found, at the point where she had crossed, a small improvement, consisting of a cabin and a little patch of clear land _ the work of hunters of the Spring before. Some corn which had been planted by them, had been destroyed by buffaloes. Mrs. Ingles was now enabled to form a pretty correct idea of the distance she had yet to travel, and the rugged aspect of the country that intervened between her and her home. By this time, her clothing was almost worn out by the thorns and brier bushes she had encountered. Her moccasins were entirely gone. To add to her distress, the weather was getting cooler; snow had commenced to fall; so that now, almost upon the threshold of her home her prospects of reaching it were almost hopeless. But her inflexible resolution bore her up under every discouragement. At night, to keep herself from perishing from the cold she would seek out a hollow log or tree, gather leaves into it, and then bury herself in them, until morning. Perils began to thicken around her. For four or five days after she had crossed New River, she journeyed on, through frosts, _ wading the cold waters, climbing around cliffs, and over ridges _ until her limbs became so benumbed and swollen, that despair, for the first time, was fast overwhelming her. It seemed impossible for her to go farther. Just at the last moment _ just as every hope had fled _ she descried a settlement, in the distance.

It so happened, at this time, that a man named Adam Harman was upon New River with two sons _ at a place where he had previously made improvements _ engaged in securing some corn. One day while all three were out hunting, they heard, to their surprise, in the distance, the voice of a woman, calling. They listened. Again and more distinctly was the call heard. Said Harman _ "that's the voice of Mary Ingles!" He was sure he could not be mistaken. But knowing she had been captured by the Indians, he was, at first, suspicious of lurking savages around her. However, with their trusty rifles in hand, they all ran towards her. The joy of the poor perishing woman, upon seeing Harman, who was one of her neighbors, knew no bounds.

Mrs. Ingles was immediately taken by Harman to his cabin and tenderly cared for. He had plenty of bear meat and venison in store, some of which he cooked for her; but, knowing of the danger of her situation, he would only suffer her to eat a few mouthfuls at a time. Her feet and limbs were bathed; and, in a few days, she has improved greatly; so much, indeed, that she was soon taken on horse back not to her old home, for all the plantations in that section were deserted _ but to the Dunkers' Bottom, where a fort had been erected at a point on the west side of New River, three miles south of English's (Ingles') ferry, in what in now Pulaski county, Virginia. There she came to meet her husband; when, but for the memory of her two boys she left among the savages, far in the wilderness _ her happiness had been completed.[17]

Chapter Seven

First Military Expedition against Western Indians
1756

Although the Seven Years War was a contest between two civilized countries _ England and France; yet so far as the Western borders of Pennsylvania, Maryland, and Virginia were concerned, it was a conflict to repel the murderous incursions of the Western Indians _ allies of and instigated by the French, and not infrequently under their immediate direction; _ until diplomacy and the triumph of the British arms upon the Ohio, brought about, in 1759, a general peace with the tribes beyond the Alleghenies.

All along the frontiers of these Colonies, in the Fall of 1755, the savages were marauding upon the inhabitants; for the defeat of Braddock and the retreat of the remnant of his army, had cleared the passages of the mountains for the ready ingress of the foe. Every where in the back settlements, terror and desolation ensued. The fear and consternation inspired by the cruel visitations of the Indians, were dreadful. The roads were thronged with unhappy sufferers flying from their homes; _ without subsistence, beds, or clothing to defend them from the cool; their houses burning, their cattle shot down, and near and dear ones wantonly slain or hurried into captivity worse than death.

As yet, no expedition, in either of the three Colonies, had been organized exclusively against Indians in the West. The most that had been done by the borderers was, to pursue war-parties making incursions into the settlements, in hopes to overtake them _ kill the marauders and release the prisoners in Virginia, as these Indians were particularly troublesome to the counties of Frederick, Hampshire, and Augusta, which in 1755, included the whole of the Colony west of the Blue Ridge. There had been, in the latter county alone, seventy of the inhabitants, killed, wounded, or taken prisoner, since the commencement of hostilities.

It was not however until urged by some friendly Cherokees that the Governor of Virginia resolved to punish the Shawnees for their audacity and bloodthirstiness. An expedition was accordingly planned against them _ to rendezvous on New River, on the west bank of the stream, at Fort Frederick, then in Augusta (now Pulaski) county. It was the intention to cross from New River to the head waters of the Big Sandy down which the stream they would march to the Ohio; thence, to the Shawnee Towns. "I think the affair very practicable;" wrote Dinwiddie , "as the Cherokees have sent in one hundred and thirty men against the common enemy; and they propose, when joined with a number of our forces , to march to the attack of the Shawnees."[1] "I must heartily wish your party of Rangers, in conjunction with the hundred and thirty Cherokees," wrote Governor Morris of Pennsylvania, to Dinwiddie, "may succeed in their proposed expedition against the Shawnee towns."[2]

As soon as Washington received information from Dinwiddie of the intended expedition, he immediately dispatched, from Winchester, Virginia, <u>Major Andrew Lewis</u> of the provincials, a resident of Augusta county, to New River, to take command of the troops destined against the Shawnees. He was ordered to follow such directions as should be received from the Governor of the Colony.[3] Dinwiddie's instructions were largely discretional. "They are not particular," wrote Lewis; _ "he has left almost every thing to my management."[4]

Beside the Cherokees, under their chiefs, Ontacite, Yellow-Bird, and Round-O _ the two last commissioned as Captains by Lewis _ there were seven companies of provincial troops and two volunteers who rendezvoused at Fort Frederick for the expedition against the Shawnees; the whole force consisting of three hundred and sixty-five men.[5] As several days were consumed in providing a sufficient number of horses for the expedition, and to prepare pack saddles for them, so as to transport provisions, ammunition, and other necessaries, the army was not ready to march until the eighteenth of February. The course taken was over the mountain to the "Bear Garden" on the North Fork of Holston, which they reached on Thursday, the twenty-third. Here they lost "sundry horses." Leaving the "Bear Garden" the next morning, they passed over two large mountains with great trouble and fatigue, reaching Burke's Garden _ so called at that date _ a remarkable spot completely surrounded by Clinch mountain, except at a narrow pass, through which flows Wolf creek, a southern tributary of New River. Here the soldiers found a plentiful supply of potatoes which they gathered from deserted plantations incipient settlement, the first within Burke's Garden. Numbers of the men went out hunting, bringing in fresh meat in abundance. That night it snowed. On the morning of the twenty-fifth, twenty Virginians and as many Cherokees, were sent forward with orders to wait for the main force either upon the head of Clinch or "Sandy creek" _ now known as the Dry Fork, in Tazewell county. The object of this movement was to range the woods in advance, as some tracks had been discovered which were believed to be those of enemy Indians.[6]

The army left Burke's Garden early on the morning of the twenty-sixth, crossing, with great difficulty, three large mountains, and arriving, after dark, at the head of the Clinch river,[7] where they met the detachment sent out the day previous, which reported no signs of enemy Indians. The whole force remained in camp the next day, some of the men spending the time hunting; _ several bears were killed. At ten o'clock in the morning, Saturday, the twenty-eighth, the army was again in motion, passing several branches of Clinch; and arriving, at length, at the head of "Sandy creek" (Dry Fork);[8] "when," wrote Preston, "we met with great trouble and fatigue occasioned by a very heavy rain and the driving of our baggage-horses down the stream, which we crossed twenty times that evening." "We encamped," adds the writer, "an hour before sunset; _ our hunters had good success _ three buffaloes and some deer."[9]

The army continued its march down the stream on the twenty-ninth; crossing it sixty-six times in a distance of only fifteen miles! The next day, March the first, they experienced "a great gust of thunder, hail and rain." Indian signs were seen, as on former occasions. On the second, their real troubles began. The men this day had but half a ration of beef, which was almost exhausted; no more was issued to them; so that their only reliance for meat, thereafter, was upon what they would kill. "This day," says Preston, "we came into the coal land."[10] They crossed the stream in a march of only three miles this day, eight miles.

On the third of March, the army was put upon an allowance of half a pound of flour for each man; and, although less than ten miles were traveled, yet the "Sandy" was crossed nineteen times.[11] Where the encampment was made that night there was no food to be found for the horses, which occasioned many to stray away. The next day, but little progress was made.[12] Before starting, a tedious search was made for the horses strayed off; some could not be found. The creek, down which the army was marching, was now considerably increased in size by several tributaries flowing in from either side; "which rendered it difficult," wrote Preston, "for our poor men to wade." "I sent out several hunters," he adds, "but they had no success; and nothing but hunger and fatigue appears for us."[13]

On Friday, the fifth of March, a little more progress was made than on the day previous; but the river being now very deep, and, in general, more than forty yards over, and often to cross, it almost killed the men. Their sufferings were the more poignant as they were in the utmost extremity for want of food. That night, they encamped not far above the junction of the stream with the Tug Fork of the Big Sandy. This day there was no appearance of a level country, although it was wishfully looked for. "My horse expired," wrote Preston, "and was left on foot with a hungry stomach, which increased my woe."[14] Indeed hunger was one of "woes" of every man in the army, at this juncture.

The Tug Fork[15] was crossed on the sixth, at a point immediately above the mouth of the Dry Fork, when the army encamped. Their horses were turned out to gain a scanty supply of food among the seeds. One of the volunteers killed an elk, but the Cherokees took half of it by force, as they were well nigh famished. "We were now," writes Morton, "in a pitiable condition; our men looking on one another with tears in their eyes, and lamenting they had ever entered into a soldier's life." "Indeed." continues the writer, "our circumstances were shocking; for, in our camps, was little else but cursing, swearing, confusion, and complaining."[16]

At this point, the Cherokees proposed to make bark canoes to carry themselves down the river. This suggestion was not lost upon the remaining officers, who immediately set men at work constructing a large one to carry down the ammunition and what little flour remained, also some smaller ones. It was, indeed, an imperative necessity; as the small number of pack-horses left was fast giving out. On account of suffering from hunger, mutiny among the men was imminent; but the Indians kept up an excellent discipline, notwithstanding the fact that starvation seemed to stare them in the face. They were accustomed to such trials. "The men murmur very much," records Preston, on that day, "for want of provisions; and numbers threaten to return home."[17] "Our strength is almost exhausted," wrote Morton."[18] Evidently a crisis was approaching. Major Lewis became very much concerned. To please the men, he ordered a cask of butter to be divided among them. But this was no more than a taste to each man. To add to the general alarm, it rained very hard all that night, and no tents to protect from the chilling storm .

The next morning, Sunday (the seventh), a council of war was called. It was agreed that a detachment of one hundred and thirty men would proceed down the stream fifteen miles, and no further, in search of hunting grounds, there to await the arrival of the commanding officer, with the remainder of the men, who were to tarry where they then were and complete the canoes. The Cherokees opposed this, but were overruled, and the advance set out with only a single pound of flour to each man to last until Major Lewis and the remainder of the men should overtake them. The party had not gone above two miles before the horsemen were obliged to leave the river and turn up a small creek, "a difficult, rocky and very bad way;" thence they passed over a steep and high mountain, to another little creek down which they pursued their toilsome course to the river again, where the found the foot men, who had made their camp at a distance of only six miles from the place of starting.

It was now evident that matters were getting worse than ever; the river had become impassable for horses; the mountains were higher and lying in larger cliffs on the stream. Those who had been buoyed up with the hopes a level country and better hunting grounds were now greatly discouraged. A great number resolved to break off homeward the next morning, but afterward condescended to continue another day _ down the river. It was proposed by one of the Captains, to kill horses for food; to this, the men objected, saying it might answer, if they were returning, to support them home; but it was not proper food to sustain soldiers encountering every hardship, on a long march against an enemy. This reasoning looked, of course, to an immediate return and a desperate alternative.

The same trials were encountered, the next day, by the detachment, in their attempts to move down the "Sandy," as on the preceding one; _ rugged mountains, steep cliffs, hunger, and despair. Luckily, however, one of the volunteers killed, that day, two elks, "to the no small joy of every man." "By that time," says Preston, "hunger appeared in all our faces, and most of us had become weak and feeble." "Had we not got that relief," he continues, "I doubt not several of the men would have died of hunger; their cries and complaints were pitiful and shocking."[19] A tedious march of seven miles _ and their camp was pitched upon the banks of the river. As they had reached the limited distance of fifteen miles from "the forks" very nearly, their marching was ended until the commanding officer could be heard from. "We can see nothing before us," writes Morton, "but inevitable destruction."[20]

On the morning of the ninth, the volunteers had the good fortune to kill two buffaloes and an elk. The men, however, still continued to murmur. Quite a number went out to hunt and view the country; some went seven or eight miles down the river and returned that night, reporting several prodigious mountains ahead; that the stream seemed to bear to the westward, and no probability of being able to travel with horses along its banks; and that no game was seen. These reports had a very dispiriting effect upon the detachment; they agreed almost to a man to set out on their return home the next morning. However, the officers made every exertion and prevailed upon their men to stay until Major Lewis should arrive with the remainder of the troops. The next day a letter was dispatched up the "Sandy," urging the commander to hasten forward, as confusion and disorder were prevailing in camp; _ that the men were suffering with hunger and nothing remained for their subsistence. During the afternoon, intelligence was received that the canoes were to leave the "forks" that morning. But there was, also, this ominous addition, _ that a horse had been killed to support the men, who were almost perished with hunger.

On the morning of the eleventh, notwithstanding their promises to remain until the arrival of the commander, the men manifested a determination at once to take up their line of march homeward. After many arguments and persuasions, they were finally prevailed upon to wait that day for the coming of Major Lewis, as also for the report of one of the men who, with a companion, had been sent down the river, and had been out three days making observations. A little venison was procured allaying in a slight degree, the pangs of hunger; and about noon two Indians arrived in a canoe from the "forks," reporting that the upper companies would be down that night. In the afternoon, the men sent below returned with the information that they had proceeded fifteen miles down the "Sandy;" saw a large buffalo path, and fresh signs of those animals and elks; that they saw great numbers of turkeys, and were of the opinion that game was plenty; that they found an old fort which they believed was an Indian hunting-fort; and that they thought the main mountains was not more than two miles beyond.

While the report from below greatly pleased and cheered the officers, it rather increased the mutiny among the men; who looked upon it as found only to draw them still farther from home. They reasoned that, _ were the game so plenty, it would be utterly impossible to support the whole army upon it as there was nothing else to depend on; and, should they proceed any farther, they would eventually perish with hunger, which they looked upon as more inglorious than to return and be of service to their country, when properly provided for. "These and many other weighty arguments," wrote Preston, "they made use of, but through the whole, they laid great part of their misfortunes on the Commissioners for not providing necessaries for such a number of men." the truth was, as the writer adds, _ "We had not above fifteen days provisions when we left Fort Frederick, to support us on a journey of near three hundred miles."[21] That night, ten of the men started off _ the beginning of the end.

A dispatch was sent, the next morning, to hasten the arrival of Major Lewis, as the men were in readiness to march homeward, despite every entreaty of their officers; some were disarmed, and brought back, by a detachment which still felt willing to obey orders. Just at this juncture, Captain Woodson arrived from the "forks," with some of his company, bringing intelligence that his canoe had overturned, losing his tents and every thing valuable in it; that the commander's was also sunk and several articles of value lost, particularly five or six fine guns. Soon after this recital, Major Lewis reached the camp with only two men. The upsetting of his canoe, he gave as the reason for his having been so long detained. He left Captain Hog with his company to bring down the baggage. He met the party of ten men who had left for home the day before. They declared they had the consent of their officers who would have gone with them but fear of their superiors.

Saturday, the thirteenth of March, brought matters to a crisis, the commander gave orders for each Captain to call his company together immediately. When all had assembled he told the soldiers he was informed of their design to go home and that he was much surprised at it. He hoped they would change their intentions of mutiny and desertion, and continue the journey. He set forth the ill-consequences that would certainly attend such conduct. He felt confident, there would be abundant supplies when they reached hunting grounds which he believed were very near. At all events, their horses would support them for some time. But starving men could not be reasoned with. Notwithstanding all that could be said, the soldiers were determined to retrace their steps. To go forward was either to eat horses or perish _ an alternative too dreadful for contemplation, while marching against an enemy.

An expression was now taken as to the number present desiring to go forward with their commander and share his fate. Only the officers and a score of the privates responded favorably. Immediately the return march commenced. Montgomery's volunteers were the first to go; followed, however, in a short time, by nearly the whole of Preston's and Smith's companies; and, in the afternoon, by Dunlap's volunteers. Major Lewis spoke to the Man-Killer, who seemed most grieved to see the men move off. The old chief said he was willing to proceed; but some of the warriors and young men were yet behind, and he was doubtful of them; but would sent a messenger to bring them down _ which he did. He said white men could not bear abstinence like Indians; "Indeed," writes Preston, "hunger and want were so much increased that any man in camp would have ventured his life for a supper." "And it is impossible," he adds, "to express the abject condition we were in both before and after the men deserted us."[22] Thus ingloriously terminated the onward movement to attack the Shawnees upon the Ohio. Upon the north bank of the Tug Fork of the Big Sandy, less than fifteen miles below the mouth of the Dry Fork, was made the last camp, outward bound, of this ill-starred expedition.

The particulars of the return of the Expedition have been vaguely preserved by uncertain traditions; but all agreeing in this, that there was great suffering for want of food. This could hardly have been otherwise, considering the want and misery which prevailed at the beginning of the journey homeward. When horse-flesh and buffalo hides were exhausted, strings of moccasins, belts of hunting-shirts, and flaps of shot-pouches were eaten. It was the first military movement ever organized upon the Western border solely against the Indians.[23] "It was an expedition," wrote Washington, from Winchester, Virginia, on the seventh of April, "from which, on account of the length of the march, I always had little hope, and often expressed my uneasy apprehensions on that head.[24]

Chapter Eight

Armstrong's Kittanning Expedition
September, 1756

The Spring of 1756, was one long remembered upon the Western borders of Pennsylvania, Maryland, and Virginia, on account of the continual depredations of the savages. Small parties of Indians _ Shawnees and Delawares; for the most formidable part of these nations had joined the French[1] _ penetrated into the settlements, struck a fatal blow, and then retreated, generally before an availing pursuit could be made. Their almost certain success only made them the more audacious. Carlisle, Frederick, and Winchester had become frontier Towns of their respective Provinces _ so great was the depopulation of the back country. Forts and block-houses were erected at the most exposed points, and were occupied by provincial troops who ranged the intervening distances. Many of the inhabitants sought these posts for their personal safety from the ferocious and blood-thirsty savages.

In Pennsylvania, the most important of these forts west of the Susquehanna were Fort Lyttleton,[2] near an upper branch of Aughwick creek, a southern tributary of the Juniata, in what is now Dublin township, Fulton county; Fort Shirley within the present limits of Shirleysburgh, Huntingdon county, on the east side of, and about one fourth of a mile from Aughwick creek;[3] and Fort Granville, on the north-bank of the Juniata, about a mile west of the present Lewistown, county-seat of Mifflin county.[4] All the forts were erected in January, 1756, and all were within what was then the county of Cumberland, which included the whole of the Province west of the Susquehanna, except the territory now constituting the counties of Adams and York.

Minor works of defense also dotted the wilderness of Cumberland, helping to form a chain of "forts," reaching from a point on the West Mohantango, near what is now the northern boundary of Juniata county, twelve miles from the Susquehanna, where "Pomfret Castle" was marked out, _ to the Juniata, in a south westerly direction; strewn thence to the Aughwick and west branch of the Conocheaque, beyond all which, there was scarcely any vestige of civilization.[5] But these fortifications, although garrisoned by four provincial companies, all proved of little avail against a foe, moving "with stealth and mystery, only to be traced by its ravages and counted by its footprints." The savages not only laid waste the exposed settlements, but occasionally appeared in the vicinity of a fort; watching an opportunity to tomahawk and scalp one or more of its garrison or take a prisoner. Sometimes they would boldly invest an out-post ,and, if the work was weak, as many were, especially such as were erected by the settlers, capture and burn it, killing or carrying off all who had taken refuge within it. Such was the case with "McCord's Fort," a private fortification, which was destroyed in April, and many captives taken.

Fort Granville, situated, as it was, upon the Juniata whose head-springs are far up the Allegheny Mountains to the westward was soon brought under the surveillance of the savages. They began to make their appearance in the vicinity of the fort as early as the last of March. Soon after, two of the garrison were wounded within sight of the post. A detachment was sent in pursuit of the enemy, but could not come up with them. The Indians thus far had not made their marauds in larger parties either in the settlements of Cumberland or near its fortifications, but distributed themselves in different places, along the frontier, in small numbers, sometimes accompanied by a Frenchman or two. As a protection to the inhabitants, parties, made up of detachments from the various companies stationed in the several forts upon the frontier, ranged the woods in various directions as far to the westward as their provisions would justify; but these scouts, the wily savages generally succeeded in eluding.

Early in July, Governor Morris, of Pennsylvania, received intelligence that a number of French and Indians would soon be on the warpath; that they were gathering to the westward and would strike the settlements, in harvest time. Orders were immediately dispatched to the forces upon the frontiers of the Province beyond the Susquehanna, to be on their guard; and directing them to be disposed in such a manner as would most effectually assist and protect the people while gathering their grain.[6] This would necessarily draw off a large portion of the garrison in some of the forts, and, as a consequence, greatly weaken theie efficiency _ possibly result in the capture of some one of them; but the commands of the Governor were nevertheless, strictly obeyed. On the twenty-second of the month, a party of sixty Indians appeared before Fort Granville, and after a vain attempt to draw out the garrison, divided themselves into small parties and fell upon the exposed settlements.

Sometime during the month, a war-party of the enemy was made up at Fort Duquesne, consisting of twenty-three Frenchmen, and thirty-two Indians, under Neyon de Villiers, a Lieutenant for a foray upon the back settlements of Cumberland county, or to attack some of the forts in the vicinity.[7] In immediate command of the savages was Captain Jacobs. On the thirtieth, they appeared before Fort Granville and immediately commenced an attack. The post at this time was in command of Lieut. Edward Armstrong who had, as his garrison, only twenty-three soldiers of Capt. Edward Ward's company of foot. The men were provincials _ all in the pay of Pennsylvania. The residue of the company, with their commander, had been drawn off to Sherman's Valley,[8] in what is now Perry county, to protect the settlers while harvesting. Besides the provincials there were, in the fort, three women and seven children. The officer next in command under Armstrong was John Turner.

The enemy attacked the fort with great energy during the afternoon and until near midnight, but they were gallantly opposed by the garrison. Lieut. Armstrong especially distinguished himself. Just at this juncture, the assailants attained a deep ravine, by which they were enabled to approach the fort completely protected by the bank, until sufficiently near to set it on fire. Through a hole this made, they killed the brave Lieutenant and one private and wounded three others who were endeavoring to extinguish the fire. The enemy now offered quarters to the besieged, if they would surrender, when Turner immediately opened the gate to them. One of the prisoners was tomahawked; the residue, loaded with burdens, were hurried off and the fort burnt to the ground. Only one of the garrison escaped.[9]

Turner's fate was a terrible one. Before the commencement of the war, he had killed an Indian, and was now recognized as the offender. He was, as a consequence, made the victim of the savages' cruelest resentment. Taken with the rest of the prisoners to Kittanning, an Indian town on the Allegheny river, _ having to carry an unmerciful burden the whole distance _ he was put to death with the most horrid cruelties. He was first tied to a black-post; then the savages danced around him; afterward, gun-barrels heated red-hot were thrust into his naked body. For three hours he was tortured and then scalped _ still alive. Finally, an Indian boy was held up, with a hatchet in his hand, who gave him a finishing stroke. On a log near by, sat his wife with an infant son at her breast, compelled to witness the shocking spectacle.

Mary, the wife of Turner, was an English woman, whose maiden name was Crosley. Her first husband was Simon Girty, an Irishman, who emigrated to Pennsylvania at middle age. Married in the Province, they lived on the Big Island of the Susquehanna, at the mouth of the Conestoga, between what are now the counties of Mark and Lancaster, where their four sons _ Thomas, Simon, James, and George _ were born. Thomas was the eldest. Simon, according to the most reliable traditions persevered among his descendants, was born about the year 1741. James was the third son; George, the youngest.[10] The father while residing upon the Island, was engaged in the Indian trade.

In the year 1746, Girty moved up to "Chamber's Mill," on the east side of the Susquehanna, near the mouth of Fishing creek, six miles above the present Harrisburg. The morals of the place were far from being strict. The pious David Brainerd who visited the settlement in August of that year wrote: "Rode this day to one Chambers', upon the Susquehanna, and there lodged. I was much afflicted in the evening with an ungodly crew, drinking and swearing."[11] Girty continued, at this point, his old occupation of Indian trader.[12]

In the Spring of 1749, Girty moved his family across the river, into a cabin on Sherman's creek, in what is now Perry county. The settlers in this valley were all trespassers upon Indian lands, and the next year were forcibly ejected by the Government, and their cabins burned. The men were held in recognizance of one hundred pounds each to appear at Shippensburg _ the then county-seat of the extensive county of Cumberland _ to answer for their trespass.[13] Thereupon, Girty returned, with his family to Chambers' Mill.. At this "ungodly" place, not long after he was killed by an Indian, known as "the Fish," in a drunken frolic.[14] Joining with him, at the time, was Turner; who, afterward, having a good opportunity, murdered "the Fish;" _ thus avenging the death of his friend and employer.[15] Turner married the widow Girty, and sometime subsequently, but previous to the attack upon Fort Granville, moved to Sherman's Valley, where his son John was born. The four step-sons _ Thomas, Simon, James, and George, with the mother and her infant, _ were all made prisoners when Turner opened the gate of the fort, and were taken, with him to Kittanning,[16] where they were unwilling witnesses of his frightful suffering.

The condition of the frontiers west of the Susquehanna, immediately following the destruction of Fort Granville, was most deplorable. One year previous, there were, in the county of Cumberland, nearly three thousand fit to bear arms; now, exclusive of the Provincial forces the number had been reduced to less than one hundred. The harvest of 1756, had been unusually abundant; but the farmers abandoned their plantations, and left what grain was not stacked or carried into barns, to rot upon the ground. The outrages of a barbarous and savage enemy upon the remaining inhabitants of York county, who had continued to hold their possessions in face of the most imminent danger in expectation of soon seeing more happy days, were distressing in the extreme. They had hoped much from the erection of the chain of forts along the frontier; but now that one of the best of these fortifications was destroyed, all their prospects of safety and protection seemed at once to vanish; especially as Cumberland was mostly evacuated, and their own county _ including, at that date, not only its present territory but also that of Adams _ the theater of daily murders and captivities. "The people west of the Susquehanna," said Governor Morris in a message to the Pennsylvania Assembly, "distressed by the frequent incursions of the enemy, and weakened by their great losses, are moving into the interior parts of the Province; and I am fearful the whole country will be evacuated, if timely and vigorous measures are not taken to prevent it."[17] Very different in spirit were the words of Montcalm, the French commander, in Canada: "Our latest news from the Ohio river is excellent. M. Dumas, a Colonial Captain, who commands there, continues to devastate Pennsylvania." "Chevalier de Villiers," he added, "has, with fifty-five men, just burnt Fort Granville."[18]

Governor Morris had received repeated information from prisoners taken by the savages, who made their escape, that the Delaware Indian Town of Kittanning, situated upon the east bank of the Allegheny river, forty-five miles above Fort

Duquesne, and fully two hundred miles from the Susquehanna _ the sight of the present seat of justice of Armstrong county, Pennsylvania _ was a most prolific hive of mischief to the western frontiers of his Province; that there the savages, many of them, were fitted out for incursions upon the back settlements of Pennsylvania and the neighboring Provinces; that many of the captives and much of the "plunder" were taken there; and that the noted Delaware leader _ Captain Jacobs _ made that village his home. This rallying point for the hostile Indians must be broken up; and, if possible, the unfortunate captives liberated. The Governor, therefore, concerted an expedition against town, to be conducted by Lieut.-Colonel John Armstrong, of Cumberland a native of county Fermanagh, Ireland, _ then in the command of the Provincial forces west of the Susquehanna, who was to have under him several companies of Colonial troops and as many volunteers as could be engaged for the enterprise. The affair was to be kept as secret as possible. Fort Shirley was fixed upon as the place of rendezvous. It would be a most desperate undertaking, but the need of punishing the enemy was so great, that the expedition must go forward at every hazard.

On the twenty-seventh of August, 1756, William Denny who had just succeeded Morris as Governor, was informed by the latter, that he given Colonel Armstrong particular Instructions with regard to the proposed expedition against Kittanning; and in consequence of his orders, and agreeable to the plan concerted, the necessary preparations had been made; and that the army was on the point of setting out upon the enterprise.[19] Three days after; the whole force, consisting of "about three hundred" men,[20] were under way. Beside Col. Armstrong's own company, there were six others, all provincials, under the command of Captains Hans Hamilton, Hugh Mercer, George Armstrong, John Potter, John Steele, and Edward Ward. Their route from Fort Shirley lay up the Juniata to Frank's Town, an Indian village, on the right bank of the stream, about two miles below the present town of Hollidaysburg, in Blair county, at the mouth of Oldtown run;[21] thence along an Indian trace, which led through a gap in the Allegheny Mountains near "Burgoon's," on to Kittanning _ about eighty miles distant.

On the third of September, Armstrong reached "the Beaver Dams, a few miles from Frank's Town," where an advanced party was overtaken.[22] Here he was informed that some of his men having been sent out on a scout had discovered the tracks of two Indians about three miles on the east side of the Mountains, and but a few miles from the camp. "From the freshness of their tracks," wrote the Colonel, "their killing of a cub bear, and the marks of their fires, it seemed evident they were not twenty-four hours before us." "This," he adds, "might be looked upon as a particular Providence in our favor _ that we were not discovered." Leaving the Beaver Dams on the morning of the fourth, they reached, the evening of the fifth; a point "within fifty miles from Kittanning."[23]

It was adjudged necessary, on the sixth to send some of the men forward to reconnoiter the Town. _ to get the best intelligence they could concerning the situation of the enemy. An officer with one of the guides and two soldiers were sent off for that purpose. These were met the day following, on their return. They declared the road entirely clear of the foe, and that they had the greatest reason to believe themselves undiscerned. But it appeared from the rest of the intelligence they gave, they had not been nigh enough to the place either to perceive the true situation of it, the number of the Indians therein, or what way it might be attacked most advantageously. Notwithstanding this; it was determined to continue the march, and not to halt until very near the village; so as to be able to effect a surprise of the enemy about day-light the next morning.

Between nine and ten o'clock, a point then called Blanket Hill,[24] about six miles east of the town[25] was reached, when one of the guides reported a fire just ahead, with two or three Indians near. Whereupon, with all possible silence a short retreat was made and a consultation held as to the best method of proceeding without being discovered. The pilot again returned, assuring Armstrong, from the best observations he could make, there were not above three or four Indians at the fire.[26] It was now proposed to surround the savages and cut them all off; but this was thought too hazardous, for if but one of the enemy should escape, it would be the means of discovering the whole design.

As the light of the moon, on which depended the posting of the men for the attack upon the town, would not continue long enough to admit of their staying until the Indians at the fire fell asleep, it was determined to take a circuit around their camp and thus avoid them altogether. Lieut. James Hogg of Capt. Armstrong's company, with twelve men and the guide who had discovered the fire, were left behind, with orders to watch the savages, but not to attack them till break of day, and then, if possible to cut them off. As it was believed the village was only six miles distant, and as the road around the Indians' camp would be rough and incommodious, on account of the stones and fallen timber, it was resolved to leave the horses _ many of them being tired _ and the baggage, so as, if possible, to prevent any discovery.

By this interruption, the march was much retarded; but still more so, as they neared the town, from the ignorance of the guide who neither knew its true situation nor the best path leading to it. On this account, after crossing a number of hills and valleys, the front of the army reached the Allegheny river some distance below the main body of the village, to which point, they were guided by the beating of a drum and the whooping of warriors at a dance, rather than by the pilots. As the moon was now almost down it behooved the commander to make the best possible use of the remaining light. Just then, an Indian whistled in a very singular manner about thirty rods in their front, in the foot of a corn field. Those in advance immediately sat down when Armstrong passed silence to the rear and asked one of the soldiers by the name of Baker, who was his best assistant, whether that was not a signal to the warriors if the approach of the enemy. Baker answered, "no; it is the manner of a young Indian calling a squaw after he is through his dance." The fellow cleaned his gun, shot it off, and then laid down to sleep.

All this while, the soldiers were obliged to lay quiet and hush; and by the time the Indian had fallen asleep, the moon was fairly set. Immediately after, a number of fires appeared in the corn field; by these, Baker said, the savages lay, _ the night being warm; and that all would quickly be extinguished, as they were only designed to disperse the gnats. Soon the day began to break; and, as the men had marched thirty miles from their last encampment, they were mostly asleep. The line being long, the three companies of the rear were not over the last bluff. Some proper persons were now sent to have them advance, while the weary soldiers in front aroused to their feet. A proper number of the men under sundry officers, was then ordered to march from the foot of the hill where they were standing along the top of it to a point not less than a hundred rods distant, and as much further as would carry them opposite the upper part, or at least the body of the town. For the lower portion and the corn field, Armstrong kept the larger number of his men, as he presumed the warriors were there. He promised those sent along the hill, that he would postpone the attack in his quarter for eighteen or twenty minutes _ until they should have time to advance to the place assigned them. _ It was now broad day light; but a death-like silence reigned in Kittanning.

The time, having elapsed, the attack was commenced in the corn field, the men with as much expedition as possible rushing through its various parts. It was now day light, and the party above rushed down to the town. The first Indian seen came out of one of the houses, held up his hand to shade the light from his eyes, and stood in that position looking at the advancing party until five shots were fired at him. He then ran and with a loud voice cried out "shewanick!" _ White men. There was in the house, a young woman, a prisoner, who came out with her hands raised; but the guns were firing so fast she got frightened and ran back. She soon afterward was slightly wounded in the arm by a swan-shot. She then came out the second time, and was secured by the Americans; there was by this time a general rush toward the houses.

Captain Jacobs immediately gave the war-hoop, and, with sundry other Indians, cried out that the White Men were come at last, and that now they would have scalps enough; but, at the same time, the squaws and children were ordered to flee to the woods; _ as was related by English prisoners who were afterward rescued. The soldiers with great eagerness passed through, and fired in the corn field, where they had several returns from the enemy, as they also had from the opposite side of the river, where the Indians had a fort wherein were kept most of their prisoners. By this time, the whole town was aroused, and several made their escape, among whom were five Canadians, one of whom was a cadet.[27] Presently after, a brisk fire begun among the houses, which, from the one belonging to Captain Jacobs, was returned with much resolution. Armstrong immediately repaired to the spot and found that from the advantage of the house and the portholes, the savages had wounded several of his men, and some killed.

The commander finding that returning the fire upon the house was ineffectual, ordered the contiguous ones to be set on fire. This was immediately done by sundry of the officers and soldiers _ the Indians continuing their firing whenever a man presented himself, and they seldom missed of wounding or killing someone. Armstrong, in moving about to give the necessary orders and directions received a wound from a large musket ball, in the shoulder. The shot was fired from the house of Captain Jacobs. The savages were now called upon to surrender, but an answer was received from only one Indian who replied that he was a man and would not be a prisoner. He was then told in his own language he would be burnt. To this he answered he did not care, for he would kill four or five before the died. The soldiers by this time generally became careful in exposing themselves as it was seen the savages were pretty well armed.

As the fire commenced to spread and the smoke grew thick, one of the warriors to show his manhood, began to sing. A squaw in the same house and at the same time, was heard to cry. For this, she was severely rebuked by the men. By and by, the fire growing in intensity, two Indians and a squaw sprung out from one of the houses and ran for the corn field. They were immediately shot down by the soldiers. Following them, came the renowned warrior-chief Captain Jacobs, who jumped from a garret window.[28] But he, too, was shot. He was identified by his powder-horn and his bullet-pouch, which some of the English prisoners who were recaptured declared he had lately got from a French officer, in exchange for Lieut. Armstrong's boots he had brought from Fort Granville after that officer was killed. His body was also recognized by these captives, from the peculiar arrangement of the tuft of hair upon his head.[29] A price had been offered for his scalp by Pennsylvania, and he was supposed to have been killed some time previous, by a friendly Indian who had claimed and received the bounty offered.

During the burning of the houses _ about thirty in number _ the army was agreeably entertained with a quick succession of reports from charged guns, but much more so with the loud explosions of sundry bags and large kegs of gun powder with which at most every house abounded. When Captain Jacob's house blew up, the leg and thigh of an Indian, also a child three or four years old, were thrown so high, "they appeared as nothing and fell in the adjacent corn field." There was a large quantity of goods burnt, which the Indians had been presented with, by the French, but ten days before.

About the time the buildings were fired, Captain Mercer, having his right wrist broken by a ball, was taken to the top of a hill, above the town; with him were a number of the men and some officers. From this point, Indians were discovered to cross the river and take a course, as thought, leading to the rear of the army, to intercept the retreat. The party sent several pressing messages to the commander to leave the houses and retire to the hill, or the whole force would be cut off. But Armstrong determined to hold his ground until all the houses were set on fire. Then a retrograde movement to the high ground was made, which prevented a thorough search in the corn field and along the river side for the savages, and doubtless caused the loss of several scalps, besides some squaws, children and English prisoners. The commander now found time to have his wound dressed.

As the provisions of the army had been placed upon scaffolds some thirty miles back, except what were in the men's haversacks left with Lieut. Hogg and his party, and there were a number of the soldiers wounded, it was deemed best not to wait to destroy the cornfield, but to commence the homeward march at once. From apprehensions of being ambushed or surrounded, it was difficult for Armstrong to keep his men together. His march, therefore, for some distance did not exceed two miles an hour. The fears of the soldiers were heightened by the appearance of a few Indians, who, for some time continued to assail both wings in a desultory manner. However, they soon desisted. The only damage done by them was the wounding of one man, Andrew Douglas, shot through both ankles.

Upon the return of the army to the place where the Indian's fire had been discovered the evening previous, a Sergeant of Captain Mercer's company and two or three of his men were overtaken, who had run away in the morning immediately after the attack upon the town. These cowards had found Lieutenant Hogg, by the side of the path desperately wounded. This gallant officer when he came to assail the Indians in their camp, at daylight, as he was ordered, found to his surprise, _ instead of three or four, as had been reported by the guide quite a large party; indeed, as was afterwards ascertained, double his own number of men, one of whom was a Canadian. Before daybreak the party crawled near the Indians. One of the savages came toward them, and was likely to come too near, so they fired and missed him; whereupon all those at the fire ran leaving their guns but soon returned and secured them. Hogg and his men fought bravely against fearful odds, for an hour; when, having lost three of his men killed, and being himself twice wounded, _ his party fled; but he to save himself, hid in a thicket. During this time, the firing at Kittanning was distinctly heard by the combatants, which greatly cheered the Lieutenant and his surviving comrades, notwithstanding they were overpowered by numbers.

Lieutenant Hogg was taken along by the run-aways, when, after moving a short distance, four Indians appeared; upon which, they all fled, notwithstanding the wounded officer urged and commanded them to stand and fight. The result was one of the number was killed and the brave Hogg again wounded; but, as he had been put upon a horse, he made his escape, rode some miles upon the trail, and then died. Such were the facts; but the Sergeant when come up with, told the army quiet a different story.

He declared there were many more Indians than had made their appearance in the attack; that he and his companions had fought five rounds; and that he had seen Lieutenant Hogg and several others killed and scalped. He also declared that he had discovered a number of Indians turning themselves before the army. This information caused considerable confusion among the soldiers; so that the officers had much trouble to keep them together. The disorder was so great that the men could not be prevailed upon to secure what horses of the army the Indians who had vanquished the Lieutenant and his party, had left behind; _ except a few, which some of the bravest were induced to collect. The baggage was also left behind.

From this point, until the army reached Fort Lyttleton, on Sunday night the twelfth of September, the men were never separated, nor were they once attacked by the enemy. No one received an injury of any kind until the Allegheny Mountains were crossed, when one Samuel Chambers, having left his coat at the "Clear Fields," desired leave of Colonel Armstrong to go back for it and to bring in three horses which had been given out. The commander advised against it, but Chambers insisted on going; and finally received permission. When he came to the top of the mountain a party of Indians fired on him but missed him; Chambers then made his way toward Big Island in the Susquehanna. The Indians pursued him and on the third day he was killed. The army brought home seven English prisoners who escaped to them when the town was attacked. From these captives it was learned that on the very day Kittanning was destroyed, two batteaux of Frenchman, with a large party of Delawares and other allies, were to have joined Captain Jacobs at his town, and to have set out early the next morning to take Fort Shirley, or, as they called it, "George Croghan's Fort," and that twenty-four warriors, who had lately arrived, had started the evening before _ for what purpose they did not know; _ whether to prepare meat, to spy the Fort, or to make an attack on some of the back inhabitants.[30] These were the savages seen on the evening of the seventh, and were assailed with so much spirit by Hogg and his men on the morning of the eighth.

Captain Mercer, as the army was preparing to march homeward from Kittanning, was persuaded, wounded as he was, to take a different route on the return than the one followed on the way out; some of his men who were traders assuring him there was a shorter way. He thus, with Ensign John Scott, and a small number of privates[31] was separated from the main force. With them went four of the rescued prisoners. The party was attacked by the Indians and Mercer came very near, at one time, being captured. The young woman who was slightly wounded and early liberated, by the Americans when Kittanning was first assailed, was recaptured. Her fate was a most heart-rending one. She was stripped naked, bound to a post, and hot irons applied to her quivering flesh. "She screamed in the most pitiful manner," relates an eye-witness, "cried for mercy, but these worthless barbarians were deaf to her agonizing shrieks and prayers; and continued their cruelty till death released her from the torture!"[32] Mercer, was fourteen days in reaching Fort Lyttleton. For ten days he lived, on two dried clams and a rattlesnake with the addition of a few berries. As he approached Fort Shirley, he found a piece of dried beef which the soldiers on their return had lost. On trial, the Captain rejected this, as the snake was better. On the route, although his wrist was broken, he applied what temporary relief he could to the wound _ he was himself a physician; so that, upon his arrival it was "in a good way" of recovery.[33] The residue of his party, including the released prisoners, reached the settlements in safety.

Mercer was afterward promoted to the rank of Lieut.-Colonel. Accompanying the army of General Forbes in 1758 to the Ohio, and being present at the reduction of Fort Duquesne, he was left in charge of that important post. He was one of the Brigadier-Generals of the Revolution; was mortally wounded at the battle of Princeton, on the third of January, 1777, and died on the twelfth, greatly lamented. In him, the army "lost a chief, who, for education, experience, talents, disposition, integrity, and patriotism, was second to no one but Washington."[34]

Of the English held in captivity at Kittanning about one hundred at the fort across the river,[35] so that only eleven were retaken at the attack, all of whom arrived at Fort Lyttleton in safety. Among them, however, were none of the family of the ill-fated Turner, except Thomas Girty. The residue were divided among the Senecas, Shawnees and Delawares.

The loss of the army, under all the circumstances, was not a severe one. Seventeen were killed out-right and three of the thirteen wounded afterward died. Of the nineteen missing, all eventually came in save one _ Samuel Chambers. It was, impossible to ascertain the exact number of the enemy killed in the action, as some were destroyed by fire and others in different parts of the corn field. Besides, several were killed and wounded in attempting to cross the river. Upon a moderate computation it was generally believed that between thirty and forty were killed or mortally wounded. "Upon the whole," wrote the commander, "had our pilots understood the true situation of the town, and the parts leading to it, so as to have posted us at a convenient place, where the disposition of the men and the duty assigned to them, could have been performed with greater advantage, we had by Divine assistance, destroyed a much greater number of the enemy, recovered more captives, and sustained less damage."[36]

The destruction of Kittanning was a severe stroke on the savages. No expedition had hitherto reached any of their towns from the frontier settlements. Upon the Allegheny, they lived in a fancied security. They believed the English would not venture so far into their country. Now, however, they were undeceived. That they should be immediately urged on by an unquenchable thirst of vengeance, to retaliate the blow, is very probable. But should they rebuild their town, what security had they that in their absence on the war path, their wigwams might not again be laid in ashes? Such of the Delawares, therefore, as escaped the attack of their village, refused again to make that point their home. The spot continued as left by Armstrong _ a desolation. The Indians who survived the shots of his army retired up the Allegheny to Fort Venango, or down that river to Fort Duquesne, choosing to live thenceforth under the protection of their Forts.[37]

The success of the Kittanning expedition was hailed with delight in all the Provinces. Before this event, all the principal movements against the enemy had proved disastrous. But here was a victory gained by the provincial arm alone, and one which, in all its details could but challenge admiration of the English nation. Honors to the victors followed. On the fifth of October, the city of Philadelphia voted one hundred and fifty pounds "to be paid out in pieces of plate, swords, or other things suitable for presents," to the officers and towards the relief of the widows and children of those who lost their lives in the expedition.

On the fifth of January, 1757, Atwood Shute, mayor addressed Armstrong an official letter. "The corporation of the city of Philadelphia," said he, "greatly approve of your conduct and public spirit in the late expedition against the town of Kittanning, and are highly pleased with the signal of proof of courage and personal bravery given by you, and the officers under your command, in demolishing that place." "I am therefore ordered," he continued, "to return you and them the thanks of the board for the eminent service you have thereby done your country." "I am also ordered," added the writer, "by the corporation to present you, out of their small public stock, with a piece of plate and silver medal,[38] and each of your officers with a medal and a small sum of money to be disposed of in the manner most agreeable to them."

The reply of Armstrong on the twenty-fourth, from Carlisle, was modest and patriotic. "The officers employed in the Kittanning expedition, have been made acquainted with the distinguished honor you have done them, and desire to join with me in acknowledging it in the most public manner." "The kind acceptance," said he, "of our past services by the Corporation, gives us the highest pleasure and furnishes a fresh motive for exerting ourselves on every future occasion for the benefit of his Majesty's service in general, and in defense of this province in particular."[39]

Colonel Armstrong and his officers while receiving such substantial tokens of the esteem of their countrymen for meritorious deeds, did not forget that the gallantry and good behavior of those under them largely contributed to the good results of the expedition. They generously gave the privates their part of the money received from the government for the scalps brought in, likewise for the released prisoners, and also what "plunder" they secured; _ "an instance of generosity this, which shows that these gentlemen did not go against the enemy from a mercenary motive, but from as regard of the service of their King and bleeding country."[40]

Colonel Armstrong did not rest upon his laurels won at Kittinning. He served during the war, in most of the campaigns to the southward; _ was honored with the command of the Pennsylvania forces; and his general military conduct and spirit much approved by all who served with him.[41] He took an active part in Pontiac's War of 1763, against the savages upon the upper waters of the Susquehanna;[42] and, at the commencement of the Revolution, having an intimacy of many years' standing with Washington, was recommended by the latter to Congress on the thirty-first of August, 1775, for the office of Brigadier-General and received the appointment, the first day of March, 1776; whereupon he was ordered to the southern Department.[43] This office he resigned on the fourth of April, 1777.[44] He was afterward made Major-General of the Pennsylvania militia and, as such, fought at the battle of Brandywine and Germantown. He was one of the Major-Generals present at the famous council of war held at Valley Forge, eighth of May, 1778, when it was determined to remain on the defensive and await the coming of events.[45] He was a member of Congress from 1778 to 1780, and died at an advanced age in Carlisle, on the ninth of March, 1795. His character is summed with great accuracy in the few laudatory words inscribed on his tombstone; "He was imminently distinguished for valor, patriotism, and piety."

Chapter Nine

Destruction of Fort Loudon by the Cherokees
1760

The Cherokee Indians from time immemorial, had their homes in what are now the northern parts of Georgia and the northwestern portions of the present State of South Carolina. Out-lying Settlements finally drew to the waters of the Tennessee, until, near the heads of this river in the Savannah, came to be located their clustering villages. Like most other savage nations, they were almost always at war with adjacent tribes; but, between then and the English, peace had generally been preserved. It was not long, however, after the commencement of hostilities west of the Alleghenies, in 1754, before they began to give indications of being tampered with by French emissaries; an easy matter for the latter, who had to travel from Four Toulouse,[1] on the Coosa, only seven days, by an Indian trace over "a good, level way," to reach the Cherokees. The Colonies whose boundaries were contiguous to the territory occupied by this nation saw at once the necessity of endeavoring to put a stop to all such machinations.

As early as July, 1755, Governor James Glen of South Carolina, held a council with the Cherokees in their own country, brightening the chain of friendship and renewing the anxious covenant of peace with them _ at the same time obtaining a cession of land of prodigious extent. Territory was also stipulated for, upon which to erect two forts near the villages, to protect them against their enemies, and to be a retreat to their friends and allies, who were to furnish them with arms, ammunition, clothes _ in short, every thing they wanted! On the east bank of the Keowee, one of the branches of the Savannah, Governor Glen, soon afterward erected Fort Prince George, in what is now Pickens county, South Carolina _ in the very heart of their Settlements upon that river, and within gun-shot of one of their towns.

The Virginians were not slow in following up the good work so unsuspiciously begun by South Carolina. In the Autumn following, Dinwiddie also held a treaty with the Cherokees; the result of which was the arrival soon after in that Province, of one hundred and thirty warriors under their chiefs, Ouatacite,[2] Yellow Bird and Round-O, _ the same party that soon after joined Major Andrew Lewis in his unfortunate Sandy creek expedition. Thus it was that the wild mountaineers were brought into closer relations with their more civilized neighbors of the English Colonies.

Upon the Hiwassee, Tellico and Little Tennessee, upper branches of the parent stream, were located the Tennessee settlements of the Cherokee. Situated upon Tugalo and Keowee, head tributaries of the Savannah, were their Carolina Towns. From the "Great Island" in the Tennessee a short distance below the mouth of Tellico, extending up the river a distance of about twenty miles, there were no less than ten villages, the chief of which was Chota, the metropolis. All these clustering homes, _ the "Over-Hills" _ were within the present county Monroe, Tennessee, and were known as the "Upper Settlements." Not far away and included therein, were two towns, upon the east side of the Tellico. There were other villages above the Over-Hills, upon the Little Tennessee, all situated in what is now the Southwestern extremity of North Carolina. The first of these were the "Valley Settlements;" still farther up were the "Middle Settlements." In the northwest corner of the present State of South Carolina were located their " Lower Settlements." _ Such were the homes of the Cherokees at the beginning of the year 1756.

On the nineteenth of May, 1756, Governor Glen started from Charleston for the Over-Hills Settlements of the Cherokees, to build a second fort upon the territory of that nation. He took with him an Independent company under command of Captain Paul Demere and two provincial companies whereof John Stuart and John Postell were Captains; the whole numbering two hundred effective men . With them went several of the soldiers' wives and children. The services , also, of a competent engineer were secured, to draw the necessary plans and superintend the building of the work. Twelve cannons _ one-pounders _ were taken along. These were carried upon horses, _ saddles having been made, specially adapted to their transportation. Other materials, as well as implements, and a supply of ammunition and provisions, helped to make up the luggage of the three companies. The distance to be traveled was more than five hundred miles as then estimated, not a small portion of which was a wild, rugged, and mountainous region.

The arrival in South Carolina of William Henry Lyttleton as the successor of Governor Glen caused the return of the latter from the expedition after it had reached Fort Prince George. Captain Demere was put in command, in his place. From Keowee, a Cherokee town immediately across the river from that post, the forward movement commenced again. After reaching the first village _ Old Steooe _ of the Middle Settlements, Demere took what was known as the "Back Path," which lay more to the southward, leading through towns upon a branch of the Hiwassee, thence to a point near the confluence of the Tellico and Little Tennessee, in what is now Monroe county; _ making the journey in ten days from Keowee.

Not long after the arrival of the South Carolina forces among the Over-Hills Cherokees, Major Andrew Lewis, with Captain Overton and an escort reached the

Little Tennessee, from Virginia, whence they came, to induce the return with them, if possible, of a large body of warriors, to assist in the war against the French and their allies. Lewis not finding the fort, projected by Demere actually commenced, concluded to erect a small fortification with his own force. It was located on the north side of the river about five miles above the mouth of Tellico, and just across the stream Chota, the metropolis, in what in now Blount county, Tennessee. _ Lewis did not succeed in his mission, owing principally to the interference of a white man, an old trader among the Cherokees, by the name of James Bramer. The Major returned the first of October, with seven men and three women only of that nation. His fort was soon after demolished by the Indians.

The arrival of Demere in the Upper Settlements was hailed with every demonstration of joy by the Indians. His first care was the selection of a proper place for building the Fort. After a minute examination of the country, he determined upon a point on the south side of the Little Tennessee just above the confluence of the Tellico, in what is now Monroe county. It was in the immediate vicinity of Toskegee, one of the Cherokee towns. Nearby was a fine level spot secured to the men for planting corn. Every thing being in readiness _ a large space being cleared of trees and the ground staked off _ on the fourth day of October, the fort was commenced. The Indians who, up to this time, appeared highly satisfied and joyous, now brought in refreshments from all parts. One hundred men were constantly employed upon the fortification until the work was completed. For the support of the garrison, South Carolina made liberal provision; and it now seemed that the friendship of the Cherokee nation could be counted upon with a great degree of certainty. To the post was given the name of Fort Loudoun.[3]

After Col. Armstrong's successful expedition against Kittanning the inhabitants of the Susquehanna, in Pennsylvania, enjoyed a season of rest from the incursions of the savages. Many of the people who has been driven from their plantations returned to them. This respite, however, did not last beyond the middle of June 1757, when the Indians resumed their visits, continuing them at longer or shorter intervals until the Autumn of 1758. Nor were their inroads less constant, at this time, upon the borders of Maryland and Virginia. It was everywhere seen that a defensive warfare afforded at best only an indifferent protection against the encroachments of the enemy. To think of defending a frontier extending from the banks of the Susquehanna in Pennsylvania to the head waters of New River, in Virginia, against the merciless foe was idle and vain. Offensive measures were necessary. Fort Duquesne must be destroyed. When, therefore, that important post fell _ as it did in November, 1758 _ then, as had been so generally foreseen, the Western Indians sued for peace. Victories at the North protected, at the same time, the frontiers in that direction; and but for a concatenation of unfortunate circumstances the Southern frontiers would also have enjoyed repose from savage marauds.

For nearly three years, the Cherokees had continued to send help to the Colonies against the French and their Indian allies. Their aid, however, had been, as a general thing, productive of little good. Besides, when traveling through the back counties of Virginia, to and from their homes, they had been guilty, at various times, of depredations upon the property of the inhabitants. One of the parties on its return from Winchester, in May, 1758, by killing cattle, destroying plantations, and carrying off horses, aroused the Virginians to revenge, by force of arms, in which some of the Indians were killed; the rest fled.[4]

The Cherokees, to avenge the slain of their nation, sent out a company of warriors to bring in as many scalps as the Virginians had taken. They were to proceed as near where their braves had been killed as safety would permit, and there take satisfaction. The party set off, but advancing pretty far into the upper parts of North Carolina, instead of Virginia, the ambitious young Cherokees could not be restrained; so, separating into small companies, they killed as many settlers as unfortunately fell into their power, belonging to the province. The number who perished far exceeded their own. Upon their return, they shot two of the soldiers belonging to the garrison of Fort Loudoun, and a traitor.

It was many months after this before a general war was brought on; _ it was not fully inaugurated until the Spring of 1760. In the mean time, South Carolina being the most intimately concerned in the quarrel of account of the proximity of the nation to her western borders, espoused to a great extent the burden of the contest . Criminations and recriminations followed. Duplicity, perfidy and treachery were resorted to, by both parties; and yet there were those on both sides who were sincerely disposed for an agreement. But one outrage provoked another, until compromises and reconciliations were out of the question.[5] Meanwhile the situations of the garrison in Fort Loudoun became a matter of much uneasiness. Surrounded, as they were, by hostile Cherokees; their line of communication cut off, it became at once a serious question how they were to receive supplies, which, owing to the great distance from Charleston, and the mountainous region to be traversed, were very difficult of transportation at any time, but now utterly impracticable. So long as the Indians kept up a show of friendship, provisions, after much trouble, had continued to reach the fort. Late in the winter a convoy of hogs had arrived _ but that was the last. The number of men constituting the garrison was still two hundred strong, commanded by Captains Demere and Stuart, Lieutenants Adamson and Anderson, and Ensigns Boggs and Wanthe.

No sooner had the war-spirit pervaded all the Settlements of the Cherokees than energetic action was taken by them against the Carolina borders. To meet the shock, active measures were concerted by Lyttleton. His object two-fold: to humble the Cherokees and to retire Fort Loudoun. In March 1760, there were detached from the British army which had marched triumphantly to the Ohio, twelve hundred veterans under the command Colonel Archibald Montgomery and Major James Grant, to the aid of South Carolina; arriving in Charleston, on the first day of April. At Ninety-Six, a post at the eastern verge of the present county of Abbeville, in that State, Montgomery was joined by seven hundred Rangers. The march thence, on the twenty eight of May, was to the Lower Settlements of the

Cherokees. It was the determination of the commander "to burn and destroy all he should meet with" of property belonging to the enemy until Fort Loudoun was reached.[6] By the middle of June the Lower Settlements were a desolation. From sixty to eighty of the Indians were killed.

On the twenty-fourth of June, Montgomery began his march for the Middle Settlements of the Cherokees; but before there could be reached, the barriers of the Alleghenies would have to be passed _ "rugged defiles, which were as dangerous as men had ever penetrated." In two days more, the army had reached the valley of Little Tennessee. The next day, at a point about eight miles above the present town of Franklin, Macon county, North Carolina, and not more than one and a half below "Smith's Bridge," _ Montgomery fell into an ambuscade.

There was no lack of bravery upon that trying occasion; and the enemy were finally beaten back; but the army did not reach the first Cherokee village until midnight; suffering in the meantime a loss of twenty men killed, besides seventy-six wounded.[7] To go forward, now, the commander must abandon his sick and wounded men as well as his luggage; for he was assured that however difficult he had found the passes to the first village of the Middle Settlements, they were not to be compared with those beyond. Although heartily lamenting the situation of the garrison at Fort Loudoun, and greatly fearing the bad consequences which might follow if it were not relieved, yet, as there was no fort wherein to lodge those who must be left behind, and to have secured a retreat, in case of defeat, it was judged impracticable to proceed further. He therefore resolved upon a retreat. On the first day of July, Fort Prince George was reached, the army arriving at Charleston on the eighth of August, bringing down to that city, one man[8] and thirty-two women of the Cherokees, the whole number taken during the expedition. Montgomery immediately embarked for New York, leaving behind four battalion companies of the Royal regiment for covering the frontiers, who were ordered to return to the Congress.

By the first of March, 1760, the garrison at Fort Loudoun began to feel the want of their usual supplies from the sea-board. On the fifth, the men were reduced to the short allowance daily of a pint of corn each with meat in proportion. In one of the chiefs of the Cherokees, Atta-kulla-kulla, or Little Carpenter, Captain Demere found a true and steadfast friend. He gave the commander timely and proper cautions and intelligence, and, when provisions grew scarce, aided in sending food secretly to the soldiers. Very different were the actions of Oconostata who surrounded the fort on the twentieth, with a large party, and for four days and nights in succession kept up a determined fire against the walls, but from so great a distance as to do little or no execution. The month of April brought no relief to the suffering garrison; the contrary, as the weeks wore away, increasing vigilance was manifested by the enemy. The determination of the Indians was to starve the fort, if possible, into a surrender. On the first of June, a friendly Indian conveyed into the fort from Hiwassee, four head of cattle _ a great relief to the suffering garrison.

On the third of June, everything seeming quiet and no Indians around the fort to be seen by the sentinels, two of the garrison, Lieutenants Morris Anderson of the Provincials and Thomas Smith of the pack-horsemen ventured out, but they had not gone above fifty yards, on the side of a hill before they were killed and scalped by some Indians who had concealed themselves behind a small log. Forty or fifty men sallied out, but too late to be of service. Immediately after, the Indians fired on the fort on all sides from the hills around, but were so well concealed that returning the fire was in vain. Great were the rejoicings in Chota over the scalps of Anderson and Smith. It gave the Cherokees so much courage that plans were laid to set fire to the fort and then take it by storm. Timely notice of these designs was sent by the Little Carpenter to Captain Demere who at once prepared for their reception; but the attempt was abandoned.

Notwithstanding the watchfulness of the savages, Captain Demere found opportunities, occasionally, to send off dispatches; but, on the fourth of June, the last one reached him from the settlements. It informed him of the march of Montgomery against the Cherokees and for his relief. The Indian sentinels, thickly posted in the surrounding woods, were eluded by the courier, and the news delivered to the eager Commander. The effect was too greatly revive the spirits of both officers and men. On the sixth, the Little Carpenter sent Captain Demere word that a runner had arrived at Chota, with an account of Colonel Montgomery's doings at the Lower Settlements and of his determination to serve the residue of the Settlements in like manner.

By the first day of July, the men in the fort were reduced to their very last shifts. They had not above about two or three weeks provisions at most and were obliged to kill what horses they could get, the flesh of which being eaten made them very sickly. Although Atta-kulla-kulla had continued their friend, they had of late, been able to procure, through him, but very little corn, as the Indians were short of that article themselves, or they had secreted it. After the seventh of the month, the garrison had nothing whatever of any bread kind.

When sufficient time had passed for the arrival of Montgomery, how eagerly the garrison peered into the dark woods around them, in hopes of catching a glimpse of his serried ranks! How intently they listened for the report of distant guns, heralding the approach of British troops! But all were doomed to disappointment. Soon, vague rumors reached the post, through Indian channels of course, of the defeat of the army. They had beaten Montgomery back, they said. They had taken from him two drums, one horse-load of ammunition, and a quantity of flour. Besides, "they had killed and scalped so many that their hands were sore." To all this, the garrison gave no credit. Yet it produced uneasiness in their minds. Captain Demere sent off, in the night, an express for their better information and satisfaction; fully expecting that the army would be met on the way. But the courier reached Fort Prince George on the tenth of July, only to learn, for the first time, of the retreat of Montgomery from the headwaters of the Little Tennessee. A suspicious circumstance in connection with the report of the defeat of he army was the activity now displayed by Oconostota, the Great Warrior. He spirited up his people by telling them he was sure of Fort Loudoun and all who were in it; "foe," said he _ and he now spoke the truth _ "they are almost starved." This coming to the ears of the garrison had a depressing effect. The Great Warrior, at the same time, followed up his words with action. He frequently caused the post to be surrounded, in expectation of its surrender.

When the men in Fort Loudoun could get no other intelligence than that the army under Montgomery had been attacked, defeated, and driven out of the Indian country, which the Cherokees continued to affirm, their hearts sank within them. South Carolina buoyed up with hopes of relief coming to the garrison from Virginia by the way of Holston river; but the promised aid never came, although strenuous exertions were put forward that end, all of which was unknown to Captain Demere. The obstacles in the way were numerous; they could not be overcome, notwithstanding the urgency was great. On the twenty-ninth of July, Demere found an opportunity to send a dispatch to Charleston. The situation of the garrison was represented as miserable beyond description. Truly did they say it almost seemed as though they had been abandoned and forsaken by God and man. They had given up all hopes of relief. They had no longer any horse-flesh to subsist upon; as the Indians, having discovered that some of the animals had been killed for food, took great care that none should come in their way.

The fort was constantly surrounded in such a manner, that nobody dared stir out of it, even for water or wood; and the paths were everywhere so well-guarded, that it was almost impossible for anyone to escape from the post. The garrison in their extremity made several ineffectual attempts to bring about a peace with the Indians; but the chiefs knew but too well that they were starving, and told them, in reply to their overtures, that they would soon be at their mercy, when it would be time to talk of peace.

The chief who had special charge of starving the garrison into a surrender was Willinwaw, head man of Toyua, a village situated between two and three miles above the fort. This chief threatened with death anyone who should carry food to the garrison; but some of the soldiers having married into the nation, continued to be recipients of small supplies of beans and poor pork, from their devoted squaws who to relieve their
husband braved every danger. They boldly told Willinwaw that they would continue their kind offices, and that if he killed them, their relations would make his death atone for theirs, according to the usual custom of the Indians.[9] Of course such precarious supplies offered but little relief.

The men were now becoming excessively weakened; and it was plainly evident they would soon be incapable of any duty. The officers had long endeavored to encourage and animate them; until, finally, every hope had fled _ no succour came. Some threatened to leave the fort; and on the nights of the fourth and fifth of August considerable parties went off; a few had previously thrown themselves upon the cruel mercy of the savages. Then the garrison generally threatened to abandon the officers and betake themselves to the woods. Captain Demere was thus reduced to the dreadful alternative of perishing by hungry or submitting to the enemy.

On the sixth of August, Captain Demere held a council of war, the object of which was to concert the best measures to be pursued in their fearful condition. After consultation, the officers gave their unanimous opinion, in writing, that it was "impracticable to maintain the fort any longer; and that such terms as could be procured from the Indians, consistent with honor, should be immediately accepted of, and the fort abandoned." Thereupon Captain Stuart was sent to Chota, the Great Warrior's town, accompanied by Lieutenant Adamson and some Indians to treat with the Cherokees. In this attempt they were successful; as quite favorable terms were obtained.

It was agreed that the garrison should march out with their arms and drums; each soldier having as much powder and ball as the officers should think necessary for the march; and what baggage he might choose to carry. It was further agreed that the troops should be permitted to march for Virginia or Fort George, as the commanding officer should think proper, unmolested; and that a number of Indians should be appointed to escort them, and to hunt for provisions on the march. It was also stipulated, that such soldiers as were lame or by sickness disabled from marching, should be received into the Indian towns; and kindly used until they recovered; then to be returned to Fort Prince George: that the Indians should provide the garrison with as many horses as they conveniently could, for the march; agreeing with the officers or soldiers for payment: and that the fort, "great guns,"[10] powder, ball, and spare arms should be delivered to the Indians without any fraud, on the day appointed for the march of the troops. On the seventh, the Articles of Capitulation were signed by "Captain Paul Demere, commanding his Majesty's forces at Fort Loudoun and the two chiefs, Cunni-Coloque and Oconostata, of the Cherokees."

On the eighth, Captain Demere sent a dispatch to Lieut. Governor William Bull, of South Carolina acquainting him with the fact of the Capitulation and the reasons therefore. The letter was entrusted to Charles McLamore, a mulatto, who had been among the Cherokees ever since the commencement of the war. Accompanying him was an Indian named Cappy, son of a Cherokee chief, Old Hop. The commandant hoped the surrender of the fort would be approved of, considering the great distress they were in. He assured the Lieut.-Governor that they would have been obliged to abandon the post that day, happen what would. The garrison he said would set out the next morning, flattering themselves the Indians would do them no harm, and that they would make all the dispatch their starved condition would admit of.

The Cherokees, in their conference with Stuart, seemed desirous of peace. They said they would expect that immediately upon the arrival of the garrison at Fort Prince George, the prisoners confined there would be released. They then hoped all thoughts of further hostilities would be laid aside, and an accommodation heartily set about; and that a firm peace and well-regulated trade established, "such as," said they, "may last forever." Nothing could be discovered in their behavior that seemed to contradict their words. By the surrender of the fort the savages would come in possession of the twelve cannon, - "great guns," as the Indians termed them _ about one thousand pounds of powder, with balls in profusion, and about eighty small arms. Captian Demere determined to march for Fort Prince George, distant about one hundred and forty miles, upon the route he had marched when coming to the Over Hills, in 1756.

On the ninth of August, the garrison marched out of Fort Loudoun with their arms and eighteen rounds of ammunition; their powder-horns full, and some buck-shot in their pouches. With them were the women and children, belonging the soldiers. They traveled that day as far Cane creek _ then so called _ about sixteen miles from the fort, where they encamped. Oconostota and Outacite promised to set out with them; but they failed; _ neither they or any other Indians accompanied them. The two chiefs said they would come to them at Cane creek. Outacite came late in the evening, and, after speaking with the officers, went off towards Tellico, one of the Cherokee villages, not very far away. Oconostata did not make his appearance according to promise. There were suspicious circumstances; and Captain Demere placed a guard around the camp.

The next morning after the reveille, and while the preparations were making for the march, suddenly two shots were fired by Indians and Captain Demere was wounded. Lieutenant Adamson who was standing near caught sight of the savages, returned their fire and wounded one. Then the war-hoop was immediately given; and volleys of small arms with showers of arrows were poured in upon the party from every side, by about seven hundred Indians. This was continued for some time as the garrison advanced, putting them into the greatest confusion. Seeing it impossible to save themselves, they called out to one another not to fire, and surrendered themselves the perfidious enemy. By this time, all the officers, except Captain Stuart and a Sergeant were killed and thirty two privates; also three women. There were many wounded.[11]

Sad was the fate of poor Demere. After receiving two wounds, he was scalped and was then made to dance around for some time! Subsequently they chopped off one of his arms; and finally his legs! _ When death put an end to his terrible sufferings. The most shocking barbarities were perpetrated upon the bodies of the others of the slain. Every Indian, as soon as the affair was over, stripped his prisoner or prisoners. They were then taken to the various towns; having, as they marched forward reeking scalps frequently thrust into their faces. Upon their arrival at the Indian villages, they were driven into the "junker yards" of the savages and there beat and abused in a most inhuman manner. To amuse their captors, they were obliged to dance for several nights; but none are known to have suffered torture except one of the women who, subsequently, was tied to a stake and shot full of arrows. In the course of time, all who survived, either made their escape or were delivered up, generally at heavy expense, to Virginia or the Carolinas.

Of all the prisoners, no one had a stranger rescue, than Captain Stuart. When first attacked on the morning of the tenth he ran towards the creek and called to the men to stand to their arms. He was soon after seized by an Indian, a brother of Round-O, and forced across the stream. On the twenty-seventh of the month, he was offered his liberty if he would, by managing the cannon taken from the fort, which in the mean time, had been moved to Chota, assist the Indians in reducing Fort Prince George. This post, they were to go against, on the sixth of September. Stuart, of course, refused to purchase his freedom in so base a maneuver; but fearing he might be compelled to aid the savages, appealed to the Little Carpenter. That chief immediately purchased him at a considerable price of the fellow who captured him and then set about devising ways and means for his escape. Upon Reed creek, in Virginia, was the camp of Colonel William Byrd _ the nearest point of safety in that direction. To that place, he resolved to pilot the Captain in person. To allay suspicion in the minds of the other Chiefs, he gave out that he was going hunting, to be absent six days, at the same time taking with him his wife and brother, two young fellows, "and a wench." He succeeded, undiscovered, in taking with him not only Stuart, but the servant of the latter, together with William Shorey the interpreter at Fort Loudoun and one Johnson. On the fourteenth of September, all arrived safely at Byrd's Camp; showing, on part of the Little Carpenter, a persistence of fidelity and attachment such as the world has rarely seen.

South Carolina again made application to the Northern army for help against the Cherokees. As Canada was now reduced and the Seven Years' War at an end, the commander-in-chief of the British forces early in 1761, dispatched an adequate detachment under Grant - now a Lieutenant-Colonel _ to the relief of that State. Aided by provincials, the Middle Settlements of the Cherokees were soon reduced to ashes, but not until the Indians had fought and lost a battle in their mountain fortresses. Then they sued for peace. It was granted; and the Cherokee War was ended.

Chapter Ten

<u>Ambuscade of the Devil's Hole</u>
14 September, 1763

On the eight of September, 1760, the Marquis de Vaudruiel surrendered Canada, with all its dependancies, to the British crown _ the end of the Old French War. It has already been shown that two years previous the Western Indians broke their alliance with the French; and but for the hostile Cherokees the borders of the English premises would have been free from the predations of the savages. With the single exception of that tribe, all the nations, upon the surrender of Canada, if they did not give evidence of active friendship continued very passive enemies. With but little show of disapprobation on their part, the British flag was soon raised over all the French posts upon the waters of the Ohio and the Great Lakes; and they saw with astonishment the scepter pass from the hands of the French without further resistance and with no attempt at retaliation.

The year 1762 was a year of repose _ but of that calm which precedes the tempest _ of that stillness which is the precursor of the hurricane or the earthquake. When, early the next year, it was made known to the Indians far and near that France had ceded all their country without saying "by your leave," there was a general burst of indignation against the would-be recipients of their soil. "A plot was matured, such as was never, before or since, conceived or executed by a North American Indian. It was determined to attack all the English forts upon the same day; then, having destroyed their garrisons, to turn upon the defenseless frontiers and ravage and lay waste the settlements, until, as many of the Indians fondly believed, the English should be driven into the sea, and the country restored to the primitive owners."[1] The arch-plotter of this deep-laid plan was <u>Pontiac</u>, principal chief of the Ottawas.

Pontiac's home was with his band, upon the eastern bank of the Detroit River, not far below the foot of Lake St. Clair. The impolitic course of the English toward the Indian tribes, _ the disorders of the fur trade, military insolence, and French intrigue, caused the savages to take up the hatchet; but how, and where, and when the blow was to be struck, was wrought out by Pontiac alone. He sent his ambassadors to different nations; to those who dwelt upon the waters of the

Ohio, to the Mississippi, and the Great Lakes. This was in the Fall of 1762. A certain time in the month of May following, the rifle, the tomahawk, and the scalping knife were to begin the works of death. The announcement that the whole territory occupied by the savages had been ceded to England, only whetted their appetite for the slaughter. English garrisons and fur traders were to be the first victims, then the horrors of indiscriminate warfare were to be visited upon the frontiers everywhere.

As the time rolled around, the storm, so long gathering, burst forth with awful fury. "At first, some trader or hunter, weak and emaciated, would come in from the forest and relate that his companions had been butchered in the Indian villages, and that he alone had escaped. Next succeeded vague and uncertain rumors, of forts attacked and garrisons slaughtered; and soon after, a report gained ground that every post throughout the Indian country had been taken, and every soldier killed. Close upon these tidings came the enemy himself. The Indian war-parties broke out of the woods like gangs of wolves, murdering, burning and laying waste; while hundreds of terror-stricken families, abandoning their homes, fled for refuge towards the older settlements, and all was misery and ruin."[2] Pontiacs war was, thus fully inaugurated.

At this era, the Six Nations _ Iroquois _ occupied what is now the central portion of the State of New York; also the western part, to Lake Erie. These were the Mohawks, Oneidas, Tuscaroras, Onondagas, Cayugas, and Senecas. South of this Confederacy, upon the upper waters of the Susquehanna, were to be found Nunticokes, Connoys, Mohicans, with a portion of the Delawares. Westward, high up the Allegheny, were located detached band of the Iroquois. Mingled with them were several villages of Delawares. Most of the latter nation, however, had their homes upon the waters of the Big and Little Beaver, and upon the Muskingum and its affluence. The Shawnees dwelt upon the Scioto and its branches. North of them, in the valley of the Sandusky were seated a portion of the Wyandot nation; others of these Indians were located in the vicinity of Detroit. The valleys of the Maumee and Wabash were dotted with the villages of the Miamis and their kindred tribes. Beyond them, upon the river which bears their name, lived the Illinois, contiguous to the Mississippi. The Michigan peninsulas held to a large extent, the Chippewas, Ottawas, and Pottawattamies. Between Lake Michigan and the Mississippi, were the hunting grounds and home of the Kickapoos, Menomonies, Winebagoes, Sacs, and Foxes. Nearly all these nations except the Iroquois joined the Confederation; _ even a few Cayugas together with all the Senecas save two small villages became hostile to the English.[3] It was a wonderful and most formidable combination; such as one, indeed, as never before had been formed by savage tribes against British interests in America.

English posts upon the Great Lakes, the Ohio, and the Mississippi, were widely scattered. Frontinac at the foot, of Lake Ontario and Fort Niagara at its head guarded the portals of that inland sea. Fort Schlosser stood sentinel at the upper terminus of the Niagara portage; while the links of the chain connecting Lake Erie with the Ohio, were Fort Presyu' Isle, Fort Le Bouf, Fort Venango and Fort Pitt _ formerly Fort Duquesne. Upon the south side of Sandusky Bay, was Fort Sandusky. The head of the Maumee river was defended by Fort Miami. Fort Detroit frowned down upon the Detroit river; while Fort Michilimackinac watched the Strait of Mackinaw. Fort St. Joseph stood about thirty miles up the river of that name in the present state of Michigan; and at the head of Green Bay, Wisconsin, Fort La Baye kept guard over the entrance to Fox River, up the waters of which, Louis Joliet accompanied by Father Marquette, many years before, paddled his canoe to the discovery of the Upper Mississippi. Fort Ouatanin upon the Wabash and Fort Chatres below St. Louis completed the list of the wilderness posts. All these forts were far beyond the then frontier settlements of New York, Pennsylvania, Maryland and Virginia.

"The intelligence concerning the fate of the traders in the Indian villages proved but too true. They were slaughtered every where without mercy, and often under circumstances of the foulest barbarity."[4] And, although more than a hundred thus miserably perished, and all their property fell into savage hands, yet this was but the beginning of the dreadful catastrophes. Every post beyond the Niagara river, situated upon the waters of the Ohio and the Great Lakes fell _ Forts Pitt and Detroit only excepted. Many were take by stratagem; others were boldly assaulted and their garrisons compelled to capitulate. The tales that are told of the horrors which followed are melancholy in the extreme. The tomahawk and the scalping-knife were every where reeking with the blood of hapless victims; but, far worse _ far more shocking _ was the awful fate of those who suffered torture at the stake; and numbers were them immolated. Destruction and death ran riot all along the back settlements, from the Delaware in Pennsylvania to the Holston in Virginia.

To check the tide of carnage now rolling down the eastern slopes of the Alleghenies, and turn it back through the passes of the mountains, to the wilds beyond, was the arduous task imposed upon Colonel Henry Bouquet, commanding the first Battalion of "Royal Americans. With a force not exceeding five hundred men, Bouquet, in July, 1763, broke up his camp at Carlisle and started for Fort Pitt. His route lay along the army road of General Forbes in his march to the reduction of Fort Duquesne, in 1758. On this line were Forts Loudoun, Lyttleton, Bellford, and Seigoiner. After relieving the latter post, Bouquet encountered the Indians in force at Bushy Run. A battle ensued _ "one of the best controlled actions ever fought between white men and Indians." The savages were defeated. This conflict occurred on the fifth and sixth of August and was the turning-point of the war. From the victorious battlefield, the gallant little army marched to the effectual relief of Fort Pitt, which the infuriated savages had in vain assayed to capture.

Fort Venango was destroyed by the Senecas. They soon after, made a weak attack upon Fort Niagara. However, they quickly abandoned the project. Ever since early in May, Pontiac himself had closely besieged Detroit. Sir Jeffrey Amherst, British commander-in-chief at New York, in sending reinforcements, and supplies of ammunition and provision, to that post had of necessity to transport them by water _ along the line of Lakes Ontario and Erie and the rivers Niagara and Detroit. The dangers of the lakes were from storms only; upon the rivers, perils of the enemy beset the transports; especially was this the case in attempts to make the passage from Lake Erie to Detroit. Serious disasters had occurred there from savage attacks; but upon the lower river, where there but two forts as safeguards and but one tribe _ the Senecas _ to annoy, little trouble had been experienced, except during the brief period of the investment, by those Indians, of its posts, _ Schlosser and Niagara. But this was suddenly changed; and the awful voice of the great cataract was, for a time, heard as if chanting a requiem over many victims slain by the savages near the wild, headlong rush of waters.

A necessary link of the chain of communication between Fort Niagara and the post to the westward was the carrying-place, or portage, around the Falls. Men, military stores, merchandise _ in short everything to be transported to the Upper Lakes _ had to be here conveyed by land, a distance of about eight miles. The road, from the earliest period of French occupation, was upon the east side of the river.[5] It commenced at a point six miles below the cataract at the head of navigation. From the water's edge to the top of the bank and thence to the brow of the ridge which, at this point, intercepted the pathway, property of every kind was drawn by capstans of windlasses on tramways laid, where required, upon inclined plains. Before the construction of these mechanical aids, the Indians and French had great difficulty in climbing the steep acclivity, under their heavy burdens.[6] This commencement of the carrying-place was known as the Lower Landing; now Lewiston, Niagara county, New York.

From the summit of the ridge, the French portage-road ran along the east bank of the river as close as the nature of the ground would permit, to the Upper Landing _ striking the stream about a mile above the cataract. When the English took possession, the route was changed so as to reach the Niagara nearly two miles from the Falls. Near this point was the French post _ Fort du Portage _ which was burned in 1759. It was rebuilt by the British in 1760, and named Fort Schlosser.[7] After the brief investment of this post and Fort Niagara by the Indians early in the Summer of 1763, a fortified camp was established at the Lower Landing for the better protection of the portage. At this time, property was transported mostly upon wagons, drawn by ox teams. Pack-horses were also employed to a limited extent. In sending trains from the Lower to the Upper Landings, squads of soldiers were detached as guards. One of the principal duties fo the commander of Fort Niagara was attending to the safety of these convoys.

Perhaps in all the world beside, there is not short a distance so abounding in the awful and sublime as that which includes the Niagara river between the points then occupied as the two landings, concerning the great Cataract itself nothing need be said. Its wonders have a thousand times been described. The river, a short distance below the Falls, "assumes an aspect scarcely less remarkable than that stupendous scene itself. Its channel is formed by a vast ravine, who sides, now bare and weather-stained, run shaggy with forest trees, rising cliffs of appalling height and steepness. Along this chasm pour all of the waters of the lakes, heaving their furious surges with the power of an ocean and the rage of a mountain torrent."[8] The Whirlpool, three miles below the cataract, is a notable place. Here the waters have boiled and foamed, eddied and whirled, until an immense basin has been scooped out, where all floating bodies passing down the stream, circle round and round _ sometimes for days, and even weeks, before making their exit.

Half a mile below the American maelstrom is a deep cleft in the almost perpendicular bank _ a wild, dark cove, of about two acres in extent, wherein, according to an Indian legend, once dwelt a demon "of aspect dire," whose furious wrath, at the approach of white men, rent the rocks asunder. This famous locality is upon the eastern side of the river. The portage-road ran so near that the passer-by could look down into the frightful gulf to its very bottom _ a distance of one hundred and fifty feet _ through the forest trees whose tops failed to reach the summit of the cliff. "The mind can scarcely conceive of a more dismal looking den . A large ravine made by the falling in of the perpendicular bank, darkened by the spreading branches of the birch and cedar which had taken root below, and the low murmuring of the rapids in the chasm, added to the solemn thunder of the cataract itself, contribute to render the scene truly awful." This spot is known as the <u>Devil's Hole</u>.[9] Approaching the place from the Lower Landing, the road, about a half a mile distant, descended a small hill and wound along a flat piece of ground which continues to narrow until opposite the chasm where there is but little space left between the brink and a ridge to the eastward. Indeed, at this point, a small spur had to be passed over, when the track entered another and smaller flat, through which ripple the waters of a brook _ now called Bloody Run (suggestive name!) _ and then fall into the abyss below.

On the thirteenth of September, 1763, a considerable train of wagons and pack-horses started from the Lower Landing for Fort Schlosser, loaded with provisions, intended for Fort Detroit. Guarding this was an escort of twenty-four soldiers under the command of a Sergeant. Nothing occurred on the way up, to excite suspicion of an enemy near. The loads were all safely delivered at the post; and, on the following morning, the convoy set out to return, with the same escort as the day previous. Accompanying them were "Captain Johnson of the Jersey Blues, going down on some business."[10] and the contractor having charge of the transportation upon the carrying-place, whose name was John Steadman.[11] The ox teams and horses moved lazily along; the teamsters in their empty wagons were "whistling for want of thought;" while the soldiers, in fancied security, marched dreamily and with but little regularity, on either side of the slowly moving throng. Tradition says the day was a beautiful one _ the sun was shining in splendor _ birds were singing upon the branches of trees _ and, save in the perturbed river far below, all was serenity and peace. At eleven o'clock the Devil's Hole was reached.

Just as the head of the army had passed the edge of the chasm _ the rear, not yet having crossed the run _ the sudden and stunning report of a hundred rifles greeted the ears of the soldiers and wagoners. Following this were the cries of wounded and frightened men, the rushing of cattle, and the bounding of maddened horses. Then came the appalling war-whoop and the furious advance of a host of Indians from their hiding places. At the first discharge, many of the soldiers were killed. So stunned and stupefied with horror were the remainder that they made not the slightest resistance.[12] They were thrown at once into hopeless confusion. The savages fell upon them like tigers, tomahawking some of the teamsters in their seats. The uproar and carnage were dreadful. Horses and cattle, wagons and men, _ went over the precipice, crashing, in one dismembered and mutual mass, upon the rocks below. Some of the men, as they fell, caught in the branches of trees and were riddled with balls.[13] All was but the work of a moment; the destruction was terrible;[14] only three persons escaped.

The Indians who had successfully ambuscaded the train and its escort, were mostly Senecas from the Genesee river,[15] within the present county of Livingston, New York. The whole force numbered less than two hundred.[16] Their right wing was posted a short distance from the road; the center, just opposite the cliff; while the left was hidden south of the run.[17] The Indians had none killed and but one wounded. They took no prisoners. The slain were stripped naked, and so mangled, as a general thing, as afterwards to be unrecognizable. Sixteen oxen were killed; the residue, with what horses were not frightened over the precipice, were laden with the "plunder" and taken to a spot about a mile and a half distant from the river, in the woods, where the savages made their camp the night previous.

Of the three who got off, one was the conductor of the train _ John Steadman. Being mounted, and seeing the fatal effects of the onset around him and the utter hopelessness of the situation, he wheeled his horse, with a determination, if possible, to break through the Indian crowd and escape. That he should have, thus far, received no injury was a marvel. One of the savages, at this juncture, caught his bridle-rein; but quickly drawing his knife he freed himself; then plunging his spurs into the side of his horse, he darted into the woods, through a shower of bullets, entirely unscathed. Making his way, at full speed, through the forest, he reached, in around-about way, Fort Schlosser in safety. A drummer-boy, whose name was Matthews, was one who made the fearful leap over the precipice; but the strap of his drum catching in the branch of one of the trees, arrested his fall, so that he reached the bottom of the chasm but slightly injured; whence under cover of the river bank, he crept safely away, and succeeded in reaching the Lower Landing. One of the wagoners, also, wounded at the first fire crawled unobserved into the woods where he lay concealed until the Indians had gone, when he managed to get in to camp.

There were, at this time, occupying the Lower Landing, two companies of light infantry. These soldiers heard the distant sound of the firing at the Devil's

Hole, and at once conjectured that the convoy was attacked. The men, under four Lieutenants sallied forth to the rescue. But the Senecas anticipating this, had already moved about a mile farther down the road; and there in three divisions as before, lay in wait for their prey.[18] The soldiers, after leaving their camp, hastily formed at the top of the ridge and at once marched forward with all practicable speed, eager to encounter the enemy. In a compact body and precipitately, they rushed into the very jaws of death. The savages from their covert poured in upon the defenseless troops a volley that killed half of their number. With wild yells they rushed upon the rest of their victims. Every officer was slain. There was repeated the scene that had so recently transpired only a mile up the road _ wanting only, to be replete with horror, the dreadful precipice. A large number of dead bodies, naked, and mutilated, soon marked the spot of this second ambuscade. A small remnant of the two companies, only, succeeded in escaping the merciless ferocity of the savages.[19] They fled to Fort Niagara. The Senecas gathering up the spoils, returned their camp; and, by night-fall, were well on their way to the Genesee.[20]

Chapter Eleven

A <u>Perilous</u> <u>Journey</u> up the <u>Maumee</u>
1764

"<u>Preamble</u>. Some reason perhaps, ought to be assigned for my troubling the public with the following narrative. I shall satisfy those who may be of that opinion x x x. The truth is this: the Journal had lain for many years in a chest among other papers, unseen either by myself or my friends. But, on a late unsuccessful event, I thought that, for the benefit of my children, I ought to attempt to repair the injury I had done them by my speculations; and, as every one who knew the story of my adventures in America, allowed that I had a claim on government, I determined to make it. I, therefore, drew up a memorial to his Majesty, setting forth, that my grandfather, my father, and myself, had all been Captains in the 17th regiment of foot, and my uncle Lieutenant Colonel to that regiment, &c. To this, I annex the following Journal.[1] But having in vain sought a mediation between Majesty and me, I dropt all thoughts of the memorial x x x. Sometime after, I spoke, by accident, [to 'a respectable gentleman of my acquaintance'], of my memorial and journal. He was surprised at my account of an adventure which, in the course of fifteen years acquaintance, he had never heard me mention. After taking it home and reading it, he advised me to print [it] x x x. I have followed his advice. This is a plain and simple tale, accounting for my presumption in offering to the public an old story relating to one whose wish used to be to lie concealed in domestic life x x x."[2]

"<u>General</u> Bradstreet,[3] who commanded an army sent against those Indian nations[4] who had cut off several English garrisons, of which we had taken possession after the surrender of Canada,[5] having to hastily determine to send an officer to take possession also of the Illinois country[6] in his Britannic Majesty's name, sent his Aid de Camp to sound me on the occasion. His Aid de Camp desired me to recommend some officer with qualities he described. I named every one that I could recollect [2]; but he always answered me shortly: 'No, no; he won't do.' I then began to suspect that he might have a design on myself. Accordingly, I said: 'If I thought my services would be acceptable' _ He interrupted me: 'That is what is wanted.' I replied: 'Why did you not say so at first?' He said, with an oath: 'It is not a thing to be asked of any man.' I answered: 'If the General thinks me the properest person, I am ready' I was immediately conducted to the General; and while I was at dinner with him, he said, in his frank manner: 'Morris, I have a French fellow here, my prisoner, who expects to be hanged for treason; he speaks all the Indian languages, and if you think he can be of use to you, I'll send for him, pardon him, and send him with you.' I answered: 'I am glad you have thought of it, Sir; I wish you would.' The prisoner, whose name was Godefroi,[7] was accordingly sent for; and, as soon as he entered the tent, he turned pale, and fell on his knees, begging for mercy. The General telling him that it was in his power to hang him, concluded with saying: 'I give thee thy life; take care of this gentleman!' The man [3] expressed a grateful sense of mercy shown him, and protested that he would be faithful: and indeed his behavior afterwards proved that he was sincere in his promise. As General Bradstreet had pardoned him on my account, he considered me as his deliverer. Little minds hate obligations; and thence the transition is easy to the hatred of their benefactor: this man's soul was of another make; and, though in a low station, a noble pride urged him to turn a heavier weight of obligation on him to whom he thought he was indebted for his liberty, if not his life; and I had the singular satisfaction of owing those blessings to one who fancied he owed the same to me.

"While I was preparing to set out, the boats being almost loaded with our provisions and necessaries [including presents for the Indians,] the Aid de Camp told me, that if the Indian deputies, who were expected to arrive at the camp that evening, did not come, the Uttawaw [Ottawa] village, where I was to lie that night, would be attacked at three o'clock in the morning; 'but that,' added he, 'will make no difference in your affairs.' I was astonished that the General could think so: but I made no reply to him, and we talked of other matters. [4] However, as I was stepping into my boat, some canoes appeared, and I came on shore again, and found they were Indian deputies who were expected.[8] This I thought a very happy incident for me; and having received proper powers and instructions,[9] I set out in good spirits from Cedar Point, in Lake Erie, on the 26th of August, 1764, about four o'clock in the afternoon, at the same time that the army proceeded for Detroit.[10] My escort consisted of Godfroi, and another Canadian; two servants; twelve Indians, our allies;[11] and five Mohawks, with a boat in which were our provisions, who were to attend us to the swifts [rapids][12] of the Miamis [Maumee] river,[13] about ten leagues distant, and then return to the army. I had with me likewise Warsong, the great Chippawaw [Chippewa] chief,[14] and Attawang, an Ottawaw chief, with some other Indians of their nations, who had come the same day to our camp with proposals of peace. We lay that night at the mouth of the Miamis river.

"I was greatly delighted on observing the difference of temper betwixt these Indian strangers and those of my old acquaintance of the five nations.[15] Godefroi was employed in interpreting to me all their [5] pleasantries; and I thought them the most agreeable ralliers I had ever met with. As all men love those who resemble themselves, the sprightly manners of the French cannot fail to recommend them to the savages, as our grave deportment is an advantage to us among our Indian neighbors; for it is certain that a renown English man differs not much more from a lively Frenchman than does a stern Mohawk from a laughing Chippawaw. The next day (27th), we arrived at the swifts, six leagues from the mouth of the river, and the Uttawaw chief sent to his village for horses. Soon after, a party of young Indians came to us on horseback, and the two Canadians and myself having mounted, we proceeded, together with the twelve Indians my escort, who were on foot, and marched in the front, the chief carrying English colors, towards the village; which was two leagues and a half distant. On our approaching it, I was astonished to see a great number of white flags flying; and passing by the encampment of the Miamis,[16] while I was admiring the regularity and contrivance of it, I heard a yell, and found myself surrounded by Pondiac's [Pontiac's] army, consisting of six hundred savages, with tomahawks in their hands, [6] who beat my horse, and endeavored to separate me from my Indians, at the head of whom I had placed myself on our discovering the village.[17] By their malicious smiles, it was easy for me to guess their intention of putting me to death. They led me up to a person, who stood advanced before two slaves (prisoners of the Panis nation, taken in war and kept in slavery)[18] who had arms, himself holding a fusee with the butt on the ground. By his dress, and the air he assumed, he appeared to be a French officer. I afterwards found that he was a native of Old France, had been long in the regular troops as a drummer, and that his war-name was St. Vincent. This fine dressed half French, half Indian figure desired me to dismount; a bear-skin was spread on the ground; and St. Vincent and I sat upon it, the whole Indian army, circle within circle, standing around us. Godefroi sat a little distance from us; and presently came Pontiac, and squatted himself, after his fashion, opposite to me. This Indian has a more extensive power than ever was known among that people; for every chief used to command his own tribe: but eighteen nations, by French intrigue, had been brought to unite, and chose this man [7] for their commander, after the English had conquered Canada; having been taught to believe that, aided by France, they might make a vigorous push and drive us out of North America.

"Pontiac asked me in his language, which Godfroi interpreted, 'whether I was come to tell lies, like the rest of my countrymen.' He said, 'That Ononteeo (the French King)[19] was not crushed as the English had reported, but had got upon his legs again,' and presented me a letter from New Orleans, directed to him, written in French, full of the most improbable falsehoods, though beginning with a truth. The writer mentioned the repulse of the English troops in the Mississippi, who were going to take possession of Fort Chartres,[20] blamed the Natchez nation for their ill conduct in that affair, made our loss in that attack to be very considerable,[21] and concluded with assuring him, that a French army was landed in Louisiana, and that his father (the French King) would drive the English out of the country.[22] I began to reason with him; but St. Vincent hurried me away to his cabin; where, when he talked to me of the French army. I asked him if he thought me fool enough to give credit to that account [8] and told him that none but the simple Indians could be so credulous. Attawang, the Uttawaw chief, came to seek me, and carried me to his cabin.

"The next day (28th) I went to the grand council, and addressed the chiefs. When I mentioned that their father, the King of France, had ceded those countries to their brother the King of England, (for so the two kings are called by the Indians) the great Miamis chief started up and spoke very loud, in his singular language, and laughed. Godfroi whispered me, that it was very lucky that he received my intelligence with contempt and not anger, and desired me to say no more, but sit down, and let my chief[23] speak; accordingly I sat down, and he produced his belts, and spoke. I have called the Miamis tongue a singular language; because it has no affinity in its sound with any other Indian language which I have heard.[24] It is much wondered whence this nation came;[25] who differ as much from all the other nations in their superstitions, practices, as in their speech; and manner of encamping. As they left the Uttawaw villages before me on their way home, we traced their encampments, where we saw their offerings of tobacco, made by every individual [9] each morning; ranged in the nicest order, on long slips of bark both on the shore, and on rocks in the river. They carry their God in a bag, which is hung in the front of encampment; and is visited by none but the priest; if any other person presumes to advance between the front of the encampment and that spirit in the bag, he is put to death; and I was told that a drunken French soldier, who had done so, was with great difficulty saved.

"When the council was over, St. Vincent changed his note, and told me that if I could ensure to him his pardon, he would go to Detroit. I answered him, 'that it was not in my power to promise it.' However, as I found that I could not well to do without him, I contrived to make him my friend. Pondiac said to my chief: 'If you have made peace with the English, we have no business to make war on them. The war belts came from you.'[26] He afterwards said to Godfroi: 'I will lead the nations to war no more; let 'em be at peace, if they choose it: but I myself will never be a friend to the English. I shall now become a wanderer in the woods; and if they come to seek me there, while I have an arrow [10] left, I will shoot at them.' This I imagined he said in despair, and gave it as my opinion, that he might easily be won to our interest; and it afterwards proved so.[27] He made a speech to the chiefs who wanted to put me to death, which does him honor; and shows, that he was acquainted with the law of nations: 'We must not,' said he, 'kill ambassadors: do we not sent them to the Flatheads, out greatest enemies, and they to us? Yet these are always treated with hospitality.'[28]

"The following day (29th) the Mohawk, who commanded the Indians in the provision-boat, stole away, without taking my letter to General Bradstreet, as he had been ordered, having, the night before, robbed us of almost everything, and sold my rum (two barrels) to the Uttawaws. The greater part of the warriors got drunk; and a young Indian drew his knife, and made a stroke at me, but Godfroi, seized his arm, threw him down, and took the knife from him. He certainly saved my life, for I was sitting, and could not have avoided the blow though I saw it coming. I was now concealed under my mattress, as all the young Indians, were determined to murder me; _ was afterwards obliged to put on Indian shoes [moccasins] and [11] cover myself with a blanket to look like a savage, and escape by fording the river into a field of Indian corn with St. Vincent, Godfroi, and the other Canadian. Pondiac asked Godfroi, who returned to the village to see what was going on, 'what he had done with the English man.' And being told, he said, 'you have done well.' Attawang came to see me and made his two sons guard me. Two Kickapoo chiefs came to me, and spoke kindly, telling me that they had not been at war with the English for seven years. Two Miamis came likewise, and told me that I need not be afraid to go to their village. A Huron [Wyandot] woman however abused me because the English had killed her son.

"Late at night I returned to Attawang's cabin, where I found my servant concealed under a blanket, the Indians having attempted to murder him; but they had been prevented by St. Vincent. There was an alarm in the night, a drunken Indian having been seen at the skirt of the wood. One of the Delaware nation, who happened to be with Pondiac's army, passing by the cabin where I lay, called out in broken English: 'D___d son of a b__ch.' All this while I saw none of my own Indians: I believe [12] their situation was almost as perilous as my own. The following day (30th) the Miamis and Kickapoos set out on their return home, as provisions were growing scarce. An Indian called the Little Chief, told Godfroi that he would send his son with me, and made me a present of a volume of Shakespear's plays; a singular gift from a savage.[29] He however begged a little gun-powder in return, a commodity to him much more precious than diamonds.

The next day (31st) I gave Attawang, who was going to Detroit, a letter for General Bradstreet, and to one of my servants whom I sent along with this chief. I gave another for his Aid de Camp.[30] And now, having purchased three horses and hired two canoes to carry our little baggage, I set out once more, having obtained Pondiac's consent, for the Illinois country, with my twelve Indians, the two Canadians, one servant, St. Vincent's two slaves, and the Little Chief's son and nephew.

"There was scarcely any water in the channel of the river, owing to the great drought, so that the canoes could hardly be dragged along empty, in some places. We passed by the Island where is Pondiac's village,[31] and arrived at a little village consisting of only two [13] pretty large cabins, and three small ones, and here we encamped: that is, we lay on the ground; and as a distinguished personage, I was honored by having a few small branches under me, and a sort of basket-work made by bending bows with their ends fixed in the earth, for me to thrust my head under to avoid musketoes or large gnats with which that country is infested. The day following (August 1st) arrived St. Vincent and Pondiac. The latter gave the former the great belt, forty years old, on which were described two hundred and ten villages.[32] St. Vincent joined us, and we set forward, and arrived at another village of the Uttawaws, the last of their villages we had to pass.[33] One of the chiefs of this village gave me his hand, and led us into the cabin for strangers, where was Katapelleecy, a chief of very great note, who gave his hand to all my fellow travelers, but not to me. This man was a famous dreamer, and told St. Vincent that he had talked with the great spirit the preceding night; and had he happened to dream anything to my disadvantage the night I lay there, it had been over with me. The Indian [Washenauits] who gave me his hand, went into the upper range of beds, and came down dressed in a laced scarlet [14] coat with blue cuffs, and a laced hat. I wondered more at the color of the clothes than at the finery; and was told that it was a present from the English, and that this Indian had conducted Sir William Johnson to Detroit.[34] The next morning (2d) he told me the English were liars; that if I spoke falsehoods he should know it, and ask why the General [Bradstreet] desired to see the Indians at Detroit, and if he would clothe them. I assured him that the General sought their friendship; and gave him, at his own request, a letter of recommendation to him.[35]

"We then continued our route towards the Miamis country, putting our baggage into the canoes, but the greater part of us went by land, as the water was so shallow, that those who worked the canoes were frequently obliged to wade and drag them along. We met an Indian and his wife in a canoe returning from hunting; and bought plenty of venison ready dressed, some turkeys, and a great deal of dried fish for a small quantity of powder and shot. The following day (3d) we were overtaken by Pondiac's nephew and two other young Uttawaws, who, with the Chippawaws before mentioned, made the party twenty-four. We met an Indian who, as we afterwards [15] found, had been dispatched to Pondiac with belts from the Shawnees and Delawares; but he would not stop to talk to us. This day I saw made the most extraordinary meal to which I ever was or can ever be witness. Till these last named Indians joined us we had killed nothing but a very large wild cat, called a pichon, which indeed was very good eating: but this day we eat two deer, some wild turkeys, wild geese, and wild ducks, besides a great quantity of Indian corn. Of the wild ducks and Indian corn we made a broth; the Indians made spices of the bark of a tree in a few minutes, and, for the first time, I eat of boiled wild duck. When we marched on after dinner I could perceive no fragments left. What an Indian can eat is scarcely credible to those who have not seen it. Indeed the Frenchmen, who had been used to savage life, expressed their astonishment at the quantity which had been devoured.

"The next day (4th) we found plenty of game, having sufficient time to hunt for it, as the canoes were for the greatest part of the day dragged along, there not being water sufficient to float them. The day after (5th) we met an Indian on a handsome white horse, which had been General Braddock's, [16] and had been taken ten years before when that General was killed on his march to Fort du Quesne, afterwards called Fort Pitt, on the Ohio.[36] The following day (6th) we arrived at a rocky shoal, where the water was not more than two or three inches deep, and found a great number of young Indians spearing fish with sticks burnt at the end and sharpened; an art at which they are very dexterous; for the chief who steered my canoe with a setting pole (no oars being used the whole way), whenever he saw a fish, used to strike it through with his pole, though the end, had been blunted and made as flat and broad as a shilling, pin it to the ground, then lift it out of the water, and shake it into the boat. I never saw him miss a fish which he took aim at.

"The day after, on the 7th of September, in the morning we got into easy water, and arrived at the meadow near the Miami's fort,[37] pretty early in the day. We were met at the bottom of the meadow by almost the whole village, who had brought spears and tomahawks, in order to dispatch me;[38] even little children had bows and arrows to shoot at the Englishman who was come among them; but I had the good fortune to stay in the [17] canoe, reading the tragedy of Anthony and Cleopatra, in the volume of Shakespeare which the Little Chief had given me, when the rest went on shore, though perfectly ignorant of their intentions; I pushed the canoe over to the other side of the river, where I saw a man cutting wood. I was surprised to hear him speak English. On questioning him I found he was a prisoner, had been one of Lieutenant Holme's garrison at the Miami's Fort, which officer the Indians had murdered, a young squaw whom he kept having enticed him out of the garrison under a pretext of her mother's wanting to be bled. They cut off his head, brought it to the fort, and threw it into the Corporal's bed, and afterwards killed all of the garrison except five or six whom they reserved as victims to be sacrificed when they should lose a man in their wars with the English.[39] They had all been killed except this one man whom an old squaw had adopted as her son. Some years afterwards, when I lay on board a transport in the harbor of New York in order to return to Europe, Sir Henry Moore, then governor of that province, came to bid me adieu, and was rowed on board by this very man among others. The man immediately recollected [18] me; and we felt, on seeing each other what those only can feel who have been in the like situations.

"On our arrival at the fort, the chiefs assembled, and passed me by, when they presented the pipe of friendship; on which I looked at Godefori, and said: 'Mauvois augre pour moi.' A bad omen for me. Nor was I mistaken; for they led my Indians to the village, on the other side of the water,[40] and told me to stay in the fort with the French inhabitants;[41] though care had been taken to forbid them to receive me into their houses, and some strings of wampum, on which the French had spoken to spare my life, had been refused. We wondered at this treatment, as we expected that I should be civilly received;[42] but soon learned that this change of temper was owing to the Shawnees and Delawares, a deputation of fifteen of them having come there with fourteen belts and six strings of wampum;[43] who, in the name of their nations, and of the Senecas, declared they would perish to a man before they would make peace with the English;[44] seven of them had returned to their villages; five were gone to Wyant;[45] and three had set out the morning I had arrived for St. Joseph;[46] (a fortunate circumstance for me for they [19] had determined to kill me.) The Shawnees and Delawares begged of the

Miamis either to put us to death (the Indians and myself) or to tie us and send us prisoners to their village, or at least to make us return. They loaded the English with the heaviest reproaches; and added, that while the sun shone they would be at enmity. The Kickapoos, Mascontins, and Wiatanous, who happened to be at the Miamis village declared, that they would dispatch me at their villages, if the Miamis should let me pass. The Shawnees and Delawares concluded their speeches with saying: 'This is the last belt we shall send you, till we send the hatchet; which will be about the end of next month (October).' Doubtless their design was to amuse General Bradstreet with fair language, to cut off his army at Sandusky, when least expected, and then to send the hatchet to the nations: a plan well laid; but of which it was my good fortune to prevent them from attempting the execution.[47]

"To return to myself: I remained in the fort, and two Indian warriors (one of whom was called Visen lair) with tomahawks in their hands, seized me, one by each arm; on which I turned to Godefroi, the only person who had not left me, and [20] cried out to him, seeing him stand motionless and pale: 'Eh bien! Vous m' abandonnez donc?' Well then! You give me up? He answered: 'Non, mon Capitaine, Je ne vous abandonneraz jamais, No, my Captain, I will never give you up; and followed the Indians, who pulled me along to the water-side, where I imagined they intended to put me into a canoe; but they dragged me into the water. I concluded their whim was to drown me, and then scalp me; but I soon found my mistake, the river being fordable. They led me on till we came near their village; and there they stopped and stripped me. They could not get off my shirt, which was held by the wrist bands, after they had pulled it over my head, and in rage and despair I took it off myself. They then bound my arms with my sash, and drove me before them to a cabin, where was a bench, on which they made me sit. The whole village was now in an uproar. Godefroi prevailed with St. Vincent, who had followed us to the water side, but had turned back, to come along with him; and encouraged Pondiac's nephew and the Little Chief's son to take my part. St. Vincent brought the great belt, and Pondiac's nephew spoke. Inananis, [21] an Indian, bid Godefroi take courage and not quit me. Godefroi told le Cygene' [the Swan], a Miamis chief, that his children were at Detroit; and that, if they killed me, he could not tell what might befall them. He spoke also to le Cygne's son, who whispered to his father, and the father came and unbound my arms, and gave me his pipe to smoke.

"Visen lair, upon my speaking, got up and tied me by the neck to a post. And now every one was preparing to act his part in torturing me. The usual modes of torturing prisoners are applying hot stones to the soles of the feet, running hot needles into their eyes, which latter cruelly is generally performed by the women, and shooting arrows and running and pulling them out of the sufferer in order to shoot them again and again: this is generally done by the children. The torture is often continued two or three days, if they can continue to keep the prisoner alive so long.[48] These modes, of torture I should not have mentioned, if the gentleman who advised me to publish my journal, had not thought it necessary. It may easily be conceived what I must have felt at the thought of such horrors which I was to endure. I recollect perfectly what my apprehensions were. I [22] had not the smallest hope of life; and I remember that I conceived myself as it were going to plunge into a gulf, vast, immeasurable; and that, in a few moments after, the thought of torture occasioned a sort of temper and insensibility; and I looked at Godefori, and seeing him exceedingly distressed I said what I could to encourage him: but he desired me not to speak. I suppose that it gave offense to the savages, and therefore was silent; when Pacanne, King of the Miamis nation, and just out of his minority, having mounted a horse and crossed the river, rode up to me. When I heard him calling out to those about me, and felt his hand behind my neck, I thought he was going to strangle me out of pity: but he untied me, saying (as was it afterwards interpreted to me.) 'I give that man his life. If you want meat (for they sometimes eat their prisoners)[49] go to Detroit, or upon the lake (meaning go face your enemies the English) and you'll find enough. What business have you with this mans flesh, who is come to speak to us?' I fixed my eyes steadfastly of this young man, and endeavored by looks to express my gratitude. An Indian then presented me his pipe; and I was dismissed by being [23] pushed rudely away.

"I made what haste I could to a canoe, and passed over to the fort, having received on my way a smart cut of a switch from an Indian on horseback. Mer. Leir, a few traders, and some soldiers, who were prisoners, came to see me. Two very handsome young Indian women came likewise, seemed to compassionate me extremely, and asked Godefroi a thousand questions. If I remember right they were the young king's sisters. Happy Don Quixote, attended by princesses! I was never left alone, as the wretches, who stripped and tied me, were always lurking about to find an opportunity to stab me. I lay in the house of one L'Esperance, a Frenchman. The next day, my Indians spoke on their belts.[50] The two wretches still sought an opportunity to kill me . The day following, the Miamis returned their answer: 'That we must go back:' shewed the belts of the Seneca, Shawnees, and Delawares; gave my Indians a small string of white wampum; and told them: 'to go and inform their chiefs of what they had seen and heard.' While the council sat I was concealed in L'Esperance's garret, as Godefroi was obliged to attend it.

"Being determined at all events to get into the Illinois [24] country if possible, St. Vincent and I agreed that he should endeavor to gain le Cygne and the young king to attend me to Wyant: but in the middle of the night, St. Vincent came and woke me, told me that two Frenchmen were just arrived from St. Joseph, and that the Delawares who were there, were coming back to the Miamis village. He advised me to send for my chief immediately, and tell him, for his own safety as well as mine, to try to get leave to go away in the morning, (for the Miamis had appointed the next day but one for our departure.) This was accordingly done, and leave obtained. I went to visit le Cygne, who told me, 'that he would have been glad to have attended me to Wyant, but that he could not think of leading me to my death: for that there were so many tomahawks lifted up there, that he should have trembled to have gone himself.' I gave notes to Pacanne and Pondiac's nephew, setting forth that they had saved my life, and entreating all Englishmen to use them kindly. (Pacanne shewed this paper to Colonel Croghan, when he made his tour through the Indian country, and the Colonel was pleased to bring him to Detroit, and, at a private meeting appointed [25] for that purpose, sent for me, and give me a very handsome present to lay at his feet.)[51] We gave all our blankets and, shirts to those Indians who had done us service; and hearing that the chiefs were in council, and talked of not allowing me to return with my party, but of detaining me prisoner; and my Indians themselves appearing uneasy, _ having left my money and baggage with one Capuain, a Frenchman, I hurried away about noon, vexed at heart that I had not been able to execute the orders I had received. I gave General Bradstreet's letter for Meusieur St. Ange, the French Commandant at Fort Chartres, to St. Vincent, to deliver to that officer;[52] and signed a certificate which he was pleased to put into my hands, specifying that, on many occasions, he had saved my life.

"Fear lent wings to my Indians this day; and we continued our march till it was quite dark, being apprehensive of an attack. We set out very early the next morning; and as nothing worthy of observation happened, my thoughts were taken up during this day's journey in admiring the fine policy of the French with respect to the Indian nations; of which, from among a thousand, I shall select two remarkable instances, [26] which I mention as not only worthy of mention, but to wear out of the minds of such of my countrymen as have good sense and humanity, the prejudices conceived against an innocent, much-abused, and once happy people; who have a deep sense of the justice and benevolence of the French, as of the wrongs and hauty treatment which they have received from their present masters.[53] The first of these is the encouragement given by the French court to marriages betwixt its subjects and Indian women; by which means Lewis [Louis King of France] got admission into their councils, and all their designs were known from their very birth. Add to this, that the French so entirely won their affections by this step, that to this hour the savages say, that the French and they are one people. The next instance is, the prohibiting the sale of spiritous liquors to Indians, under pain of not receiving absolution: it is what the French call a <u>cas reserve'</u>; none but a bishop can absolve a person guilty of it. This prevented many mischiefs too frequent among the unfortunate tribes of savages, who are fallen to our lot. From drunkenness arise quarrels, murders, and what not? For there is nothing, however shocking and abominable, that the [27] most innocent of that innocent people are not madly bent on when drunk. From imposing on the drunken Indian in trade, abusing his drunken wife, daughter, or other female relation, and other such scandalous practices, arise still greater evils. When such things are done (and they are done) can we wonder that the Indians seek revenge? The ill conduct of a few dissolute peddlers has often cost the lives of thousands of his Majesty's most industrious subjects, who were just emerging from the glum of toil and want, to the fair prospect of ease and contentment.

"The following day, while we were shooting at some turkeys, we discovered the cabin of a hunting party on the opposite side of the Miamis river;[54] the men were in the woods; but a squaw came over to us who proved to be the wife of the Little Chief. Godefroi told her that I was gone to the Illinois country with her son. She informed us that the Indians [Attawang, Wasson, and others] were not returned from Detroit; and added that there were four hundred Delawares and three hundred Shawnees (as she had been told), at the Uttawaw villages, who wanted to go and set fire to that place. We were sure that this piece of news about the Shawnees and Delawares was false as the Uttawaws [28] themselves wanted provisions: but my Indians: believed it, and it served to bring them over at once to my way of thinking, which was; to pass through the woods, and avoid the villages of the Uttawaws. They were all much alarmed, but in particular the Huron of Loretto.[55] This degenerate monster of the church, this Christian savage, who spoke French fluently, had the cruelty and insolence to tell me, that as I could not march as fast as the rest, I must take an old man and a boy (both lame) and make the best of my way: that the chief would go with me, and he would conduct the others, who were eleven in number, and all able men. I spoke to him with gentleness, and begged that he would not think of separating from us; on which he said something that I did not understand, in his language which resembles that of the five nations,[56] and of course was understood by my chief, and which vexed him so much, that he told me, 'I might go by myself;' but I found means to pacify him. I now told Godefroi, who was of himself so determined, that he would of course go with me. Upon this the Huron gave us very gross language; and indeed such stubborn impudence I never saw. He told the [29] chief that if he suffered me to take my horses with me, we should be discovered, but I obtained the chief's consent to take them a little way. I then proposed going into the wood to settle the distribution of our provisions and ammunition; but the Huron would listen to nothing: so leaving him and his party, consisting of ten, with my best horse, which he said he would turn loose as soon as he should get a little way further, I struck into the wood with Godefroi, the chief, the old Indian, and the Indian boy; Godefroi and myself on horseback.

"We went North East from twelve o'clock till two; from two to five went North; and finding a pool of water, we took up our lodgings there. The next day we continued our route North, North East, being as nearly as we could guess in the course of the Miamis river. We endured great thirst all this day. About three o'clock we reached the swamps, which, by the dryness of the season, might have passed for meadows, and not finding any water, about five o'clock we made a hole, two feet deep, with our hands, (for we had no kind of tool fit for that use) where some tall broad grass grew; and getting good water, though very muddy, we made a [30] fire, and determined to pass the night by the side of our little well. We traveled in the swamps the following day till half an hour after one o'clock, at which time we came to open woods, having found water in two places on our way; but we could find none when we wanted to prepare ourselves at the close of the day. We therefore set to work, as the day before, and made a hole four feet deep in a place which must be a swamp in the wet season: but it was three hours before we got a drought of what I might rather call watery mud than muddy water. We were forced from want of water to stew a turkey in the fat of a raccoon; and I thought I had never eaten any thing so delicious, though salt was wanting: but perhaps it was hunger which made me think so.

"We heard four shots fired very near us just before dark; we had a little before discovered the tracks of Indians, and they undoubtedly had discovered ours, and supposing us friends, fired to let us know where they were. Three shots alarmed our chief, and he told me that I must leave my horses behind. I bid Godefroi drive them some little distance from us, and let them go: accordingly he went towards the place where we had left them, as if he [31] intended to do so; but, unknown to me, wisely deferred it till morning, hoping our chief would change his mind. This night the chief, seeing me writing by the light of the fire, grew jealous, and asked if I was counting the trees. The next morning the chief being a little intimidated, instead of going East North East, as agreed on the night before, in order to draw near the Miamis river, went due North; by which means he led us into the most perplexed wood I ever saw. He had my compass, which I asked him for, and wanted to carry about me, as he very seldom looked at it; but this gave great offense, and he told me I might go by myself. In short, he was grown captious beyond measure. In order to please him, we had put his pack on one of our horses; but we were forced to take it off again, as a loaded horse could not force its way through the thick wood we were in. I found such a difficulty in leading my horse (for it was impossible to ride) through this part of the forest, that I called out to the party for God's sake to stop till I could see them, or I should never see them more: at that time I could not be more than fifteen yards behind them. They had hurried in pursuit of a rattle-snake.

"The chief [32] now told me again, that I must let my horses go; but Godefroi convinced me, that I could not reach Detroit without them. I therefore resolved if he persisted, to quit him, to take Godefroi, with me, and to kill one of my horses for a supply of food, for we had very little ammunition left, and no provisions. However, the chief grew good-humored by Godefroi's management; and as he now thought himself out of danger, changed his course, going East, North East. We soon got into a fine open wood, where there was room to drive a coach and six. Here we halted to refresh ourselves by smoking our pipes, having nothing to eat, the old Indian, who always ranged as we traveled on, having found no game that morning. As I had not been used to smoking, I desired to have sumach leaves only, without tobacco; but, after a few whiffs, I was so giddy, that I was forced to desist: probably an empty stomach was the chief cause of this unpleasant effect of smoking. Soon after we came into extensive meadows; and I was assured that those meadows continue for a hundred and fifty miles, being, in the winter, drowned lands and marshes. By the dryness of the season they were now beautiful pastures: and [33] here presented itself one of the most delightful prospects I ever beheld; all the low grounds being meadow and without wood, and all the high grounds being covered with trees, and appearing like islands; the whole scene seemed an Elysium. Here we found good water, and sat down by it, and made a comfortable meal of what the old Indian had killed, after we left our halting-place. We afterwards continued our route, and at five o'clock discovering a small rivulet, which gave us all, and me in particular, inexpressible pleasure, we made a fire by the side of it, and lay there all night.

"The day following, we crossed the tracks of a party of men running from the Uttawaw villages directly up into the woods, which we imagined to be those of the Huron's party who might have lost their way; as it proved. I laughed and joked a good deal with Godefroi on this occasion; for when the Huron left us, I asked in a sneering manner, 'if he had any commands, in case I should get before him, to Detroit:' and he answered one in the same tone, 'if when you arrive, you don't find me there, you may safely say that I am gone to the devil.' Soon after, to our great joy, we fell into the path leading from the Uttawaw [34] villages to Detroit, and struck into a by-path to avoid meeting Indians; but unluckily stumbled on that which led from the great path to Attawang's village. We met three Hurons on horseback, who told us peace was concluded,[57] that the Uttawaws had returned the day before to their villages, and that General Bradstreet was to be at Cedar-Point that night on his way to Sandusky.[58] One of these Indians had been present when I was prisoner at Attawang's village; and though I was dressed like a Canadien, and spoke French to Godfroi to prevent discovery, recollected me to be the Englishman he had seen there. I gave him a letter from St. Vincent to Pondiac which I had promised to deliver. They then took their leave of us; and as soon as they where out of site, we turned into the great path, and putting our Indians on our horses, Godefroi and I walked at a very great rate.

"We arrived at the Potiwatamy [Pottawattamy] village at a quarter past three, where I had the pleasure of seeing English colors flying. I wanted to avoid the village; but the chief, being very hungry (for we had eat nothing that day) fell into a passion, and asked what we were afraid of. He knew he ran no risk here. I was a [35] little vexed, and mounting my horse bid him follow. I went to the village, where I bought a little Indian corn and a piece of venison; and then Godefroi and I rode on until it was dark, in hopes of reaching Detroit the next day; and finding water, made a fire near it, and passed the night there, having left our fellow travelers to sleep with the Pottiwatamies; who, as none of them knew me, were told by Godefroi that I was gone to the country of the Illinois, and that he growing tired of the journey, and wanting to see his children, was on his return home. The next morning we set out at the dawn of day; and, to save ourselves the trouble of making a raft, took the upper road, though the journey was much longer that way, hoping to find the river fordable, in which we were not disappointed. We traveled this day a great way, and our horses were so much fatigued, that they were hardly able to carry us towards the close of the day. We found fresh horse dung on the road, which Godefroi having curiously examined, knew that some Indians had just passed that way; and by their tracks he was sure they were before us. He therefore made an excuse to halt for about an hour, endeavoring to conceal the truth [36] from me; but I was no stranger to his real motive. However, about seven o'clock we arrived at Detroit;[59] whence I was fifty leagues distant when I left the Miamis river and struck into the woods: and by the circuit I was obliged to make to avoid pursuit, I made it at least four score leagues, or two hundred and forty miles.

"The Huron and his people did not arrive till many days after, and in three different parties. They had lost their way; were obliged to divide themselves into small bodies in order to seek for game; had suffered extremely by fatigue and hunger; one having died by the way, and all the rest being very ill when they reached Detroit. The Huron I imagined would have had died. I gave him, as well as all the others, all the assistance in my power; but could not help reproaching him with his barbarity to me, and reminding him 'that the Great Spirit had protected one whom he had abandoned, and punished him who had basely deserted his fellow-warrior.'

"Immediately after my arrival at Detroit, I sent an express to General Bradstreet, with an account of my proceedings,[60] and to warn him of the dangerous situation he was in, being advanced some miles up the Sandusky river[61] and [37] surrounded with treacherous Indians. The moment he received my letter,[62] he removed, falling down the river, till he reached Lake Erie:[63] by this means he disappointed their hopes of surprising his army.[64] This army however suffered extremely afterwards, and great numbers were lost in traversing the descent, many of their boats having in the night been dashed to pieces against the shore, while the soldiers were in their tents. The boats were unfortunately too large to be drawn out of the water. The sentinels gave the alarm on finding the sudden swell of the lake, but after infinite labor, from the loss of boats, a large body of men were obliged to attempt to reach Fort Niagara by land, many of whom perished.[65] It is worthy of remark, that, during this violent swell of the waters, soldiers stood on the shore with lighted candles, not a breath of wind being perceived. This phenomenon often happens. Another curious fact respecting the waters of these lakes is, that they rise for seven years and fall for seven years; or in other words, there is seven years tide. I have read from somewhere, that the Caspian sea overflows its banks once in fifteen years. This, however, is derived elsewhere. But, if the former [38] opinion be really the case, as the American lakes and the Caspian sea are in parts of the same earth almost opposite to each other, it might be worth while to inquire, whether, when they are at the lowest in one place, they are at the highest in that which is opposite, or both rise and fall at the same time?[66]

"The Natchez Nation, mentioned in the letter to Pondiac, which he shewed me, and who were blamed by the rest of the Indian army for having fired too soon on the English who were sent to take possession of Fort Chartres by way of the Mississippi river, no doubt did it by design, that the troops might have an opportunity of retreating; for the French had formerly endeavored to extirpate that nation, and had nearly succeeded in the undertaking, a small number only having escaped the massacre. It is not probable such an action could ever be forgiven; especially by savages.[67] This nation has a perpetual fire; and two men are appointed to watch it. It has been conjectured that their ancestors were deserters [descendant?] from the Mexicans who worship the sun.[68]

"The Miamis nation, of whom I have spoken so much, and into whose hands I fell after leaving Pondiac's army at the Uttawaw villages, are the very [39] people who have lately defeated the Americans in three different battles;[69] and when the last accounts from that country reached us, they were encamped on the banks of the Ohio, near the falls or cataracts of that river.

"It may not be improper to mention, that if I could have completed the tour intended,[70] viz. from Detroit to New Orleans, thence to New York, and thence to Detroit again,[71] whence I set out, it would have been a circuit little short of five thousand miles.

"Detroit, September 25, 1764."[72]

Chapter Twelve

Logan, the Mingo Chief
1710 - 1780

During the last half of the sixteenth century, long and bloody wars were waged between the Five Nations of Indians and the white inhabitants of Canada. The savages killed or captured _ as was ever their wont _ regardless of age or sex. Among their prisoners was a boy, born in Montreal of French parentage,[1] and baptized in the Roman Catholic church,[2] who, after being adopted into a family of Oneidas,[3] of the Wolf clan,[4] and given the name of Shikelimo,[5] eventually married a wife of the Cayugas.[6]

Shikelimo became the father of several children,[7] who according to the Indian rule, were of the same tribe as the mother.[8] In the course of time, he was raised to the dignity of a chief among the Oneidas[9] _ the nation of his adoption. In the year 1728, having been by the Grand Council of the Iroquois "set over" the Shawnees,[10] who then occupied contiguous territory to, and were held in subjection by the Five Nations. Shikelimo removed with his family to a small Indian village on the east side of the West Branch of the Susquehanna, at a point about fourteen miles above its junction with the Northeast Branch, near the mouth of Warriors Run, in what is now Northumberland county, Pennsylvania;[11] _ removing, about ten years after to Shamokin, now the city of Sunbury, where he made his future home;[12] and where, at an advanced age,[13] he died, in December 1748.[14]

Shikelimo filled for more than twenty years, a large space in the Indian history of the country he may be said to have ruled over; for, in the course of time, his office became greatly extended. He swayed almost a vice-regal scepter over all the inferior tribes south of the Iroquois who paid tribute to that powerful League, or were held by it in subjection. He became a kind of resident ambassador of the Five Nations, in Pennsylvania. He frequently acted as the agent of that Province in their dealings with that famous Confederacy. That he dealt out justice even-handed to the savages over whom he was placed, is evident from their high estimation of him, frequently expressed. That his conduct was satisfactory to the Grand Council of Onondaga, is established by the fact of his being continued so many years as its representative and agent abroad. The government of

Pennsylvania was ever loud in their praise of "Shikelimo, the true friend of Englishmen." Taking into consideration its complicated character, it is doubtful if any such office had ever before been created by North American Indians; or one so important, filled with more satisfaction to all concerned.

Shikelimo was, of course, unlettered. He was tutored only in Indian craft. In all respects, except the color of his skin, he was a savage _ but of the highest type of the race. Revenge, a passion so strong in the breast of the Indians, he seemed incapable of. The use of intoxicating liquors, he held in utter abhorrence. There is an abundance of recorded evidence of his fine personal appearance, of his genial manners, of his shrewdness as a diplomat, and of the firmness and nobility of his character. By the Moravians, he was held in high esteem; a few words of his once moved several of their young men to consecrate themselves to the work of missions among the North American Indians;[15] indeed, wherever known, he seems to have been a general favorite.

Logan,[16] whose Indian name was Tuck-neck-du'-rus,[17] _ "the branching oak of the forest"[18] _ was the eldest son of Shikelimo.[19] He was known, however, for many years, to white people, especially to Pennsylvanians, as John Shikelimo.[20] He was born in the Oneida country, now an interior portion of the State of New York,[21] about the year 1710. Although his father was a white man, Logan was, agreeable to the Indian rule, by birth-right a Cayuga _ to which nation his mother belonged;[22] although, as already explained, Shikelimo was, by adoption, an Oneida.[23]

Concerning Logan's minority, history is entirely silent. That he grew to manhood in possession of superior talents is evidenced by the early recognition of his abilities in council.[24] He unquestionably inherited the talents of his father, but not his sobriety. His passion for strong drink, which, in the end, so overcame him, was largely due to his residing, for so many years, at or near Shamokin _ "the very seat of the Prince of Darkness."[25] Situated about midway of the Province of Pennsylvania, at a point one mile below where the northeast and west Branches unite to form "the winding river" _ Susquehanna, it had a very commanding and accessible position. It was directly on the route from Philadelphia to the Grand Council House of the Six Nations. Its situation was delightful. An early writer was enraptured with "the charming plain of Shamokin, two miles long and above one broad, skirted on the west and north by the river, and encompassed east and partly south, with lofty hills."[26] In strange contrast with the magnificence of the natural scenery was the immorality of its savage occupants. "The Indians of this place," wrote the pious Brainerd more than three years before the death of Shrikelimo, "are accounted the most drunken, mischievous, and ruffian-like fellows of any in these parts."[27]

Logan had four brothers. The youngest died in 1729, at Shamokin. "You are very sensible of our love and our care," wrote the Governor of Pennsylvania, to the father upon the sorrowful event, "for all the good Indians, our brethren, that live amongst us or near us." "We send," he added, "a straw to cover Shikelimo's son."[28] The brother next to Logan was Lay-ugh-to-wa,[29] known to the English as "James Logan."[30] He was thus named by his father in honor of a warm friend, James Logan, a learned writer and statesman, born in Lurgan, Ireland on the twentieth of October, 1764, of Scotch parentage, _ who died at Stenton, near Philadelphia, on the thirty-first of October, 1751. He landed in Pennsylvania as the Secretary of William Penn early in December, 1699; and after the return of the latter to England, in 1701, he was invested with many important offices, which he discharged with fidelity and judgment. He was provincial Secretary, Commissioner of Property, Chief Justice, and upon the death of Governor Gordon, in October, 1736, governed the province of Pennsylvania for two years, as president of the Council. He was the friend of the Indians, possessed uncommon abilities, and great wisdom and moderation.

The Indian name of Logan's second brother _ the third son of Shikelimo _ was Sa-go-gegh-ya-tu. He was known to the English as "John Petty," or "John Petty Shikelimo;"[31] having been named after a trader of some prominence in the early days of Pennsylvania.[32] Shikelimo's fourth son bore the dolorous name of "Unhappy Jake."[33] He was killed by the Catawbas in 1744, with five others of the Six Nations. "As this is a great stroke to our friend Shikelimo," wrote Conrad Weiser, on the second of January, 1745, to the Secretary of Pennsylvania, "who is, for the trust put in him by the Council of the Six Nations, and our government, worthy to be taken notice of. I thought it my indispensable duty to inform you of this; and to lay it before the Governor, whether or no he thinks fit to send to Shikelimo a small present, in order to wipe away his tears and comfort his heart, and enable him, by so doing, to stand to his charge; which would be not only satisfactory to him, but very agreeable and pleasing to the Council of the Six Nations; _ and, consequently, some little service done to ourselves."[34]

Of the sisters of Logan, but little is known. The eldest, who was married to an Indian named Cajadis, in 1731, lost her husband in 1747.[35] He was reckoned the best hunter among all the Indians at Shamokin. There was one sister living among the Conestoga Indians, near the Susquehanna, at no great distance from the town of Lancaster, Pennsylvania, in the year 1756,[36] who, seven years after, fell a sacrifice to the wild ferocity of the Paxton rioters, along with the residue of those peaceable and friendly Indians.[37]

Of the thirty-seven years that Logan resided upon the waters of the Susquehanna _ from 1728 to 1765 _ seventeen of them were to him, years of great activity and responsibility. In 1747, a Cayuga Chief, known as Sca-yen-ties, bore to him a message from one of the tribes of his nation of great importance. He was found, in company with his father, at the house of Joseph Chambers, on the east side of the Susquehanna, about six miles above the present city of Harrisburg, Pennsylvania. He was informed that he had been nominated and appointed one of their Counselors. He was desired to apply himself to public business.[38] This was the commencement of his long official career, _ greatly augmented, in its importance, upon the death of Shikelimo. The instruction of the father had not been thrown away upon the son. From this time forward until the day of his death, Shikelimo was always accompanied by him, wherever absent on public business.[39] It was no new custom, however, as the records of previous public meetings and treaties abundantly prove.[40] Scarcely had Logan entered upon his duties as Counselor for the Cayugas than he was called upon to mourn the death of his wife.[41]

Logan was sent by his father, to the Six Nations, on business connected with public affairs, in 1748.[42] Shikelimo was too feeble to attend the Great Council at Onondaga in person. He died soon after. Logan and his brothers were the recipients of many messages of condolence upon the occasion of his death. One came from the bishops and Synod of the Moravian church, "sympathizing with them in their loss, telling them of their father's faith in the Lord Jesus Christ, and urging them to follow in his footsteps."[43] "I returned from Shamokin," wrote Conrad Weiser, Indian agent for Pennsylvania, to the Governor of that Province, on the twenty-second of April, 1749, from Heidelberg, in the present county of Berks, "on the eighteenth instant. I happened to meet the oldest and youngest son of Shikelimo, at the trading house of Thomas McKee, about twenty-miles this side of Shamokin." "All I had to do was," continues the writer, "to let the children and grandchildren of our deceased friend, Shikelimo, know that the Governor of Pennsylvania and his Council condoled with them for the death of their father."[44]

Weiser then gave them a small present in order "to wipe off their tears," according to the custom of the Indians. After this, and in the name of the Governor, and on behalf of the Council, of Pennsylvania, he desired Logan to take upon himself the care and responsibility of a chief instead of his deceased parent, and to be the true correspondent of the government, until there should be a meeting between the same and the Six Nations, when he should be recommended by the Governor and confirmed, if he would follow the footsteps of his departed father. "He accepted thereof," says Weiser, "and I sent a string of wampum to Onondaga to let the Six Nations know of Shikelimo's death and my transactions, by order of the Governor."[45] There was a necessity for expedition in this appointment of a successor to the Iroquois "vicegerent" at Shamokin; for the Indians were getting very uneasy about the white people settling beyond the "Endless Mountains," on the Juniata, on Sherman's creek, and elsewhere, west of the Susquehanna. It was their only hunting ground for deer; _ farther to the northward, they were very scarce. Five years before, a deputy from the Grand Council of the Six Nations, addressing himself to the Governor of Pennsylvania, desired that the people who were then located upon the Juniata might be removed; "for," said he, "we have given that river for a hunting-place to our cousins, the Delaware Indians, and our brethren, the Shawnees,[46] and we ourselves hunt there sometimes."

Logan was soon raised by the Grand Council of Onondagas to the dignity of "Sachem or Chief of the Shamokin Indians,"[47] an office, in all that appertained to the government of the various Indian tribes represented in that place, equal in importance to the one held by his father; besides, he was made one of the ten Sachems of the Cayugas[48] _ the nation to which he belonged. Logan heeded the advice of Conrad Weiser and became a "true correspondent" of Pennsylvania, acting as its agent frequently in its intercourse with the Six Nations. To conciliate the Indians and give them assurance that those who settled upon their lands on the Juniata should be speedily removed, a conference between them and the Government of Pennsylvania was held on the seventeenth of May, 1750, at Pennsboro, Cumberland county. Logan was present and took part in the proceedings.[49]

In 1754, the Governor of Pennsylvania informed its Council that, having standing instructions from its Proprietary to take all opportunities of making a purchase of land from the Iroquois which was every day becoming more urgent by the great number of people settling beyond the Blue Hills over the Susquehanna, contrary to the stipulations of the government with those Indians which might create differences with them, _ he had recommended the Proprietaries to try by all the means in their power to make a purchase; and to facilitate the necessary work, he had, by the advice of Conrad Weiser, dispatched Logan _ "John Shikelimo" _ early in the Spring with a message to the Six Nations, informing them of the necessity of their selling, by reason of the increase of the inhabitants, and the impossibility of restraining them from making settlements beyond the boundaries previously established; and desiring they would enter into a treaty with the Proprietaries whose agents would be at Albany in the ensuing Summer.

Logan conducted the negotiation, preliminary to the treaty, to the satisfaction of both parties. A vast extent of land west of the Susquehanna, including the whole territory watered by the Juniata, was secured and the Indian title quieted, on the sixth of July, at Albany. "As to Wyoming and Shamokin and the land contiguous thereto, on the Susquehanna," said the Indians, "we reserve them for our hunting ground and for the residence of such as in this time of war shall remove from among the French and chose to live there, and we have appointed John Shikelimo to take care of them. He is our Representative and Agent there, and has our orders not to suffer either the Pennsylvania people or the New Englanders to settle any of those lands; and if any shall presume to do it, we have directed him to complain to Pennsylvania, whether it shall be their own people or those from other provinces; and to insist on their being turned off; and if he shall fail in this application, we will come ourselves and turn them off. No body shall have this land." Logan was present at the treaty and signed the deed as one of the Sachems of the Cayugas.[50]

Trouble soon arose in Logan's "dominions" after the meeting at Albany. Connecticut people began to crowd in upon the Wyoming lands. He thereupon sent a message with a belt to the Governor of Pennsylvania: _ "When the great treaty," said he, "was held at Albany this Summer, the Six Nations in their council appointed me to the care of the lands at Wyoming and north of the Western

Branch of the Susquehanna which they kept for the use of the Indians who are daily flocking there from all parts, and acquainted the Commissary of Pennsylvania in the presence of all the people that I was their agent; that they put those lands into my hands; and that no white men should come and settle there; and ordered me, if they did, to complain to Pennsylvania; and to get them punished and turned off." "In virtue of this appointment," continued Logan, "I complain to Pennsylvania that some foreigners and strangers who live on the other side of New York and have nothing to do in these parts, are coming like flocks of birds to disturb me and settle those lands; and I am told they have bought those lands of the Six Nations since I left Albany, and that I have nothing further to do with them." "I desire you," he said, in conclusion, "to send to these people not to come; and if you do not present it, I shall be obliged to complain to the Six Nations."

This was the commencement of the difficulty between "The Susquehanna Company" _ formed in Connecticut the year previous, for the purpose of establishing a settlement in Wyoming _ and Pennsylvania, which afterward bore bitter fruit, but was now interrupted by the coming on of the French War. The Connecticut people claimed that they had already purchased, by deed only executed of the "chief sachems and heads of the Five Nations," the lands spoken of by Logan. But the latter continued his complaints to the Governor of Pennsylvania, _ insisting, the next year, as in 1754, "that people were beginning to settle to the northward of the Albany purchase." "I have laid your complaint," wrote the Governor, "before the Council in which you set forth that sundry people have settled beyond the line of the late purchase made at Albany, upon lands not yet conveyed by the Six Nations; and it is determined that the line shall be run that it may be known for certain where the limit extends: and when this is done, I will issue a Proclamation prohibiting all persons from settling to the north of that line, and I hope this will have its effect. You shall have notice when the line is run that you may be present and see that all things are done right. If, after this any shall presume to settle there, they will be punished."[51]

After the defeat of Braddock in July, 1755, French interests began largely to prevail among the Indians of the Susquehanna. "You and the French," said a recalcitrant chief afterward in addressing Sir William Johnson, "quarreled for the lands on Ohio, and the French came there with a large body of men and beat yours off; and so the Indians on the Ohio were, in a manner, obliged to come into their measures. They were persuaded to take up the hatchet against the English; and, as they came in small parties to the Susquehanna river, they prevailed on the Susquehanna Indians to go with them, _ they being related to one another. Many had their fathers, mothers, sons and daughters, on the Ohio, and could not withstand their request; being one people, they could not resist."[52] Logan, for months, opposed the tide there setting in so strongly at Shamokin. Finally, in the Fall of that year, it became too powerful to be resisted with safety; and, as a consequence, he and his family, together with his two brothers, were swept away from their town by the storm of war now raging so fiercely around them. They moved up the Northeast Branch of the Susquehanna to a hostile village; a report being circulated among the Delawares that the Pennsylvanians were coming in large numbers to destroy them, and Logan's life being threatened if he did not at once leave Shamokin.[53] He even went so far, it was afterward reported by a friendly Indian, as to consent to take the war-path against the English; but fortunately, at this crises, and while at Wyoming, whither he had gone and was waiting to be joined by eighty Delawares to go against the back inhabitants, he was met by two Indian messengers who had been dispatched to the Six Nations by Pennsylvania and were then on their way to the Onondaga Council. These Indians upbraided him for his ingratitude to the English who had ever been extremely kind to his father when alive, and to him and his family and relatives, since his decease; and charged him not to go along with the war-party which would soon set out, but rather to join some friendly Indians _ about thirty in number _ who were then in the village, and who disapproved of the measures of the Delawares.[54] Logan took their advice; remained in the town; and firmly resolved never to strike the English; _ to which resolution, so long as the war lasted, he steadfastly adhered: and also during the continuance of Pontiac's war. His well known declaration made in 1774, was true: "during the course of the last long and bloody war, Logan remained idle in his camp, an advocate for peace."

Early in 1756, two Indians of the Six Nations were sent by the Governor of Pennsylvania up the Susquehanna, to gain intelligence of the motions and number of the enemy Indians, and to try to find out Logan and his brothers, and, if possible, bring them to Conrad Weiser's, that the former might consult with his white brethren upon the present state of affairs. This was a fortunate circumstance. It confirmed Logan in his loyalty to the English. He and his wife returned with the messengers, to "a fort at Hunter's Mill near the place where the Blue Hills crossed the Susquehanna," _ generally known at that time, as McKee's fort _ where a guard was ordered to escort them to Tulpehocken, Weiser's residence. But Logan declared positively that he would not go there; being apprehensive that the "Dutch" would fall upon him and either kill him or do him some mischief. He would go, he said, through Lancaster to Philadelphia and deliver what he had to say to the Governor in person; and insisted that the commander of the fort _ Captain McKee _ should go along and protect him. At Harris', now Harrisburg, they were joined by three other Indians, when they all made their way to Lancaster. Here Logan sent for his sister, who was living among the Conestoga Indians, not far off. She and the Conestogas joined the party and all journeyed thence to Philadelphia, when they arrived, _ men, women, and children _ on Saturday, the twenty-first of February.

On Monday morning following, the Governor sent his Secretary to welcome the Indians to town and in particular, Logan; and to make them the usual compliments of drying up their tears and taking away the grief out of their hearts, that they might be at liberty to declare the business they came upon. After they had returned thanks, and made the Governor the same compliments, they said the two messengers and Logan whom they had brought with hem, would go directly to the Governor and tell him in person what they had to say. However, before the meeting, Logan sent a message by Weiser who was present, to the chief executive: "My father, who," he said, "it is well known was all his life a hearty and steady friend to the English, and to Pennsylvania in particular, charged all his children to follow his steps and to remain always true to them, who had ever been kind to him and his family." "Upon the troubles first breaking out," continued Logan, "between the Indians and the white people, the former came to Shamokin and obliged me and my brothers against our inclinations to stay with them; but I had the good fortune to get from among them, which I was glad of; and I am now come to my brethren to assure them that, though I have been absent some time, and among their enemies, yet it was against my will, being forced to it." "I was still your good friend," he added, "and would live and die with you. I desire you should receive me as a friend." The Governor ordered his Secretary to return his answer to Logan, and assure him he was glad to see him; that the government gave him a hearty reception, and would make every thing agreeable to him, and take care of his family.

Logan afterwards reported that the two messengers found him at Wyoming; that he and his brethren and others of his friends were informed that when the Delawares upon the Ohio proclaimed war against the English, they forewarned all the Indians to come away from the latter; desiring them to move up the Northeast Branch of the Susquehanna; whereupon, a council was called at Shamokin, and it was agreed, by the Indians there present, chiefly Delawares, to go up that stream for safety. "I and my family," said Logan, "intended to go to the white settlements, but the Delawares would not let us. They said the white people would certainly kill us. I therefore went with them and took my family with me." "After a while," continued he, "I found that these Indians were in the French interest. Then, I began to be afraid. I, with my brethren and others, would have gladly gone to the English, but we dared not venture, being afraid of the back inhabitants, and much more afraid of the Delawares, who told us, in plain terms, that if we offered to go down the river they would look upon us as brethren to the English and as their enemies." When the Delawares began to bring in English scalps, Logan left the town and went to Wyoming, where the government messengers found him and induced him to return with them to the white settlements.

Logan had not been long in Philadelphia before he began to grow uneasy lest some mischief might befall his family in his absence. He feared that the enemy Indians, if they should hear of his journey to the settlements, might take revenge upon them. He therefore desired to return at once to Wyoming; and promised to bring them and his brothers down into the province.[55] So he and his wife hastened back to the Northeast Branch of the Susquehanna. By the fifth of April, Logan had again reached McKee's fort, a few miles above the present city of Harrisburg, with his family and his two brothers. He brought an account of there being great confusion among the Indians up the Northeast Branch; the Delawares were all moving from there to the Ohio, and were trying to persuade the Shawnees to go with them; but the latter declined, as they would rather join the English, and were going up to Tioga where there was a body of the Six Nations, and there they intended to remain.[56] Logan again asked the commander to conduct him, as he had previously done, through the white settlements, at least as far as Conestoga where his sister and children lived; but this officer, Captain McKee now declined; and Logan and his family remained in the fort, _ only, however, for a brief period; for, being ill treated and threatened by the people,[57] he made his escape without even his gun; and after enduring many hardships and much suffering from hunger, again reached one of the Indian towns upon the Northeast Branch, whence, soon after, he made his way to Tioga.

Early in June, 1756, the Governor of Pennsylvania, ever mindful of the previous services of Logan and indignant at the treatment he had received at Fort McKee, sent him a message, with a string of wampum, to Tioga, expressing his concern that he should have been the recipient of such abuse; and assuring him that it was entirely unknown to the Government; and requesting that he should come with the messenger to Philadelphia, and he should receive a kind welcome and receive sufficient proofs of the friendship of the Governor.[58] Conrad Weiser also sent him a pressing invitation to return. Logan could not resist these importunities notwithstanding the indignities heaped upon him at "the fort near John Harris'; so, with his wife he immediately started upon his journey to see the Governor, taking Bethlehem on his road to Philadelphia.

Reaching Bethlehem on the first day of September, Logan was carefully questioned by David Zeisberger, who spoke the Indian language well. He obtained much information as to the feeling and determination of the Delawares and Shawnees as well as the Six Nations, which he communicated at once to the Governor of the Province. Logan told the worthy missionary the story of his leaving "the fort near John Harris'; that it was because the Irish people did not use him well and threatened to kill him; that, therefore, he went away leaving his guns, clothes, and all that he had. He also informed Zeisberger that, fifteen days before, he had left the Cayuga Lake, where he had been all the time; that all the Delawares and Shawnees up the river were now for peace; and that a great many intended to come and live again where they lived before; that the previous winter the Six Nations had sent many belts of wampum to those Indians and desired them to leave off doing mischief; and at last they were obedient to them. Logan and his wife reached Bethlehem nearly starved; they received from the Moravians every attention; and, on the third, they started, under the care of two of the brethren, for Philadelphia, abundantly refreshed with "eating bear; and rum."[59]

Logan reached Philadelphia in safety and at once waited on the Governor in Council to acquaint him that he had received a string of wampum from him, and a belt from his friend Weiser, with invitations to come and speak with him. He was kindly received; and, at his instance, an express was dispatched for Weiser. Upon his arrival, Logan thus addressed him; "Uncle! here I show you the belt of wampum you sent me, and my brethren, and my whole family. By this belt you reprimanded myself and my family from running away from Shamokin last fall into a wilderness, where we must certainly perish for the want of the necessaries of life; and you told us that it was a very wrong step to run away from our friends; and you charged us, your cousins, to come back either to Shamokin, or to your own house Tulpehocken, or elsewhere in your neighborhood, so that you could have an opportunity to help us with some provisions, and have an open eye over us, who were like little children and knew not what was for our own good. Uncle! I assure you, that I and my brethren have often repented that we came away from Shamokin, and fled up the river, when we were assured of your friendship, and should have fled to your house. It is true what you have said _ we have lost ourselves; but we have been deceived by our near neighbors the Delawares, and my brother Say-ugh-to-wa suffered himself to be led astray. He repents now and sees his error; and we all have agreed to come down either to Shamokin, our old place, if we can be protected there, or to your house, as soon as we can with safety; and that some other friendly Indians will join us who already promised to come down with us."[60]

At the very time Logan was professing his attachment to the Pennsylvanians in such an artless but effective manner, the Governor of that Province was engaged in erecting a fort at Shamokin, where he could be "protected" in his old home. But the glory of that village as an Indian residence had departed. Its cabins had been burned; and the sons of Shikelimo never again made it their place of abode. For the next nine years Logan, after his return from Philadelphia, continued to live upon the waters of the Northeast Branch; and, although the Seven Years' War and the sanguinary conflict which followed it, disturbed, at times, the "Shamokin country," yet he "remained idle in his camp, an advocate for peace." On the twenty-eighth of January, 1760, the commandant of the post at Shamokin sent word to Conrad Weiser that a Mingo Indian had, the day previous arrived at that place with a message from Logan desiring to meet him there in ten days from that time. Weiser being disabled, sent his son Samuel to see Logan _ "now a noted man among the Indians on the waters of the Susquehanna." There was to be a Grand Council of the warriors of the Six Nations and he had been invited to attend. Knowing that the Governor of Pennsylvania was desirous of having a road cut from the settlements to the post _ Fort Augusta _ at Shamokin, he thought it a good time while meeting with the assembled Indians in conference, to suggest the matter to them if it would be desired he should do so, by the Governor. So he came down from his town, to Shamokin, to lay the subject before his old friend Weiser, whom he was in hopes to meet there. But as that could not be, a conference was held with the authorities at the Fort, acting under instructions from the Governor.

Logan was told that Governor Hamilton thought it exceedingly kind of him to send information of his having been invited to a Grand Council of the Six

Nations and that he returned him thanks for his offer of mentioning to the Onondaga Council his design of cutting a road from the frontier to Fort Augusta; and he looked upon it as a fresh instance of his steady friendship, and sincere attachment to the Province. The result of the conference was that Logan should carry a message giving as a reason why it was desirable that a road should be opened, "that the Indians might be supplied with goods at Fort Augusta _ Shamokin _ at all times in the year, by a nearer, safer and more commodious way than by the dangerous and round about way of the river Susquehanna, which is sometimes impassible in Summer and all the winter admits of no transportation of goods or provisions." Logan promised that he would deliver this message; that he would use all the arguments and efforts in his power that the opening of the road should meet with the approbation of the Onondaga Council; and that, if he should succeed, he would be down again in two months at farthest with the news. Logan, after the conference was over, requested a small supply of provision to carry him home, "which," writes the commander of the fort, "I have ventured to comply with, though it is not customary and is without orders."61

No recognition of Logan's official duties is to be found after August, 1762. In that month he attended, along with his two brothers, a treaty held with the Northern and Western Indians at Lancaster, Pennsylvania. After the public business was over, Logan, together with another Cayuga chief and three Senecas, had a private interview with Governor Hamilton. They entered complaints against the agent at Fort Augusta, as a man who always treats the Indians who come there with ill usage and bad language, in so much that they were often so provoked as to do him violence; and they entreated the Governor to remove him and put a more quiet man in his place. They said further that as the Governor had acquainted them that the war had occasioned a rise in the price of goods, they hoped he would give orders that the Indians be paid a higher price for their skins and furs. Hamilton made answer that he would take the matter into consideration and do in it whatever was thought reasonable.[62]

For the next ten years of Logan's life, his history is partly traditionary. He makes his appearance, after the close of Pontiac's War and the return of peace, no longer as agent of Pennsylvania in its intercourse with the Six Nations, nor as the representative of the Indian Confederation in their dealings with that Province or their rule over the Susquehanna tribes, _ but as a hunter, simply, and with his habitation changed from the Northeast Branch of that river to the delightful valley of the Kishacoquillas, in what is now Mifflin county, Pennsylvania. The Kishacoquillas creek is a beautiful, never-failing stream, fed by surrounding mountains. It breaks out of its fertile valley by a deep gorge, when it enters the Juniata, from the north, at the present site Lewistown. Immediately after the purchase of the land from the Indians, by the treaty of Albany in 1754, settlements began in this region; but the Seven Years' Conflict and Pontiac's War depopulated the Juniata country; so that when Logan in the year 1765 first made his camp near the Kishacoquillas, the valley was as desolate and lonely as when the Indians claimed it as their own territory. But settlers soon began to arrive. By midsummer of 1766, six or seven families had located there.[63]

A writer of early times records that, in the year 1765, he was living in Raccoon Valley, near the foot of the Tuscarora mountain, in what is now Perry county, Pennsylvania, _ when, upon a certain Saturday evening a report came that the Indians had begun to murder the white people. The next day in the forenoon, while the children of the family were outside the house, they espied three Indians coming across the meadow, a few rods from them. They ran in and informed their parents, who were considerably alarmed. The Indians, however, set their guns down on the outside of the house, and went in. They were invited to take seats which they did. After dinner, they sat a considerable time. One could speak tolerable good English. The other two spoke nothing but their own language. They appeared to be making observations on the large wooden chimney, _ looking up it, and laughing. This the family supposed was on account of a man, on the Juniata, not far distant, having made his escape up one when his house was attacked by Indians. One of the little girls, a sister of the narrator, then a child of three or four years, having very white curly hair, _ they took hold of it, stretching it up, and laughing. It was conjectured they were saying "this would make a nice scalp," or that they had seen such. Otherwise, the Indians behaved with civility.

After some time, when it was seen that the three visitors had no hostile intentions, one of the boys took the bible and read them two or three chapters from the book of Judges, respecting Sampson and the Philistines. The one that could speak English paid great attention to what was read. The father of the family, upon observing this, took occasion to mention to him what a great benefit it would be to the Indians to learn to read. "O!" said he, "a great many Indians on the Mohawk river can read the book which speaks of God." After remaining in the house about two hours, they took their departure towards the Kishacoquillas Valley. In a few days, the family was informed that the Indian who spoke the English language was a chief _ Captain John Logan.[64]

Many are the legendary tales told of Logan during his five years residence _ from 1765 to 1770 _ in the valley of the Kiskacoquillas. He seems to have been a general favorite with the early settlers there. One of these, while in pursuit of a bear, came suddenly upon a fine spring, and being thirsty laid down to drink. Just then he saw reflected in the water, on the opposite side, the shadow of a tall Indian. He sprang up. When the savage gave a yell, _ whether for peace or war, the hunter was not just then sufficiently master of his faculties to determine. However, upon seizing his rifle, and facing the Indian, the latter knocked up the pan of his gun, threw out the priming, and extended his hand. It proved to be Logan _ the best specimen of a man, white or red, the relator declared, he ever met with. Logan "could speak a little English" and told the hunter there was another one a little way down the stream, and offered to guide him to his camp.

Another settler once shot at a mark with Logan at a dollar a round. The Chief lost four or fives shots in succession, and acknowledged himself beaten. He thereupon went into his cabin; brought out as many deerskins as he had lost dollars, and handed them to his opponent, who refused to take them, alleging that he was simply his guest and did not come to take his property; that the shooting was only a trial of skill between them; and the bet merely nominal. Logan drew himself up with great dignity, and said: "I bet to make you shoot your best. I am a gentleman, and would have taken your money had I won." So the settler was obliged to take the skins or affront his friend, where nice sense of honor would not permit him to receive even a horn of powder in return.

While in the Valley, Logan supported his family by killing deer, dressing the skins, and selling them to the settlers. He had disposed of a number to a tailor who lived in an adjoining valley. Tailors, in those days dealt extensively in buckskin breeches. Logan received his pay in wheat, according to an agreement. The grain upon being taken to the mill, was found so worthless that the miller refused to grind it. Logan was much chagrined, and attempted in vain to obtain redress. He then took the matter before a magistrate. That officer questioned him as to the character of the wheat, and what was in it, but Logan sought in vain for words to express the precise nature of the article with which the grain was adulterated, but said it resembled in appearance the wheat itself. "It must have been cheat," said the magistrate. "Yes," said the chief, "that is very good name for it!" A decision was rendered in Logan's favor and a writ given him to hand to the constable, which, he was told, would bring him the money for the skins. But this the chief could not comprehend. He could not see by what magic the paper would force the tailor against his will to do him justice. The magistrate showed him his commission, having the arms of the King upon it, and explained the first principles and operations of civil jurisprudence. "Very good law," said Logan, "it makes rogues pay!"[65]

One of the early occupants of the valley was a neighbor of Logan's. One day, during the absence of the settler, he came to his house and having gained the confidence of his little son, carried him off through the woods to his cabin. The lone and terrified mother dared not resist; but after several hours of fearful anxiety, she determined to follow at any risk and rescue her child. Her relief can scarcely be imagined when she met the friendly chief bringing her little boy in his arms, having on his feet a pair of beautiful beaded moccasins _ the gift of Logan.[66] Another mother had a similar experience; but it was a little daughter, this time, that was carried off. She was just beginning to walk; when the parent expressed her regret, in the chief's presence, that she could not get a pair of shoes to give more firmness to her little steps. Logan stood by, but said nothing. Soon, however, he asked the mother to let the little girl go with him and spend the day at his cabin; but her cautious heart was alarmed at such a proposition. With apparent cheerfullness but secret reluctance, she complied with the request. At sundown the child was brought back shod with a dainty pair of moccasins, wrought by Logan's own hands.[67]

The course of the Indian, like that of empire, is westward; _ and Logan turned his eyes toward the region of the setting sun. Leaving the valley of the Kishacoquillas, he moved up the Juniata to the Standing Stone,[68] now Huntingdon, Pennsylvania. Before taking his departure, he carved, it is said, with his hatchet, on the trunk of a royal oak, the full-length image of an Indian, brandishing, in his right hand, a tomahawk. This "monarch of the forest trees" stood there, long after the chief had gone, attracting the attention of the curious.[69] A fine spring in the valley still perpetuates the name of Logan.[70] Crossing the Alleghenies, the son of Shikelimo did not rest his feet until the Ohio was reached; which was, at least, as early as the Summer of 1772.[71] Upon the "Beautiful River" or some of its branches, Logan spent the residue of his years.

Upon the arrival of Logan in the trans-Allegheny country he made his camp at the mouth of Big Beaver, upon the northern or right bank of the Ohio, at a point at or near the present site of Beaver, Pennsylvania.[72] He was a frequent visitor at Pittsburgh, then an insignificant village of about thirty log houses.[73] A pious missionary, who was then visiting that town, was not favorably impressed with the moral condition of things. "About every day," says he, "since our arrival, we have had the disagreeable sight of drunken Indians staggering through the streets; _ as this is the most frontier settlement of the English, and the chief place of rendezvous where the miserable creatures frequently meet for the sake of a drunken frolic."[74] Logan's appetite for rum had already become his besetting sin. His indulgence was so great as to bring on occasional attacks of delirium tremens. "Wherever I go," said he, at this time, when suffering from a debauch, "the devils are pursuing me. If I go into my cabin, it is full of them; and the air itself is full of them. They hunt me by day and by night. They seem to want to catch me and throw me into a great deep pit of fire!"[75]

The Spring of 1773 found Logan farther down the Ohio than the mouth of Big Beaver.[76] At this time, there was a village of Mingoes _ Iroquois _ at Mingo Bottom, on the west or Indian side of the Ohio, nearly three miles below the present city of Steubenville, in Jefferson county, Ohio. By the Fall of that year, these Indians _ off-shoots or colonists of the Six Nations _ had left that locality, removing to Pluggy's town on the Sciota. But Logan and his friends and relatives _ also Mingoes[77] _ remained upon the Ohio; where, at or near the mouth of Big Yellow Creek, fifty-five miles below Pittsburgh, they had, in the Spring of 1774, "a hunting camp composed of men, women and children."[78]

For ten years subsequent to Pontiac's War, there was peace all along the frontiers from Lake Erie to the Gulf of Mexico, but in reality a nominal one only; for, as the natural result of the ever increasing numbers of one race crowding in upon the ever decreasing population of another _ "while neither the savages of the one, nor the hardy woodsmen of the other were prepared, by continuous forbearance, to avoid a conflict." _ murders were frequent. Here, a trader was killed; there, a peaceable settler. Here, an Indian was shot while hunting in the forest or paddling his canoe upon the Ohio; there, another was slain in the cabin of the white man. Then, whole parties were killed, on either side; culminating, finally, in the Indian war of 1774, generally known as Lord Dunmore's War.

Pennsylvania was not brought as close to the western Indians as Virginia; and her intercourse with the savages was mostly through the channels of trade. She enjoyed, therefore, a large immunity from savage atrocities. With Virginia, the case was very different. Her borders were the Ohio, _ her settlements crowding down that river, out-running treaties with the Indians, and rapidly moving toward Kentucky. Besides, she then claimed Pittsburgh and its surroundings. So, while Pennsylvania strove to conciliate the savages thereby to avoid their wrath, Virginia, goaded by their hostilities, determined to punish them for their continued aggressions; _ for such they seemed to her Government.

Logan, at Yellow Creek, was not an indifferent spectator of the events transpiring around him; yet he counseled peace. "I admit," said he to the assembled Mingoes, "that you have just cause of complaint." "But you must remember," he added, "that you, too, have sometimes been in the wrong. By war, you can only harass and distress the frontier settlements for a time; then the Virginians will come like the trees in the woods in number, and drive you from the good lands you possess _ from the hunting grounds so dear to you." Meanwhile, the contest was gradually increasing in intensity and drawing nearer and nearer to the camp of Logan. Unfortunately, his endeavors to restrain his followers did not succeed; as some of them soon determined to take up the hatchet _ at least, to the extent of killing a family of Virginians the nearest to their locality;[79] the members of which were Joshua Baker, his wife and children, then living just opposite the mouth of Yellow Creek. A friendly intercourse had been kept up between these people and the Mingoes,[80] until the evening of the twenty-ninth of April, when one of the squaws who had been particularly befriended by Baker's wife came over the river and after considerable hesitation disclosed to her that the Indians the next day were going to kill her and all her family. Just what particular act or acts, prompted this sudden determination of the friends of Logan, it is left to conjecture to determine. Indians had very recently been killed upon the Ohio below them, and only the night previous, it is said, two had been shot close to Logan's camp.[81] The warning of the friendly squaw was at once heeded by Baker, who, before morning, had several frontiersmen, well armed, gathered at his house, where they were secreted to await the coming of events.

Early in the morning of the thirtieth, a party, consisting of four unarmed Indians and three squaws _ one of whom brought with her a child two months old _ came over the river to Baker's cabin. Among them was John Petty, the youngest brother of Logan; also his mother and sister. The child was the daughter of the latter. The Indians, except Logan's brother, having obtained some rum, soon became excessively drunk. It had been previously arranged that two of Baker's friends should not conceal themselves but remain with him to watch the course of events. After some time, John Petty took down a coat and hat belonging to Baker's brother-in-law and putting them on strutted about the room; then, coming up abruptly to one of the borderers addressed him with very offensive language and attempted to strike him. The frontierman thus assailed, kept out of his way for some time; finally, becoming irritated, he seized his gun and shot him as he was rushing for the door. The report of the rifle brought the hidden party at once from place of concealment. In a few moments every Mingo was killed, except the child. Thus perished the relatives of Logan _ all but his "cousin," as he was wont to call his little niece.

While these events were transpiring two canoes were observed putting out from the Mingo camp and steering across the river. In one, there were two Indians; in the other, five; all were naked, painted and armed. The frontiermen thereupon ranged themselves under cover of some bushes along the bank ready to receive the canoes. The foremost one carried the two Indians. Both these were killed at the first fire of the bordermen. The other canoe then went back. After this, two other canoes started across, one containing eleven, the other seven Indians, painted and armed as the first. These attempted to land below; but being fired upon, they retreated, with one of their number killed, at the same time, returning the fire, but with no harm to the Virginians.[82]

Logan now smothered down the promptings of his better nature. He gave full play to his savage instincts. Vengeance was his from the moment he heard the sad news of the killing of his relatives. Woe to the hapless victim upon the frontier, young or old, male or female, who should be startled by his war cry! Woe to the father or mother, brother or sister, _ decrepit age or the tender babe, who should come in the way of his brandishing tomahawk! He was no longer "an advocate for peace." Now, was for war _ war to the knife.

Upon the west side of the Muskingum river at a point near the sight of the present town of Dresden, Ohio, there was located in 1774, the Shawnee village of Wakatomica.[83] Here lived many of the friends of the slain at Baker's.[84] Hither hastened Logan, breathing destruction and death to the Virginians. The Mingoes _ mostly Senecas _ followed him to the Muskingum.[85] The news they brought caused lamentation in the Shawnee town.[86] So enraged was Logan that he raised a party to cut off some traders among the Shawnees at a place then known as Canoe Bottom on the Hockhocking, where they were pressing their peltry preparatory to transhipping it to Pittsburgh; but the Indians with whom they had been trafficking protected them, else even Pennsylvanians would have suffered from the wrath of the Mingo Chief. Indeed one was barbarously slain.[87]

On Monday, the nineteenth of May, 1774, Logan with a small party of Mingoes and Shawnees, for the second time started upon the war-path, from Wakatomica, now, however, on a maraud into the Virginia settlements _ the first overt act of war, on his part, against the border. A still smaller number soon followed the others, making, in all thirteen warriors. It was their intention to strike their blows on that part of the Ohio near where their friends had been killed or some where else below that point if practicable. They declared as soon as they had taken revenge for their people, they would then home, set down and listen to their chiefs who advised against their taking up the hatchet.[88]

Logan and his warriors were out about two weeks before a good opportunity to commence the work of death; and, instead of the Ohio, it was upon the west side of the Monongahela in the settlement on Tenmile, Dunkard, Whitely, and Muddy creeks _ then claimed as a part of Virginia _ that their depredations began. Stealthily they came upon the settlers. The first fell victims to their vengeance were a man by the name of Spicer, his wife and five children, living at Meadow Run on Dunkard creek. Two others of the children _ Betsy, a girl eleven years of age, and William, nine years old _ were taken prisoners. The former was afterward given up; the latter spent most of his life with the Indians. After the taking of sixteen scalps in all, Logan and his warriors, with their two prisoners, returned to Wakatomica. His success had now somewhat appeased his wrath; and he seemed ready to listen to the councils of the Shawnee chiefs who had vainly endeavored, before his setting out, to restrain his bloodthirsty animosity against the Long Knives.[89] By this time, however, _ the last of June _ even the Shawnees were beginning to waiver. So Logan, in a few days, was again upon the war-path.

On the twelfth of July, as William Robinson, and two others, a Hellen and Coleman Brown were pulling flax in a field upon the West Fork of the Monongahela, opposite the mouth of Simpson's creek, in what is now Harrison county, West Virginia, Logan with a party of seven warriors approached unperceived and fired at them. One by the name of Brown was killed; the others were made prisoners. The Indians now set out on their return to Wakatomica, taking with them a horse belonging to Hellen. They reached the village on the eighteenth when both prisoners were compelled to run the gauntlet. Ever since the capture, Logan had manifested a friendly disposition to Robinson who, having been tied to a stake, preparatory to be tortured, had his life saved by that chief. He was then adopted by Logan in place of a warrior killed at Baker's; his intention being, should an opportunity present itself, to have him exchanged for his "cousin" _ the young child saved from the general massacre on the thirtieth of April; but such an occasion not occurring, Robinson was finally delivered up under other stipulations. Logan, thereupon, made immediate preparation for another war-expedition. On the twenty-first, he brought Robinson, who was then in a Shawnee village near Wakatomica, a piece of paper and told him he must write a letter which he intended to carry with him and leave in some house where he should kill some one. After making ink of gun powder, he instructed his amanuensis to address the note to Captain Michael Cresap, who he supposed _ but in this he was mistaken _ had killed his relatives at Baker's Bottom, or commanded the party upon that occasion. Robinson, from Logan's dictation wrote as follows:
To Captain Cresap.

What did you kill my People on Yellow Creek for? The White People killed my Kin at Conestoga at great while ago & I thought nothing of that; but you killed my Kin again on Yellow Creek, and took my Cousin Prisoner: then I thought I must kill too; and I have been three times to War since; but the Indians is not angry only myself.

Captain John Logan.
July 21st Day, 1774.

With this letter _ "savagely circumstantial and circumstantially savage" _ Logan started upon his fourth maraud.[90]

The settlements next to suffer from the malignity and implacable animosity of Logan were in the Southwestern corner of Virginia, upon the waters of the Holston and Clinch. This region was a long distance from Wakatomica; and Logan and his party did not reach it until near the middle of September. The letter written by Robinson was left in the house of John Roberts, upon Reedy creek a branch of Holston. It was found tied to a war- club among the mangled remains of the slain family. The presence of the hostile savages caused great excitements among the settlers. Several were killed, while a son of Roberts and two negroes belonging to a man by the name of Blackmore living upon Clinch, were taken prisoner.[91]

With his captives and booty, Logan retraced his steps to the Ohio, crossing that stream about the middle of October. In the meantime, the Shawnees and Mingoes had been driven from the Muskingum to the Scioto by the Virginians; so Logan and his party sought their friends upon that river, at Chillicothe,[92] the principal Shawnee village, _ now Westfall, Pickaway county, Ohio. The son of Shikelimo had by this time fully "glutted his vengeance" upon the hated Virginians. He brought with him not less than five scalps from this his last foray. These were not exhibited as trophy of his prowess, but to show his deadly thirst for revenge upon the people who had slain his relatives.

Great were the events which had occurred upon the Muskingum and the Ohio during the absence of Logan. His raids upon the Monongahela settlements had hastened the Virginians in their resort to arms. The Shawnees, as well as the Mingoes, had become involved in the contest. Late in July, four hundred men crossed the Ohio under Major Angus McDonald and early in August laid waste not only Wakatomica but several contiguous villages of the Shawnees.[93] This had aroused that nation to a most determined effort. Sympathizing with them and indeed finally coming to their aid against the Long Knives, were warriors of the Delawares upon the Muskingum, of the Wyandots upon the Sandusky, of the Ottawas upon the Maumee, and of the Miamis upon that river and the Wabash. The vagrant Mingoes, who had villages upon the Scioto, were, of all the Indians, the most vindictive against the Virginians. A few renegade Cherokees also took part in the war. No nation however as a whole took up the hatchet except the Shawnees.

Logan, upon his arrival at Chillicothe learned that Lewis' army was rapidly approaching the Scioto. He saw around him every where that active war-like preparations had been made to meet the expected coming of the Long Knives. He heard the tales of the warriors, concerning a great battle they had fought a few days previous _ October the tenth _ at the mouth of the Great Kanawha. He knew but too well they must have been discomfited by the Virginians. The Shawnees had seen that a conjunction of the two parties was inevitable; so they made haste to treat with Lord Dunmore. Conferences had been held preliminary to a treaty. Some distance from the spot, Logan, to one of Dunmore's interpreters, spoke the following speech, desiring it might be delivered to the Governor;[94]

"I appeal to any white man to say that he ever entered Logan's cabin but I gave him meat; that he ever came naked but I clothed him. In the course of the last war, Logan remained in his cabin an advocate for peace. I had such an affection for the white people, that I was pointed at by the rest of nation. I should have ever lived with them, had it not been for Colonel Cressop, who last Spring cut off in cold blood, all the relations of Logan, not sparing women and children: There runs not a drop of my blood in the veins in any human creature. This called upon me for revenge; I have sought it, I killed many, and fully glutted my revenge. I am glad that there is a prospect of peace, on account of the nation; but I beg you will not entertain a thought that any thing I have said proceeds from fear! Logan disdains the thought! He will not turn on his heel to save his life! Who is there to mourn for Logan? _ No one."[95]

"I may challenge," says Jefferson, "the whole oration of Demosthenes and Cicero, and of any more eminent orator _ of Europe has furnished any more eminent _ to produce a single passage superior to this speech."[96] "Nothing can be imagined," are the words of an American historian, "more venerable than the strain of tender and lofty sentiment running through this short address. Parts of it rise into the highest order of moral sublimity. It reminds us of Ossian, 'the last of his race;' of Tingal, 'in the last of his fields.'"[97] "It was uttered," writes a learned jurist, "in accents dictated by an abiding sense of his wrongs, and in tones expressive of the hopeless desolation of his heart. It was its last passionate throb. The man was done with impulses, even of revenge."[98]

"I alone am left on earth!
To whom nor relative nor blood remains,
No! _ not a kindred drop that runs in human veins!"[99]

And thus an accomplished scholar of our own times; "The speech was repeated throughout the North American colonies as a lesson of eloquence in the schools, and copied upon the pages of literary Journals in Great Britain and on the Continent. This brief effusion of mingled pride, courage, and sorry elevated the character of the native American throughout the intelligent world."[100]

The treaty entered into between the Shawnees and Lord Dunmore adjusted all important differences; but the Mingoes were not a party to it. They stood aloof. They did not share in the sentiment of their chief as to the "prospect of peace." They wanted none. Thereupon the Virginia Governor resolved they should be pursued up the Scioto. Major William Crawford with two hundred and forty men marched against them. Seekunk was destroyed. Six Mingoes were killed and a number made prisoners. A considerable amount of plunder consisting of Indian goods, horses, silver trinkets and other articles, were captured.[101] Thus ended the Indian war of 1774. The Virginians returned to their homes; and their Assembly declared Dunmore's conduct in the campaign "noble, wise, and spirited." Time has confirmed its judgement.

From Chillicothe Logan made his way to Pluggy's town. To this village, the Mingo prisoners captured by Crawford and taken to Fort Pitt for safe keeping, returned after several months detention,[102] _ their people, in the Spring of 1775, manifesting a sincere desire for peace,[103] and joining in the Autumn of that year with other nations in a treaty with Virginia[104] and Congressional commissioners. But this friendship was of short-duration; for the very next year they had again become troublesome to the Virginian border, being now under British influences.[105]

Logan carried with him to Pluggy's town the same feelings _ the same spirit _ manifested in his speech to Lord Dunmore. He no longer sought revenge against the Virginians; he brooded over his misfortunes; he became more intemperate; he often repeated, the story of his wrongs and as often recounted his exploits connected with their requital.[106] When in 1776, his people again began to show their animosity, he apologized for their conduct and remained in his cabin. "We hear bad news," said he, "some of us are certainly threatened. We are informed that a great reward is offered to any person who will take or entice either of us to Pittsburgh, where we are to be hung up like dogs by the Big Knives. This being true, how can we think of what is good. That it is true, we have no doubt."[107]

Although Lieutenant-Governor Henry Hamilton, in the service of Great Britain, had as early as September, 1776, exerted himself at Detroit _ then the center of British influence in the Far West _ to organize small parties of savages against "the scattered settlers on the Ohio and its branches," yet the war upon the Western border was not fully commenced by British Indians for nearly a year afterward. But the frontiers of Virginia, in the mean time were sorely afflicted with savage incursions, mostly by the lawless gang of Mingoes of Pluggy's town. These Indians having in reality no tribal organization, marauded upon the settlements independent of surrounding nations. It is not known, however, that Logan took part in any of their raids. The death of their leader _ the Mohawk Pluggy _ who was shot at the attack upon McCelland's fort, in Kentucky, at the close of 1776,108 somewhat abated their activity; but their depredations were sufficiently galling in the Spring of 1777, to induce the Governor of Virginia to organize an expedition against them; which was abandoned, finally, for fear of a general Indian war, should the Mingoes be attack.

Afterward, the machinations of the British, through the instrumentality of agents and traders, having secured the alliance of the Shawnees and Wyandots in hostility to the Americans, the Mingoes joined these confederated nations. Meanwhile Pluggy's town was deserted by its occupants, Logan and his friends moving still farther up the Scioto _ near the head springs of that river, in what is now Hardin county, Ohio; also upon the upper waters of Mad river in the present county of Logan, adjoining Hardin on the south.

In the Fall of 1778, Logan occupied "a little winter town used for hunting" on the Scioto. It was situated on the Indian trace leading from the Indian village of Wapatomica, in what is now Logan county, to the Wyandot town of Upper Sandusky; in the present county of Wyandot, Ohio. Simon Kenton, who was then a prisoner among the Indians, saw the chief at his village. Logan, learning his fate, and commiserating his condition, said, "I will send two men to Sandusky to speak a good word for you." He did so; and the prisoner who had been condemned to be tortured at the stake was, through his instrumentality, taken safely to Detroit, where he was out of danger from the infuriated savages.[109] Logan continued his good offices to prisoners captured by the British Indians. In 1779 he adopted in his family a white female captive as his sister, in place of the one killed at Baker's.[110]

It was not until the Western border war of the Revolution had continued fully three years, that Logan appears as an actor on the side of the British Indians, against the Americans. In 1780 the plan of an expedition was laid by the British at Detroit, to break up the settlements in Kentucky. To effect this project, a force of British Indians with some soldiers of the regular army and a number of Canadian volunteers, marched for the Ohio. With them was Logan. The whole was under the command of Captain Henry Bird. After crossing into Kentucky, the army ascended the Licking river and captured Ruddell's and Martin's Stations. The enemy then re-crossed the Ohio, without further molesting the settlements. Many prisoners were carried into captivity by the savages.[111] Logan had frequent conversations with some of these unfortunate persons. His remarks, afterward related by one of the captives, concerning his disposition and belief, are of interest; "I know," said he, "that I have two souls; the one good, the other bad. When the good soul has the ascendant, I am kind and humane. When the bad soul rules, I am perfectly savage and delight in nothing but blood and carnage."[112]

Soon after the expedition into Kentucky Logan visited Detroit. On his journey homeward, at a noted camping-place, four miles south of Brown's town, on the bank of small creek, upon the trace leading to Sandusky and his town upon the Scioto, he was killed, because of an insult, fancied or real, by one of his own friends _ a Mingo. The next morning, one of the party returned to Brown's town and gave information of what had happened. A number of leading Wyandots went out, brought in his body and buried it in the burial-place of their village.[113] Thus miserably perished Logan _ the Mingo Chief as renowned as Indian, perhaps, as the world has ever known.

Logan was a tall man considerably above six feet in height, strong and well proportioned. He had a brave, open, manly countenance. He was as straight as an arrow, and to appearance would not be afraid to meet any one in a personal encounter. He weighed about two hundred pounds, _ had a full chest, and prominent and expansive features. To those who were ignorant of his paternity, his complexion very white for a savage. His talk and actions showed the effects of his intercourse with the English. He was, when sober, dignified and reserved, but frank and honest; when intoxicated, he was vain, boastful and foolish."[114]

Chapter Thirteen

Indian Eloquence — Speeches of Garangula, Pontiac, Shegenaba, Skenaudo, and Big Elk[1]

At the period of 1684, the French in Canada availed themselves of a temporary peace with the famous Iroquois Confederacy, to establish forts and trading houses at several important localities. The Confederates opposed these stealthy movements. M. de la Barre, the Governor of Canada, complained to the English of some infringements on the part of the Iroquois, hoping they could restrain their allies; and, moreover, took measures, by placing vessels on the Lakes, and embodying a large force at a convenient point to strike the Indians, with a view of menacing them into peace and friendship. He invited them to a council with the haughty Garangula, the pride of the Onondagas, though then well advanced in years, attended by thirty of his warriors, met the French Governor, who made an insinuating speech, closing with a demand that the Confederates make restitution for the injuries they had done, or he would at once invade the country of the Iroquois, and take full vengeance by the destruction of their villages.

Garangula, who had listened to these threats with contempt, now stepped forward, and addressed the Governor, seated in his elbow chair, as follows:

"Younondio![2] _ I honor you, and the warriors that are with me all likewise honor you. Your interpreter has finished your speech; I now begin mine. My words make haste to reach your ears _ hearken to them.

"Younoundio! _ You must have believed when you left Quebec, that the sun had burnt up all the forests, which render our country inaccessible to the French, or that the Lakes had so far overflown the banks, that they had surrounded our castles, and that it was impossible for us to get out of them. Yes, surely you must have dreamed so, and the curiosity of seeing so great a wonder has brought you so far. Now you are undeceived, since that I and the warriors present, are come to assure you, that the Senecas, Cayugas, Onondagas, Oneidas and Mohawks, are yet alive. I thank you in their name, for bringing back into their country the calumet, which your predecessor received from their hands. It was happy for you, that you left under ground that murdering hatchet, so often dyed in the blood of the French.

"Hear, Younondio! _ I do not sleep. I have my eyes open. The sun, which enlightens day, discovers to me a great captain at the head of a company of soldiers, who speaks to me as if he were dreaming. He says, that he only came to the lake to smoke on the great calumet with the Onondagas. But Garangula says, he sees to the contrary; that it was to knock them on the head, if sickness had not weakened the arms of the French. I see Younondio raving in a camp of sick men, whose lives the Great Spirit has saved by inflicting this sickness upon them.

"Hear, Younondio! _ Our women had taken their clubs, our children and old men had carried their bows and arrows into your camp, if our warriors had not disarmed them and kept them back, when your messengers came to our castles. This done, and I have said it.

"Hear, Younondio! _ We plundered none of the French, but those that carried guns, powder and balls to the Twightwies and Chictaghicks, because those arms might have cost us our lives. Herein we follow the example of the Jesuits, who break all the kegs of rum brought to our castles, lest the drunken Indians should knock them on the head. Our warriors have not beaver enough to pay all the arms they have taken, and our old men are not afraid of war. This belt preserves my word.

"We carried the English into our lakes, to trade there with the Utawawas and Quatoghwees, as the Adirondacks brought the French to our castles, to carry on a trade, which the English say is theirs. We are born free. We neither depend on Younondio or Corlear.[3] We may go where we please, and carry with us whom we please, and buy and sell what we please. If your allies be slaves, use them as such; command them to receive no others but your people. This belt preserves my word.

"We knock the Twightwies and Chictaghicks on the head, because they had cut down the trees of peace, which were the limits of our country; they have hunted beaver on our lands; they have acted contrary to the customs of all Indians, for they left none of the beavers alive _ they killed both male and female; they brought the Latanas into their country, to take part with them, after they had concerted ill designs against us. We have done less than either the English or French, that have usurped the lands of so many Indian nations, and chased them from their own country. This belt preserves my word.

"Hear, Younondio! _ What I say is the voice of all the Five Nations. Hear what they answer. Open your ears to what they speak. The Senecas, Cayugas, Onondagas, Oneidas and Mohawks say, that when they buried the hatchet at Cadarackui, in the presence of your predecessor, in the middle of the fort, they planted the tree of peace to be there carefully preserved: That in the place of a retreat for soldiers, that fort may be a rendevous for merchants: that in place of arms and ammunition of war, beavers and merchandise should only enter there.

"Here, Younondio! _ Take care for the future; that so great a number of soldiers as appear there, do not choke the tree of peace planted in so small a fort. It will be a great loss, if, after it had so easily taken root, you should stop its growth, and prevent its covering your country and ours with its branches. I assure you, in the name of the Five Nations, that our warriors shall dance to the calumet of peace under its leaves. They shall remain quiet on their mats, and shall never dig up the hatchet, till their brother Younondio, or Corlear, shall either jointly or separately endeavor to attack the country which the Great Spirit has given to our ancestors. This belt preserves my words, and this other the authority which the Five Nations have given me."

Then addressing himself to the interpreter, he added: "Take courage _ you have spirit _ speak! Explain my words. Forget nothing. Tell all that your brethren and friends say to Younondio, your Governor, by the mouth of Garangula, who loves you and desires you to accept of this present of beaver, and take part with me in my feast, to which I invite you. This present of beaver is sent to Younondio on the part of the Five Nations."

De la Barre, when this harangue was explained to him, was struck with surprise at its wisdom, and with chagrin at his ill success. He quietly left the council, and withdrew to his tent; while Garangula feasted the French officers, and then retired to his own country. The Governor returned to Montreal, disbanding his troops, thus ingloriously terminating his vaunted expedition against the Iroquois.

Garangula's speech evinces sagacity, spirit, courtesy, and self-possession couched in the most effective imagery, and pointed with the sting of sarcasm in marked contrast with the pompous parade and boisterous threat of the Governor. De Witt Clinton, a statesman and scholar of acknowledged reputation, has placed this forensic effort in the same rank of that of Logan's.[4]

The success of Bouquet in bringing the Delawares and Shawnees to submission in the fall of 1764, virtually ended Pontiac's War. Nevertheless, there still remained, so long as England had not taken possession of all the western posts, to that chief and his warriors farther to the westward, "the phantom hope of French assistance, to which they cling with infatuated tenacity." The English commander having determined to send, by way of Fort Pitt and the Ohio, a force to the Illinois, which still remained under control of the now humbled rival of England _ George Croghan, a deputy of Sir William Johnson, was dispatched in advance to clear the way if possible by reasoning with the Indians; _ by softening "their antipathy to the English, to expose the falsehoods of the French, and to distribute presents among the tribes by way of preparation." After many difficulties, he succeeded in accomplishing, in the main, the object of his mission. Upon the Wabash he met Pontiac and the Illinois chief, which rendered it needless for him to advance farther upon his journey in that direction; so, with the renowned Ottawa chief and many of his followers, he directed his course to Detroit, where he arrived on the seventeenth of August, 1765.[5]

On the twenty-seventh of August, Crogan had a meeting with Pontiac and all the Ottawa tribes, Chippewas and Pottawattamies, _ with the Hurons of Detroit, and the chiefs of those settlers at Sandusky and the Maumee river. "We are glad," said he, " to see so many of our children here present at your ancient council-fire, which has been neglected for some time past, since those high winds arose and raised some heavy clouds over your country. I now, by this belt, dress up your ancient fire and throw some dry wood upon it, that the blaze may ascend to the clouds, so that all nations may see it and know that you live in peace and tranquility with you fathers the English.

"By this belt[6] I disperse all the black clouds from over your heads, that the sun may shine clear on your women and children, that those unborn will enjoy the blessings of this general peace, now so happily settled between your fathers the English and you and all your younger brethren to the sun setting.

"Children: By this belt I gather up all the bones of your deceased friends and bury them deep in the ground, that the herbs and sweet flowers of the earth may grow over them, that we may not see them any more.

"Children: With this belt I take the hatchet out of your hands and I pluck up a large tree, and bury it deep, so that it may never be found any more; and I plant the tree of peace, where all our children may sit under it and smoke in peace with their fathers.

"Children: We have made a good road from the sun rising to the sun setting; and I desire that you will preserve that road good and pleasant to travel upon, that we may all share the blessings of this happy union. I am sorry to see our children disbursed through the woods; I therefore desire you will return to your ancient settlements, and take care of your council fire, which I have now dressed up, and promote the good work of peace." To these words Pontiac replied

"Father" We have all smoked out of the pipe of peace; it is your children's pipe; and as the war is all over and the Great Spirit and Giver of Light, who has made the Earth and everything therein, has brought us all together this day for our mutual good, to promote the good works of peace; _ I declare to all the nations, that I have settled my peace with you before I came here. And I now declare my pipe to be sent to Sir William Johnson that he may know I have made my peace, and have taken the King of England for my father, in presence of all the nations now assembled; and whenever any of those nations go to visit him, they may smoke out of it with him in peace."[7]

In 1775, at the dawn of the Revolution, the Colony of Virginia as well as the Continental Congress turned anxious eyes to the westward _ to the Indian tribes beyond the Ohio. As it was already apparent that they were being tampered with by agents of Great Britain, it was thought best to hold a treaty with them at Fort Pitt. The Delawares, Shawnees, Mingoes, Wyandotts and Ottawas were invited to be present. Among the chiefs of the latter tribe was Shegenaba, a son of the renown Pontiac. The Commissioners of the treaty, which was held in the Autumn of that year, addressed him a speech of condolence because of the death of his father, taking occasion at the same time to thank him for having preserved the life of a young man by the name of Field who had been captured by the Indians. To this speech Shegenaba replied:

"Fathers: From the information I had of the commandant of Detroit, with distrust I accepted your invitation, and measured my way to this council-fire with trembling feet. Your reception of me, convinces me of his falsehood, and the groundlessness of my fears. Truth and him have long been enemies. My father and many of my chiefs have lately tasted death. The remembrance of that misfortune almost unmanning me and filled my eyes with tears. Your kind condolence has lightened my heart of its heavy burden and shall be transmitted to my latest posterity.

"Fathers: I rejoice to hear what I wish they have heard, and do assure you it shall be faithfully be delivered to my nation. Should you want to speak to me in future, I shall joyfully attend, and thank you for the present invitation. The particular favor showed me, in the gun you have given me for the kindness showed your brother, claims my warmest acknowledgments. I am conscious I did but my duty. He who barely does his duty, merits no praise. If any of your people hereafter visit mine, whether through curiosity or business, or both motives, or if unwillingly compelled by the strong hand of the victor, they shall find the entertainment your brother found. You informed me, if my people visit yours, they shall have met an hospitable welcome. My fears are done away; I have not one doubt remaining _ I will recommend it to my young men to visit and get acquainted with yours.

"Fathers: What has passed this day is too deeply engraven on my heart for time itself to erase. I foretell that the sunny rays of his day's peace shall warm and protect our children's children from the storms of misfortune. To confirm it, I present to you my right hand _ that hand which never yet was given but the heart consented, which never shed human blood in peace, nor ever spared any enemy in war _ and I assure you of my friendship with a tongue which has never mocked at truth since I was at age to know falsehood was a crime."[8]

Speech of John Skenaudo, head chief of the Oneidas, delivered about 1812, when he was blind, and near a hundred and six years old, on discovering that the lands and improvements at the Castle were sold to the State by the intrigue, as he asserted, of certain white men. Taken from his lips by a missionary, who stated that tears ran copiously from his eyes, and from the eyes of many who heard him.

"My warriors and My Children _ Hear! _ It is cruel _ it is very cruel! A heavy burden lies on my heart _ it is very sick! This is a dark day. The clouds are black and heavy over the Oneida nation; a strong arm is heavy upon us, and our hearts groan under it. Our fires are put out, and our beds are removed from under us. The graves of our fathers are destroyed and their children are driven away. The Almighty is angry with us, for we have been very wicked _ therefore his arm does not keep us. Where are the chiefs of the rising sun? White chiefs now kindle their anxious fires. Here no Indian sleeps, but those that are sleeping in their graves. My house will soon be like theirs; soon will a white chief here kindle his fire! Your Skenando will be no more, and his village no more a village of Indians.[9]

"The news that came last night by our men from Albany made this a sick day in Oneida. All our children's hearts are sick, and our eyes rain like the black cloud that roar on the top of the trees of the wilderness. Long did the strong voice of

Shenando cry _ "children, take care! be wise! be straight!" His feet were then like the deer's, and his arms like the bears! He can now only mourn out a few words, and then be silent; and his voice will soon be heard no more in Oneida. But surely he will long be in the hearts of his children _ in the white man's land Skenando's name has gone far and will not die. He has spoken many words to make his children straight. Long has he said, drink no strong water, for it makes you mice for White men, who are cats. Many a meal have they eaten of you. Their mouth like a snare, and their way like the fox. Their lips are sweet, but their heart is wicked. Yet there are good whites and good Indians. I love all good men; and Jesus, whom I love, sees all. His great day is coming _ he will make all straight; he will say to cheating whites and drinking Indians: Begone ye! _ begone ye! _ Go! go! go! Certainly my children he will drive them away. In that day I will rejoice. But, oh! great sorrow is in my heart, that many of my children mourn.

"Hearken, my children, when this news sounds in the council house towards the setting sun, and the chiefs of the Six Nations hearken, and they send to the council by the Great Lake near the setting sun, and they cry _ make bows and arrows _ sharpen the tomahawk _ put the chain of friendship with the Whites into the ground _ warriors, kill! kill! The great chief at the setting sun won't kill any of the Six Nations that go into his land, because they have a chain of friendship with the whites; and he says the whites have made us wicked like themselves, and that we have <u>sold</u> them our land. We have <u>not</u> sold it _ <u>we have been cheated</u>; and my messengers shall speak true words in the great council toward the setting sun; and say yet, bury the tomahawk _ Oneidas must be children of peace."

On the night of the fourteenth of July, 1815, the Black Buffalo, principal chief of the Teton tribe[10] of Indians died at Portage De Sioux, on the upper Mississippi. The succeeding day he was buried with the honors of war. On his grave, spoke <u>Black Elk</u>, another chief:

"Do not grieve. Misfortunes well happen to the wisest and best men, death will come, and always comes out of season. It is the command of the Great Spirit, and all nations and people must obey. What is past and cannot be prevented, should not be grieved for. Be not be discouraged or displeased then, that in visiting your father here,[11] you have lost your chief. A misfortune of this kind may never again befall you, but this would have attended you perhaps at your own village. Five times have I visited this land and never returned with sorrow or pain. Misfortunes do not flourish particularly, in our path. They grow everywhere.

"What a misfortune for me that I could not have died this day, instead of the chief that lies before us. The trifling loss my nation would have sustained in my death would have been doubly paid for by the honors of my burial. They would have wiped off every thing like regret. Instead of being covered with a cloud of sorrow, my warriors would have felt the sun-shine of joy in their hearts. To me it would have been a more glorious occurrence. When <u>I</u> die it will be as humble. Instead of a noble grave and a grand procession, rolling music and thundering cannon, with a white flag waving at my head, _ I shall be wrapt in a robe (an old robe perhaps) and hoisted on a slender scaffold to the whistling winds, soon to be blown to the earth; my flesh to be devoured by wolves and my bones rattled on the plains by the wild beasts!"

Chapter Fourteen

Dunmore's War
April - November, 1774

    During the Spring session of the Virginia Assembly of 1774, of which Andrew Lewis was a member representing Botetourt county, and his brother, Charles Lewis, representing Augusta county, intelligence was received of Indian hostilities, and a further threatened out-break, which prompted these patriot brothers, as commanders of the militia of their respective counties, to send an express to the frontier settlements, warning them of their danger, and directing the militia officers to send out scouts to watch the warriors' paths, and put their several localities in a posture of defense . On the twenty-sixth of May, Lord Dunmore, Governor of Virginia, dissolved the Assembly, for having passed resolutions sympathizing with their oppressed fellow citizens of Boston, whose port had been ordered by the British Parliament to be closed as a fitting punishment for their recent destruction of tea in that harbor _ their sturdy protest against taxation without representation. The Lewis brothers now repaired to their homes to lead forth their people in defending the frontiers from the capacities of a savage enemy.[1]

    The tocsin of a border war resounding through the land, with the usual sickening details of murders, scalpings, captivities, burning and desolation of once peaceful homes, very naturally aroused Dunmore to a sense of the situation and exposure of the widely-extended frontiers of the Province confided to his charge. On the tenth of June, he issued a manly circular; well benefitting the occasion, declaring as the late Assembly had neglected to provide for the exigency, though sufficiently apprised of it, and the disposition of the Indians gave no longer any hope of a pacification, that recourse must now be had to the only means available to extricate themselves from so calamitous a situation. He, therefore, directed the commandants of the border counties to forthwith embody the militia of their respective localities, to erect small forts for the protection of the frontiers, and secure the important passes, especially recommending the establishment of a fort at the confluence of the Ohio and Great Kanawha; to march as occasion might require, to the assistance of other threatened settlements; to unite for the public good, their respective militia corps in one body, and follow the enemy into their own country, striking such a blow as might prove effective; to keep open the communications between the mouth of the Great Kanawha and Fort Pitt; leaving it to their zeal and discretion to provide extraordinary means for extraordinary occasions. And he closed by adding, that he should, at his own risk, supply them with ammunition as expeditiously as possible.[2]

On Sunday, July tenth, the Governor left his palace at Williamsburg, and proceeded to the frontiers, the better to acquaint himself with the most effectual measures necessary to suppress the cruelties of the savages. He reached Rosegill, in Middlesex county, the seat of Ralph Wormley, one of the Governor's Council, on the twelfth of that month, and Fredericksburg on the fifteenth; and thence made his way to Old Town, in Maryland, and finally entered the Virginia Valley. When writing from Rosegill, July twelfth, to Colonel Andrew Lewis, he contemplated raising no special command of his own. The idea of a second or Northern division, under his immediate direction, with Lewis and his Southern force to join him down the Ohio, must have been the result of an after thought.

On the twenty-fourth of July, his Lordship wrote Colonel Lewis from Winchester, stating that the general confederacy of the different Indian nations, their repeated acts of hostility, their discovery in, and the universal alarm throughout, all the frontiers of the Colony, and the unhappy situation of the divided people west of the Alleghenies, rendered it necessary for him to go in person to Fort Dunmore, at Pittsburgh, to put matters in the best shape for the defense of the country, and give the enemy such a blow as would break their confederacy, and render all their schemes abortive. "I intend," he continued, "to take as many men from this region as I can get in order in a short time; and desire you to raise a respectable body in your quarter, and join me either at the mouth of the Great Kanawha, or Wheeling, or such other point on the Ohio as may be most convenient for you to meet me."[3]

The Wakatomica expedition, next in the order of time, deserves an appropriate notice. Angus McDonald, a Major of militia, of Frederick County, had, in April, been down the Ohio, taking up and improving lands, in the region of the Great Kanawha. On the occurrence of the Indian difficulty at that period, he returned home; participated, on the eighth of June in a popular meeting at Winchester; and by authority of the Governor, embodied a considerable force, and proceeded in the early Summer, to Wheeling, where aided by William Crawford, Captain of a party of militia, he erected Fort Fincastle; after which, in accordance with the Governor's orders, he was to descend the river and join Colonel Lewis.[4]

As early as June twentieth, Lord Dunmore approved an expedition against the Shawnee towns, suggested by Major Connolly, who had the command of Fort Dunmore; and recommended the appointment of Captain Crawford as a proper person to conduct it;[5] but Major McDonald either took it upon himself, or had Connolly's authority, to carry it into effect. His force consisted of eight companies, numbering about four hundred men, who descended in boats from Wheeling, twenty-four miles, to mouth of Fish Creek, where they encamped on Tuesday, the twenty-sixth of July. Here it was determined to make a strike at the Wakatomica towns of the Shawnees, on the Muskingum, about ninety miles distant, as estimated by the zigzag route of that day; and Jonathan Zane, Thomas Nicholson, and Thady Kelly, were chosen the pilots.

With seven days' provisions assigned to each man, McDonald crossed the Ohio with his little force, and took up the line of march for the Indian country. A violent storm was encountered on the way, which lasted a whole night; and as a matter of precaution, the men were directed, the next morning, to discharge their guns in a hollow log, to deaden the sound, and load afresh. Nothing further of moment occurred till the following Sunday, when the advance discovered three Indians approaching on horseback; who on observing the Virginians, and a single shot being fired at them, wheeled and rode off. On Tuesday, the second of August, three others were seen in front, supposed to be spies of a larger force not far distant; and were promptly fired on by some of McDonald's men, when uttering war-whoop, they quickly disappeared.

The Virginians were immediately formed into three parties, and advanced, in parallel columns, some distance apart, about a half a mile, when they crossed a branch _ perhaps the northern prong of Simms' Creek _ and passed along its first bottom, with a view of finding a suitable place to cross a swamp between the first and upper bottoms. At length discovering a trace across the swamp ground, the heads of the three columns were thrown together in the passage; and, as they reached the base of the second bottom, on the top of which the Indians, under Captain Snake and other Chiefs, to the number of fifty or sixty, were lying in ambush, and fired on the advancing Virginians. The troops immediately deployed to the right and left, under the bank, and commenced ascending it, taking trees, and fighting the Indians, for some thirty minutes, in their own peculiar mode of warfare.

As Nathaniel Fox and a man named Martin were ascending a point, formed by a ravine from the Second bottom, aiming to gain the cover of a large oak on the top, both were fired at and both fell _ Martin to rise no more; while Fox received a shot in the breast, penetrating the bone; the ball was drawn out of the wound with a fragment of the clothing forced in with it. An Indian chief, concealed behind the oak whose shelter these two unfortunate whites were seeking, had shot them both, being in range, with a single ball. A soldier named Wilson having seen the chief when he discharged his gun, and dodged behind the tree, watched his opportunity; and, while the Indian was yet loading his rifle, with his ball only half down, he could not refrain from peering out to take a survey of the situation, when the vigilant frontiersman shot him dead. Four Indians, at least, were killed, and many wounded, while McDonald had two killed, and five wounded _ among the latter, William Linn, and John Hardin, who recovered and became noted in the subsequent border wars, though both eventually fell victims to savage warfare. This engagement took place about six miles _ apparently nearly east _ of a point on the Muskingum, opposite Wakatomica; and near the close of the day.

The Indians were driven about a mile and a half, firing upon their pursuers from every rising ground or covert, when they at last disappeared. During this exciting pursuit, Captain Teabaugh, an experienced soldier and fine marksman, brought down an Indian some distance in his advance. The men, who had become much scattered in the woods, pressing after the Indians, and endeavoring to outflank them, were now collected by McDonald and the other officers; and, leaving a party with the wounded, the main body hastened forward, some four and a half miles, to the river. Here the Indians were discovered, posted on the western bank, to dispute the passage of the whites, each party resorting to such protection as trees, logs, and banks afforded them; and watching for opportunities to fire on each other. John Hargus, of Captain Cresap's company, discovering an Indian on the opposite shore, occasionally popping up his head in the fork of a low tree, to get a view of the whites, loaded his rifle with an extra charge of powder, and two balls; and, when the warrior next raised his head, Hargus instantly fired, sending both balls through the fellow's neck, killing him on the spot. The Indians dragged off and buried the body, which was found the next morning, and scalped by Hargus.

There was a wide difference of opinion expected as to the feasibility of crossing the river, in the face of the enemy, who seemed determined on defending Wakatomica which lay directly in their rear. Not only the officers, but the men, entered warmly into this discussion; when Patrick Haggerty, a brave Irishman, of Captain James Wood's company, exclaimed, "Captain, wherever you'll lead us, even to the hot region below, I'll follow you!" The shades of night, however, were now rapidly approaching, and the hazardous attempt of crossing the Muskingum at that time was abandoned.

It was proposed in council by McDonald and his officers, to cross farther down the river in the night, meanwhile, to amuse the Indians. Just after dark, one of the interpreters called out to the Indians, in their native language, to come over the river; when a Delaware replied, by asking his name? It turned out that they were personally acquainted; and, on assurances of safety and good treatment, the Delaware came over. Major McDonald told the Delaware that Lord Dunmore had given him special instructions not to molest any Indians at peace with whites, especially the Delawares. This Indian recrossed the river, and soon returned accompanied by two of his countrymen, and a Mingo warrior, and much friendly talk transpired. To prevent the whites from destroying the Wakatomica towns, the Mingo consented to bring over two or three young Shawnee warriors to serve as hostages, till a council could be held with the chiefs. The Delawares also left in the most friendly manner. It was generally believed, that their chief object had been to befriend the Shawnees, and enable them to remove their aged people, women, children, and effects, from their villages.

Captains Michael Cresap and Henry Hoagland had been ordered to cross the river before day some considerable distance below Watatomica, cover the bank, and secure the landing of the remainder of the troops. Cresap, an old Indian fighter, was up all night, cautioning his men to keep themselves and arms in readiness for a morning attack, which he confidently expected; and, about two hours before day, silently formed by command, examined their rifles, and led them across the river. The others soon followed, meeting with no opposition. The Mingo not returning as promised, the whole body moved up the river towards Wakatomica; and, when within two miles of the town, they were met by the Mingo ambassador, who reported that the Indians declined to furnish any hostages.

Proceeding not over two hundred yards, the whites discovered a party of the enemy in ambush under a bank. While endeavoring to surround them, they fled, hotly pursued by Cresap, and about thirty of the men, when a skirmish ensued, Cresap overtaking and tomahawking one of the Indians. From the signs of blood, many others must have been wounded. Wakatomica, and its neighboring villages, five in number, were all burned; and saving only some corn, and a cow, for their own use, they destroyed about five hundred bushels of old corn, and cut down about twenty acres yet unmatured in the field. As the Mingo must have known of the ambuscade prepared for the whites that morning, and did not apprise them of it, he was secured; but under the circumstances of his friendly offices, he was spared, but retained as a prisoner. Passing through a deserted Delaware town on their return, nothing in it was injured, and only a little corn taken, of which the men were much in want. The men became much famished on their homeward march, subsisting on weeds, one ear of corn each per day, with a scant supply of game.[6]

Including the party already in service on the Ohio, under Major McDonald and Captain Crawford, Governor Dunmore, now that the grain harvest was over, succeeded in raising a force of some twelve hundred men. Those of them embodied in the counties of Frederick, Berkeley, and Dunmore, were put under the command of Angus Stephen as Colonel. They marched near the close of August, accompanied by the Governor, and Major Connolly, for Pittsburgh; and there, in September, his Lordship held a council with several of the Delaware and Mingo chiefs, in which he recounted a number of murders committed by the Shawnees, at different times, since Bouquet's treaty in 1764, and various robberies they had perpetrated. This, said the Governor, as our dispute with the Shawnees, "and I leave it to you to judge what they want." The Delaware and Mingo chiefs returned conciliatory speeches, conveying the impression that Cornstalk, head chief of the Shawnees, and that nation generally, were peaceably disposed, and that it was only a few of "the foolish young warriors who may have found a war-tomahawk hid in the grass, and may have made use of it."[7]

Dunmore, with seven hundred of the troops, descended the river in canoes to Wheeling; while Crawford, now advanced to the rank of Major, went down by land, with the remaining five hundred, serving as a convoy for the beeves for the use of the expedition. They arrived at Wheeling on the thirteenth of September; and, the next day, Crawford resumed his march by land, with the same force, on the southern side of the Ohio, escorting two hundred bullocks, and fifty pack-horses; proceeding to a point opposite the mouth of the Big Hockhocking, a distance of one hundred and ten miles below Wheeling, where men, cattle, and horses, swam the river. Just above the junction of the Hockhocking, Crawford and his men erected a block-house, with some stockading, which was designated with the name of Fort Gower, in honor of the Earl Gower, of England.[8] About twenty acres of ground were partially cleared[9] for timber for the block-house, stockading, and fuel; and to some extent to remove protection, for a suitable distance, to any approaching enemy.

Dunmore, with the troops under his command, arrived in one hundred canoes, including a few boats of large dimensions,[10] in a few days after. One evening his Lordship prevailed upon Simon Girty, and his half brother, John Turner, together with Joseph and Thomas Nicholson, who had all been prisoners with the Indians, to perform some of the Aboriginal war-dances, which they did, with accompanying war-songs, kicking fire-brands about the camp in lively Indian style, to the no small amusement of the Governor and the whole army.[11]

While at Hockhocking, the friendly Delaware Chiefs, White Eyes and John Montour, joined Dunmore's forces[12]: White Eyes was at once dispatched by the Governor to invite the Shawnees to a treaty, who soon returned, reporting that they would not listen to any propositions for an accommodation; but in the figurative language of the Red Man, the Delaware chief informed his Lordship, that "seven hundred warriors had gone to the southward to speak to the army there, and they had been followed by another nation; that they would begin with the Virginians there in the morning, and their business would be over by breakfast time, and then they would speak with his Lordship."[13] This shows the confidence of the confederate Indians in their ability to beat, first Lewis, and then Dunmore, in detail; particularly designing to make quick work with Lewis _ a sort of morning diversion before breakfast.

On the tenth of October, Dunmore was observed, as he had been on previous occasions, to place his ear now and then at the river's surface, and said he thought he heard the roaring of guns; when Abraham Thomas, a young soldier, placed his ear, at the Governor's suggestion, in the same position, and declared he "distinctly heard the report of musketry"[14] __ an intervening distance of sixty-six miles by the bend of the river, but twenty-eight only by a direct course across the country from the mouth of Hockhocking to Point Pleasant. In view of White Eyes' information, and these supposed evidences of a conflict, it is neither strange, nor suspicious of any treachery on the part of Dunmore, that he should have remarked to Major Connally and the officers on the day of the battle, that he expected by that time that Lewis had hot work.[15]

Why, under such circumstances, his Lordship did not hasten to the support of Lewis, history and tradition are alike silent. It can only be surmised, that believing White Eyes report of the strength of the Indian army correct, he would conclude it inferior to that of the Virginians; and that, on any thing like an equal footing, Lewis' frontiersmen, accustomed from boyhood to the use of the rifle, and familiar with the methods of Indian warfare, were well able to cope with the savage enemy. That this was the conclusion reached by Dunmore, is well attended by his own independent action with about the same number of them as composed at Point Pleasant.

The refusal of the Shawnees to meet Dunmore at Fort Gower to settle all differences by amicable terms of peace; and learning of their movement in force against Lewis, who, he believed, was fully able to repel them, his Lordship had only to push on to the Scioto towns, and lay them waste in the absence of their warriors; and, should the Indian army return while they were invading their country, to fight them till they were completely subdued. On the next day, October eleventh, the army accordingly set out for the Indian country, having first dispatched instructions to Lewis to join him on the way.

Immediately after the battle at Point Pleasant, Lewis sent an express to Hockhocking to inform Dunmore of his operations; but on arriving at that point, it was found that the Governor had marched with his troops across the country for the Shawnee towns on the Scioto, each man carrying a supply of flour for sixteen days. Captain Kuykendall, considerably advanced in years, was left in command of Fort Gower, having in charge the cattle and supplies. The army camped the first night at Federal Creek[16], the second at Sunday Creek, both in Athens County, Ohio; and the third night a few miles apparently west of the present village of Nelsonville, in the same county, where Lewis' messenger overtook his Lordship, with the intelligence of the signal victory gained at Point Pleasant over the combined warriors of the North Western tribes, which, when announced, produced a thrill of joy throughout the camp of the borderers.[17] The next night they stopped at the Falls of the Hockhocking, a mile above the present village of Logan; and, near there, left the river, camping once, if not twice, between that point and their final location on Sippo Creek, in what is now Pickaway County, Ohio.

During this march of Dunmore up the Hockhocking Valley, and thence across to the waters of Scioto, no incident of importance occurred. Once, Simon Girty, one of the scouts and pilots shot at, and wounded an Indian spy, who, however, escaped, leaving signs of blood behind him. Defiles were passed, where parties of the enemy were posted in the rocky cliffs to annoy the advancing army, but they shrunk from making any demonstration; and, on one occasion, the line of battle was formed, when the Indians hastily decamped.[18] It is quite probable, that the governor profited by the useful suggestions of the friendly Delaware chiefs; and thus, perhaps, avoided the snares and ambuscades of the wily Shawnees.

Lord Dunmore occasionally indulged in a bit of fun and humor. His Scotch friend, Colonel Stephen, was quite corpulent, and was the only officer who enjoyed the luxury of a horse; for even the Governor trudged along on foot, with his knapsack on his back. But of mischief, he prevailed upon Nathaniel Fox, one of McDonald's men, who had been wounded on the Wakitomica expedition, to spirit away the Colonel's horse, which necessitated his marching on foot for several hours till he was well nigh exhausted, when the horse was kindly restored to its owner. When about to cross the Hockhocking at a place called "the Press," within the present limits of Hockhocking county, where traders had formerly pressed their skins preparatory to packing, John Stevenson, one of the Captains, a man of strong and vigorous frame, tendered his good services to carry his Lordship over on his back. "Hoot mon," retorted the sturdy old Scotchman, "I'll gang over as the ithers do," and dashed across the stream.[19]

Cornstalk and his Indian army, having met with signal discomfiture, made haste for their towns. They had no heart either to renew the contest with Lewis and his Long Knives, or make the promised visit to Dunmore. The morning call on Lewis at Point Pleasant had proved a more disastrous undertaking than the confederate Indians had anticipated; and when defeat came, the neighboring tribes who had joined the Shawnees, including even the fierce Mingos, now abandoned them and their villages to their fate. Dunmore was marching direct for their towns, and all their stratagems to entrap him had proved ineffectual; and they had, moreover, every reason to expect a further invasion from the victorious troops at Point Pleasant, who had their revenges to satisfy.

Another council of the Shawnees was called by Cornstalk. It presented a very different aspect from that held just before setting out on the campaign, when they were so hopeful and defiant. Now they were surly and dejected. Cornstalk, the father of his people, now addressed them, with less formality than effect. He reminded them of their late ill-success; that they would give no heed to his admonitions, for he had counseled peace, and they were now suffering the consequences. He touchingly alluded to the loss of Captain Dickson, Puck-e-shin-wa and other valiant warriors in battle; to their wigwams and cabins filled with their wounded, and to the one depicted in every family circle. "What," he earnestly inquired, "will you do now? The Big Knives are pressing upon us with two powerful armies, and we shall all be killed. Now you must fight, or we are undone." No one answered. "Then," said he, "let us kill all our women and children, and fight until not one shall be left to tell the sad story of the once proud Shawnees." Still all were silent. "Then," exclaimed Cornstalk, striking his tomahawk in the post, in the center of the council-house, "I will go, and make peace."[20]

It was then agreed to send Matthew Elliott, a white trader, well befitting the character of a go-between, with a flag, begging Lord Dunmore to withdraw his army from their country, and appoint commissioners to meet their chiefs at Pittsburgh, and arrange terms of peace. At Chillicothe, on the west bank of the Scioto, the Indians had cleared the woods to a great distance, so as not to prove a means of protection for the Virginians, should they advance so far; they had yet plenty of ammunition and provisions; and resolved, if Elliott should fail in his mission, that, after sending off their women and children they would steal up in the night and attack Dunmore's camp; then fall back over the Scioto to Chillicote, and there make a stand; if pursued, they would fire on the whites, doing all the damage they could, and then make a final retreat.[21]

At dusk of the evening, of about the sixteenth of October, when the army had just halted for the night's encampment, Elliott made his appearance. To the request for a treaty at Pittsburgh, the Governor replied that he was well inclined to cease hostilities and make peace; but as he was so near their towns, and within convenient distance of the other hostile tribes, it would be best to negotiate at once, and not delay it; so, if proper terms could not be agreed upon, he should be forced to carry on the war. He then named a place, to which he would march the next day and encamp, and would there receive and listen to their proposals. John Gibson, a well-known trader and Simon Girty, were dispatched with Elliott on his return, to give assurances of his Lordship's good intentions.

The next day the army reached the point in the northern bank of Sippo Creek eight miles east of Chillicothe, upon a pleasant piece of ground, in view of the Pickaway Plains: It was without any defenses, natural or artificial, and was only selected as a convenient locality for holding a council with the Indians. The creek in front was too small to form any impediment to an approach from that quarter, and the country was level and accessible in all other directions. In the center of the camp, a small pole-building was improvised for the occasion, not much more than a pen, some twenty by twenty five feet in size, which was stockaded; & there the Governor made his head quarter; around it the army encamped.[22] Dunmore peeled a large white oak, and wrote on it with red chalk "<u>Camp Charlotte</u>," in honor of the popular Queen of England.[23]

Cornstalk soon made his appearance, preserving his natural dignity, in his defeat, and evincing every disposition to do what he could to accommodate matters; but frankly acquainted the Governor, that none of the Mingoes would attend, and he was apprehensive that a full council could not be convened. Dunmore requested that he would send runners, and convoke as many chiefs of the other nations as he could, and bring them to the council fire without delay. With Cornstalk came his sister, the Grenadier Squaw, somewhat of a diplomat, and her graceful daughter, Fauny - both mother and daughter quite tall, and riding fine horses, with elegant saddles.[24]

On the third day after Dunmore and his army had formed their camp on Sippo Creek, Cornstalk re-appeared, having eight chiefs with him. The Governor addressed them, and, from a written memorandum, recited the various infractions, on the part of the Shawnees, of former treaties, and of different murders of white people they had committed in the most unprovoked manner. Cornstalk made a manly reply, mingling not a little of recrimination with his defense of the Indians; and when he had concluded, a time was set for holding the treaty, and the chiefs again urged to bring forward a suitable representation to attend it.

Anxious to have the Mingoes represented at the contemplated treaty, eight of whose implacable leaders the Governor then had in confinement, and learning that Logan had returned on the twenty first of that month, from a bloody foray on the frontiers of Holston, with several scalps and three prisoners, his Lordship dispatched Gibson to urge his attendance on so important an occasion; but he replied surlily, that "he was a warrior, not a counselor, and would not come;" but, at length, so far relented, as to send in his place - offering his simple and sublime appeal to the white man in his own vindication, and expressive of the joy it would give him to witness the return of peace.[25]

Shortly after, Cornstalk and the other chiefs repaired to Camp Charlotte, and entered into negotiations. Quite a large number of Indians attended __ all, apparently, Shawnees; and a place was designated outside the camp, where they were to deposit their guns. Captain Hoagland, who commanded the guard stationed there, had some difficulty in enforcing the order; for several of the Indians urged, in vain, the privilege of taking their arms into camp with them under the pretense of trading them off to the soldiers. One of the chiefs who accompanied Cornstalk, was quite aged, and was observed sitting a long time with Lord Dunmore, conversing in French.[26]

An incident is related, showing the unity of the frontier people of that day against the Indians generally, without much regard whether the nature of their mission was one of peace or war. While three prominent chiefs __ Cornstalk, very likely, one of the number _ were sitting with the Governor in his tent, a backwoodsman having then concluded he could kill them all at a single fire; so passing around the tent, when he thought he had them in range, he discharged his rifle through the canvas, and instantly disappeared among the crowd. No one knew who committed the dastardly act, or, at least no person was willing to reveal the name of the guilty actor. Fortunately, nobody was hurt. It was, however, a narrow escape for the three Shawnee ambassadors. Lord Dunmore was shocked at such treacherous conduct; but punishment, under the circumstances, could not be inflicted. With increased precaution, the good work of peace proceeded.[27]

In these negotiations, Cornstalk displayed remarkable skill; and enforced his views with the persuasive oratory of a "forest Demosthenes." He evinced the sincerest patriotic devotion to his country and people; and, in strains of commanding eloquence, he recapitulated the accumulated wrongs which his fathers had suffered, and his people were now suffering, at the hands of the Virginians. He boldly charged the white people with having precipitated the present war by the massacres at Pipe Creek, and Baker's Bottom. With masterly power, he sketched the once happy and powerful condition of the Indians, and strikingly contrasted it with their present fallen fortunes and unhappy destiny. He accused the white race of perfidiousness in their intercourse with the Indians, and charged the traders with the most flagrant dishonesty; and proposed, as the basis of a treaty, that no persons should thereafter be permitted to carry on trade with the Shawnees for individual profit; but that the Government should send to them such articles as they needed, by the hands of honest men, who should be directed to exchange, at fair prices, for their furs and peltries, and that no spirituous liquors of any kind should be sent among them, as from the "fire-water" of the whites proceeded only evil to the Indians.[28]

Cornstalk's speech was lengthy; and delivered in so loud a tone of voice that he was heard all over the camp. Benjamin Wilson, one of the officers present, declared of this great effort of Cornstalk, that "when he arose, he was in no wise confused or daunted, but spoke in a distinct, and audible voice, without stammering or repetition, and with peculiar emphasis. His looks, while addressing Dunmore, were truly grand and majestic, yet graceful and attractive." "I have heard" continues the narrator, many years after, "the first orators in Virginia, Patrick Henry and Richard Henry Lee, but never have I heard one whose powers of delivery surpassed those of Cornstalk on that occasion,"[29] Such testimony from one who afterward, served with Henry, Wythe, Pendleton, Mason, Madison, and Marshall, in the Virginia Convention of 1788, and with Richard Henry Lee on other occasions, deserves to be regarded in the light of the most unstinted praise.

In the midst of these peaceful negotiations, after the Governor and Cornstalk had mutually indulged in charges of hostile acts on the part of each others' people, yet agreeing to forget and forgive _ or, in Indian parlance, to bury the bloody tomahawk so deep that it should never again be disinterred, Indian messengers came rushing into camp, announcing the near approach of Lewis and his army, "like so many devils, and would kill them all."[30]

After the battle at Point Pleasant, Lewis and his men were busily occupied, for several days, in caring for the wounded, collecting the scattered beeves and working on the store-house, bastion, and other defenses, in progress of erection, which, by subsequent enlargement, became a small stockade fort, rectangular in form, about eighty yards long, with block-houses at two of its corners. Early on the morning of the thirteenth of October, messengers previously sent, returned with letters from Dunmore to Lewis, with instructions to march as soon as possible, with all his disposable force, towards the Shawnee towns, and unite with his Lordship at a designated point, some twenty to twenty-five miles from Chillicothe _ perhaps on Salt Creek. The next day, Francis Slaughter, with his small force, arrived with the remaining beeves, from the mouth of Elk. Every preparation for the march of the troops into the Indian country was now prosecuted with the utmost vigor, in addition to the work of completing the defenses, and clearing the undergrowth some distance from the lines.[31]

By the evening of the seventeenth Lewis' troops, with their supplies, had crossed the Ohio, and camped that night on its northern bank. The men numbered about eleven hundred and fifty, all eager to fight the Shawnees and their allies, and lay waste to their towns as with the besom of destruction. They drove one hundred and ten beeves, and carried a ten days' supply of flour, with half a pound of powder, and a pound and a half of lead cast into bullets, to each man, and a horse assigned to each company for the conveyance of tents. William Fleming, Colonel of the Botetourt troops, who had been severely wounded in the action, was left in command at Point Pleasant, with Captains Dickinson, Lockridge, Herbert, and Slaughter, and two hundred and seventy-eight men, of whom seventy-one were wounded, and the rest generally sick, lame, or otherwise unfit for the hardships of active service.[32]

Lewis moved forward, on the eighteenth, for the Shawnee towns, some eighty miles distant - perhaps something more by the zig-zag trails they had to pursue. The army was piloted by that brave soldier and superior woodsman, Captain Arbuckle; and the line of march was kept as compact as possible. When only a mile and a half from the Ohio, a deserted Indian camp was discovered, in which were sundry articles, showing haste on the part of the enemy in their homeward flight after the battle. The next day, while marching, a wild deer ran through the ranks, which tempted one of the men to shoot at it, wounding James Newell through the knee. That night the army camped about twenty miles from the Ohio. Early the ensuing morning, a large body of Indians were seen by the scouts, and the whole camp was called to arms, forming a circle, and keeping their ranks about an hour and a half, when no enemy appearing, and having sent back the wounded man Newell, the army re-commenced its march.[33]

Advancing cautiously, in a north-westerly direction, on an average of some eleven miles a day, and following, apparently, an old Indian trail, the army reached the well-known Salt Licks, near the head of the southern branch of Salt Creek, in now Lick township, not very far from the county seat of Jackson county, Ohio, and about thirty-five miles from Point Pleasant. From this locality, they probably descended the Salt Creek valley to the Scioto, and thence to a prairie on Kinnickinnick Creek, where, in sight of an Indian village, whose inhabitants had just deserted and fired it, and while yet some thirteen miles south of Chillicothe, now Westfall, they were met early on the twenty-fourth of the month, by an express from Lord Dunmore, ordering him to halt where they were, as he had very nearly concluded a treaty with the Indians. As the troops had been fired on that morning, and their present locality was unfitted for a camp, Lewis concluded to march on to a more suitable position, where they would have the convenience of good water, as well as a more safe encamping place; and thus he ventured to take the liberty of seeking better quarters.

The Indian spies reporting the near approach of Lewis and his army to their towns, Cornstalk and his associates, alarmed at the threatening aspect of affairs, quickly fled from Camp Charlotte, to the relief of their wives and children, leaving the treaty incomplete. Dunmore dispatched another express, who met Lewis troops on their march that day, with information that peace was, in a measure concluded, the Shawnees having acceded to his terms, and he again ordered Lewis to encamp where he was; but that he, and such officers as he felt disposed to indulge with the privilege, might visit his Lordship at Camp Charlotte.

Lewis did not deem it prudent to go to the Governor's camp with only a few officers, and therefore marched his whole force with the design of uniting with the northern division, but the guide mistaking the path, took the one that led between Camp Charlotte and Chillicothe _ the trail, in fact, lead directly to the Grenadier Squaw's Town,[34] and thence on to Chillicothe; and camped at the close of the day on the west bank of Congo Creek, two miles above its mouth, and five and a quarter from Chillicothe, with the Grenadier Squaw's Town nearly half way between

Not only were the Indians startled by this bold march of Lewis and his men, heading for the principal towns; but the Governor, too, evidently began to surmise, that, smarting under their losses at Point Pleasant, they were determined on taking ample revenge, now almost within its very accomplishment. So he set out in person, riding over to "Camp Lewis," six miles distant, accompanied by the Delaware chief White Eyes, the trader Gibson, and some fifty of his men. White Eyes, knowing full well that Dunmore had ordered Lewis to stop his march, and had not been obeyed, asked in his simplicity, if one big man could stop another big man?

His Lordship, on reaching Lewis, just at dusk of the evening, not a little nettled at the independence of his subordinate, inquired why he had not halted when repeatedly order to do so; or whether it was his purpose to push on to the Shawnee towns? Lewis informed his Lordship the reasons for not having stopped, and how it happened that he got between him and the towns, supposing that Camp Charlotte was nearer Chillicothe than it really was, and had missed the proper trail; but that he need not be apprehensive of his attacking the towns after having received his Lordship's orders to the contrary.

Lewis designed, in good faith, to have marched to Camp Charlotte, but his troops, and those of Dunmore's division also, murmured that they could not be permitted to attack the towns of the treacherous Indians; and, it is related, that Lewis had to double and triple his guard that night, to prevent the men from killing the Governor and White Eyes.[35]

Very soon after the troops had formed their evening camp, it was discovered that there was a great number of wild turkeys in the neighborhood. A strong party sallied forth, and soon came upon the uncautious turkeys, who, standing aghast, with heads erect, suddenly received a heavy fire, killing not a few of the innocents. The survivors fled, only to be closely pursued, through copse and glen, over hill and dale, in the course of which many other fell victims to the deadly rifles of the Virginia marksmen; and the victors at length returned to camp, in high glee, laden with the spoils of war, recounting their exploits in "the battle of the turkey gobblers," and enjoying throughout the camp an evening repast of the richest viands of forest-life.

While on the way, the Governor and escort had heard the firing, and some supposed that the Indians and whites had gotten again embroiled in battle. All however, was quiet before their arrival; and the Red Stone boys, as Dunmore's men were called _ a fine set of fellows they were, better uniformed that the West Virginians _ gladly partook of the hospitality of their fellows, and listened, with thrilling interest, to the story of the battle of Point Pleasant fought two weeks previously, with its many strange incidents and romantic adventures.[36] They in turn, related the story of Logan's extraordinary speech, which had just been delivered, and was fresh in the minds of all; several attempts at its rehearsal were made during the evening _ some of the most striking passages of which, were so strongly impressed upon the memories of those who had heard them, that they referred to them a quarter of a century thereafter.[37]

The next morning, Tuesday, the twenty-fifth, the Governor requested Lewis to introduce him to his officers. They were accordingly ranged in rank, and had the honor of a formal introduction. His Lordship politely thanked them for the important services they had rendered their country on so momentous an occasion, and tendered them his high esteem and respect for their gallantry and good conduct. He assured them that the Shawnees were completely subdued, and had agreed to all his terms; and that, as the presence of Lewis and his troops could be of no benefit, but rather a hindrance, he ordered them to return to Point Pleasant, and leave a small garrison of fifty men there under William Russell, a Captain of one of the companies, the rest to retire to their respective localities. They took up the line of march that day, reaching Point Pleasant the night of the twenty-eighth, whence they marched by companies, and early the ensuing month were welcomed at their several homes by their families and friends.[38]

The departure of the Long Knives re-assured the Shawnees of the entire good faith of Lord Dunmore, and they again repaired to Camp Charlotte to complete the treaty. Learning that the Mingoes generally designed to slip off to the Lakes with their prisoners and stolen horses, his Lordship detached, on the night of the twenty-fifth, Major Crawford, with two hundred and forty men, to surprise a settlement of these implacable Indians called Seekonk, on the Salt Lick Town _ sometimes the Hill Town _ some thirty or forty miles above, on the waters of the Scioto, reaching there the following night undiscovered; and the next morning, before day, surrounding the principal town, with one half his force, and sending the remainder to a smaller settlement, half a mile distant. The Indians were taken by surprise, six of whom were killed, several wounded, fourteen, mostly women and children, were captured, the rest escaping under cover of the darkness. These Mingoes, from every indication, designed speedily deserting their towns, which Crawford's party burned, and returned in triumph with their prisoners and plunder.[39]

Under the circumstances, it is not strange that the Shawnees threw themselves on the Governor's mercy. They had been beaten in the severest battle they ever fought. The warriors of the neighboring tribes, who had joined and encouraged them in the war, now left them to shift, as best they could, for themselves _ Logan alone sending his manly acquiescence. These earnest efforts at pacification were not in vain. The Shawnees frankly told the Governor to dictate the terms, and they should be complied with. In these he was not severe. He simply required that they should surrender all prisoners, return, or pay for, all horses stolen since the last war, and never more commence hostilities; that, henceforth, the Ohio should be the boundary between the Virginians and Indians, and the latter should not hunt on the south side of that river; that they should not only not molest any persons on the Ohio, but should render them every assistance and protection; that they should consent to such regulations concerning trade as should thereafter be submitted to them, and for the fulfillment of the stipulations regarding the surrender of white prisoners, and return of stolen horses, six chiefs _ or two chiefs, and four sons of chiefs _ should be given as hostages; while some unsettled points, and minute details, should be refined for future discussion to a treaty to be held at Pittsburgh the ensuing Spring.[40] Quite a number of prisoners were then surrendered.

There were two persons accompanying Lord Dunmore, who, doubtless, had a marked influence and deservedly so, upon his actions _ Colonel Stephen and White Eyes; and to them should be accorded no little credit for the peaceful solution of the campaign: Stephen, who had been in command on the frontiers from 1754 to 1764, was thoroughly acquainted with Indian wars and their causes; and he was constrained to declare, when preparing for this expedition, that the Indians were a brave people, and, in his opinion, would behave well, were their minds not poisoned by the blackguard traders allowed freely to go among them.[41] So the representative of the Delaware Council, White Eyes used every means to prevent further bloodshed, and induce the Governor to relinquish his plan of scouring the forest on his way from the Ohio to the Scioto; and urged that the mere presence of so large a force in the midst of their country would yet bring the Shawnees to terms. The result fully justified the wisdom of his course; and, at the close of the treaty, Lord Dunmore took occasion to pay a deserved compliment to White Eyes and his people. They had been, he said, the unflinching advocates of peace, he and they were one body; and the Shawnees must remember that only out of regard, for these, their grandfathers; had he treated them so leniently.[42]

Dunmore's conduct in making peace has been charged as strange and mysterious[43] _ his actions the subsequent year in Virginia serving to give color to these views. It must be confessed, that he boldly accused the Indians of inciting the war by their murders and robberies. Looking impartially at all the facts a century afterward there is really nothing to be found which would justify any suspicions that he catered to the passions or prejudices of the Indians with a view of conciliating them, and securing their cooperation in a possible war between the mother country and the colonies. Though there were unhappy forebodings, yet few if any anticipated open hostilities. Lord Dunmore's sole objection in making this long and hazardous expedition, in which he had so nobly borne his share of fatigue and self-denial, was to compel the savages to cease their inhuman barbarities. Lewis and his brave army had convinced them that the Virginians could not only beat them in open conflict, but could press their way to the very thresholds of their cabins in the wilderness. When asked by an humble and prostrate foe, what brave man would refuse to that foe life and peace? Lord Dunmore was both brave and generous; and if he could bring about peace, with promised security to the frontier inhabitants from future aggression, it was all he desired. He did not seek the destruction of a brave people because they had been his enemies.[44]

The treaty once happily concluded, the Shawnee hostages, and eleven Mingo prisoners _ the other Mingo captives having been released __ were assigned two to a company; and the army returned by its outward route to Fort Gower. There, a popular meeting was held, on the fifth of November, addressed by one of the officers, contending for of the Colonies. They adopted two resolutions _ one, renewing their allegiance to the King, yet pledging themselves to exert every power at their command for the defence of the rights and liberties of America; the other expressive of the greatest respect for their royal Governor, Lord Dunmore, "who, we are confident." they declared, "underwent the great fatigue of this singular campaign for no other motive than the true interests of the country." This compliment to his Lordship, without a dissenting voice, and by those who had the best opportunities of judging correctly of his conduct must forever stand as his triumphant vindication against the vague surmises of later years, that he designedly permitted the Indians to attack Lewis, presuming they would annihilate his army, and thus seriously cripple the strength of Virginia, and then he would treat them leniently with a view of conciliating them to his Majesty's interest in the expected contest with the Colonies.

If further evidence were wanting of the universal opinion of that day of Lord Dunmore's patriotic motives in conducting the campaign, it is to be found in the unanimous vote of thanks to him by the Virginia Convention, of March, 1775 _ "a tribute justly due for his truly noble, wise and spirited conduct on the late expedition against our Indian enemy." Beside Washington, Jefferson, Henry, and Dr. Walker, than whom none in Virginia were better acquainted with Indian affairs, there were Andrew Lewis, Adam Stephen, William Christian, and Samuel McDowell, who had served on the campaign against the Indians, all heartily uniting in this public expression in his Lordship's favor. The respective addresses of the Mayor, Aldermen, and Common Council of Norfolk; and of the freeholders of Fincastle, express a grateful sense of his services on the expedition against the Shawnees.[45]

Cornstalk, with several Indians, and the Grenadier Squaw,[46] accompanied the army on its return march to Fort Gower; the old chief making his lodge at night with Captain Michael Cresap, with whom he was on terms of friendly familiarity. Thence the troops divided into squads, some returning in canoes up the river, and others by land. Some of the parties nearly starved, relying upon such game as chance threw in their way; others, of which John Guin's mess was one, occasionally had the good fortune to secure a plentiful supply, having killed eighteen turkeys on a single small island in the river.

This Indian war, though of limited duration, cost Virginia, in addition to many precious lives, nearly £150,000.[47] It served only as a temporary check on the Indians; holding them back two of three years after the outbreak of the Revolution _ a consideration, however, well worth the large outlay which it cost the people of that Colony. It had another important bearing on the subsequent contest for independence _ it served as a school for not a few ablest military leaders whose experience and prowess were recognized on almost every battle-field in the Central and Southern States, and even to the bank of the Mississippi.

Chapter Fifteen

<u>Battle</u> <u>of</u> <u>Point</u> <u>Pleasant</u>
10 October 1774

During the ten years succeeding Bouquet's Treaty, in 1764, there had been as previously noticed, frequent murders on the frontiers committed alike by colonists and Indians. The number slain of both races was scarcely less than those resulting from the entire war of 1774. Sometimes the mischief-making and life-destroying 'fire water' was the traceable cause; sometimes mercenary motives; while the breaking of plighted faith had much to do in bringing about these sanguinary occurrences. A singular instance maybe cited of several Cherokees killed by border Virginians, near Staunton, in May, 1765, which the Indians agreed with John Stuart, Superintendent of the Southern Indian Department, to condone for five hundred dressed deer-skins for each person so slain, but the payment having been long delayed, the surviving friends of the murdered Indians retaliated, in 1768, by killing five Virginia traders in the Cherokee country; and, when upbraided for the act, they urged this want of faith of the part of the English as their justification. In contradistinction of such faithless promises, it is related that certain families had obtained, by private treaty with the Indians permission to settle and hunt on the Monongahela river; and when the war now broke out, Governor Dunmore sent a message to warn them, that, if they remained, all would be killed. An Indian who happened to hear it delivered, replied indignantly to the messenger, "Tell your King he is a liar; Indian no kill these people." And the families in fact remained there unharmed throughout all the horrors of the bloody war that followed.

These mutual aggressions of the white and red race for a long decade of years _ here a trader or borderer murdered, and there an Indian slain _ culminated in the killing of some of Logan's family and others at Baker's Bottom. The bad blood, once stirred, on the frontiers, in the Spring and Summer of 1774, and the vindictive feelings in return, engendered by the Mingoes and Shawnees, very naturally eventuated in an open Indian war, with all its concomitant horrors.

Lord Dunmore, the Virginia Governor, ordered Andrew Lewis, Colonel of the militia, of Botetourt county, to raise such body of men as he might think necessary, and march at once at their head to the mouth of the Great Kanawha, and there erect a fort; and, should he deem his force sufficient, to proceed directly to the

Indian towns, destroy them, their crops and supplies; prevent the enemy, if possible, from crossing the Ohio, and keep the communication open between his command and Forts Wheeling and Dunmore _ the latter at Pittsburgh. Such were the Governor's orders as late as July twelfth, at which time he contemplated no distinct expedition of his own; for he mentioned having ordered a large body of men to join Lewis, alluding to the troops under Angus McDonald, who was Major, and, added, that he should lend more, if fit men could be obtained for the service.[1]

Changing his plans, and resolving on a separate expedition, Dunmore, on the thirtieth of August, directed Lewis to meet him at the mouth of the Little Kanawha. To this Lewis replied, that it was then too late to make the change suggested; and hence should proceed, with all possible dispatch, to the mouth of the Great Kanawha, and there await his further orders on arrival.[2]

On the first day of September, Lewis reached what was then known as the Big Savannah or Great Levels of Greenbrier, where Lewisburg is now situated, and found most of the Augusta regiment, under his brother, Charles Lewis, already there, together with a part of the Botetourt regiment under William Fleming. Their encampment, where the several bodies of troops united for the campaign, was not inaptly denominated Camp Union. William Christian, with a portion of the Fincastle troops; John Field, with some forty men from Culpeper, and Francis Slaughter, with about the same number, from Dunmore, afterwards Shenandoah county, soon after arrived.

Charles Lewis was detached, on the sixth of September, with his Augusta troops, numbering about six hundred, with a drove of one hundred and eight beef cattle, and four hundred pack-horses, laden with fifty-four thousand pounds of flour, to proceed to the mouth of Elk, and there make canoes for transporting the supplies to the mouth of the Kanawha. He was soon after followed by Field's company. On Saturday, the tenth of that month, two of Field's men, named Coward and Clay, left the company to hunt deer, on the waters of Little Meadow River. Two Indians, one past middle life, the other his son, a youth of thirteen, first discovered the white hunters, and concealed themselves under a large fallen tree; and as the whites passed, unconscious of danger, around the roots, the elder Indian killed Clay, and running up to take his scalp, Coward, some distance behind, shot and killed the Indian, so that both the red man and white fell very nearly together. A bundle of ropes was found where the Indians were concealed, which proved that stealing horses was their purpose. The young Indian escaped, and hastened to the Indian towns, giving the Shawnees the first notice of a large army moving against them.[3]

Colonel Andrew Lewis marched on the twelfth with about 450 men, consisting of Fleming's Botetourt troops, with the companies of Evan Shelby and William Russell from Fincastle, Thomas Buford from Bedford, and Slaughter's from Dunmore, conveying the remaining beeves, and 200 pack-horse loads of flour, leaving Christian with the rest of his Fincastle men at Camp Union, to guard the residue of the provisions, and hasten them forward, as soon as the brigade of horses should return from the mouth of Elk.

Thus were nearly five weeks consumed in transporting the troops, and their supplies from Camp Union to Point Pleasant, a distance of one hundred and sixty miles; an entire wilderness route, through defiles and fastnesses, in the rough and mountainous region of West Virginia. They were piloted by Matthew Arbuckle and his company of pioneers, and at length reached Point Pleasant on Thursday, the sixth of October, not a little wearied from the hardships and exposures of the long and tedious march.

Anthony Bledsoe, with his company of Fincastle troops, was left in charge of Camp Union, with the sick of the regiment, when Christian moved forward; and to Slaughter was assigned the command at the mouth of the Elk. The little army, on reaching Point Pleasant, numbered upwards of eleven hundred effective men, consisting of the Augusta and Botetourt regiments, the independent companies of Field and Buford, together with the three Fincastle companies, from the lower Holston country under Shelby, Russell, and Wm. Herbert. All these distinctive companies, save Herbert's, were attached to Fleming's Botetourt regiment. "With such a force," wrote that officer, "would the Shawnees and Mingoes be more than a breakfast for us?"[4]

On the beautiful promontory of Point Pleasant, between the two rivers, the army encamped, pitching their tents from the fork up both streams near half a mile. The ground was covered with a gigantic forest, thickly studded with a vigorous undergrowth, and presented an extensive and variegated prospect, on either hand _ hills, valleys, cliffs, and plains, picturesque and magnificent; embosomed in their native wildness.

Though a few Indians had been seen by the scouts and stragglers on the route, yet no danger was apprehended from an attack by the enemy. On arriving at Point Pleasant, Lewis found an advertisement indicating dispatches from Lord Dunmore deposited in a hollow tree, brought by Simon Kenton and two fellow messengers, directing him to join his Lordship at the mouth of Hockhocking, where the Governor's advance, under Major Crawford, was engaged in erecting a small fort. The first step was to provide shelter for the flour and stores, and pens for the security of the cattle at night. Spies were sent out, but no Indians were discovered. On the morning of the eighth of October, further dispatches arrived from Lord Dunmore, then at the mouth of Hockhocking; and one of the messengers, named William McCullock, an old Indian trader, mysteriously hinted Lewis' men might soon expect hot work; but the vague remark made no serious impression. To the renewed orders to move up to Hockhocking, Lewis replied that he would do so as soon as the remainder of the food supply, and powder, and the rear troops under Christian should arrive. The men, however, complained that it was over sixty miles by the river and nearly half that by land, to the mouth of Hockhocking; when it was, really nearer to the hostile towns from their present locality than from Hockhocking _ and to leave Point Pleasant unprotected, would be to leave open one of the most important thoroughfares of the Indians to the back settlements of Virginia. The messengers returned with these tidings written a few hours after their arrival.

It is recorded by one present, that on Sunday, the ninth, after the troops had heard a good sermon from their chaplain, they retired peacefully to their night's repose.[5] This fancied security, as the sequel will show, had well-nigh proved the ruin of the army.

Every movement of these border men, from Camp Union to Point Pleasant was doggedly watched by the sleepless spies of the enemy; and these couriers of the wilderness quickly threaded the intervening country, and reported accurately to the Shawnee towns, both the strength and progress of the bold invaders.

The hot-headed Mingoes, who had early in the war, been urged on by the grief-stricken and revengeful Logan, exerted their influence upon the surrounding tribes, to take up the tomahawk, and hurl it, with all their maddened fury, at the detested Long Knives. The younger warriors of the Shawnees, and other neighboring tribes, were not slow to take up the quarrel, and adopt it as their own. In response to their runners, a dusky Indian army quickly assembled on the plains of Scioto, headed by Cornstalk, who had scoured the Greenbrier and Carr's Creek settlements in the preceding war, well-seconded by Blue Jacket, Black Hoof, Red Hawk, Captain Dickson, Puck-e-shin-wa, the father of Tecumseh, El-i-nip-si-co, and other Shawnee braves; aided by bands of Delawares, Miamies, Wyandottes, Ottawas, and the Mingoes of the Ohio country.

Of all the Indian tribes, the Shawnees were reputed the most intrepid warriors, and Cornstalk stood confessedly at the head of his people as an experienced and successful war leader _ "the bravest of the brave." At the grand council that now assembled, he calmly, but eloquently appealed to his warriors not to act rashly _ not to embroil the nation in a war which would be sure to eventuate in their discomfiture and humiliation; that it were wiser to seek an honorable peace, taking a hickory withe, he deftly wound it around his finger, saying the Indians could once have thus easily mastered the Virginians, and have done almost as they pleased with them. "But," said he, "the circumstances are changed. Do you see that towering oak?" _ pointing to a noble tree before them _ "thus are the whites now grown strong, and we cannot now uproot that monarch of the forest." "The Long Knives," added Cornstalk, "now gathering to march against us, have with them not only their long knives, but their long rifles, too; and something tells me that we had better make peace." A Mingo chief[6] present boldly charged Cornstalk with cowardice; that he dared not fight the Long Knives. "I am no coward," calmly but nobly replied Cornstalk; "my life _ my acts _ attest my character; if my people resolve on war, I will myself lead them to the battlefield, and it shall be seen who the cowards are."[7]

An impassioned appeal to an excited assemblage of Indian warriors, to glut their revenge, and seek imperishable renown, is always more effective than any suggestions in the interests of peace, however wise and just; and the decision, on this occasion, was no exception to that general rule. The Indians, stung, no doubt, by a deep sense of real or imaginary wrong and injuries, went forth fully resolved on victory _ feeling it, they thought they could achieve it. They were led by some of the bravest and most skillful war-chiefs that their peculiar methods of warfare had produced.

While the echoes of the chaplain's voice, on the Sabbath of the ninth of October, were yet reverberating from the thickly studded shores opposite to "the Point," and the dying cadences of the sacred songs of the frontiersmen were yet faintly resounding along the valley where solemn praise was never heard before, Cornstalk's Indian army, fully eight hundred strong, were ready, with a quiet yet determined view, to meet their invading foe. Their first intention was, it is said, to attack the army while crossing the river; But this plan was changed, so as to permit its undisturbed passage, and then ensnare them into a fatal ambuscade, with the re-crossing of the river to impede their retreat. Two circumstances tended to interfere with this well-laid scheme; first, Lewis and his men remaining quietly in camp at "the Point," and, secondly, that the Indians, each of whom carried but a scanty supply of provisions, began to apprehend an immediate scarcity, which would compel the dispersion of their force.

A council of their Chiefs was, therefore, called, when it was proposed to cross the river some miles above Point Pleasant, march down in the night, attack the camp at break of day, carry it by surprise. Cornstalk, whose sagacious view had, from the first, foreseen the disastrous consequences of an unequaled war with the whites, opposed the proposed plan of operations, again declaring that war was not their true policy, and strongly advised that overtures for peace should yet be made, of which he would be the bearer. Overruled by numbers, he acquiesced, reminding the council that they who had now renewedly declared for war, were responsible for the result; that as they had resolved to fight, they must make up their minds to fight with the most determined bravery, while he would lead them to the onset, and share in their perils and hardships.[8]

They at once set about preparing to cross the Ohio at the mouth of what has ever since been called Campaign Creek, on the northern shore of the river, four miles above Point Pleasant. Here they divested themselves of their silver trinkets and ornaments, as well as of every other unnecessary article, hanging them upon bushes, and leaving a small guard for their protection.[9] During the silent hours of the night, they constructed wide rafts of dry sticks and poles, with grape-vine fastenings, and commenced their passage to the southern shore, a mile above Old Town Creek _ a locality with which they were intimately acquainted, for just above the mouth of that stream was once the Upper Shawnee Town, which was deserted shortly before Lewis' Sandy Creek Expedition, in he early part of 1756. But so slow and tedious, was the process of crossing the river, that the Indian army consumed the entire night and landed the last of their frail rafts on the southern bank of the Ohio about day-light _ too late, as Cornstalk subsequently confessed to Isaac Shelby, to rush up and surprise Lewis' men, in their camp while yet enjoying their morning slumbers.

It is well known to hunters, that deer have alike their hours of repose and of feeding; and about daybreak is one of their feeding periods. Then, too, while the leaves are yet wet with the night dew, the experienced hunter sallies forth in quest of his game, when the dampened leaves make no noise to disturb the wary animals. So the hunters, desirous of delicious venison, set out from the camp at "the Point" before day on the memorable tenth of October _ some in one direction, and some in another. James Mooney, of Russell's company, a spy on this campaign, went up the Ohio with a young man named Joseph Hughey, one of them had killed a fawn, and threw it over his shoulder, when reaching the mouth of Old Town Creek, three miles away, the Indians were discovered, a little after daybreak, crouched in the tall grass, on the high ground just above. Young El-i-nip-si-co, Cornstalk's son fired the first shot, quickly followed by the discharge of the rifle of Tavenor Ross, who had lived with the Indians from his youth, killing Hughey on the spot.[10] Mooney fled with all haste to the camp, where he arrived just before sun-rise, declaring that he had seen an Indian army that thickly covered above five acres of ground, a report that was very generally discredited.[11] While he was yet relating his marvelous story, James Robertson and Valentine Sevier, sergeants in Shelby's company, both of whom subsequently became distinguished pioneers of Tennessee,[1] who had gone out early that morning to procure fresh meat for soup for the nourishment of James Shelby, a son of the Captain's, then sick of fever, now came rushing into camp, and reported that at a ravine, about a mile distant, they came upon the extreme left of the enemy, and Robertson fired upon one of them who was slaking his thirst at a spring or rivulet _ the first gun on the part of the part of the whites on that memorable day. These hunters fully confirmed the mere presence of a large body of hostile Indians.

Others were almost simultaneously chased into camp by the Indians. William Casey, then a youth of eighteen, one of Shelby's men, went out a little distance, in company with others, to bring in some horses which had been hobbled out for feeding. They were unexpectedly fired on, and Casey, though wounded in the side, and knocked down, jumped up and tried calling out to his fellows to take trees also, assuring them that he was not killed. One followed his example, while the rest fled; the Indians, however, disappeared. Casey and his companion now retired to camp, and helped to confirm the report of the enemy close at hand. Casey met with a narrow escape, for the ball that struck him, first passed through an ashe-cake in his shot-pouch, which so broke its force, that it barely penetrated under the skin, from which he easily extracted it.

Though imagining this to be a mere scouting party of the enemy, Colonel Lewis, as a matter of precaution, had the drums beat to arms, as many of the men were yet asleep in their tents; and, while smoking his pipe, calmly ordered a detachment from every company of the Augusta troops, to the number of one hundred and fifty men, under Captains John Dickinson, Benjamin Harrison, and John Skidmore,[12] with Colonel Charles Lewis at their head to march to the right, near the foot of the hills skirting the east side of Crooked Creek, a small stream flowing from the north into the Kanawha; and as many more from the other regiment, under Captains Shelby, Russell, Buford, and Phillip Love, with Colonel Fleming as their leader, to move to the left; each detachment pushing forward pretty briskly, nearly two hundred yards apart. The one the right encountered the enemy about a quarter of a mile from camp, and a half a mile from the junction of the two rivers, lurking behind trees, logs and bushes, along the hill on the east side of Crooked Creek; while the detachment on the left moved up the Ohio to a pond, just a mile from the fort, and three fourths of a mile in advance of the camp. The enemy's line was found to extend from the Ohio to the pond, which was one of the sources of Crooked Creek, and nearly fifty rods from the river, and thence along the creek about half way to its mouth.

As Dickinson's men were hastily preparing for the conflict, their experienced leader, now past fifty years of age, and who had participated in many an Indian fight, addressed them, in an informal manner, in this wise: "Now, my brave boys, screen yourselves as much from danger as possible, and pull away but you know just as well how to do it as I can tell you." But the brave Indian fighter did not succeed in screening himself from Indian bullets, for he was wounded during the course of the engagement.

The rays of the Autumn sun were first beginning to shed their brightness upon that strange scene in the wilderness, when the enemy gave the Augusta line on the right, three scattering shots, instantly followed by a heavy fire, which was quickly returned by the Virginians, when volley rapidly succeeded volley, attended with the loss of many on both sides. Nor were the Indians less tardy in their attack on the left column under Fleming, who had briskly advanced along the Ohio to the pond already mentioned. Both of the scouts in front of the two lines were killed at the first fire.[13] The peals of musketry, intermingled with the terrific yells of the savages was now heard from one extreme of the line to the other. Most of the officers, and many of the men, accustomed to backwoods warfare, recognized the necessity of resorting to trees and other modes of protection. Observing this, the Indians endeavored to thwart their purpose by rushing forward, and forcing both lines of their opponent to fall back; in which they succeeded, compelling the Virginians to retreat one hundred and fifty or two hundred yards under a heavy fire, attended with the most dismal screams and yells.

At the very commencement of the action of the right, Charles Lewis received a mortal wound, while exposed in an open piece of ground, not having taken a tree, encouraging his men to advance. Calmly handing his gun to someone near him, he walked into camp, supported by two of his men, remarking to his soldiers as he passed, "I am wounded, but go on, and be brave." His brother, Andrew, met him before reaching camp, and remarked, "I expected something fatal would befall you"; to which he calmly replied, "It is the fate of war," and to Charles Simms, one of the commissaries, he observed, with his last words, that he had sent one of the enemy into eternity before him, and died in a few minutes after. His early fall was severely felt, and the partial advantage gained by the enemy, near the commencement of the action, was largely attributed to the depressing influence caused by the loss of so bold, animating, and experienced a leader.

Colonel Fleming, on the left, not very long after the fall of Lewis, received two balls through his left arm, below the elbow, breaking both bones; but he continued to encourage his men, exhibiting the most advisable coolness and presence of mind, and frequently repeating, in a loud voice, not to give back an inch, but continually advance and outflank the enemy, and, possible, get between them and the river. He, at length, received a thin shot, penetrating his left breast, and lodging in his body; but his unconquerable spirit would not permit him to retire, and his men, conforming to his advice, continued slowly to advance from tree to tree, pressing back the enemy. So severe was his last wound, that he was soon compelled to retire from the field; and found, on reaching the camp, a portion of his lungs, protruding through the orifice, which were, with difficulty replaced. His wounds once dressed, he insisted on visiting his friend, Charles Lewis, whose life was fast ebbing away, and who breathed his last at noon-day. Though Colonel Fleming eventually recovered, his was a double loss to the army; for he had been an officer of much experience in the former Indian war, in whom great confidence was reposed, and he was, withal, an able and skillful surgeon.[14] He, too, as he retired from the field, animated his officers and men in the calmest manner to the pursuit of victory.

At the critical period, when the enemy was forcing back both lines, John Field was promptly ordered out with a reinforcement of two hundred men to support the right wing; consisting of his own company, with those of Captains Samuel McDowell, George Matthews, and John Stuart, of Augusta, and Henry Pauling, Matthew Arbuckle, and Robert McClanahan, of Botetourt; Field acting as Colonel on the occasion. These men went into the action with such determined valor, that the enemy, in turn, were forced back till they were in line with those opposing the left wing. It was in this precipitate retreat of the enemy; driven from tree to tree, that Colonel Field was killed. He was protected for the moment, by a large tree, with an Indian amusing him with talk on his left, and while the Colonel was endeavoring to get a shot at him, two others on his right fired upon, and killed him. A faithful mulatto servant of the Colonel's, now rushed up to save his master's body from savage mutilation, for several Indians were already there, one of whom he knocked down; and possessing uncommon strength, he instantly threw the Colonel's body on his shoulder, and ran off with it to camp. The Indians were in the act of shooting the devoted servant, when one of their chiefs, who witnessed the scene, bade them desist; that one of a color so similar to their own, and so faithful to his fallen friend, ought to be permitted, on such an occasion; to retire, in safety. On the fall of Colonel Field, Captain Evan Shelby succeeded him in command of the left wing.

Other companies were, from time to time, sent forward from the camp, till fully two thirds of the troops were in the field, including all the Captains of each line, except Alexander McClanahan, of Augusta, who was upon guard duty, and

John Lewis, of Botetourt, who had command of the line for the double service of defending the camp, and erecting a suitable breastwork for its protection.[15] One of the re-enforcing companies, after running about half a mile, joined the advance by a hill, while the Indians were yet sullenly retiring, and forced them back till a small ridge was reached, where, ensconced behind logs, they fired upon the Virginians, who still pressed their advantage from the Ohio to the extreme right wing; and, at length, dislodged the foe from the fine long ridge which they had endeavored so tenaciously to hold, which stretched from a small opening in the woods near the river towards the hills, discontinued by a small wet bottom, and rising and continuing again to the hills, half a mile or more from the river. This advantageous position was gained by the Virginians about one o'clock; and all subsequent efforts on the part of the enemy to regain it, of which there were many daring dashes made with such force as they could muster, were unavailing. During all these long hours of bloody strife and carnage, "the hideous cries of the enemy, and the groans of the wounded, were enough to shudder the stoutest heart."[16] The Indians now fell back another position, so advantageous, protected by logs and natural locality, that it was not deemed prudent to attempt to dislodge them from it.

Many an act of heroic daring was performed that day by both the contending parties. During the first three or four hours of the conflict, the enemy, before all the reinforcements had been sent out from the camp, were much superior in numbers, and disputed every inch of ground with the greatest obstinacy, often running up to the very muzzles of the guns of their antagonists, this not unfrequently falling victims to their reckless intrepidity.[17]

The Virginians, particularly of Fleming's regiment, at the suggestion of the Colonel himself, resorted to a stratagem that deceived not a few of the enemy. Among them Richard Burk, a droll and fearless Irishman, of Shelby's company, while on the flank of his company, and having a log for his protection, placed his hat on the end of his ramrod, and elevated it slightly above the log, when an Indian fired at it and the hat disappeared; and, to complete the deception, Burk commenced floundering, kicking and struggling, when the elated red man, confident of his success, ran up to secure the scalp, but lost his own instead, for he instantly fell a victim to the rifle of his more wily antagonist. Burk succeeded in killing another Indian in the same way. At noon, under little or no military restraint, he remarked, "Well, I believe I've earned my dinner;" and away he darted to camp, refreshed himself, returned to the battle-field, and before night sent another of the hated Red Skins to his long home.[18]

A similar incident occurred in the right wing. Capt. Harrison, while passing along these lines, observed a mere youth, of awkward appearance, behind a tree, intently watching a not very distant brush-wood, from which he noticed several shots had been made. Sheltering himself, for the moment, behind the same tree with the lad, Harrison finding him though apparently only half witted, yet cool and anxious for a shot at the concealed Indian, suggested to him to adopt the expedient of putting his hat on the end of his ramrod, and push it out slowly from behind the tree, which the Indian would very likely take to be his head. The Captain had scarcely departed, when the young hero put the expedient into practice, with complete success; for though the Indian put an ugly hole through his hat, he, in turn, sent a bullet through his antagonist's body, which put an end to shots from that particular covert.[19]

Nor was this the only lad who deserved to be ranked among the heroes of that day. There were several who did good service, William Stephen, at the tender age of fourteen, anxious to serve his country, though the only support of his aged and infirm father, went on the campaign, and lost his life in the bloody contest.

Another youth, John McKinney, then only fifteen, was badly wounded early in the engagement, while the morning's fog and powder smoke settled and intermingled, under cover of which, an Indian seeing the prostrate young soldier, rushed up, and stabbed him; but before he had time to secure his scalp, the object he evidently had in view, he discovered several whites endeavoring to get a shot at him , more than half enveloped in the fog and smoke, he scampered off. McKinney recovered, and lived to a good old age.[20]

John Frogg, a prominent citizen and magistrate of Staunton, went on the campaign in some official capacity. To encourage his friends and neighbors, he rushed among the foremost into the battle, under the gallant leadership of Charles Lewis. He unfortunately wore a bright scarlet vest, which attracted the attention of the Indians; and, early in the action, he fell mortally wounded. So eager was the Indian who shot him to secure his scalp for a trophy, and perhaps the gay garment too, evidently supposing him to have been a more conspicuous officer than he really was, that he rushed up to his victim, who was able, by a desperate effort, to raise himself sufficiently to grapple with his foe; at which critical juncture, William White, a noted Indian fighter, watched his chance, and shot the red warrior dead. Another Indian now attempted to perform the feat in which his fellow had failed; but White's rifle was by this time reloaded, and this adventurous Red Skin shared the fate of the other; and a third one also, in a few minutes after.

By this time, Frogg was dead, but the enemy failed to secure the much coveted scalp and red jacket; and White gained no small renown among his fellow soldiers. And after the battle, on examining the features of one of the three dead Indians, one of them, when the paint was washed from his face, was recognized by his own brother, as George Collet, who was early captured by the Indians, and was heard repeatedly, during the contest, urging on the enemy, and exclaiming, "Fight on!. Fight on! We will soon whip them all."[21]

George Cameron, an assistant commissary possessed of the most chivalrous feelings, seized his gun when the men were fast gathering to go out and greet the enemy; but his brother, Charles Cameron, the Lieutenant in Dickinson's company, dissuaded him from it, as he might be needed to attend to the special duties of his station, and he put his weapon aside. As the battle raged, however, and his brother and friends were exposed to its dangers, he sprang up, declaring he must go and share the dangers with the others. He fought well, but lost his life towards the close of the action.

When orders were given, on the left line, to advance and dislodge the Indians from one of their fastnesses, Isaac Shelby, the intrepid Lieutenant who had succeeded to the command of his father's company, when the latter assumed the direction of the left wing on the disability of Colonel Fleming, now exclaimed, "let us push forward, my brave boys, right and left, and drive them," and fearlessly dashed ahead himself to a spreading elm that had large roots projecting considerably above the surface, and prostrated himself behind the rooty barriers; when a fellow soldier, named Walker, who aimed for the same covert, reached there a moment after Shelby, but being more exhausted, was instantly killed by some Indian sharp-shooter.[22]

An incident is related of William Clendenin, of Stuart's company, who went into the action with Field's re-enforcement early in the day. During the battle, Clendenin picked up a fanciful Indian cap, and quickly thrust it into his bosom. The Indians, then retreating, were trying to get shots as they retired; one of whom, behind a log, aimed at Clendenin, the ball cutting obliquely across his breast, and probably would have killed him, but for the cap in his bosom partially checking the force of the bullet. Clendenin, momentarily stunned by the shock, reeled, but recovered; when the Indian rose from his covert, and leaned forward, intently gazing to see his supposed victim fall, that he might secure another scalp _ the warrior's richest trophy; but he presumed too much on the fatality of his shot, for Clendenin, once fairly on his feet again, whipped his gun to his face, and, the next instant, the Indian fell dead; and, in his shot-pouch, five fresh scalps were found all apparently taken that day. The soldier was but slightly wounded; from which he soon recovered.[23]

Another episode of that eventful day so prolific of stirring adventures, deserves a passing notice. William Bryan, of John Lewis' Botetourt company, while standing guard that morning before day, had loaned his fine rifle to one of the early hunters, taking a poor shot-gun in its place till the sportsman should return. He consequently went near to the scene of action with his almost worthless piece, with which he could scarcely expect to perform any essential service; so he concluded he would take a position some little distance in the rear, reasonably secure from danger, and render such service as chance might throw in his way. Discovering an Indian in the act of shooting at his young friend, Thomas Lewis, son of Colonel Andrew Lewis, who seems to have gone on the campaign as a sort of volunteer cadet in his brother's company, Bryan hallowed to him, apprizing him of his danger, which gave him barely time to dodge, which he so far effected as to escape with only a slight graze on the bridge of his nose; and, in turn, instantly discharged his rifle, sending his antagonist sprawling upon the ground in the agonies of death.[24]

William Moore, of the Augusta division, observing his fellow soldier, John Steele, disabled at his side, seized his fallen companion, at much personal risk, being in full view of the enemy's line, and bore him on his shoulders to the camp, escaping the balls of the enemy; and, placing his charge in the care of attendants, he returned to the battle-field, which he did not again relinquish till victory declared in favor of the Virginians. Steele, though desperately wounded, having been shot quite through the breast, and his wound at first deemed mortal, at length recovered; and subsequently distinguished himself at Germantown, and became Secretary, and Acting Governor of the Mississippi Territory. This was but one of many similar instances of personal daring, prompted by the noblest impulses of humanity, that occurred during the battle; and, it is a remarkable fact, that not a solitary soldier disabled or otherwise, fell into the hands of the enemy throughout all that terrible conflict.

Lieutenant William Bracken, a noted hunter and backwoodsman, went over the Ohio spying early in the morning, and had extended his route several miles, when he heard the distant report of firearms, an hastened back. Reaching the camp, he dashed into the fight, upbraiding some of the men for so carefully protecting themselves behind logs, like so many cowards; when he was admonished for unnecessarily exposing himself, but kept on, up the rising ground, behind which, the Indians were posted, and was soon shot down. Another scout, named Fowler, of Harrison's company, a brave and stalwart fellow, seven feet in height, was also employed as a scout that morning, on the northern side of the Ohio; and, when the battle began, waded the stream at a shallow point, the river then being low, and warmly engaged in the conflict.

During the day, the Indians, at times, indulged, in their rude manner, in no little bravado, "we'll learn you how to shoot" _ and "why don't you whistle now?" _ alluding to the fifes of the musicians. The stentorian voice of Cornstalk was repeatedly heard, high above the din of the conflict, commanding his warriors, in their native language _ which Jacob Persinger, and others, who had formerly been captives among the Shawnees, readily understood _ "to lie close _ shoot well _ be strong, and fight!" He everywhere exhibited prodigies of valor; and in whatever part of the line his voice was heard, from thence issued a thick and deadly fire. Towards the close of the day, the Indians boasted of having "eleven hundred warriors as well as the whites, and would have two thousand for them the ensuing day;" and made no little merriment about a treaty.[25]

Among the Indians was a young Cherokee, who had been early captured, and mostly raised by the Shawnees, who had long carried on an embittered warfare with their Southern neighbors. About the middle of the day, Tavenor Ross, then one of the Indian army, got his rifle choked, and retired a little distance, partially behind some rising ground, where he could safely unbreach and clear it; and, while there, saw two prominent Indians successively fall, and wondered at it. Seeing no opponent, when at length he detected the Cherokee in the rear, as he proved to be, shooting down a third one. Ross immediately ran up, and brained him with his war-club. This, at first, caused no little commotion among the Indians; who, upon examining the three slain warriors, were satisfied that they had all, indeed, been shot from behind, and they not only acquitted, but warmly commended their adopted brother for this prompt act of retribution. The cause of the strange conduct of the young Cherokee can only be accounted for by supposing, that those whom he had so treacherously dispatched, had, during the battle, or on some previous occasion, either slighted him, or impugned his character for bravery,

In the course of the battle, the young adopted white warrior, Ross, still farther endeared himself to his Shawanese friends by his constant acts of sagacity and valor. Discovering the smoke of a discharged gun emerge from behind a cluster of bushes two or three times, and an Indian fall on each occasion, he watched closely, and soon caught the dim outline of a Long Knife through the bushes, fired on, and "silenced him," as he expressed it.[26]

Cornstalk and Blue Jacket were particularly on the alert in spiriting on their warriors, and thwarting the bad examples of the timorous. Blue Jacket promptly killed a fellow who exhibited signs of cowardice; and during the battle, Cornstalk kept his vigilant eye on the haughty Mingo chief, who had previously charged him with timidity; and discovering him in the act of skulking from danger, sternly admonished him that he must not repeat it, or his life would pay the forfeit. Before the close of that memorable day, the Mingo chief was again seen to shrink from the contest, when Cornstalk instantly cleaved his skull with his tomahawk.[27] He also whipped a warrior for the same cause, who had been clamorous to be led into battle,[28] using his ramrod freely on others who were tardy or timid in advancing on the whites.[29]

It had been the purpose of the enemy to drive the Virginians completely into the two rivers. They had placed a select body of warriors, _ two hundred in number, including some squaws and Indian youths _ on the western bank of the Kanawha, and northern bank of the Ohio, so as effectually to have cut off all who might succeed in reaching those respective shores. "We drove you in the morning," said Cornstalk subsequently to Isaac Shelby; "and we thought we could, by a desperate effort, spirit on our warriors, and drive you into the river like so many bullocks." By one o'clock in the afternoon Cornstalk and his war chiefs became convinced of the utter futility of such efforts, and ceased to mass their warriors, and urge them on to destruction.

For several hours, little was done save to watch each other intently, interchange occasional shots; and mutually indulge in low blackguardism and bravado. About three or four o'clock in the afternoon, the Indians evidently growing quite dispirited, all the attempts of their leaders to rally them proving useless, they were seen carrying off their dead and wounded, giving their antagonists now and then a shot to prevent immediate pursuit.

Another movement was now made which hastened their retreat. The east or upper side of Crooked Creek was bordered by quite a ridge, which the Indians, by their actions, indicated an intention to regain. Colonel Lewis ordered a detachment under Captains Matthews. Isaac Shelby, and Stuart, to make a division under cover of the bank of the Kanawha, and up Crooked Creek some little distance, and thence to the right of the ridge, with a view of gaining the rear of the enemy, or, at least, securing a point from which they might enfilade their line, and prevent their occupation of this advantageous position. This was nearly effected when the design was discovered; and the Indians, at half an hour to sunset, supposing Colonel Christian's reinforcement had arrived, darted off, raising a loud yell as they retired, as if to convey the impression that they were about to renew the conflict.[30] They had, by this time, been forced back to the site of the old Shawnee Town, well protected by a thick undergrowth, where they made a stand, daring the Virginians to "come on;" but as night was rapidly approaching and Old Town Creek separated the parties, the whites retired to their camp unmolested.[31]

They had been nearly all the afternoon amusing the Virginians with a tame defense, in order to conceal their real purpose of dragging off their dead, securing the safety of their wounded, and, after nightfall, re-crossing the river. It was highly creditable to Cornstalk's generalship, that, in the very face of a brave, vigilant, and victorious adversary, all these designs were successfully accomplished.

What a sense of relief came to the hearts of the Virginians when they fully realized that the enemy, with whom they had so desperately contended that day, had finally skulked away from their rude lines of defense, confessedly yielding the palm of victory to the more skillful and persistent pale faces. One cause of the failure of the Red Men, was their deficiency in mechanical skill requisite for keeping their rifles in order; and they, moreover, exposed themselves too recklessly in the hope of securing a worthless scalp, or some tempting plunder. They probably realizing the need of an excuse, attributed their lack of success to the mercenary deportment of the Chillicothe band of Shawnees, who abandoned their places in the line, and gave themselves largely up to plundering their fallen foes _ especially in the earlier part of the action, when the Virginians were forced back a considerable distance; and, but for this un-warrior-like conduct, they would, they contended, have rushed their half-demoralized enemies, like a flock of frightened sheep, into the two rivers.[32]

But in this, the Indians were evidently mistaken. They were ignorant of the real facts in the case; for after the several reinforcements had been sent out, Colonel Lewis still retained in camp fully one third of his force, not only as a reserve to meet contingencies, but to erect a breastwork across the peninsula for the protection of his whole army, should those in the field be forced to retire, and to repel the enemy should they succeed in getting between the troop engaged and the camp. From the earliest morning's alarm, the reserve corps were working energetically in cleaning a line from river to river, at the upper extremity of the tents, half a mile above the point of the junction of the two streams, and making a breastwork of trees and brushwood, thus effectually protecting the camp, the supplies, and the wounded.[33]

As the setting sun was shedding its departing rays upon the scene of this remarkable conflict, the wearied backwoodsmen slowly wended their way back to camp. A heavy guard was now mounted, and the appropriate watch-word was "Victory." But it was a dearly-bought triumph; for forty six non-commissioned officers and privates, and nine commissioned officers, were killed in the conflict, and ninety-two wounded, of whom about fifteen subsequently died. Thus nearly one-fifth of all those actually engaged were either killed or wounded _ a fact which sufficiently attests the severity of the losses incurred in that memorable action. The entire camp was little else than a hospital, and the groans and sufferings of the disabled officers and soldiers were heartrending in the extreme; and all the more so, since there were no surgeons of skill, nor any proper comforts for persons in their unhappy situation. Poultices of slippery elm bark for their wounds, and broth made of beef or wild game for their nourishment, constituted about all that could be done for these brave and patient sufferers.[34]

A somewhat ludicrous incident connected with that day's history, may be briefly be related. An old Dutchman named Kishioner, together with his son Andrew, suffered their fears to get the better of their judgment; and they skulked away at first alarm in the morning, and hid themselves under some driftwood on the beach of the Ohio. as night approached, and the din of battle ceased; the old man crawled from his hiding place, and casting about his wary eye, and seeing danger was over, bawled out to his hopeful son, "You may come out now, Andy; all is safe!"[35]

During the course of the day, a messenger had been dispatched over the Kanawha, who eluded the Indians posted there _ or they chose not to make their presence known _ with orders to Colonel Christian, who had with him two hundred and twenty of his regiment, convoying some beeves, and a supply of powder, to make a forced march to Point Pleasant. In the evening, when he had proceeded about fifteen miles from the Point, the messenger met the party, who left their convoy, and hastened forward with all possible dispatch, reaching the camp about midnight. Christian's arrival imparted to all a new impulse of hope and safety. Among his captains were William Campbell, subsequently distinguished at King's Mountain, and James Harrod and John Floyd _ names intimately associated with the early history of Kentucky.[36]

At the earliest morning's dawn of the eleventh of October, the camp at Point Pleasant was all astir. Strong parties were sent out, under Colonel Christian and others, to carefully reconnoiter, and ascertain whether the enemy had retreated across the Ohio. Eighteen or twenty dead Indians were found scattered over the battle-field, and twelve others were discovered in one place partially covered; while the trails where many were dragged, and thrown into the Ohio, were numerous. They had scalped some of their own dead, to prevent the Virginians from doing so. While the latter lost but three scalps, they secured eighteen or twenty of those of their enemies, which they dressed after the Indian style, and displayed the next day on a pole by the river bank.

It was fully believed by all who had participated in the engagement, and corroborated by McCulloch, and other Indian traders, that the Indian loss was considerably greater than that of the Virginians. It was observed, that almost all the killed and wounded on either side, were shot in the head or breast, showing with what precision the respective marksmen hit that part of the body exposed to the range of their deadly rifles. Many of the trees on the battle-field were found bespattered with the blood of the combatants. Proceeding above Old Town Creek, Lewis' men found twenty-eight rafts, on which the Indians had crossed and re-crossed the Ohio. During this and the succeeding day, there were collected on the battle-fields twenty-three guns, twenty-seven tomahawks, eighty blankets, with war-clubs, shot-pouches, powder-horns, match-coats, deer-skins, and other articles, which brought at auction near one hundred pounds.[37]

Colonel Lewis, on the eleventh, returned hearty thanks to the brave officers and men who distinguished themselves in the battle of the day previous, by whose gallant behavior a victory, under God, was obtained. "Let us," he continued, "not be dismayed by the loss of our brave officers and soldiers who fell in the conflict, though we can not help regretting their loss; but rather let us be inspired with a double degree of courage and earnest desire to give our perfidious enemies a thorough scourging."[38] This day, with many a sorrowful heart, the lamented dead were buried. The officers were interred in the magazine, near the fork of the rivers _ Colonels Lewis and Field, Captains Wilson, and Murray; together with the latter's half brother, Assistant Commissary George Cameron, Lieutenant Allen, and John Frogg.

No engagement between Colonists and Indians was ever more obstinately contested than the memorable conflict at Point Pleasant. "Never did Indians stick closer to it." wrote Colonel Fleming, "nor behave bolder."[39] Their loss, never certainly known, was reported at two hundred and thirty-three killed and wounded. Certain it is, that not very long after Dunmore's treaty, and while the Sciota villages were still hospitals for their wounded, some white traders approaching Chillicothe came near losing their lives, having been chased off, and shot at, by the Shawnees, who declared that they came merely to discover how many wounded the Indians had, and to deride them for their signal discomfiture and losses.[40]

So decisive was the defeat of the Shawnees on the tenth of October, 1774, that they hastened to their towns, and supplicated peace at the hands of Governor Dunmore on any terms. For severity and persistency, this engagement will always stand out in bold relief in the annals of border warfare. As long as any of its actors survived, it was fame enough that they were accorded the proud distinction of having been among the heroes of Point Pleasant.

Chapter Sixteen

Dunmore and his Field Officers

John Murray, the fourth Earl of Dunmore, was born in Scotland in 1732, descending in the female line from the house of Stuart, and related to many of the crowned heads of Europe. His father, the third Earl, was pardoned by the King for his share in the Scotch rebellion of 1745, and died in 1756, when he was succeeded by his son. The young Earl was married, in 1759, to Lady Charlotte Stuart, daughter of the Earl of Galloway. From 1761 to 1784, he was one of the representative peers of Scotland; and, in 1770, he was appointed Governor of the Colony of New York. In July, 1776, he was transferred to the Governorship of Virginia, upon which he entered early the following year. So jealous was he after royal prerogative, that he thrice dissolved the popular Assembly; once for recommending a committee of correspondence with the patriots of the other Colonies, and again for setting apart a day for fasting, humiliation and prayer in consequence of the closing of the port of Boston. His services on the Indian campaign of 1774, and his unwearied efforts to protect the exposed frontiers of Virginia during that year, greatly merited the thanks of his army, and of the Assembly of that Province.

In his zeal for his royal master, he removed the public powder from the magazine at Williamsburg to the Fowey man of war in the spring of 1775; the people, however, under the leadership of Patrick Henry, compelled the Governor to compromise the matter by paying for the powder. He fled to the Fowey, with his family, and , with other naval vessels, carried on a petty warfare; and finally, January first 1776, fired Norfolk, then the most populous and flourishing town of Virginia. In the following July, he was dislodged from Gwynn's Island, in the Chesapeake, by his subordinate of 1774, General Andrew Lewis, being wounded in the leg by a splinter. He shortly after returned to England, and was, in 1776, chosen one of the sixteen peers of Scotland in the place of Lord Cassilis, deceased; and, in 1787, was appointed Governor of the Bahama Islands, serving ten years. It was creditable to Lord Dunmore's good sense, that when British emissaries among the Creek Indians, in 1792, instigating them to hostilities against the Americans, induced a party, of that nation to visit him at Nassau, he gave them no presents, and but little countenance.

Retiring from the Governorship of the Bahamas, his Lordship died at Ramsgate, England, March 5, 1809, in his seventy-eighth year. He was a short, and thick-set man, simple and unpretending in his manners, and carried his knapsack on the campaign of 1774, like the common soldiers. His grandson, Hon. Charles Augustus Murray visited, this country, some forty years since, and published an interesting account of his travels.

Adam Stephen, a native of Scotland, and an accomplished physician, early migrated to Virginia, where, early in 1754, he joined the forces under Colonel Joshua Fry as the eldest Captain of the regiment, and continued to serve prominently till the close of the French and Indian was. On the death of Fry, on the thirty-first of May, Washington succeeded to the command, when Stephen was promoted to the rank of Major, and served as such in the action at the Great Meadows, July the third, 1754; and at the close of that year, and beginning of 1755, he acted as Paymaster to the Virginia troops. Under General Braddock, he served as Captain commandant, and was desperately wounded at the memorable defeat at the Monongahela, on the ninth of July. He could only cleanse his wound in the abdomen by drawing a silk handkerchief through it. In August following, he was selected by Washington as Lieutenant Colonel of the regiment, performing good service the remainder of that, and the ensuing year, on the frontiers of Virginia. He led a detachment of two hundred men to the relief of South Carolina in 1757; and served under Colonel Byrd on Forbes' campaign in 1758, on the frontiers in 1759, and against the Cherokees in 1760-61; succeeding Byrd in command of the regiment in 1762. Peace being restored, his troops were disbanded, but he was again called into service during the Pontiac outbreak.

In 1764, he was appointed one of the Justices of the County Court of Frederick; and when Berkeley county was set off from Frederick, in 1772, he became the sheriff of the new county, in which he resided; and the county town, Martinsburg, was laid off from his hands.

On the campaign of 1774, he ranked next to Lord Dunmore. He was, it would seem, the officer, who, at Fort Gower, made the speech maintaining the rights of the Colonies. His letters, at this period, to Richard Henry Lee, evince his unselfish patriotism in the popular cause. "Lord Dunmore orders me to the Ohio," he wrote on the twenty-seventh of August, 1774; which "prevents my attending the General Congress, where, I would expect to see the spirit of Ampyctions shine, as that illustrious council did in their purest times, before debauched by Persian gold. The fate of America depends upon your meeting, and the eyes of the European world hang upon you, waiting the event."[1]

He was a member of the Virginia Convention of March 1775, and took an active part with the prominent leaders of the Colony. He was appointed one of the Virginia commissioners to hold a treaty with the Indians at Fort Pitt in the autumn of that year, and soon after was chosen to the command of one of the Virginia regiments. Promotions followed rapidly, for, in 1776, he was made a Brigadier General; and, in December of that year, Dr. Benjamin Rush wrote to Richard

Henry Lee, "Stephen must be made Major General; he has genius as well as knowledge." He appears[2] to have participated in the battles of Trenton and Princeton; and, for several months thereafter, was busily employed in harassing the enemy's foraging parties in New Jersey, sometimes successfully attacking the Royal Highlanders, who were regarded as obstinately brave.[3]

In February, 1777, Stephen was elevated to the rank of Major General. He behaved well at Brandywine, and cooly inquired of an officer near him, if he did not hear the leaden travelers "whistling for want of thought?" But yielding to a bad habit, though a brave and tried officer hitherto, he used his canteen too freely on that same morning of the battle of Germantown, and was chastised for misconduct on the retreat, and for intoxication.

He retired to his home at Martinsburg, Berkeley County, Virginia, where he lived neighbor to two dishonored brother soldiers, Charles Lee and Horatio Gates. Once Lee sarcastically observed to his military associates in retirement, that Berkeley county was pre-eminently noted as the asylum of three unfortunate Generals. "You, Stephen," said he, "were broke for getting drunk, when every man should be in his senses; I for not fighting when I was sure to be beat; and you, Gates, for being beat, when you had no business to engage."

General Stephen enjoyed the confidence and respect of his fellow citizens, frequently serving them in civil capacities; having been a prominent member of the Legislature from 1780 till January, 1785, and of the Virginia Convention. He died at Martinsburg, July 16, 1791, at an advanced age. He was distinquished for his medical acquirements, industry, and mental culture.

Angus McDonald was born in the Highlands of Scotland in 1727, of the clan of Glengarry; but was raised and educated in Glasgow. At the age of eighteen, he engaged, with his father, in the Scotch rebellion of 1745; and, the next year, having been left fatherless by the war, and probably attainted of treason, he fled to Virginia, and early settled in Frederick county. He took quite an active part in the old French and Indian war, in the defence of that frontier country, retiring with the rank of Captain. He became a Justice in 1765; Major of the militia in 1769; Lieutenant Colonel, in 1774, and Sheriff in 1775. In 1776, he was re-commissioned a Justice, and made Deputy Sheriff; and again a Justice in 1778. Though an ardent friend of the popular cause, he refused to accept a Lieutenant Colonelcy of a regiment under Parson Thurston, who had seen no active service, though urged to do so by General Washington.

His military services in 1774 were useful and important. He was regarded as a good disciplinarian; and it is related of one of his captains, who was twice guilty of disobedience of orders, on the Ohio campaign, that he had him tried, and sentenced to be tied to a tree, for several hours, his own company by their actions approving the sentence. The insubordinate officer learned a lesson which proved a real service to him ever after.

Colonel McDonald died early in 1779, leaving three sons and three daughters. He was a man of commanding presence, being six feet two and a half inches in height. His son, of the same name, served as a Captain of the regulars in the war of 1812. His eldest daughter, Mary, was married to Maj. Elias Langham, a Revolutionary officer of Fluvanna county, Virginia, and subsequently one of the early settlers of Clillicothe, Ohio.

William Crawford was born in Westmoreland county, Virginia, about the year 1722. His parents were of Scotch-Irish origin. The father died when William was young, leaving also another and younger son _ Valentine. The mother remarried again; her second husband was Richard Stephenson, with whom she lived until five sons and one daughter were born, when she died. The family was then living upon Bulls Bin creek in Frederick county, Virginia, in the present county of Jefferson, West Virginia.

William Crawford had an early acquaintance with Washington. He learned of him the art of surveying. During the year 1755, he gave up the double occupation of surveyor and farmer and entered the service, receiving from the governor of Virginia a commission as Ensign. For gallantry displayed upon the frontiers, he was promoted, the following year to a Lieutenancy. He was employed until 1758 in garrison duty as a scout upon the borders of Pennsylvania and Virginia.

Crawford was now commissioned as Captain. He raised a full company of hardy, stalwart farmers and hunters, from his own neighborhood, to augment the regiment of Washington which was marching under General Forbes to the reduction of Fort Duquesne. On the twenty-fifth of December, 1758, that post was reached and occupied by Washington. Crawford, after this event, remained in the service of Virginia three years, when he returned to his home. He took an active part against the savages during Pontiac's War, which so soon followed after that of the Seven Year's contest between France and Great Britain.

Early in the Summer of 1765, Crawford started on a horse-back trip over the Alleghany mountains to seek a home in the Western wilds. He chose a spot for his residence upon the Youghiogheny river at a point known at that day as "Stewart's Crossings." It was in Augusta county, Virginia, as claimed by that Commonwealth; afterward in the District of West Augusta, and finally, in Mohogania county, until Virginia relinquished her claim to what is now Southwestern Pennsylvania. As claimed by Pennsylvania, it was in Cumberland county; subsequently in Bedford; afterward in Westmoreland; and, finally, in Fayette county. It was opposite the present town of Connellsville, where the village of New Haven is now located. Crawford did not settle here until the Spring following, when, with his wife and three children, he made his permanent home.

The intimate relations between Crawford and Washington were not broken off by the removal of the farmer west of the mountains. They frequently corresponded. Most of the letters passing between them related to lands, which Crawford was securing for his friend upon the waters of the Ohio, and over which he continued, as long as he lived, to exercise a general supervision. Until the year 1770, he employed his time in various ways: he also engaged in trade with the Indians. During the year just mentioned, he was appointed one of the justices of the peace for his county _ Cumberland, as the jurisdiction to the region of county where he resided was not, in 1770, seriously disputed by Virginia.

In the Autumn, he received a visit at his home in the Youghiogheny from Washington. The latter was then on a tour down the Ohio, with a view to select lands for himself and others, entitled thereto as officer and soldiers in the French and Indian War, under an order of the Council of Virginia, and a proclamation of Dinwiddie, governor of that commonwealth. Washington reached Crawford's cabin on the thirteenth of October, and was welcomed to his humble but hospitable home. Crawford accompanied his distinguished guest down the Ohio; embarking at Pittsburgh in a large canoe on the twentieth, destined for the Great Kanawha, which they reached on the last day of the month. On the twenty-fourth of November the party returned to "Stewart's Crossings." The next day, Washington took leave of Crawford, and pursued his journey leisurely homeward.

On the ninth day of March, 1771, Bedford county, Pennsylvania was formed from a part of Cumberland, and a few days afterward Crawford was appointed by Governor Penn to be a justice of the peace for the new county within which was his residence. By virtue of that office he became one of the judges of the Bedford courts. Upon the erection, in 1773, of Westmoreland his commission was renewed for that county, and, being first mentioned, he was, by courtesy and usage made its presiding judge. He was also appointed, in place of Christopher Gist deceased, surveyor of the Ohio company. He was visited during the Summer of this year by Lord Dunmore, governor of Virginia.

Although for several years the country about the head-waters of the Ohio had been a subject of dispute between Pennsylvania and Virginia, yet the quarrel did not assume a very threatening aspect until the erection of Wesmoreland county by the former Commonwealth; the whole of the disputed territory being included therein. Lord Dunmore, as Governor of Virginia, then attempted, by violent measures, to enforce jurisdiction over the same territory. Crawford, although a Virginian by birth, remained loyal to the Commonwealth he was serving, until Dunmore was drawn into the War of 1774 with the Shawnees and Mingoes, when his ardent love of adventure got the better of his Pennsylvania loyalty; and he joined in the contest as already narrated. At its close, he returned to more peaceful employments upon the Youghiogheny. Pennsylvania could not forgive his dereliction. He was, as a consequence, soon after removed from all positions held by him in Westmoreland county. He never again accepted office under that Commonwealth.

Virginia was not unmindful of the services rendered by Crawford. On the sixth of December, 1774, he was commissioned by Dunmore, as a justice of Oyer and Terminer for the county of Augusta, Virginia, although he did not qualify until the May following. In the Spring of 1775, he took an active part in the Virginia side, in the boundary controversy; opening a land office, and, as deputy surveyor, making surveys, overriding Pennsylvania claims. After the erection of Monogalin county, in November 1776, by Virginia, he was appointed one of its deputy-surveyors, and was sworn in as chief of that office on the twenty-eighth of September, 1779. This position he continued to hold until his death in 1782. He was one of the judges of Yohoganier, sitting as such at intervals during the year 1777 and 1778. In the mean time, he had become an actor in other scenes; at home and abroad, which reconciled such of his old friends as had been alienated by his active partition in the boundary troubles. As the day of the Revolution began to dawn, he sank his partisan feelings in the nobler impulses of the patriot. He struck hands with Pennsylvanians in the cause of liberty.

In the Fall of 1775, Crawford raised a regiment for the defense of the Colonies, and on the twelfth of January, 1776, entered the Revolutionary service as Lieutenant-Colonel of the Fifth Virginia regiment, commissioned by Congress, as such, on the nineteenth of February following. He afterward was in command of the Seventh Virginia; but in order to raise a new regiment west of the mountains _ the Thirteenth Virginia _ he threw up his command of the Seventh. This latter regiment was intended for home protection; but Congress, on the eighth of January, 1777, ordered it "to march immediately by the nearest routes to join General Washington, in New Jersey." What recruits had been collected were thereupon marched over the mountains.

Crawford again returned to Fort Pitt, reaching that post about the first of March 1777, employing his time in collecting together the new recruits of the Thirteenth Virginia regiment, and placing them at points upon the frontier where, in his judgment, they could most effectively protect the inhabitants who had already begun to feel, early as it was in the season, the effects of Indian depredations. About the middle of August, he with two hundred of his men joined the main army near Philadelphia. The residue of his recruits he left west of the mountains. In the preliminary movements which resulted in the battle of Brandywine _as well as in that conflict _ he took an active part. He was also in the battle of Germantown. Late in the year he again returned home, Congress meanwhile having requested Washington to send him "to Pittsburgh to take command, under Brigadier-General Hand, of the Continental troops, and militia in the Western Department."

Crawford's duties in the Spring of 1778 were various. He marched with General Hand upon the inglorious "Square-Campaign," in February. Sometimes he was employed at Fort Pitt sitting as president of courts-martial; at other times, attending to his own affairs at his home upon the Youghiogheny. It was not, however, until the arrival of General McIntosh in the Western Department, early in August, that Crawford had very active employment in a military way. In September, he was appointed commander of the troops from the western counties of Virginia, and had in charge the building of Fort McIntosh near the site of the present town of Beaver, Pennsylvania. He was Acting Brigadier in command of the militia in the expedition from that post into the Indian country in the Autumn of that year, which resulted in the erection of Fort Laurens upon the Tuscarowas, in the present State of Ohio. When the militia were finally discharged by General McIntosh, Crawford was left without a command. Although retaining his commission as Colonel until his death in 1782, yet he never again was placed at the head of a regiment of regulars. During the years 1779 and 1780, he contented himself as best he could at his home upon the Youghiogheny. Sometimes he pursued small Indian parties who committed their ravages upon the exposed settlements. In these expeditions he was generally successful. At other times, he took an active part in the organization of campaigns against the western savages. Finally however, the expedition against Sandusky, in May, 1782, found him its leader. This campaign proved disastrous; and Crawford, on the eleventh of June, 1782, on the banks of Tymuche creek one of the tributaries of the Sandusky river, in what is now Wyandot county, Ohio, suffered death in the most horrid aspect, by being tortured at the stake.

Chapter Seventeen

Field Officers of Point Pleasant

    The grandfather of <u>Andrew</u> <u>Lewis</u>, who had the same name, was a French Protestant who fled from France to Ireland to avoid the religious persecutions of the times, and there married Mary Calhoun. Their son, John Lewis, was born in Ireland in 1678. He intermarried with Margaret Lynn, also a native of Ireland, but of Scottish descent _ from the Lynns, of Loch Lynn, so famous in Scottish clan legends. John Lewis settled down upon a farm in Donegal county, where several of his children were born _ among them, the second son, Andrew, October ninth, 1720. When he was some six or eight years of age, an unhappy incident occurred which changed, not only the residence, but the whole tenor of the lives of the father and his family. Remonstrating with Sir Mungo Campbell, a young scion of aristocracy, for his insolence, Samuel Lewis, a sick brother then living with John Lewis, was killed by the impulsive young Lord, John Lewis at the same time receiving a wound in the hand; when the enraged husband and brother quickly resented the injury, and mortally wounded Campbell.[1]

    There was no alternative for Lewis. Should he remain, the prospect of justice being administered was exceedingly improbable, for the young Lord's connections were rich and powerful. So, disguised in female apparel, he sought Londonderry, the nearest sea-port, designing to reach Oporto, in Portugal, where William Lynn, a brother of his wife, was established in trade. Let down from an upper window upon the deck of the first vessel that sailed, though not bound for Oporto, he was rejoiced to get to sea, beyond the clutches of tyranny; and after various adventures, in different countries, he at length arrived at Oporto, in the year 1729. His brother-in-law promptly advised him, in order to elude the vigilance of his enemy, to sail for the New World, and there await the arrival of his family, whose good health he now learned, and whose removal to America his brother-in-law undertook to effect.

    Following this advice, Lewis proceed to Philadelphia, where, the following year, he was made happy in greeting the arrival of his family; and learning from them of the unwearied efforts made to trace the place of his flight, he resolved to penetrate deep into the American forest. With his family, he spent the winter of

1731-2 in Lancaster, and thence in the ensuing summer, removed to the then remote region, the Valley of Virginia. His first temporary location where he built a cabin, was on the bank of what was long known as Carthrar's, now Middle Creek, in then Beverly Manor; and not long thereafter he removed to the spot where he made his permanent home, on a stream which bears his name, two miles east of Staunton. The Lewis family were among the earliest to locate in that part of Virginia, and proved themselves efficient leaders in every good word and work. This was indeed, at that day, a beautiful country, in its native wilderness, with its flowing streams, flowering meads, and laurel-crowned hills; and, throughout all this rich valley, the brusque buffalo, stately elk, and graceful deer roamed in countless numbers.

Amid such surroundings and influences, Andrew Lewis, from the age of twelve grew to years of manhood, securing a very respectable education, well fitting him for the duties of a surveyor, and for the many important positions he was called to fill during the ensuing forty years. As early as 1736, Benjamin Burden, it is related, accompanied John Lewis on his return from a visit to Williamsburg, and spent several months in the Virginia Valley, making his home with his friend. He enjoyed many an exciting buffalo hunt with young Andrew Lewis, capturing, on one occasion, a young buffalo calf, which Burden took with him, and presented to Sir William Gooch, Governor of Virginia, and which served him a good turn in securing from that official a large grant of rich land in the Valley.

In 1742, when but twenty years of age, he was honored with a Captain's commission in the new county of Augusta, but which he did not see fit to accept. In 1743, he received a bounty for killing a wolf __ an additional evidence of his early love for the chase. As he gradually developed a fitness for the public service, he was chosen to fill places of trust and responsibility. While thus honored by his neighbors, it is not strange that he attracted the attention of at least one estimable young lady __ Elizabeth Givens, of Augusta county; to whom he was united in marriage in 1748. In 1750, he was appointed a justice of the peace, and member of the County court.

His elder brother, Thomas Lewis, who was County Surveyor of Augusta, appointed him Deputy Surveyor in 1751; and he was selected, towards the close of that year, as the agent of the Greenbrier Land Company, which had secured a grant for one hundred thousand acres on the waters of that river, and went in person to superintend the surveys, which were continued from time to time, till the subsequent Indian war arrested their completion. While engaged in this service, he came across two strange adventurers in that region, who, as they themselves related, had separated on account of a difference of opinion. In the dark recesses of the wilderness, many miles in advance of civilization, and only two of you, what could you possibly find to quarrel about? "Religion," drawled out one of them. But they became sufficiently reconciled, so that when one emerged from his cabin in the morning, and the other from his hollow tree residence, within view, they would condescend to salute each other with "good morning Mr. Martin," and a "good morning Mr. Sewell." They at length separated _ Sewell removing forty miles farther west, where the Indians found and killed him. Martin's Bottom, and Sewell's Creek, serve to commemorate the names of these singular but adventurous men.

Andrew Lewis must have taken some active part in the militia organization prior to 1752, since in that year, he was appointed Colonel of the several cavalry companies of the county _ of which, in 1744, there were eight in number, while there were eleven foot companies. When the long and sanguinary French and Indian war broke out, in 1754 _ that frontier school for many of the best officers of the Revolution _ young Lewis was, in some measure, prepared for the arduous duties he was destined to perform. On the eighteenth of March in that year, he was appointed a Captain of the Virginia troops, and that year, he raised one of the first companies with which he hastened to join the youthful commander, Washington, to aid in resisting the encroachments of the French on the Ohio. This little force advanced as far a Gist's plantation, near where the village of Counellsville, in Fayette County, Pennsylvania, is now located; whence Captain Lewis was detached with Lieutenant Waggoner, Ensign Mercer, two sergeants, two corporals, a drummer and sixty men, to endeavor to extend the road as far as the mouth of Red Stone Creek _ a little above which is situated the present town of Brownsville. Learning of the advance of a superior force of the enemy against him, Col. Washington called in his detachments, and retired to the Great Meadows, some thirteen miles, dragging their nine swivels by hand over a rough and mountainous region, the whole distance, nearly exhausted from fatigue, having been eight days without meat.

At the Great Meadows, where they arrived July first, they found only a few bags of flour which had been sent forward to meet them, some horses and milch cows; and here, awaiting reinforcements, they hastily constructed Fort Necessity. On the third of that month, a very rainy day, they were attacked by the French and Indians, and after several hours of severe fighting, in which the Virginia regiment lost twelve killed and forty three wounded, not including Mackay's South Carolina Independents, Washington was compelled to surrender, from want of supplies, and the superiority of the enemy. He secured favorable terms _ including permission to retire on parole. During the engagement, Lewis behaved with becoming bravery, receiving two wounds, one of then in his leg. During the intermixture of the parties the evening of the parley and surrender an incident occurred which might have proved fatal to Washington and his party, had it not been for the great presence of mind exhibited by Captain Lewis. An Irish soldier in the crowd, seeing an Indian near him, became uncontrollably excited, swearing, in the vigorous style of his countrymen, that he would send his yellow brother to a warmer climate, when Lewis, who was limping near him, from the effects of his wound, had barely time to knock up the muzzle of his gun into the air, thus saving the Indian's life, and probably the most disastrous consequences.

Though permitted by the capitulation to retire to the frontiers, yet Washington and his party were put on their wit's ends to accomplish the purpose. Their horses and cows had all been killed by the enemy during the action; and, after they had surrendered, they were plundered by the Indians of almost every article of personal comfort remaining; so that the four wounded officers and soldiers, who were unable to travel, had to be carried on the backs of those who had been so fortunate as to have escaped injury, fifty miles, to Wills' Creek _ taking their turns in this work of mercy. Recovering from his wounds, the incursions of the enemy on the Virginia parties furnished Captain Lewis with ample employment in vigilant endeavors to check their hostile purposes.

In the early Spring of 1755, he was ordered with his company of Rangers to Greenbrier River; there to erect two stockade forts, in one of which he was to remain himself, and to detach to the other a subaltern and fifteen men. These forts were designed to cover the western settlements of Virginia from the inroads of the Indians. And here, so far as the records show Captain Lewis remained during the Spring and Summer, keeping out scouts, and rendering every service within his power. But he was not in the disastrous battle of Monongahela, as has been asserted.[2]

About the close of August, a party of fifty Indians, supposed to have been Shawnees, devastated the settlement on Greenbrier, killing and capturing fifteen people, burning eleven houses, and driving off five hundred head of cattle and horses. Several of the people fled to a small post they had built in the neighborhood, where they were four days besieged by the enemy. Lewis, who was then on Jackson's River, seventy miles distant, received intelligence of this irruption, and hastened with his company to the relief of the survivors; but the Indians had retreated two days before his arrival.[3]

On the re-organization of the Virginia regiment, in August of this year, Washington selected Lewis for his Major, and sent him to recruit in the Fredericksburg region. In writing to him the following month, Washington, who was a good judge of men, paid him the high compliment _ "I know your diligence and punctuality require little or no spurs." His unfortunate Sandy Creek expedition, early in 1756, destined against the Upper Shawnee Town, on the Ohio, miscarried, in consequence of the misconduct of his guides, and the loss of provisions and ammunition; but the very hardships he and his heroic men underwent, inured them the better to bear other privations in the cause of their long services in defence of the Virginia frontiers. In the Summer of this year, Major Lewis and Captain Overton, with one hundred Virginians, were sent to the Cherokee county to build a fort near Chota, and also embody a large force of Cherokees, and return with them to Virginia. The fort was erected, but the South Carolina force expected, failing to reach there in season, and the "villainous traders" exerting their influence to prevent the Cherokees from engaging in the service, Lewis returned in October with only seven warriors and three women.

It is related, that during one of Washington's visits to the Augusta frontiers, probably about this period, to inspect forts, and learn the condition of affairs, a party of seven Indians had a special mission to secure Washington's scalp, and bear it in triumph to their people. They had, probably through some captive, learned of this tour of Washington on the part of the Virginia Colonel; and, to carry out their purpose, had selected a suitable place for ambushing the main road leading to a fort near the Roanoke. Weary of watching for two successive days and nights, the Indian leader suggested that he would hasten across a mile to view a shorter but more mountainous road, which was possible Washington might have taken; but enjoined them, during his few minutes' absence to fire on no one who might pass. It so happened that while he was gone, Washington, accompanied by Major Lewis and William Preston, a Captain of Virginia Rangers, passed by on the lower road, and were unmolested _ a singular and narrow escape for them all.

The year 1757, and early part of 1758, required the continued vigilance of Lewis on the Virginia frontier; sometimes, heading parties of friendly Cherokees on scouting excursions; sometimes employed by Washington fifty miles in advance of Winchester; and, at others, visiting the border garrisons of Augusta, directing the local officers, and suggesting specific services. An Indian inroad would necessitate an immediate pursuit, which sometimes proved successful in overtaking and chastising the marauders, and causing them to be more cautious in venturing into the settlements.

At length, a strong force was embodied, destined for the reduction of Fort Duquesne, under General Forbes; Colonels Washington, Bouquet, and Grant serving conspicuously under him. Major Lewis was ordered to join the expedition, which he did with such "extraordinary despatch," as to attract the particular attention of Bouquet. Lewis' battalion numbered two hundred men, all neatly attired in hunting shirts. "Their dress," wrote Bouquet, "should be our pattern for this expedition; it takes very well here, and, thank God, we see nothing but shirts and blankets."[4]

While slowly approaching Fort Duquesne, Grant was detached with a select body of eight hundred and forty men, composed of three hundred and thirty Highlanders, one hundred and seventy six Virginians, one hundred and fourteen Royal Americans, one hundred and twelve Pennsylvanians, ninety five Marylanders, and thirteen Carolinians. Lewis commanded the Virginians, and the object was to reconnoitre the French fort. It was ill-concerted expedition _ at least, so far as Grant, in its execution, was concerned. As they drew near the fort, undiscovered _ the prize so long sought by the English _ the vain-glorious Highlander conceived the idea of surprising the garrison, and appropriating to himself all the honors of the conquest. In vain did Lewis remonstrate, representing that the garrison had been reinforced by French and Indians, and that it would be almost an impossibility to reach the fort without discovery. But Grant was too self conceited to be diverted from his purpose; so he advanced leaving Thomas Bullitt, one of the Virginia Captains, some distance in the rear with two subalterns and fifty men, to guard the baggage; and moved forward with the main body, in the night, some two miles, to the hill since bearing his name, within sight of Fort

Duquesne.

At break of day, on the morning of the fourteenth of September, Grant detached Lewis with his two hundred Royal Americans and Virginians, to ambush the trail, a mile and a half in their rear, to prevent the enemy from making a dash at the baggage; while he sent Captain McDonald, of the Highlanders, with some fifty men, to march directly to the fort, with an engineer to take a plan of the works, and to attack any Indians they might find outside of the garrison. They found none, nor were they challenged by any sentries. McDonald's party marched with beating drums, and their only exploit was setting fire to a large log storehouse near the garrison, which was extinguished soon after they left it. As if this impudence and temerity were not sufficient, Grant had the reveille beaten by all the drums and bag-pipes of the detachment in several places, at the same time.

Four or five hundred men were posted along the base of the hill, facing the fort, to cover McDonald's retreat, and receive the enemy. But, instead of only two hundred French and Indians in the fort, as Grant had deceived himself into the belief that there were, a recent re-inforcement of four hundred men under Aubrey from the Illinois country, enabled the French commander to send out a strong force, accompanied by several hundred Indians; and, the result was, that McDonald and two columns of Highlanders posted further down the hill, as well as those on its brow, exposing themselves without cover, were rapidly shot down, and the survivors compelled to retreat. The Royal Americans and Pennsylvanians, Marylanders, and Carolinians, concealing themselves behind trees and brush, made a good defense for a time, and Grant exposed himself in the thickest of the fire, endeavoring to rally his panic-stricken men, but all to no purpose, as they were by that time flanked on all sides.

Lewis soon perceived, by the retreating fire, that Grant was overmatched, and in a bad situation. He advanced with his two hundred Provincials, and met a Highlander running at the top of his speed, of whom he inquired how the battle was going? He tersely replied, that they were "a' beaten, and he had seen Donald McDonald up to his hunkers in mud, and a' the sheen of his heed" _ this scalping, or skinning men's heads, was a novel mode of warfare with which the Highlanders were quite unacquainted in all their European experience. Lewis and his reinforcement came up, fell upon the rear of the Indians, and made way for Grant and some of his men to escape; but Lewis was soon obliged to fall back, the enemy having the advantage of the hill, and flanking him on all sides; and a number of his men were driven into the Ohio, most of whom were drowned. Lewis himself was exposed to great and imminent perils. He was for some time engaged in a personal combat with an Indian whose repeated blows he had successfully parried; and, at length, was so fortunate as to extricate himself by the death of his enemy. But his place being immediately supplied by others, he retreated until he reached each detachment, to whose commander he surrendered himself. The Indians desire to put him to death, but the French, with difficulty, saved him, with the loss however, of all his clothes, save his shirt, before he reached the fort. An elderly Indian seized hold of this remaining garment, but Lewis resisted, with the tomahawk drawn over his head, when a French officer, by signs, directed him to deliver it to the Indian, and then took him into his private room, and gave him a complete suit of clothes.

Major Grant did not seem disposed to stop and assist Lewis in his unequal contest, when he came to his relief; but retreated to where Bullitt was posted for the protection of the baggage, and there endeavored to rally the flying soldiers, by entreating them, in the most pathetic manner, to stand by him. But all in vain, for the enemy were too close at their heels. As they came up, Capt. Bullitt attacked them very furiously for a time; but the most of his men unsupported, were soon killed, when the gallant Captain and few survivors were compelled to fly for their lives. The vigorous attack, like that of Lewis, checked the pursuit of the enemy for a time, and enabled Grant, and some others, who became separated from Bullitt, to make off. Wandering all night in the woods, with seven or eight soldiers, Grant, the next morning, thinking discretion the better part of valor, since he was utterly ignorant of the wilderness, made his way to the fort, and surrendered himself and little squad to a French officer, who had the utmost difficulty in saving him from the tomahawk of a savage who insisted on killing him; but the Frenchman was firm in maintaining his pledge of protection, in accordance with the usages of civilized warfare. But his companions fell victims to the fury of the Indians. In this adventure of Major Grant, no less than twenty-six officers, and two hundred and seventy three privates, were either killed, wounded or taken; of these, the Virginia regiment lost six officers and sixty-two privates _ Captain Bullitt and Stewart escaping. No other corps, save the Highlanders, suffered in the same proportion.

After the French had blown up the fort, in November, and were wending their way up the Allegheny River towards Canada, with their prisoners, the weather was very cold, and Grant lay shivering in the boat, cursing the Americans and their country; threatening, that, if he ever returned to England he would let his Majesty know their insignificance,
and the useless trouble and expense to the nation in endeavoring to protect such a vile country and people. Lewis retorted with great severity upon such pusillanimous exhibition of himself, and made a manly defense of his countrymen from the dastardly attack of this supercilious and ungrateful officer,

They met with rather a rough reception from M. Chauvignerie, the French commandant at Venango, until he received a letter from his son, who had the previous year gone out at the head of a scouting party of Indians to the Susquehanna region, where he got separated from his detachment, and surrendered himself to the English, rather than starve in the woods. He wrote his father how kindly he had been treated by the English, and begged him, in turn, to alleviate the distresses of such of their number as should happen to fall into his hands. This produced a great change in the treatment extended to Lewis and his fellow prisoners.[5]

Smarting under the denunciations he had received on the Alleghany from a hated Provincial officer, the haughty and unprincipled Grant, while imprisoned at Quebec, had the effrontery, in a communication he addressed General Forbes, to ascribe the whole disgrace of his defeat to the misconduct of Lewis and his Provincial troops. As such letters had to pass the inspection before they were sealed and sent off, the French officer, who discharged that duty, immediately carried the letter to the Virginia Major, who, indignant at such a scandalous and unjust misrepresentation, accused Grant of his duplicity, in the presence of the French officers, and challenged him; but Grant prudently declined the combat, even after Lewis had spit in his face, and still further taunted him with insulting language.

Towards the close of 1759, Major Lewis was exchanged, and resumed his services on the frontiers of Virginia, scouting after the Cherokees, who had been incited to war against the Colonies by the machinations of French emissaries, and assisting Colonel Byrd, who then commanded the Virginia regiment, in his campaign during 1760-1, against those Indians _ a campaign of much frontier hardship and privation, though productive of no brilliant results. When the regiment was disbanded in 1762, Major Lewis was voted, in common with his fellow officers, one year's extra pay for faithful services to his country. In the new regiment raised this year, he declined to serve, and retired from military employment.

In a letter of Francis Fauquier, Governor of Virginia, in July, 1761, Major Lewis is designated with the title of Colonel _ either a brevet honor, or else he had succeeded to that rank in the militia. In the years 1762-4, during the Pontiac outbreak, the Indians visited the Virginia frontiers with a great slaughter and barbarity, when he was appointed Lieutenant of the militia for Augusta _ commanding all the forces of that county; garrisoning the forts, and directing the Rangers, in a defensive warfare, carried on with various success, but with great vigilance, efficiency, and prudence.

On the application of Colonel Bouquet, sometime in August, 1764, to Francis Fauquier, Governor of Virginia, for men for his contemplated expedition against the Ohio Indians, Colonel Lewis was directed to raise a corps of volunteers, which he soon accomplished, and joined the army at Pittsburg towards the end of September. Though raised in Virginia, they were designed to complete the Pennsylvania troops, and were in the pay of the last mentioned Province. Lewis' men, from the frontiers, and accustomed to Indian fighting, formed the scouts and pioneers of the army. At the close of the expedition, Bouquet acknowledged his "particular obligation to Colonel Lewis for his zeal and good conduct during the campaign."[6] Colonel Lewis had served as a member of the County Court over seven years, when, in 1757, finding his active military employment prevented his proper attendance on its duties, he declined further service. He was again placed in the commission of Justices, in 1766; and, in the same year, was made sheriff of Augusta, serving till the close of 1767, and then as Justice again in 1768 and the following year.

Sir Wm. Johnson and the Six Nations, at a treaty in 1765, discussed the question of a boundary line between those tribes and the Colonies, but without definite action. In accordance with the policy of the British Government to establish a definite Indian boundary, John Stuart, the Indian Agent for the Southern Colonies, concluded a treaty with the Cherokees, in October, 1768, by which the line between that tribe and Virginia was fixed, running in a straight course from Chiswell's Mine, on New River, opposite the mouth of Cripple Creek, about thirteen miles easterly from Wythe Court-House, Virginia, to the confluence of the Ohio and Great Kanawha. This alarmed the Virginians, for they claimed the valleys of the Upper Holston and Ohio as embraced within their territory. At this period, too, there was considerable uneasiness on the part of the Indians on account of the encroachment of white settlers on the Monongahela and Yohioghany.

When the grand council at Fort Stanwix, on the Mohawk, was called, in November, 1768, Colonel Lewis was appointed one of the Virginia commissioners. The important treaty concluded, served to quiet, for the time, the complaints of the Indians, extending the western boundary down the Ohio as far as the mouth of the Tennessee. Colonel Lewis returned, by special order, to Fort Chiswell, to treat with the Cherokees with reference to a new boundary between them and Virginia; and in the ensuing winter, he was sent on a mission to Charleston, to confer with the Agent of the Southern Indians on matters connected with the same subject. These efforts eventually brought about a new treaty with the Cherokees, in October, 1770, by his Majesty's orders, when a new line was established, beginning where the boundary between North Carolina and the Cherokee hunting ground terminates, thence by a west course to a point six miles east of the Long Island, in Holston, and thence to the confluence of the Ohio and Great Kenawha. Thus were the settlements on the Holston recognized as within the Colony of Virginia.

Colonel Lewis removed in 1770, to the neighborhood of Salem, on the Roanoke, within the bounds of the county of Botetourt organized that year; and of which he was appointed the County Lieutenant, and placed at the head of the commission of Justices, thus making him the presiding officer of the County Court. In the Spring of 1774, he, with an associate, represented his county, in the Virginia Assembly, and hastened home to defend his exposed frontier from the attacks of the hostile Indians, and led the expedition to Point Pleasant, as already narrated. His faithfulness in enforcing discipline, was the cause, in after years, of the propagation, to some extent, on the part of thoughtless men of the report that he had lingered in camp during the entire day of the tenth of October, while others encountered the dangers, and won the victory.[7] It may be truly said, that all great commanders in battle, take a position where they can best learn the movements of the contending forces, and supply such aid from the reserves as the exigencies may require. But the inuendo, that Lewis remained in camp, in any sense shirking his duty, is not justified by the facts in the case. One of the most prominent and experienced officers under him on that day, states most emphatically, that neither the commander-in-chief nor his officers expected a general engagement; that he behaved with the greatest bravery and prudence, that he was fully employed in sending out reinforcements, from time to time, where needed in different quarters, superintending the hasty erection of a breast-work by the felling of trees, and caring for the wounded, and thus, "under God," preventing the enemy from breaking into camp, and finally securing the victory.[8]

In March, 1775, he was chosen, with John Bowyer, to represent Botetourt county in the Virginia Convention, called by the people to oppose the tyrannical acts of the British Ministry. The instructions given their representatives by the people of that county, while quaint their style, were singularly suggestive of great earnestness, without the least effort to conceal their sentiments. "When the honest man of Boston," they said, "who has broken no law, has his property wrested from him, the hunter of the Alleghanies must take the alarm, and, as a freeman of America, he will fly to the representatives, and thus instruct them:, "Gentlemen, my gun, my tomahawk, my life, I desire you to tender to the honor of my King and country; but my Liberty to range these woods upon the same terms my father has done, is not mine to give up. It was not purchased by me; but purchased it was. It is entailed upon my son, and the tenure is sacred. Watch over it, gentlemen, for to him it must descend unviolated, if my arm can defend it; but if not, if wicked power is permitted to prevail against me, the original purchase was blood, and mine shall seal the surrender."

Colonel Lewis was a conspicuous member of this convention of the patriot men of Virginia, and, in accordance with Patrick Henry's celebrated resolutions for immediately putting the Colony in a state of defense, he was associated among others, with Henry, Washington, Jefferson, Stephen, and Christian, in preparing a plan for embodying, arriving, and disciplining a sufficient number of men for that purpose. It was a bold measure, but the Virginia patriots did not shirk their duty. Colonel Lewis was chosen one of the Virginia commissioners for holding a treaty at Fort Pitt, in the autumn of this year, for ratifying the former treaty of Camp Charlotte, and pacifying the Western Indians generally. Having accomplished the object, he returned to Williamsburg, and resumed his seat in the Convention. When Lord Dunmore, it was thought, in December of this year, after the repulse of his detachment at the Great Bridge, meditated an attack on the defenseless towns of York and Williamsburg, the few military companies within reach were called into requisition, who, with an armed association of private gentlemen _ and members of the Convention, repaired to York, and were placed under the command of Colonel Lewis. They remained there till the threatened danger was over.

On the first of March, 1776, Andrew Lewis was chosen a Brigadier General by Congress, and assigned to the command of the Continental forces in Virginia. Among his subordinate officers were Colonels Woodford, Scott, Weedon, and Christian, who had seen service in the old French and Indian war, and the latter on the Point Pleasant campaign also. His first business was to guard against Dunmore's improvised naval force, which was hovering on the coast of Virginia;

and he succeeded, July ninth, in dislodging his old commander from Gywnn's Island, and driving him from the continent. On that occasion, having erected two batteries nearly opposite the point on the island where the enemy was encamped, Lewis gave the signal for attack, by applying a match himself to an eighteen pounder, the ball passing through the hull of the Dunmore, five hundred yards distant; a second and third shot also proving effective slivering one of her timbers, a splinter from which wounded Lord Dunmore in his leg. The batteries pouring their shot upon the Governor's fleet and camp, compelled him to embark, slip the cables of his vessels, burning several which got aground, and then put to sea.

On the twenty-fifth of July, he shared in proclaiming the Declaration of Independence to the rejoicing troops at Williamsburg. Other duties also fell to his lot _ forwarding several tons of powder to South Carolina _ sending two battalions of Continental troops, under General Mercer to join Washington in New Jersey; and, early in 1777, he was directed to send forward all the Continental troops in Virginia to the main army, and fitting the newly raised troops for effective service.

The promotion of Adam Stephen by Congress to the rank of Major General, February nineteenth, 1777, had an unhappy effect on the sensitive nature of Andrew Lewis, who thought he had been overlooked and neglected. Washington, anticipating the effect, wrote him, on the third of March, a patriotic and soothing letter, expressing the wish that the neglect might not induce him to abandon the service, and beseeching his old friend to stand at his post at that critical juncture, when "gentlemen of ability," especially in the military line, were indispensable to the success of the patriot cause; and closed by inviting him to repair to headquarters, take a command in the main army, and trust to the results of the approaching campaign to secure him the rank to which he was entitled.

But Lewis, conscious of unsullied integrity, patriotic motives, large experience, and extended services, felt constrained, from a nice sense of honor, to send in his resignation to Congress, which he did on the twenty-first of March, and which was on the fifteenth of April, accepted by that body. Washington, in a letter, written a year and a half thereafter, alluding to this matter, said: "if Congress are not convinced of the impropriety of a certain irregular promotion, they are the only set of men who require further and greater proof, than have already been given, of the error of the measure."

It was perhaps, after all, not alone the offence which the promotion of others of less merit gave him, that caused his retirement from the service."He was grown old," says Colonel Stuart, and "his ardor for military fame had abated." But his love of country still burned as warmly in his bosom as ever; and his counsels of wisdom were always at the service of his struggling countrymen. In the summer of 1778, Congress having requested the Governor and Council of Virginia to appoint two commissioners, to join others from Congress, and from Pennsylvania, to hold a treaty at Fort Pitt with the Delaware, Shawnee and other Indians, General Lewis, and his brother, Thomas Lewis, were appointed for that purpose.

Towards the close of August, and early in September, a treaty was held with the Delawares, but the cold-blooded murder of Cornstalk, and his associates, had served to intensify the already embittered and alienated feelings of the Shawnees, and the "fire-water" and machinations of the British had so wrought upon the prejudices of Logan, that it was not strange that neither the Shawnees nor the Mingoes were represented at the council-fire. As Washington had apprehended, the end designed was not answered by the pains taken to effect it.

During the Revolution, the Indians made several attempts to kill General Lewis, by waylaying the paths near his residence. They well understood his high character and influence, and were, doubtless, instigated by British emissaries to secure his scalp, if possible, with the promise of some large reward. While watching the trails in his neighborhood _ particularly in 1778 _ though they failed in the special object of their search, they succeeded in killing and wounding a number of people, including several children.

In July, 1779, he was appointed by the Congress and Council, in conjunction with Colonels Fleming and Christian, to report on the proper posts to be supported on the south-wester frontiers of Virginia, and in Kentucky, and the complement of men for their respective garrisons; and, in December one of the commissioners, on the part of Virginia, to consider a proper boundary line between that State and Pennsylvania _ an effort to obviate the difficulties growing out of the conflict of jurisdiction on the western borders of the respective States. At the May session of the Virginia Assembly, of 1780, while serving as one of the representatives of Botetourt, he was chosen, by the joint vote of the two Houses, a member of the Privy Council of State _ a position of great importance, and never more so than during his term of service in that and the ensuing year.

He was called to attend a special meeting of Governor Nelson and the Council, at Richmond, early in September, 1781, to prepare for the expected arrival of the French fleet; and to make, as well, the necessary military preparations, which soon after eventuated in the capture of Lord Cornwallis and his army. It was supposed, that feeling the first symptoms of a bilious fever, he hastened to reach is home in the more elevated and healthful country, and reached Capt. Talbot's, in Bedford County, about twenty-eight miles from his residence, on the twenty fourth of that month, but could proceed no farther. A messenger was promptly despatched to his family, and the next day his sons, Thomas and Andrew, arrived, accompanied by Colonel Fleming. But human efforts could avail nothing, for he was already speechless, and in the agonies of death, and breathed his last the same evening.

Thus died General Andrew Lewis, September the twenty-fifth, 1781, at the age of nearly sixty-one years. Measuring his life by his usefulness, it was a long career of honored deeds and services. Two days after his decease, his remains were consigned to the grave, beside those of his youngest son, Charles, at his homestead, on the elevated ground skirting the Roanoke, adjacent to Salem, in the present county of Roanoke. The silent grief of his kindred and friends best attested their strong attachment to him.

General Lewis was, in person, upward of six feet in height, well proportioned, and singularly imposing and symmetrical in his appearance. He was possessed of uncommon strength, activity, and powers of endurance. His face was full and florid with a dark brown eye; stern, austere, invincible, and reserved, he was seldom known to smile _ he seemed, indeed, like one "born to command." Stuart states, that one of the Colonial Governors at the treaty of Fort Stanwix _ doubtless William Franklin, of New Jersey, the only Governor present _ attracted by the dignity and grandeur of his presence, remarked that "the earth seemed to tremble under him as he walked along;"[9] and the same high authority asserts, that when Washington was nominated for General-in-Chief of the army, in June, 1775, distrusting, in his great modesty, his own ability, he recommended Lewis to one of his Virginia colleagues as the foremost military man in the Colonies, and the fittest person for that high command.

His independent spirt despised sycophantic means of gaining popularity; and hence an army of volunteers, without discipline, experience, or a proper sense of estimating his real worth, never rendered more than his merits extorted. Some would take umbrage because they were required simply to do their duty; others questioned whether the routine drudgeries of the common soldier were not beneath the dignity of the volunteer; and thus many imaginary complaints were made. Yet on all occasions of great emergency, the people invariably looked to him to guide and lead them through their difficulties and dangers. Colonel Stuart, who knew him well, declared that his departure was "lamented by all who were intimately acquainted with his meritorious services and superior qualities."

It was a fitting recognition of the transcendent merit of Andrew Lewis, that he should have been selected by his adopted State as one of her representative men whose statues, placed on monuments, adorn the capitol square in Richmond.

William Fleming was the third son, and fifth child of Leonard Fleming, whose ancestors were long settled in Westmoreland county in the north of England, not far from that beautiful sheet of water, Winandemere. His mother was of the Satterthwaite family. Becoming straitened in their circumstances, Mr. Fleming sold his paternal estate, on the road leading from Kendal to Ambleside, about 1728, and moved to Scotland with his wife and four children, where he was appointed to a place in the excise , the salary of which, together with an annuity enjoyed during his wife's life-time, enabled them to live in easy circumstances, and give their children a respectable education.

William Fleming was born in Jedburgh, the principal town of Roxburgshire, Scotland, Feb, 18, 1729. Having early finished his classical studies, in Dumfries, his inclination led him to the study of the physic, which in the army or navy, would enable him to gratify a strong curiosity he cherished for travel. He passed the usual term of three years as an apprentice to a surgeon, Dr. McKee, first in Dumfries, and then in Kirkendbright whither the Doctor removed; but instead of then going immediately to a medical school to study the theory of medicine under different professors for a brief period, as was the usual course at that day, young Fleming wisely judged that a thorough knowledge of materia medica and pharmacy would have a far better preliminary preparation. He, therefore, went to Kendal, near his father's former residence in England, and entered the apothecary store of Christopher Brown, eminent in his line, with whom he remained till he became thoroughly proficient in this branch of the profession. While there, the Scotch rebellion of 1745 occurred, and he witnessed a body of Highlanders while marching through Kendal on their route to Derby. The next year he went to Edinburgh, where he finished his professional course at the well known medical college in that city, and graduating with the brightest prospects.

About 1747, he entered the British navy as a surgeon, and entered upon the career to which he had long been looking forward with the fondest anticipations. For the ensuing seven or eight years, nothing is definitely known of his services, save that he largely gratified his desire to travel and see the world; but, in doing so, passed through many toils and perils. He saw considerable actual service; receiving, in one action, a sword-cut across the bridge of his nose; and suffering several months as a prisoner of war with the Spaniards. But the peace of Aix-la-Chapelle, in October, 1748, and the final accommodation of difficulties with Spain in 1750, left matters quite too peaceful a condition to suit such a roving spirit as young Fleming, in quest of danger and adventure.

The troubles that were breeding between the Colonies and the French on the Ohio, held out to him a bright prospect for active service, with every opportunity for studying a new phase of human nature in the wild backwoods of America. The story of the Indian race, always full of romantic interest, had its charms for the young physician. There was, moreover, a fine opportunity for one of his experience and culture, to serve his King and country; and, at the same time in the new country where he proposed to cast his lot. He sailed for the Colonies, landing at Williamsburg immediately after the disastrous defeat of Braddock; and, on the twenty-fifth of August, 1755, was commissioned an Ensign by Gov. Dinwiddie to serve under Washington, and made himself also useful as an assistant surgeon. He was promoted to the rank of Lieutenant in the same regiment, May twenty-sixth, 1757, still acting in the additional capacity as a surgeon; and served on Forbes' campaign in 1758, and under Colonel Byrd against the Cherokees in 1760. On the reduction of the old regiment, and the formation of a new one under Colonel Stephen, Fleming was, in May, 1762, promoted to the rank of Captain. He saw much hard frontier service; stationed, at one time at Voss's Fort, on the Roanoke; and, at another, at Stalnacher's, on the Holston.

In April, 1763, Captain Fleming was married to Annie Christian, daughter of Israel Christian, of Augusta county. At the period of 1766-7, he served as a Justice of the Peace for Augusta. In a letter written by Patrick Henry, June tenth, 1767, it appears that he was solicited by him and Dr. Walker, to visit the country near the junction of the Ohio and Mississippi, with a view of examining and describing it, so as to attract adventurers there, and found a new Colony; but the scheme seems to have failed, probably for the reason that the British Ministry were opposed to the extension of English settlements so far to the westward, having rejected Colonel Charles Lee's application, about 1763, for a grant of lands to settle one Colony on the Ohio below the Wabash, and another on the Illinois;[10] though Walpole's proposed Ohio Colony, backed by the powerful influence of Franklin, met with a tardy sanction at a subsequent period.

About 1768, Dr. Fleming removed to the neighborhood of the present city of Christiansburg, in a region which successively became Botetourt, Fincastle, and Montgomery county, Virginia, where he settled down in the double capacity of a farmer and physician. On the organization of Botetourt, early in 1770, he was continued in the commission of Justices, and appointed Colonel of the militia; and, in May, 1774, he was promoted to the full rank of Colonel, commanding the Botetourt regiment, as well as some other companies assigned him, on the Point Pleasant campaign. The distinguished part he acted in the memorable engagement of the tenth of October, and the severe wounds he received have been fully narrated __ wounds that crippled him the remainder of his days.

When Andrew Lewis was chosen a Brigadier General in Continental service, early in 1776, Col. Fleming succeeded him as County Lieutenant of Botetourt, and during the most, if not the whole, of the Revolutionary war, his duties were various and arduous; filling quotas of men for the service, providing against Indian irruptions, and carrying on an extensive correspondence with the Governor and Council of Virginia, the Generals in command of the Western Department, and the commandants of the neighboring counties, relative to the situation and defence of the frontiers. During 1778-9, he represented the district, composed of Botetourt, Montgomery, Washington, and Kentucky, in the Virginia Senate, and, in July, of the latter year, he was, by appointment of the Governor and Council, associated with General Lewis and Colonel Christian, to determine what posts and garrisons were necessary for the protection of the western counties, including Kentucky, and the number of men requisite for their defense.

Shortly after performing this service, he was appointed by Jefferson, who was then Governor, one of four commissioners to visit Kentucky, and adjust land claims, and settle accounts against the State, which had proved a very trying undertaking, and especially during the ensuing "hard winter," in that newly settled region, where the necessaries of life were scant in the extreme. From this service, he returned home the last of May, 1780, after an absence of nine months.

Early in 1780, Colonel Fleming was chosen, by the joint action of the Legislature, to a seat in the Privy Council of State. There was a vacancy in the office of Governor for a short period, in 1781, owing to the invasion of Lord Cornwallis, when Fleming, as the only acting member of the Council present, called out the militia, and performed other acts essential to good government, which though of doubtful legality, were yet so necessary and proper, that the Legislature promptly passed an act for his indemnification. In November of that year, he resigned his seat in the Council, probably because Cornwallis; having been captured, and the war virtually ended, gave him an opportunity to retire from the public service, and spend the evening of his days with his family. But this was not altogether permitted; for the Governor and Council appointed him at the head of a board of commissioners for the settlement of unadjusted claims against the State in the western counties, which he accepted in December following. Colonel Fleming and his associates entered upon their duties in the autumn of 1782, and did not complete their arduous and complicated labors, at the various stations and settlements in Kentucky till the ensuing March. In 1778, he served as a member of the Convention for the ratification of the Federal Constitution; and this worthily concluded his long and useful public services _ it having been more than forty years since he entered the British navy, and thirty-three since he first engaged in the protection of the border settlements of Virginia.

Colonel Fleming never fully recovered from the severe wounds he received at Point Pleasant. Both bones of his left arm were broken between the wrist and elbow, and the nerves and cords so injured, that the little finger, and the one next to it, on that hand, ever hung uselessly thereafter. For many years that arm was regularly bandaged, supported by a leather stay; and it was always somewhat crooked. The bullet which lodged in his body was never extracted; at times it would seem to work up some distance, causing much pain until it would again recede to its former position. But at length it caused his death, August twenty-fourth, 1795, in the sixty-seventh year of his age.

He was a man of great goodness of heart and benevolence of character, frequently, when in the army, dismounting from his horse to accommodate and relieve some weary or feeble soldier. His medical practice was extensive and laborious; and, though desperately wounded, he was enabled to give such directions at Point Pleasant, where so many others needed attention, that not a few men there acquired useful lessons in dressing gun-shot wounds, that proved of service in their frontier localities during the ensuing twenty years of border warfare. In size, he was of ordinary height, thick-set, fair complexion, with a fine blue eye. He was connected with the Episcopal church, and was strongly religious in his character. His widow survived him till November, 1811, and their seven children, worthy members of society, nearly all lived to a good old age.

<u>Charles Lewis</u> was the youngest of the sons of John Lewis, and was born in Augusta county, Virginia, in 1733. From his early youth he seems to have possessed a daring nature, which attracted the admiration of his friends and acquaintances. There is preserved a tradition of him, that he was once captured by the Indians while on a solitary hunting expedition. After having been taken about two hundred miles, with his arms pinioned behind him, and goaded on by the threats of his captors, he managed to effect his escape, by suddenly bursting the cords which bound him, and plunging down a steep precipice of some twenty feet, into the bed of a mountain torrent. The Indians hesitated not to follow; and in a long race, Lewis had gained a little upon his pursuers, when, upon leaping a fallen tree in his path, his strength suddenly failed by the exertion, and he fell prostrate

among the luxuriant weeds which grew thickly around its body. Three Indians sprang over the tree within a few feet of his place of concealment; but one by one, to his great relief, they disappeared in the dark recesses of the forest. When about to rise from his uneasy bed, a new an unexpected enemy appeared in an enormous rattlesnake, which had thrown itself into the coiling attitude of attack, his fangs within a few inches of his face, and his rattles loudly ringing out the preliminary to the deadly onset. The slightest contraction of the body, or relaxation of a muscle, would have provoked the fatal spring. In this situation he lay for several minutes, when the snake, meeting with no opposition, crawled over his body, and slowly moved away. "I had eaten nothing," said Lewis on his return, "for many days; I had no fire-arms, and I ran the risk of dying with hunger before I could reach the settlement; but rather would I have died than to have killed and made a meal of the generous reptile."

At the opening of the French and Indian war in 1754, Charles Lewis was just the age to enter into it with all the zeal of youthful ardor; and the traditions are, that he and his brothers served together, especially in the earlier stages of the border difficulties. It may, therefore, be presumed, that he was in the company of his brother, Andrew Lewis, in the affair at Fort Necessity, in July, 1754; and on the frontiers with him during that and the following year, as well as on the Sandy Creek expedition early in 1756. In November, in the latter year, he was assigned, by Major Lewis, as a Lieutenant of William Preston's company, which was ordered to the relief of Miller's Fort, and Wilson's Fort on the Bull Pasture, and to give attention to scouting in that quarter. Washington, in October, 1757, refers vaguely to "Captain Lewis being attacked," but gives no particulars. It is quite probable, that he served on Forbes' campaign of 1758, and on Byrd's Cherokee expedition of 1760-1.

When the Pontiac war broke out in 1763, Captain Lewis was again called into active frontier service. At this period, he was residing on the Cow Pasture River, in the present county of Bath, a region greatly exposed to the inroads of the enemy. When Captains Moffett and Phillips were defeated, in September of that year, the companies of William Christian, Charles Lewis, and John Dickinson were united, comprising altogether one hundred and fifty men and went in pursuit of the enemy, overtaking them, October third, on the head waters of Back Creek, killing several, putting the survivors to rout, and recovering much valuable plunder.[11]

The next year was no less troublesome on account of savage visitations. Fully one hundred people, on the borders of Virginia alone, were either killed or carried off by the Indians within a brief period succeeding the twenty-second of May. Early in June, a party of Indians, with two Frenchmen, did much mischief on the frontier of Augusta; when Lewis with a company took their trail, and soon overtook the marauders. They killed one of the Frenchmen and two Indians, and put the rest to flight, recovering some prisoners whom they had taken, from whom they learned that the Frenchman slain was the leader of the party. So vigilant was

Captain Lewis, that no sooner had he returned from this successful foray, than he had occasion to enter upon another; and, on the 13th of that month, he encountered another band of the enemy, killing five of their number.[12]

During this season, Joseph Mayse, a youth of some twelve years, whose parents resided on the Cow Pasture, while a short distance from home was punched down by a large Indian with the muzzle of his gun, and made prisoner. He was placed up on a horse, with his feet tied under the animal's belly; and, after five days journey towards the Ohio, the party thinking they were beyond the reach of pursuers, untied their little captive. While passing along, unconscious of danger, they were overtaken by that energetic Indian fighter, Charles Lewis, with a party, who fired on the enemy. Mayse's horse took flight, and dashed into the bushes, when the lad was knocked off by his body coming in contact with the limb of a tree _ luckily for him, that he was not then fastened to the horse, or the consequences might have been fatal. As it was, he lay in the underbrush where he fell, till the pursuing party came in sight, when he jumped up and ran to them. It was but a slight skirmish, for the Indians decamped. Mayse, ten years thereafter, was a soldier under Lewis at Point Pleasant, and received a severe wound in the engagement.

Captain Lewis, in the autumn of this year, joined Colonel Bouquet on his campaign against the Ohio Indians, which eventuated in a treaty on the Tuscaroras, pledging renewed fidelity to the English, and surrendering their white captives. The Virginia volunteers, Colonel Andrew Lewis, Major Field, and Captain Lewis, went to the Lower Shawnee Town, to receive their friends and relations who were prisoners there; and Benevissica, a noted Shawnee chief, fulfilled his promise to accompany them from the treaty ground to get their captive friends, and saw them safe to Fort Pitt. This was the last service of Lewis. In the long Indian war, with but temporary intermissions, for over ten years, during which he was not permitted to remain a single month at a time with his family.

During the ensuing ten years, a period of comparative peace, Charles Lewis rose to the rank of Colonel in the militia; and, in the Spring of 1774, was chosen a representative from Augusta to the Virginia House of Burgesses, and hastened home, at the close of the session, for the defence of the frontiers. He lost his life at the battle of Point Pleasant, animating his men to the last. He was among the most skillful of the Virginia leaders in border warfare. During his life it was his lot to have frequent skirmishes with the Indians, in which he was always successful; had gained much applause for his intrepidity, and was greatly beloved by his troop. He had been the hero of many a gallant exploit, and his death was sincerely lamented by all classes of people. "You have lost a brave leader," said Andrew Lewis, to the Augusta troops, two days after his fall, "and I the loss of a brother." He left three sons and two daughters.

Abraham Field was among the earliest settlers of that part of Spotsylvania, which became first Orange, and the Culpeper county, Virginia, and was a respectable farmer in early circumstances. He had by his first marriage four sons;

and by his second several sons and daughters. His son, John Field, was born, in what is now Culpeper, about 1720. His education was limited; such only as the "field schools" of that day afforded. He grew up to years of manhood, fond of sports and pleasure _ the turf and the gaming table; he was cheerful, social, and popular. He early married Ann Clift, and settled down as a farmer _ devoting as much time to the occupation as his fondness for companionship and hilarity would permit.

He early evinced a partiality for military life, which was developed by the French and Indian war, and was ever after his ruling passion. It is difficult to trace many of his services in that war. He was in command of a company, in the autumn of 1756, on the frontiers of Virginia, and was engaged, in conjunction with Captain Robert Spotswood, in a conflict with the Indians near the foot of the Alleghenies, in which he acted a conspicuous part, and the enemy were routed with loss. His company, at Fort Cumberland, in August, 1758, numbered ninety-eight men, forming a part of Byrd's regiment; and he was engaged on Forbes' campaign against Fort Duquesne, in that year, commanding a party of pioneers, "blazing" out the road for the advancing army. During the ensuing three years, he was, it seems with his regiment guarding the frontiers, on scouting parties, and taking part in the campaign against the Cherokees. In the autumn of 1763, he joined Major Campbell with about one hundred volunteers, in escorting a convoy to Fort Pitt; and, in 1764, served under Colonel Lewis in the Virginia volunteers, with the rank of Major, on Bouquet's campaign against the Ohio Indians. The ensuing year, he was a chosen member of the House of Burgesses from Culpeper county; and, not long after, was made Colonel of the militia. About 1766, he made a trip of exploration to Florida, but did not like the country.

In the spring of 1774, anxious to locate a new home in the rich valleys of the west, he started for the Kanawha country. Accompanied by his eldest son, Ezekiel, his kinsmen Daniel and Reuben Field with a negro man and woman for cooks, and reached the settlement of Walter Kelly, about twelve miles below the Great Falls of the Kanawha. Here, on the eastern side of the river, about half a mile above Kelly's, Colonel Field made an improvement and planted some corn, with a view of having a crop in readiness when he should move out his family, as he contemplated, in the autumn.

Towards the close of June, Captain John Stuart, of Greenbrier, sent an express to Field and Kelly, advising them to remove immediately, as there was great danger of an Indian war. Kelly gave heed to the advice, and sent off his family in charge of his younger brother; and while Field was combating the idea of danger, a party of Indians came upon Field and Kelly, while they were taking some leather from a tan-trough, a short distance from the cabin, and fired on them, killing Kelly on the spot. Field ran to the cabin, where the guns were, but unloaded; and seizing one, he ran into an adjoining corn field, leaving a Scotch boy and the negro crying at the door. The boy was killed, and the girl captured. Field made his escape. The Kelly family were still within hearing distance, when the guns fired;

and they fled with all haste to Greenbrier. Captain Stuart, on their arrival, hastened with ten or fifteen men, towards the Kelly settlement, and when ten miles on the way, they met Colonel Field with only his shirt on his back, having run eighty miles through the woods, brush, briers, tearing off his clothes and severely lacerating his limbs. He was down with fatigue and hunger.

His two kinsmen, and the negro man, some way effected their escape; while Ezekiel Field, had left his father only a short time before the attack, with some message, perhaps for his kinsmen, and had gone less than half a mile when he discovered ten or a dozen Indians, within twenty or thirty steps of him. Too late to try to elude them, he surrendered himself a prisoner. It may be added, that when the Indian party captured the negro girl, and secured their plunder, they packed the two prisoners with the spoils they had taken. After proceeding eight or ten miles, the poor girl became faint and weary under her load, when the tomahawk ended her suffering. Young Field was taken to the Detroit region, and was brought into the Fort Pitt treaty, in the autumn of 1775, by Shegenaba, son of the famous Pontiac, and returned to his friends, married his relative, Eliza Field, and removed to Kentucky about 1780. He lost his life, at the fatal battle of the Blue Licks, August the nineteenth, 1782, leaving a widow and several children.

Colonel Field, exasperated by the captivity of his son and negro girl, returned to Culpeper, raised a company of forty active men; and, with the approval of Lord Dunmore, hastened to join Colonel Lewis, evidently believing his division would be more likely, than that under his Lordship to penetrate to the Indian towns, where he hoped to recover the prisoners from their savage captors. But he did not live to see the end of the war nor his son's return; for he fell as already mentioned, on the well-contested field at Point Pleasant, October tenth, 1774, where he but confirmed his reputation of ranking among the bravest of the brave.

He left three sons and three daughters. He was a man but little short of six feet in height, with broad shoulders, a compact frame, and a piercing black eye; possessing a hardy, vigorous constitution, active, resolute, and brave. Such a man, with his determined spirit, military experience and popular address, would undoubtedly have become a conspicuous leader in the war of Independence, had he been spared to participate in its dangers and glories.

Evan Shelby, was born in Wales in 1720, and while a youth, migrated with his father, about 1735, and settled near the North Mountain, in what subsequently became Frederick, and then Washington County, Maryland. During the period of the conflicting claims of Pennsylvania and Maryland to the territory where he resided, in 1738, his father, Evan Shelby, was prosecuted on the part of Pennsylvania with reference to his land title.

Possessing an iron constitution, and great endurance, Evan Shelby, the younger, early became a noted woodsman and hunter; so that when the French and Indian war broke out in 1754, he was chosen one of the border leaders of his region. Early in May, 1757, Captain Richard Pearis and Evan Shelby, a Lieutenant under him, headed a party of about sixty friendly Cherokees on a scout from Fort

Frederick; and, after pursuing the trail of the enemy four days, they fell in with another party of fifteen Indians in the Allegheny mountains, at the head of Denning's Creek, near Ray's Town, eating their breakfast, killed four of their number, captured two, and put the others to flight.[13] It was such successful adventures that gave Evan Shelby prominence as an Indian fighter. In the summer and autumn of of this year, Lieut. Shelby was serving in Capt. Alexander Beall's company, and was almost constantly engaged in ranging through the wilderness in quest of the enemy.[14]

In 1758, he raised a company of forty four volunteers, besides officers, to serve on General Forbes' campaign against Fort Duquesne. They were composed of hardy frontier men, inured to backwoods life, equipped with each a blanket, moccasins, a pair of leggin and one half of the number with a tomahawk.[15] Washington mentions Captain Shelby's active and important services on that expedition. Colonel Bouquet had repulsed a large body of French and Indians at Loyal Hanning, on the twelfth of October, after four hours hard fighting; but they still hovered around the army to take any advantage that might present itself. On the twelfth of November, Colonel Washington, while out with a scouting party, fell in with a considerable force of the enemy, about three miles from Loyal Hanning, when a skirmish ensued. The friendly Cherokees wore a white scarf around their foreheads to distinguish them from the enemy, but the latter noticed the mark, and one of their leading chiefs adopted it as a mode of deception. Thus protected, he approached so near without being suspected, that he had already shot one of Washington's men, when Captain Shelby discovered the trick, and instantly rushed up with his tomahawk to attack him, when the Indian fled; but Shelby, as fleet of foot, overtook him, driving the deadly instrument to its very handle under the fellow's shoulder blade, where it became so firmly imbedded, that, holding fast by the handle, they ran several hundred yards between the lines of the opposing forces, until the loss of blood on the part of the chief enabled Shelby to release the tomahawk, when the Indian, exhausted, fell, and a second blow dispatched him. This exciting adventure was witnessed by many of the troops, and elicited general admiration.

During the Pontiac outbreak, Captain Shelby, who, with his associates in mercantile affairs, lost heavily of goods in the Indian trade _ June 3, 1763, goods lost and destroyed by the Indians at Fort Bund, on the Monongahela, as per invoice, # 420, 17, 4; eight horses taken by the Indians, #80, goods taken by the Indians at Fort Augustus, Green Bay, #1440. These heavy losses did not dispirit Captain Shelby and his partners; for besides their large home trade at Fort Frederick, they dispatched eighteen horse-loads of goods, in 1764, under the charge of one of the firm, Edmond Moran, to Fort Pitt, with two of which he followed Colonel Bouquet's troops to the Tuscaroras.[16]

At the beginning of December, 1763, Captain Shelby's residence, near Fort Frederick, was unfortunately burned by accident, by which he lost nearly everything he possessed. In May, 1764, he was usefully employed scouting in the Great

Cove, on the frontiers of Pennsylvania, notifying the people when signs were discovered of approaching parties of the enemy. His services, of which but few details are preserved, were important, and recognized by the people.

When an effort was made, at the November session of Maryland Legislature, for 1765, to liquidate debts incurred during the late war, some of which were for money advanced, by different officers, to fit out or supply their companies, it was particularly designated, that among them was "Captain Evan Shelby, to whose services the House bore ample testimony,"[17] Yet from a difference between the two houses, because some equally deserving were not included, the whole subject was postponed to some future day. The people of the Frederick region, who were principally interested in these claims, were indignant at this treatment, and gathered at Frederick to the number of three or four hundred, armed with rifles, and tomahawks. They chose their officers, and threatened to march to the seat of government, to demand a redress of grievances. These frontier people were patriotic in their impulses, denouncing the Stamp Act and protesting against any future attempt to deprive them of their liberties. Captain Shelby took part in these popular movements; but it had its origin by men in their cups, and, on their cooler moments, more prudent counsels prevailed. The people were quieted, and the matter was finally adjusted the following year.[18]

In 1772, Captain Shelby removed to the then remote frontier, on the border of the Cherokee country, settling in the rich valley of Beaver Creek, an affluent of Holston, just over the present State line, in what is now Sullivan county, Tennessee. The locality was long known as King's Meadows, now Bristol. On the 1st of March, 1774, he was commissioned a Captain in the Fincastle county militia.[19] His company of forty-nine, officers and men, played a conspicuous part in the battle of Point Pleasant; where, after Colonel Fleming was disabled, Shelby, as the oldest Captain, succeeded to the command of the left wing, and rendered good service throughout that eventful day of strife and carnage. Five of his company were killed, and a few wounded.

Upon General Washington's appointment to the command of the army, in June, 1775, such was his appreciation of Captain Shelby's merits, that he would have secured for him the rank of Lieutenant Colonel of the Rifle Battalion, had he not have resided at so great a distance from the scene of action, and so much time would have been consumed before he could have joined the army at Boston.[20]

Early in 1776, he was advanced to the rank of Major of the militia of Fincastle County, Virginia, and, in July of that year, he hastily raised a hundred men, and went to the relief of Watauga Fort, then besieged by the Cherokees, who fled before his approach. He served as a Major on Colonel Christian's expedition against those Indians the ensuing autumn. When Washington County, Virginia was organized, in January, 1777, Colonel Shelby was placed in the commission of Justices, and commissioned Colonel of the militia. He was, early in the year, directed to draw out four hundred men for the protection of the south-western frontiers, and charged with the care of several garrisons; and was subsequently appointed one of the commissioners for holding a treaty with the Cherokees, which was effected at the Long Island of the Holston in July of that year, and served to restrain those barbarians for a while.

The Chickamauga band of Cherokees, under their restless chief, Dragging Canoe, declined all overtures for peace, and sent out their war parties to murder and plunder wherever they could successfully do so. In April, 1779, Colonel Shelby and Lieutenant Colonel John Montgomery led a joint five hundred[21] bordermen from South-West Virginia, and the East Tennessee settlements, against those troublesome neighbors; who fled in all directions, without giving their invaders battle _ a few were overtaken and killed in their flight, eleven of their towns burned, and twenty thousand bushels of corn and other articles of provisions destroyed. A portion of the plunder taken consisted of a store of British merchandise valued at £20,000, one hundred and fifty horses, one hundred cattle, and a large quantity of deer skins. These trophies of war were sold at vendue, and the proceeds divided among the troops.

By the running of the boundary line between Virginia and North Carolina, Colonel Shelby was found to reside in the latter; and, in March, 1780, he was chosen to represent Sullivan county in the Senate of North Carolina. At the close of that year, extending early into 1781, Colonel Arthur Campbell led a force into the Cherokee country; and so effectually chastised them, that they begged for peace; when Shelby was appointed by General Greene, commanding the Southern army, one of the commissioners to hold a treaty with them. In 1786, he was appointed Brigadier General; and, in March, 1787, he was requested by Governor Caswell, of North Carolina, to exert his friendly offices in endeavoring to quiet the prevailing difficulties with reference to the independent State movement then in partial operation under the leadership of Governor Sevier. This he effected by a compromise, which subserved a temporary purpose; and this mission of a peace-maker was his last act of public service. In September following, he requested Governor Caswell to relieve him of the cares of General of the militia, as his advanced years rendered the request proper.[22]

General Shelby continued to live in his rude log dwelling, in the simplicity characteristic of the times, till he closed his long and useful life, December 4th, 1794, at the age of seventy-four years.[23] It has worthily been recorded of him, that he "was high in the confidence of his countrymen, and remarkable for his probity, candor, good sense, and patriotism,"[24]

Chapter Eighteen

Sketch of Cornstalk
1759 —— 1777

    The early history of Cornstalk[1] is involved in obscurity. During those eventful years of Indian attack and massacre between 1754 and 1763, there can be no doubt that he was a prominent leader. His forays were directed against the frontier settlements of Virginia, as most approachable from the Scioto country, where the Shawnees were then mostly concentrated.

    The earliest of these expeditions, of which there is any word, was one he led against several families of the name Gilmore, and others, who resided on Carrs's Creek, in what is now Rockbridge County. Suddenly and unexpectedly Cornstalk and his war-party fell upon these people, October tenth, 1759, and massacred ten persons, men, women and children, with the usual shocking barbarity attendant on Indian warfare; among them, John Gilmore, wife and son, and the wife of William Gilmore. While an Indian was scalping Thomas Gilmore, he was knocked down by Mrs. Gilmore with an iron kettle; when another Indian ran, with uplifted tomahawk, to kill her, and was only prevented from doing so by the Indian who lay bleeding from the blows she had given him, claiming quickly, "don't kill her; she is a good warrior," and this magnanimity in a savage saved her life. A little girl whom they tomahawked and scalped, and left for dead, recovered, and lived thirty or forty years. They burned and laid waste the homes of six of the settlers, killing many cattle, carried off eleven unhappy prisoners, and many horses laden with the spoils they had taken.

    Captain Christian pursued the marauders with a party of militia, who were joined by an equal number of the frontier battalion under Captain Thomas Fleming, stationed at Fort Dunlop; and after following the trail several days, they finally overtook the enemy west of the Alleghanies. It was intended to have attacked them in their night camp, but the accidental discharge of a musket, gave the Indians an opportunity to escape, which they improved in such hot haste, that they abandoned all their prisoners, seventeen horses, and all the stolen goods, save money, beside match-coats,[2] blankets, and many other articles. Six white scalps were recovered. From the prisoners they learned, that there were two

Frenchmen with the Indians; and in the baggage were found the French orders, directing the expedition, dated at Scioto. The loss of the people whose property was devastated, exceeded £2000; but it was no small matter of congratulation; in the midst of their sufferings. That the prisoners were rescued from an unhappy captivity, and that Cornstalk and his warriors were sent home without any trophies; and destitute of many articles of their necessary clothing. The "Carr's creek massacre," with its honors and its acts of heroism, was long kept in remembrance by the people of that region and their descendants.[3]

At length the storm of war ceased, and peace again smiled in the Western valleys. It was only, however, temporary _ more deception than real. Cornstalk evidently dissatisfied, and became a party to the grand Indian combinatimon under Pontiac in 1763. He sallied forth from the Scioto towns, at the head of about sixty warriors, aiming to strike the border settlements of Virginia before the news should reach them of the simultaneous attack on the frontier posts and the capture of many of them. In this he was but too successful. Reaching the nearest Greenbrier settlement in June, which was a German one, on Muddy creek, where the new settlers had raised but two crops, the Shawnee warriors boldly entered the people's houses, under the guise of friendship, and received every civility of personal attention and entertainment; when, on a sudden, they killed the men, captured the women and children, plundered the houses, and reduced them to ashes. Except a few who had charge of the prisoners, Cornstalk's passed over to the Levels of Greenbrier, where some seventy-five people had collected at Archibald Clendenin's, within two miles of the present locality of Lewisburg, and where, Ballard Smith long resided. Here, or at Muddy creek, the Indians were hospitably entertained; for none suspected any hostile intentions, save Clendenin's wife alone, who did not like the manner in which they were painted as it differed from what she had been accustomed to see.

Clendenin had just returned from a hunt, having killed three fat elk; and, as the warriors asked for something to eat, a plentiful feast was promised them. As he had been very successful of late in killing large numbers of buffalo, elk, and deer, he cut off the clear meat and salted it down for future use; while the bones and fragments were boiled up in a large kettle for the present supply. His wife was at that time cooking a kettle full, under a shed near the house. Handing her infant to her husband, she took a large pewter dish and meat-fork in her hand, and went out to bring some of the food to the Indians.

At this juncture, an old woman having a diseased limb, aware of the medicinal virtues of the wilderness supposed to be known to the Indians, explained her distress to one of the warriors, and asked if he could not suggest or administer some relief? He promptly said, that he thought he could; and drawing his tomahawk, he instantly killed the poor woman, which was the signal for them to engage in the bloody work assigned them. Nearly all the men were quickly dispatched. Conrad Yoakum, who was some little distance from the house, being alarmed by the outcries of the women and children, made his escape. A negro woman, who, with her husband, was working in a field near by, started to run away, followed by her crying child; she tarried long enough to kill her little one, to stop its noise and save her own life. With her companion, she made good her escape to Augusta.

Clendenin might have saved his life, had he either surrendered himself, or not been encumbered with the child; for he started to run, and was making an effort to reach the fence, that separated the door-yard from a corn-field. Had he gained the field, he would doubtless, have eluded the pursuit of the Indians, as the corn was high enough to have concealed him; but he was killed in the act of climbing the fence, he falling on one side, and the child the other.

Mrs. Clendenin had scarcely left the house, when she heard Mr. Clendenin exclaim "Lord have mercy on me!" when she dropped her dish and fork; and turning back, saw an Indian with her husband's scalp in his hand, which he held up by the long hair, shaking the blood from it. She rushed upon the murderer, and, in a fit of frenzy, asked him to kill her too, even spitting in his face to provoke him to do so. She did not fail to reproach him and his fellows with baseness by every epithet known to her_ even charging them with being cowards, the worst accusation that could be made against a warrior; and though the tomahawk was brandished over her head, and she threatened with instant death, and her husband's bloody scalp thrown in her face, she nevertheless fearlessly renewed uttering the severest invectives her ready tongue could invent. Her brother, John Ewing, who was spared from the general massacre, said to the Indian, "Oh, never mind her, she is a foolish woman." Following the suggestion, the warrior desisted from making the intended tomahawk stroke.

Yoakum fled to Jackson's River, alarming the people, who were unwilling to believe his terrible report, until the approach of the Indians convinced them of its fearful reality; many saved themselves by flight, while not a few of the aged and helpless fell victims to their fury. The newspaper accounts of the time only refer to the Greenbrier and Jackson's River settlements having been cut off, in June, 1763; but Carr's Creek received another visitation, and there, too, many families were killed and taken.[4]

Near Keeny's Knob, not very far distant from Clendenin's, resided a family of the name of Lee, who shared the fate of the others_ some killed, and others captured. All the prisoners, taken at the several places, were hurried over to the Muddy Creek, where they were detained till the main body of the warriors returned from Jackson's River, and the Carr's creek settlement with their prisoners and booty. An old Indian was left in charge of the captive women and children, Ewing's having been taken with the war party. Mrs. Clendenin made up her mind to kill the old Indian, if the other women would aid her. Her first effort was to ascertain if the old fellow could speak or understand English; but making no reply to her inquiries, she took it for granted that he could not. She consequently made her proposal to her sister prisoners, but they were to timid to consent to any such heroic attempt. During the few days absence of the warriors, Mrs. Clendenin was too narrowly watched by the vigilant old guard to effect anything. He had evidently overheard her proposition, and sufficiently comprehended its import; for when their ears were saluted with the whooping of the returning warriors, with the jingling bells of the horses, the old fellow sprang to his feet, exclaiming in plain English, with an oath, "Yes, good news!" Mrs. Clendenin now expected nothing but death for plotting his destruction, but she heard nothing further of it,

The war party had been successful in their foray, for they returned with many additional captives, and a large number of horses loaded with booty; and every horse had an open bell. Mrs. Clendenin still resolved on effecting her escape, even at the risk of her life. As they started from the foot of Keeney's Knob, the Indians mostly in the front, the prisoners next, and the horses with their tinkling music bringing up the rear, and one Indian behind them all. She managed to hand her infant child to a fellow prisoner to carry; and when they came to a very high precipice on one side of the route, and the Indians carelessly pursuing their way, she watched her opportunity, when unobserved, to jumped down the precipice; and crept under a large rock. She lay still until she head the last bell pass by; and concluding they had not yet missed her, she began to hope that her scheme was successful. After some little time elapsed, she heard footsteps approaching very distinctly and heavily. They drew near the place of her concealment; and in her leaning posture, on her hands and knees, with her head bent forward and to the ground, she awaited the fatal stroke of some unfeeling pursuer. She ventured, however, to raise her eyes, and behold a large bear was standing over her! The animal was as much surprised as she was, for it gave a fierce growl, and ran off at its best speed.

Soon missing her, the Indians took her child, and laid it on the ground, thinking its cries would induce her to return; but she was too far away for this, when the wretches, would torture and beat the little thing, saying "make the calf bawl, and the cow will return." At length they unfeelingly beat out its brains against a tree, and went on without the mother; who remained under the rock till dark, when she sought her way back. Traveling all that night, she concealed herself the next day, and during the second night reached her desolate habitation. As she came in sight of the place, she thought she heard wild beasts howling in every direction; and thought she heard voices if all sorts, and saw images of all shapes, moving through the cornfield _ and, with an almost overpowering sense of mingled fear and desolation, she imagined she saw a man standing within a few steps of her. She withdrew to a spring in the forest, and remained there till morning; when she visited the place, found her husband's body by the fence, with his body shockingly mutilated, and her lifeless child near by, and covered them, as well as she could, with a buffalo hide and some fence rails, finding her strength unequal to the task of covering them with earth.

Resuming her journey, Mrs. Clendenin directed her course for the nearest settlements in Augusta, from which the Greenbrier emigrants had originally set out. At Howard's Creek, some ten miles from the present locality of Lewisburg, she met a party of several white men, who had heard, by the two negro fugitives, that every soul was killed at the Greenbrier settlements, and came to drive away the cattle, and save whatever else was spared by the Indians. Among these men was one who was heir-at-law of the Clendenin family, who was evidently much disconcerted that she had escaped the general massacre. This wretch offered no sort of sympathy, nor any relief whatever. Some of his companions, however, gave her a piece of bread, and a cooked duck; but the half-famished condition of her stomach loathed food, and she wrapped them up in her petticoat, and pursued her journey by herself, expecting she would enjoy them when her appetite should return. Unfortunately she lost them, without ever tasting a single morsel.

While pursuing her lonely journey, she had the good fortune to find an Indian blanket, which proved of great service to her; as, when her clothes became torn, and her limbs lacerated, by briers and brambles, she was enabled to make leggins of it for her protection. After nine nights' painful journeying, secreting herself by day, to avoid the danger of recapture, she at last reached the Dickinsion's, on the Cowpasture River. During all this time, she ate nothing but an onion and a little salt, which she found on a shelf, in a spring-house, at a deserted plantation.

The history of the two children of Mrs. Clendenin who had been captured _ a boy and a girl _ requires a brief mention. Her brother, surrendered probably at Bouquet's treaty the following year, narrated the particulars of the untimely fate of the little boy. He e had been formally adopted by an aged Indian couple, all of whose children were dead, who became very much attached to the lad, and he in return to them. But one day, the old man became displeased with his wife on some account, and told the child, whom she directed to get some water, not to go; for if he did, he would kill him. At length the old Indian went out to the field, and the child, glad of an opportunity to please his mother, picked up the vessel and set off for the spring; but the surly old fellow seeing him from where he was, walked up behind the unsuspecting lad, and gave him a fatal blow with a tomahawk. I was obliged, said the conscience-stricken Indian, "to approach him behind, that I might not see his face; for if I had, I could never have had the courage to kill him."

The little girl was seven years with the Indians, and when brought to her mother, the latter could recognize nothing whatever to indicate her as her child, and she disowned her, saying, "she is not mine." The little waif scampered off among other captive children, who had not yet been reclaimed. Thinking over the matter, the mother called to mind a mark on the body of her daughter, when she ran to her to see if she could find this evidence of identity. Upon examination, she found it. Her long-lost child was indeed restored to her; but with such thorough Indian habits, that it was a long time before the mother felt any particular attachment for her. It need only be added, that Mrs. Clendenin, returning from her captivity to her old neighborhood in Augusta, subsequently married a man named Rogers; and, when peace was restored, she settled on the place where the massacre occurred, and, on looking about the old premises, Mrs. Rogers found the dish and meat-fork where she dropped them on the day of her former husband was killed; and there she resided till 1817, when she died at the age of seventy-nine years. She is represented to have been a woman of strong mind, invincible courage, and of unequalled fortitude. Her daughter, an heiress to a valuable landed estate, had many suitors when she grew to womanhood, and at length gave her hand to a man by the name of Davis. One of her daughters became the wife of Ballard Smith of Greenbrier, one of the first lawyers in the western country, and six years a representative from his district in Congress.[5]

It is related, that when the captive survivors of the Carr's Creek massacre, reached the Shawnee towns, the Indians, in cruel sport, called on them to sing, as they had done at their evening camps while journeying through the wilderness. Unappalled by the bloody scenes they had already witnessed, and the fearful tortures that might yet be in reserve for them, within that dark forest where all hope of rescue seemed forbidden, and undaunted by the fiendish revellings of their savage captors, they sang aloud, with the most pious fervor, from Rouse's version of the one hundred and thirty-seventh psalm, as they had often done, in more hopeful days, within the sacred walls of old "Timber Ridge Church," near which they lived:

"On Babel's streams we sat and wept when Zion we thought on,
In midst thereof we hanged our harps the willow trees among,
For then a song required they who did us captive bring,
Our spoilers called for mirth, and said _ a song of Zion sing."[6]

It were difficult to judge, whether the captive Jews, or the captives of Carr's Creek, felt the most poignantly their desolate condition; but Time, that sweet restorer of hopes and joys, eventually brought them alike out of their unhappy bondage. What particular part Cornstalk enacted in all this, save that he was the leader of the foragers, history is silent.

When Colonel Bouquet, the ensuing year, penetrated the Ohio country, and compelled the Indians to make pace, Cornstalk was one of the designated hostages, on the part of the Shawnees sent to Fort Pitt, in fulfillment of the terms of the treaty, but they soon afterward managed to effect their escape.[7] Nothing further is heard of him, during the long interval of nominal peace which followed, till the war of 1774, already related, and with which his name and fame as so intimately interwoven.

At a critical period of this border outbreak, in the month of May after the alarming affair at Captina and Yellow Creek were well-known in the Indian towns, and while Logan was upon the war path, the head Shawnee chiefs of the Scioto towns shielded Richard Butler and other Pennsylvania traders among them from the fury of the Mingoes; and when the latter, towards the close of that month, were ready to depart with their goods, Cornstalk sent his brother, Silver Heels, to protect them on their homeward journey. On the return of this chief, with two Indian companions, from this friendly mission, they were waylaid and fired on, by a party of frontiersmen under William Lynn, near the mouth of Beaver, and

Silver Heels dangerously wounded. Nor was this all. Cornstalk, at the same time, sent a speech, by the united advice of several of this associate chiefs, addressed to the Governors of Pennsylvania and Virginia, and the commandant at Pittsburgh, entreating to put a stop to any further hostilities, and they would endeavor to do the same.[8]

The invasion of the Ohio country by Bouquet and Bradstreet, in 1764, served to convince this sagacious chieftain, that neither his own nation, nor indeed the confederated tribes of the North West, were able to cope with the strong and growing power of the Colonies; and, hence it was, no doubt, that he so readily yielded himself as one of the hostages on that occasion in order to secure an honorable peace for, his people. In 1774, he had a trying part to perform _ in earnest endeavors to pacify both the frontier settlers and Indians, and restrain if possible, the half-smothered fires, ready to burst along the whole border. His experience and observation taught him, that peace was the true policy of both races. But he soon found that these counsels of the wise and aged were utterly lost on the fiery and turbulent young spirits of his nation. Though he failed in dissuading them from the folly imbruing their hands in the bloody contests, he was too much of a patriot to forsake his people, heady and reckless though they were, and went forth with them to battle. His whole conduct evinces the highest exhibition of tact and wisdom in council, with the loftiest trails of bravery in the field. He fought like a hero; and yielded with becoming and dignity when fighting was no longer of any avail, giving up his own son, the Wolf, at the treaty at Camp Charlotte, as one of the hostages for the faithful fulfillment of its stipulations.

Captain Wm. Russell, who was left in command of Fort Blair _ afterwards called Fort Randolph _ at the mouth of the Great Kanawha, proved himself a wise and discrete officer. Cornstalk frequently resorted to brighten the chain of friendship, and sometime, to deliver up horses in accordance with the stipulation of the treaty of Camp Charlotte. During the winter of 1774-5, he made such a visit. On the fourth of June, 1775, he again arrived at the fort, and spent four days with Captain Russell, reporting that the news of the affairs at Concord and Lexington had been received at the Shawnee towns eight or ten days before his departure. The Mingoes, according to Cornstalk's information, were behaving very indolently, calling the Shawnees the Big Knife people and upbraiding them with having in a cowardly manner, made the treaty with Lord Dunmore. The Picts, or Miamis, were also represented as unfriendly in their feelings towards the Colonies.

Cornstalk had scarcely returned to his people, when he sent a very friendly letter to Captain Russell, written at the chief's dictation, by a trader, in which he assured the Captain that the Shawnees were always willing to comply with any reasonable request that the Big Knife should ask; that a negro woman had been returned as desired, but her two children were retained, as the Indians claimed them as their own "flesh and blood," and could not consent that they should be enslaved, and that they had sent in all the horses they had taken from the white people. He expressed the hope, that the Shawnees would not be charged with having taken all the horses the Virginians may have lost, as several other nations took horses as well as they. He further said, that he, his brother Nimwha, and his son would soon start for Fort Pitt to confirm the treaty made at Camp Charlotte, by which the Shawnees expected to abide.[9]

The contemplated treaty at Pittsburgh, was at first intended to elaborate minor details for which time did not permit at Camp Charlotte, but which, in the changed circumstances of the country was more particularly designed to satisfy the former treaty,[10] and conciliate the Western tribes generally. It was at length held in the autumn of 1775. Cornstalk's participated in it, and, as an assurance of keeping plighted faith with the Colonies, he cited the fact that when some of the Cherokees robbed the new settlers in Kentucky the preceding Spring, he and his people wrested two of the stolen horses from the plunderers, and delivered them at the mouth of the Kenawha, whither they had likewise returned a negro woman; and claimed that they had been all the past winter delivering up horses taken from the white people. Colonel Andrew Lewis, one of the commissioners at the treaty, remarked that Cornstalk was the most dignified Indian chief, particulary in council, he ever knew.[11]

In June, 1776, William Wilson was dispatched by the Indian Agent, Colonel George Morgan, to visit the Western tribes, whom Cornstalk cheerfully aided in every measure calculated to preserve the neutrality of the Indians, accompanying him to the Wyandots, near Detroit, for that purpose. In November of this year, Cornstalk again visited the fort at Point Pleasant, then commanded by Captain Arbuckle. But the storm was fast gathering, which was soon to burst with all its fury, upon the frontier settlements. British presents and British influence were too powerful with the fickle Indian tribes, the younger portions of which were always but too ready to be enticed into war, when the double prospect of glory and plunder was glitteringly held out before them.

Trusty messengers were dispatched to the Indian country, and treaties appointed, with the fond hope of averting the impending storm; but all to no purpose. It was as much as Cornstalk could do, to restrain his own particular tribe of the Shawnees, from engaging in the war; all the others took up the tomahawk; ammunition was forwarded to them, early in 1777, from Detroit, and hostile parties were quickly on the war-path. In his intercourse at the Moravian mission Gnadenhütten, on the Tuscarawas, Cornstalk had formed so great a regard for John Jacob Schmick and wife, that he adopted them both into the Shawnee nation as his brother and sister. But all whose hearts were poisoned with British Lieutenants were proof against the good principles of peace inculcated by the noble and disinterested Cornstalk.

On the nineteenth of September, two prominent Shawnees, Red Hawk's son, and a one-eyed Indian, familiarly called Old Yie, arrived at Point Pleasant with a string of white wampum, which they delivered with a speech replete with strong protestations of friendship. They them submitted a suspicious black string, which they said was sent to the Delawares by George Morgan, the American Indian agent, and forwarded by the Delawares to the Shawnees, the significance of which they professed to be desirous of learning. Their understanding of it, however, they sufficiently explained, when they confessed, that on the receipt of the black string, with information of an army about to invade their country _ referring doubtless to an intended expedition by General Edward Hand, then in command at Pittsburgh, the Indians embodied themselves. They concluded by begging strenuously that Cornstalk and his particular tribe might be exempt from any hostile blow. Under the circumstances, Captain Arbuckle, suspecting them to be spies, felt himself justified in detaining the Indian messengers.[12]

Some eight days after, Cornstalk's son, El-i-nip-si-co, and an Indian youth of some twelve years, made their appearance on horseback, on the northern bank of the Ohio, opposite to Point Pleasant; and hallooing over, the interpreter, Scoppathaw, an old German and his wife, formerly prisoners with the Indians, assured them that they could safely visit the fort and depart unmolested whenever they pleased. El-i-nip-si-co's errand was, to learn why the messengers were detained, giving assurances that his father, as well as the Hardman and other chiefs, would soon pay the garrison a friendly visit.[13] El-i-nip-si-co remained but a brief period.

What message Arbuckle sent to Cornstalk can only be conjectured. Writing to General Hand at this period, he gave the reason for detaining the Indian messengers, adding that he should in custody as many more as should fall into his hand, save those engaged in carrying intelligence, until he should receive further instructions. Duplicity on his part, was, perhaps, being fair in war-time _ the end justifying the means. At all events, Cornstalk, sometime in October, with his heart filled only with good will to his Big Knife friends, came fearlessly to the garrison, to renew pledges of his friendship, and report the movement of the Indians in the British interest. With his open-hearted frankness, he made no effort at concealment of the hostile disposition of the Indians generally; declaring that, for himself, he was opposed to joining the British in the war; but that all his nation save his own tribe, were fully resolved, despite all his efforts to the contrary, to engage in it; and that, of course, he and his clan would have to run with the stream as he expressed it. Cornstalk was now, with the others, detained as a hostage for the neutrality of his people; Capt. Arbuckle assuring them that no other violence should be offered them, provided the treaty of 1774 should still be observed by the nation.[14]

During this visit, Captain William McKee, one of the officers assembled there for Hand's intended campaign, had frequent conversations with Cornstalk with reference to the antiquities of the West, in which the old chief evinced much intelligence and reflection. In reply to an inquiry respecting the mound and fort-builders, he stated that it was the current and assured tradition among his people, that Ohio and Kentucky had once been settled by a white race possessed of art of which the Indians had no knowledge; that, after many sanguinary contests with the natives, these invaders were at length exterminated. McKee inquired why the

Indians had not learned these arts of those ancient white people. Cornstalk replied indefinitely, relating that the Great Spirit had once given the Indians a book which taught them all these arts; but they had lost it, and had never since regained a knowledge of them. What people were they, McKee asked, who made so many graves on the Ohio, and at other places? He declared that he did not know, and remarked that it was not his nation, or any he had been acquainted with. The Captain next practically repeated a former inquiry, by asking Cornstalk if he could tell who made those old forts, which displayed so much skill in fortifying? He answered that he only knew that story had been handed down from <u>a very long ago people</u>, that there had been a white race inhabiting the country who made the graves and fort, and added, that some Indians, who had traveled very far west, or north-west had found a nation or people, who lived as Indians generally do, although of a different complexion.[15]

On the ninth of November El-i-nip-si-co came on the filial errand to learn if his revered father was alive and well. Arriving at the river, opposite the fort he hallooed over, desiring that a canoe might be sent for him. Cornstalk was, at the moment, by request of the officers, in the act of delineating, with chalk upon the floor, a map of the country between the Shawnee towns and the Mississippi. Recognizing the voice of his son, he arose, went out, and answered him. When El-i-nip-si-co landed, the father and son embraced each other in the most tender and affectionate manner.

The next day a council was held, at which Cornstalk was present. His countenance was dejected, as if he had some terrible presentiment of evil. He made a speech which indicated an honest and manly disposition. He frankly acknowledged that he expected that he and his party would have to run with the stream _ an expressive phrase he was want to utter; for, he said, all the Indians on the Lakes and northwardly were taking up the hatchet for the British. He averted to his efforts, in the interests of peace, both before and after the battle of Point Pleasant. At the conclusion of every sentence, he would sadly repeat this expression: "When I was young and went to war, I thought that each expedition might prove the last, and I would return no more. Now I am here amongst you; you may kill me, if you please; I can die but once; and it is all one to me, now or another time." His repeated declaration seemed, in the light of subsequent events, almost a revelation of his impending fate.

Within an hour of the conclusion of the council, Ensign Robert Gilmore of Captain John Hall's company of Rockbridge men designed to take part on Hand's expedition _ one of the Gilmore connection who suffered so severely in the Carr's Creek massacres by Cornstalk's party in 1759 and 1763 _ together with a man named Hamilton, straggled over the Kanawha to hunt. Soon after crossing the river, they separated, and Gilmore was shot and scalped, within a short distance, by some of the enemy concealed in the weeds and willows on the bank of the stream. Hamilton escaped. A party of Hall's men crossed over and soon returned with the bleeding corpse of their late comrade. They had scarcely touched the shore, when they raised the retaliatory shout _ "let us kill the Indians in the fort."

Hearing this ominous out-cry, the wife of Scoppathaw, the interpreter, ran with all haste to the cabin where the hostages were, for whom, having once lived among them, she retained a kind regard, and informed them of Gilmore's death, that the soldiers charged the act upon Indians, who, they averred, must have come with El-i-nip-si-co the previous day, and the maddened white people were now coming to kill them by way of retaliation. El-i-nip-si-co, trembling exceedingly with emotions of fear and terror, utterly denied that any of the enemy accompanied him, and declared that he had nothing whatever of them. Cornstalk calmly encouraged him not to be afraid, for the Great Spirit had sent him there to die with him, and shamed him for showing a disposition to hide in the loft; that he had but once to die, and should die like a warrior. The Great Spirit, he added, knew better than they did when they ought to die; and as they had come there with good intentions, the Great Spirit would do good to them.

Unhappily none of the militia officers who had assembled there for Hand's expedition, save Captain Stuart, were present, at the moment, to aid Arbuckle in restraining the enraged men, and they were powerless for good. Headed by their Captain, the infuriated soldiers rushed, with rifles in hand for their devoted victims _ stopping only a moment, when appealed to by Captain Arbuckle and Stuart, cocking their guns, and threatening them with instant death, if they interposed to save the Indians. As they reached the cabin door, Cornstalk rose up and met them, bearing his breast, and remarking, "if any Big Knife has anything against me, let him now avenge himself," when a volley was fired, seven or eight balls passing through his body. He fell lifeless upon the floor. El-i-nip-si-co was shot dead, as he sat upon a stool, awaiting his inexorable fate. The Red Hawk's son, who attempted to climb up the chimney, was pulled down and shot, while the other Indian _ Old Yie _ was shamefully mangled and was long in the agonies of death.[16]

Thus fell the great and noble Cornstalk _ whose name was bestowed upon him, by the consent of the nation, as their great strength and support.[17] It was a sad and sickening tragedy _ one of those frenzied acts that occasionally grow out of the frequent contact of impulsive men with unnatural scenes of war and its consequent desolations.

Eight days after this tragic event, General Hand arrived at Point Pleasant, and was much concerned to learn of the unhappy occurrence. Though the officers united in expressing the greatest abhorrence of the deed, yet he was convinced from the actions of the soldiers, that it would be in vain for him to try to bring the perpetrators to justice _ so he wrote to Patrick Henry, the Governor of Virginia; but suggested that Colonels Dickinson and Skillern, who were present, knew the most active of the participants. Governor Henry's letters, at that time, evinced the strongest determination that the offenders should be brought before the court, on their return home, and the guilty punished. It was not only a flagrant crime against humanity, but one highly detrimental to public policy. The few troops assembled at Point Pleasant, altogether too inadequate for the contemplated expedition, were discharged; and, arriving at Rockbridge, some of the ring leaders fled the country to avoid prosecution, and none were ever brought to justice.

"From this event," wrote General Hand, "we have little reason to expect a reconciliation with the Shawnees, except fear operates on them; for, if we had any friends among them, those unfortunate wretches were so; Cornstalk particularly appearing to be the most active of the nation in promoting peace."[18] The Indians, in this instance, were at a loss to determine on whom the blame should be laid; whether on the perpetrators of the act, or on their superiors for not using their authority in preventing it; and their accusations against the white people at Point Pleasant were the more severe, since they knew the friendly disposition of their chief towards them, and the important errand on which he was engaged at that time.[19]

In all the long line of Shawnee chiefs, the one in whom was most blended the sterling qualities of bravery, eloquence, wisdom and justice, was unquestionably Keigh-tugh-qua _ the Cornstalk. His noble personal appearance, as well as his many brave and manly acts, combine to constitute him one of the most remarkable men savage life has yet advanced. In 1774, when his nation, rushed headlong into war, in opposition to his vehement protestations, he nevertheless risked his life in leading them into battle, and, by his powerful personal presence, kept them totally engaged the whole day; and, in 1777, when they again resolved on hostilities, against his strong admonitions, he made the mission of peace and good will to Point Pleasant, pleading in their behalf, and sealing his devotion to his people by the sacrifice of life itself. Such a man was truly a hero and a patriot, though not educated in the schools, nor trained in military academies. Whoever visits his grave, yet pointed out at Point Pleasant, may worthily drop a tear to his person.

Chapter Nineteen

Tragical Death of Jane McRae
26 July, 1777

The next year after the declaration of American independence, the British ministry tried to separate New England from the rest of the Colonies, by taking military possession from Canada of the valleys of Lake Champlain and the Hudson, and thus open the way to New York.

In pursuance of the scheme which was to dismember the Colonies and thereby suppress the rebellion, a large force under Lieutenant General John Burgoyne assembled at St. Johns, preparatory to a movement southward. Near the river Bouquet, on the west side of Lake Champlain, in what is now Essex county, New York, the British army was joined by a considerable number of Indians. Early in July, 1777, Burgoyne took possession of Ticonderoga, a post situated near the foot of Lake George,--it having previously been abandoned by the Colonial troops and militia under General Arthur St. Clair.

About the middle of July, the American troops reached Fort Edward, situated on the east bank of the Hudson, the site of the present village of that name, in Washington county, New York. On their retreat from Ticonderoga, portions of them were engaged with the enemy in two separate battles, the British being victorious. At this time General Phillip Schuyler was in command of the Northern Department. At and around what is now Whitehall lay the army of Burgoyne for some days before advancing against the Arebels. Meanwhile every exertion was put forth by Schuyler to impede his march to the Hudson. As a consequence he did not reach the banks of that river near Fort Edward until the twenty-eighth of July; the American general, deeming his own forces insufficient to oppose so powerful an army, had abandoned his position and retreated down the river.

Editor's note:
There is a short note in the August 22, 1777 edition of the *Virginia Gazette* which cited two previous articles, one a letter from Moses's creek, dated July 26 and the other from Fish-Kill dated July 31, stating:
"We have just had a brush with the enemy at Fort Edward, in which Lieutenant

Van Veighten was most inhumanely butchered and scalped. Two sergeants and two privates were likewise killed and scalped, one of the latter had both his hands cut off. They took a young woman, Janey McCrea by name, out of a house at Fort Edward, carried her about half a mile into the bushes, and there killed and scalped her in cold blood. They have killed and scalped another woman near the same place."

In the service of Burgoyne was a young royalist, David Jones, a Lieutenant in Peters' corps, in the division of Brigadier-General Simon Fraser, commander of the grenadiers and light infantry. His home was in the vicinity of Fort Edward on the west side of the Hudson and half a mile below that post. He was a young man of handsome features and graceful form, possessing an easy and affable manner; and a generous disposition. For more than year after the commencement of hostilities, Jones maintained a neutral position. To outward appearances, taking part on neither side in the great questions then agitating the public mind. In the Autumn of 1776, he resolved to remain no longer an inactive spectator of the stirring scenes around him. He proffered his services to the mother country, reaching St. Johns in the Spring of 1777; was made a Lieutenant; and, as pilot, approached the vicinity of his home, in July, with the British army, in its march to the Hudson river from Canada.

The van of Burgoyne's forces, having reached a point then called Pine Plains, now Moss street, about four miles north of Fort Edward, had there encamped. With these troops was Lieutenant Jones. From the British camp to the American post, stretched an old military road. It was a broad well-beaten path, crossing a level and sandy table-land, until it reached the brow of a hill whose side drops abruptly to the bank of the Hudson. About half-way down grew a large pine tree which was on account of its height, a conspicuous object. Directly at its foot, gurgled a never failing spring. While the British van in encampment was awaiting the approach of Burgoyne, the main body of the Americans had abandoned the fort, moving about five miles down the river, halting at Moses' creek, on the east side of the Hudson; _ a rear guard of one hundred men having been left in the fortress.

At dawn on the twenty-sixth of July, a picket of the Americans, under the command of Lieutenant Van Vichten, upon the brow of the hill, was on the lookout for the advance guard of the British, now constantly expected, and prepared on its first approach, to convey the intelligence to the patriots in the fort. A few hours brought the enemy _ not a civilized foe, however, but a bunch of savages under command of The Wolf, followed by a discharge of musketry and the terrible war whoop. --

"A wild and fearful yell !
Rushed the Indians from the brake !
Fled the guard, in fright or fell !"

Not far from the scene on the hill-side where the Americans were being pursued toward the fort by the savages, and directly in their path, a young lady was seen flying for her life to a house nearby. It was Jane McCrea.

At Lamington, New Jersey, in 1757, lived James McCrea, a Presbyterian clergyman, _ a native of Scotland. About this date, his daughter Jane was born. The latter, at an early age, met with an irreparable loss in the death of her mother. When she had reached the age of sixteen, her father also died. Jane, soon after, went to reside with a brother, John, who had settled upon waters of the Hudson some six or seven miles below Fort Edward on the west side of the river. Among the father's neighbors in New Jersey, was a family _ a widow Jones and her six sons, one of whom, David, who was the young man who has been previously mentioned, as a Lieutenant in Burgoyne's army of invasion. This family also ascended the Hudson, and located a few miles north of John McCrea, on the same side of the river, at a point just below Fort Edward, where they established a ferry.

Having been children together in New Jersey, a mutual affection had grow up between David Jones and Jane McCrea. When the latter came to reside with her brother, their attachment was strengthened _ much of their time being passed in each other's society. It was soon well understood among the scattered inhabitants for miles around that "David" and "Jenny" were betrothed. She who was so dear to the heart of young Jones, was of middlng statue, finely formed, _ had very dark and long hair, and beautiful features. "As the day approached which was to witness the consummation of their hopes by the ceremonial of marriage, they gave themselves up to delightful anticipations. In the morning of life, full of health and vigor, confident in the knowledge of reciprocated affection, and unconscious of impending danger, there was indeed no apparent reason why they should not indulge the most sanguine dreams."

But the troublous times of the Revolution were at hand. From the first, John McCrea favored the patriots. Not so David Jones; he leaned to the Tory side. The one joined the army under Montgomery in its invasion of Canada, only to return, and meet the scoff and scorn of his Royalist neighbors; the other, finally, as already mentioned, allied himself with the British under Burgoyne. The sisterly attachment of Jane McCrea to her brother and her affection for her affianced, were not shaken by the estrangement which had gradually separated the two, who of all the world, were the nearest and dearest to her. So she continued faithful to David Jones though he left his home to aid in "crushing the rebellion" and afterward joined the army which invaded their country; and she continued to reside with John McCrea, who nobly took up arms against the invaders.

The lovers met to take leave of each other at the house of a mutual friend, close to Fort Edward; where it was arranged that they should communicate as frequently as opportunity afforded by letter, through the agency of a man in whom they reposed implicit confidence; _ and having renewed their vows of perpetual constancy, they separated; Jane to return to her brother's family, on the west side of the river, young Jones to start for the north to ally his fortunes with the cause of the King against the Colonies.

Occasional messages were received by Jane from young Jones down to the time of his arrival with the British army at what is now Whitehall. A letter of the eleventh of July, 1777, from that point, which was safely delivered to her, expressed the opinion of her lover, that the army would, in a few days, reach Fort Edward, when he would have the happiness of seeing her, if she did not remove south with her brother to avoid danger, which he hoped she would not do, but would remain at the house of her friend where they had separated, where he would soon meet her.

John McCrea apprehensive for the welfare of his family, had already made preparations to remove to Albany. Various causes contributed to prevent his carrying his design into execution as soon as he desired, _ the principal one being the reluctance which Jane exhibited to leaving their home. He was unconscious of the secret information she had obtained from Lieutenant Jones. He knew nothing of the importunities she had received from him to remain at Fort Edward. When, therefore, the van of the British army made their encampment within four miles of that post, John McCrea was still at his home, and with him was his sister.

Another missive from young Jones now reached the agitated girl. It was an "affectionate an glowing epistle," "suggesting a scheme that would relieve them from the unhappiness of longer separation, and appealing to her to unite in it. It contained such an alluring and romantic proposition, and abounded with so many warm and endearing terms, that the confiding, but distracted girl finally resolved to accede to it." It was no less a proposition than that she should meet him within the British lines and at once be united with him in marriage. At least, such was the plan in its full development. After the ceremony, she could remain temporarily at her friend's house where at last the two had seen each other, or join the officers' ladies who accompanied the army.

The details of the arrangement which were to result in conducting the confiding girl to the British camp where the marriage ceremony was to be performed by the chaplain of the regiment to which Lieutenant Jones belonged, were these: Jane was to go to Fort Edward, thence to the house of a widow McNiel, a staunch Loyalist in sentiment, a cousin of General Fraser. Her house stood about sixty rods north of the fort. She was the person who has previously been spoken of as a friend of the lovers; she was an old acquaintance; and it was at her residence they parted. Thence the girl was to make her way toward the British lines unattended. Two miles from Fort Edward, on the road to the British camp lived William Griffin, a royalist who had a protection from Burgoyne. Once at his house, and the remainder of the distance would be comparatively free from danger. That every emergency might be prepared for, a small party of Indians, under Duluth, a trusted warrior, was to steal cautiously through the forest, from the British camp at Pine Plains avoiding all encounters however tempting, with the Americans, to a point within sight of the house of widow McNeill. On displaying a certain signal, Jane would walk forth alone along the road toward Griffin's, _ the Indians keeping pace with her as they returned; so near as not to lose sight of her, and so distant as to avoid observation.

Jane left the home of her brother, without any suspicion on his part of her determination. She gave out that the object of her visit was, to bid farewell to the widow McNiel and another friend. She stopped on the road at the widow Jones, the home of her lover. She was accompanied by a lady as far as Fort Edward. On the way, she confided her secret to her companion. John McCrea expected the return of his sister the next day, but she came not. Early on the morning of the second day after her departure, he sent a messenger to conduct her immediately home. She framed excuses and the man returned without her. So great was the alarm, however, on account of the proximity of the British, and so certain was her brother of danger, that the messenger was again dispatched for her, but the second time returned unaccompanied by the determined girl.

The Indian_ Duluth_ who was employed by Lieutenant Jones to take charge of the savages going out as Jane McCrea's invisible guides and protectors, was, as first intimated, a warrior in whom he reposed the utmost confidence. All were promised a suitable reward if his soon-to-be bride was brought unharmed to his keeping. On the morning of the twenty-sixth of July, they departed upon their romantic expedition; such an one, indeed, as, it is believed, no other savages, before or since, have undertaken. They reached the point unobserved where they had been directed to secrete themselves; _ it was between the tall pine tree and the river, at a spot where a signal could be seen from the residence of widow McNiel. Soon came forth, at the sign agreed upon, the dauntless girl arrayed in wedding attire. Her long glossy tresses were arranged in a graceful and becoming manner. She moved forward "quietly and undisturbed, and had partly ascended the first rise of ground, when to her utter astonishment, and to the astonishment of Duluth and his party, who were watching her from their place of concealment," down the hill-side came that rushing tide of destruction _ the savages, under The Wolf, chasing the picket-guard of Lieutenant Van Vichten. The affrighted girl instantly turned and ran as fast as she could, back to the house of her friend.[2]

The savages under the lead of The Wolf were a band that had left the British camp sometime before on a marauding excursion into the settlements to the south eastward of Fort Edward. In the course of their wandering they came to the home of John Allen, a royalist, in what is now Argyle, in Washington county. Soon nine ghastly and bloody corpses lay stretched upon the floor _ the inanimate bodies of Allen, his wife, sister-in-law, three children, and three slaves; all were scalped. Directly from this scene of carnage, came The Wolf and his followers, on their way to the British camp. They had stolen a number of horses which were loaded with the spoils of war. The scalps of the murdered Royalist and his family dangled conspicuously from their war-belts. On their way back they had approached so near Fort Edward as to discover Van Vichten and his party upon the hill which as has been before stated they proceeded to attack. The Lieutenant, two sergeants and as many privates were killed and scalped.

Such of the picket as had not fallen under the well-directed aim of the Indian's rifle or had been cut down by the keen-edged tomahawk escaped to Fort Edward, followed close to the ramparts by the savages. One of the guard, however, Samuel Standish, was wounded in the fort and made a prisoner. Meanwhile Jane had been perceived by a number of them as she ran for life to the house of her friend, and they pursued her, reaching the dwelling but a few moments after she had entered it. The inmates consisting of the widow McNeil, Jane, two small children, and a black servant girl, had secreted themselves in the cellar; but the first two were quickly dragged forth; while the others remained unobserved. Jane McCrea was now a captive in the hands of The Wolf.

The savages had no sooner secured their prisoners and such plunder as could be quickly collected, than they hurried away, clearly appreciating that, in consequence of their proximity to the fort, their own safety, demanded the utmost expedition. Before the soldiers behind the ramparts could fairly comprehend what was transpiring before their eyes, the Indians were beyond the reach of their fire. They soon came to the spring under the tall pine; here the path divided. At this point, they halted; when the widow McNeil was seized by two Indians, and hurried up the right-hand path which led toward the house of the royalist Griffin. Jane was placed upon one of the stolen horses; when Duluth and his braves made their appearance, demanding the privilege of escorting her to the British camp. At once an angry contest ensued. The Wolf, anxious for the reward which Burgoyne had offered for prisoners, denied the right of Duluth to the possession of the unfortunate girl. While thus contending, it became manifest to both, that a detachment from the fort was in pursuit. Soon was heard the report of firearms, succeeded by the whistling of bullets and the shouts of the advancing Americans. There was no time for words now. The horse upon which Jane sat was urged forward by The Wolf, but Duluth, notwithstanding the approaching danger, clutched the bridle-rein, determined to escort her himself to camp. Maddened with this pertinacity, The Wolf shot the poor girl in the breast. Falling to the ground, she was at once scalped by the infuriated savage who uttered a yell of exultation at the deed.[3] His warriors tore the dress from her lifeless body, leaving the latter shockingly mangled with their tomahawks. Duluth, more compassionate, bore her remains a short distance away, and covered them with brush; _ then the whole party hurried quickly forward.[4]

The mangled corpse of Jane, wept over by her sorrowing brother, was, together with the body of Lieutenant Van Vichten, borne, by a small detachment, on the evening of the same day she met her untimely death, to Snook Hill, three miles south of Fort Edward, where, the next day, it was buried.[5] Here it rested for fifty years when it was disinterred and again buried; _ this time in the burial ground of the village of Fort Edward, "near the ruins of the old fortress, in the presence of young men and maidens, and a vast multitude of people that the unusual ceremony had attracted thither." In 1852, they were a second time exhumed and tenderly laid in "the beautiful cemetery just over the brow of the hill at whose base the clear water of the spring still gurgles up;" and there a tasteful monument is seen which sufficiently explains that lying beneath, is all that remains of one whose untimely death was indeed a fearful tragedy of the times that tried the souls of men.

Duluth, upon his arrival in the British camp, recounted to Lieutenant Jones, the particulars of the tragedy. The story well-nigh dethroned him of his reason. From a laughter-loving young man, he at once began to tread the path of gloom and despair, which, so long as he lived, he never forsook. He remained with the army until its surrender, when bidding adieu to the valley of the Hudson where he had suffered more than death itself, he retired into Canada. "There he selected a secluded residence, and passed, unmarried, the remainder of his life in solitude." He ended his existence in sorrow and misery. To the day of his death, he never once rallied from the awful shock which he received when Duluth narrated to him how, by the savage blows of The Wolf, miserably perished, beneath the tall pine tree where the pure waters still flow from the spring on the hill-side C the unfortunate Jane McCrea.

The event produced so much commotion in the British army, that Burgoyne instituted an inquiry into the matter. He summoned his Indians to council and demanded the surrender of The Wolf to be punished as a murderer. The savage was sentenced, but afterward pardoned. "He certainly should have suffered an ignominious death," wrote Burgoyne, "had I not been convinced, from my circumstances and observation, beyond the possibility of a doubt, that a pardon under the terms which I presented and the Indians accepted, would be more efficacious than an execution to prevent similar mischiefs."[6]

In the patriot army upon the Hudson, and throughout the Northern settlements, details of the sad affair spread quickly, and was everywhere related with horror. It was soon known all over the land. It aroused a more determined opposition to the invaders, and alienated the feeling of many royalists from the British. General Horatio Gates, who superceded Schuyler in command of the Northern Department, took advantage of the tragedy, in arousing the patriots of the North to a more effectual resistance. In a letter to Burgoyne, he recited the particulars in language, well suited to the times: "Miss McCrea, a young lady, lovely to the sight, of virtuous character, and amiable disposition, engaged to an officer of your army, was taken out of a house near Fort Edward, carried into the woods, and there scalped and mangled in a most shocking manner." "The miserable fate of Miss McCrea," continued the writer, "was particularly aggravated, by her being dressed to receive her promised husband, but met her murderer employed by you."[7]

"In regard to Miss McCrea, her fall wanted not the tragic display," was the response of the British General, "you have labored to give it, to make it as sincerely abhorred and lamented by me, as it can be by the interest of her friends." "The fact was no premeditated barbarity. On the contrary, two chiefs who had brought her off for the purpose of security, not of violence to her person, disputed which should be her guard; and in a fit of savage passion in one, from whose hands she was snatched, the unhappy became the victim."[8]

In Europe, the story awakened deep indignation against the employment of savages in civilized warfare; in America, it revived the drooping spirit of Liberty. It will continue to be a theme which eloquence and sensibility will alike dignify; _ one, which "has kindled in many a breast the emotions of a responsive sympathy."

Chapter Twenty

Battle of Oriskany
6 August, 1777.

Simultaneously with the invasion, by Lieutenant-General Burgoyne, of the valley of the Hudson, Lieutenant-Colonel Barry St. Leger, an officer of the regular army of Great Britain, holding the local rank of Brigadier-General, entered the borders of New York from Canada, by way of Lake Ontario, "to make a diversion on the Mohawk;" enjoined "to proceed forthwith to, and down that river, "to Albany, and put himself under the command of Sir William Howe."[1]

St. Leger's white men numbered over seven hundred and fifty; his Indian warriors more than eight hundred; and, having collected his army from Montreal to Three River Point, at the junction of the Oneida and Seneca rivers in New York, he marched with his motley force, early in August, 1777, to penetrate the country, by way of Oneida Lake and Wood creek, to the Mohawk river.[2]

In the year 1772, all that part of New York lying west of a line running north and south through the center of the present county of Schoharie, was included in Tryon county, so called in honor of William Tryon, then governor of the province. It was at this county, numbering in 1777, not far, it is presumed, from ten thousand inhabitants, that was invaded by the army of St. Leger. At the commencement of the Revolutionary struggle, the extreme western outposts of this county were Oswego and Niagara. The most westerly settlement, however, was at the head of navigation on the Mohawk river, at the site of the present village of Rome, Oneida county. Here, during the year 1776, a fortification was commanded by continental soldiers and militia of Tryon county, to which was given the name of Fort Schuyler.[3] From this post, extending across to Wood creek, was the ancient carrying-place, or portage, between the waters of the Hudson and those of the Great Lakes and the St. Lawrence. Fort Schuyler lying directly in the path of St. Leger must of course have early engaged the attention of that officer. He was, indeed fully apprised of its condition before leaving Canada.[4]

As early as April, 1777, Colonel Peter Gansevourt succeeded to the command of Fort Schuyler. He was reinforced, by the arrival on the twenty-ninth of May, of Lieutenant-Colonel Marinus Willet with the third New York regiment. His garrison was augmented on the second of August, by the arrival of two hundred state troops, so that the next day when the post was fully invested by the British army, he had under his command, seven hundred and fifty men. Upon and examination, it was found that there was provisions enough to sustain this force for six weeks. The fortification was, however, not completed. There was fixed ammunition enough for the small arms of the garrison; but for the cannon, it was lamentably deficient.

    The army of St. Leger, composed of detachments of the eighth and thirty-fourth regiment of regulars; of Sir John Johnson's regiment of New York _ the Royal Greens; of Hessian riflemen; of rangers, royalist, and Canadians; and, last, but not least, of Iroquois and Canada Indians managed by Colonel David Claus,[5] son-in-law of Sir William Johnson, and by Major John Butler;[6] this army, passing through Oneida lake along Wood creek, and across the carrying-place to the Mohawk, completely invested Fort Schuyler, on the third of August, 1777[7] _ the commencement of a memorable siege, which, with its attending circumstances, forms an important feature in the Northern border warfare of the Revolution.

    It was in June of that year _ 1777 _ that the patriot citizens of Tryon county, heard with alarm of the intended invasion of their homes by the enemy. It was pleasant for Lord George Germain to authorize St. Leger to "act as exigencies might require, and in such manner as he should judge most proper, for making an impression on the rebels, and bring them to obedience;"[8] quiet otherwise, for the freemen of the Mohawk valley to know their country was about to be overrun by a brutal soldiery and blood-thirsty savages. At a late hour, the militia arose in their might, determined to succor the garrison of Fort Schuyler.

    Nicholas Herkimer, Brigadier General of Tryon county, issued a proclamation on the seventeenth of July, announcing his determination to call out the militia, as soon as the enemy should approach from Oswego. While St. Leger, therefore, was marching from that point on his "diversion," over eight hundred patriots were assembling at Fort Dayton, now Herkimer, in Herkimer county, to march to the relief of Gansevourt, whose post, it was now certain, would be immediately invested.

    St. Leger employed his time until the afternoon of the fifth of August, so far as the siege was concerned, first in the summoning the post to surrender, which was declined; then, in ordering his Indians who had surrounded the fort, to keep up a constant fire from behind logs and hillocks, at the garrison, so as to prevent them from working at the fortifications. His cannon were not yet in position. At the expiration of that time word was brought by savages sent by a sister of Thayendanegea,[9] that a body of "rebels" _ Herkimer and his force _ were on their march to relieve Fort Schuyler and would be within ten or twelve miles of the British and Indian encampments that night. Immediately, St. Leger determined to attack them either openly or covertly, as circumstances should offer. The Indians were, at once, ordered out.[10] Sir John Johnson asked leave to join his company of "Light" Infantry and head the whole, which was granted.[11] Butler and other white officers were sent with the savages. Not above eighty white men, rangers and troops included, marched upon the expedition. Johnson in command of the whole, moved from the vicinity of the fort that afternoon at five o'clock. "This evening," afterward wrote Willett, "indicated something in contemplation by the enemy. The Indians were uncommonly noisy."[12]

General Herkimer, on the fourth day of August, with his men of Tryon county, took up his line of march from Fort Schuyler. All were eager to meet the enemy. Crossing the Mohawk at or near where the city of Utica now stands, the army encamped on the fifth in the neighborhood of Oriskany, in what is now Oneida county, whence three messengers were dispatched to Gansevourt to apprise him of the approach of the militia and that Herkimer proposed to force his way to the post; also requesting him to announce the arrival of the express by three successive discharges of cannon, which it was presumed, could be heard at the encampment, distant about eight miles. As will readily be imagined, the messengers met with much difficulty in approaching Fort Schuyler; so much, indeed, that they did not place Herkimer's letter in the hands of its commander until eleven o'clock in the forenoon of the next day.

The Indians ordered out to oppose Herkimer made the welkin ring with their horrid yelling the greater part of the evening of the fifth. The woods resounded with their war-cries. They were lashing themselves into a wild state of excitement, preparing for the expected contest. Stripping themselves of their blankets and robes, they became impatient for the fray. Armed with spear, tomahawk, and musket they at length moved cautiously toward Oriskany; going "in their shirts or naked" to the field of strife. Johnson, when within two miles of Herkimer's encampment, called a halt. At ten o'clock, the Americans being discovered on the advance, the Seneca chiefs formed an ambush. Across the path which all knew the "rebels" would take, were stationed the men under Johnson's immediate command. The Indians with twenty rangers were moved some distance eastward, flanking to the right and left, and then concealed behind trees and logs, leaving an open space towards Oriskany.[13] Thus was completed almost a circle _ a well-planned ambuscade. Silently and eagerly they awaited the coming of the "Mohawk-river militia" with a convoy of fifteen wagons of provisions and stores.

It was not until the forenoon of August sixth was somewhat advanced that Herkimer from his encampment gave the word to march.[14] Misinformed as to St. Leger's strength, the Americans moved forward with a feeling of security. About two miles brought them to a deep ravine which crossed their path, _ "sweeping toward the east in a semicircular from, and bearing a northern and southern direction." Beyond this the ground was elevated and level. It was here the ambuscade of the enemy was laid _ into which, the ill-starred forces of Tryon county were unsuspectingly rushing. The whole number marched through the narrow opening purposely left by the savages, except the rear-guard, before they became aware of any danger but for the uncontrollable impetuosity of the Indians, all would have been in a few moments surrounded; as it was, one regiment with the baggage and ammunition wagons was left outside the fiery circle. Then the contest began.

It was not a long while after Herkimer found himself beset on every side by the foe, that his three messengers succeeded in getting inside of Fort Schuyler with the news of his movement for the relief its garrison. During the afternoon, by Gansevourt's order, two hundred and fifty men, half of New York, half of Massachusetts, under Lieutenant Colonel Willett, made a sally in the direction of Oriskany. They passed through the quarters of the Royal Greens, as well through those of the rangers and savages. They drove before them a few white men and red men; also some squaws and their children. They captured Johnson's papers, five British flags, the gala-robes, the blankets, the kettles and trinkets of the Indians, and four prisoners. Then they returned pursued by St. Leger with some regulars, to the fort with their spoils, without the loss of a man. The British colors were displayed under the continental flag, _ "the first time a captured banner had floated under the stars and stripes of the republic."[15]

The force led by Herkimer across the ravine into the jaws of death belong to several regiments of militia. There were also a few volunteers. The rear-guard, composed of men of a single regiment, cut off from the rest of the army by the premature movement of the savages enclosing up the circle, immediately retreated,[16] perused however by a portion of the Indians who inflicted a considerable punishment upon the flying party. The fire upon the flanks, upon the advance, and upon the rear, was opened almost at the same instant. Its suddenness and destructiveness threw the Americans at once into disorder. It was close and brisk from every side. For a while the whole body seemed destined to be utterly destroyed. But the bloodthirstiness of the savages, impelling them to rush forward to tomahawk and scalp those who fell although causing the death of many who were not fatally wounded, yet, in the end, brought the militia to a realizing sense of their danger and aroused them to heroic deeds of valor. It soon, therefore, became largely a hand-to-hand conflict. Gradually the enemy closed in upon the patriots. But the work of death soon began to recoil effectively, upon the advancing host. Under the direction of their General, the Americans now took possession of an advantageous piece of ground and formed themselves into a circle. There stood the desperate men, determined to sell their lives as dearly as possible. In the early part of the battle, it had been observed by Herkimer that frequently when one of his men standing behind a tree, discharged his gun, an Indian would rush up and tomahawk him before he could re-load. He ordered, therefore, for the future two men to a tree, one only to fire at a time, _ the other reserving his shot until the savage made his appearance.

With wild fury the conflict continued. The death-dealing rifle flashed from behind trees and fallen logs. Single-handed a militia-man fought with a ferocious savage or with a hated Tory. Mortal wounds were made with bullet, with spear, with bayonet, and with the blood-dripping tomahawk. So raged the strife; _ but so deadly a contest must of necessity be of short duration.[17] The enemy, finding their ranks diminishing, lost heart. Finally, the savages raised the retreating cry of

Oonah! and fled, leaving the men of Tryon county in possession of the field. _ The bloodiest battle of the Revolution _ considering the numbers engaged _ was ended.

No sooner had the enemy disappeared than the Americans set themselves at work to construct rude litters upon which to bear off the wounded. Between forty and fifty were removed in that manner. The entire loss of the militia and volunteers was not far from one hundred and sixty killed, wounded and taken prisoners.[18] Most of the latter were inhumanly killed by their savage captors. Just after sunrise the following morning, several were made to run the gauntlet, near Fort Schuyler. Those who were forced to this ordeal were clubbed to death.[19] It is probable that others were subsequently tortured at the stake.[20] _ All thoughts of continuing the march to the relief of Gansevoort, had now, of course, to be abandoned; the army, therefore, returning upon their trail, soon re-crossed the Oriskany. Numbered among the slain of all of the regiments were one Colonel, one Lieutenant-Colonel, three Majors, and eight Captains.

The British loss including white men and Indians was, in killed and wounded not much less than one hundred. Over thirty of the Senecas, among them some of their chief warriors, lay dead upon the battle-field. Two Captains _ Indians officers _ were killed, also a Captain-Lieutenant of Johnson's regiment. The number of privates, together with the specific number of Indians of other nations, that fell, is not told.[21] "I should not do justice to the Indians in general," afterward wrote one of their officers, "and to the Senecas in particular, was I not to acquaint you, that their behavior in the action exceeded anything I could have expected from them."[22]

The return of Johnson from the battlefield was in time to see his camp sacked by the irresistible Willett. That he ingloriously fled when that officer sallied forth from Fort Schuyler is established beyond a reasonable doubt.[23] But St. Leger, as has been shown, came with his regulars to the rescue of the fugitives. The Indians upon their return from the red field of Oriskany were astonished to find their quarters had been despoiled. Gone were their "packs, with their clothes, wampum, and silver work," to gladden the hearts of the "rebels." Their resentment was soon visited upon their unhappy prisoners. "The disappointment was rather greater to the Indians," wrote Claus, "than their loss; for they had nothing to cover themselves at night or against the weather, and there was nothing in our camp to supply them."[24] Afterward, upon the arrival of the Senecas at their villages, loud was the howling by the relatives of the fallen braves, for their irreparable losses. The hatchet that had been accepted from the British was red with the blood of slaughtered chiefs of their own nation.

General Herkimer was badly wounded in the early part of the action by a musket ball which shattered his leg just below the knee. His horse fell dead under him, killed by the same shot. The General was afterward bolstered up, as comfortably as possible, in which position, he continued, with great coolness to give orders to the end of the conflict, notwithstanding his suffering the most excruciating pain. He was conveyed to his own house near the Mohawk river, a few miles below the Little Falls where his limb was unskillfully amputated. It was found impossible to staunch the blood. He soon after died greatly lamented by his country.[25]

While the battle raged, Major Butler attempted a stratagem against the Americans which well-nigh succeeded. He sent, suddenly, from the direction of Fort Schuyler, a detachment of the Royal Greens disguised as American troops, in hopes they might be mistook as a timely reinforcement from the garrison of that post. Lieutenant Jacob Summers was the first to descry their approach, in the direction of a body of men commanded by Captain Jacob Gardenier _ an officer who during that memorable contest performed many acts of valor. Perceiving that their hats were American, Summers informed Gardenier that succors from the fort were coming up. The quick eye of the Captain detected the deception, and he replied _ "Not so: they are enemies; don't you see their green coats?"

The detachment continued to advance until hailed by Gardenier at which moment one of his own soldiers, observing an acquaintance, and supposing him a friend, ran to meet him, and presented his hand. It was grasped but with no friendly grip; and the credulous fellow was dragged into the opposing line, and informed that he was a prisoner. He did not yield without a struggle; during which Gardenier, watching the action and the result, sprang forward and with a blow from his spear, leveled the captor to the dust; and liberated his man.

Others of the foe instantly sprang upon Gardenier, of whom he slew one and wounded another. Three of the disguised Tories now rushed forward to seize or kill him. His spurs became entangled in their clothes and he was thrown to the ground. Still contending, however, with almost super-human strength, both of his thighs were pinned to the earth by the bayonets of two of his assailants while a third one presented his weapon at his breast as if to thrust him through. Seizing this bayonet with his left hand; by a sudden wrench he brought its possessor down upon himself, where he held him as a shield against the arms of the others, until one of his own men, Adam Miller, observing the struggle ran to the rescue.

As the assailants turned upon their new adversary, Gardenier arose, and although his hand was severely lacerated by grasping the bayonet which had been drawn through it, he seized his spear lying upon the ground, and quickly planted it to the barb in the side of the Tory with whom he had been clinched. The man fell and expired. He proved to be Lieutenant McDonald, one of the loyalist officers from Tryon county. While engaged in this struggle, some one of his own men called out to Gardenier _ "Captain, you are killing your own men!" "They are not our men," he replied, "they are the enemy _ fire away!" The undaunted courage of the Captain infused fresh spirits into his men. Several of the disguised loyalists paid the penalty of their rashness with their lives.

It happened during this hand-to-hand contest _ that three of the royalists rushed within the circle of the militia and attempted to make a prisoner of Captain Andrew Dillenback. One of his assailants seized his gun, but he suddenly wrenched it from him, and felled him with the butt. Another he shot dead, and then thrust the third through with his bayonet; but a ball soon laid this brave man low in the dust. _ Many are the heroic deeds handed down to future generations _ by the industry of historians _ of the brave Tryon county militia on the red field of Oriskany.

A few days after the contest, an American was crossing the battle-field. "I beheld," says he, "the most shocking site, I had ever witnessed. The Indians, and white men were mingled with one another, just as they had been left when death had first completed its work." There they lay, "their left hands clinched in each others hair; their right grasping in a grip of death, the knife plunged in each others bosom!"

Chapter Twenty One

Ambuscade at Fort Henry - Wheeling
1 Sept., 1777

Fort Henry _ Wheeling _ was built in the Summer of 1774, under the immediate direction of Major William Crawford and Angus McDonald, the latter having been sent over the mountains by Dunmore for that and other purposes. It received at that time the name of Fort Fincastle, being situated in what was then the county of Fincastle, Virginia _ the most westerly one in the colony; which name was changed to Fort Henry, in honor of Patrick Henry, first Governor of Virginia, after the flight of Dunmore.

The fort stood upon the bank of the Ohio river, about one fourth of a mile above the mouth of Wheeling Creek, in open ground, and included an area of something more than a half acre. In shape, it was a parallelogram; it was substantially built of squared pickets pointed at the top, and furnished with bastions and sentry boxes at the angles. The interior contained a store-house, barracks for the men, a house for the officers, a garrison-well, and a number of cabins for the use of families. Between the fort and the base of the hill in the rear, the forest-trees had been cleared away and a few log dwellings erected, which constituted all that there was then of Wheeling.

Being, when completed, next in strength and importance to that of Fort Pitt, it is not surprising that Fort Henry should have attracted the attention of the Western Indians soon after the commencement of their hostility against the border; which was in the year 1777.

The Delawares as a nation, including the "Moravians," all of whom lived upon what is now the Tuscarawas and Muskingum, Ohio, were well-disposed toward the Americans during the year 1777. Runners were frequently dispatched by them to General Hand or George Morgan, at Pittsburgh _ the former, commandant, the latter, Indian agent, at that post _ with information as to the hostile intentions of the Wyandots and Mingoes, and with whatever of important news could be gleaned from persons visiting Detroit. It was through this channel that word was brought to Fort Pitt that a large force of these Indians and others were going to strike the Virginians; that is, to attack the border at some point across the Ohio below Pittsburgh. On the second day of August, General Hand dispatched a letter to David Shepherd, Lieutenant of Ohio county, Virginia, the one in which Wheeling was situated, informing him of the fact; _ "which," responded that officer, on the fourth, "will tend to put our country to its utmost endeavors."[1]

The express sent by General Hand to Colonel Shepherd carried, beside the letter of advice, orders for him to leave his own fort which was about six miles distant from Fort Henry and take command at Wheeling. He was also directed to issue orders to all the militia captains between the Ohio and Monongahela rivers to rendezvous at that post with all possible dispatch, bringing the whole number of their men. Accordingly, several companies finally assembled at the fort.[2] Shepherd was also admonished to put the post in as good a condition for defense as practicable. Immediately, therefore, great activity prevailed at Wheeling. The work of repairing the stockade was pushed forward rapidly. Meanwhile scouts were sent up and down the Ohio, upon both sides of the river,[3] but no Indians were seen. Lulled into a false security by the non-appearance of the enemy, several companies were allowed to return; the general impression being that the report concerning the intended attack was an erroneous one. However, Shepherd did not relax his efforts to make Fort Henry "Indian proof," as he styled it. By the close of August, he was able to facilitate himself upon its being "in some better posture of defense than it was before."[4] On the last day of the month two companies _ those of Captain Joseph Ogle[5] and Captain Samuel Mason _ alone remained in the fort; two others left that very day. That evening scouts reported no appearance of Indians.

During the night of the thirty-first, the enemy consisting of Wyandots and Mingoes with a few Shawnees and Delawares, numbering in all about two hundred,[6] approached Fort Henry undiscovered. After leaving Cashocton,[7] they had, with their accustomed shrewdness and sagacity, suspecting that their movements might be watched, abandoned the traces usually followed, and, dividing as they approached the river, into small parties, afterward consolidated their force about two miles below Wheeling,[8] crossed the Ohio, and cautiously took up a position under cover of the darkness, beyond the brow of the hill to the eastward.[9] A few Indians, said to have been six in number,[10] were placed in advance of the main body toward the fort. With their plans all completed they awaited in silence the approaching daylight. It was the first incursion of savages in force across the border since the commencement of hostilities. Not a white man was among them.[11] The warriors from each tribe had chosen their own Captains. Their organization was completed with no ordinary skill.

The few families occupying the cabins at Wheeling, had, upon receipt of information as to the contemplated invasion, betook themselves to the fort for safety. The night of the thirty-first of August, 1777, found them, fortunately, still occupants of the post, notwithstanding the general belief that immediate danger had passed. About sunrise the next morning _ September the first[12] _ Andrew Zane, young John Boyd, Samuel Tomlinson, and a Negro set out from the fort to hunt the horses of Dr. James McMechen,[13] then ranging in the woods. McMechen was intending to move that day to the older settlements.[14] The party had reached the top of the hill back of Wheeling, at the spot where the National Road now passes it, when they were attacked by the vanguard of the enemy. Boyd was caught after running about eighty rods, tomahawked and scalped.[15] Zane made his escape by jumping over a cliff of rocks of considerable height,[16] _ the Indians who were chasing him not choosing to risk the perilous leap. He was much bruised in the fall and his gun broken in pieces. In the course of the day he reached Shepherd's fort without further mishap. Tomlinson[17] and the Negro also succeeded in alluding the savages, reaching Fort Henry in safety and giving the alarm. A small party immediately sallied forth and, unharmed, brought in the remains of Boyd.[18]

The enemy rightly judged that the commander of the fort would send out a party to pursue the few Indians seen. They determined, therefore, at once to form an ambuscade. The whole force thereupon descended to the creek bottom and followed the bend of the stream until the flat piece of ground at the south end of the hill was reached. In this place a line was formed crescent-shaped, with its convexity towards the creek, its points resting within a short distance of the foot of the eminence. A number of savages also secreted themselves among the bushes on the western side of the hill. The Indians took the precaution to make a very plain trail leading from the vicinity of the spot where Zane and his party had been surprised. Their plans thus skillfully arranged, they quietly awaited the appearance of the Americans. They did not long remain inactive.[19]

Colonel Shepherd, as soon as the lifeless body of Boyd had reached the fort, dispatched Captain Mason with a few men[20] in pursuit of what he had no doubt was a small party of lurking savages. They soon fell upon the trail of the enemy, when two were selected to follow directly on the trace while the others, divided into two equal parties, marched in single file several steps apart, at the distance of about seventy yards to the right and left of the track. When the men had progressed some distance into the very jaws of the ambuscade, a soldier who was marching next to Captain Mason, discovered an Indian whom he quickly shot.21 Instantly the contest commenced. At the first fire, Mason was wounded in the hand. Seeing the impossibility of maintaining a conflict with the Indians who nearly surrounded his small party, he gave orders to retreat to the fort; but the attempt cost the lives of several of his men.[22] He was himself wounded a second time. So enfeebled was he from the loss of blood, and faint from fatigue, that he almost despaired of reaching the post; yet he pressed forward with all his powers, closely pursued by a savage and expecting every instant to be struck down by his tomahawk. Suddenly wheeling to shoot his pursuer, he found him so close that he was obliged to thrust him back with all his force. The weapon in the hand of the Indian, in its decent, missing its aim, gave Captain Mason an advantage. The next moment the ball from his gun had done its errand and the savage fell lifeless to the ground. But Mason was only able to proceed a few paces farther. Concealing himself as best he could, he succeeded in remaining unobserved until the Indians had gone, when he made his way into the fort[23]. The commandant of the post lost a son _ William Shepherd _ in the sortie. Hearing the uproar, but, on account of a dense fog which overhung the creek bottom, unable to see the effect of the conflict, _ Captain Ogle, with a party still smaller than the one headed by Mason, advanced to his relief. Of course this sally was only another holocaust to the demoniac fury of the savages. Several were killed and scalped. Ogle made good his escape by secreting himself in a cluster of tall weeds, in a fence-corner. While thus concealed, two plumed warriors seated themselves on the fence above him, one of whom was severely wounded and cried piteously with pain. The Captain saw the blood running down one of his legs. They soon moved off, but Ogle was compelled to remain in his hiding-place until the enemy had disappeared, when he regained the fort.[24]

Although fortunate in their ambuscade, the savages did not venture an attack upon the fort. They contented themselves with erecting some rude breastworks and blinds; scalping the dead; killing all the cattle, sheep and horses within reach; and, after dark, in setting fire to the unoccupied cabins and burning them to the ground. They then left _ recrossing the Ohio and returning to their homes. The Americans loss during the day was fifteen killed and five wounded.[25] The savages had but one killed and nine wounded; two of the latter were Delawares.[26] The next day the garrison was reinforced. Thus ended "the first siege of Wheeling;" which, though intended by the Indians when they crossed the river to be an attack upon Fort Henry, resulted, in the end, only in a skillfully laid plan to entrap small numbers of its garrison, as the exigencies of events would naturally compel the commander to send out, either as relief parties or scouts. Their success, fortunately, did not exceed the scope of their finally limited designs.[27]

Chapter Twenty Two

Foreman's Defeat
27 Sept. 1777.

    After the withdrawal of the savages from Wheeling, on the night of the first of September, 1777, the borderers saw nothing more of them, or heard of their movements, and the impression became general that they had returned to their home. This conclusion was a correct one.[1] Nevertheless, forty Wyandots, under the lead of the Half King, head-chief of that nation, left Sandusky, not long after, to strike the Virginia settlements in the vicinity of Fort Henry.[2]
    On the morning of the twenty-sixth of September, Captain William Foreman who had recently arrived from Hampshire county, to join General Hand's expedition,[3] started with twenty-four men, _ Captain Joseph Ogle with ten men, and William Linn with nine men, on a scouting-party, from Fort Henry.[4] They proposed reconnoitering as far as Captina creek, and to make their return in three or four days.[5] Linn led the force,[6] he being recognized as an adept in Indian craft. _ Their course lay down the Ohio to the mouth of Grave creek, about twelve miles distant, where they intended to cross the river. Thence to Captina was a distance of only eight miles.[7]
    Nothing worthy of record occurred to the party on its way down to the proposed place of crossing. To the surprise of all, they found upon their arrival there, the "fort" burned, the standing corn cut up and destroyed, and all the canoes and other craft missing. The place had been abandoned before the appearance of the savages at Wheeling on the first of the month; and now, it was evident, its destruction had been completed by the enemy. As there were no facilities at hand for getting over the Ohio, a resolution was taken of returning to Fort Henry the next day.[8]
    Remaining over night at Grave creek, the party the next morning, in accordance with the determination arrived at the evening previous, started to return to Wheeling. Advancing up the river until the foot of the Narrows[9] was reached, the party halted. Linn with three of his men[10] here separated from the main body and took to the hills on the right. He did not care to risk himself in so dangerous a pass as the one which, for some distance, they were now required to go through. He had his suspicions, it is said, that Indians were near.[11]

The forty men under the lead of Foremen and Ogle entered the narrow defile with little regard to discipline. The two Captains did not share with Linn his apprehending of encountering savages. Along the river bank, their path was skirted with a thick growth of willows, buckeyes, and pawpaws. They marched in single file, bandying jokes with each other as they passed along. They had now reached the head of the Narrows _ the point where the river approaches the hill _ where the bottom is very narrow. Just here to the left, hidden from view by the bushes and bank, lay the Half King and his forty warriors, thirsting for the blood of their victims. Never were contending enemies nearer equal as to numbers, never more unequal as to preparation. A few scattered Indian trinkets, it is said, now attracted the foremost of the Americans. Soon the whole force was huddled together looking at them. A few Indians stepped into the path before and behind them. At that moment came the deadly discharge from the ambuscade; _ then wild yells and a headlong rush: it was about eleven o'clock in the forenoon.[12]

Several were killed the first fire. The only avenue of flight for those who were not at once shot down was, up the steep acclivity to the right. This was a difficult and hazardous undertaking for the fugitives, but the only chance left. Some were shot in the attempt and others severely wounded. Fortunately, Linn and his comrades, over the brow of the hill, had not made as rapid progress as those in the Narrows; and, as a consequence, had fallen somewhat behind. Hearing the firing of the savages, they ran along the ridge until opposite the spot of the deadly ambuscade. Here Linn and one of his companions saw a man, as they reached the bank, with his right leg broken.[13] They lifted him up; carried him to a place of safety, and then made all haste to Fort Henry.[14] Linn's party, with one man from the principal force, who had escaped with two wounds, was the first to bring the news of the sad result of the scout to Colonel Shepard, the commandant.[15]

Captain Foreman and twenty others, including his son[16] and six of Linn's company,[17] were killed[18] and one captured.[19] There were several wounded but none fatally. All the latter eventually reached Fort Henry; and most of them, with all those unhurt, came in during the afternoon and evening. "There are wounded men," wrote Shepherd a few hours after the massacre, "who lie in the woods, particularly one with a broken leg, and some others."[20] It was four days after _ when Major James Chew had arrived from Fort Pitt with reinforcements _ before a detachment under command of that officer and Colonel Shepherd ventured from the fort to bury the dead;[21] the impression being general that the scouts had been attacked by the savages in force _ the same who had assailed Wheeling on the first of September.

No censure fell upon Shepherd because of the fatal result of the movement of the twenty-sixth of September from Fort Henry, which post he then commanded. "The party that went out in the late unfortunate excursion," he wrote, a week after, "went not at my request or order, but from motives of their own, as they were tired of being cooped up in the fort idle, and proposed the same several times before I would at any rate consent." "I myself," he continued, "thought their force was sufficient for any scouting party of Indians they might fall in with; as it was hardly to be supposed that forty-six of our best riflemen, well equipped, should be overpowered by numbers of Indians, from the known manner of their sending small parties to annoy the settlements."

The spot where the twenty-one men met their fate was two-thirds of the distance from Wheeling to Graves creek _ about eight miles below the former and four miles above the latter place (now Moundsville,) in what is the present county of Marshall, West Virginia.

Chapter Twenty Three

<u>Battle</u> <u>and</u> <u>Massacre</u> <u>of</u> <u>Wyoming</u>
3 July, 1778

    The State of Pennsylvania is chiefly drained by the Delaware, Susquehanna and Ohio rivers. The Susquehanna "drinks up the waters of more than one half the Commonwealth's wide area. Its chief tributaries are the Tioga, Northwest Branch, and the Juniata, all flowing into the parent stream from the west or northwest. In the northeast part of the State, lying below the first mentioned tributary but above the second, is the present county of Luzerne. The Susquehanna sweeps through it, first in a southeast and then a southwest direction. Its territory is mountainous; its ranges running in a northeasterly course, the main one crossing its northwestern portion. Two inferior chains cross near its center: while parallel with these and about six miles distant are two other ranges. In the intervening space lies a lovely valley.

    The Susquehanna enters the valley through a gap in the western mountain and flowing in a serpentine course about twenty miles, leaves it through another opening in the same range. The river is, in most places, about two hundred yards wide, and flows _ except near the center of the valley, where is a rapids with a very gentle current unless swollen with rains or melting snows. Along the river, on both sides, extending in some places nearly a mile and a half from its margin, are level plains; then commence small hills stretching to the mountains; the stream sometimes washing the base of the hills on one side, and sometimes on the other. The surface of the plains is in some parts of the valley, elevated about ten feet higher than in other parts, forming a sudden declivity from one to the other. _ The name of this valley _ one of the most charming names, and yet the most melancholy, to be found upon the pages of American history _ is Wyoming.

    Connecticut, whose charter from Charles the Second was older than that of Pennsylvania, using its prior claims to land north of the Mamaroneck river, had colonized this beautiful region and governed it as its county of Westmorland. The settlements, begun in 1754, increased in numbers and wealth till their annual tax amounted to two thousand pounds in Continental currency. In the winter of 1776, the people aided Washington with two companies of infantry, though their men were all needed to protect their own homes. Knowing the alliance of the British with the Six Nations, they built a line of ten forts as places of refuge.

The upper settlements in Pennsylvania in 1778 _ those nearest to Wyoming _ were Easten and Bethlehem, about sixty miles away. Down the Susquehanna, about the same distances, at the confluence of the Northwest Branch with the North Branch were a small number of persons in the town of Sunbury _ formerly Shamokin. North and northwest of the isolated valley of Wyoming, was the home of the Iroquois; _ not a single tribe, but the most potent confederacy of Indians the white man had ever encountered on this continent. Their dreaded arms reached to the Catawbas of Carolina, dealt blows of vengeance to the Mohicans of New England, drove the Wyandots from Lake Simcoe, Canada, and struck down with remorseless cruelty, the clans upon the Illinois. They were at once the most powerful and the most warlike of the red race. This Confederacy inhabited the upper waters of the Susquehanna, the whole of the Lake and the Genesse country. They were in force at Oyuago, at Arnadilla, at Tioga, and at Newtown. From Tioga where they could rendezvous, at a moderate rise of water, boats could descend to Wyoming in twenty-four hours. This descending water communication rendered an attack from them sudden and easy. It placed the county of Westmorland in a more exposed position on account of the assured hostility of most of the Six Nations, than any other portion of the American frontier. A numerous, implacable blood-thirsty enemy was within striking distance. Thus near was the danger. Thus exposed was Wyoming.

The two companies raised in Westmorland in the latter part of 1776, were to be stationed in proper places, for the defense of the inhabitants; but, being on the continental establishment, and Washington had pressed, they were ordered to join his army. The exigencies of the country below _ the state of the continental forces _ their defeat at White Plains _ the surrender of Fort Washington _ Cornwallis' march from New York, pressing in the rear of the American army, _ all these events justified Congress in ordering the two companies to join General Washington with all possible expedition, although it left Westmorland unprotected. The year 1777 came and went and still they could not be sent back to the Susquehanna. A storm-cloud was gathering in the North in May, 1778, and yet they were absent. Wo to Wyoming!

Early in the Spring of 1778, Congress was apprised of a meditated attack on Wyoming. Westmorland was rife with rumors that the British and Indians were preparing an expedition for the destruction of the settlement. Defenseless as the position was known to be, and exasperated as the enemy were, by the efforts of the people in the cause of Independence, nothing could be more probable than that such a design was contemplated. It was therefore resolved that another company of men should be raised for its protection. _ But what of the valley that was thus to be so faintly guarded?

The first bright beams of a January sun _ 1778 _ leading up the new year, lighted a scene at Wyoming, of white and cold and placid beauty. Hill and valley were clad in virgin snow. Smoke rose clinging to the skies from hundreds of cottages. Barns surrounded by stacks of wheat showed that the staff of life was abundant. Cattle and sheep fed _ direct from stacks in the meadow, or sheltered in rude sheds, sleek and thriving, gave evidence that they shared in the super-abounding plenty of these fertile plains. The deep-mouthed watch-dog barked fiercely as the sled drawn by a smart span of horses with jingling and its merry load of girls and lads, going to some quilting, singing meeting, wedding, or other merry-making, passed swiftly by. The soldiers' wives and the soldiers' widows were well provided for. Coffee was little known, but the fragrant and exhilarating cup of tea graced the table on which smoked the buck-wheat cake, and the luscious honey-comb, the venison-steak and well preserved shad. If perchance, a furlough had granted some of the men of the two absent companies to visit their wives and little ones, the broiled chicken, the well-fatted roasting pig, or the delicious turkey, bade them a thousand times welcome. Neighbors would flock in: to hear how they whipped the British at Millstone, and took a hundred horses! _ how General Washington, at Germantown rode right into the mouths of the enemy's cannon, as it were. The wearied scouts would come in, while others set off on tours of duty, creating little excitement, as no danger impended, all seeming quiet up the river. Meanwhile the flail sounded merrily on the threshing-floor _ the flax-break and hatchel were in active requisition _ the spinning wheel buzzed its normal _ while the shuttle sped its rapid flight. Such was the dawning of 1778 upon Wyoming.

"Fair Wyoming! beneath thy skies,
The happy shepherd swains had nought to do
But feed their flocks in green declivities.
Happy valley! How long before thy babbling streams
Ran red with gore! How long before in desolation
Cold the death serpent dwelt alone
Where grass o'er grew each mouldering stone?"

The settlement of Wyoming was made by the people of Connecticut, on grant of lands purchased by the inhabitants of that colony of the Indian proprietors, under sanction of the government; and these lands falling within the limits of the Pennsylvania claim, a dispute concerning the right had arisen between the two governments, causing frequent acts of hostility. When it was at a height that threatened the disturbance of the other governments, Congress interposed, by whose recommendation and authority the decision of the dispute was suspended till that with Great Britain was concluded, when there might be more leisure to attend to the other, and consider the justice of each claim.

On this footing, the dispute lay dormant for two or three years. The inhabitants as has been shown lived happily, and the settlement increased, consisting of the townships of Lackawana, Exeter, Kingston, Wilksbarre, Plymouth, Nanticoke, Huntington and Salem, each containing five miles square. The six lower townships were pretty full of inhabitants; the two upper ones had comparatively but few, and thinly scattered. The settlement had lately supplied the continental army with three thousand bushels of grain, and by the first of July, 1778, the ground was loaded with the most promising crops of every kind. There were, in the valley, upwards of a thousand families numbering about twenty-three hundred inhabitants. In the townships of Lackawana, Exeter, Kingston and Wilksbarre were four forts garrisoned by citizen-soldiers: Fort Jenkins, Fort Wintermoot, Forty Fort, and Fort Wilksbarre.

The Tories and Indians had given some disturbance to the settlements in 1777, before the battle of Oriskany and the skirmishes soon after at and near Schahasie where they were dispersed. Then Burgoyne surrendered, which event released from service in the northeast many savages. The Spring of 1778, therefore, found the wilds of western New York thronged with enemies ready for deadly strife and carnage in the exposed settlements of the "rebels." But the storm was some time gathering which hung by the first of July so darkly over the valley of Wyoming.

The people had frequent intimations that the Indians had some mischievous design against them; but their fears were somewhat abated by seeing them seemingly solicitous to preserve peace. They sent down the river several times, different parties with declarations of their peaceable disposition towards the settlers, requesting a return of friendship. They were always dismissed with assurances that there were no designs to disturb them. In March, 1778, appearances became more alarming, and the scattered families which were located, for thirty miles up the Susquehanna, were collected and brought into the more populous parts. In April and May, strolling parties of Indians and Tories made frequent incursions into the settlement, robbing and plundering the inhabitants of provisions, grain, and live stock. In the latter month, scouting parties of the settlers began to be met by those of the enemy. The latter hovered around this settlement at a distance of twenty miles, seeming intent on preventing all communication with the upper country. They attacked no families; they burned no houses. Shots were rarely exchanged, as the foe rather kept aloof than courted battle. It was the ominous calm before the coming storm.

Soon one of the settlers _ William Crooks _ was shot dead. This was the first life taken by the Indians at Westmorland _ the first gust preceding the dreadful hurricane. A few days after, a party of six, out on duty were fired upon; two were wounded, one of whom died the next day. These incidents increased the alarm already distractingly painful. But an event soon occurred of more exciting importance. Two Indians, formerly residents of Wyoming, and acquainted with the people, came down with their squaws on a visit, professing warm friendship; but suspicions existed that they were spies, and directions were given that they should be carefully watched. An old companion of one of them, with more than Indian cunning, asserting his attachment to the redmen, gave his visitor drink after drink of his favorite rum; when, in confidence and the fulness of his maudlin heart, he avowed that his people were preparing to cut off the settlement; the attack to be made soon; and that he had come down to see and report the present state of affairs in the valley. And he told the truth. Then the alarm and distress rose almost to phrensy. Something must be done quickly or the Happy Valley would become a desolation.

Mention has been made of a determination to raise another military company in the valley. Now that the danger was become imminent a Captain was appointed to enlist men to fill its ranks. This like the other two was to be a Continental company. About forty men were finally mustered into its ranks. In June, several persons being at work on a farm from which Tories had gone to the enemy, were attacked and one man was killed. Soon after, a woman and her five children were murdered, her house plundered of all that could be taken away and the rest destroyed. These depredations greatly increased the excitement, which now arose to a white heat in the valley.

Early in May, 1778, Major John Butler, in conformity to instructions received from Guy Johnson, commanded at Niagra, to prepare for an expedition against the "post and settlements at Wyoming." To that end, he assembled Rangers and savages. The Seneca Indians to the southeastward had kept fresh in their memory; their chiefs and braves who fell at Oriskany. Besides, their head sachem or king _ Gi-en-guah-toh _ the foremost man at that time of all of the Iroquois, was the implacable foe of the Americans. So, by the blandishments of gifts and pay bestowed by Butler, and by the influence of their leader _ lured, also, by the chances of revenge, the Senecas were induced to join the expedition which marched across the Genesee on its way to the Susquehanna. Reaching the head waters of that river towards the last of June with a force of not less than five hundred, Butler prepared to descend the stream to Wyoming. He had with him, besides the Rangers and Seneca Indians, a few savages of other tribes.

That the enemy were assembling in force in the wilds of the north was soon known at Wyoming. As a consequence, every man who could bear arms was called into service and trained. Scouts were sent up the river to observe the motions of the foe. The forts were now filled with women and children. Every company of militia was ordered to be ready at a moment's warning. It was known that the attack would soon be made; but the precise time could not be calculated. Butler landed his forces on the west side of the river, about twenty miles above the Valley, in a direct line, where, securing their craft, they marched across the bend of the river and the last day of June found them on the western mountain. "I encamped," says the commander, "on an eminence which overlooks the greatest part of the settlement, from which I sent out parties to discover the situation or strength of the enemy." "These parties," adds Butler, "brought in eight prisoners and scouts."[1] This was the opening scene of the bloody drama. The lovely and unprotected valley, thus invaded, was in all its blooming beauty. The fields were waving with the burden of an abundant harvest.

On the first day of July, Major Butler entered the Valley through a notch in the mountain and marched within a half mile of Fort Wintermoot, when he halted and sent Lieutenant John Turney of Captain Caldwell's company of Rangers, with a flag, demanding immediate possession, which was soon agreed to. The

Captain himself was then sent to Fort Jenkins with a detachment, which soon capitulated. Butler the next day commanded Fort Forty; but now, for the first time, there was a refusal. A surrender of all of the forts, all the public property, the company of regulars, and the Valley, was, the morning of the third, demanded. Again there was a refusal.

In the valley of Wyoming, at the moment of the invasion, was Colonel Zebulon Butler of the Continental Army, just from Yorktown, on a visit to his family. By common consent, he assumed command of the company of regulars and of the militia. On the first of July, his whole force was in Fort Forty. On that day, he marched to the place where the first blood had been shed by the enemy since their advent into the valley. It was up the river, in Exeter, after removing the bodies of nine men killed while hoeing corn, to the vicinity of Fort Jenkins and there burying them, the little army returned _ the militia to their homes for provisions, to muster again at Fort Forty on the third of July. When they had assembled, there were six companies including the regulars; the whole numbering not less than three hundred men.

After the reception of the last summons from the enemy to surrender, Zebulon Butler called a council of war, when it was determined to sally forth, march up the river, and attack the foe, who were in force near Fort Wintermoot, before they had advanced any further down the valley. So, on the third of July, 1778 _ a memorable day in the annals of Wyoming, as, indeed, in those of the country at large _ old men and young, militia-men and regulars, all that were in the fort, marched out to give battle to the Indians and Rangers, _ in numbers, as it proved, nearly, if not actually, double their own; and equally, if not more skilled, in the woods, than themselves. "Parties," says Major John Butler, "were sent out to collect cattle, who informed me that the rebels were preparing for an attack." "This," continues the writer, "pleased the Indians highly, who observed that they should be on an equal footing with them in the woods."[2]

The enemy were stationed at Fort Wintermoot, which was built about eighty rods distant from the immediate bank of the river, and about a mile below the head of the Valley. The foe, until they discovered the approach of the Americans, were in camp around that post. Finding the settlers determined to offer battle, Major Butler ordered the fort to be set on fire, intending thereby to deceive the approaching force into a belief that a retreat had taken place. He then posted his army _ his left resting virtually upon the river; his right, upon a swamp. His opponents marching up the stream formed their line of battle some distance from, but immediately in front of, the enemy; the latter, for greater safety, lying flat upon the ground, waiting the approaching column. Between four and five o'clock, the Americans advancing to within two hundred yards of the foe, opened fire. Three volleys were fired by the Americans on the advance before the enemy replied. The lines were then only one hundred yards asunder. Gi-en-guah-toh, with his Seneca braves upon the right, began now to respond to the fire of the settlers. They were immediately seconded by the Rangers on the left and the battle became general.

Colonel Zebulon Butler, in immediate command of the American right, pushed the white troops of his namesake until they were on the point of giving away. Just then, through some mistake, the left wing, which was gallantly resisting the attack of the savages, gave way. The utmost pains were taken by the officers to rally the settlers, but in vain. After less than an hour's fighting, the day was lost. Then commenced the massacre of Wyoming.

The Senecas gave no quarter. Until darkness ended the pursuit, the tomahawk, the spear, and the scalping-knife, did their work. Nor could the whites have shown mercy; for, while two hundred and more scalps were taken, only five prisoners remained alive. One Lieutenant-Colonel, one Major, ten Captains and ten Lieutenants were killed. These scenes enacted upon the banks of the Susquehanna at the close of the day _ July third, 1778, as the fugitives rushed from the battle-field, pursued by the yelling and blood-thirsty savages, were revolting in the extremes. Many were tortured at the stake that night. The victory of the Indians and Rangers was complete. Of the former, one was killed and eight were wounded; of the latter, two were killed. Colonel Zebulon Butler escaped the fury of that dreadful discomfiture.

On the day after the battle, the remaining forts of the Valley capitulated. In the meantime, fugitives were flying _ and they continued to fly _ to the wilderness. All was confusion, consternation and horror, in the settlements. The only hope of safety seemed to be in flight; and in that flight, what suffering! Every fort, every dwelling, before the enemy finally departed, were burned down. "About one thousand head of horned cattle and sheep and swine in great numbers, were driven off." Wyoming was a desolate place! Her sons, many of them, slept the sleep of death, or were wandering in the circumjacent wilds. And her daughters, _ what a long, what a wailing procession was flying from the once Happy Valley! Wyoming was destroyed!

Chapter Twenty Four

Clark's Conquest of the Illinois
July, 1778

Spotswood, one of the ablest of the Colonial Governors of the Old Dominion, proposed, as early as 1711, the incorporation of a Virginia trading company, to extend its operations, promote settlements, and sustain fortified posts, as far west as Kaskaskia, thus practically supplanting the claim of France to the rich Valley of the Ohio. He was, however, ahead of his time, the people opposing his scheme of a privileged monopoly.[1] The conquest of the Illinois country was reserved for another generation.

In 1744, the Iroquois Indians deeded, at the treaty of Lancaster, to Virginia all their right by conquest to the lands in the Ohio Valley. At Logstown, eight years later, the Ohio tribes confirmed the grant made at Lancaster.[2] The treaty at Camp Charlotte, in October, 1774, fixed the Ohio as the boundary between the Shawnees and Virginians; while the treaties of Fort Stanwix, in 1768, that with the Cherokees in 1770, together with the Cherokee grant to Henderson and company, in March, 1775, with the confirmation of the Ohio as the boundary, by the Ohio tribes, at Pittsburgh, in October of that year, virtually extinguished the Indian title to the Kentucky country as far as the Tennessee River. But for the Indian disturbances, in 1774 the settlements commenced that year in Kentucky would have been permanent. Indian hostilities only temporarily postponed them; for in the Spring of 1775, they were renewed with increased vigor, and a new colony was planted in the wilderness.

These settlements very naturally excited the ire and jealousy of the British leaders in Canada, Detroit, and the Illinois country; and soon the Indians were hounded on to cripple and annoy them. Some slight attacks were made on the settlers during 1775 and 1776, which became quiet formidable in 1777; Harrodsburg, Boonesborough, and Logan's Fort, all having been the objects of Indian vengeance, succeeded in repelling their savage assailants.

George Rogers Clark, a native of Albermarle County, Virginia, who had served as a Captain on Dunmore's campaign of 1774, wended his way to Kentucky in 1775. "I have come out," he said, to young James Roy, whom he met in the woods, "to see what you brave fellows are doing, and to lend you a helping hand, if necessary."³ He was then twenty three years of age, over six feet in height, with a florid complexion; and well-calculated, by his native talents and popular address, to attract attention, and became a leader of the people. He at once enlisted hardily in their defenses against the Indians, and studied how best to subserve their interests. In 1776, he was chosen a delegate, in conjunction with Gabriel John Jones, to represent them in the Virginia Convention; but was not admitted to a seat, as the Kentucky region, forming a part of Fincastle County, was already represented in that body.

While at Williamsburg, he applied to the Governor and Council for a supply of ammunition for the defense of the infant settlements of Kentucky, and drew out from them an expression of regret that they were unable to grant his request; but, at length, moved by his powerful appeals, they so far relented, as to agree to loan the Kentuckians five hundred pounds of powder, on his personal security, and issued an order to the keeper of the public magazine to deliver that quantity to him, to be transported at his own expense. "The country that is not worth defending is not worth claiming!" exclaimed Clark, indignantly, as he declined the useless order; for, he frankly informed them, that it was utterly out of his power alone to convey military stores many hundred miles through an enemy's country. But he was recalled, and an order was passed for the conveyance of the powder to Pittsburgh, there to be delivered to Clark for the use of the people of Kentucky. Remaining several weeks for the meeting of the Virginia Legislature, Clark and his colleague, Jones, succeeded in obtaining in the creation of the County of Kentucky; then hastened to Pittsburgh, and procuring a few men to aid them, descended the Ohio with their precious charge of the powder in kegs, which they hid on the lower of the Three Islands, a few miles above Limestone, now Maysville, and went across the country by land to Harrodsburg. A party was sent back with horses for the powder; but they encountered a Mingo force under Pluggy, when a skirmish ensued, in which two of the Kentuckians were killed, and two made prisoners. The powder, however, was saved, which enabled Clark and others at McCelland's Station, near the present locality of Georgetown, Kentucy, to make a gallant defense when attacked, a few days later, by Pluggy's band, repelling them, with the loss of their noted leader.⁴

In April, 1777, Clark, who had been serving as Major in the military organization of the new county, concluded to send a couple of trusty spies to reconnoiter the British settlements in the Illinois country, whence issued many of the Indian parties that invaded and harassed Kentucky. He selected Samuel Moore, Benjamin Linn, Silas Harlan, and Simon Butler, _ afterwards better known by his real name of Simon Kenton, _ as superior woodsmen for the purpose, who cast lots, and it fell upon Moore and Linn to perform the service. Clark gave them such verbal instructions as were suited to the occasion. They soon reached Kaskaskia, representing themselves as wandering hunters; Philip Rocheblave the British Lieutenant Governor, promptly employed them to procure game for his table. In the course of a couple of months, having learned all there was necessary, steered their course for Harrodsburg, with the intelligence that there were no troops stationed in the Illinois settlements, but that a considerable quantity of military supplies were stored in the fort of Kaskaskia; that the principal French inhabitants were quite inimical to the Americans in consequence of their ignorance of the causes of the rupture between them and the mother country, but were apprehensive of no danger from the Bostoni, as they denominated the Americans; and that the Lieutenant Governor was constantly inciting the Wabash Indians, by large presents and promised rewards, to make inroads on the Kentucky settlers, and procure as many of their scalps as possible.[5]

Strongly impressed with the importance of the capture of Kaskaskia and its dependent settlements, or, in less than in a twelve month; it would become necessary to send an army, at a far greater expense, to chastise the Wabash Indians, Clark made, in the autumn, a journey to Williamsburg, and laid his plans before the Governor and Council of Virginia. The result was, the authorization, January second, 1778, of a secret expedition for the purpose, with Clark as its head as Lieutenant Colonel Commandant. Twelve hundred pounds were advanced to Clark with which to raise, on the frontiers, seven companies, of fifty men each; with one set of instructions, for the public eye, that the force was destined for the protection of Kentucky, there to obey the further orders of the commanding officer; but with a set of secret instructions, to push on to the Illinois country. William Bailey Smith was appointed Major of the regiment, with orders to repair to the Holston country to recruit four companies from among the hardy frontiersmen of that region, and lead them through the wilderness route to the Kentucky settlements.

After encountering many difficulties, and discouragements, Clark at length descended the Ohio in May, with about one hundred and fifty men, under Captains Joseph Bowman, Leonaid Helm, and William Harrod. Early in June they landed on a small island, of some seven acres, at the head of the Falls of the Ohio, where they encamped, built a blockhouse for the protection of their stores; and the ten or a dozen families, who had accompanied the expedition; erected cabins, cut down the cane and planted a crop of corn _ hence the name of Corn Island. From the mouth of Kentucky River, expresses had been sent to the stations in the country, requesting Colonel John Bowman, the military commandant of Kentucky, to meet him at the Falls, as he had an object in view of the utmost importance. He was also desired to bring with him all the men. Major Smith's command, who might have arrived, with as many volunteers as could be induced to repair to his standard, and could with safety be spared from the several stations.

Clark was mortified to learn that none of Smith's recruits had reached Kentucky, but that a company under Thomas Dillard, from Pittsylvania county, had arrived in March, to serve a tour of duty in protecting the settlements and beyond these, but few men could be spared for the expedition. Nothing daunted, Clark still determined to carry forward his long cherished enterprise. He regarded the adventure as a desperate one; but, if successful, it would prove the salvation of the country. Instead of first striking at Vincennes, much the strongest settlement with the Piaukeshaw Indians at hand to aid in its defense, he resolved to direct his attention to the Illinois settlements, more scattered, and with fewer Indians to lend them any assistance.

Captain Dillard had resigned before reaching Clark's encampment,[6] leaving Lieutenant Hutchins in command of the detachment; which together with a squad of ten or a dozen men who had been making salt at Drennon's Lick about forty miles north east of the Falls, near the Kentucky River, with Captain John Montgomery, and a few other volunteers, made up the fourth company of Clark's command numbering seventy-five men.[7] Montgomery was placed at its head. Lieutenant Levi Todd, and nine others were assigned to Helm's Company[8] _ Todd also serving as adjutant or aide to Colonel Clark.[9]

Much attention had been devoted to drilling the men. Time for action had come. Clark now presented to his little band of followers the real object of the Expedition, with the urgent necessity for it, and that it was now in their power to render their country an inestimable service, and put a stop to the merciless Indian depredations from the Illinois and Wabash country. The officers and all the men, save Hutchins' party, heartily approved the proposition; and the next day was set for their departure. But an untoward event occurred, which caused some disappointment, and a day's delay in the setting out on the expedition. The next morning before day, Hutchins and the most of his men silently stole from the camp, waded the stream separating the island from the main land, and directed their course towards Harrodsburg. As soon as their desertion was discovered, a party was mounted on the horses of the visitors from the stations, and the runaways were overhauled after a pursuit of twenty miles; but they scattered in the woods, and only eight were taken and returned. The others were nearly starved before they reached Harrodsburg and so indignant were the people there of their treachery, that they would not, for some time, permit them to enter the fort and relieve their wants. There was some excuse for their conduct; they alleging that the time of their term service had expired and that they were being forced on the expedition without their consent. On the return of the party in pursuit of the deserters, the soldiers hung and burnt the runaway Lieutenant in effigy.[10]

Five keel boats,[11] and the necessary provisions were made ready, and a few invalids left to protect the island and families, and attend to the corn crop. It being observed that Clark and his men were without a flag, one of the dames of the garrison made the patriotic sacrifice of one of her undergarments, from which an ensign was soon improvised, which was elevated on a pole and placed at the prow of the foremost boat, where it was hoisted with much good cheer, the men declaring they would conquer, or die under the banner presented to them.[12]

Clark's little flotilla set sail from Corn Island, during the forenoon[13] of Wednesday, June twenty-fourth, bearing about one hundred and seventy-five men,[14] working up the river something like a mile in order to gain the main channel, when they passed in safety over the Falls, some two miles in extent, during a notable eclipse of the sun. Some of the party were apprehensive that this phenomenon of nature, at the very out-set of the expedition, was a warning _ and omen of evil; but Clark every ready to turn the events of the moment to the happiest account, assured his followers, that they should rather regard it as an indication of Providence, that, after a little darkness, a brighter sky and more auspicious prospects awaited them. So, full of hope, they floated down the river. They were overtaken on the way by William Linn, with a letter from Colonel John Campbell[15] at Pittsburgh, giving intelligence of the alliance with France, which served Clark an important purpose in his subsequent intercourse with the French inhabitants of the Illinois and Wabash country.

Landing on the lower and larger of the two islands, which Clark denominated Baritania, at the mouth of the Tennessee, to prepare for the land march upon which they were soon to enter, they, not very long thereafter, hailed a boat of hunters, among whom were John Duff, John Saunders, Nicholas LaPlant, Parfait Dufore, but eight days from Kaskaskia. Clark first administered to them the oath of allegiance, and then, apart from his men, examined them concerning the situation of affairs in that quarter, which they reported not as favorable as he could have wished, as Rocheblave had received some rumor of a visit from the Americans, and had French and Indian spies on the alert in various directions; but being instructed by Clark to relate to the soldiers only such views as were of a hopeful character, on pain of punishment, they proved equal to the occasion, giving such rose-colored representation, as served greatly to elate the spirits of the little army. No part of the information derived from these hunters pleased Clark so much as that the leading French people regarded the Long Knives or Bostoni as more barbarous than the surrounding Indians; for he was determined to profit by it, should he succeed in capturing their town and making them prisoners. Duff and his party of hunters volunteered for the Expedition. Descending the river nine miles, Clark ran his boats up Massac Creek, a small stream, half a mile above the long abandoned locality of old Fort Massac _ Massacre[16] of the French _ where they were sunk for concealment. Thus, in five days, a distance of three hundred and fifty-two miles had been accomplished.

After a night's bivouac, Clark and his men took up their line of march, June twenty-ninth, by sun-rise from Fort Massac. Their scanty provisions were parceled out for a four day's supply, the supposed time necessary to reach Kaskaskia; and this, with the gun, accouterments, ammunition, and butcher-knife, dressed pretty much after the Indian style, made up the equipment of each man of the party. No artillery _ no pack-horses _ no markees _ no military supplies, accompanied the adventurers. There were two routes from Fort Massac to Kaskaskia. One, quite circuitous, bearing largely to the right, over dry ground, heading the streams that flow into the Mississippi, and reckoned at one hundred and fifty miles; the other called the Hunter's Trail, was more direct, passable only at dry seasons by footmen, over low grounds, crossing the heads of the Cache

River, and Big Muddy, not very far below the junction of Beaucoup Creek, and Mary River, a few miles below Kaskaskia; an estimated distance of eighty or ninety miles.

John Saunders, one of the hunters who joined Clark at the mouth of the Tennessee, was selected as the principle guide. On the third day of the march, he failed to recognize the trail, and became quite bewildered and Clark, suspecting treachery, threatened his life if he did not soon find the Hunters's Road. After two hours search, he recovered the trail, when all parties felt relieved from a heavy weight of anxiety and apprehension. It was, at best, during the heat of Summer, a very fatiguing journey; fifty miles through a wilderness _ the remainder, a prairie country, scant of both water and game. Ponds, lagoons, and water-courses had to be waded; and they could only spread their blankets where night overtook them, and, with fighting mosquitoes, get such rest as they could. Instead of four days, six were consumed in reaching Kaskaskia; the last two, almost without food, excepting roots and a few berries. This condition added to the determination of the whole party to take Kaskaskia, or die in the attempt.[17]

On Saturday evening, July fourth, they arrived within three miles of the town, not having met on the route from Fort Massac, a solitary hunter nor a straggling Indian. They laid by till after dark, to avoid discovery, when they marched to a farm on the east side of the Kaskaskia River, just below the ruins of the old wooden fort, on a rocky imminence, which had burned down twelve years before. Clark was now within a mile of his coveted prize on the opposite side of the river, with intervening bottoms skirting either shore, thickly overgrown with umbrageous trees and bushes. From the occupant of the farm, it was learned, that on a recent alarm, the Lieutenant Governor had assembled the whole male population under arms, but soon dismissed them.[18] Hearing a noise in the village, Clark inquired the cause, when the French rustic replied that it was probably proceeded from some hilarious Negroes enjoying a dance on the green.

It was a beautiful night, the moon shining brightly; and, having obtained from the farmer several boats, in two hours Clark and his men were all safely across the stream, eighty yards wide at that point. The little force now all sat down in a circle to hold a consultation as to the future operations. Clark, in a low, earnest manner, said to his men:

"Soldiers! We are near the enemy who have so long annoyed us, and whom we have been for years endeavoring to reach and punish. We are not fighting alone for liberty and independence but for the defense of our own frontiers from the tomahawk and scalping-knife of the Indians. We are virtually defending the lives of our women and children, although a long distance from them. These British garrisons furnish the Indians with powder and lead to desolate the frontiers; and they pay gold for human scalps. We must take and destroy these garrisons. The fort before us is one of them, and it must be taken. We cannot retreat. We have no provisions, and must conquer or starve. This is the Fourth of July. We must act to honor it. Let it not be said, in after times, that Virginians were defeated on that memorable day. The fort and town, I repeat, must be taken at all hazards."[19]

Clark was gratified to find the troops in fine spirits, perfectly according with him in the opinion, that "the place must be taken at all hazards."[20] It was now near midnight, when drums were heard beating near the fort, and it was feared, they had been discovered. Clark hurriedly divided his men into three parties; one of which he was himself to lead against the fort, while the others were to surround and attack the town, which was adjoining the fort on the west and north-west. If successful in capturing the Lieutenant Governor, who, it was known, occupied apartments in the fort, Clark's party were to raise a loud hurrah, which was to be the signal for the others to subdivide _ into squads and with a shout, rush upon the place. The fort at Kaskaskia _ sometimes referred to as Fort Gage _ was located near the river bank, on the west side of the stream, a little below the ferry. It was not a very formidable affair. After the destruction of the old fort on the East side of the river, a British officer and twenty soldiers were quartered in the village for several years; and the old Jesuits' lot and buildings, which had been abandoned, were used as the commandant's head-quarters, and the yard picketed in.[21] Here Rocheblave, the Lieutenant Governor, resided, but without any soldiers to maintain a garrison.

Clark's party, piloted by one of the hunters, passed between the fence east of the fort, and the river, when the barking of dogs saluted them from every part of the town.[22] They soon reached the posterior gate on that side of the fort which had been left open for water purposes[23] when about entering this unguarded avenue, a light was discovered in a small house nearby, and a few men were dispatched to surround it; the occupant of which proved to be a Pennsylvanian, who, disliking the British, was but too ready to lend whatever aid he could. He said there were no sentinels, and lead the way to a place where the pickets were so rotten as to be easily broken down.[24] Thus were two entrances made into the fort almost simultaneously.

Rocheblave was found in bed, fast asleep in an upper room of the fort building. Suddenly aroused from his slumbers, Levi Todd and other officers informed him that he was a prisoner of war, and when he began to realize the situation, he presented a most ludicrous appearance of mingled grimaces, amazement, and distress.[25] From him were taken the keys of the magazine, with his military instructions from his superiors at Mackinaw, Detroit and Quebec, including orders to set the Indians on the Americans, offering them rewards for all the scalps they should produce.[26] As Mrs. Rocheblave was, from motives of delicacy, left undisturbed that night, and her trunks never examined, it was suspected that many other important papers were concealed or destroyed by her[27]. Rocheblave was taken below; and Clark, next hauled down the British ensign, and ran up the American flag, in its place.[28]

Thus, with the utmost quietude, was the fort, together with its commandant, transferred to the possession of Clark, before the citizens of the place had the least intimation of the presence of an enemy, save half a dozen loiterers who had been taken up in the street and immediately put under guard to prevent any alarm being given; for even the frolicking Negroes had previously retired to their homes, and were sharing in the profound slumber of the people generally. The signal shout of Clark's party now suddenly resounding through the village, was instantly caught up by the others in every part of the town, and was well calculated to startle the sleeping populace, filling their minds with intensest wonder and apprehension. By pre-concerted arrangement, the hunters and others with the invaders, who could speak the French language, ran through the several streets proclaiming the capture of the fort and Lieutenant Governor, warning the people to keep within their domiciles; should any appear in the streets, or attempt to escape, they would be instantly shot down.

The soldiers patrolled every part of the town, keeping up a succession of shouts and hurrahs, indicating the presence of a large army. Though there were two hundred and fifty families in the place, and about four hundred men bearing arms, yet not a solitary one escaped to give notice to the neighboring settlements. Everywhere the French inhabitants maintained the utmost seclusion and silence. They had been taught by the British, that the Long Knives, or Bostoni, as they were indifferently called by the Creoles of the country, were savage and unmerciful; and they painfully awaited the final result, whatever it might be.

When parties were sent out during the night to bring the principle citizens before Clark, it was not calculated to allay the fears of the people. To obtain additional information was the object; but little, however, was learned beyond what was already known. Clark himself, at the head of a detachment, appeared at the residence of Gabriel Cerre'; one of the principal merchants of the place, who was particularly inveterate of his feelings against the Americans _ perhaps in consequence of his frequent visits to Mackinaw and Detroit where he heard and imbibed the malicious stories invented by the British officers and their numerous emissaries. Clark peered in at the window. When Mrs. Cerre', a spirited woman, jumped up from her bed, seized an iron poker, threatened to break his head; when the Colonel called his interpreter Michael Perrault, who explained the turn affairs had taken, assuring her that Colonel Clark was only seeking her husband, intending no harm to her or her children. After some search, Clark became satisfied that M. Cerre' had gone to St. Louis, on his way to Mackinaw with a cargo of furs and peltries.[29] In the course of the night, the arms of the inhabitants were demanded and conveyed to the quarters of the Virginians.

This was an extraordinary conquest _ not a gun fired _ not a drop of blood shed; achieved by considerably less than half the number of armed citizens- soldiery of the place. A man of military genius had planned and executed the expedition. He had yet a difficult task to perform _ to win over the people to his interests; but he was equal to the emergency. The next morning, after a plentiful repast, provided for the troops by Richard Winston, and Daniel Murray, two American residents there, several of the principal militia officers of the place were apprehended, and put in irons. Soon after, Pierre Gibault, the village priest, waited upon Clark, accompanied by five or six elderly gentlemen. They were shown into the room where Clark was sitting with his officers, all of whom were in a most dilapidated condition, dirty, unshaven, and unkempt; but little clothing, and that badly torn by briers and bushes on their journey, with blankets thrown over their shoulders fastened with thorn pins. The good priest was at a loss whom to address, when Clark invited him and his associates to seats, and inquired the object of their mission. Gibault frankly said, that as the inhabitants expected to be separated from their families, and perhaps from each other, he begged that they might be permitted to spend some time in the village church on that Sabbath morning, and take their leave of each other. Clark carelessly remarked that he had nothing to say with regard to their religion; that he had no objection to the meeting being held as requested, but desired that the people be informed, that they must not venture out of town. Attempting additional conversation, Clark pretended that he had not leisure to hear them further, and curtly dismissed them, leaving on their minds the impression that any further interviews would not be agreeable to him. The whole town gathered at the church; Clark, meanwhile, forbidding his men to enter the temporarily abandoned houses of the people. After the dismissal of the meeting, Priest Gibault, with a deputation of the principal men, again repaired to Clark's quarters to return grateful thanks for the indulgence afforded him and his people; and while recognizing their present situation as the result of war, and yielding uncomplainingly to the loss of their property, they pled that the fathers might not be separated from their families; that the women and children might be permitted to retain some of their clothing together with a small quantity of provisions. In behalf of the people, Priest Gibault declared, that their conduct had been influenced by their commandant's, whose orders they had been taught they were bound to obey; that their opportunities of information were indeed limited, and they knew but little of the causes of the American war, and had even expressed their sympathies in behalf of the Colonies so far as they dared do in their situation. The great burden of their hearts was to secure lenity for the women and children.

Clark, of all of the western leaders of his day, had the clearest insight into human nature; and could best adapt himself to the management of men, whether his own troops, the Illinois French, or the yet simpler Indians. The opportunity had now arrived for which he had been directing all his artful maneuvers _ when the people felt that they had little to hope from their savage and unmerciful conquerors. He now abruptly addressed them in a tone of mingled surprise and kindness:

"Do you suppose," he inquired, "that you are addressing savages? I am certain you do, judging from the tenor of your conversation. Do you suppose that we mean to strip women and children of their clothing, or take the bread from their mouths; or make war on helpless innocency, or on the church? It was to put a stop to the effusion of blood by the Indians, instigated by the British commandants and their emissaries, that constrained us to visit you, and not the prospect of plunder; and, as soon as this object is obtained, we shall be perfectly satisfied. As the good King of France has joined the Americans, there is a probability of the war being brought to an early and successful close."

After explaining the nature of the dispute as clearly as he could, Clark continued: "I am sorry to find you have been taught to harbor so base an opinion of the Americans and their cause. It is certain that as a conquered people, you are, by the fate of war, at my mercy; but it is my purpose not to enslave you, as you imagine. Give me some surety of your zeal and attachment to the American cause, and you shall immediately enjoy all the privileges of our Government, and your property be fully secured to you.

"I will be more liberal still. You and your people are at liberty to take whichever side you please _ that of the Americans and King of France, or of Great Britain _ without any danger of losing your property, or having your families distressed at our hands. As for the church, all religions are tolerated by the new Republic; and so far from our intermeddling with it, any insult offered would be promptly punished. And to convince you, that we are not the savages and plunderers you were taught to believe, return to your families and friends and inform them to go and conduct themselves as usual, with all freedom, and without the least apprehension of danger. From the information I have obtained since my arrival among you, I am convinced that you have hitherto been influenced by false representations from your leaders. I am willing to forgive everything of the past; and your friends in confinement shall be immediately liberated, the guards withdrawn from every part of the town, excepting from the house and goods of M. Carre'. I shall only expect a strict compliance with a Proclamation I shall immediately issue."[30]

The delegation of Kaskaskians were very sensibly effected, both by the strange news of the French alliance, and Clark's unexpected generosity to them. They hastened away at Clark's suggestion, to relieve the anxieties of the people; and in a few minutes the good news spread from house to house, when the deepest dejection was changed to the most enthusiastic delight. The bell was rung and the church quickly crowded with excited, happy people, returning thanks to God for their deliverance. Clark adds, that their expressive joy may be more easily imagined than described.

The American commander now promptly set free the militia officers and restored their arms to the people, who, with hardy unanimity, took the oath of allegiance to the United States _ the friend and ally of their beloved France. That evening Captain Bowman set off, with thirty men, and a few volunteer Frenchmen, all mounted on French ponies, for Prairie Du Rocher, St. Phillips, and Cahokia, the latter some sixty miles up the country; the two former he reached the first night and Cahokia the next, the people of all of these settlements quickly submitting to the new order of things.[31]

Nor was Clark's success less decisive with the Indians, who, from enemies were soon converted into friends, by his peculiar tact and management. Thus was a peaceful conquest of the Illinois country effected, and the American Flag floated over the land unstained by human blood. The Indians in all that quarter were either pacificated or disconcerted, while the British at Detroit were not a little vexed and perplexed at the turn affairs had taken.

Henry Hamilton, the British Lieutenant Governor of Detroit, alarmed at Clark's conquest of the Illinois settlements, from which Detroit was largely dependent for food supplies, resolved upon their recapture. Clark had, in the Summer, sent Captain Helm to command at Vincennes, unable, however to supply him with any troops for a garrison; and this officer was necessarily compelled to yield to Hamilton's superior force in December. The moment Clark heard of this advance of the British, he clearly realized the situation and his duty; "I must either take Hamilton," he said, "or he will take me." Should Hamilton's plan prove successful, not only the Illinois country, but the Kentucky and other frontier settlements would, in all probability, fall into his hands.

So Clark, early in February, 1779, set out with one hundred and seventy six men, sixty of whom were French volunteers; forty six of the number were dispatched under Lieutenant John Rogers in a large batteau, with artillery and stores to go around by water;[32] while he and the remaining hundred and thirty commenced their march by land across the country, nearly a hundred and fifty miles, at a season of the year when much of the route was submerged by water. Sixteen days were consumed in this remarkable march _ wading "sometimes to the neck for more than a league" _ sometimes, even, breaking the ice before them _ carrying those exhausted, or benumbed with cold, in their two canoes _ many days without food of any kind _ Clark always plunging into the water, and leading the van, sometimes placing the drummer boy on the shoulders of a stalwart sergeant, beating the charge from his lofty perch, and sometimes directing his best singers to lead off in a spirited song to animate the men in their trying situation. No murmur escaped their lips, though encountering indescribable difficulties and hardships, far surpassing anything they had ever experienced, though they had passed all their lives on the frontiers. "No provisions of any sort now for two days. Hard fortune!" Such is an entry in Captain Bowman's Journal. The next day they fortunately killed a deer _ a single deer for one hundred and twenty-eight half starved men, for two of their number had left them to meet and hasten forward Roger's batteau party. Then followed another long fast, Bowman recording, the second day: "No provisions yet. Lord help us!" But, the next day, they reached Vincennes, the French people residing some distance outside the fort, relieving their distresses. Then, forgetting all of their sufferings and without awaiting the arrival of the artillery, they laid siege to Fort Sackville, plying their sharp-sighted rifles with such dexterity and success, that Hamilton, after a two days' attack, was compelled, on the twenty-fifth of February, to surrender himself and eighty officers and men prisoners of war, though having several mounted cannon to aid them in their defense.

Whether viewed from the stand-point of desperate daring, the uncommon sufferings of the men composing it, or its important political result, this expedition must ever be regarded as one of the most singular and adventurous, from its inception to its termination, recorded in the annals of American history _ appropriately compared, by John Randolph, of Roanoke, to Hannibal's celebrated passage of the Thrasimiine marsh.[33] Clark, in 1778, conquered the Illinois country, but, in 1779, he saved it _ completely turning the tables on his enemies, capturing those who had planned his destruction; confounding the British authorities, and disconcerting their Indian allies.

Washington spoke of his "activity and address;" "I know the greatness of his mind," exclaimed Jefferson; Marshall commended his "great courage, uncommon hardihood, and capacity for Indian warfare;" while Patrick Henry, Mason and Madison, united in expressing their high appreciation of the importance of his services. Even the British recognized the "extraordinary activity and unwearied spirit"[34] of Clark. And Franklin, in after years, greeted him with the high compliment _ "You have given an empire to the Republic!" That empire is the opulent North West, between the Ohio, the Great Lakes, and the Mississippi, in which hundreds of millions of dollars have been realized by the General Government from the public domain, while Clark, by whose genius it was acquired, died in poverty and neglect.

Chapter Twenty Five

<u>Indian</u> <u>Attack</u> <u>on</u> <u>Boonesboro</u>
September, 1778.

 <u>Daniel</u> <u>Boone</u>, the hero of the "Big Siege of Boonesborough," in September, 1778, as it was ever after designated by the pioneers of Kentucky, was a native of Oley, Berks County, Pennsylvania, born October twenty-second, 1734.[1] In his youthful days, his parents removed first to Virginia, and then to the western part of North Carolina. For many years he indulged in the chase, ever seeking out new regions where game abounded in the sylvan forests.
 After a variety of adventures consequent upon his settlement in Kentucky in 1775, repelling several Indian attacks on Boonesborough, he at length, in February, 1778, led a party of twenty-six men to the Salt Springs on Licking, since better known as the Lower Blue Licks, to procure a supply of the necessary article of salt for the use of the garrison. Leaving his companions busily engaged in evaporating the saline waters, Boone strolled away some miles distant hunting game for their food; and, while thus employed, all unconscious of danger, he was surprised by a party of Shawnees under Black Fish, and a few Frenchmen from Detroit. Not willing to yield himself a prisoner without an effort to escape, he made a rapid race for his liberty; but after running half a mile, in a blinding snow storm, hotly pursued by three fleet young warriors, who fired several ineffectual shots at him, he was at length compelled to surrender.
 Boone was peculiarly a man of policy, when he had reason to believe it would stand him a good turn. Happily adopting himself to his situation, and learning that the enemy were destined against Boonesborough, he set his wits at work to change their purpose. He knew that the picketing of the fort was in a weak and decayed condition; that but few men were there, to resist the attack of such a force; and, moreover, they might well be taken by surprise, in an unguarded condition in the midst of winter, when Indians were seldom known to engage on a distant hostile expedition. He finally told Black Fish that all his young men were making salt near by; these, he would induce to give themselves up as prisoners without resistence; but insisted, that, to undertake to convey the old people, women and children from Boonesborough, at that inclement season of the year,

through a wilderness of nearly two hundred miles, to the Shawnee towns, would be attended with the greatest suffering, and many would perish by the way. He contended if he surrendered to them his young men at the Salt Springs, they ought to be satisfied; and, in the coming Summer, he would accompany them to Boonesborough, and then the people could be removed without distress or serious inconvenience. Boone's diplomacy, enforced, with his persistent earnestness and apparent candor, prevailed; and, piloting Black Fish's party to the salt boilers, explained to them what he had done, and the reason for it, when they reluctantly surrendered themselves prisoners of war. After a tedious march, they at length reached the Indian towns in a half starved condition.[2]

Black Fish adopted Boone as his son, and dignified him with the new name of Skel-ton-ee, or the Big Turtle. For several months, he bore his captivity with great equanimity, conciliating the Indians by his success as a hunter, and ready adaptation to the Indians' modes of life. A fellow captive, William Hancock, restive under his own condition, wondered that Boone could go about whistling and apparently contented, while torn from his family and friends, and living on food prepared so filthily. During this period he was taken to Detroit, where he so impressed Lieutenant Governor Hamilton with the idea of his loyalty _ justifiable duplicity, Boone thought, in war-time _ that he made an earnest effort to redeem him from captivity, offering Black Fish one hundred pounds sterling for his release, with a view of sending Boone home on parole. The old chief's refusal of this liberal reward, is decisive evidence of the strong attachment he had formed for his adopted son. Sometimes, to while away the time, Boone would go out into the field, and voluntarily assist in planting or hoeing corn; observing which, Black Fish, regarding such labor as unbecoming men and warriors, would remark: "My son; you need not engage in such drudgery; your mother can easily raise corn enough for my family; and for yours also, when we bring them from Kentucky."

It was now arranged, by the Shawnees, that they would carry into effect the scheme of transferring the Boonesborough people to Chillicothe. By the middle of June the Indians began to gather for the expedition to Kentucky, when Boone concluded that it was now time to make his escape, and apprise his friends of the impending danger. Seeking the earliest opportunity, and taking with him an old gun, with a few charges of powder and ball, he dashed off, near night, on an Indian pony. He rode rapidly all night, and till about ten o'clock the next day, when his horse gave out and he abandoned him. After crossing the Ohio on a raft, constructed of dry saplings, he reached, on the fourth day of his flight, the forks of the three branches of the Flat Fork of Johnson's creek, about three miles southeast of the present village of May's Lick, Mason County, Kentucky, where he killed a deer, struck fire, and roasted some of the venison, enjoying his only meal from the time he escaped from the Indians till he reached Boonesborough, where he arrived the next day _ a distance traveled of one hundred and eighty miles.[3]

The startling intelligence brought by Boone, roused the occupants of the garrison to the greatest efforts to prepare for the coming storm. Ten days were spent in repairing the decayed picketing, and spies were kept on the alert. On the seventeenth of July, William Hancock, one of Boone's fellow salt-boilers, reached Boonesborough, not being so good a woodsman as Boone, he had been twelve days, enduring much suffering in accomplishing the journey. He reported, that, in consequence of Boone's escape, the Indians had postponed their march three weeks; that, on the fifth of July, the principle Indians of the different tribes had assembled at Chillicothe, where they were met by twelve Frenchmen from Detroit, two of whom were Captains, and one an Ensign, who distributed many British presents among the warriors; that it was resolved to embody four hundred men to march against Boonesborough, with four swivels, which latter were to be transported in boats down the Miami and Ohio, and up the Kentucky. Upon their arrival at the point of destination, they were to make a tender of the British flag; if not accepted, to batter down the fort or lay around it living on the cattle and crops, and starving out the garrison. The next day, Boone wrote to the nearest settlement on Holston in Virginia, over two hundred miles distant, that they expected the enemy in twelve days, and would lay up supplies for a siege; that they had good crops growing, and were resolved to fight hard to secure them; and that if relief could be sent them within five or six weeks, it would be of infinite service[4] _ thus intimating that he thought the garrison could stand a siege of three or four weeks.

Six weeks had elapsed since Hancock's arrival, and yet no indication of the enemy. It became apparent, that they had either still further postponed their expedition, or abandoned it altogether. Weary of the uncertainty, and anxious to unravel it, Boone led a party of nineteen men, toward the close of August, across the Ohio, against the Shawnee town on Paint Creek, a western tributary of the Scioto, hoping to take a prisoner and learn the intentions of the enemy. Within four miles of the town they met a party of some thirty warriors, evidently on their way to join the main body on their march from Chillicothe; the enemy were repulsed, losing one killed and two wounded. Hastening back, Boone passed, undiscovered, the enemy army on the fifth of September at the Lower Blue Licks, and reached Boonesborough the next day.

On Monday, the seventh of September, about ten o'clock in the morning, the Indian force, having crossed the Kentucky a mile and a half above Boonesborough, at a point ever since known as Black Fish's Ford, made its appearance, marching along the hill south of the fort, in single file, some on horseback, displaying English and French flags, the whole numbering about four hundred,[5] including several Frenchmen, and a Negro named Pompey, who had long lived with the Indians. Black Fish, Moluntha, Black Hoof and Black Beard were the principle Indian leaders, and Captain Isidore Chêne, of the Indian Department, represented the British authorities. They brought no swivels to assist in the siege.

Boone, with his rifle in hand, was outside the fort when the enemy marched within view. Soon Pompey, playing the part of interpreter, presented himself with a white flag, a hundred and fifty yards off, and mounting the cornfield fence, inquired in a loud voice, if Captain Boone was there? Boone replied affirmatively. Pompey then announced that Black Fish had letters for him from Governor Hamilton, of Detroit; and that the Governor and Indians expected him to fulfill his promise of peacefully surrendering the fort and garrison. Directed to return and bring the letters, Pompey repaired to the Indians, when Black Fish sent an urgent message to Boone to come out to him _ and, as a token of good faith, sent him seven roasted buffalo tongues. Black Fish, though a considerable distance away, discovering Boone, called out, addressing him by his adopted name of Skel-towee, and renewing the invitation to come out to him. Boone now resolved, with the approval of his friends, to venture to have an interview with the chief; and designated a certain stump between them, where he would meet him and receive the letters. Boone went forth fearlessly to where Pompey was, at the cornfield, thence both went together and met Black Fish.

After a cordial hand-shaking, the old chief chidingly inquired: "My son, what made you leave me in the manner you did?" "I wanted," Boone replied, "to see my wife and children so much, that I could not stay any longer." "Had you only told me so," responded Black Fish, "you could have gone at any time and I would have rendered you every assistance." The old chief, having an eye to business, reminded Boone of his promise to surrender the fort and people, and demanded its fulfillment. He now delivered Hamilton's letter and proclamation, advising Boone to give up the fort in accordance with his pledge; that it would be folly for him and his friends to attempt resistance against so powerful a force; that should they have the temerity to offer opposition, the massacre of men, women, and children would be the probable consequence. Should he and his people quietly submit to be taken to Detroit, and become British subjects, they would be treated well and, such of them as held offices should be continued in the same rank with the loss of all property in making the transfer of residence made good.

When Boone had perused the documents, Black Fish eagerly asked how he liked them? Boone adroitly replied that the Indians had detained him so long a prisoner, that other commanders had been appointed, and he must consult with them before an answer could be given. Black Fish then said: "My son, there is a heavy cloud hanging over this country. This is called the Bloody Land, you know; we have had much war, and whoever gets the first fire, always beats. Now I am come to take you easy; I have brought forty horses for the old people, women and children to ride."

Meanwhile, the chief, Moluntha, had made his appearance, and said, abruptly: "You killed my son the other day over the Ohio River." Boone answered that he had not been there. "It was you," replied Moluntha, "I tracked you here." Some conversation followed about the nature of the war. Boone finally demanded two days for himself and people to read and consider the letter and proclamation, which was agreed to. Boone's object was to gain time, as he expected re-inforcements from the Holston. Black Fish remarked that his warriors were hungry, when

Boone, knowing full well they would take what they wanted, concluded to make a merit of it, and said: "There, you see plenty of cattle and corn; take what you need _ only let none be wasted." Both parties now retired. The Indians immediately commenced whooping and yelling, some shooting down cattle and others gathering corn.

Hamilton's letter and proclamation were now submitted to the people. As to himself, Boone declared that he had never the remotest idea of giving up Boonesborough to the enemy, that what he had said to the Indians and Hamilton on that head, when in duress, was only to curry favor and win confidence and that he was for resisting to the last extremity. Squire Boone, his younger brother, said, warmly, "he would never give up; but would fight until he died." Richard Calloway, William Bailey Smith, John Holder, David Gass, and, indeed, all the leading men _ and women too, for that matter _ were decidedly opposed to accepting the invitation to take a trip to Detroit, or yielding to the enemy in any particular. "Well, well," responded Daniel Boone, "I'll die with the rest of you." It was now agreed, as a stroke of policy, to amuse the Indians as long as possible in order to gain time for the hoped-for succor from Holston.

Some further interviews took place that day between the respective diplomats _ Boone asking for explanations of the submitted documents, and declaring that his people demanded plenty of time to consider matters of such grave importance. Black Fish, who at first seemed to put confidence in Boone's surrender of the fort and garrison, now began to give evident indications of distrust and urged his compliance with his former promises; and exhibited a wampum-belt, having a white, red, and black row of beads, indicative of either peace, war, or a solemn warning of evil. During the ensuing night, great vigilance was exercised, lest a surprise should be attempted; but the Indians remained quiet. Nor did anything material transpire the next day, save that the respective parties became quite familiar, the Indians complementing some of the women as "pretty squaws," who fearlessly sauntered out to the spring, about one hundred and fifty yards west of the fort for water and to which the Indians also appear to have resorted for their supply. The officious Pompey twice that day rode up a very indifferent pony, offering to trade him for a rifle, in which he met with no success. Some of the men in the fort could scarcely be restrained from shooting him.

Boone recognized it as a critical period with the garrison. Old and young, white and black, they numbered sixty persons capable of bearing arms; only forty, however, were really effective.[6] "Death," said Boone, "was preferable to captivity." They resolved to make a determined defense. A portion of the cattle and horses were brought into the fort; and a supply of wild meat and of corn from the fields, had previously been provided. To impress the enemy with the strength of the garrison, the men were mounted on the walls and cabins with their rifles in hand, while the women, dressed in surplus hats and hunting shirts, armed with guns, powder horns and bullet-pouches, marched and countermarched within the fort, with the big gate open so the Indians at a distance could plainly observe their evolutions. And still further to inculcate on the minds of the enemy the idea of a numerous garrison, mere women and children at Boone's suggestion repeatedly united in raising their loudest yells of defiance.

Black Fish and his warriors began to exhibit signs of uneasiness and called out to Boone to give a definite answer to their summons to surrender and march to Detroit. Finally, towards evening, Boone, Colonel Callaway, and several others, went out about thirty yards, within the protection of the guard of the garrison, however, and met Black Fish and an Indian deputation. Both parties were unarmed, as they had previously agreed upon. Boone frankly informed the Indians that his people would not consent to go to Detroit, and were determined to defend the fort while a man was living. "Now," he continued, addressing Black Fish, who stood an attentive listener, "we laugh at all your formidable preparations; but thank you for giving us notice and time to provide for our defense. Your efforts will not prevail, for our gate shall forever deny you admittance."

The Indian deputies now appeared disappointed and surly. The apparent strength of the garrison, the new palisades and bastions, must have had a disheartening affect on Black Fish; so he thought it the wiser course to resort to stratagem. He declared that Governor Hamilton did not wish to destroy their lives; and, since they seemed averse to going to Detroit, if nine of the principle men of the garrison would come out to the Indian camp, or within the enclosure, he and his associates would meet them, enter into friendly negotiations and retire with his warriors to their villages. "This," observed Boone, "sounded grateful to our ears, and we agreed to the proposal;" and, all the more readily since the Indians of the Illinois country had just entered into treaties of peace with Colonel Clark. Black Fish might be sincere; at all events, it was the wiser course to exhaust all the resources of diplomacy and strategy.

Some difficulty ensued in agreeing upon a proper place for holding the treaty; Boone declaring it would not do to have it held in the fort, as the women and children were afraid of Indians, but the real objection was, that it might end in a surprise and massacre, as at Mackinaw, fifteen years before, and as attempted at Detroit by Pontiac. Nor would he consent to meet beyond the reach of the guns of the fort, at the Indian camp. A green plot, about sixty yards distant, directly in front of the big gate, and near a Lick, was chosen _ "on purpose," says Boone, "to divert them from a breach of honor, as we could not avoid suspicions of the savages." This conference lasted a considerable time, during which Squire Boone took occasion to remark, that an army was then on its march from Virginia under Colonel Clark; which information, though not strictly sure, so far as Clark was concerned, excited manifest uneasiness. The wily Black Fish insisted on being accompanied at the treaty by eighteen Indians, so that each town or village of the Indians should be represented, otherwise the treaty would not be regarded as binding. Boone combated this proposition for a while; but finally yielded to it, under the belief, that while treachery was contemplated, yet he trusted to the superior strength and dexterity of himself and associates. That evening Black Fish was seen walking around the fort and viewing it carefully; and, soon after, the Indians were observed holding a council, and performing the war-dance. All these were regarded as additional evidences of hostile designs on the part of the enemy.

On Wednesday, the ninth of September, this singular diplomacy was renewed _ wiles and stratagems on the part of the stoics of the woods, successfully counteracted and supplemented by Boone and his vigilant companions. That morning the cattle were hovering around the fort, exhibiting signs of uneasiness, as usual, when Indians were about; when a few of the enemy were seen loitering in the neighborhood, they were told that the "white squaws" were afraid to venture out to milk the cows, they had the gallantry to aid in driving the stock into the fort. Once there, they were of course, retained; securing, altogether, about sixty head. They were thus saved from wanton destruction and from furnishing support to the enemy, and at the same time, providing additional subsistence for the garrison.

But few Indians were anywhere seen, which Boone regarded as ominous of the expected attack. The forenoon was occupied in preparing the dinner for those who were to participate in the treaty. Tables, chairs, knives, forks and pewter plates were taken out; and among the nicely cooked dishes were bear and buffalo tongues. The good house-wives of the garrison made an extra effort to provide a plentiful repast, in the best style, so as to impress the Indians with the fact that they had a great abundance of food in the fort _ sufficient for any emergency. At noon the dinner was partaken of by the white and Indian commissioners, with an evident relish on the part of Black Fish and his red comrades; after which, the furniture was taken back to the fort.

Associated with Boone in making the treaty, were Colonel Callaway, Major Smith, Captain William Buchanan, Squire Boone, Flanders Callaway, John Smith, Sen., Edward Bradley and a man named Crabtree, who far surpassed ordinary men in size, strength and action. As the day was warm, they had divested themselves of any unnecessary clothing before leaving the fort, that they might be the better prepared for any rough-and-tumble work, if forced upon them; and Boone had taken the precaution to give the most explicit orders, that every part of the stockade should be strictly guarded, and the port-holes, in the bastion nearest the treaty-ground, manned with twenty-five of the very best marksmen, with their rifles ready loaded and primed, their eyes on the sites and fingers on the triggers. They were specially charged, the moment the Indians should betray the least treachery, to fire at the group, whites and Indians, as they would be more likely, two to one, to hit an Indian than a white man. So sudden and well-directed a volley, it was thought, would throw the enemy into confusion, and cover the retreat of Boone and his companions to the fort.

Observing two or three Indians hanging about, Boone called Black Fish's attention to their presence, who promptly ordered them away. When reminded that young warriors had been substituted for old chiefs at the council board, Black Fish adroitly replied that the change had been made to gratify the young men, who were anxious to witness the proceedings of the treaty. All were at length seated, two Indians on each side of every white man, and the customary pipe was smoked by each of the respective parties. Black Fish proposed to bury the tomahawk, make a lasting peace and thence forward live like brothers; but, as a necessary condition that the people of Boonesborough should agree to abandon the country, which was the Indian hunting ground, and retire to the old settlements. To this requirement, Boone and his friends said they could not consent. Black Fish then asked by what right the white people occupied Kentucky? He was answered that Richard Henderson and company had fairly purchased it of the Cherokees and paid them for it. Turning to a Cherokee Indian present, Black Fish inquired if this were so? The Cherokee frankly admitted it. After a little pause, as though somewhat disconcerted at this turn in the discussion, the old chief remarked, that this being so, the white people might live there in peace; only they must take the oath of British allegiance, submit to the authority of Governor Hamilton of Detroit; that while the Ohio should be the boundary between them, yet both parties might peaceably hunt on either side of the river; but there should be no robbery of each other's hunting camps, or stealing of horses. To these terms, the white diplomats agreed, seeming to regard the transfer of their allegiance as a mere subterfuge for the occasion. Black Fish declared, in the usual Indian style, that the treaty should be alike binding on both parties as long as the trees should grow, or the water run down the Kentucky.

A good deal of ceremony was used, as is generally the case in Indian treaties, shaking hands, smoking pipes, and making speeches. One of the white party, on this occasion, acted as secretary, putting the articles into writing which were formally signed. Black Fish, who was the guiding spirit of his people, and took the entire lead of the Indians at this treaty, remarked, that it remained for him to step aside a little distance and "give out the big talk to his young men, that they might fully understand that a firm peace had been made." Taking his position, he made quite a lengthy speech in his native language, in a very loud, impassioned manner, as if addressing his warriors at a considerable distance from him; but few of whom however, were anywhere to be seen during the treaty. He spoke in finely modulated tones, exhibiting much of the grace and ease of an accomplished orator.

Returning to the treaty circle, Black Fish requested both white and Indian deputies to rise up, cautioning Boone and his fellow commissioners not to be afraid; that it was usual with the Indians when exchanging tokens of friendship to shake hands singly; but when they concluded a treaty designed to be long and lasting, they shook "long hands" _ two Indians embracing each white man, so as to bring their hearts close together. This seeming friendship, but really dissembled treachery, however cunningly devised and carried into effect, deceived no one. Boone and his companions resolved to see the strange performance through, whether comedy or tragedy, feeling themselves fully equal to the occasion. So, suiting the action to the word, Black Fish and another Indian advanced, with extended arms, towards Boone, who evinced no distrust; and while the old Indian chief interlocked his right arm in Boone's left; and with his left hand seized Boone's left one, the other Indian did the same on Boone's right; and thus were all the whites embraced, or attempted to be, by their allotted opposing deputies, in this singular mode of confirming the treaty. At this moment, Black Fish exclaimed, "go!" _ when an Indian rose up at some little distance, from his place of concealment, and quickly drawing a gun from under his blanket, fired it in the air as a preconcerted signal to all the Indians to be ready for the conflict. The Indian deputies instantly attempted to drag the white men down the clay bank, a few steps off, under cover of which they would be protected from the guns of the garrison; but in this effort they were completely foiled.

The moment the perfidy was apparent, the marksmen in the bastion fired a volley at the Indians, which prostrated with a mortal wound one of those who had hold of Major Smith, and evidently had its effect in disconcerting the others. Colonel Callaway was the first to break loose from the Indians. Boone, in the excitement of the moment, threw Black Fish flat upon the ground, and pretty hard at that; when the other Indian let go of his hold. At this instant, a disengaged savage, who had carried around the pipe-tomahawk for the treaty-makers to smoke in council, and had no special part assigned him in the "long hand" _ shaking ceremony, aimed a blow at Boone with the tomahawk, which, however, partially missed its object, as he was in a posture bending forward, ready to run, the handle striking across the back of his head, cutting a gash through the scalp two inches in length while the tomahawk edge inflicted a lesser wound between the shoulders. A second blow aimed at him, he dexterously avoided, Major Smith, passing rapidly by at the moment, receiving it, the force of which, however, being almost spent, caused but a slight wound.

John South, a large, fleshy man, who had passed middle age, came very near being dragged into a gully leading to the Lick flat; but, with a powerful effort, he sent one of the Indians whirling fully a rod from him down the descending ground, and escaped from the grasp of the other. Crabtree, Squire Boone, Bradley, Gass and Flanders Callaway, renewed by the unusual excitement of the occasion, shook of the Indians almost as easily as though they had been so many children; and, thus extricated, they quickly made their way to the fort. When some fifteen paces from the council table, Squire Boone received a ball grazing one shoulder and the back-bone, and lodging in the other shoulder, knocking him down. He fell partly on the fort side of a small hickory tree but instantly recovering himself, he ran for the gate, through which all had passed, save himself and South, and which was now closed. Quickly repairing to the door of a cabin, between the gate and the bastion nearest the treaty-ground, which had previously been designated in case the gate was shut, they were admitted.

As the parties to the treaty were precluded from carrying their arms, Boone had instructed his fellow deputies to leave their guns loaded, close to the gate, where they could snatch them up conveniently on their return to the fort; so well persuaded was he of a hostile result to all these anxious efforts. He always contended, that it was the timely volley from the garrison, and perhaps the fall of their old war chief, supposing him killed, that so confused and dismayed the Indians as to enable him and his associates so successfully to extricate themselves from the grasp of their enemies, and escape without receiving a single fatal wound. This was indeed wonderful, as not less than two hundred shots were discharged at them by the Indians, who were concealed behind the clay bank, bushes, logs, stumps and fences, in every direction, where they had carefully secreted themselves the preceding night, and the few loiterers who had been seen carelessly sauntering around some little distance away, now seized their arms where they had conveniently deposited them, and instantly took part in the contest. Under all circumstances, with such fearful odds against them, the escape of the nine treaty-makers seemed almost miraculous.

The action of Boone and his associates, in thus risking their lives, might seem a reckless adventure; but the fact that every expedient was resorted to by these sagacious men, to gain time for the expected succor from Holston, was unknown to the early writers on Western history; and, wherever known, must completely exonerate Boone and his companions from any hasty and unmerited censure. "They may say what they please of Boone," said Simon Kenton, "he acted with wisdom in that matter!"[7]

The first gun fired after the Indian's preconcerted signal was by William Stafford. He was posted on the south-west bastion, which was nearest the treaty ground, and had his gun ready poised, pointing at an Indian sitting on a log some little distance beyond the council, witnessing the proceedings, and awaiting, as he no doubt expected, a tragic result. The savage was well bedecked with brooches, half-moons, and other silver ornaments; and Stafford was thinking what a conspicuous mark he would make, when the signal gun fired, and amid the yell that attended the attempted seizure of the white deputies, he discharged his rifle, instantly killing the chief, for such his appearance proclaimed him. His body lay where it fell till carried off by his companions the ensuing night. A counterpart to this incident occurred at the same moment at the south-east bastion. Ambrose Coffee lay stretched at full length on the upper log of that bastion, carelessly viewing the progress of the treaty, little dreaming that he was the target for concealed Indian marksmen; for no less than fourteen bullet holes at the first general fire, were made in his clothes, when he tumbled down into the building unhurt, and was subsequently no little jeered for the folly of his unconcerned exposure.

Soon after the attack commenced, Pemberton Rollins had a bone of his arm broken above the elbow; the ball having passed through the thin part of two adjoining pickets, not sufficiently protected by a third one overlapping the joint.

The suddenness of the attack, the rushing into the fort of the treaty commissioners, some of them wounded, the almost simultaneous accident to Coffee, together with the terrific yells of the savages without, and the answering shouts of the men within, all combined to alarm the more timid of the women and children, who cried and screamed piteously; supposing the place was being stormed, and all would become victims to the merciless knife and tomahawk. To add to the excitement of the scene, the dogs raised a furious baying, while the cattle in the fort ran about in wild confusion.

Upon reaching the garrison, from the treaty so suddenly broken off, Daniel Boone at once went around from point to point, encouraging the men. All had previously had their places assigned them, in case an attack should be made on the fort; and, in accordance with this arrangement, Squire Boone, seizing his loaded gun as he entered the fort, ran to his designated place in the south-west bastion, and soon discharged its contents at the enemy. While reloading, in attempting to push down the ball, he discovered his shoulder pained so much, that he requested his brother, now coming in, to ram down the bullet for him. But the pain of his wound increasing, he was compelled to retire to his cabin, where his brother, when a lull occurred in the firing, extracted the ball from his shoulder, and the invalid had a light broad axe placed beside his bed declaring he would wield it as long as he could in case the Indians should break into the fort. Not until he had gone the rounds of the garrison, and, by his cool intrepidity, had re-assured all classes, did Daniel Boone have his own wound dressed.

During the afternoon, the Indians made a rush towards the fort, as though they designed scaling the pickets, but were soon beaten back to their lurking places. Proper care had not been taken to cut down all of the trees and bushes within shooting range and burn up the logs and stumps. At the base of the hills, southeast of the garrison, the Lick Branch took its rise, passing through the flat south of the stockade, and entering the river eight or ten rods below; and along the Branch, just above the spring, west of the fort, were a few sycamores. A couple of small hickories were standing near the treaty ground and about forty yards above the south-east bastion, stood the "divine elm tree," under which the law-givers of the Kentucky settlements had assembled in 1775. There were also quite a number of trees beyond the big elm, in the same direction, some on the hill-side to the south-east, and along the river opposite the stockade. The abrupt clay bank skirting the Lick Branch, next the fort, was some half dozen feet high, with the open flat beyond, affording ample concealment for the Indians, extending almost from the Indian encampment a little below the high land, south-east of the garrison, circling partly around the fort to the river below; and the river bank also furnished a place of convenient shelter. The locality of the fortification was injudiciously chosen, as the enemy from the hills, on either side of the Kentucky, could command a full view of what transpired within the enclosure. The fort was a parallelogram containing fully three-fourths of an acre of ground, located on a second bank, nearly sixty yards from the river; which was about a hundred yards wide. From the high bluff on the northern bank of the stream. with no intervening bottom as on the south side, the Indians could send an occasional ball within the stockade. As they could also from the hill beyond the Lick, which was a somewhat longer shot than the other.

Among the inmates of the fort was an old Dutchman named Matthias Prock, a potter by trade. A coward by instinct, disliking the smell of gunpowder, the moment the attack commenced, he hid himself first under a bed at Colonel Callaway's, and then under the bellows in Squire Boone's adjoining gun-smith shop, from both of which places the courageous Mrs. Callaway drove the coward with her broomstick. Determined to keep himself out of harm's way, he next took refuge in a new well near the old one, and which had been sunk only a few feet deep. At this juncture Boone and Callaway came up, severely reproaching him for his cowardice, which constitutional failing he frankly confessed, pleading his occupation of life as an excuse _ that he was only a potter, and not a fighter. He was then told if he would not aid in defending the fort, he should dig in the well. He plied the pick and shovel with considerable zeal so long as he thought he was in the least exposed to the shots of the enemy. When the firing slackened, he ventured to leave his prison-hole, declaring he would not work while the others were resting. Colonel Callaway again ordered him to his task to which Prock demurred, whereupon the Colonel drew his tomahawk, which he always carried in his belt at his side, and gave chase to the delinquent, who, true to his non-resistant principles, betook himself to his heels. He ran directly to the well, jumping into it at a single leap, then some ten or twelve feet deep where he kept himself busily employed a considerable time.

During the first day and night, as well as the second day, of the siege, the enemy kept up a warm and steady fire on the fort, with but few and brief intermissions. Making no apparent impression, new schemes were devised on the part of the Indians and their white allies. The Boonesborough people had that year raised some flax, which was stacked near by; this the Indians, in the night, scattered along a fence running from the lower part of the Lick plot, near the river, to Henderson's Kitchen, which formed the north-west corner or bastion of the fort, and set the flax and rails on fire, expecting the flames would communicate to the buildings; but a hole was dug under the outer wall of the kitchen, through which several men crept, pulled down that end of the fence connecting with the fort, and returned in safety.

On Friday, the eleventh of the month, the river below the stockade was observed to be quite roily, and a noise was heard under the river bank like cutting of roots, while the end of a cedar pole was seen moving, as if used to loosen the dirt. It was at once suspected, that the Indians, led on by their French assistants, were pushing a mine towards the fort from under the river bank, where their operations were concealed, and were throwing the dirt into the stream. Various were the conjectures as to the object they had in view. Some thought a passage-way was intended, to convey powder under the fortification to blow it up; others surmised it was their purpose to construct a tunnel, through which to march a large body of warriors and capture the fort. Two plans were immediately set on foot to frustrate the enemy's purpose, whatever it might be: One, to erect a battery on the top of Henderson's Kitchen, for the double object of observing these new movements of the enemy, and try to dislodge them; the other, to commence in the Kitchen cutting a deep trench or countermine of considerable length, running parallel with the river. The battery was accordingly erected on the Kitchen roof house, six feet high, when something of the enemy's operation was observed and dirt was seen as they cast it from the mine into the river.

The firing that night was the severest on both sides that occurred during the siege. The mingled reports of the fire-arms, echoing back from the surrounding hills, and the vivid flashes of powder, in quick succession, partially displaying the dark forest in the distance, imparted an indescribable solemnity and grandeur to the scene. So constant and bright were the flash of the guns, that the smallest article could be seen in every part of the fort. In the course of the night, an Indian crept to within fifteen steps of the north-west bastion, and posted himself behind a tree, near where the fence had been consumed the preceding night. He there succeeded in maintaining so warm a fire on the garrison, as to attract the particular attention of London, a Negro servant belonging to Nathaniel Henderson,[8] and who was every inch a soldier. Posted in the passage-way dug the previous night under the hill of Colonel Richard Henderson's Kitchen, he there watched his opportunity, in a prostrate condition, to get a good shot at the bold warrior, and fired at the flash of his gun; and London, in turn, became similarly a target for his foe. They snapped their guns several times at each other, only igniting the powder in the pan, and finally the Indians fired clear, and London was hit in the neck, killing him instantly. It was a chance shot, aimed only at the flashing of London's gun, but it proved fatal; and the loss of so good a soldier was a source of unfeigned regret to the whole garrison. During that busy and exciting night, David Bundrin, a Dutchman, who was posted in the south-west bastion, was looking through a port-hole, partly closed with a stone, when a ball stuck on it and split, one part penetrating his forehead, causing his death in a few hours. A little before day, Boone directed the men to cease firing, as they were necessarily shooting at random, uncertain of producing any good effect. The Indians observing the cessation, followed the example.

Perseveringly did the enemy labor at their mine, not venturing, however, to expose themselves as they had done before the erection of the battery. On Saturday morning, Pompey was seen in the aperture of the excavation, near the river, occasionally thrusting up his head to make discoveries, or gratify his curiosity. Two or three ineffectual shots were fired at him from the fort, and in each case the balls were observed to strike the water in the river below. At length William Collins, a fine marksman, took careful aim when Pompey's head next appeared, and fired; the bullet did not, as the others had done, strike the water, and the officious interpreter was neither seen nor heard any more. During the attack, he had frequently called, in a loud voice, upon the garrison to surrender, and sometimes engaged in a species of blackguarding, or bandying words with the men in the bastions. Hearing no more from that loquacious and important personage, and presuming he had been killed, the men in the fort would call out jeeringly, "where's Pompey?" In broken English, it would be replied, that he had gone after more Indians, or that he had gone hog-hunting; and sometimes, "Pompey ne-pan" _ i.e. asleep; but, before their final departure, the savages frankly acknowledged "Pompey nee-poo" _ that he had really been killed.

Boone and his companions prosecuted their countermine with energy. It extended from Henderson's Kitchen or block-house up the river under several adjoining cabins, some two or three feet wide, and several deep; and, while they kept steadily at work, with a relay of hands, they at the same time acted in the additional capacity of a guard against any sudden emerging of the enemy, like so many locusts, from the bowels of the earth. While in the trench, the digging of the Indians could be distinctly heard. Boone had a box so adjusted with ropes and fastenings, as to be able to raise a portion of the dirt to the top of the palisades and throw it over, that the Indians might be convinced that their scheme was fully understood, and the proper means taken to counteract it. In response to inquiries what they were doing down there, the Indians would reply that they were digging a hole, and would blow the garrison to a pretty hot region before morning. "And what are you doing," they would retort. "O, as for that," responded the white people, "we are digging to meet you, and will make a hole large enough to bury five hundred of your Indian carcases."

Holder and some others possessing strong muscular powers, cast large stones, over the cabins and palisades, and down the river bank, which would elicit hearty curses in return, on the part of the Indians, taunting the garrison to "come out and fight like men, and not try to kill them with stones, like children." Old Mrs. South, in the simplicity of her heart, earnestly besought the men "for God's sake not to throw stones at the Indians, for they might hurt them, make them mad, and then they would seek revenge." The good old lady's humane remark, evincing her tender regard for the feelings of the Indians, caused many a jibe and jeer among the men at her expense.

The work on the mine progressed steadily, on the part of the enemy, though it must have been prosecuted under discouraging circumstances, with only sticks and tomahawks for their implements. They had penetrated about forty yards, fully two thirds of the distance from the river to the fort. Fortunately for the beleaguered garrison, there were a succession of showers almost every night; during one of which, near the close of the siege, the earth became so saturated as to cause large portions of that over the subterranean passage to cave in, and thus put an end to the scheme, whatever may have been its purpose. They probably designed by springing a mine to blow up a portion of the works and secure an easy entrance; and, failing in this, to penetrate upwards to the surface near the fort, and thrust through the aperture poles and rails, covered with flax and the dry scaley bark of the hickory tree securely fastened on to be set on fire and leaned against the outside of the cabins, and palisades, and produce a general conflagration. Such huge torches, ready for use, were subsequently found near the entrance of the passage, and this, it was conjectured, was the object for which they were intended. But all these ingenious plans of the enemy, attended with so much toil, and fraught with so much evil, came to naught.

Failing in their underground operations, they again relied chiefly upon their guns, with which they were much more familiar. In the center of the fort stood the flag staff, some fifty feet high, from which defiantly floated the American colors; and, on the top of the staff, was a small wooden gun, made by Squire Boone, which served the purpose of a weathercock. For several days, the Indians directed no little of their firing at the standard, and at length cut off with their repeated shots, the small stem just below the flag, and raised a great rejoicing when it fell to the ground. The men in the fort, not to be thwarted in this way, soon took down the pole, replaced the ensign, and again it floated proudly over their heads, when they in turn raised a loud hurrah. At this demonstration the Indians remained quiet, and made no further attempts to shoot it down again.

Prior to the siege, Squire Boone had directed his ingenuity in the construction of a wooden cannon from a tough black-gum tree, strongly banded with iron; but when tested, it cracked. Making another, still more effectually banded, it was twice tried, and found to answer a very good purpose. Some two hundred yards distant, south-east of the fort, at the lower end of the nursery, the Indians had made quiet a temporary breastwork of rails, behind which a group of them were gathered. By this time Squire Boone, uneasy to share in the excitements and dangers of the contest, though not yet fully recovered of his wound, had ventured out; and, discovering that cluster of warriors, thought it a good opportunity to bring his black-gum cannon into requisition. While Squire was charging it with a swivel ball and some twenty slugs and leaden bullets, his brother opened a sufficient hole in the pickets through which to fire its contents at the enemy. "Those fellows," said Squire Boone, "must be driven from that position." His words were scarcely uttered when he applied the match; and, as he expressed it, "O Lord! how I made the rails and the Indians fly." The Indians, indeed, made a prodigious scampering in every direction, as though a mine had exploded beneath their feet; several of them were thought to have been killed and wounded, and certainly very considerable havoc was made in the peach nursery in that quarter.[9] Either at that shot, or a second one, the cannon cracked, and was necessarily laid aside; but the Indians were afterwards very cautious about collecting together within shooting range of the fort. Sometimes they would inquire, "Why don't you fire your big wooden gun again?" Suspecting, it would seem, its composition from the dullness of its report. They were told in reply, that they would hear from it whenever any considerable number of them should be found together; but that it was not worth their while to be shooting the cannon at a straggling Indian dodging and running about.

Besides preparing refreshments for the men, the women were much employed during the siege, in running bullets, and preparing ball-patches. While Daniel Boone's daughter, Jemima, the wife of Flanders Callaway, was standing in her cabin door, which opened within the fort, with her face inside, busily engaged in suppling her father with ammunition, she was struck in the back by a spent ball, which partly buried itself in the flesh, carrying with it a very small portion of her linen undress, in withdrawing of which the ball fell out. During the whole siege, she partook largely of her father's fearlessness, and seemed to expose herself more than other females in serving the brave defenders of Boonesborough with ammunition and refreshments.

Between the adjoining cabins, doors were cut during the siege, so that a passage could be effected easily around the fort without exposure to the rifles of the Indian sharp-shooters. But there was no protection for the horses and cattle, a few of which were killed, and others wounded, by shots from the bluff over the river, and from the hill south-west of the Lick. Having had but little food and water for many successive days, the cattle had become thin and gaunt; and, poor as they were, the men would dress the beef of nights, thus killed by the enemy, and divide it among the garrison. They did this the more readily as the buffalo meat they had provided for the siege was scant in quantity; and killed in the Summer, was of a poor quality. At one time, the Indians wounded a cow outside of the fort; the frightened animal running to the fort gate, was let in, and slaughtered, furnishing the best meat the garrison had during the attack.

Anticipating the probable attempts of the Indians to fire the fort, Squire Boone had, previous to their arrival, unbreeched several old musket barrels, and provided them with pistons, which would force out from a pint to a quart of water at a time. These squirt-guns were distributed among the women in the different parts of the fort so that they might be prepared to extinguish any fire the enemy might communicate to the roofs of the cabins; and these roofs for additional safety, were generally put on in shed style, sloping but one way, and that within the stockade. Covered with long shingles, which were fortunately fastened but slightly _ with a single wooden peg at the upper end, and a weight-pole at the lower, they could readily be forced off from within.

For several successive nights, the Indians made the greatest efforts to fire the fort. They would collect the long, dry, loose bark of the hickory intermingled with splints, and sometimes flax, all well rubbed with dampened powder, the whole made fast around one end of a stick. The other end serving for a handle, the torch end of the fagot being left loose, like a broom, with which to apply the fire. With these combustible instruments, the enemy would approach as near the fort as they would dare venture and protected by some tree, or the river bank, would aim to hurl them upon the roofs of the cabins. Almost invariably they were sent with such force that they would pass entirely over the cabins into the fort; and, if they happened to lodge, the squirt-guns or punching-poles were brought into a position, thus easily thwarting the designs of the enemy. These torches were well calculated to produce mischief, prepared, as they were, with much care, and from such inflammable materials, a foot and a half or two feet in length, and five or six inches in thickness. On one occasion, such a torch lodged against the outside door of a cabin, when John Holder, seizing a bucket of water, opened the door, and dashed out the blazing fagot and the fire it had ignited; but, in doing which, amid the excitement of the occasion, he made use of some rough language, for which the good Mrs. Colonel Calloway _ then, or shortly after, his mother-in-law _ who was as much shocked at hearing profanity as she was pained at witnessing Prock's cowardice, touchingly chided him for want of proper reverence to his creator.

Another plan of the Indians was, to fasten smaller torches of similar structure to arrows and shoot them from the bluff over the river. One day such an arrow struck a cabin roof and lodged, with a small quantity of powder fastened to it in a rag, and a piece of lighted punk-wood attached. It had scarcely found a lodgement, when the powder ignited, setting the shingles on fire. The Indians over the river raised a triumphant shout and at once commenced firing rapidly at the spot, to deter the garrison from venturing there to extinguish it. But the burning shingles were, in a few moments, loosened from their wooden fastenings, and slid off harmlessly to the ground. The enemy were evidently not a little dispirited with their repeated failures to fire the fort. The showers which so fortunately fell almost every night, served to keep the cabin roofs more or less dampened and thus rendered them more difficult to set on fire. These rains, too, and more especially towards the close of the siege, enabled the garrison to catch water for the half-famished cattle, while the old well furnished a bare sufficiency for drinking and cooking purposes.

In these night attacks, the Indians would sometimes attempt to conceal their torches under their blankets, and rushing up as near as they thought it prudent to venture, would hurl the fagots into the fort. Several in this way lost their lives, as the blazing torches served to render their bearers visible to the marksmen in the bastions. William Hays, Boone's son-in-law, one night observed three Indians approaching with their fagots, and fired at them; they disappeared, and the signs at the spot, the next morning, indicated that one of them must have been killed. One of the enemy, more daring than his fellows, had the presumption one night to run up directly under one of the projecting bastions, and kept so near the wall that none of the men could get a fair chance to shoot him. He at length passed beneath where Stephen Hancock was posted, who fired, when the Indian fell beside a stump as though dead, but was seen to drag himself up behind it. Hancock directed a young man near him, whose gun was charged, to shoot the fellow through the head, in which he succeeded; at that as a subsequent examination proved, was the only ball that touched him.

Another adventurous Indian had erected a scaffold behind a large white oak, on the summit of the bluff over the river, so as to avail himself of a convenient fork of the tree, through which to send his whizzing messengers into the fort. Sometimes he would change the scene, and, from his eyrie, exhibiting his person in a bantering, derisive manner. Several shots had been ineffectually fired at him, when Daniel Boone brought his famous "Tick-Licker," as he termed it _ a rifle of more than ordinary calibre, carrying an ounce ball _ with an extra charge of powder, to bear upon the bold, saucy warrior; and, as the old pioneer described the result, twenty eight years thereafter, "the Indian fell, taking his scaffold with him, evidently the effect of my powder and ball." The dead body rolled down the hill, well nigh two hundred yards, to the margin of the river. Such a fatal shot deterred the enemy from attempting to remove the remains of their fallen comrade, till after nightfall, the hogs meanwhile rooting the swollen corpse about.

Near the river bank, a hundred yards or more above the fort, was a large prostrate sycamore, which afforded shelter for the Indians in their attack on the garrison. They aimed to watch, as well as they could, when a gun was discharged from a port-hole, so as to fire back through the aperture before the gunner had time to close it with a stone or knotty plug; and, it was in this manner that Burdin had been mortally wounded. Of two Indians posted behind the sycamore, one had a wooden false-face, which he would adroitly expose as though taking a preliminary peep in order to secure a good shot, and, in this way, draw the fire of one of the garrison in the nearest bastion, when the sham Indian would disappear, and make way for a real one to fire into the port-hole. After a few such demonstrations, the man in the fort began to comprehend the situation, discovering the live Indian, partly exposed to view, intent on exhibiting to good advantage his wooden humbug; the white marksmen now directing his efforts at the right one, took good aim, _ not at the false-face, as the victim supposed, but at that part of his body in view _ and killed him on the spot. The surviving Indian, evidently alarmed for his safety, betook himself to his heels, and disappeared. After the siege, signs of blood were found behind the sycamore as well as the veritable false-face, punctured with two or three bullets holes.

William Hayes, discovering an Indian ensconced behind a stump, sitting upon the ground, loading and shooting frequently, with one of his knees exposed to view, fired at the unsheltered limb; when it became apparent from no more shots proceeding from that quarter, that he was disabled _ and so it was afterwards learned; for his knee was so badly shattered, that it eventuated in his death. At another time, an Indian was observed sitting carelessly on the fence, near the place where the Indian flag-staff was planted, about three hundred yards from the stockade. Three men of the garrison putting heavy charges in their rifles, fired simultaneously at him, when he tumbled off the fence, apparently dead. Repeated instances of similar fatal marksmanship, had the effect to make the Indians, towards the close of the siege, extremely wary of exposing their persons, and probably hastened their departure. At first, they had been very profuse in the use of blackguarding and tantalizing language, frequently calling upon the garrison to surrender, freely promising all sorts of good treatment; but at length they seemed to get out of heart, and said but little.

On Thursday night the seventeenth of September, the enemy made their expiring efforts. They appeared fully determined to fire the fort at all hazards; and would boldly rush up with their torches, and hurl them with their might towards the roofs of the devoted cabins. Their frightful shrieks and yells, were answered by the repeated defiant yells and screams of the garrison; who, after the first day's attack, were in high spirits, confident that they could successfully repel any assault, or frustrate any stratagem of their enemies. So light was it that night, from the blazing fagots, and the constant discharge of musketry, that, it was said, a pin could have been seen anywhere within the palisades.

But the enemy's desperate efforts were of no avail, and they were thought to have lost several warriors during these operations. William Patton, who lived at Boonesborough, but was out hunting when the Indians first appeared, afterwards approaching the fort, discovered their presence. He lingered nearby till this night's attack, when he ascended a neighboring hill, from which he witnessed, as well as he could in the darkness, and at a considerable distance, the repeated rush of the Indians with their torches, and hearing the frightful yells and screams, he sorrowfully concluded that the fort was taken, and the whole garrison, men, women, and children, had fallen victims to savage vengeance. With this belief he hastened to Logan's Fort, a mile west of the present town of Stanford, Lincoln county, and some thirty-five miles distant from Boonesborough, with the alarming intelligence.

Early the next morning, the eighteenth of September, but few Indians were to be seen. They killed some cattle that had not been taken into the fort, to provide themselves with a supply of meat for their homeward march. They did not all depart at once, but gradually, and in squads; the few remaining occasionally firing a gun to keep up the appearance of a continuance of the siege; and, by an hour after sunrise, not an Indian remained, and a few guns only were heard far away in the distance. The last squad that left were about thirty in number, who crossed the river and bent their course up the stream; and, as their trail was found to continue many miles in that direction, they were believed to have been Cherokees. It will be remembered, in this connection, that Black Fish appealed to one of that nation in the treaty council.

Again Boonesborough was free, having passed through the longest and severest ordeal of any attack ever made in Kentucky. It proved the last effort of the savages against the home and fortress of Daniel Boone. Black Fish and his warriors retired to their villages with no trophies to grace their return _ not a solitary scalp, nor a lonely prisoner; and no tidings of victory to convey to their "father," Governor Hamilton, of Detroit; only a few remaining to disperse themselves around other stations, and waylay their straggling hunters.

When the Indians had scarcely departed, and before the garrison was fully confident of it, some of the men ventured into the garden, adjoining the fort, procured a quantity of cabbages and fed the half-famished horses and cattle. During the siege, but little corn had been doled out to them, as, being scarce, it was carefully husbanded, not knowing how long they might be compelled to remain cooped up in the stockade. Of the cattle driven away by the enemy, probably for a food-supply on their return march, a young cow, on the third day after their departure returned with a buffalo tug, three feet in length, dangling from her horns, with which she had evidently been tied of nights, and managed to get away; and when the poor creature reached the fort, she capered about, manifesting the greatest possible delight.

During the eleven day's siege, nine days and nights of which were employed in almost continuous fighting, the garrison lost but two killed and five wounded; while Boone and others thought that thirty-seven of the enemy were slain, and a great many wounded. The buzzards and vultures for many days circled around and fed upon the dead carcases, which had been thrown into the crevices of the rocks, or floated down the river.

The Indians had been prodigal in the use of ammunition, of which they must have had a bountiful supply, and which they wasted in the most careless manner, frequently burning and squibbing the powder to no possible purpose. Boone relates that one hundred and twenty-five pounds of bullets were picked up after the siege. The upper bastion, nearest the river, which was commonly referred to as Phelps' house was thought to have had a hundred pounds of lead shot into it _ sufficient evidence of the industry of the Indians in burning powder and whirling leaden balls from behind the large fallen sycamore in that direction. Around the port-holes particularly, the bullets were thickly studded, _ and had so often struck upon each other and fallen to the ground, that whole handfuls of these battered balls could be scraped up beneath the port-holes of the bastions.[10]

The name of Daniel Boone has become synonymous with all that is romantic and adventurous in Western history. A child of Quaker parentage, he grew up to years of manhood under the peaceful teachings of that religious order and never seemed to take delight in war or human carnage. He simply regarded himself an instrument, in the hand of Providence, in the exploration of the beautiful land of Kentucky, and in pioneering the way for the early settlement of the country. His religion, as he himself defined it, taught him to reverence God, love his fellow men, and do as little harm as possible.[11] In all his wanderings whether in his native region on the waters of the Sakuylkill, in the valley of Virginia; on the Yadkin, in North Carolina; in Kentucky, West Virginia, or Missouri; he was every where pre-eminently a man of peace _ never ambitious of military fame, nor even taking part in hostilities against the Indians, save when self-defense, or the protection of his family and neighbors, required it. This accomplished, he invariably turned his attention again to the indulgence of his love of the wilderness, and his passion for the chase. "He loved the solitude better than the towered city or the hum of business;" for there

"He held unconscious intercourse with beauty,
old as creation."[12]

Boone died at old Charette Village, St. Charles County, Missouri, September twenty-sixth, 1820.

Chapter Twenty Six

<u>Captivity</u> <u>of</u> <u>Simon</u> <u>Kenton</u>
September, 1778 - June, 1779

<u>Simon</u> <u>Kenton</u>, born in Fauquier County, Virginia, in 1753, grew nearly to manhood with few or no opportunities of learning letters. In March, 1771, piqued at the result of a love affair, in which a rival carried off the prize, a severe encounter ensued between him and a brother of the successful suitor. Supposing he had killed his antagonist, he fled to the deep recess of the Western wilderness, changing his name to Simon Butler.

Hunting for three years along the Kanawha and its tributaries, as well as down the Ohio Valley, and serving as a scout during the Indian war of 1774, he was among the earliest to share in the settlement and defense of Kentucky. Aiding in repelling the two attacks on Boonesborough in the spring of 1777, and taking part in Clark's Kaskaskia campaign in the summer of 1778, he returned to Kentucky in time to participate in Boone's expedition in September following to Paint Creek, a western tributary of the Scioto, to discover whether the Indians were marching against Boonesborough, as they had planned to do sometime before; and then to engage with George Clark and Alexander Montgomery, to visit the Shawnee town of Chillicothe, on the Little Miami, a northern affluent of the Ohio. This mission was designed for the double purpose of regaining some horses captured from the Kentucky settlers and at the instance of the Lieutenant of the county of Kentucky, Colonel John Bowman, to ascertain the situation of those villages, and the best route to reach them.

These expeditions for the return of stolen horses were prompted by the sternest necessity; for the pioneers could not settle the wilderness, and support their families, without these animals to bring in the wild meat from the woods, and break up the ground for their crops of corn and vegetables. When, in after years, the thoughtless or the ignorant would refer to these forays for recovering their own stolen property or replevying others in their stead, as horse-thieving expeditions, Kenton would indignantly resent it. "I never in my life," he would declare, "captured horses for my own use, but would hand them over to those who had lost their animals by Indian thefts; nor did I ever make reprisals upon any but hostile tribes, who were at war against the white settlers.".

Kenton and Montgomery, when at the Paint Creek town with Boone, remained behind to secure horses, of which, after watching all day, they obtained four; and, making a rapid night's march for the Ohio, they swam it with ease, reaching Logan's Fort, near Stanford, in the present county of Lincoln, with their booty the second day afterwards. About the nineteenth of that month, Kenton and Montgomery took a jaunt to Boonesborough, to learn whether Boone and party had safely returned; and were the first to visit the fort after the termination of the siege, a day or two before, of which they were surprised to learn the particulars.[1] Returning to Logan's, Kenton, Clark, and Montgomery, towards the close of the month, set out for Chillicothe, on the Little Miami.

With a suitable supply of salt and halters, they started on their mission, and arrived at Chillicothe without any adventure, and without discovery. In the night, they took seven horses from a neighboring pound; but caught them with considerable difficulty, and attended with some disturbance, which aroused the Indians from their slumbers, who sallied out to learn the cause. Kenton and his friends now rode off at their horses' best speed, each mounted, one leading the way; the younger horses following their file leader, and the rear rider plying his whip freely to urge on the whole troop before him. The first night they never once stopped to rest; and about two o'clock in the afternoon of the second day, reached the Ohio at what was, subsequently named Logan's Gap, about a mile and a half above the mouth of Eagle Creek, in what is now Brown County, Ohio, and about four and a half miles below Herndon.

In consequence of the agitation of the water, caused by a high wind, the horses could not be induced to swim the river. It was hoped the wind would lull by sunset. The horses had cost them too much toil and effort to think of abandoning them on a mere suspicion of pursuit by the Indians; and Kenton and friends did not seem to realize that they would lessen the danger to which they were exposed by promptly moving up or down the river _ a sad mistake, as the event proved. So they hobbled the horses, and turned them out to graze in one of the neighboring ravines of Cedar Hill, here skirting the river while they took their position in an adjoining wood. Several hours were spent in retracing their trail, and way-laying it, but no pursuers appearing, they became careless. Though the wind had measurably abated by the following morning, the horses still refused to take the water, timid from the difficulties they encountered the preceding day. In this dilemma, the adventurers resolved to select each a good horse, and make their way down the Ohio to the Falls, where Colonel Clark had established a garrison. After they had made their selection, and turned the others loose, the spirit of greed suggested that they might as well take them all. Considerable time was consumed in retaking the horses, which caused a separation of Kenton and his comrades.

While thus engaged, Kenton heard a distant yell; he left his horse, and ran to the top of the hill, when he discovered five Indians approaching on horseback up the northern side of the Gap. Without a moments delay, he took deliberate aim at the foremost of the party, but his gun, wet from exposure while he was attempting to cross the river on a raft when the horses refused to follow, now flashed. Quickly retreating through some fallen timber, overgrown with young trees and bushes, the Indians divided, and rode rapidly on either side; and as Kenton emerged from the thicket at the foot of the hill near the river, he discovered that one of his pursuers had nearly overtaken him. He was about to make an effort to regain the timber patch, when the Indian leaped from his horse, and ran towards him with up-lifted tomahawk, calling out, "brother!" "brother!" as an invitation to surrender. Regretting that his gun was not in a good condition so that he could have given him a warm "brotherly" reception, he was in the act of raising it in self-defense, when Bo-nah, a stalwart Shawnee warrior, sprang up in his rear unperceived, clasping him around his arms and body, placing one knee in the small of his back, threw him suddenly upon the ground. The other Indian now rushing up, Kenton, overpowered, was forced to yield himself a prisoner. His arms were bound with tugs to a pole across his breast, and then he was seated beside a tree, to which he was firmly fastened.

 Montgomery, hearing something of the fray, and evidently suspecting its nature, now made an appearance, and fired without effect at the Indians with Kenton. One of these warriors who had been on the march for Kenton's associates, now joined the two with the captive; when one was left in charge of him, the other starting after Montgomery, who now fled. One of the Indians fired at him ineffectually, but the shot of the other proved fatal. The two warriors soon returned with his reeking scalp; and seizing it by the long hair, they took turns in slapping it in Kenton's face, exclaiming indignantly at each repetition, "Steal Indian horse, ha?" Weary, of this operation, they wound up with cursing him roundly for a rascal, "and a white man."

 Clark, from the first seeing how unequal would be the contest, as he and his fellows were, betook himself to flight, till weary, and beyond immediate reach, when he secreted himself under some driftwood. Satisfied that he was not pursued, he at length rafted himself over the Ohio, and returned to Logan's Station with the unhappy tidings of the capture or destruction of his companions.

 Not very long after these exciting adventures, Black Hoof, a chief of the Shawnees, arrived upon the spot with a small reinforcement of warriors. That night Kenton was placed flat upon his back, and very uncomfortably pinioned to stakes driven in the ground, on the bank of the river, near the spot where he was taken. To the stout stick across his breast, to which his extended arms were fastened with buffalo tugs, a strong rope was attached, bound so firmly around his body and arms as to render it scarcely for him to move hand or foot in the slightest manner; and, as a final precaution, a halter was tied around his neck, and made fast to a convenient sapling. During all this time, he was alternately kicked, and cuffed and flouted; and constantly berated with a re-iteration of their limited vocabulary of abusive epitaphs, interlaced with choice bits of profanity as they had picked up from the traders and rougher class of frontier settlers. Painful as his bodily situation was, his mind was almost overwhelmed with still greater sufferings, in apprehension of the terrible tortures which he had but too much reason to believe were in store for him at their villages.

The Indian is fertile in plans and inventions for torturing his enemies; and he regards all as adversaries who venture to lay violent hands on his horses _ next to his gun, his most valued property. One of the animals captured by Kenton and his associates was young and unbroken. This was chosen as most fitting for their purpose. So they drove it into a fallen tree-top and caught it. And, on this wild, young steed, they fastened their forlorn prisoner. It required several of them to hold the restive colt, while the rider was being properly adjusted on him. His feet were tied under the horse's belly, his hands pinioned behind him, and a tug made fast in its center, around his neck, with one end firmly attached to the animals breast, and the other under his tail. "They tied his hands, Mazeppa-like, and set him on a steed, wild as the mustang of the plains _ and, mocking, bade him speed! Then sped that courser like the wind, of curb and bit all freed, o'er flood and field, o'er hill and dale, wherever chance might lead."

While this was sport for his tormenters, it was misery intensified for poor Kenton. The terrified colt at first made desperate efforts to rid itself of its unusual encumbrance by rearing, kicking and plunging; then dashing through thickets, and under low boughs of trees, endeavoring to brush off the rider; but all to no purpose. The Indians enjoyed the scene in a high degree _ laughing and yelling; and every now and then, sarcastically enquiring, if he wished to steal any more horses from the Indians? On the whole, Kenton escaped with fewer bruises and scratches than could have been expected; and, at length, weary of his ineffectual efforts to shake off the rider, the subdued colt quietly submitted to his fate, and fell into the rear of the cavalcade entirely avoiding the bushes and brambles by the way-side.

On each successive night, Kenton was securely fastened as on the first, to stakes and saplings, exposed to the weather, gnats, and mosquitoes; submitting, by day with the best grace he could, to the strokes, kicks and cuffs of his whimsical captors. On the night of the third day from the Ohio, when they had accomplished a journey of some seventy miles, they arrived within a mile of Chillicothe, where the Indians encamped for the night, and the prisoner was properly secured. His grand entry into the Shawnee capital was reserved, with appropriate ceremonies, for the morrow; and a runner dispatched to the village to announce the return and success of the party. The Indians sallied out from the town, to the number of about one hundred and fifty, to welcome the return of Bonah, Black Hoof, and their successful associates, and gratify their curiosity over the prisoner.

Black Fish, the Shawnee chief, who had recently returned with his warriors from the expedition against Boonesborough, was among the first to arrive; and, viewing Kenton somewhat sternly, said, inquiringly, in pretty good English: "Young man, you have been stealing horses?" "Yes," was the frank reply. "Did you not know it was wrong to steal Indian horses?" "No, I did not, for you come and steal horses from the white people." "Did Captain Boone send you here to steal our horses?" "No, I did it of my own accord because you steal our horses."[2] "Don't you know," continued Black Fish, "that the Great Spirit don't love people who steal?" "No; did you ever know it?" "Yes," responded Black Fish, "twenty years ago."

"The Indians," continued the old Chief, "have no cattle about their doors like white people; the buffalo are our cattle; but you come here to kill them. You have no business to kill Indian's cattle. Did you know that?" "No, I did not," replied Kenton. Black Fish then said to him, that he was sorry he was taken; that if a white man stole horses from one of his fellows, white man's law would hang him; but that Indians, from the same offense, don't hang, "only hawk him," indicating by gesture the act of tomahawking. He then repeated his regrets to Kenton that he had been captured; would rather he had escaped. Unused to hearing any expression of sympathy during his captivity, Kenton now began to hope that Black Fish would prove to him a kindhearted friend, and perhaps deliverer. But this faint hope was instantly dispelled; for the old chief raised his cane or stick, and gave him a severe cudgeling until poor Kenton thought every bone in his body would be broken. Then the old fellow, in accordance with his ideas of Indian courtesy, hardily shook the prisoner by the hand, renewing his regrets that he had been taken.

For three long hours the Indians indulged themselves in dancing, singing, and yelling, in the most approved savage style, around the helpless prisoner, stopping occasionally to bestow upon him a passing kick or stroke, partly for their amusement, and partly as a punishment for his temerity in running off from under their very noses, a squad of their much prized horses. His tormenters at length, retiring to the village, Kenton was left, exhausted and forlorn, staked to the ground, to suffer the remainder of the night from the attacks of voracious insects.

There was no peace for the lone prisoner. At the dawn of the ensuing day, Chillicothe was all astir. From tottering age down to the smallest child that could wield a stick or bramble, all appeared, excited with rage, whooping, yelling, and clapping their hands, pouring out upon Kenton's devoted head the most envenomed words at their limited command. Preparations were now made for running the gauntlet. All were arranged in two rows, facing each other, some six feet apart, each armed with a switch, ramrod, wiping stick, or gad from four to six feet long; the rows extending from the foot of what is now known as Reed's Hill, south-east of Chillicothe, to the council-house, near the base of the northern termination of the ridge, a distance of some eighty rods. A Negro named Caesar, who had long lived with the Indians, and was familiar with their customs, ventured stealthily to suggest to Kenton, that could he succeed in breaking through their lines, and reaching the council-house without being overtaken, he would not be required to go through the trying ordeal again at that place. Kenton determined to profit by this hint.

An athletic Indian stood at his side to start him off with a vigorous application of his tough hickory whip. The moment the signal was given _ the tap of a rude drum at the council-house door _ Kenton, started off at his best speed expedited by the expected blow from the warrior designated to administer it at the starting point; receiving now and then comparatively mild strokes, the heaviest from a squaw. At length, eyeing an Indian in advance, of more than common presence, he managed to plant a sudden blow with his fist between the fellows eyes as he came within reach, felling him to the ground. Jumping over his prostrate body, he renewed the race towards the council-house, the refuge of safety; and, when nearly there, he was met by a warrior leisurely approaching him _ apparently the drum-tapper _ who, throwing aside his blanket, and being fresh, while Kenton was by this time well-nigh exhausted, soon overtook and knocked him down with a club. The whole party now coming up with yells and shrieks, like so many enraged demons, they fell to cuffing, kicking, and beating the unlucky prisoner at a fearful rate, tearing off his clothing, and leaving him nearly naked, and almost helpless. For some cause, he was not required to repeat the race _ because, perhaps, he was manifestly too badly beaten to renew the effort. After he partially recovered from his enfeebled condition, someone brought him water and food. Kenton had now another, and very different, ordeal through which to pass _ a trial for his life, without having the slightest chance of submitting any justification for his conduct. For the lone prisoner, there could be no hope with those grim warriors, possessing no very nice perceptions of justice, and in whose estimation it was highly honorable for them to steal horses from the white people, but criminal in the extreme for the frontiermen to recapture their stolen property. His condemnation was a foregone conclusion.

But the forms and decorum of an Indian trial were as rigidly adhered to, as in similar cases in a civilized community. Kenton was taken into the council-house, and permitted to sit down in one corner of the earthen floor with his body made fast to a post or a log. The warriors formed a circle within the judgement-hall, and an old chief _ Black Fish, it is believed _ took his place in the center, with a war-club as a sort of voting instrument, and a knife and piece of wood to record the final decision. Passionate speeches now quickly followed each other, and Kenton, though he understood not a word the speakers uttered, had no difficulty in perceiving by their fierce looks and animated gestures, that a large majority were contending that the stake and fagot should be his fate. These expressions were greeted by the excited audience with many a grunt of approbation, while a few pleas for mercy were raised cooly with few and faint indications of approval.

When the harangues ceased, the old chief who sat in the inside the circle, arose, and passed the war-club to the warrior next to the door, the formal decision was now to be made. Those favoring the death, struck the club with violence upon the ground; and those who favored mercy, passed the club, without striking, to the one next to him, the old chief watching the result and cutting a notch on one side of his record-stick for condemnation and on the other for acquittal. Before the decision was announced, Kenton discovered that a large majority had voted against him; and, when the result was proclaimed, shouts of savage joy made the welkin ring.

The next consideration was to determine the place of execution. Some were quite urgent that it should take place at once, and at Chillicothe; while others appeared to think that his death, at the stake, should be at a central point accompanied with all the solemnity that could be accorded to so interesting an occasion. Wapatomica[3] was the place finally selected. A white renegade present informed the prisoner where he was to be taken. Any postponement was regarded as hopeful to Kenton; but anxious to learn what was in reserve for him, he inquired of the white man what the Indians designed to do with him on reaching the appointed place. "Burn you," accompanied with a bitter oath, was the ferocious reply.

Kenton's clothing was now restored to him. The next morning he was hurried away, under a strong guard, on his route to Wapatomica. He resolved in his own mind, that he would, the first good opportunity that should present itself, make a desperate effort to escape; well judging that should he fail, his case could be no worse. The first town reached was Piqua, about thirteen miles distant, nearly due north, located on the northern branch of Mad River, five miles west of the present city of Springfield, in Clark County, Ohio. The usual ceremony of running the gauntlet _ a sort of introduction of a prisoner to each Indian community _ was again Kenton's fate; in which he underwent much the same treatment as at Chillicothe _ switchings, cudgelings, and poundings, laid on with little or no regard to mercy, the more pain inflicted on the helpless victim, the greater the rejoicing on the part of his tormentors. He was then, for several hours, fastened to a stake near the council-house door and around him the warriors encircled themselves performing their exciting dances, and screeching like devils incarnate, giving the poor prisoner a faint foretaste of the yet greater sufferings in store for him at Wapatomica.

Leaving Piqua for Mack-a-chack,[4] some twenty-eight miles distant, the trail soon passed to the east side of Mad River, crossing Lagonda or Buck Creek, thence on, some half a dozen miles, through what is now known as Moore's Prairie. It continued on for several miles in a northerly direction, to where Urbana was subsequently located, the trace leading near the eastern margin of the wide bottom skirting Mad River on the east; and, from long use, it had, in many places, worn several inches deep. Reaching the stream known as King's Creek, some three miles north of Urbana, the Indians treated their prisoner with the greatest severity, rolling him in the water and mud, and making a bridge of his prostrate body. He thought he was, for the first time in his life forsaken of God and men. A Negro of the party, as unfeeling as the rest, attempted to crow, in imitation of a rooster, over Kenton's humiliation, when the Indians would ask him to "chicken again;" and thus could savages extract amusement out of the sufferings they had inflicted upon a helpless fellow creature.

About two and a half miles south of the present village of West Liberty, in Logan County, was a small Indian town called Wapakoneta,[5] where Kenton had to make a display of his agility in the inevitable gauntlet race. At length the Indian guard with its forlorn prisoner reached the Mack-a-chack, located on a rich second bottom on the northern side of the beautiful stream of that name, near its junction with Mad River. They were met by the denizens of the village now the race-path on the prairie, before reaching the creek; and Kenton was made to run the gauntlet at a small mound a little to the right of the road after crossing that outlet of the stream from West Liberty.[6]

All now passed over to Mack-a-chack village. As if the Indians, old and young, were not already surfeited with this cruel amusement, the prisoner was again required to run the race between parallel rows of whips and thorns, and cudgels. Ever since his condemnation to the stake at Chillicothe, he had been almost constantly resolving in his mind the idea of attempting his escape. At night, he was too firmly fastened, hand and foot, to render it practicable, and watched as he was, by day, by many vigilant eyes; an effort at best would be but a desperate undertaking. Seeing a tree, a cluster of bushes, or other conspicuous mark, some distant ahead on the trail, he would resolve that on reaching that point to make a bold dash off for life and liberty; but on the nearing the spot, his heart failing him, he would abandon the intention; only, however, to renew it again and again, and as often shrink from its execution. He had now run the gauntlet so frequently, that he was measurably used to it, and knew how to take advantages whenever he thought best to do so. Thus, on this renewed occasion at Mack-a-chack, as the drum beat the starting signal at the council-house, he darted off under high excitement and, perhaps, receiving some smarting reminders to bid adieu to such heartless cruelty, he, when near the end of the line, suddenly broke through the ranks directing his course at his best speed for the woods beyond. So unexpected to the warriors was this bold movement on the part of Kenton, that they for some moments stood in mute astonishment which enabled him to get quite a good start in the race. He had, indeed, so far out-stripped them, in running a couple of miles, he was entirely out of their sight. But now his high hopes were suddenly dashed to the ground; for he met a party of mounted Indians on their way to Mack-a-chack, headed by Blue Jacket, a Shawnee chief, who, at once comprehending the situation, gave him a hot chase, soon overtaking him. One of them dealt a severe blow on Kenton's head with the pipe end of his tomahawk, cutting through the scalp to the skull. He was felled to the ground senseless and bleeding; but soon recovering, his captors hurried him back towards the village. On the way they encountered the panting warriors in pursuit of the fugitive who fell to beating him in a most unmerciful manner, until he was again rendered insensible. When, at length, he became, in some measure, resuscitated, he found some of the them were throwing water in his face for his restoration.

From Mack-a-chack he was conveyed to Wapatomica, about eight miles up Mad River, and about two miles below the present village of Zanesfield, in Logan County. This town was situated on a beautiful plateau, on the western side of the river, with a fertile bottom intervening. On the west, the village was skirted with quite an elevated ridge, from which issued crystal springs and rivulets. Here was a large council-house, about one hundred and fifty feet in length, seventy-five in width and sixteen in height, built of split poles, covered with bark. The Indians of the place, of whom there were one hundred and fifty warriors alone, rushed out with their various instruments of torture, to greet the prisoner with a gauntlet reception; which was accorded him with the usual vigor and hilarity, he running something like a quarter of a mile south of the town to the council-house.

Preparations were now made for the last ordeal _ burning the prisoner. His face was blackened as a mark that the sentence of death had been pronounced on him; and the stake and fagots were being made ready. Fastened in the council-house, he was the object of the jeers and torments of the savage crowd. Among others, an Indian lad, anxious to practice in the exquisite art of inflicting pain and suffering on a helpless prisoner, would run up to Kenton, and apply to the exposed parts of his body the ignited end of a stick, when the poor victim, watching his opportunity, gave the youthful tormentor a kick that sent him whirling some distance. Not long after, an enraged squaw, made her appearance, and applied a thornbush pretty briskly on the hated white man who had dared to show such indignity to her promising young warrior.

Something of an excitement in the village now attracted the attention of the council. Simon Girty, with a party of white renegades and Indians, had just returned, uttering the scalp-halloo, having brought in Mrs. Rachael Kennedy as a prisoner, together with seven children and seven scalps. These were the fruits of a foray upon the waters of Racoon Creek, in Washington County, Pennsylvania _ between the present villages of Florence and Burgettstown, two miles from the former, and three from the latter. Robert Kennedy and other members of his family were also taken, but separated from Mrs. Kennedy. Kenton was now recovered from the council-house, without hearing Girty's name mentioned, and a council held whose deliberations were protracted to a late hour, determining the disposition to be made of the newly arrived prisoners, as well as making the necessary preliminaries for Kenton's execution. He was, at length, summoned to appear before the council. He had, by this time, become quite calm and indifferent, having put forth his best effort to escape without success; and it now seemed to him that it was his inexorable fate to die: all he could do was to meet death with manly firmness.

Entering the council-house he was greeted only with savage scowls, auguring no good to the wretched prisoner. He instantly recognized in Girty, his old friend and comrade on Dunmore's campaign four years previously. With mingled pent up feelings of hope and fear _ a trembling hope now suddenly revived _ he concluded to patiently await the unfolding events. He had not long to wait. Girty, throwing a blanket upon the floor, rudely ordered Kenton to take his seat on it; suiting the action to the word, perhaps impatient that he did not instantly comply, seized him by the arm, and jerked him down pretty roughly. In a threatening, imperious tone, he demanded to be informed of the condition of Kentucky. To the inquiry how many men there were in the several stations and settlements, Kenton, obedient to the suggestions of patriotism, thought it best to resort to subterfuge and evasion. "It is impossible," he said, "to answer that question; but I can tell you the number of officers, their respective ranks, and you can then judge for yourself;" and proceeded to do so, many of whom enjoyed military titles from mere courtesy, and of course had no command. After some other inquiries, Girty asked _ "What is your name?" At first Kenton hesitated, but finally responded, "Simon Butler." _ the name which he had adopted as previously stated, and by which Girty knew him when they served together. The renegade keenly eyed him for a moment, not at first recognizing him in his blackened and changed condition; and then, with his athletic frame, strongly agitated, he threw himself into Kenton's arms. "Oh! he was mighty glad to see me," in describing the scene; "He threw his arms around me and cried like a child. I never saw one man so glad to see another." Recovering somewhat from this paroxysm caused by the sudden and unexpected meeting with one, whom he had long ago plighted unalterable friendship, and reverting in his mind to the tragical fate impending over Kenton, Girty said earnestly, "Well, my friend, you are condemned to death; but I will use every means in my power to avert it."

This affecting interview must have touched the hearts of the savages, and prepared them, in the same measure, to extend that mercy to the prisoner they had hitherto denied him. Girty now turning to the council, under a high state of excitement, made undoubtedly one of the most impassioned appeals ever presented to such untutored minds. His very soul was stirred with him, so that the deep earnestness of his plea, and the energy of his gestures, rendered his effort both eloquent, and effective. He informed his astonished spectators, that the prisoner before them, condemned to the stake, was his old comrade and bosom friend; that they had, after the Indian custom, while serving under Lord Dunmore, selected each other as an especial friend, and had pledged their mutual devotion; and he appealed to his Indian brothers, who knew the sacredness of this relationship _ a sacredness excelled only by the ties of consanguinity _ to respect it in this instance. He averted the fact, that he and the prisoner had traveled in the same war-path, eaten with the same spoon and out of the same kettle, slept under the same blanket, dwelt in the same wigwam and their hearts had long beaten in unison. He entreated them to have compassion for his feeling _ to spare him the terrible agony of witnessing the torture of an old friend by the hands of his adopted brethren _ and plead with them not to refuse so small a favor as the life of a white prisoner to the special intercession of one who, on the war-path, and at the council-fire, had on all occasions proved his sincerity and devotion to the interests of the Red Men, and the cause of their good King George.

While several of the chiefs and principal warriors uttered a deep guttural approval, others objected, urging that his fate had already been determined in a full council at Chillicothe, and that they would be acting like squaws to change their minds with every veering wind; insisting that the prisoner was an acknowledged horse thief, and had actually flashed his gun at one of their warriors when he was taken; that so bad a man could never become a good Indian at heart, like their brother Girty; that the prisoner was one of the hated Kentuckians, a very bad people, who ought to be killed as fast as they were taken. Moreover, many of their people had come a long distance to share in the torture of the prisoner; and, if he were now reprieved, they would be deeply chagrined and disappointed.

Girty now renewed his efforts, urging his former request with singular earnestness of purpose. Adverting again to his own services, and the many instances of attachment he had given them, he described what he had risked and suffered in escaping from the white people; and asked, if, under such circumstances, he could now be suspected of partiality to them in general? When had he before interceded for any of that detested race? Had he not just returned from a long and tedious journey on the war-path to the frontiers of Pennsylvania, bringing seven scalps as trophies of his success over their enemies; and had he not also freely delivered up to them the eight prisoners that very evening for their disposal? Had he evinced the slightest desire that a single one of the captives should be spared, or assigned to himself? This was his first, as it should be his last, request; for if they refused him what had always been freely granted to one of their chiefs, he would construe the act as an evidence that he was no longer worthy of their confidence, and stood disgraced in the eyes of their people. Who of their warriors had been more zealous in the cause than himself? When they had danced around the council-fire, and sang their war songs, had he shrunk from striking the war-post, and enlisting for the expedition? What white man had seen his back, skulking away from danger? Whose tomahawk and scalping knife had been bloodier than his? He would only add, that he asked that the life of his bosom friend and pledged brother might be spared, as a first and last favor _ as an evidence that they approved his zeal and fidelity. After a further heated debate the war-club was handed around, the vote taken, a large majority passed it in silence thus securing the prisoners acquittal.

Kenton had watched the progress of the deliberations with thrilling emotions, and the results when announced, produced in both him and his deliverer the most rapturous delight. Girty's two white comrades on the Raccoon Creek foray, his brother James Girty, and John Ward _ the latter of whom, captured when only three years old, had been living with the Indians for over twenty years _ rendered every personal effort in their power to bring about this happy result.

Girty's singular devotion to Kenton on this occasion, deserves a fitting recognition. It was no ordinary friendship that prompted his action. Offended with his countrymen, whether with or without cause; for supposed slights and neglects, Girty became a fugitive _ a deserter _ a renegade; and, like all of that character, his hatred of them in general became deep-seated and intense; and, under the excitement of liquor or passion, his temper was perfectly ferocious. But the moment he recognized in Kenton his old friend, with whom he had formed that sacred union of pledged friendship, whatever might betide them, in weal or in woe _ an excellent custom he had learned during his former adoption and residence among the Indians _ he was prompt, and in no half-hearted manner, to redeem the sacred pledge.

A similar usage prevailed among the ancient Greeks, two young men after assuming this obligation of brotherhood, taken with peculiar ceremonies, and maintained inviolate through life. The Mohawk chieftain, Brant, had early adopted such a friend _ the counterpart of his very self, producing a romantic attachment, sharing each other's secrets, and participating in each others joys and sorrows."[7] "I will venture to assert," declares Heckewelder of the Indians, "that there are those among them who, on an emergency, would lay down their lives for a friend.[8] How touchingly Kenton has described this vow between himself and an early comrade: "Girty and I, two lonely men on the banks of the Ohio, pledged ourselves one to the other, hand in hand, for life and death, where there was nobody present in the wilderness but God and us!"[9]

A reprieve upon the gallows to one under sentence of death, could not produce a more striking transition of feeling than was now felt by Kenton in the changed situation of himself so suddenly effected by the powerful and successful interference of Girty in his behalf. The stake, the fagot, and death in its most terrible form, seen but a little while before staring him grimly in the face; everything, indeed, being in readiness for his immolation _ even a horn containing a small quantity of water having been attached to the stake, to enable him in the early part of his fiery ordeal, to assuage his burning thirst. And now he was set free! Even the stern countenances of his recent implacable enemies relaxed their vigor, as they extended their hands for a hearty shake, saluting him as "brother," while so recently they had for him only savage kicks and bitter jeers, denouncing him as an unmitigated horse-thief.

Led to Girty's wigwam, Kenton was now once more a free man. He was washed up and had conferred on him the name of Cut-ta-ho-tha, the Blackened or Condemned Man. From a British trading establishment located at Wapatomica, Girty procured for his friend a full suit of clothes, for he was well nigh naked; hat, coat, moccasins, breech-cloth, leggins, a handkerchief for his neck and another for his head. He was also provided with a horse and saddle. Girty bade him cheer up, as he appeared too downcast to suit the Indians.

During a period of twenty days, while recovering from his bruises and harsh treatment, and roaming from town to town, at his convenience, with Girty, he visited McKee's Town, on a beautiful ridge, on the eastern bank of a small purling stream, bearing that name, about two and a half miles nearly north-west from Wapatomica; and thence in the same direction, and about the same distance they reached Blue Jacket's Town, on the site of the present Bellefontaine, Logan County, Ohio. Other Indian villages also in that region were visited. Kenton met Alexander McKee, one of the renegades who had fled from Pittsburgh with Girty, who treated him pleasantly enough in his presence, but cast slurs and innuendoes at him behind his back. Once, while traveling together, Kenton pressed Girty with the inquiry, referring to his late murderous incursion into Pennsylvania, whether it did not hurt his feelings to engage in such bloody raids into regions where he was formerly so well acquainted? Hesitating at first, he at length replied, that "they were only Scotch-Irish" _ implying that they were an humble people, of not much account in his estimation.

A war party, who had been worsted in Western Virginia, now returned to Wapatomica chagrined and sullen; and learning about Kenton, obtained a re-hearing of the case, when a deputation was dispatched for him. He was found with Girty at Solomon's Town,[10] a Mingo village, about nine miles north of Blue Jacket's Town. The party, headed by Red Pole, a Shawanese chief, at its approach, uttered whoops of peculiar intonation. Girty informed Kenton that it was the distress halloo, and they must obey it. When Red Pole came up, he shook hands with Girty, but refused to do so with Kenton, scowling ominously upon him. To Wapatomica they were summoned, where a new council was to be held to determine Kenton's fate. On entering the crowded assemblage, the prisoner offered his hand in friendship to the savages, but six successively rejecting it, he gave up in despair.

The war-chief of the defeated party opened the debate with a bitter invective against Kenton; declaring that the manes of his slain warriors in Virginia could only be appeased by the sacrifice of the hated pale-face before them. In this trying situation, Girty did not desert Kenton, but renewed his appeal for his salvation. He asked, he said, for none of the spoils of war _ they were welcomed to all he should capture for he fought alone for the destruction of their enemies; and now he entreated that his old comrade might be spared to him _ the pledged friend of former years, for whom he had recently, under peculiar circumstances, of which they were the witnesses, renewed his old attachment _ thus forming a double tie of friendship and affection; and closed with a touching appeal to grant him this last request, solemnly declaring that he would never again ask them to spare the life of a hated American.

Appealing to the jealousy of the warriors, the hostile chiefs charged Girty with exerting too much influence, and assuming too much importance, for one who had been scarcely eight moons among them. An overwhelming majority voted to reverse the last decision and remand the prisoner to the stake. Kenton was dumbfounded at this sudden reversal of his fortune. Girty, sad and dejected, turned to him and said: "Well, my friend, you must die. I do not see what more I can do for you; but I will not cease to use every exertion." On the spur of the moment, he gained an important point. Reminding the council that there were large numbers of Indians at Sandusky receiving British presents, Girty urged that the execution should there be carried into effect, where so many assembled tribes could witness the solemn scene. This was agreed to and five warriors designated to convey the prisoner there.

While the guard were on horseback, Kenton was driven before them on foot, strongly pinioned, with one end of a long rope fastened around his neck, the other held by one of the guards. When they had traveled but two and a half miles to

McKee's Town, Girty passed them, encouraging Kenton with the hope that he might accomplish something for his benefit at the next village, Blue Jacket's Town; but on arriving there, and finding that he could effect nothing, he abandoned all hope and returned to Wapatomica by a different route to avoid the necessity of a painful interview with the hapless captive.

Passing through Blue Jacket's Town, without stopping there, the guards and prisoner kept on two and a half miles beyond, where a squaw was busily engaged, near the trail, plying her squaw-axe in chopping wood with her indolent Indian husband sitting on the log, leisurely smoking his pipe, and directing her labors. Seeing the guard approaching, he enquired about the prisoner, and was informed that he had been caught stealing their horses, when the excited warrior snatched the axe from his squaw, aiming a deadly blow at the head of Kenton, who raised his pinioned arms, as well as he could, to ward off the stroke; but he could not altogether avert its force. It fell upon his left shoulder, cutting into it deeply and breaking the bone. The enraged Indian would have repeated the blow, but for the prompt interference of Kenton's conductors, who severely reprimanded the fellow for attempting to deprive them of the amusement of torturing the prisoner at Sandusky. In this wretched condition, and without any attention to his wounds, Kenton was compelled to prosecute his painful journey through the wilderness, goaded on by savage masters whose hearts were calloused to every generous feeling of sympathy or humanity.

Misfortunes did not come singly to poor Kenton. Hurried forward some sixteen and a half miles further, in a northeasterly direction, Kenton and his escort reached a small stream, near its head, now called Silver Creek, an unimportant tributary of the Scioto, where they stopped for a few minutes to drink. Kenton was the first to arise after satisfying his thirst and barely stepped over the rivulet and sat down on its opposite bank, when one of the warriors, seeming to think that he had moved without orders, jumped forward, striking him violently with a war-club, fracturing his arm.

After traversing a distance of some twelve miles from the place of this last unfortunate occurrence, they reached the village of Logan, the Mingo chief, on the northeastern side of the Scioto, apparently at or near the crossing of that stream by the old road leading to Sandusky, about six miles below the present town of Kenton. After learning from the guard the object of their mission, Logan walked gravely up to Kenton, and said: "well, young man, you have been stealing these people's horses and they are mad at you." "Yes," he responded, "they seem very mad." "Well," rejoined Logan, "don't be disheartened; you are to go to Sandusky _ they talk of burning you there; but I am a great chief, and will send two runners to-morrow to speak good for you."

These words fell upon Kenton's ears like "good news from a far country." His spirits instantly revived on the friendly assurance of the benevolent chief to speak good for him in a quarter where only powerful influences could possible avert the dreadful sentence which impended over him. That night the party shared the hospitality of Logan's wigwam. The good chief extended to Kenton every attention, conversing freely with him. The next morning, Logan detained the escort so that he could send the messengers to Sandusky, some twenty-two miles distant. They faithfully accomplished the journey, returning that evening, and were closeted some time with Logan.

Perhaps from prudential motives, the old chief _ for now he was well stricken in years _ did not see proper to communicate the result to Kenton. It was apparent that he did not wish the guard to know what instrumentalities he had used, and proposed to use, to befriend the prisoner; perhaps wisely concluding, that should he impart the secret to Kenton, his escort, on the way, might extort it from him by means of such brutal treatment as they could inflict upon him, and thus possibly defeat the object he had in view. The next morning, when about to start, Logan presented himself, shaking hands with Kenton, giving him some bread and meat. He simply informed him that he was immediately to be conducted to Sandusky,[11] but gave no intimation, by word or look, as to the fate that awaited him there.

Kenton was again depressed in spirits, judging from Logan's silence that his intercession had proved unavailing. Long before reaching Sandusky _ which was located on the eastern bank of the river of that name, about three miles above Upper Sandusky of the present day _ a troop of boys, some twenty or more in number, painted black, and mounted on horses, met the prisoner; and, after riding around him, would dart off, uttering the most terrific screams and shouts. Something like half way from Logan's village to Sandusky, they came to an Indian race-path, in a beautiful grove, where a number of Indians had gathered including the troop of young warriors; and there, without regard to his broken arm Kenton was made to run the gauntlet. When, forty-nine years thereafter, he pointed out the spot to a friend, who expressed surprise at his ability to recognize the locality after so long an intervening period _ "Ah!" replied Kenton, "I had a good many reasons laid on my back to enable me to remember it." He was driven into Sandusky without a renewal of the gauntlet ordeal _ to which he had already been subjected thirteen times. But the stake and fagot were promised him the next morning. As the time approached, however, a severe storm arose _ an indication to the superstitious Indians that the Great Spirit was angry with them. So they desisted from their purpose for the time being, and repaired to the council-house to consider the matter. The storm passed over _ they soon forgot its supposed admonition; and reached the conclusion, that as sentence of death had already been formally pronounced on the prisoner, it only remained for them to put it into execution.

At this juncture, Peter Druillard strode into the council. He was a British interpreter, attached to the Indian department, dressed in a tinseled red coat, and recognized by all the tribes in the quarter as one clothed with authority. He was the person to whom Logan had sent his messengers to intercede for Kenton. Druillard was the man, of all others, who knew how to manage Indians, favored, as he was, with his official position to aid him.

He was, moreover, possessed of humane feelings, and readily entered into Logan's scheme to save Kenton, with a firm determination not to be thwarted in his purpose. He told the Indians that General McIntosh would soon approach, with a large army, from Pittsburgh, invading the Indian country; and that he, as an officer of the Indian department, had been specially ordered to Sandusky, to secure and convey to Governor Hamilton at Detroit, any white captives taken on the frontiers as the information which might be extorted from them relative to the plans and movements of the Long Knives, might prove of some benefit to the British cause than the lives of twenty prisoners. That, in this case the Indians had been revenged on the Kentuckians by killing one of their number, and rescuing all their horses. As a recompense, however, for their fatigue and trouble, he would pay the party, who had Kenton in charge, a hundred dollars worth of rum, tobacco, powder, or any other articles they might choose, if they would permit him to take the prisoner to Detroit, for examination by the Governor, when he could be restored to them to be dealt with in any manner they should think proper.

The Indians at length acceded to this proposition, and Kenton was turned over to Druillard, who promptly paid the Indians the amount promised; one of the Chiefs was, by arrangement, to accompany the captive to Detroit and take him in charge on his return. Proceeding some forty miles to Lower Sandusky, now Fremont, the county-seat of Sandusky county, Ohio, they went thence by water to Detroit. On the way, Druillard took occasion to impress Kenton with the important service he had rendered him, and informing him of the promise he had made, under the necessities of the case, to return him to the tender mercies of the Indians; which pledge, however, he declared was made with no intention of its fulfillment, and that no consideration could induce him to abandon a prisoner to such unfeeling wretches. This was Kenton's first knowledge that the sentence of death at the stake was still hanging over him; but so many unexpected interpositions had occurred in his behalf, that such a contingency now no longer excited his fears.

It was early in November when they reached Detroit, the eleventh day after Kenton's shoulder had been broken; which, with the ease he had enjoyed during his canoe voyage on Lake Erie, had, during the last two days, began to knit together. He was taken the next day before Governor Hamilton, who elicited nothing from him of any consequence, as he was really ignorant of McIntosh and his movements; and, with reference to Kentucky, he resorted to the old subterfuge of specifying the numerous military officers there, leaving the Governor to judge, from their rank and number, the strength of the many forts and settlements in that country. The chief who accompanied him was plainly told that the prisoner could not be taken back to Sandusky for the purpose of savage torture; and the Governor ordered some additional presents as a ransom, which the Indian reluctantly accepted, and went off grumbling and disappointed.

Kenton was now sent to the hospital, where the surgeon, on examining the disabled shoulder, found it was displaced and required to be broken apart, and properly re-adjusted. Kenton experienced more suffering in this operation than he did when originally injured. Governor Hamilton directed Captain McGregor, the commissary, to supply him with necessary clothing for his comfort during the approaching winter. He soon recovered. He had the liberty of the town reporting daily to the commandant of the place. While he could not reasonably complain of his treatment, he still realized that he was a prisoner of war, and longed to enjoy the society of his old friends, and the freedom of Kentucky. One McKenzie, a Scotch trader at Detroit, quietly remarked one day in Kenton's presence, and apparently for his benefit, that American prisoners made a great mistake when they undertook to escape by going south through the country of the hostile Indians, where they were liable to be retaken; but were they to direct their course south-west to the Wabash country, they would encounter fewer Indians, and consequently be far less likely to be intercepted. Kenton determined to profit by this hint. Having concerted a plan to escape, with two fellow prisoners, Nathaniel Bullock and Jesse Cofer, they were aided by the good Mrs. Rachel Edgar, and indirectly by her husband, John Edgar, an Indian trader at Detroit, who procured for them guns, ammunition, moccasins, and other needful supplies. Pretending to engage in a duck hunt, they took their departure on the third day of June, 1779; and, after thirty days travel through the woods and prairies, with various mishaps and adventures, securing occasionally a buck or an opossum, by the way, they at length, to their great joy, reached the Falls of the Ohio in safety.

Bonah, Kenton's captor, used to visit him in Ohio, long after the old Indian wars, and received valuable presents at his hands. Kenton, by way of bothering him, would ask, if it was because he kicked, cuffed, and abused him so savagely, that he should now bestow these gifts upon him? The old warrior, after thoughtfully contemplating the matter a while, would reply, with the satisfaction of one who had made an important discovery, "No, that is not the reason; but because I did not kill you."

To his dying day, Kenton would never fail to recognize Girty's almost super human efforts in his behalf_ "Yes, I tell you," he would declare, "Girty was good to me."

Poor Logan! Kenton had not the satisfaction of meeting this faithful friend after parting with him on the Scioto; but he never wearied in speaking of his kindness to him at the time of his direst necessity.

When Druillard, who rescued Kenton from the stake at Sandusky, subsequently became poor, Kenton presented him a fine tract of land in Kentucky, a horse to ride, and for many years furnished him and his family their chief support.

From Dunmore's campaign in 1774, to that of Harrison on the Thames, in 1813, Simon Kenton ever proved himself ready for his country's service, taking a foremost rank for activity and enterprise _ excelled by none, and equaled only by his great compeer, Daniel Boone. Promoted successfully to the rank of captain, major and general, and serving under Clark, Wayne, and Harrison, he died at his cabin-home, near the head of Mad River, three miles north of Zanesfield, Logan County, Ohio, April twenty-ninth, 1836, at the ripe old age of eighty-three years, "The wheels of weary life at last stood still."[12]

Chapter Twenty Seven

<u>Bowman's</u> <u>Expedition</u> against <u>Chillicothe</u>
May - June, 1779.

In the month of October, 1776, the Commonwealth of Virginia passed an act dividing the county of Fincastle _ then the most westerly of any in its jurisdiction _ into three distinct counties, to one of which they gave the name of Kentucky, being, substantially, the present State so called. The act took effect on the last day of the year.[1] On the twenty-first of December, <u>John</u> <u>Bowman</u> was appointed by Patrick Henry, Jr., then Governor, to the office of Colonel of its militia.[2] In the Summer following, he arrived out, reaching Harrodsburgh on the second of September, when he took upon himself the duties of his office.[3] The Colonel was made Lieutenant of the county, in 1778, receiving his commission from Thomas Jefferson who had become Governor.[4] By virtue of his office, he had the general direction of military affairs, at that date, in that distant region.

By the terms of the treaty made by Lord Dunmore with the Shawnees in the Autumn of 1774, on the banks of the Scioto, that nation was to give up all the prisoners ever taken by them in war both white people and Negroes and all the horses stolen or taken by them since the close of the war of 1764; and further, no Indian of that nation for the future was to hunt on the Virginia side of the Ohio nor any white man on the other side of that river. This agreement at once opened the pathway for an advance of emigration into the region which soon after became the county of Kentucky. However, even before the treaty _ in June, 1774 _ James Harrod and others had erected a cabin in that country, upon the site of the present Harrodsburgh, Mercer county, _ only to be deserted shortly after, because of the hostilities of the savages.[5]

The adventurers who came to the Kentucky country in 1775, enjoyed, for that season, almost entire immunity from savage aggression; only a few were killed and wounded; enough, however, to induce the settlers to be watchful _ ever on their guard. But the next year _ 1776 _ the Indians were more emboldened. With an increase of immigration came an increase of their attacks. The machinations of the British began to have an effect upon the Shawnees; and the Mingoes, who, it will be remembered, were not a party to Lord Dunmore's treaty, were avowedly hostile. Already the pioneers had availed themselves of the advantages of rude forts as protection against the savages: one was commenced and completed in the early part of April, 1775, near the mouth of Otter creek in what is now Madison county, and was known as Fort Boone.[6] Others were built as the exigency of the settlements seemed to demand; among them, that of McClelland's, adjoining the site of the present Georgetown, Scott county, which, on the twenty-ninth of December, 1776, was assailed by the Pluggy's-town gang of Mingoes and their famous leader killed[7] _ the first regular attack upon any fort in Kentucky.

Early in 1777, the Indians commenced their depredations in the settlements south of the Ohio. More of the Shawnees now started upon the war-path from their towns upon the Scioto and Miami. Before the end of the year, a large portion of that nation had taken up the hatchet. In the Spring, as there were but very few men interested in keeping possession of the posts on the north side of the Kentucky river, they broke up _ their occupants removing, on the thirtieth of January, either to Boonesborough or Harrodsburgh. The whole population was then in these two forts and did not exceed one hundred and fifty men fit for duty, with about forty families. As the months scud away, both posts were attacked,[8] but neither taken. In the meantime, Logan's fort near the site of the present town of Stanford, Lincoln county, was occupied;[9] it, too, was assailed by the savages, but their attack proved unsuccessful.[10] So troublesome had been the Indians throughout the year _ so discouraging had their hostilities proved to immigration _ that, at its close, the settlements were restricted to the three forts just mentioned.

The siege of Boonesborough was the great event of the year 1778, in Kentucky. Preparations for this, at the principal town of the Shawnee Indians north of the Ohio,[11] operated for a length of time to restrain small parties of savages from their incursions into the settlements. Still, there were Indian depredations before and after that event. As to the siege itself _ it is more notorious for what was not accomplished than for any particular success of the enemy. That three hundred and thirty Indians with eight Canadians,[12] one of whom _ Isadore Chêne[13] _ commanded the expedition, should, for eleven days and nights, beleaguer the rude stockade causing a loss of only two killed[14] and four wounded, notwithstanding at one time nine men were outside negotiating with the enemy, _ is something bordering on the marvelous. This occurred in September. The savages then dispersed to the different forts, waylaying hunters but captured no posts.

The time had arrived with the opening of the Spring of 1779, when it was very evident to the settlers of Kentucky that, all the Indians who were at that time infesting the country, the Shawnees were the most active and bloodthirsty. It seemed exceedingly plain to them that from Chillicothe, on the Little Miami, came most of the war-parties marauding in the now rapidly increasing settlements.[15] "Why should not that prolific hive of mischief be destroyed?" was a question then frequently asked. And it was finally determined by the settlers, to free themselves from danger and their settlements from savage inroads, to carry an expedition against it. John Bowman, residing at Harrodsburgh, as Colonel of militia and Lieutenant of Kentucky, called for volunteers, resolved to take the command of them in person; _ the first regular enterprise to attack, in force, the Indians beyond the Ohio ever planned in Kentucky. Bowman, the year previous, had contemplated an expedition to the same town, and sent Simon Kenton with two others to Chillicothe to make discoveries. The settlers were to plant their corn and be in readiness to rendezvous in May at the mouth of Licking. The Shawnees seem not to have had any apprehensions of such a retaliation for their frequent invasions of the Dark and Bloody Land. The place of meeting for the volunteers of the interior was fixed at Harrodsburgh; whence, under Benjamin Logan and Silas Harlan as Captains, they marched to Lexington, meeting at that point a company from Boonesborough commanded by Captain John Holder. These two companies were there reinforced by another headed by Captain Levi Todd. They marched from Lexington by way of the Little North Fork of Elkhorn, encamping the first night near its mouth. Their second encampment was on a small branch of Mill creek about two miles northward from Lee's Lick. Thence, they went down the Licking, until they finally reached its mouth _ opposite what is now the city of Cincinnati, then a howling wilderness _ the place appointed for the general meeting of the army, the site of the present city of Covington, Kentucky.[16]

Previous to this time, William Harrod as Captain had reached the place appointed for the general meeting with a company of men from the Falls of the Ohio _ Louisville. To stir up the people that volunteering might go forward with alacrity, Harrod took "the stump," while his company was forming, haranguing the settlers, showing the necessity of the expedition and that the settlements in the other parts of Kentucky were desirous of promoting the enterprise. With his force, when it arrived at the mouth of Licking, were a number of men from Redstone Old Fort, on their way home, but who proposed to go upon the expedition. They had visited the Big Bone Lick and had with them a canoe-load of specimens from that interesting locality, which they were transporting up the river. Harrod had been ordered by Bowman to meet him with boats to enable the troops to cross the Ohio _ two keel-boats and three canoes were brought up for that purpose to the place of rendezvous. The men from the Falls employed their time until the arrival of the other companies in hunting _ killing buffalo, bears, and deer, for provisions. They had killed some game while at the Big Bone Lick.

Colonel Bowman left the men from Lexington, on their way to the Ohio, _ turning off to the right, to go to Licking _ afterward Ruddell's Station. Here he found a few men under Lieutenant John Haggin. With this force, he started for the mouth of Licking where he arrived on the twenty-seventh of May, and immediately began preparations for crossing; as the troops were now all present and eager to be led into the wilderness. "I had gathered," afterward wrote Bowman, "two hundred and ninety-six men."[17]

Early in the morning of the twenty-eighth of May, 1779, immediately below the mouth of Licking river, Colonel John Bowman and his army crossed the Ohio. Thirty-two men remained to take care of the boats; _ two hundred and sixty-five, including officers, formed into marching order with George M. Bedinger as Adjutant and Quarter Master, commenced their march along an Indian trace for the objective point of the expedition _ the Shawnee town, on the east side of the Little Miami, distant about sixty-five miles in a northeast direction, _ piloted by George Clark and William Whitley. The men were mostly on foot, not very heavily encumbered with provisions _ a peck of parched corn and some "jerked" meat to each man was all. Firing was interdicted after crossing the river and the whole force marched rapidly on their way, making directly for the Little Miami, which stream they were to follow to the Indian town. One of the pilots upon the expedition was William Whitley. The volunteers were armed with rifles and tomahawks. They arrived within ten miles of Chillicothe at dusk, on the twenty-ninth when a halt was ordered. During the whole journey not an Indian had been seen, and the Commander was sanguine of being able to surprise the savages.[18]

A council was now called to determine upon the time of attacking the town. It was resolved to march that night, and invest the place and commence the attack at day-break the next morning. A point a few hundred yards south-west of the village, in a prairie, was reached a little after midnight. Bowman and his Captains now went forward to reconnoiter. They were gone about an hour. Upon their return, a disposition of the force was made preparatory to the attack.[19] The men were separated into three divisions: one under Captain Logan was to march to the left of the town: another under Captain Harrod to the right until they met on the north side. The other division under Captain Holder was to march directly in front of the village, but to stop some distance away. By this arrangement, there would be an opening south of the two first mentioned companies through which, when the alarm was given, the Indians might escape; _ they would be allowed to go some distance from their cabins before encountering, immediately, before them, the company of Holder. This was a very ingeniously contrived plan; for, if all the men were to rush up at once, the enemy would be forced to remain in their wigwams where they could fight their assailants at a great advantage on their side. Silently and undiscovered, the three divisions took the positions assigned them and impatiently awaited the appearance of day, so as to begin the work of death. The men under Harrod and Logan, at a given signal, were to commence the attack; while Holder's were to lie in ambush, to await the out-rushing of the frightened savages and pour in upon them, as they appeared, a deadly fire. It was understood if the men should be discovered before daylight _ Holder's division was to endeavor immediately to fire the cabins. It was not long before the Indian dogs set up a loud and persistent barking. Their owners would come out, in some instances, and encourage them on as if they were apprehensive of danger.

The town thus silently encompassed by two hundred and sixty-three backwoodsmen anxious for daylight to appear, was the Little Chillicothe of the Shawnees; known, however, to the frontiersmen of that day, as New Chillicothe. The center of the village was about one hundred and twenty rods east of the Little Miami. Skirting along on the east side of the town was a small stream, afterward called Old Town Run, which, with a course nearly north, empties its tribute into Massie's creek at no great distance away. On the west side of the village was a fine spring, the waters from which run in a southwesterly direction, soon to mingle with those of the Little Miami. A prairie lay adjoining the town, on the south; and cabins were built some distance upon one, on the north. A ridge south of the spring, extended from the skirts of the village in a southwest course to the river; another, just across the run to the east, has a north-east trend to Massie's creek.[20] The site of the village is about three miles north of the present town of Xenia _ county-seat of Greene county, Ohio.

At the time of this expedition against the Shawnees their whole number of warriors at Wapatomica, Mack-a-chack and Piqua[21] on Mad river and at Chillicothe on the Little Miami was about five hundred, of whom one hundred were in the latter village with about two hundred squaws and children. About a month previous, true to the wandering instincts of that nation, four hundred of their warriors with their families, under their chiefs Black Stump and Yellow Hawk, accompanied by the French trader, Laramie, migrated west of the Mississippi, settling on Sugar creek, a little distance above Cape Girardeau in what is now the State of Missouri, then under Spanish rule. The principal chief of the Shawnees at Chillicothe when the town was invested by Bowman, was Black Fish. His subordinates were Black Hoof and Black Beard. Northeast of the center of the town stood the council house _ a large building, said to have been sixty feet square, built of round hickory logs, one story high, with gable ends open and upright posts supporting the roof. Black Fish's cabin was some thirty yards to the west of this structure. There were several board houses or huts in the south part of the village _ some ten or twelve.[22]

Now it so happened while the army of Bowman lay quietly around Chillicothe, a Shawnee hunter was returning, on its trail excitedly of course to the threatened village. As he neared Holder's division, "puffing and blowing," fearful of falling into a trap, he suddenly stopped, and made a kind of interrogative ejaculation, as much as to say, "Who's there?" _ when one of the men very near him, shot, and the savage fell, at the same time, giving a weak, confused yell. Immediately another soldier ran up and tomahawked and scalped him.[23] The firing of that gun set at naught many of the wise plans and well-laid schemes depending upon day light for their execution. A few Indians, came in the direction of the report, to ascertain the cause. As they approached Holder's line the men laid close and still only cocking their guns. But this was enough to alarm the vigilant savages who hastily retreated, receiving a volley as they fell back, wounding Black Fish severally, the ball ranging from his knee along up his thigh and out at the joint and shattering the bone; showing that he received the wound in a squatting position. He was taken to his cabin, by three warriors. He called upon them not to leave him but to stand their ground and all die together.[24]

The return of the party of observation and the volley fired by Holder's men, fully aroused the slumbering occupants of Chillicothe. There was immediately a great out-cry and confusion. About seventy-five warriors taking advantage of the darkness escaped through the lines which surrounded the town. The squaws and children with a few men made a rush for the council house. According to previous orders Holder's division now advanced to set fire to the town. The men reached the board shanties on the south, and at once began the work of plundering, giving the savages ample time to fortify themselves by fastening securely the door of the huge building they had congregated in. The houses were set on fire as fast as they were plundered. This attracted the attention of the other divisions, portions of which, without orders, left their positions and joined in the work of securing valuables.

No sooner were the cabins all ablaze than an attempt was made to capture the Council house; but the assailants were so warmly received that they were glad to fall back. It now began to grow light in the east and Bowman satisfied that it would be impossible to capture the strong hold of the enemy sent word to Logan's and Harrod's division to fall back to the south of the town. Meanwhile, in front, a desultory fire was kept up between some of Holder's men and those within the Council house; the stragglers from the other divisions also took part. When it became broad daylight, a few men, in their endeavors to get as near the building as possible in hopes of killing some the inmates, found themselves so much exposed that to attempt a retreat would be certain to draw upon them a volley from the Council house. They had a position behind a large white oak log not over thirty yards from the enemy. Some of the party in moving their bodies to get a good position for delivering their fire, were killed. The survivors finally heard a voice calling to them to retreat; but how this was to be done was the question. Adjutant Bedinger concluded to make the attempt. The spot where the men lay was south east of the Council house. Bedinger sprang up, ran a very zigzag race across the stream east, and escaped unhurt, although a volley was fired at him. The rest of the party immediately ran to an empty cabin near by reaching it before the enemy had time to re-load their rifles.

The men remained in the hut some time, trying to devise means to escape. Finally a novel plan was hit upon. Each one provided himself with a plank and holding it upon his back, slantingly so as to protect his body from the bullets of the savages, started upon the run. This memorable backwork _ rather than breastwork _ proved amply sufficient to save the lives of all; for they all escaped over the path of Massie's creek near by; dropping, each one, his puncheon as he entered in safety the corn field at that point.[25]

During all this time the scenes being enacted within the council house were of a strange character. Assatakoma, a conjurer, nearly one hundred years old kept constantly calling out, encouraging the few warriors congregated there _ not over twenty-five in number, with about fifteen boys who could shoot; but quiet a number had no guns to use. The squaws and children kept up a great noise _ screaming and whooping. The Indians managed to make what answered for port-holes, between the logs and in the roof of the building, through which they fired. Joseph

Jackson who had been a prisoner to the Shawnees since February of the preceding year, calmly surveyed the scene _ tied as he was to a post in the midst of the shrieking crowd. At the first alarm, he had seized a rifle and started for the woods, but was overtaken by a warrior, brought back, and secured, as just related.

As soon as Bowman determined not to attempt to capture the Council house, deeming it too strong to be assailed with rifles only, and had called back the divisions to the southwest of the town, the principal effort was to secure horses _ a large number being found near by in a kind of commons _ evidently driven in from the woods by the flies. One hundred and eighty were captured.[26] The army was thus engaged when the surviving stragglers who had been in such close quarters behind the oak log, arrived. The sun was then about two hours high. The amount of plunder taken from the cabins that had been burned and from others on the west side of the town not fired, was considerable, consisting of silver ornaments _ of which a large number was found _ and clothing. By nine o'clock, every thing being arranged marching orders were given and the army started upon its return having lost eight men killed in exposing themselves to the fire of the savages within the Council house and one wounded. The trail out was the route taken; the men, as is usual with volunteers and militia upon such occasion, being at first in considerable confusion. The principal cause, however, was this: soon after day light a Negro woman came out of the council house as if having escaped the savages, and reached the army without harm. She declared that Simon Girty with one hundred Shawnees from Piqua _ twelve miles distant _ was hourly expected. The commander gave little credence to this tale; but the story getting among the men and the number of Girty's savages increasing to five hundred by the time of starting, caused some consternation _ resulting in a disposition of many to be off regardless of the manner of their going; but order was soon restored and the march continued.

After making fourteen miles, Indians were discovered in pursuit, soon commencing an attack. Bowman with great courage and steadiness called a halt, formed his men into a hollow square _ ready to meet the savages should they appear in force. It was soon discovered there were but few of them; but as they continued their annoyance, wounding some of the men, a small detachment charged out and routed them. One of their number was killed and scalped. Bowman had three of his men wounded, in all, during the afternoon, _ none killed. After this, they were not again molested by the Indians. The army reached the Ohio just above the mouth of the Little Miami, early on the first day of June, where they found the boats in waiting. The men were soon conveyed across the stream _ the horses swimming. The number of the latter captured from the savages, reaching the Kentucky shore, was one hundred and sixty-three.[27] The boatmen, while the army was about, had remained in their batteaux and canoes moving up and down the river, for greater safety.

The army now feeling greatly at ease moved leisurely some three or four miles to the rear of the elevated hills which skirted the Ohio until a fine spring was reached when it halted. Hunting and fishing soon supplied the camp and what with rest and sleep enjoyed, soon gave new life and vigor to all. They were again in Kentucky where pea-vines, wild clover and wild rye furnished an abundance of food for the half famished horses. It was now agreed to have a sale of the horses and other booty; and then, an equal division was to be made of the amount realized. The Captains were to keep the account of the amount purchased by their respective companies and when it should be ascertained that anyone had bid in property exceeding the amount of his dividend he was to pay the surplus _ having a credit of one year _ to his commanding officer. The several sums thus collected were to be divided among such as did not purchase to the full amount of their dividend. The vendue realized a little over thirty two thousand pounds giving to each one of the two hundred and ninety-six, about one hundred and ten pounds Continental currency.[28] Many purchased more than that amount; but, as these debtors were scattered afterward from Redstone Old Fort on the Monongahela to the Falls of the Ohio and Boonesborough, no collections were ever made, or if made were never paid over to those who were justly entitled thereto; so, it resulted in each one securing, in most cases, just what was struck off to him at the vendue.

The Monongahelaeans now took to their canoes and made their way up the Ohio to their homes; while the residue scattered to their various places of abode _ the general impression being that the expedition was far from a failure. The amount of booty obtained was large; the march had been conducted outward with great secrecy; and it was evident to all, but for the accident of the return just at that inauspicious moment of the Shawanese hunter, the whole village would have been captured, _ as it was, not only many of their cabins were burned, but much corn was destroyed. It is very evident from the journals of that day, that the enterprise was looked upon as a success.[29] The noted leader of the Shawanese nation, Black Fish, died of his wound in about six weeks from that date. One of the assailants supposed to have been killed behind the white oak log near the council house and numbered among the dead of the expedition was found soon after the return march began, fast asleep and entirely free of any wound. An aged warrior begged to have the opportunity of killing him; as it would be, doubtless, the last chance he would ever have of wreaking his vengeance upon the foe. The request was granted, and he tomahawked the soldier, who made not the slightest resistance _ who uttered not a single word _ as the old savage assailed him with the instrument of death; _ a priceless boon to the unhappy man, who no doubtfully expected, as his fate, horrible tortures at the stake.

Chapter Twenty Eight

Roger's Defeat — Remarkable Adventure of Basil Brown and Robert Benham.

When the mighty struggle for independence was forced upon the American people in 1775, they were illy prepared for it. They were poor; they had no accumulated wealth _ no supply of arms and munitions of war _ no manufactories. It was the policy of the mother country to blockade the ports of the rebellious Colonies, and cut of all supplies from abroad.

Not unfrequently the patriot army was scantily provided with arms and ammunition. At the battle of Honing Rock, Sumter's men went into the fight with scarcely two rounds of powder per man, re-supplying themselves from their vanquished foes. During the terrible winter of 1777-78 at Valley Forge _ a winter of great severity _ Washington's army suffered greatly from hunger and nakedness, and could be tracked by their bleeding feet. No less than two thousand eight hundred and ninety-eight men were in camp unfit for duty, because they were barefoot or otherwise naked; and, for want of blankets, many were obliged to sit up all night by fires to keep themselves comfortable. For three days successively, the troops were without bread, and two without meat; and these were no uncommon occurrences. Washington declared, that he could not enough admire the incomparable patience and fidelity of his army.[1]

Nor did the troops encamped on the Highlands of the Hudson that winter suffer less terrible privations. "There is not one blanket," wrote General Putnam, "in Colonel Dubois' regiment; very few have either a shoe or a shirt; and most of them have neither stockings, breeches, or overalls."[2] At a later period of the war, it is related of Greene's Southern army, that all were in clothes nearly worn out, many in tatters, many with but a remnant of some garment pinned around their waists with the thorn of the locust tree. The heavy musket bruised sorely the naked shoulder. The cartouch-box pressed roughly upon their unprotected loin. More than a thousand were so naked that they could not be put on duty of any kind; three hundred were with out arms.[3]

The people throughout the country resorted to every make-shift to supply their own and the pressing wants of the army. Some fabrics were woven in the rude looms of their own construction; even the wild nettle, in some instances, was brought into requisition as a substitute for flax. But while these proved essential aids, they did not lessen the necessity for resorting to additional sources of supply, and especially for the more important munitions of war. The ambassadors were dispatched to foreign countries, to enlist their sympathies, and invoke their assistance. A million of francs were given from the French treasury in 1776; while cannon and military stores, to the value of a million of dollars, were placed at our disposal. Spain, the same year, sent the revolted Colonies a free gift of a million of francs; and cargoes of military stores from the port of Bilboa.[4]

Important supplies came from an unexpected quarter. Oliver Pollock migrated from his native Ireland several years before the Revolutionary war, and settled in Carlisle, Pennsylvania, in the humble capacity of bar-keeper to his brother James, who kept a tavern there.[5] In 1769, he arrived in New Orleans, in a brig from Baltimore, with a cargo of flour, at a time of great scarcity when the price had risen to twenty dollars a barrel. He sold the cargo to Governor O'Reilly, for military supplies, at fifteen dollars a barrel, which so much pleased the Governor that he promised the enterprising adventurer free trade to Louisiana as long as he lived and a favorable report to the King.[6]

Establishing himself as a merchant in New Orleans, and marrying a Spanish lady, a friend of the subsequent Governor Galvez, he acquired wealth and influence. The Spanish Government had not only sent to the American Colonies a present of money, and military stores from Bilboa, but tendered a gentle hint that there were three thousand barrels of powder stored at New Orleans which should be at their service; and, as early as August, 1776, on application of Patrick Henry, Governor of Virginia, through the friendly intercessions of Mr. Pollock, a cargo of this precious article, consisting of ninety-eight barrels, aggregating about ten thousand pounds, was despatched by Governor Unzaga, passing up the Mississippi and Ohio, under the charge of Lieutenant William Linn, in safety, and proving of essential service to the country.[7]

The sufferings of the troops at Valley Forge, and the extreme difficulty of procuring military supplies, induced Governor Henry again to look to New Orleans for succor in this time of sore distress. Colonel David Rogers was selected as a proper person for this delicate and important mission. A native of Ireland, he had migrated to this country when quite young, settling himself as a merchant at Old Town, Maryland; and subsequently, in 1775, making a settlement five miles above Wheeling on the Ohio.[8] In the fall of this year, he marched a company to Pittsburgh; and in 1776, was chosen to represent the district of West Augusta in the Senate of Virginia.[9] In December, 1776, while a Major of militia, he was appointed a Captain in one of the six Virginia regiments on Continental establishment, but did not qualify.[10] Retaining his position in the militia service, he was ordered, in February, 1777, to station fifty men at the mouth of Wheeling, and as many more at the mouth of the Little Kanawha, properly officered, for the defense of those posts, and the protection of the neighboring settlements.[11] When Ohio

County, Virginia, was organized, he was appointed its County Lieutenant, March 4, 1777; and, the next month, was re-elected to the State Senate. But shortly after, the incursions of the Indians broke up the settlement where he resided.[12]

Colonel Rogers sojourned a while at Mount Braddock, half a dozen miles north-east of Union Town, Fayette County, Pennsylvania; but returning to the Potomac region, he married the widow of Captain Michael Cresap, and located on the Potomac, in Hampshire County, Virginia, opposite to Old Town. Changing his residence from Ohio County, resigned his commission as County Lieutenant; and was succeeded in June, 1777, by Colonel David Shepherd.[13]

Proving himself active and energetic in the public service, Col. Rogers was prevailed on by Governor Henry to convey, by the way of the Ohio and Mississippi, a letter to Bernardo de Galvez, the Spanish Governor of Louisiana. He was authorized to engage a Lieutenant, Ensign and twenty-eight men, with directions for General Hand, at Pittsburgh, to assist in supplying boats for the expedition. In addition to conveying dispatches to Governor Galvez, he was to act in the capacity of private ambassador in behalf of Virginia, consulting with the Governor as to the most suitable point on the Mississippi for the establishment of an American garrison; making to him a full representation of the resources, strength and condition of Virginia, the progress of the war, together with any additional information he might desire. Colonel Rogers was, on his return, to take into his care such supplies as Governor Galvez, Mr. Pollock, the American commercial agent, might have to transmit for the use of the State. He was, furthermore to be the bearer of dispatches to Colonel G. R. Clark, connected with his expedition against the Illinois country; who, when Rogers should ascend to the Ohio, was directed to furnish him a proper escort for the safety of his vessels and cargo. These instructions, which met the approval of the Council, were given January fourteenth, 1778; and, six days thereafter, the sum of six hundred and twenty-five pounds, Virginia currency, was advanced to Colonel Rogers to defray the expenses of the expedition.[14]

He raised his little company of thirty men in the Red Stone region. Isaac Collyer was appointed Lieutenant, Patrick McElroy, Ensign, and Robert Benham commissary. Two keel boats were built at Pittsburgh, one of which was taken to Red Stone Old Fort, for the baggage and supplies of the party; and, in June, 1778, Colonel Rogers set out on his voyage down the Ohio and Mississippi, encountering many hardships in descending those rivers. With a plentiful stock of flour, the commissary had to rely for wild meat upon the success of squads of hunters, who took their turns, in following along the margin of the streams, while the boats were being carried down by the current, aided by the oarsmen of the party.

Arriving, at length, at the Arkansas Post, fifty miles up the Arkansas River, where a Spanish garrison was established, Rogers and his party were kindly received by the commandant, and informed that the goods he sought had been sent up to St. Louis; but that it would be necessary for him to go to New Orleans to get the proper order for them. Selecting half a dozen of his men, among whom were Robert Benham and Basil Brown, Colonel Rogers descended the Arkansas and Mississippi in a canoe, and narrowly escaped capture in passing the British post of Manchac in the night.[15]

He at length reached New Orleans, about the twentieth of September, where he met a very cordial reception by Mr. Pollock and Governor Galvez. Rogers had confirmed to him what he had learned at Arkansas Post, that a very considerable quantity of goods had been sent up the river by Pollock, for the use of Congress or Virginia _ having, apparently, like the Governor, no very clear distinction between the States in their separate and federal relations. As Governor Henry had been the medium of former negotiations for supplies, and renewed dispatches now coming from him, there was no difficulty in securing an order for the goods. As for the loan Governor Henry solicited in behalf of Virginia, Galvez had to defer that matter to his superiors at Madrid _ a request which, he was quiet confident, would be granted.[16]

There was a British sloop of war in port; the Captain of which, suspicious of the presence of Colonel Rogers and his American party, watched their movements closely, ready to take any advantage if any infringements were made on the treaty relations existing between the courts of London and Madrid. While this state of affairs was perhaps some what perplexing, yet the fact that the goods and military supplies for which Rogers was in quest, were out of the reach of British interference on the Mississippi, rendered the espionage less harmful than it otherwise might have been. As the Spanish Government, from motives of public policy, was privately disposed to promote the interests of the new Republic, Colonel Rogers found no difficulty in holding such interviews with Governor Galvez as he saw fit to solicit. Benham was sent with despatches, it is conjectured, to Governor Henry, and probably to Colonel Clark and General Hand, through the long intervening wilderness; and, with the hardihood characteristics of the times, subsisted principally on Indian corn boiled in lye, to preserve it from the weevil. He went first to Kaskaskia, and proceeded thence to the Falls of the Ohio.[17]

It was near the close of the year before Colonel Rogers took his departure from New Orleans, going about ninety miles by water, to the point where Plaquemine village is now situated, a little distance below Manchac; thence by land, to avoid the English garrisons at Manchac and Natchez, where all passing boats were rigidly overhauled; and the bare suspicion that any party was friendly to the American cause, was very certain to subject them to seizure and imprisonment, with the confiscation of all their property. After leaving the river, their course led them about sixty miles to Opelousas, and thence about one hundred and twenty miles to Natchitoches on Red River, where arrived on the first of February, 1779. Their journey had been much impeded by almost continual rain, and consequent high waters, which compelled them to tarry a couple of weeks at Natchitoches. Resuming their toilsome travels through the wilderness _ partly by canoe, and partly by land _ in a north-eastern direction, over two hundred miles, and, at length, after great hazard and fatigue reached their point of destination. Over this route, some goods were conveyed, which seemed to have been brought from New Orleans.[18]

From Arkansas Post, Rogers and party descended the Arkansas River to the Mississippi, and thence on the slow and tedious manner of that day, they proceeded up the latter stream to St. Louis, where the goods, for which they had orders were

Editor's note: At this point the text of this unfinished chapter ceased.

Chapter Twenty Nine

Andrew Poe's Desperate Encounter with two Indians.
September, 1781

Andrew Poe was born the thirtieth of September, 1742, in Frederick county, Maryland. George Poe, the father of Andrew, died while the latter was in his teens. He remained at home until he became of age, living with his mother and an elder brother. Not long after the termination of Pontiac's War, he came to the neighborhood of Pittsburgh, where he remained some time; when, in company with two others, he commenced the first settlement on Harmon's creek, in what is now Washington county, Pennsylvania, at a point about twelve miles from the Ohio river. Two years after, he returned to Maryland, and induced his brother Adam, who was some years younger than himself, to go with him to his new location. Andrew had already selected a tract of land for a farm and made improvements; Adam, upon his arrival out, also secured a piece not far from his brother's. Here the two continued to reside. Andrew was five feet eleven and one half inches in height; and his usual weight, two hundred and five pounds. He was a man of unnatural strength and activity.

On the twentieth of September, 1781,[1] a party of Wyandot warriors, seven in number, was sent by the Half King, principal or head chief of that nation, from the banks of the Walhonding, where the latter then was on his way to the Sandusky, on a maraud upon the white settlers to the eastward of, and across the Ohio river. Among the braves were three sons of that sachem, the oldest of whom was Scotash who afterward became a chief of the Wyandots. The latter was put in command of the party,[2] which reached and crossed the river near the mouth of Tomlinson's run, a distance of about twelve miles from the settlement of the Poes on Harmon's creek.

The Wyandots came within one mile of Adam Poe's about midnight, capturing one Jackson, a man about sixty years of age, whom the savages found alone in his house. With their prisoner, they immediately set off for the Ohio, but the fact of the incursion of the Indians into the settlement having been discovered just after they had departed, a small number at once assembled, and made preparations to pursue the marauders as soon as it was light enough to see their trail. Andrew

Poe was chosen a Lieutenant _ to lead the party.³

That night there was a sharp frost _ the first of the season; so that the borderers, in pursuit, as soon as the morning dawned, had but little difficulty, although all were mounted, in following the tracks of the savages. Rapidly they approached the Ohio. On the river hill, half a mile from the stream, they dismounted and tied their horses. They were now a short distance below Tomlinson's run,⁴ the trail at the bottom of the hill turning down the river. Here fresh signs of the Indians were discovered. Some of the men were now cautioned by their leader to march quietly; as they were making considerable noise with their feet in running. The fear was that the Indians would discover them and at once kill their prisoner. But one of the men, in particular, was not to be restrained; so Andrew Poe turned squarely to the right, leaving his company, and, making his way cautiously, took a straight course to the immediate bank of the Ohio.

The residue of settlers, with whom was Adam Poe, followed the trail of the retreating Wyandots to the river, where they discovered five Indians and the prisoner, Jackson. Four of the savages were making a raft which they had quite completed; while the remaining Indian stood sentry and also guarded their captive. The borderers got within twenty-five yards of the warriors before they were discovered. Jackson saw them at the same moment, and sprang forward to escape to his deliverers, but his savage keeper seizing a tomahawk pursued him instantly and succeeded in striking him in the back with the weapon, fortunately, however, inflicting not a very serious wound. Before the Indian could repeat the blow, he was shot dead by one of the settlers. Thereupon, the rescued man ran up and embraced one of the borderers _ William Castleman, crying out, "Oh! Castleman; Oh! Castleman;" seeming all unconscious of his wound; so over-joyed was he to escape.

In the meantime, the bordermen had fired upon the four Wyandots and the latter returned the fire. The Indians all sprang into the river; one only escaped, and he _ Scotash _ badly wounded in the hand. He was the elder of the three sons of the Half King, and leader of the party. One of the settlers was shot _ a young man by the name of Cherry. He sat down by a sugar-tree, expressing a hope that, his companions would not let the Indians scalp him. His wound was in his left side cutting away the lower part of his left lung. Thus ended the contest with the five savages, which, of itself, would have been a memorable one; but, as will now be seen, it had already been eclipsed by a hand-to-hand conflict up the river a short distance, wherein the leader of the white men was performing prodigies of heroic daring.

Andrew Poe, when he left his companions, and had reached the river bank peered cautiously over it. He discovered two Indians near the water's edge, both half bent, with their guns in their hands, and looking intently down the river. The two savages were brothers of Scotash and sons of the Half King; neither was remarkable for size;⁵ one, however, was a trifle smaller than the other; nor was either of them a chief of the Wyandots; but their father being head-sachem of the nation, they, of course, were men of distinction and importance.[6] When first discovered by Poe, they evidently were alarmed at the noise of the approaching party farther down the stream.

Andrew Poe instantly concluded to shoot the larger Indian and then, with his butcher-knife, jump down the bank _ about fifteen feet at that point to the water's edge _ and attack the other before he could turn and use his gun. It was a most desperate resolve. He had not been discovered; so taking deliberate aim he pulled the trigger _ but his gun misfired. Both Indians at once turned around with a "Waugh!" of surprise. Poe, as quick as thought, dropping his gun, jumped down the declivity, intending first to dispatch the larger savage, with his knife, and then the smaller one. As he alighted upon them, he caught each around the neck. His weight and the force acquired from the distance he had jumped, brought the larger Indian upon his back with Poe upon his breast, the other savage being brought down, also, and held there by Poe's right arm and his right leg over the fellows body. Both their guns fell from their hands as Poe descended upon them.

The smaller savage made violent efforts to disengage himself from the clasp of his antagonist; but he was held by Poe as in a vise; meanwhile, the latter tried to reach his knife which was in a scabbard attached to his shot-pouch and was partly under him as he lay upon the larger Indian. The savage comprehending his intention, seized his left hand; the other Indian all the while struggling to get loose. Poe now thought he would make a desperate effort to get hold of his knife handle and draw the weapon from its sheath with his right hand, even if, in so doing, he should release the smaller savage, trusting to his efforts and prowess with the weapon to dispatch the two. He had, however, no sooner loosened his right hand grip and seized hold of his knife with his thumb and finger, and made a jerk, than the Indian under him let go his left hand _ the knife came easily from its scabbard; so easily, if fact, that the jerk caused it to fly several feet from him upon the shore. This effort of Poe necessarily gave the smaller Indian a chance to free himself from his foe.

The chances now were decidedly in the favor of the Indians. The larger one clasped his strong arms around Poe holding him fast, while the other seized a tomahawk lying upon a raft which was fastened to the shore not more than six feet away, and aimed a blow at the head his antagonist; seeing which, the latter threw up his right foot, the toe of his shoe striking the Indian's wrist as the weapon was descending _ sending the tomahawk flying into the river. There was still one in reserve upon the raft, which the savage lost no time in securing and after two or three feints, leveled another blow at Poe's head. The latter threw up his right hand and received the weapon on his wrist cutting off one of the bones and the cords of three of his fingers. The tomahawk sticking fast among the sinews, was drawn from the Indian's hand as Poe threw back his arm, dropping some distance away upon the ground.[7] The larger Indian now loosened his hold of Poe who immediately, jumped up, seizing one of the guns as he rose, with his left hand and it being already cocked, he shot the smaller Indian dead. This somewhat lessened the odds against him.

Scarcely had the fatal shot been fired, when the other Indian jumping to his feet, seized Poe and threw him into the river; but the latter, at the same time grasped the savage's breech-clout with his left hand and brought him tumbling along with him into the stream. The water was deep and both went under. Now a mighty struggle was made by each to drown the other. Sometimes one was under, sometimes the other, and frequently both. Poe getting his antagonist by the tuft of hair upon his scalp held his head under the water until he thought him drowned. They had been by this time, carried by the current quite a distance from shore. Letting go the savage's hair and pressing him down with his right arm over his neck, Poe endeavored to swim with his left hand, getting at the same time his head above the surface to breathe. But the Indian immediately slipped out from under his arm, rose to the surface, also, and swam for shore with all possible speed, followed by his disabled antagonist who was unable to overtake the uninjured savage.

The moment the Indian reached the shore, he sprang for the loaded gun, seeing which Poe quickly turned and swam back into the current, to escape the shot. The savage in cocking his gun broke the lock. Throwing it down, he picked up the empty gun and sprang to the raft for a shot-pouch and powder horn and commenced loading. Meanwhile Poe continued to swim away from shore, turning upon his back and exposing only his face; at the same time calling aloud for his brother, Adam, whom he supposed could not be far away; and he was not mistaken; for the latter, after the contest was over with the Indians down the stream, missing his brother and hearing the report of a gun up the river, hastened to the spot. It was a very opportune arrival; for he reached the top of the bank with his gun, unloaded however, and caught sight of the savage just as he was in the act of commencing to load. Adam remained unperceived by the Indian but was discovered by Andrew in the water who called to him to load quickly.

It was now a question whether the savage would shoot Andrew or Adam the savage: it all depended upon who should load first. The Indian would have had the first shot, had he not, in drawing the ramrod let it fly from his hand upon the beach. This gave his unseen antagonist the advantage; for, by the time he had recovered the ramrod, rammed down the ball, and raised the gun to shoot, the crack of Adam's rifle brought him down, mortally wounded, but able to spring into the river where he struggled as if in the agonies of death. Seeing this turn in affairs, Andrew commenced swimming again towards the shore; at the same time calling to his brother to catch the savage or he would get away. While Adam was descending the bank and endeavoring to reach the Indian, others of the party who had made their way up the stream after the conflict with the five Indians, now espying Andrew in the river and supposing him to be an Indian, shot at him; _ one ball splashing the water into his face, another cutting his hunting-shirt, while a third one wounded him dangerously.

Adam observing the accident paid no more attention to the savage, but sprang into the river and assisted his wounded brother ashore. The Indian sank and was seen no more. All things considered this encounter must be set down as one of the most remarkable ever known to have taken place upon the border in all the wars with the savages of the West. As soon as it was over, young Cherry was brought up and placed beside Andrew upon the beach; he died in half an hour. The wounded man and the dead one were taken up the hill and back to the spot where the horses were tied, when a litter was made and Andrew placed upon it. Both were carried to the settlement where Cherry was buried. Andrew Poe did not get well of his wounds for nearly a year; indeed, he never fully recovered, as he lost the use of the three injured fingers; and his right hand became smaller than the other. He died in Green township, Beaver county, Pennsylvania, on the fifteenth of July, 1823.

Scotash, the Wyandot who escaped, although badly wounded in the hand, as has been shown, swam the river and hid until night came on when he re-crossed the stream, found the dead body of his brother who was shot by Andrew Poe on the shore, and buried him as well as he could where a tree near by, had turned up the earth.[8] He then made his way homeward, communicating the news of the disaster to the Half King.[9] The sachem afterward took ample revenge for the death of his two sons, by his unremitting hostilities to the Americans; but that the nation at large ever attempted to requite the injuries done them by sending one of their number to murder Andrew Poe, after peace had been declared or at any other time, is a prevailing tradition, _ but one wholly unworthy of credit.[10]

Chapter Thirty

Gnadenhütten

The Moravian Indians from the Susquehanna river, who appeared upon the banks of the Tuscarawas, in the present county of that name, in the eastern part of what is now the State of Ohio, in 1772, to locate there, were under the guidance of David Zeisberger, a Moravian missionary, assisted by John Heckewelder. Two villages _ Schönbrunn and Gnadenhütten _ were built upon the eastern bank of that river, upon territory set apart for them by the Delaware Indians, who then occupied the valley, having their principal town some distance down the stream, near the site of the present Newcornerstown, in Tuscarawas county. This village was, however, not long afterward, removed to what is now Coshockton, Ohio, at the confluence of the Walkonding and Tuscarawas, which together form the Muskingum, _ so called, at that date, as far up as the present northern boundary of Tuscarawas county.

At the commencement of their labors, Zeisberger and Heckewelder were assisted by John George Youngman. There was at this time, a village of Moravian Indians upon Beaver river, called Friedenstadt, in what is now Lawrence County, Pennsylvania, under the charge of John Roth, the occupants of which in the Spring of 1773, joined their brethren in the two towns upon Tuscarawas, accompanied by their leader. In August of that year, another missionary, John Jacob Smick, reached the valley: so that the whole corps now consisted of Zeisberger, Heckewelder, and Roth, at Schönbrunn; of Schmick and Youngman, at Gnadenhütten.

Schönbrunn, the upper Moravian town, was situated about three miles southeast of the present New Philadelphia, in what is now Goshen township, Tuscarawas County, Ohio. Gnadenhütten, the lower village was located in the outskirts of the present town of the same name, in Clay township. In both villages, the Indians built themselves log houses to dwell in. The occupants were a mixture of Stockbridge, Mingo and Delaware Indians, from the Beaver river and from two Moravian Indian villages situated in what is now Bradford County, Pennsylvania.

The Delawares in the valley of the Tuscarawas, were located in New Comer's town in White Eyes' town. The latter was situated across the river from the former and farther down, on the left side, in what is now Oxford township, Coshocton County; while New Comer's town was identical in location or nearly so, with the present village of that name in Tuscarawas County. There was, likewise, a small village between the two. The Delawares at this date, had a town at Standing Stone, near the present Lancaster, county-seat of Fairfield County, Ohio. Upon the Licking river to the northward of this, there was likewise a village, occupied in part by Indians of that nation. There were also two towns upon the Walhonding: one, a few miles above its mouth, the home of Wingemund, a war-chief of the nation; and one, some distance above the latter, the residence of another Delaware war-chief known as Captain Pipe. The principal sachem of the Delawares, King New Comer, resided at New Comer's town. A war-chief, White Eyes, lived at White Eye's town. The Delawares claimed, at this date, by virtue of a grant from the Wyandots, their Uncles, the whole of what is now the State of Ohio, east of the Sandusky and Hocking rivers; or at least, to the eastward of the former river and the Muskingum; but their right to this domain was disputed by the Six Nations.

The locating of the Moravian missions in the valley of the Tuscarawas, was a measure inaugurated upon the banks of the Susquehanna, by the missionaries and other authority of the Moravian church, to the end that a safe asylum could there be found for their Indian converts. It was not alone the founding of a mission among, or the preaching of the gospel directly to, the Delawares of that country, that induced the movement. The Indians upon the river were generally averse to both. It was their opinion that the Great Spirit did not intend the religion of the whites should be their religion; that if He had intended it, He would have informed them long ago; _ that it was not their interest to appear so friendly to them, for they had already crowded too fast upon them and driving them from their hunting-grounds; _ that what the white people wanted, was, to get their lands and bring them to slavery; _ and that the English religion would take them off from their knowledge of war, and then they would be an easy prey to their enemies.

Their land was their idol; and their fears were that in every proposal to send missionaries among them, there was, at the bottom of it, a design to rob them of their possessions, and bring their nation to subjection, which they dreaded more than death itself.[1] But, in the settlement of their own kindred and members of other tribes near them, though directed by missionaries, they saw no danger; on the contrary, these came by an express invitation; for they looked upon the Moravians as white people of another kingdom from that of English and (being from Germany) who would never oppress Indians.[2] By the end of January, 1774, as many as twenty of the Delawares of the Valley, had been baptized by the missionaries. In May, there were two hundred souls at Schönbrunn; at Gnadenhütten, probably half as many. The Delawares took no prominent part in Lord Dunmore's war of 1774, except that of mediators. They strongly and persistently advocated peace. In this they were visited by Sir John Johnson and by his deputy George

Croghan, at Pittsburgh. But the Virginians on the one hand and the Mingoes and Shawanese on the other, for various causes and in various ways, became involved in hostilities _ ending, after the sanguinary battle of Point Pleasant; on the tenth of October, in a treaty at Camp Charlotte in what is now Pickaway county, Ohio between Dunmore and the savages; which, but for the coming on of the Revolutionary conflict, would have proved a lasting one, there is no reason to doubt. The Moravian missionaries assisted the Delawares in the interest of peace. During this year, more of the nation were baptized as converts.

The opening of the year 1775, brought with it upon the Tuscarawas news of an approaching crisis between the American Colonies and the mother country. As the year advanced, so did the Revolution. On the nineteenth of April, the valiant sons of Massachusetts fought the battle of Lexington. Following this, Ethan Allan and his Green Mountain Boys surprised Ticonderoga _ its surrender being demanded "in the name of Great Jehovah and the Continental Congress." Then Bunker Hill awakened a general enthusiasm among the patriots of the country. The appointment of George Washington as commander-in-chief by the Colonial Congress, which had made haste to reassemble, was followed by the organization of three Indian Departments, to the end that the neutrality of all the tribes might be secured if possible, and the conflict now begun. To the first Department belonged the Indians of the East and North; to the second, the tribes of the West; to the third, all the nations south of Kentucky. George Morgan was afterward appointed agent for the Department of the West, with his headquarters at Pittsburgh.

"It was high time to adopt such measures. Not content with honorable warfare, Great Britain had inaugurated a policy of blood and cruelty against which the good of her own nation protested. In the previous year, the Governor of Quebec had been empowered to raise Indian levies and march them 'into any of the plantations of America;' and, recently, arms had been forwarded to Dunmore with which to equip the savages; while the King himself had sent instructions, in his own name, to the Canadian agent to persuade 'his faithful allies, the Six Nations,' to take up the hatchet against the rebels. Through the baneful efforts of Colonel Guy Johnson, the son-in-law and successor of Sir William Johnson, who had died suddenly in July of 1774, this policy was, in part, successful, and after the battle of Lexington, all the Iroquois, except the Oneidas and Tuscaroras, espoused the British Cause." During this year, the principal town of the Delawares _ New Corner's town _ was removed to the confluence of the Tuscarawas and Walhonding, now Coshocton, Ohio.

The establishment of Western or Middle Department was followed in the Autumn of 1775, by a treaty at Pittsburgh with the Indians living beyond the Ohio and to the Northward; that is, with as many as could be induced to attend, consisting of a large body of Delawares, some Shawnees and a few Senecas. The Delawares pledged themselves to a strict neutrality; but the policy was a difficult one for these Indians to adhere to. A party of Delawares, in 1776, headed by

Captain Pipe, removed to the Northward making their homes upon the Cayahoga River. This boded ill to the nation; as it placed the clan nearer the British influence. Meanwhile, their principal chief, New Comer, died and was succeeded by Captain Killbuck. At the commencement of the year, the missionary establishments upon the Tuscarawas were in a thriving condition; quite a number of the Delawares of the valley had been baptized. An additional village was founded to accommodate the converts at a point two and a half miles below the principal town of the Delawares; it was located upon the east bank of the Muskingum and was called Lichtenau. On the fourth of November, another missionary, William Edwards, an Englishman, arrived in the valley, but, as Roth with his family had returned to the east upon the commencement of hostilities in 1774, the core of teachers was not thereby enlarged.

In the Autumn, of 1776, a second treaty was held at Pittsburgh with the Western Indians. The object of this treaty was the same as the one the year previous: To keep the Indians quiet, and persuade them, if possible, not to molest the border inhabitants. Members of the Six Nations, Delawares, Mohicans, and Shawnees, to the number of six hundred and forty-four, with their principal chiefs and warriors, gave every assurance to the commissioners of the general government who treated with them, of their resolutions to preserve inviolate, peace with the United States; but the Mingoes, Wyandots, Ottawas and Pottawattamies, living near the British post of Detroit, stood aloof _ declining to meet the Americans.

The Spring of 1777, brought with it a change for the worse to the Western border. British influence had alienated from the Colonies all the Indian nations of the West, except the Delawares and a fragment of Shawenese. The latter nation, not long after, was a unit in their hostility to the Americans; while the former was held to a neutrality only by the uncertain tenure of the ability of the general government to furnish them with necessaries. As early as April of this year, their principal war-chief, Captain Pipe, declared that his nation laid great stress on the inability of the United States to supply their wants. And he added these ominous words: "We are ridiculed by our enemies for being attached to you, who cannot even furnish us with a pair of stockings or a blanket; this obliges us to be dependent, in a great measure on them." It was this dependence on the British and the plentiful hand of the commander at Detroit which, in the end, as will be shown, alienated most of the Delaware nation, from the Americans. In 1777, Captain Pipe was a friend to the borderers _ but largely from mercenary motives; while White Eyes, a war-chief of equal authority, was one from principle. Before the beginning of September, such was the complications and dangers which beset the missionaries that Schönbrunn and Gnadenhütten were deserted, and all the teachers except Zeisberger and Edwards at Lichtenau, gone back to Pennsylvania.

It was fortunate for the western border of Pennsylvania and Virginia that Zeisberger was, at this time, upon the banks of the Muskingum. He was the firm friend of the colonies in their struggle for independence. Equally reliable in his friendship to the Americans was Captain John Killbuck of the Delawares, "a sensible Indian who spoke good English." As early as the second of July, 1777, Zeisberger informed George Morgan, at Pittsburgh what was passing in the wilderness; and again, five days after, at the request of Captain White Eyes, gave him much additional information concerning the doings of the hostile nations against the border, and the efforts of the Delawares in the interest of the Americas. A month previous to this, Captain Killbuck from Coshocton, wrote to Morgan: "We know that our Uncles, the Wyandots, have started from home. We sent two of our young men to tell them to come here, that we wanted to speak to them. As Captain White Eyes and Wingemund are gone to you to consult with you, _ when we hear from you at their return, we shall send again to the Wyandots."[3] But British machinations at Detroit proved stronger with the latter tribe than the importunities of the Delawares. On the twenty-ninth of July, Zeisberger wrote Brigadier-General Edward Hand, then in command of the Western Department, at Pittsburgh: "On the twentieth of this month, the Half King of the Wyandots, with nineteen of his men, arrived at Coshocton, where they had a great council and after they had delivered several speeches, the Half King drew out the war-belt with the tomahawk _ told the Delawares that all the nations on the other side and this side of the Lake had joined and taken hold of it; that the Delawares only had refused. He then delivered the belt to them. After they had consulted about it, they returned it to the Half King, telling him that they would sit still and hold fast to peace and friendship."

"They also said," continues Zeisberger, "that they had promised at a treaty when peace was concluded after the last war, that they would never fight any more against the white people, as long as the sun shone and the rivers ran; and that they would keep. The Half-King, not being pleased with this answer, returned the war-belt and compelled the Delawares to take it; nevertheless, they are determined in their mind and stood fast. After the Wyandots were gone, the Delawares gathered all of their men and women and admonished them not to have any thoughts of going to war, nor to join any of the warriors when they should pass by their towns."

"We now expect," adds the writer, "nothing else but that after these Wyandots get home, their warriors will march into the settlements very fast. The Delawares desired them not to let their warriors come through their villages but compelled them to march another way; but they did not consent to it; and said they should go to the border through Coshockton. Captain White Eyes will inform you of everything that has passed and how matters are. No doubt but you will encourage the Delawares to be strong and stand fast; for if they should give out, we, with our Indians, could not maintain here any longer. We wish that an army might soon come out from Fort Pitt; this would, in my opinion, be the only method to get peace settled among the nations."

"Twenty-three warriors returned lately from the settlements," are the closing words of Zeisberger, "with three prisoners and as many scalps; also with seven or eight horses. Last night we got intelligence by an Indian who came from

Sandusky, that a party of thirty Wyandots and French among them, were not far on their march to the settlements, and will come to Coshocton perhaps to-day. The Delawares flatter themselves that an army will soon come out from Fort Pitt, which is their only hope; but should that fail, I am afraid they cannot stand; and then surely all the nations that have not yet joined and taken the war-belt will unite with them."[4]

It was thus that the faithful Zeisberger put into the possession of General Hand all the information he was possessed of, of the doings and plottings of the enemy in the Western wilderness; and, as will be hereafter shown, he continued his kind and faithful offices to the Fort Pitt commanders, so long as he remained upon the Muskingum or Tuscarawas. His position was very far from a neutral one in the conflict then raging between the Colonies and Great Britain. To the last, his letters were of the greatest value to the suffering border. And he never hesitated to communicate whatever, in his judgement, tended to put the Americans on their guard against British plots or savage encroachments. He proved himself in every sense a thorough patriot _ a real lover of his adopted country.

In August, 1777, General Hand made a requisition of two thousand men from the several frontier counties of Virginia and Pennsylvania: _ "If I get them," he wrote, "I have no doubt of reducing the Wyandots and Pluggy's Town Confederacy, at present our most troublesome neighbors." The importunities of the Delawares and the suggestions of Zeisberger were not lost upon the Fort Pitt commander, it will be seen. "By information of a white man from Detroit," wrote Zeisberger from Coshocton, to Hand on the twenty-third of September, "who came here two days ago, but does not choose to have his name mentioned, I can give you the following account: There are at that point six companies of militia, amounting to about three hundred men in all. About seventy men, only, are in the garrison. An entrenchment is around the fort, on the land side and about fifty pieces of cannon are inside the post, and seven on the wharf. If an army should come against the fort, every man is to march out to meet it and they are to be reinforced from Niagara. They have a great store of provision and large number of cattle. At Sandusky, there are one hundred head of cattle. There are six vessels on the lakes; the largest two of sixteen guns. If an army should march there late, there will be a large cargo of goods at Sandusky."[5] With this intelligence as to the state of affairs upon the Sandusky, where the Wyandots were located, Hand made every exertion to carry forward an expedition against them; but his labors in the end proved abortive; and he was compelled to remain at Fort Pitt acting only on the defensive.

On the sixteenth of November, 1777, Zeisberger from Coshocton, wrote John Gibson who had been in temporary command of the Western Department just before: "As Captain White Eyes is going to Fort Pitt, I will not fail to acquaint you how matters are here now with us. Since my last, we have had quiet; no warriors have passed here, except a small party of Mohicans, _ also fourteen Wyandots with two whites in company, who came from Detroit. Sometime ago, fifty

Frenchmen, as we heard, came over the Lake to Cuyahoga and gave the Delawares and Mouseys who live there the tomahawk and desired them to go with them to Ligonier. Captain Pipe not being at home, they consented, and forty men went with the French; but Pipe met the French on the road, reproved them for deceiving his people in his absence and told them they were only servants and had no power to hand the tomahawk to them: Nobody could force him, either, to take it. Whereupon the greater part of the Indians turned back."

"Captains John Killbuck and Pipe," he continued, "are gone to Detroit _ upon what business, Captain White Eyes can tell you better than I can. The Shawnees _ Cornstalk's people will perhaps remove from their place and come to Coshocton this winter. They lately sent messengers who consulted with the chiefs here about that matter. Of the Mingoes we have heard nothing since the Half King was here. It seems as if they were tired of going to war, or, rather, as if they were frightened. We heard that after their last return they went over the Lake and asked the Wyandot chief's counsel and advice as to what they should do, because the Virginians would, as they thought, soon be upon them. He answered them, that they had begun the war and had always encouraged others to engage in hostilities. They had now brought it to pass what they always wished for. He therefore advised them to be strong and fight as men."

"Captain White Eyes," concluded Zeisberger, "intends to stay at Fort Pitt two or three days and I wish you would let him return again as soon as possible; for none of the councillors are at home to do business; if anything should happen; but if occasion should require to detain him longer, please to let the people here know of it, that they may not be uneasy about him; for some apprehend because the Cornstalk is taken at the Kanawha, White Eyes may be served so to. If he, therefore, stays away a longer time than he has appointed, they will surely think so."[6]

Previous to this time, although he had exacted hostages of the Delawares to secure their friendship, General Hand tried the efficacy of flattery to spirit them up: "Brothers, Captain White Eyes, Captain Killbuck and other chiefs of the Delawares at the Coshockton." _

"I have again the pleasure of sending you good news by James Elliott and James Kelly. They will pass through Captain Pipe's town, whom I have requested to accompany them to your town; or if he judged it best, to carry the news himself and leave them at Kuskusky.

"Brothers! I beg that my messengers may not be long detained and that you will write by them to me and tell me the news.

"Brothers! I rejoice with you that you will shortly be a great people; for the day is near when all nations will ask your advice and follow your wise councils. I know you will not be tired of good works, especially when you may have it in your power to save many nations from ruin."[7]

The Spring of 1778 was a gloomy one not only upon the western border of Pennsylvania and Virginia but in the Valley of the Muskingum and Tuscarawas. Zeisberger was still at Lichtenau but Edwards had returned to Gnadenhütten, and taken charge of that forsaken station. Captain Pipe in the northern wilderness was growing restive under his peace policy with the Americans; but White Eyes, at Coshocton, was true as the Pole-Star in his integrity. The slumbering embers of the hostility of the former, was now fanned almost into an open flame; while the fixedness of the other's friendship was well nigh broken asunder. The cause was this: the escape from the frontiers of a number of Tories and disaffected persons and their arrival in the Valley among the Delawares.

At Pittsburgh and vicinity in March of this year, lived Alexander McKee, Matthew Elliott and Simon Girty. McKee, before the Revolution had been a deputy Indian agent under Sir William Johnson. Being suspected of Tory proclivities he had, as early as 1776, been put upon his parol which was renewed the next year. On the seventh of February, 1778, General Hand, under the direction of the Board of War ordered him to York, Pennsylvania; but, pleading indisposition he still remained at Pittsburgh. Elliott, claiming to be a prisoner, recently from Quebec, on parol, but who in reality had a British commission as Captain in his pocket, had returned to the West, whence he had gone, as he said, on a trading expedition, and had been captured by the Indians and taken to Detroit. Girty was in the employ of the Americans as Indian interpreter. These three men, with other disaffected persons, on the twenty-eighth of March, 1778, fled to the wilderness, _ making their way directly to the Delawares, where they boldly threw off the mask and declared themselves enemies to the United States.

The machinations of these men came well nigh alienating the Delawares from their peace policy _ from what was, practically, a league with the Americans; but the opportune arrival from the East of Heckewelder and another Moravian at Coshocton, with advices from Hand and Morgan at Fort Pitt, soon after the departure of these renegades to the Shawnee towns upon the Scioto, re-assured the nation. On the ninth of June, Zeisberger from Coshocton informed Morgan concerning the state of affairs in the Indian country. "The Half King, of the Wyandots," he wrote, "with all his men and Mingoes with him, a hundred in all, are gone to the fort at Kanawha." "We learned since," added Zeisberger, "that after they had killed one white man there, and had three of their men wounded, half of the party went home again, and the other half down the river."[8]

On the nineteenth of July, the faithful missionary wrote General Hand from Coshocton: "White Eyes is of the opinion that the only course left is for you to march a large army against the Wyandots and other hostile Indians. He strongly urges that course. He and I are blamed and accused before the Governor of Detroit, for giving you intelligence of the affairs in the Indian country; but I believe all this is the fruit of McKee's labor at Detroit." "All thoughts," continues Zeisberger, "of bringing about a peace with the nations, especially with the Wyandots are in vain."[9]

All of the Moravian Indians were now gathered below Coshocton, at Lichtenau, under the combined care of Zeisberger, Edwards and Heckewelder. Zeisberger wrote that he hoped to be able to hold his place until the end of the war; but if it should prove impossible, he would put himself at the head of his converts and lead them to the south country far beyond the reach of danger.

Stirring events were at this period transpiring in the West. Commissioned by Virginia, Lieutenant-Colonel George Rogers Clark set out, on the twenty-fourth day of June, 1778, from the Falls of the Ohio, with a small force of Virginia State troops, nearly all of whom were native Virginians, to capture the British post on the Mississippi. At midnight on the third of July, he took Kaskaskia by surprise and sent the commandant, together with important papers, to Williamsburg, the Virginia capital. In the same way, Prairie du Rocher, St. Phillips, and Cahokia, fell into his hands. Vincennes, where there was a preponderance of French element, voluntarily yielded as soon as he had conveyed to its inhabitants the news of the alliance between France and the American states.

These unexpected disasters roused Hamilton at Detroit, who was holding a treaty with the Indians. He gave them the hatchet anew, and urged them to more general and violent assaults upon the frontiers. There were some Delawares at the council, who, in vain, attempted the advocacy of peace. Hamilton afterward made strenuous efforts to induce the nation to join the confederate tribes. Failing in this and well knowing the attitude of Zeisberger, he planned an expedition against both the Delawares and the "Moravians," which, however, was not carried out. It was full time, therefore, that the alliance of this nation should if possible be firmly secured to the Americans by a new treaty with them; so, on the seventeenth of September, one was held, with that tribe at Pittsburgh. It was stipulated that a perpetual peace and friendship should hence forth subsist between the Delawares and the United States; and, if either should be engaged in a war with any nation or nations, then each was to assist the other in due proportion to their abilities; and if either should discover any hostile designs forming against the other, they should give the earliest notice thereof, that timely measures might be taken to prevent their ill effect. The agreement was entered into between their three principal chiefs, Captain John Killbuck, Captain Pipe and Captain White Eyes on the one part, and Andrew and Thomas Lewis, Commissioners of the United States on the other part. None rejoiced more than the Moravian missionaries that the neutral Delawares had now become the allies of the Americans.

Early in August, previous to the signing of the treaty, Brigadier-General Lachlan McIntosh, with a small force of regulars, superceded Hand in command of Fort Pitt. His policy was not only to carry on defensive measures for the frontier, but also to promote ulterior operations. His plan, ostensibly, was to attack the Wyandot towns; but, in reality, his ultimate designs were against Detroit. McIntosh was present at the treaty of September seventeenth. In marching westward from Fort Pitt, no sooner would the river be crossed than the territory claimed by the Delawares would be entered upon; so, to the end that no obstruction should be placed in his way, a clause was inserted in the articles agreed upon at the treaty, to the effect that a free passage should be given the troops while passing through their country.

McIntosh did not propose to enter the western wilderness in a hap-hazard way. His army, largely re-inforced by militia from the Western Counties, of Virginia and Pennsylvania, must have depositories erected on its line of march; besides, there must be an occasional fortification for resort in the event of disaster. All these were demanded on strict military principles and usage. It was necessary, therefore, that at least one fort should be erected in Delaware territory, and the consent of that nation was obtained, at the treaty, for that purpose; but the reason given was, "for the better security of the old men, women and children," of the Delawares whilst their warriors should be engaged against the common enemy; for these Indians at the same time agreed to join the troops of the United States with as many of their best and most experienced warriors as they could spare consistent with their own safety.

Colonel William Crawford, under orders from McIntosh, "by fatigue of the whole line" proceeded to the erection of a strong post upon the Indian side of the Ohio, near the mouth of Beaver, in what is now Beaver County, Pennsylvania, which, in honor of the Commanding General, was called Fort McIntosh. It was the second permanent foot-hold gained by the United States upon the territory of the great Northwest, now teeming with its busy millions _ the Illinois country, conquered by Clark, being the first. During the month of October, the headquarters of the army were removed from Pittsburgh to the new post.

On the fifth day of November, McIntosh, deceived by Intelligence received from the wilderness that the enemy were embodying in force upon the Tuscarawas, commenced his march into the Indian country, with his whole army except one company. With him was a small party of Delawares. For fourteen days it was continued; so slow was the movement, before the valley of that river was reached. It was now too late in the season to proceed farther; a fort was commenced upon the west side of the stream, just below the mouth of Sandy creek, near the site of the present town of Bolivar, in Tuscarawas county, Ohio; in which, when pretty nearly completed, there was left a detachment of one hundred and fifty men under command of Colonel John Gibson; and McIntosh, with the residue of his army, returned to Fort Pitt. The post received the name of Fort Laurens. Early in 1779, Simon Girty and a few savages, principally Mingoes, drove back with loss a relief party returning from that post. Soon after, a detachment from the garrison was ambushed and nearly all killed. The fort was there upon besieged by the British Indians and the garrison reduced to terrible straits. A short time after, when the siege had been abandoned, McIntosh arrived with supples and a relief of men. Major Frederick Vernon was placed in command of the post and McIntosh again returned to Pittsburgh, where he was soon after relieved by Colonel Daniel Brodhead. Fort Laurens was evacuated during the Summer, and never after occupied.

The Spring of 1779 found the Moravian missionaries and their flock still at Lichtenau; but in April, Edwards with a part of the converts re-occupied Gnadenhütten; Zeisberger, with another party, proceeded to Schönbrunn, which had been previously destroyed, and encamped amid its ruins; the rest stayed at Lichtenau in charge of Heckewelder. Zeisberger soon began a new town on the western bank of the Tuscarawas, which was completed before the close of the year and called New Schönbrunn. It was situated in what is now Goshen Township, Tuscarawas county, Ohio, a quarter of a mile from the present Lockport and one and a quarter miles south of what is now New Philadelphia, county-seat of the county. Zeisberger removed his little flock, in December, 1779, to New Schönbrunn.

Whenever practicable a correspondence was kept up between Colonel Gibson at Fort Laurens and the Delawares farther down the Tuscarawas; also with the Moravian missionaries. Information thus received was sent to McIntosh, at Fort Pitt. "The Moravians," wrote Gibson, on the thirteenth of February, 1779, "wish a fort built near their town, as they could then assist with provisions and men." "Should the other nations continue to strike us," adds the Colonel, "we shall, in my opinion, only have the Moravians upon whom to depend."

Captain White Eyes, having joined McIntosh before the first march of the General to the Tuscarawas, caught the smallpox and was taken to Pittsburgh where he died, on the seventh of November, 1778. This left Captain Killbuck and Captain Pipe as the two principal leaders of the Delawares, at the commencement of 1779. The former, on the thirtieth of January, 1779, informed Gibson of the fact that it was Girty who led the savages to Fort Laurens, where they attacked the relief party as previously mentioned. Similar information, with additional news and some of importance was communicated to the same officer by Heckewelder ten days after: "Your letters," he wrote, "were taken in the engagement." On the fifteenth of March, Killbuck wrote the commandant at Fort Pitt that he was discouraged at his poor success in holding the Delawares firmly to the American cause: "Brother! It is now past two years, since you told me you were quite ready, and held your horse by the bridle, with one foot in the stirrup, and your gun on your shoulder, ready to mount, when the first murder should be committed, in order to pursue the enemy. Now, brother, I am sorry to tell you, that, as this has been made known to the nations, and they finding nothing has been done by you, all this time, they mock and make all the game of me they can. They try all they can to disturb and convince my people that you are telling them that which is not true, pointing to your not having fulfilled your promises, and saying you were not able to do it, there being but a few of you."[10]

Thus, wrote Heckewelder, from Coshocton three days previous: "The Delaware chiefs have turned back a large party of Indians who aim to attack Fort Laurens." "I hear," continues the missionary, "that the French at Detroit, are working strongly, already, but privately, to join the United States, and forsake their former master." Heckewelder added that he thought the best and cheapest way to convey prisoners to Fort Laurens was by water; "but the headmen here think the boats ought to be well guarded."[11] The same writer to Colonel Gibson at Fort Laurens in a letter dated at Coshocton, on the nineteenth of March, says:

"Since the English see that their giving goods to the Indians at Detroit to go to war, helps them but little, _ the most of them contenting themselves with the presents, forgetting they are to do something for them, _ they have found out a better way. They now bring the goods to this side of the Lake, where they will be nearer the place the stroke is to be made, and where they will know better who will fight and will not."[12]

On the twenty-third of March, 1779, Colonel Brodhead from Fort McIntosh wrote Heckewelder, for information concerning the plans of the enemy and their operations in the wilderness. The missionary replied, on the ninth of April: "The following parties have come from war through our towns within a fortnight _ First a party of Mingoes with three children prisoners; a party of ten Delawares and Shawnees with two scouts and two children prisoners; they also brought off a sucking child, which, always crying, they killed at Little Beaver creek; a party of Shawnees with three prisoners, one an old man of eighty-four years, who was taken while boiling sugar, near Wheeling; another party of two Shawnees, one having received a shot through his arm, the bullet lodging in his body. _ This day six warriors came in here, all Wyandots, and three of them the Half King's sons; _ they killed two men somewhere above Redstone." On the twenty-eighth of April, Heckewelder sent information to Fort Pitt of the capture of Hamilton from Detroit, at Vincennes, by George Rogers Clark, in the latter part of February previous, the news he had received through Indian sources. On the fourth of May, he wrote: "I heard a few days ago that a party of warriors had killed two men and taken one prisoner at or near Fort McIntosh."[13]

The response of Colonel Brodhead from Fort Pitt, on the thirteenth of May, was of a character well calculated to reassure the Delawares: "I have no doubt but the Mingoes (being the greatest villains of all the nations) have endeavored to excite the Wyandots and Shawnees to strike the Delawares, but I will venture to predict they will not do it." On the twenty-eighth, Heckewelder cheered Brodhead with hopes of a peace with the Wyandots; but it proved a fallacy. Brodhead was informed also that the renegade, Simon Girty, was acting wickedly.

The Fort Pitt commander, exceedingly desirous of getting correct knowledge of the strength and designs of the enemy Indians, especially of the number of refugees and Rangers at Sandusky, interrogated Heckewelder, upon the subject, on the twenty-ninth. On the third of June, he informed the missionary that he had a party of warriors out toward the Mingo towns, and that others were preparing.

Heckewelder, on the twenty-ninth of June, from Coshocton, gave Brodhead the following account: "As I am come to this place last night, on my own private business, I thought proper to acquaint you with the true situation of the Wyandots. It is my opinion they are not inclined to make a proper peace with the Americans at present. They only mean to deceive you awhile until such time as their corn gets hard and they have taken it out of your way; after which their tomahawks will be as sharp against you as ever." And he was right, as the events of the next few months clearly demonstrated. Heckewelder added: "There are two of the largest vessels from Detroit, named Dunmore and Gage, cruising upon the Lake, in order to discover your coming against them. This information which I have now given you is certainly to be looked on as facts, and I assure you, should anything of consequence come to my knowledge hereafter, I shall, if in my power, inform you of it."[14]

The interest of Heckewelder in the American cause, seemed, at this time, always on the alert _ never to flag. On the thirtieth of June and on the eighth of July he wrote Brodhead at Fort Pitt giving all the particulars of the plottings and schemes of the enemy and particularly of the Wyandots. It was still his belief that they were only time-serves, that they were in fact enemies. Alexander McCormick, then at Coshocton, declared to him that the only way to bring about a peace with that nation was, to march an army against them from Fort Laurens. "March two days beyond the fort towards them," said he, "and there will be speeches enough carried from them to you for peace."

On account of reports in circulation as to the credibility of Heckewelder, the patriotic missionary wrote Brodhead, from Coshocton, on the ninth of August, 1779: "I have understood by some Delawares who came from Philadelphia that I have been represented as one who listens to any story he may hear, and for that reason have sent such fearful letters to several officers in the service of the United States. I, therefore, think best, to leave the communication of all news to the Delawares themselves, and not to trouble myself further about such matters; as they are indeed not properly my business. I thought to do some service to my country to which I am closely attached; and always have made it a rule to write nothing but what I had from a trusty body; likewise to distinguish my news by the words facts and reports. I think the most I have written has appeared to be true already, and the other part may yet so appear." But the patriotism of the missionary soon gets the better of his ill-determined resolution, for, on the twenty-third of October he not only wrote a letter for Captain Killbuck to Brodhead but added a postscript over his own signature recounting particulars of the attach by the savages upon Colonel David Rogers early in the month, a short distance above the mouth of Licking, on the Ohio river. On the tenth of August, Brodhead marched from Fort Pitt against the Seneca and Mousey towns upon the upper waters of the Allegheny. His army was composed of over six hundred men. With him went sixty Delawares. The expedition proved a complete success.

"I am very anxious to know the strength of the garrison at Detroit," wrote Brodhead to Zeisberger, on the twenty-sixth of November, 1779, "and likewise the strength of the works." He also desired him to employ a proper person to go and bring the intelligence if one could be obtained and he would pay him well for his labor; _ "the fitness of a person," he wrote on the twelfth of December, "for this undertaking must be left to you. I hope you have already sent a man that can be relied on for his integrity as well as ingenuity."

Throughout the year 1779, a faction of the Delawares headed by Captain Pipe was growing more and more unfriendly to the Americans; although that chief continued his protestations of friendship. He was seldom at Coshocton. About the first of June, he sent thither a belt asking that his clan might remain at Pluggy's Town, at the present town of Delaware, Delaware County, Ohio, the place where he was then gathering his people together. But Killbuck and the other Delaware chiefs thought "it very wrong in him to ask to stay at Pluggy's Town; we know his old town, Walhonding, was very good for him before he went away and left it; and we know no reason why he should not return there, if his heart is good; as we hope it is; and therefore we desire that he may come and sit down there." But the heart of Captain Pipe was not good _ towards the Americans; hence, he was desirous of keeping away from the councils of the other Delaware chiefs who were really friends to the new government.

In the Spring of 1780, another change was made in the Moravian Indian villages. Lichtenau was abandoned by Heckewelder, who removed his charge up the Tuscarawas on the west bank, where, in what is now Salem Township, Tuscarawas County, Ohio, one and a half miles southwest of Port Washington, a new town was founded which was called Salem. The number of missionaries was now increased by the arrival of Gottlob Lenseman; and in the Autumn following, Michael Young arrived as assistant to Edwards. At the close of the year, Lenseman had charge at New Schönbrunn; Edwards, at Gnadenhütten; Heckewelder, at Salem; while Zeisberger, as superintendent, itinerated from village to village.

During the year 1779, Brodhead had proposed to Zeisberger that he should remove his villages nearer the settlements and he also conferred with Captain Killbuck and Captain Pipe relative to the Coshocton Indians coming to live on Big Beaver. "They seem to think," wrote Brodhead to Zeisberger on the tenth of February, 1780, "it would be of advantage for them to do so, but wish your people would likewise form one or more towns in their neighborhood." "I sincerely wish," he continues, "your congregation could be prevailed upon to move nearer to us, where it would be more convenient for us to give them every necessary support." "Your situation at present," he added, "is on the road which the enemy Indians travel; you are often encumbered with them and must feed them for sake of your own preservation; which circumstance alone must be very disagreeable; but it must be very mortifying to you to see prisoners and scalps carried through your towns. Besides, I can not with safety, send parties to pursue the murderers to a sufficient distance lest they might accidentally, either early in the morning or late in the evening, fire upon some of the hunting-parties of our friends; and if such an accident should happen, it would hurt my feelings."

Brodhead began now to suspect that all was not well with the Coshocton Indians. On the twenty-second of March, he wrote Zeisberger: "My not having received a line from you or Mr. Heckewelder in answer to my several letters, induces me to apprehend that the Delawares are hostile and has almost determined me to carry on offensive operations against them, and I can no longer credit their declarations of friendship. I wish you would give me your sentiments in writing, and lest your letter should be made a bad use of, you need only say 'yes' or 'no', by way of nota bene or post script to the question put with respect to the Delawares."[15]

"We have not heard anything at all this whole winter," wrote Heckewelder, on the thirtieth of March, "what the enemy are about. The snow being so deep, and the weather so continually cold, has, I suppose, been the reason;" _ but he gave Brodhead the intelligence that warriors that very day were on their way to the settlements. He informed him also what course they had taken.

Zeisberger, who, for a length of time, had been silent, so far as corresponding with the Fort Pitt commander was concerned, now sent Brodhead a long message. It was dated at Tupaking (New Schönbrunn) on the second of April, 1780. He says:

"You desired me to procure you some intelligence from over the Lake; it was not in my powers to do; and much less now; as I live such a distance from Coshocton, where I might, perhaps, bring it about, one way or other. But hearing that a white man, who was a prisoner among the Wyandots and who was well acquainted, as I was told, with all the particulars at Detroit, went by Gnadenhütten to Fort Pitt last winter, _ I thought he could and would give you more intelligence than any Indian could procure, because Indians have not knowledge about such matters; and I thank it would be of very little service to send an Indian on such an errand, who is a stranger to the place.

"You proposed that our Indians might move nearer to Fort Pitt. Sir, this indeed would not only be very hard and difficult, but impossible for us to undertake now, except our people would leave all behind that they have; for they are not like the rest of the Indians, who can take their whole estate on their backs and go where they please; and, though they might go round by water, we would not be able to procure such a number of canoes as it would require.

"Our people have been traveling and moving from one place to another, till we at last came here to this place, where we hope to remain in possession of our settlements, and enjoy the fruit of our labor, at least for a good many years. I dare not think about moving, nor even propose it to our people; for it would quite discourage them, except there was great necessity. Therefore, pray Sir, let us remain in possession of our settlements. As we have held out so long, I hope, with the help of God, we shall get over it, till peace is again restored. Neither warriors nor other Indians come to our towns now because it out of their way, and we live very quiet."

"I have not heard," continues Zeisberger, "of hostile thoughts among the Coshocton Indians yet, and if I should perceive any thing of that kind, I would give you intelligence by express."[16]

Brodhead informed Heckewelder on the fourteenth of April, that an expedition against some of the Western nations would soon be carried into execution; but his sanguine expectations were not realized. The next day he wrote Zeisberger: "It gives me pleasure to find that your congregation is less scattered than it was some time ago, and I am far from insisting on your removal with loss or much inconvenience; but I wish you to excite your people to have an eye upon the conduct of the other Delawares and inform me from time to time of their particular conduct."

Brodhead was well aware of the duplicity of many of the Delawares. In an answer to a letter of Heckewelder's of the twenty-second of April giving him information of the doings of the Council at Coshocton Brodhead on the fourth of May says: "The Delawares have acted a double part long enough, and that at a considerable expense to the United States." In particular was this true of Captain Pipe and his clan. Brodhead continued his importunities to Zeisberger for information. On the eighth of May he wrote: "Colonel John Gibson has brought from Lancaster three letters directed to you which I enclose. A French officer who has some message to the Council at Coshocton, will do me the honor to deliver them, and I wish the Brethren to show him every mark of respect." "Perhaps," continues the writer, "it may be necessary for some of the principal men of your congregation to accompany him to the Council; but of this you must be the best judge. Should you think it best to send some with him you will be enabled to write me particularly what passes there and what is your opinion of the intentions of the Delawares in general."

In July, 1780, a party of Wyandots crossing the river on rafts below Big Beaver, were attacked by the whites and defeated. The particulars, Heckewelder wrote Brodhead as he received them from Indian sources. The Fort Pitt commander now proposed to make the Moravian Indians even more active allies than before; so he wrote Zeisberger on the second of December: "Being desirous of laying in a larger supply of salt provisions than from the present appearances will be laid in by the commissaries for the supply of my troops, I take the liberty to propose to you the sending fifteen or twenty of your best hunters to the best and nearest place of hunting buffalo, bear and elk, near the Ohio River, and salting the same in canoes made for that purpose." "If you approve of this proposal," continues the commander, "please send two or three of your people, with some horses to take out the salt that may be necessary to preserve such quantity as they may engage to lay in; and upon their delivering the meat to a party of men that I shall send to receive it, they shall be paid the full value, on my order at this place." "Should your people," concludes Brodhead, "exert themselves in laying in a large quantity of meat, they will particularly recommend themselves to the esteem of their countrymen."

The proposition of Brodhead to obtain by agency of the "Moravians" a quantity of wild meat, was not acceptable to Zeisberger and he so wrote the commander, before the end of the month. Such an overt act while in consonance with the feelings of Zeisberger, would nevertheless almost certainly become known to the Delawares, who were now on the very brink, nearly all of them, of going over to the enemy. It would, therefore, expose him and his converts to the wrath of the confederate tribes and the British, which, of course, was much to be feared, in view of their exposed position. Brodhead was satisfied, upon reading the letter of the missionary that his reasons for declining the undertaking were judicious; and so informed him by communication of the twenty-first of January, 1781.

That the Delawares as a nation should have remained so long the friends and allies of the Americans is a matter of wonder, all things considered. "Their chiefs came here," wrote Brodhead from Fort Pitt, as early as the twenty-second of November, 1779, "a few days ago and intend to wait upon Congress, to complain of their failure of a promise that they would supply the Indians with goods." "The poor wretches," added the commander, "are quite destitute of clothing and, unless a speedy supply is afforded them, they will, of necessity, be compelled to join the enemy on any terms, or perish." On the eleventh of February, 1780, Brodhead again wrote: "The Delawares continue their professing of friendship and talk of coming to settle near us. Again, on the thirteenth of May, he says: "The Delawares continue to be friendly; and some of them are now with my scouts; but, having nothing but fair words to give them, I expect they will be soon tired of this service. On the sixteenth of September, he informed the Governor of Pennsylvania, that "if the friendship of the Delaware Indians is thought to be valuable, it is time that goods should be forwarded to clothe them; otherwise they will be compelled to go where they can be supplied." "The Indian Captains," is his language on the twenty- second of January, 1781, "appointed by the British commandant at Detroit, are clothed in the most elegant manner, and have many valuable presents made them. The Captains I have commissioned by authority of Congress, are naked and receive nothing but a little whisky, for which they are reviled by the Indians in general; so that, unless a change of system is introduced I must expect to see all Indians in favor of Britain, in spite of every address in my power." From necessity, the "change of system" was not "introduced" and the Spring of 1781 saw "all Indians," as Brodhead had foreseen, "in favor of Britain." _ The Delawares except a small number of them took up the hatchet _ against the Americans.

But the faithful Killbuck gave Brodhead timely warning: "The Council of Coshocton," said he, writing from the Moravian Indian town of Salem on the twenty-sixth of February, 1781, "have entirely stopped my ears, so that I know nothing. But, brother, a bird has whispered something to me and this I shall acquaint you of: Some days ago a Mingo came to Coshocton and received a speech from the Council there, which made him go home laughing. The speech was to this purpose: "We are your friends and on this side; and only wait to see what you are about and then we shall join you. There is none of us here who think of being friends to the Virginians. There is one man who is a friend to them, namely, Killbuck." "Again," he added, "everybody here knows that the Coshocton men are getting ready to go and fight you; and a party of five are gone off already; the course they took was towards Wheeling." Upon the same day, Heckewelder, from the same place, also wrote the Fort Pitt commander: "I believe the greatest part of the people at Coshocton will be upon you in a few days. They have already been stopped once or twice, but I daily hear they will go soon; they have ranged themselves into three parties, and, if I am right, one party is gone already; but I hope they will receive what they deserve." Brodhead determined at once to circumvent these Coshocton savages; _ to carry the war to their town. Indeed, the idea was, possibly, suggested to him by Heckewelder himself: "If it should be concluded on," wrote the ardent missionary, "that a body of men should march to Coshocton to punish these wicked people, I trust that your honor will do all that lies in your power to prevent molesting anybody belonging to our towns." As will be presently shown, this suggestion as to the "Moravians" was not lost upon Brodhead.

When the Delaware council resolved to take up the hatchet against the Americans, Killbuck and those who sided with him, to the number of thirty, left their town and erected huts upon the site of their old capital _ New Comers town; so that Coshocton was only inhabited by such Delawares as were hostile to the Americans. Captain Pipe built a village upon the Tymuchtee, one of the branches of the Sandusky, where, having removed from Pluggy's town, he was in close league with the Half King and the confederate tribes generally. The "Moravian" Indians and their ministers, when the alienation of the Delawares became known, renounced all further fellowship with them. Very different was their action in 1778, when these Indians became the allies of the Americans and joined, some of them, the standard of McIntosh and subsequently that of Brodhead. Then, although Zeisberger did not approve of putting the tomahawk into the hands of that nation, the missionaries did not complain of it.

In the Spring of 1781, Zeisberger determined to pay a visit to his friends in Pennsylvania. About the first of April; on his way eastward, he called upon Brodhead at Fort Pitt, and put him in possession of all necessary information concerning the Delawares and the Moravian Indians. He was requested by that officer to go to Philadelphia and lay before Congress, the Board of War, and the Executive Council of Pennsylvania, all the particulars of his mission and the disposition of the Indians in general. "He is a faithful man," wrote Brodhead, "and what he says may be relied upon."

Brodhead did not rush headlong in the movement against the Delawares. On the twenty-seventh of March, he wrote Washington: "A number of Delaware Indians from Coshocton have been here since my last, and appear to be as friendly as ever; I am persuaded that a few are well affected, but they are now put to the trial by being ordered to remove hither without the loss of time and remain under our protection, where their daily transacting will be seen and known." "I have called upon the county Lieutenants," adds the writer, "and, if I am not disappointed as usual, I intend to surprise the Indian towns about Coshocton."[17]

His circular to the County Lieutenants was dated on the eighth of March. "I have just received letters," he wrote, "by Captain Montour, which inform me that the Delawares of Coshocton, very few excepted, have declared in favor of the British and that some of them are already come against our settlements. I believe this intelligence to be authentic and that we shall now experience what I have long strove to avoid, a general war with the savages. If we have any friends among them, besides the Moravian Indians, I expect they will be with us in a few days and that they will be useful.

"My force being much reduced," continues the commander, "cannot extend the protection I would wish to every part of the frontier, but so far as I am enabled, I am, as usual, determined to give every countenance to the inhabitants. Although it is to be wished that our endeavors to raise supplies within this Department might not be interrupted, yet at this crisis, it is highly expedient that those inhabitants who live in places of security should step forward and lend immediate aid to the frontier."

"I have in contemplation," adds the writer, "an enterprise against the deceitful Delawares at and near Coshocton; but I am much at a loss for supplies; therefore I have thought it advisable that the County Lieutenants and such commanding officers of battalions as may be desirous of giving their attendance, do assemble at my quarters on the fifteenth instant at ten o'clock in the forenoon, in order to deliberate upon ways and means to obtain supplies for an expedition, and to form suitable plan or plans for the security of the inhabitants."

"In the mean time," concludes Brodhead, "encourage the frontier inhabitants to make a stand by collecting into forts or strong houses, and by ranging in sufficient parties with great vigilance and industry; and let all the militia in your county be in readiness to repel invasion."

On the sixteenth of March, the commander wrote David Shepherd, Lieutenant of Ohio county, Virginia: "You are requested," said he, "to procure sixty men, including officers, from the militia, to go upon an expedition. Both officers and men must be furnished with at least twenty days provision each, and a good horse, saddle and bridle; and they are to be well armed and accoutered and to rendezvous at Fort Henry (Wheeling) on the fifth day of next month.

"Thirty horses, saddles, and bridles." continued the writer, "will likewise be necessary from your county to enable me to take out a part of the regular troops. The provisions and any unavoidable loss of horses or furniture, will be paid for by the public." "You will be pleased," he added, "to let me know by the first of next month whether this requisition can be complied with. I hope there cannot be any difficulty respecting it; but our force must be ascertained, to prevent the expedition falling through, to the discouragement of the inhabitants."

Besides, a regular requisition was made by Brodhead upon Shepherd, as Lieutenant of Ohio county, for three thousand pounds of beef, pork or bacon for the use of the regulars intended to be employed upon the expedition.

On the seventh of April, 1781, Brodhead left Fort Pitt with over one hundred and fifty regulars, dropping down the Ohio river to Wheeling, where Shepherd had collected one hundred and thirty-four of the militia including officers, into four companies. On the tenth, the united force made its way across the Ohio, taking the nearest route for Coshocton. The savages had received no warning of the approach of an enemy. They evidently felt secure in their wilderness home. With Brodhead was a few friendly Indians who evinced a keen desire for the scalps of the hostile Delawares.

As the army neared the objective point of the expedition an Indian was captured from whom was obtained some valuable information. Soon afterward two others were discovered and fired upon. One was wounded but both succeeded in making their escape. Fearing lest these Indians should give the alarm, Brodhead, although in the midst of a heavy fall of rain, ordered a rapid march for the town, in hopes of surrounding it before any of the savages had news of his coming. The troops marched in three divisions. The right and left wings approached the river a little above and below Coshocton, while the center moved directly upon it. The Coshocton Indians were completely surprised and their town laid waste; also two and a half miles below, on the same side of the river, Lichtenau, now occupied by them, fifteen warriors were killed and over twenty prisoners _ old men, women and children _ taken. Large quantities of peltry and other stores were destroyed and about forty head of cattle killed.

About four miles above Coshocton, on the march down, Brodhead had detached a party to cross the river and attack about forty warriors who had just before crossed over with some prisoners and scalps and were then drunk, as he learned by the Indians whom the advance guard had taken prisoner; but the excessive hard rain had swelled the river bank high. It was found impracticable. Brodhead then marched up the stream about seven miles with a view to send for some craft from the "Moravian" towns with which to cross the river, so that he could pursue the Indians; but when he proposed his plan to the militia, he found they conceived they had accomplished enough and were determined to return; whereupon he marched to New Comers town, the home of Captain Killbuck and his followers. This chief and another had no sooner heard that Brodhead was upon the river than they pursued the fleeing Delawares, "killed one of their greatest villains," and brought his scalp to the American commander.

At the request of Brodhead, the missionaries and some of their converts from the "Moravian" towns visited him before he left the river. He renewed to them his proposition that they should break up their establishments and move to the border _ urging them to accompany him to Pittsburgh. But this well-meant overture they declined. They, together with Captain Killbuck's band, supplied the army with corn and meat enough to subsist both men and horses to the Ohio River.

The Moravian Indians had become objects of suspicion to many of the frontiermen, some of whom were of the militia in Brodhead's army. Among the prisoners captured at Coshocton were five of those Indians who, of course, were immediately released by the American commander; as they were simply visitors at their former home. As they were going up the river in a canoe on their way to Salem, some of the militia, contrary to express orders, followed them and in such a menacing manner as to induce them to leave the stream and take to the hills. They were in fact fired upon by those in pursuit and one of their number wounded though they all succeeded in reaching their town. So, also, while Brodhead was receiving the visits of the Moravian missionaries and some of their converts, as just described, there was manifested a strong desire upon part of some of the militia to march to their settlements for the purpose of destroying them; but the movement was quickly repressed by those in command.

A proposition made by Brodhead to Captain Killbuck and his band to put themselves under the protection of the Americans and march with the army upon its return to the border, was gladly accepted; so, with this accession, and a large amount of plunder captured from the "Coshocton" Indians, the troops returned to Wheeling, where the spoils were dispersed of, netting quite a considerable sum. Both regulars and militia, upon this expedition, behaved with much spirit; and though there was considerable firing between them and the Indians not one was killed or wounded. Brodhead with his troops, accompanied by the friendly Delawares, then made their way back to Fort Pitt while the militia were disbanded and returned to their several places of abode.

A circumstance thought by some damaging to the reputation of the enterprise was that all the warriors killed had been captured in the assault upon the town. These were pointed out by Pekillon, a friendly Delaware, who was with the army of Brodhead. A council of war was called to determine their fate. The fact that they had raided upon the border, killing indiscriminately the old and young of either sex was clearly established; and this, too, at the very time when others of their clan were making protestations of friendship to the commander at Fort Pitt. Their crimes were thought sufficient to justify a decree of death, by the council; and, in ordering the carrying out of that decision, Brodhead, himself a humane and chivalric officer, only acted upon the idea of a complete justification according to the usages of war. The warriors were bound, taken a little distance below the town, and dispatched with tomahawks and spears, and then scalped.

Another transaction _ one of those unfortunate ones that the moralist must condemn, and which is too often seen in border warfare _ was the killing, by the militia, to whose care they had been committed of the residue of the prisoners, the women and children excepted. It was done immediately after the return march had commenced and without the knowledge of Brodhead or his principal officers. The women and children were taken to Fort Pitt. An incident occurred on the march to New Comers town which brings out in strong light the deep seated hatred lurking in the breasts of some of the border men to the savages at that period _ a frenzy of revenge, which only their extreme and long-continued cruelties and ravages could have engendered. An Indian presented himself on the opposite bank of the river and asked for the "Big Captain." Bradford responded with the question as to what he wanted. To which he replied in substance that his desire was for peace. "Send over some of your chiefs," said the American commander. "Maybe you will kill them," was the response. He was answered that they should not be killed. One came across, a fine looking man, and entered into conversation with Brodhead. But while thus engaged, Lewis Wetzel, one of the militia-men, came up behind the chief with a tomahawk concealed in the bosom of his hunting shirt and struck him on the back of his head with the weapon causing instant death.

A few days after the return of Brodhead from Coshocton, eighty hostile Delawares came up the Tuscarawas in search of Captain Killbuck and his band, breathing destruction to all of them. It was not, by any means, that they wished only to take them prisoners, especially Captain Killbuck and other chiefs and counselors, that they could thus have them under their control and prevent them governing the nation while the war lasted; it was, that they thirsted for their blood. The scalps of Captain Killbuck and his clan who had continued the allies of the Americans would have been esteemed as delectable prizes as those of any of their white enemies; for had not that chief already taken up the hatchet against them? From that moment, he was proclaimed _ he and all his followers. Not knowing of their leaving the valley with Brodhead, they felt sure of finding them. They finally reached Gnadenhütten but, of course, the objects of their search were not there. They were told by the Moravian Indians that all had gone off with the Americans. The Delaware band then endeavored to convince the "converts" that their only safety was in seeking a refuge to the westward farther away from the border. Precisely the same advice had been given them by Brodhead when upon the Coshocton expedition, only with this difference, that they should go with him to Pittsburgh. It was thus that the belligerents saw, what it needed no prophet to foresee, the danger there was in the missionaries and their flock remaining in the valley of the Tuscarawas _ literally between two fires, for although they were to all intents and purposes the allies of the Americans, they were too far away from the border for any advantages of protection by them.

The Delaware band was not entirely unsuccessful in their endeavors to persuade the "Moravians" to remove; as more than a dozen of those living in Salem concluded to go with them, "renouncing the gospel and falling back into heathenism." It was thus that there was to be found among the hostile Delawares a considerable element of what may be called "Moravianism;" false, of course, but such as enabled these before-time "converts" to appear, at least, to captives taken afterwards, as veritable Moravian Indians; the deception being helped on, frequently, by their calling themselves such and by their ability, in some instances, to speak pretty good German.

The Delaware warriors, before leaving, made several attempts to take the life of Heckewelder, rightfully considering him as a chief obstacle in the way of inducing the removal of the "Moravians. It is probable they would have had still farther success in inducing the "converts" to leave the valley had it not been that a report reached their ears of an American army being again on its way to the Tuscarawas. So the warriors departed, leaving the "Moravian" villages again in peace _ but only for a short time as small parties of Delawares continued to prowl through the valley, stealing the horses of the "converts" and whatever else they could find. One of these bands lay in ambush near a field at Gnadenhütten, into which came the missionaries Edwards and Young and began to plant potatoes. "Instantly seven of the savages cocked their rifles, took aim, and were upon the point of shooting them down," when their Captain, seized by a sudden impulse of mercy, made a sign for them to desist. "The band crept away, and the two missionaries continued working in the field, ignorant of the death which had threatened them."

The object of Zeisberger's return to Pennsylvania was to attend a synod of his church at Bethlehem. After its adjournment, he proceeded to Philadelphia where he was thanked by the President of the Supreme Executive Council of the State _ the Governor in fact as well as in law of that commonwealth, "in the name of the whole country, for his services among the Indians particularly for his Christian humanity in turning back so many war-parties that were on their way to rapine and massacre." On the fourth of June, 1781, Zeisberger was married to Miss Susan Lecron, at Litiz, Pennsylvania, from which place, on the twelfth of that month, they set out in company with John Youngman and wife who were to resume their missionary labors for the valley of the Tuscarawas. Leaving his party at New Stone on the Monongahela, Zeisberger went on to Pittsburgh alone. Danger apprehended from the savages was the cause of journeying without his wife and friends, any farther than the Monongahela. At Fort Pitt an escort of twenty "Moravian" Indians awaited him. The whole arrived at New Schönbrünn, on the fifteenth of July, in safety. Afterward came the residue of the party; so that there were now six missionaries in the valley: Zeisberger and Youngman at New Schonbrüm, Lenseman and Edwards at Gnadenhütten; Heckewelder and Young, at Salem.

In the valley of the Tuscarawas and Muskingum, there were now no longer any savages save the Moravian "converts." They were gone, too, from the tributaries of these streams. Wingemund had left his village ten miles up the Walhonding, with his clan, and drawn back to the upper waters of the Sandusky where he made his camp upon the south bank of that stream near a fine spring, at a point two and a half miles northwest from the present village of Crestline, in Crawford county, Ohio. Captain Pipe, as previously mentioned, had with his clan left Pluggy's town and traveled north to the Tymochtee creek, a western tributary of the Sandusky, where he built a village a short distance below what is now Crawfordsville in Wyandot county, Ohio. Others of the hostile Delawares settled upon the Scioto and Mad rivers among the Shawnees. Captain Pipe and Wingemund were located upon Wyandot territory not far from the home of the Half King, the principal sachem of that tribe. Thus it happened that the Sandusky and Scioto bounded the enemy's territory on the east, while the Allegheny and Ohio circumscribed that of the Americans on the west; between which, for many miles, was the ranging-ground of the belligerents, _ a howling wilderness save where the missionaries and their flock made the fertile valley of the Tuscarawas in three separate localities to "blossom as the rose."

Notwithstanding the neglect of the American Congress toward the Delawares, their alliance, finally, with the British was not secured without much diplomacy upon the part of Major Arent Schuyler De Peyster, who commanded at Detroit. His "speeches," sent across Lake Erie, thence up the Sandusky and across to the head waters of the Walhonding and down that stream to the Delaware capital, were models of simplicity and tact.

"Indians of Coshocton!" said he, writing to them on the twelfth of April, 1781, "I have received your speech sent me by the Half King of Sandusky. It contains three strings; one of them white, and the other two checkered. You say that you want traders to be sent to your village, and that you are resolved no more to listen to the Virginians, who have deceived you. It would give me pleasure to receive you again as brothers, both for your own good, and for the friendship I bear to the Indians in general, being allied to them." "Send me," continues the writer, "that little babbling Frenchman, named Monsieur Linotot, he who poisons you ears, one of them who says he can amuse you with words only _ send him to me, or be the means of my getting him, and I then will put confidence in you. I then will deal with you as with other Indians whom I call our friends, my brothers, and my children; and to whom I request of you to give free passage and kind entertainment." "If you have not the opportunity," concludes De Peyster, "to bring me the little Frenchman, you may bring me some Virginian prisoner. I am pleased when I see what you call live meat, because I can speak to it and get information. Scalps serve to show you have seen the enemy, but they are of no use to me; I can not speak with them. I request of you to give free passage to such Virginians as have a mind to speak with me; _ that you will not offer to stop them, but make a straight and even road for them to come to Detroit."[18] This "speech" intrusted to the renegade, Simon Girty, was dispatched too late to be read by the assembled chiefs at Coshocton. Brodhead and the friendly Delawares had sent such of the savages as escaped the sacking of their town, flying, "in hot haste," up the Walhonding to escape the "Long Knives," upon the banks of which stream the message reached them. Captain Pipe, upon the Tymochtee, afterward wrote De Peyster. His "speech" reached Lower Sandusky on the seventh of June where it was placed in the hands of one of that officer's agents and transmitted to Detroit. The reply of De Peyster was transmitted to the Delawares on the fourteenth of June.

"My Children! _ You see," wrote the commandant, "at length I call you children. It is owing to the enemy that I have it in my power to do you a piece of kindness." "You must not make," continues the writer in an under-tone of sarcasm, "so great a merit of a real act of necessity. I am sensible could the Americans have supplied your wants, and had they not in the most treacherous manner butchered you, you would, to this day, have listened to them. You see, at length, they have proved themselves like unto bad bees; they have kept the hives hidden from you, and have stung whilst you have listened to their honey-buzzing note." Accompanying this "speech" was a vessel with clothing and provision for the dejected nation. "Be strong," concludes De Peyster, "and thankful for what I send you and you may ever afterwards look upon yourselves as my friends and allies."[19] As long as the war continued they remained faithful to the interest of the nation which was ably represented by De Peyster at Detroit: but, though firmly adhered to, the alliance was, after all, rather more compulsory, than otherwise.

In all their actions, from the commencement of the Revolution down to the time when they were left with their converts the sole occupants of the valley of the Tuscarawas, the missionaries continually manifested in their confidential correspondence, the utmost zeal and love for their adopted country. They heartily espoused, though secretly in many instances, the cause of the struggling colonies, so far as they could without imperiling too greatly the welfare of the mission. Their policy was not a neutral one; _ very far from it. It was, first, to preserve their establishments; second, to give every possible aid to the Americans, consistent with their safety. They not only wrote letters to the authorities at Pittsburgh and to the officers at Fort Laurens and Fort McIntosh, of their own free will and in their own names, but also without compulsion for the Delaware chiefs. These letters conveyed information, frequently, of much importance. They were relied upon at Fort Pitt as the principal source of getting news of the movements of the savages and of the enemy at Detroit. To all intents and purposes, the Moravian missionaries and their "converts" were the secret allies of the United States.

That the successful expedition of Brodhead against the Coshocton Indians in April, 1781, should call forth as soon as possible retaliatory measures on the part of the British and their Indian allies, was a very natural consequence. That such an expedition should march, first to the villages of the Moravian Indians was consequent upon their location _ lying as they did nearly in the path leading from the principal towns of the British Indians to the most assailable points upon the border. The leading spirit in the movement was the renegade, Captain Matthew Elliott. He succeeded in gathering some of the Wyandot Indians from the vicinity of Detroit; some of the same nation from Lower Sandusky, now Fremont, Ohio, under command of Abraham Kuhn, a white man, who had been captured by the Indians and was now a captain among them; others also of the same tribe from Upper Sandusky, not far from the present town of that name, county-seat of Wyandot county, Ohio, following the lead of the principal sachem, the Half King, and of their war captain named Snip; Mouseys from Upper Sandusky; and Shawnees from the Scioto, commanded by John and Thomas Snake, chiefs, so called by the traders; Delawares from their new homes upon the upper waters of the Sandusky, led by Captain Pipe and Wingemund; six Englishmen and Frenchmen; also Alexander McCormick, a trader from the Half King's town, acting as ensign under Captain Elliott and bearer of a British flag. There were, besides, stragglers, as was usual upon such enterprises, from various tribes; some Mohicans and Ottawas.

This motley assemblage of warriors came first to Salem from the Walhonding, down which stream there was a trail from their villages to the westward. Most of the force was mounted. Their arrival was on the tenth of August, 1781, and their whole number one hundred and forty men. They wisely kept the secret of their destination to themselves, having sent in advance two runners, dispatched by the Half King, announcing that he and his warriors were on their way to have a talk with their father, Zeisberger, and with their cousins the "Moravian" Indians, and requesting to be informed in which village they should encamp. This message being referred to Zeisberger, he designated Gnadenhütten. Thither moved the troop which by the seventeenth of the month was augmented by other parties of Delawares and Wyandots, who had arrived from time to time, until it numbered besides the usual complement of old men and squaws, about two hundred and fifty warriors. An encampment had been put up west of the town on a green which covered the bank of the Tuscarawas, one part being occupied by the Wyandots, the other by the Delawares. In the center was the tent of Captain Elliott, surmounted by a British flag.

In the week which had elapsed since the arrival of the British Indians upon the Tuscarawas, Zeisberger, ever faithful and true to the suffering border, had managed to find out their designs, especially the points they intended to attack. On the eighteenth, he dispatched two "Moravian" Indians in the greatest secrecy to the Fort Pitt commander with a message of warning; so secret, indeed, that none of the other missionaries knew of it. It was dated at "Tuppaking" _ New Schönbrunn, and was delivered in safety. With it he sent an open letter to Bethlehem.

"By the bearer," said Zeisberger to the commander at Pittsburgh, "I acquaint you that a number of Indians, about two hundred and fifty in all, are approaching toward you. As much as I could learn, it is their intention to go to Wheeling; they also said to Fort McIntosh and Fort Pitt." "The first place," he continued, "I am apt to believe most is the one where they will go. They will try to decoy the garrison out where they lie in ambush ready for them, or drive some cattle or horses that they shall be followed, and so cut them off. The party is headed by Matthew Elliott and a few English and French; but I believe some of them will turn back from Gnadenhütten, where they are at present and not go to war." "We wish," added the missionary, "they were gone from us for they are very troublesome."

But Zeisberger was not content to give only general information as to the designs of the enemy. The friendly Delawares who as followers of Captain Killbuck had accompanied Brodhead to Fort Pitt on his return from the Coshocton campaign, were at this time, encamped on a small island opposite Pittsburgh (Smoky or Killbuck's Island, since gone) which fact was known to the Missionary, who wrote: "You will have the Indians to remove from the Island, that they may not be in danger to be cut off in the night, at which the enemy aim." And he continued: "Be on your guard at Fort Pitt, as well as at other parts, _ on your Boat Yard and New Store, if they should venture to go so far." Then he mentioned what he had gleaned as to the intentions of the British abroad: "Guy Johnson, it is said, is coming down by Presque Isle, with a thousand men to make a diversion, and stop General Clark's proceeding down the river; because they had intelligence that he would come to Detroit with an army." Of the composition of the force upon the Tuscarawas, Zeisberger wrote: "The party consists of Wyandots, Delawares, Mouseys, and a few Shawnees. They carry the English flag with them."[20]

Now, the faithful missionary was wide awake to the risk he was running in giving this intelligence; so he concluded his message, in these words: "You will be careful not to mention abroad that you had the intelligence from our Towns; for it would prove dangerous for us if the Indians should get intelligence of it; which might happen by a prisoner, if they should take one." It was thus the humane, watchful, and Christian patriot thwarted the purposes of the British Indians; but here, it may be premised, that just what Zeisberger so much feared, actually happened: the writing of that letter proved the ruin of the Mission upon the Tuscarawas.

The information received at Fort Pitt from Zeisberger was not lost upon its commander who immediately took the most energetic measures to thwart the designs of the savages and their white leaders. "I have this moment received certain intelligence," wrote Brodhead, on the twenty-fourth of August, to Captain John Clark, commanding at Fort McIntosh, "that the enemy are coming against us in great force, and that particularly against your post." "You will immediately put your garrison," he added, "in the best posture of defense and lay in as large a quantity of water as you can; clear the brush from about you, and receive them cooly; they intend to decoy your garrison; but you will guard against stratagem, and defend the post to the last extremity." At the same time, Brodhead wrote the officer in command at Fort Henry, (Wheeling.) After informing him of the enemy's designs, he added: "You must not fail to give the alarm to the inhabitants in your reach and make it as general as possible, in order that every man may be prepared at this crisis." He sent, also, at the same time a circular to each of county Lieutenants in the western counties: "By the enclosed copies of letters just come to hand, I am convinced the enemy are approaching in force. You will, therefore, give immediate orders for the militia to assemble and hold themselves in readiness to march to the frontier at a moment's warning." "Whether," he continued, "the enemy will divide their force and attack the settlements, or endeavor to starve us out of our works, is uncertain; but if it is certain (as I have long suspected from former intelligence) that a serious force is coming by way of Presque Isle or Conewango, then the force coming from the Westward will only harass the settlements, and attempt some of the weaker posts; at any rate let us be prepared to repel the enemy. I am confident that with proper exertions they will soon be routed and the country saved." "This is the time," added Brodhead, "that the friends of this country will shine in opposition to the disaffected; _ and I am confident that every man who prefers freedom to slavery will step forth to defend his property, his innocent wife and children, or dear relations." But, to these noble words, the commander, unfortunately, added indirectly, but with the best of motives, this post-script: "The letters received are from the Reverend Mr. Zeisberger, an honest man, and faithful correspondent, but his name must remain a secret, lest his usefulness be destroyed."

The whole western frontier was, of course, greatly alarmed by the intelligence so generally disseminated and several hundred men were soon under arms. All the posts were put at once in as complete a state of defense as was possible. Meanwhile to add to the general alarm and to stimulate to the utmost endeavor the frontiermen in their preparations, _ was the fact that spies of the enemy had already crossed the Ohio and were murdering unprotected persons in various places. Brodhead at once sent spies up the Allegheny river, with orders to proceed to Presque Isle, now Erie, Pennsylvania; and further if practicable to discover the enemy, should they actually be on the route, and if possible to bring him a prisoner. His circular letter sent to David Shepard at Wheeling, who was then county Lieutenant of Ohio County, Virginia, was duly received by him but the contents were not kept as secret as was desired by the writer. It soon became known to all in Fort Henry from whom the information came; that is to say, all were aware that it came from the Moravian towns and that it had been sent by the missionaries. Such was the state of affairs when the enemy made their appearance upon the border.

As Zeisberger conjectured, the enemy resolved to strike their first blow at Wheeling where, not long after full preparations had been completed to receive them, they made their appearance in force, being a portion only of the whole troop; for some, although they did not turn back from Gnadenhütten, as the missionaries suggested, they might, did "not go to war." Of three boys outside the fort at the time of the arrival of the savages, one was killed, and one _ David Glenn _ made a prisoner. The other effected his escape inside the fortification slightly wounded. The garrison being on the alert were ready in a moment to receive the Indians. The latter seeing that full knowledge of their coming had evidently been in some way communicated to the Americans and that the frontiermen were fully prepared to receive them, soon disappeared, doing but little mischief, except killing all the cattle they could find. Their depredations, however, up Wheeling creek, and Buffalo were serious, killing and capturing several persons, before they re-crossed the Ohio. However, except in this immediate vicinity, the enemy made no further effort against the border. They readily comprehended the situation _ that the whole country was in arms and on the alert. Their advanced party on the return reached Gnadenhütten on the second of September having with them David Glenn, the boy-prisoner whom the enemy captured at Wheeling, as just related.

There had long been a feeling of suspicion at Detroit that the missionary establishment upon the Tuscarawas was militating against the interests of Great Britain in the West; and, of course, the alienation of the Delawares and their withdrawal from the valley, intensified the conviction that the Moravian teachers were secret emissaries of the Americans, as that tribe, declaring themselves the allies of the English, was made the occasion by the missionaries of no longer holding fellowship with them; besides, their chiefs knew very well that when the whole tribe was outwardly friends to, and, in reality, allies of the borderers, information was carried backward and forward between the authorities at Fort Pitt and the Moravians. It is not surprising, therefore, that the Indian troop upon its arrival at Gnadenhütten, should have made the suggestion that the "Moravians" and their teachers moved further back from the border. Besides, they knew very well that, if the missionaries and their flock did not give aid and comfort to the frontier settlements, their towns at least, were very much exposed, _ lying, as they did, between the eastern frontier of the Confederate tribes and the western frontier of the Americans. It was, however, no part of their plan, upon their arrival, to break up by force, if mild measures should fail, the missionary establishment. That resolution was, as will now be shown, put into actual execution by their getting knowledge of the fact that word had been sent to the border from the Moravian towns of their proposed raid upon the frontier.

When Zeisberger dispatched, by the two "Moravian" Indians, his message to the Fort Pitt Commandant warning him of the danger to the border from the enemy, he at the same time in his open letter sent a letter to his brethren at Bethlehem, Pennsylvania, informed them of the state of affairs upon the Tuscarawas. The savages at Gnadenhütten up to the time of him sending his express to the border had proved themselves, as the missionary stated _ "very troublesome" and it was no wonder that he should so heartily wish "they were gone." On the twentieth of August, the Half King made known that on the morrow he desired to meet the principal men of the three towns as he had something to communicate to them; requesting that they should assemble at Gnadenhütten for that purpose. On the twenty-first, they met accordingly, when the Wyandot sachem addressed them to the effect that they were living between two armies which were fighting against each other, from one or the other of which or possibly both at the same time, they might be destroyed. His advice, therefore, was that they remain no longer upon the Tuscarawas. He offered them his own country as an asylum of safety, where they would find plenty of provisions; besides, their Father at Detroit would look after them. The "Moravian" Indians, in reply said to the chief that they did not see the danger they were said to be in, declaring at the same time they had too much immovable property to go with him; they added, however, that they would consider what he had said to them and return an answer between that time and the ensuing spring. This seemed to be satisfactory not only to the Half King but the greater part of his warriors; and the subject was dropped; but the suspicion of collusion with the borderers still haunted the minds of the savages, and some days were spent in secret consultation about the matter.

By some means not long after the departure of the two "Moravian" Indians with Zeisberger's letters, their absence was discovered; and it was immediately suspected by the leaders of the Indian troop at Gnadenhütten that they were gone either to Pittsburgh or some other fortification on the border, to draw a body of troops into the wilderness across the Ohio, to attack them; so a strict watch was kept on the trails leading to the eastward. Both, on their return, fell, of course, into the hands of the watchful savages before they had reached their homes. They were immediately searched but no writing was discovered in their possession. They were kept as prisoners; and being separated, were brought to Gnadenhütten and there examined in the Indian council by the Half King of the Wyandots. Nothing being found upon them and both maintaining that they took only a package to the Fort Pitt commander to be sent to Bethlehem, which they really believed was the fact, they were discharged from custody. Zeisberger was much more cautious in transmitting intelligence than the authorities at Pittsburgh were in keeping it secret.

On the twenty-fifth of August, the Half King made another attempt to persuade the "Moravian" Indians to leave their settlements and go with him on his return. This time his language was rather more emphatic than upon the previous occasion. He held up the probability of their being attacked by other tribes. The Six Nations he declared would not permit them to remain longer in the valley; or, if they escaped from all these, the Virginians would sooner or later fall upon them. But the reply was that the "converts" had a considerable harvest out which would be all lost in case of an immediate removal; and, to deprive their women and children as well as themselves of the necessaries of life, when to them there really seemed no occasion for it, was asking too much. However, by dint of much talking and persuasion some of the "Moravians" began to waver and finally consented to accompany the troop upon its return; but the number was only a small portion of the whole. Encouraged somewhat by this and determined to make a last effort to induce the "converts" to remove from the valley, a meeting was called by the Half King for the second of September for another "talk." On the morning of that day, unfortunately for the mission upon the Tuscarawas, the boy-prisoner, David Glenn, was brought into Gnadenhütten from Wheeling. The artless youth, told a straight-forward story. He explained why it was that some preparations had been made at Fort Henry and other points on the frontier. Without hesitation, he revealed the fact that the warning came from the Moravian missionaries. The Half King and his fellow-counselors were satisfied when, therefore, the principal of the "Moravian" Indians assembled on that day at Gnadenhütten, together with the missionaries Zeisberger, Lenseman, Edwards, and Heckewelder, _ Youngman remaining at New Schonbrum and Young at Salem, _ they were met by the troop with angry frowns. By night-fall, "Gnadenhütten presented a dreary scene of rioting and ruin. Savages filled it, running about with terrific war-hoops, dancing and singing, shooting down cattle and hogs and leaving the carcases to rot in the streets and the stench to infest the air." Late at night, one of the "Moravian" Indians begged the missionaries to flee to Pittsburgh. But they declined.

At eleven o'clock, on the third of September, the Half King with his counselors and captains, repaired to the Mission House where he met the missionaries and principal "converts." He gave them to understand that their last speech was not acceptable to him and that he called them together in order to give them an opportunity to yield voluntarily to his demands. They must leave their villages immediately and accompany him to the Sandusky. If they refused, he would not be responsible for the consequences. The reply of the "Moravian" Indians was that they could not leave their towns; they asked for time at least to bring in their harvest. The meeting then broke up. The fate of the Tuscarawas mission was sealed. Zeisberger, Lenseman and Heckewelder were, soon after, secured and the Mission house sacked by the Wyandots. Edwards thereupon voluntarily gave himself up. The missionaries were strictly guarded; and it was not long before Young from Salem and Youngman from New Schönbrunn, were brought to Gnadenhütten. Youngman, however, was soon set at liberty. The others regained their freedom after three days confinement, upon their representations that they were willing to do what was required of them; that is, that they would go to Sandusky and encourage their flock to go also. This was on Tuesday, the sixth of September, 1781.

The day after the missionaries had been arrested another party of those who had gone against the border arrived at Gnadenhütten having in charge a white man who had been captured by them some distance from Wheeling. He was examined as the boy-prisoner had been. He corroborated the latter in every particular. He declared that the missionaries had sent word to Fort Pitt that the warriors were at their towns. This, of course, only made the Half King and the other leaders all the more determined to go forward with their work of breaking up the mission and removing the "converts" and their teachers where they could not be a correspondence with the borderers kept up. What added to this determination still more, was the fact that, following the examination of the prisoner, came the discovery that Captain Pipe's famous riding horse, the fleetest of all belonging to the troop, was missing and that one of the "Moravian" Indian women had ridden the animal away at the top of its speed in the direction of Pittsburgh. The woman was followed in hot haste by a party of warriors; but she succeeded in making good her way to Fort Pitt. "By an Indian woman," wrote Colonel John Gibson, then in temporary command at Pittsburgh, "who made her escape from the Moravian towns and came in here, we received the intelligence that some of the party of warriors mentioned in Mr. Zeisberger's letter, to be at their towns went to
Wheeling where they took a boy prisoner who informed them that the garrison at Wheeling and the country in general were alarmed and on their guard; that they had been informed of their intention by letters sent to this place by the Moravian ministers. This exasperated the warriors so much that they took the missionaries prisoners, tied them, and destroyed everything they had, and ordered the whole of the Moravian Indians to get up and move off with their families or they would cut them all off which they were obliged to consent to."

"By the enclosed extract of a letter just come to hand by express," wrote Colonel Daniel Brodhead from Fort Pitt, to the county Lieutenants on the seventh of September, 1781, "you will learn the fate of the Moravians on the Muskingum and the dangers to which our independent posts and the settlements are exposed." "I think it probable," added Brodhead, "that this large party of Indians would not have remained so long at the Moravian town had they not expected a greater force from another quarter down the Allegheny river to cooperate with them." "It will therefore be highly expedient for the militia," continued the Colonel, "immediately to assemble in bodies consisting of at least one hundred men, and march to the frontiers to cover them and keep out spies and small scouts at least for a few days, or until we can ascertain what the principal object of the enemy is. The fears entertained at Fort Pitt of a contemplated diversion of the enemy from Canada by way of Presque Isle, now Erie, Pennsylvania, down the Allegheny, with a thousand men under Guy Johnson were based upon information given in Zeisberger's letter of the eighteenth of August, preceding. There was, however, no real cause for apprehension on that score, as the report proved groundless. And, as has already been seen, the reason for the detention of the enemy upon the Tuscarawas was their determination to break up the Moravian mission there. The news brought by the "Moravian" Indian woman of its virtual accomplishment reached Fort Pitt in advance of her, it having been sent by the commanding officer at Fort McIntosh, who despatched an express for that purpose, immediately upon her arrival at that post.

On Monday morning, September 11, 1781, the "Moravian" Indians in a body, with the missionaries and their families, left Salem on their journey to the Sandusky country guarded by some Delaware and Wyandot warriors. Everything belonging to them was left behind or had been destroyed by their captors, except what few things could be carried on pack horses or stowed in canoes. Their course was down the Tuscarawas to the mouth of the Walhonding, thence up the latter stream and Vernon's river and across the country to the Sandusky, in what is now Wyandot County, Ohio, where they arrived at noon on the first day of October and soon after erected a small number of huts at a point on the east bank of the river about two miles and an half above the present town of Upper Sandusky.[21] Fourteen days after their arrival, the missionaries were summoned to Detroit by the commandant of that post.

On the twenty-fifth of October, Zeisberger, Lenseman, Edwards, and Heckewelder, started for Detroit to answer the summons. At the same time, Schebosh[22] led a party of the "Moravians" back to the valley of the Tuscarawas for corn, as there was a great scarcity upon the Sandusky _ indeed actual famine was raging among the newcomers upon that stream. Upon the arrival of the missionaries at Detroit they were closely questioned by De Peyster, _ finally dismissed and sent back to their flock with injunctions not to meddle with the war. He informed them at the same time that he would at a future date confer with them as to the final place of abode.[23] They reached the Sandusky on their return on the twenty-second of November.

The winter that followed was one of uncommon rigor. A bushel of corn in the Wyandot town sold at eight dollars. The missionaries were placed upon the most scanty allowance. The cold became extreme. The "Moravian" Indians often had nothing to eat but wild potatoes and the flesh of their dead cattle which had miserably pined away and perished. Finally, the famine increasing, about one hundred and fifty of the converts _ men, women, and children _ by permission of the Half King, set out for the Tuscarawas to gather corn. Others visited the Shawnees; and still others roamed through the woods, boiling maple sugar. Those who reached the Tuscarawas valley scattered to their towns, each family occupying its former house, and began at once the work of gathering corn which had been left standing in the fields _ the remains of their last year's crop. "Some gathered the corn in heaps; some bagged it; while others stored what could not be transported, in such rude but safe garners as the forest afforded."[24] While thus engaged, and expecting the very next morning to complete their labors, there burst upon them what proved in the end to be a most pitiless destroyer.

The small party led by Schebosh from the Sandusky to the Tuscarawas in the last days of October, previous, while engaged in their labors in the valley of the last mentioned stream, were all captured by a body of bordermen. In pursuit of marauding savages[25] whose trail led to the Moravian towns, they came upon the converts unawares, but finding them "Christian" Indians, did them no harm, but held them prisoners because of unfavorable reports being in circulation against them. They were taken to Fort Pitt by their captors where they were very kindly treated by the commanding officer _ Brigadier General William Irvine, who finally set them all at liberty, leaving them to return to their homes when they pleased. No fact was, therefore, better known upon the border than that the Moravian towns in the valley of the Tuscarawas were deserted by their former occupants _ the "Moravian" Indians.

The year 1782, opened inauspiciously for the border settlements of Pennsylvania and Virginia. The weather during the month of February was unusually fine, so that war-parties of the savages from the Sandusky country were enabled to visit the exposed settlements and commit their depredations earlier than usual.[26] Many were the sufferers by the tomahawk and scalping knife. There was great alarm in all quarters, especially in Washington County, Pennsylvania. It was reported in the settlements upon the Monongahela that the Moravian towns were again occupied _ this time by "enemy Indians"[27] and the report was very generally believed. It seemed, indeed, very plausible; as the trail of marauding savages all led in that direction. An expedition was, therefore, determined upon by James Marshal, Lieutenant of Washington County, against the hostile savages supposed to be upon the Tuscarawas _ then known as the Muskingum _ in the three villages formerly occupied by the "Moravian" Indians; and a number of militia were ordered out for the expedition.[28] "Some time in February," recites the first account of this expedition carried eastward over the mountains, "one hundred and sixty men living upon Monongahela, set off on horseback to the Muskingum, in order to destroy three Indian settlements of which they seemed to be sure of being the towns of some enemy Indians."[29] The men composing the expedition were properly armed and equipped and assembled early in March, 1782, upon the bank of the Ohio river at a point a short distance below the present city of Steubenville, Ohio, but upon the east side of the stream. It was their intention to cross over to what was then known as "the Mingo bottom" _ once the site of a Mingo Indian village, but then deserted. The commander of the party was David Williamson, Colonel of one of the battalions of the Washington County militia. At this time the water in the Ohio river was very high, and the weather cold and stormy. There were no facilities for transporting the party to the opposite side of the river. The outlook was, indeed very unpropitious and several of the men turned back. Notwithstanding all the discouragements, about one hundred succeeded in crossing the stream. At the Mingo bottom proper preparations were made for the enterprise and the men took up their line of march along a well-known trail leading westward to the middle Moravian town _ Gnadenhütten.[30] The vicinity of the town was reached on the evening of the second day, _ the party not having been discovered by the "Moravians."The borderers encamped for the night about one mile from Gnadenhütten. Early the next morning, every preparation was made for an attack of the supposed enemy. Scouts were sent out who returned with reports that Indians were seen on the opposite side of the Tuscarawas gathering corn. The men were formed into two divisions, of which one received orders to cross the river and gain the fields on that side the stream, while the other was to advance upon the village itself by a circuit through the woods.[31]

On reaching the Tuscarawas, the first division found no means of transportation across the river. What appeared to be a canoe was seen fastened to the bank on the opposite side. One of the men swam the stream and brought back, not a canoe but a trough for maple-sap, large enough to accommodate two persons only. In order to expedite their passage, a number of the men stripped off their clothes, put them into the trough, and, holding fast to its side with one hand, swam with the other until they had reached the opposite bank. Sixteen had passed over in this manner when an Indian was seen coming towards the place of landing. The party "laid themselves flat on the ground, waiting till the Indian was nigh enough, then one of them shot the Indian and broke his arm." Thereupon, "three of the militia ran towards him with tomahawks. When they were a little distance from him, he asked them why they fired at him; he was Minister Schebosh's (John Bull's) son; but they took no notice of what he said but killed him on the spot. They then surrounded the field and took all the other Indians prisoners."[32]

The Indians told them they were Christians and made no resistance.[33] The whole party then recrossed the river to Gnadenhütten where they found the second division, which had meanwhile quietly possessed itself of the vacant huts, killing but one Indian, who was crossing the river in a canoe. Among the captured, were a few warriors who had recently returned from a raid into the settlements. The "Moravian" Indians were now informed that they would be taken as prisoners to Fort Pitt. They were ordered to prepare themselves for the journey and to take all their effects along with them. At this decision of the borderers, the Indians were not at all depressed in spirits; on the contrary they were open in their expressions of joy. They well knew that the commander of that post would treat them kindly, judging from his past conduct. They there upon commenced preparations of the journey. News was carried to the lower town _ Salem _ of the capture of their friends at Gnadenhütten, by the borderers, and of their contemplated removal to Fort Pitt.

Why the "Moravians" were held as prisoners and not at once set at liberty, is easily explained. Several reports unfavorable to them had been in circulation for some time in the border settlements. One was, that the night after those were liberated at Fort Pitt, by General William Irvine, the commandant, in the previous Autumn, they crossed the Monongahela river and killed or made prisoners of a family.[34] It was also charged that prisoners had but a short time previous been hurried into the wilderness by parties of warriors among whom were "Moravians," who had treated their captives with particular indignity.[35] So now, as in the previous fall, the militia determined to place the "converts" under charge of the military authorities at Pittsburgh, expecting that this time they would be kept secure from any mischief, should any be intended by them.

Most unfortunately, during the day, a discovery was made which changed the whole aspect of affairs so far as the kind treatment of prisoners was concerned. Blood-stained garments were discovered in the possession of the "Moravians" which were quickly recognized as being those of persons who had recently been killed by savages in the settlements. One husband found the clothes of his wife but a short time before tomahawked and scalped by the murdering and pitiless foe.[36] Many of the frontiersmen were, in consequence, seized with a sudden frenzy. Friendly Indians were at once transformed, in their heated imaginings, into blood-thirsty warriors. The "Moravians" were questioned sharply; but their replies were, to the now aroused and excited borderers, only evasions. They demanded, in retaliation, the lives of all the prisoners. The result was a council of war was called by the commander, in the evening, who "told his men that he would leave it to their choice, either to carry the Indians as prisoners to Fort Pitt, or to kill them."[37] The decision of the council was that all should be killed. That the finding of the bloody garments was the principal cause of this sudden and most unfortunate determination there can be no doubt.[38] Two other causes in the meantime operated to prejudice the minds of the borderers: one was the fact that some of the captured were, beyond all question warriors;[39] another was, the uncertainty that existed in the minds of frontiersmen as to the stability of the Indians' faith, even admitting that they were not and had never been, as "Moravians," hostile to the border settlements. It was well known that some at least had relapsed into "paganism" and again put on the war-paint. The conclusion arrived at by the council was far from being unanimous. It seems indeed to have been carried by only a small majority;[40] and that in the minority was Colonel Williamson, the commandant. Sometime during the day or evening two of the "Moravians" in attempting to escape were shot by the guard. Of the resolution of the council, the Indians were informed by two messengers, "who told them that as they had said they were Christians they would give them time" to prepare for death. "Hereupon, the women met together and sung hymns and psalms all night and so did likewise the men."[41] "In the morning, the militia choose two houses, which they called the 'slaughter houses,' and then brought the Indians two or three at time, with ropes around their necks and dragged them into the slaughter houses where they knocked them down."⁴²

Involved in the general massacre were the Indians who, when the borderers reached the Tuscarawas, were at Salem. Not so, however, with those at New Schönbrunn. Williamson had dispatched a party to the former place to bring the "Moravians" there employed to Gnadenhütten, soon after the capturing of their friends in the morning. Meanwhile the Indians at New Schönbrunn had taken the alarm and fled; those at Salem came readily with their captors, and all perished. Of the "Moravians"; twenty-nine men, twenty-seven women, and thirty-four children.⁴³ Four warriors also were massacred, so that the whole number of prisoners put to death, including the two shot upon the first arrival of the borderers and also the two that who were killed in their attempt to escape, were ninety four. It is said but few of the militia took part in this bloody work.

Two boys escaped the common fate. One received a blow that merely stunned him, and before night-fall he revived. Hearing footsteps approaching he gave no signs of life. A militia-man entered the house to view the bodies, dispatching one of the Indians who had likewise only been stunned and was in the act of rising. The other boy kept close amid the ghastly corpses until it was dark, and then made his way to the forest, although suffering excruciating pain from the loss of his scalp. The other boy, slipped, unobserved, from the house in which the women suffered, into the cellar by means of a trap-door, and when the blood began to stream upon him through the floor, forced an exit out of a narrow window, concealed himself in some hazel bushes, and at night also gained the forest.⁴⁴ Both these boys afterward reached the Sandusky in safety. Late in the evening, the two "slaughter houses" were set on fire, as were the residue of the houses, in Gnadenhütten, and burned to the ground. Those at Salem had been reduced to ashes by Williamson's detachment.⁴⁵

On the morning of the next day,⁴⁶ Williamson and his men, after securing what plunder could be readily transported, commenced their return march to the Monongahela, "where they kept a vendue among themselves."⁴⁷ They brought with them ninety-six scalps _ two of which had been taken from the heads of the lads who had survived the massacre. Thus ended an expedition which has given to the pages of American history the saddest of all its words _ Gnadenhütten!

Chapter Thirty One

Crawford's Campaign against Sandusky

The expedition of Williamson to the Moravian towns which terminated, so disastrously to the Christian Indians found therein, did not allay in any wise the excitement caused by the savage depredations upon the border; its tendency was, on the whole, rather to increase it. Alarm and dismay were in every quarter; and this is not to be wondered at; for warriors were making their way stealthily into the settlements _ the settlers were threatened on all sides, with massacres, plunderings, burnings, and captivities. The people of the border were forced into "forts" which dotted the country in every direction. These were in the highest degree uncomfortable, _ they consisted of cabins, block-houses, and stockades. Near these the borderers worked their fields in parties guarded by sentinels. Every necessary labor was, as a consequence, performed with great danger and under difficulties hardly to be imagined at the present day. It is not surprising that there was a deep and wide-spread feeling of revenge against the hostile and marauding savages. The horrid scenes of slaughter which frequently met the view of the frontiermen were well calculated to arouse such passions. From Pittsburgh east to the valley of the Ligoneer; and south-east and south, including the valley of the Youghiogheny and Monongahela; also the territory west of these rivers to the Ohio; and down that stream on the east side for a considerable distance, held quite a numerous population: nevertheless there were few families who had lived in this region any considerable length of time, that had not lost some relative near or remote, by the tomahawk and scalping-knife of the merciless Indians.

Every precaution was taken to guard against surprises by the enemy; yet it was clearly seen that a defensive policy, with whatever care plans might be laid, would prove ineffectual against frequent inroads of the wily, prowling savages, who, in spite of the utmost watchfulness, would cross the Ohio or Allegheny, fall suddenly upon helpless victims, and then quickly re-cross these rivers into the wilderness beyond. Positive security, it was universally understood, could only be obtained by carrying the war into the enemy's country, _ especially was it desirable to destroy the Wyandot towns upon the Sandusky river, in what is now the north-west part of the state of Ohio, as thence came a large portion of the marauding parties devastating the exposed settlements in southwestern Pennsylvania and northwestern Virginia. Several undertakings had already been planned against these towns; but from a variety of unforseen causes all had failed of being carried forward. The time had now arrived for another and more effectual effort.

James Marshal, the lieutenant of Washington county, Pennsylvania, early in April, 1782, importuned Brigadier General William Irvine, then in command of Fort Pitt, Pittsburgh, for leave to carry forward an expedition against the Wyandot towns. "The people in general on the frontiers are waiting with anxious expectation to know whether an expedition can be carried against Sandusky early this spring or not," he wrote.[1] That the resolutions of congress appointing Irvine to the command of the western department and the powers therein granted, authorized calling out the militia of the border counties upon such an occasion if it were deemed necessary for the protection of the country, was not for a moment doubted by the commandant; yet he proposed not to exercise the authority thus conferred, even though he should conclude to favor the enterprise; all must volunteer and place themselves under his orders the same as if drafted. Satisfactory explanations having been made and assurances given by the principal citizens of the frontier as well as by the military officers of the various counties, that in the proposed enterprise, the people had nothing in view but to harass the enemy; with an intention to protect their settlements,[2] Irvine finally gave his consent to the proposed undertaking. Any conquests they might make should be in behalf of the United States; they must be governed by the laws regulating the militia in actual service; they must collect such numbers to go upon the expedition as would probably make it a success; and they must equip and victual themselves at their own expense.[3] The twentieth of May was the time fixed upon for the rendezvous; the place, the Mingo bottom, a point on the west or Indian side of the Ohio, a short distance below the present city of Stubenville, Jefferson county, Ohio. Irvine thought strongly at one time of taking command of the expedition; but, upon reflection, concluded it would not be prudent to leave his post, _ his instructions would hardly justify his so doing. He, however, gave the enterprise every encouragement in his power; suggested a person, believed by him to be well qualified, to take command; arranged the details connected with the march; and finally issued instructions to guide the officers who might be chosen to lead the expedition. The project was as carefully planned and as authoritatively carried forward, as any military enterprise in the west during the revolution. It was intended to be effectual in ending the troubles upon the western border.

Up and down the Youghiogheny and Monongahela and westward to the Ohio, in nearly all the settlements, there was now an unusual stir, it becoming generally known that the expedition against the Wyandots was to go forward. Volunteering was very brisk. So eager were some that by the 15th of May their arrangements were all made. Some, however, were unable to equip themselves for the campaign; these generally found a friend to loan a horse or furnish supplies for the occasion. It was not doubted by anyone that, notwithstanding the general government through General Irvine at Fort Pitt, could not promise any remuneration, the state of Pennsylvania would reimburse all who should sustain losses; and in this belief they were not mistaken, as the sequel shows. It was arranged that the volunteers were to select their own officers and that each one should receive a credit of two full tours of military duty, providing he furnished himself with a horse, a gun and one month's provisions. It was also agreed that any one having been plundered by the Indians should, if he volunteered, have his plunder again if it could be found, first proving it to be his property. Horses lost on the expedition by unavoidable accident were to be replaced by others taken from the enemy.[4] Irvine was of the opinion that not less than three hundred should march into the wilderness, _ less than that number would place the lives of all in jeopardy. It was indispensably necessary that all should be mounted.

By Friday morning, May 24, there had assembled at the appointed place of meeting, preparatory to marching to the Sandusky, four hundred and eighty volunteers: two thirds of whom were from Washington county; the residue, except about twenty from Ohio county, Virginia, were from Westmoreland _ mostly from that part included the next year in Fayette county, Pennsylvania. In the afternoon the organization took place, by the election of company and general officers. The volunteers distributed themselves into eighteen companies, having a captain, one lieutenant and one ensign for each. Of the general officers, there were chosen one colonel-commandant, four field majors, and one brigade major. Accompanying the expedition were three guides, one surgeon and one aid to the colonel-commandant. The chief officer elected was Colonel William Crawford[5] of Westmoreland. The field majors to take rank in the order named were Colonel David Williamson[6] of Washington county, Thomas Gaddis of Westmoreland, John McClelland and of the same county, and James Brenton of Washington county. Daniel Leek of Washington county was elected brigade major. The three guides were John Slover, Jonathan Zane, and Thomas Nicholson. John Knight, an assistant surgeon at Fort Pitt, and John Rose, aide of Irvine, at that post were sent by him _ the former as surgeon, the latter as aid to the colonel-commandant.

Early on the morning of Saturday May 25, the army under Crawford began its march from the Ohio river for the Wyandot town of Sandusky, in what is now Wyandot county, Ohio. Its route lay through the present counties of Jefferson, Harrison, Tuscarawas, Holmes, Ashland, Richland, Crawford, nearly to the center of Wyandot county. The volunteers took, at starting, nearly a due west course moving along on the north side of Cross creek in Jefferson county as at present defined; thence into what in now Harrison county, but soon after, deviating from their course, to the south-westward, until the Tuscarawas river was reached, then known as the Muskingum as far up as the mouth of Sandy creek. The river was crossed at a point just below the upper Moravian town, on the afternoon of the fourth day of their march. That evening, the army encamped among the ruins of New Schönbrunn. Up to this time little worthy of note had transpired, except that, at the third encampment, a few men lost their horses and were, as a consequence, obliged to turn back. At New Schönbrunn, a reconnoitering party discovered two savages and fired upon them, but without effect. It was now known for the first time, _ that the movements of the army were being watched by the enemy. All hopes of effecting a surprise had, therefore, to be given up.

Crossing from the Tuscarawas to the Killbuck they passed up the latter creek until a larger spring was reached, now known as Butler's or Jones' spring, in the present county of Holmes. Their route lead westward from this point, along the north side of what is now known as Odell's lake to what was afterward the Indian village of Greentown in Ashland county; thence across to the Rocky fork of the Mohican, up which they traveled until they came to what is now the sight of the present city of Mansfield in Richland county. Their march was then resumed to the westward until the waters of the Sandusky were reached at a point immediately east of the present village of Leesville in Crawford county. A south-westerly course brought the volunteers to the mouth of the Little Sandusky creek in what is now Wyandot county, through the Sandusky plains crossing the Sandusky in the forenoon of June 11, the army marched down that river on the east side until a point was reached three miles above the present site of Upper Sandusky, the county-seat of Wyandot county, where the Wyandot Indian town _ the objective point of the expedition was located; when, to the astonishment of all, it was found deserted. It had evidently not been occupied for some time.

The army was now in the country of the Wyandots, which nation, driven from their ancient seat near Lake Simcoe, Canada, by their rapacious kindred, the Iroquois or Five Nations, finally, after many wanderings in the far west, located upon the Detroit and Sandusky rivers, in a country uninhabited; and, upon these streams, they had resided ever since. To the south of the Wyandots, whose village south of Lake Erie were at this date upon the Sandusky river exclusively, were the Shawnees, located upon the upper waters of the two Miami rivers in the south-west part of the present state of Ohio, where, in towns upon the Mad river, known as the Mac-a-chack (now Mac-a-cheek) and upon the parent streams, as Chillicothe and Upper and Lower Piqua, they then resided. The Delawares, under their war chief Captain Pipe, had a village upon the Tymochtee a western tributary of the Sandusky and another small one far up the waters of the latter stream where Wingemund, another one of their chiefs, held sway. At this date, there was, also, a village of this tribe located at the present site of Delaware, county-seat of Delaware county, Ohio, and a few dwelt near the head springs of the Scioto, where, too, were living a number of Mingoes _ off-shoots from the Iroquois, mostly of the Senecas. Here their famous leader Logan, spent the last days of his eventful life.[7]

The commandant at Detroit, A. L. De Peyster, was fully aware of the fact that expeditions had previously been contemplated from the American settlements against the Wyandot towns, and the savages themselves were constantly on the alert. When, therefore, early in May, a general stir was observed upon the border and the frontiermen were seen by war-parties in agitation, as if preparing for some enterprise, the news was soon carried by swift-footed braves to the Miami and the Sandusky. When the borderers had assembled upon the Ohio preparing to cross that river; Indian runners struck swiftly into the wilderness to carry the tidings to their towns. Couriers were dispatched to the British commander at Detroit, imploring help; as it was now evident that some portion of the Indian territory was to be invaded _ either that of the Wyandots or Shawnees. As the Americans marched from the Ohio, their movements were closely watched by skulking savages, reports constantly sent to the Sandusky of their progress. De Peyster lost no time in dispatching a company of one hundred rangers under command of Captain William Caldwell, together with what few lake Indians could be gathered, to the assistance of the Wyandots. Meanwhile, the Shawnees, Mingoes, Delawares, and Wyandots were in the greatest excitement; all were calling in their braves as rapidly as possible; and preparations were hastily made to repel the invaders, who had already reached the Sandusky country.

A brief hour terminated the halt of the Americans at the deserted Wyandot town, which they had reached at one o'clock of the fourth of June. The march again commenced, as it was believed Wyandot settlements would soon be reached. Crossing the Sandusky to its west bank and moving along past the present site of Upper Sandusky, Crawford struck out into the plains to the northward soon after calling a halt when it was determined that the march should continue that afternoon but no longer, if the enemy were not encountered. However, spies soon brought word of the presence of the foe, rapidly approaching in order of battle. Preparations by the Americans were immediately made for the conflict. When first discovered by the borderers, the savages were taking possession of a grove of trees immediately in their front. Crawford instantly detecting the advantage this would give the enemy, ordered his men to dismount. A quick forward movement and the firing began. The Indians were driven in a brief time from their shelter into the open prairie. They numbered as many as the Americans. Captain Caldwell, with his rangers, arrived just in time to take part in the contest. The action now became general, close and hot. The foe were sheltered by the high, rank group of the plains; Crawford and his men by the grove they had so bravely secured. The fighting continued until dark, and the victory was clearly with the Americans; still, the Indians and rangers were far from being dispirited. Expected re-enforcements on the morrow, stimulated their courage. The loss of the frontiermen was five killed and nineteen wounded; that of the enemy is not known. Both parties lay on their arms during the night and both adopted the policy of kindling large fires along their lines and then retiring in the rear of them to prevent surprise. The battle was fought in what is now Crane township, Wyandot county, Ohio, three miles north, and half a mile east, of the court house in Upper Sandusky _ the county-seat of that county.

On the next day while Crawford was caring for his wounded and making preparations for an attack in the evening, some desultory firing, was indulged in by both sides. In the afternoon, a large re-enforcement of Shawnees was observed to have arrived in aid of the enemy. This changed the whole aspect of affairs so far as the Americans were concerned. As help continued to arrive in support of the foe, it was resolved to retreat in the evening instead of attacking the enemy as had been determined upon in the morning. Preparations were accordingly made; but when the hour arrived considerable confusion ensued and the lines were attacked by the Shawnees and Delawares, but it was a feeble effect as the savages were in doubt as to whether the movement was a genuine retreat or only a ruse. In the conflict that ensued several parties became separated from the main army _ with one of which were Colonel Crawford and Dr. Knight. The Americans collected their somewhat demolished forces early the next morning at the deserted Wyandot village, and the retreat was resumed in better order, upon the route taken by the troops on their inward march, _ Colonel Williamson, in the absence of the colonel-commandant, having assumed the leadership of the retreating army.

In the afternoon, just as the Americans had reached the eastern verge of the Sandusky plains, in what is now Whetstone township, Crawford county, Ohio, they were overtaken by the pursing savages in force; with the latter, also, were some of the rangers. A battle ensued; the enemy attempting to surround the borderers. In less than an hour, the foe, whose exertions had been daring and furious, and who attacked the front, the left flank, and the rear, of the retreating force, gave way on all sides, owing to the coolness and steady firmness of Williamson and his men. The Americans had three killed and eight wounded in this contest. The loss of the enemy was probably greater. No sooner, had the wounded been cared for than the retreat again commenced. The enemy observing the movement, rallied their scattered forces in the plains, and renewed their pursuit, but kept at a respectable distance.

At day-break June 7, the retreat was renewed, the enemy appearing in the rear of the army and opening fire. Two of the borderers were, at this juncture, unfortunately captured, and probably immediately tomahawked. However, now, to the great relief of the army the pursuit was abandoned. The last hostile shot was fired near where the village of Crestline, Crawford county, Ohio, now stands. Not a savage or ranger was seen afterward. The homeward march was along the trail of the army when outward bound _ to the Tuscarawas which stream was crossed on the tenth of June. From this point to the Mingo bottom on the Ohio, a plain Indian trail was followed _ the same one taken by Williamson and his men when marching to the Moravian towns early in March. The army crossed the Ohio immediately upon reaching the river and on the fourteenth of June was disbanded; the volunteers making their way home as best they could; some in squads, some alone. The wounded who were able to ride were soon at their several places of abode; but such as could not be moved except on litters, were taken to the nearest settlements and tenderly cared for by sympathizing settlers. Thus ended the campaign against Sandusky. The whole loss, including those who were killed in battle, those who afterward died of their wounds, and such as were captured and tomahawked or tortured by the savages, _ was less than seventy. _ Before closing this narrative, we must again return to the wilderness; following stragglers in their toilsome and devious routes towards the Ohio and their homes; _ recounting the escapes of two from the hands of the savages; and the awful sufferings of the unfortunate Crawford by the hands of the maddened Delawares upon the banks of the Tymochtee, in what is now Wyandot county, Ohio.

Some of the stragglers from the army, who became separated from it on the night the retreat began, got very much confused, as might be expected, in their endeavors to find the trail of the retreating troops. A few in despair of regaining it, and others out of abundant caution, struck directly through the wilderness, taking a due east course for the Ohio. Some, however, became completely bewildered. Among the number was James Workman, a volunteer from Washington county. He was discovered by Nicholas Dawson and another, going exactly <u>from</u> the Ohio and <u>towards</u> Sandusky. These men endeavored to persuade him that he was wrong; but Workman with equal pertinacity insisted that he right. Finding their attempts to convince him fruitless, they told him he would certainly be killed if he continued upon the course he had been traveling and as he had better be shot by white men than be tortured by savages, they would kill him to prevent his falling into their hands. This argument proved successful and they all arrived home in safety.

Philip Smith, with a companion named Remkin, in the confusion attending the retreat on the night of June 5, became separated from the main army. Both lost their horses, though they had their rifles and ammunition; but neither had any provisions. In their journey homeward they came across an Indian pony which they killed _ the meat of which was a savory dish indeed to the two hungry men. They were afterward overtaken by two men on horseback and all traveled on together when they fell into an ambuscade and the two mounted men were shot by the unseen savages; Smith and his companion succeeded in escaping unhurt. Subsequently, they came upon a deserted Indian camp, where a white man lay scalped _ his body still warm; doubtless some straggler who had been captured and then tomahawked. The two continued their journey homeward, reaching the settlements in ten days from the time of leaving the battle-ground, _ foot sore, nearly naked and well nigh perishing with hunger.

John Sherrand of Westmoreland was another of the volunteers who became separated from the main force upon the night of the commencement of the retreat. He was in company with an acquaintance named Conrad Harbaugh; they made very slow progress owing to the darkness; but finally succeeded the next morning in finding the trail of the retreating army. Riding along together, Harbaugh was shot by an Indian and immediately expired. Sherrand, however, was unhurt and succeeded in reaching the retreating army in safety.

Not so fortunate in the end, was another volunteer named Thomas Mills. He had become separated from his companions and had made his way nearly to the Ohio river when his horse gave out. This was near where St. Clairsville, countyseat of Belmont county, Ohio, now stands. He left his horse at what was known as the "Indian Spring" about nine miles from the Ohio _ then in the wilderness of course, now on the national road. Mills soon after reached Wheeling in safety. He then proceeded to a fort in the neighborhood, when, after resting a day or two he began to think of returning for his horse. At this time there was at the fort _ Van Metre's _ that famous hunter and Indian fighter, Lewis Wetzel. The latter was, induced to accompany Mills in search for the animal. They had no trouble in finding the spring where the horse had been left, and they soon discovered the animal they were in search of _ but tied to a tree. Wetzel at once comprehended the danger, signaled his companion, and ran for life. But Mills disregarding the warning, rushed up to unfasten his horse and was shot dead by unseen savages, four of whom now rose and pursued the fleet Wetzel. The latter being pressed turned and shot on of the Indians that had nearly overtaken him. He then re-loaded his rifle as he ran, and turning shot another of his pursuers. Again his trusty weapon was loaded and again suddenly turning about he shot a third Indian; when the fourth one concluded to abandon the dangerous pursuit; and Wetzel reached the fort he had left, to recount his exploit.

The army in retreating from the battle-field on the evening of June 5, marched in three divisions, one of which, soon after, struck a swamp into which a number of men rode, some losing their horses, which were stuck fast in the mire. Among the number of volunteers who were unfortunate in this respect, was James Paull, of Westmoreland county. He and six others, all on foot, being pressed by the savages, struck off together, from the division to which they belonged. These men succeeded after a devious course in getting within about twenty miles of the Tuscarawas, in what is now Wayne county, Ohio, one of their number having straggled away from the party, when they were ambuscaded by some Shawnee Indians who had tracked them all the way from the Sandusky plains. Two were killed; three made prisoners, but Paull, running for life, escaped, though closely pursued by several fleet savages who, as they saw he gained upon them, fired at him, but without effect. Coming soon to a steep bluff bank, Paull leaped down, gun in hand, without injury, but the savages did not choose to follow, and relinquished the chase. He finally reached his home in safety.

Of all the volunteers who fell into the hands of the savages only three are known to have escaped the tomahawk or the stake. One was taken prisoner to Detroit; the other two, succeeding in breaking away from their captors, reached the settlements, after much suffering. The reason given for this unusual barbarity of the savages was the killing of the "Moravian" Indians at Gnadenhütten, by the party who marched under Colonel Williamson to the Moravian towns, early in March preceding. These "Moravian" Indians being mostly Delawares, the warriors of that tribe determined upon revenge. Not only were none spared who fell into their hands, but they demanded from the Shawnees and other tribes, any prisoners taken by them. Among the captured was the colonel-commandant of the expedition _ William Crawford, and the surgeon, Dr. John Knight, by a party of Delawares. It happened in this wise. When the retreat commenced, Colonel Crawford missed his son, John Crawford; his son-in-law, William Harrison; and his name-sake and nephew, William Crawford. In endeavoring to find them, he fell behind the divisions of the army as they began the march. In attempting to regain his position, at the head of his men, his horse gave out nearly; so he was left considerably in the rear. Dr. Knight coming up, the two moved on in company, when the savages commenced an attack. By this time they were joined by two others and the four rode off to the northward to escape the fury of the enemy.

The party after a while changed their course to the eastward, passing out of what is now Wyandot into Crawford county, Ohio; meantime one of those who had joined them lagged behind and was finally lost to view. In the forenoon of the next day, June 6, they fell in with one of the captains _ John Biggs, and a lieutenant, the latter was dangerously wounded. Adding another straggler to their company, now numbering six in all, they encamped early in the afternoon, to give the wounded officer rest and care. The next morning, they again started, coming upon the paths by which the army had gone out, about two o'clock in the afternoon, some distance to the eastward of the Sandusky plains. Proceeding onward to the point where the army first saw the Sandusky when outward bound _ just across the stream from the present village of Leesville, Crawford county, Ohio _ they were beset by a party of savages, Crawford and Knight captured, but the other four escaping, at the time. The two prisoners were taken to the Wingemund's camp, which was but a short distance away, and securely bound. The Delawares had nine other prisoners at this camp. On the tenth of June, they were all marched westward to the deserted village of the Wyandots except Crawford who was conducted at his own request to the village of the Half King located on the west side of the Sandusky about five miles below the present county-seat of Wyandot county, Ohio. The object of Crawford's request was that he might see Simon Girty whom he formerly knew, who was now a renegade from the Americans living among the Indians, being in the employment of the British Indian department. Girty was seen by Crawford at the Half King's town and promised to do all he could for his old acquaintance.

All the prisoners were assembled at the old town up the river, June 11, and marched towards the village of Captain Pipe upon the Tymochtee. On the way they were all tomahawked except Crawford and Knight who were reserved for a far more cruel death. Knight was to be taken to the Shawnee town to be tortured there while Crawford was doomed to death upon the bank of the Tymochtee. Upon the arrival of the two in the afternoon near Pipe's town, Knight was compelled to witness the awful sufferings of the colonel-commandant at the hands of the infuriated and merciless Delawares. The doctor was then taken to the house of the chief of that tribe, where he remained all night securely bound. The next morning, being put in charge of a savage to be conducted to the Shawnee towns, where he was to be burned at the stake, the journey to the headwaters of the Miami was commenced, but Knight at day-break the next morning, watching his opportunity seized the end of a dogwood fork and struck his conductor so severe a blow as to stun him at first and then send him howling in a fearful manner into the wilderness; and the doctor escaped, arriving at Fort Pitt in a famishing condition on the fourth of July.

One of those who were captured by the Shawnees when James Paull made his escape, was John Slover, the guide to the expedition. He had previously lived with the Indians and could speak their language fluently. He and his two companions were taken to the Indian villages upon the Mad river, in what is now Logan county, Ohio, when one of the captives, and old man, was set upon, beat, wounded, and finally killed, his body being cruelly mangled. At Wapatomica, one of the Indian towns, Slover saw the bodies of William Harrison, the son-in-law of Crawford, also that of William Crawford, the colonel's nephew. He also saw what he believed to be the remains of John McClelland, fourth in command of the expedition, who had been captured the night of the retreat from the first battle ground. All these bodies were black, bloody and burnt with powder. Their limbs and heads has been stuck upon poles. This was the work of the exasperated Delawares. After a length of time, Slover was doomed to die; was tied to the stake, the fire kindled, but a sudden rain extinguished it. His torturing was then postponed for the next morning. Just at day-break, he managed to get his limbs free from the rope which held him so tightly to the stake, and stepping over the sleeping warriors made his way into a field, where, mounting a horse _ entirely naked as he was _ made eastward for life! After his horse had become exhausted, he hastened forward on foot and finally reached the settlements _ the last of all the arrivals from the wilderness.

There was a fire burning at the spot where, on the eleventh of June in the afternoon, Crawford was to be immolated to satisfy the revengeful thirst of the Delawares for blood of the Americans. Around that fire was a crowd Indians _ about thirty or forty men and sixty or seventy squaws and boys. Simon Girty and Dr. Knight were also spectators of this dreadful scene. Crawford was stripped naked and ordered to sit down. The fatal stake, a post about fifteen high, had been firmly set in the ground. Crawford hands were bound behind his back and a rope fastened, one end to the foot of the post, and the other to the ligature between his wrists. The Indian men then took up their guns and shot powder into his naked body from his feet as far up as his neck. They then crowded about him and cut off both his ears. The fire was about six or seven yards from the post to which he was tied. It was made of small hickory poles burnt quite through in the middle. Three or four Indians by turns would take up, individually, one of these burning poles and apply it his naked body, already burnt black with powder. Some of the squaws took broad boards, upon which they would carry a quantity of burning coals and hot embers and throw on him. At length being almost spent he laid down upon his stomach. He was then scalped, and an old squaw got a board and laid a parcel of coals and ashes on his back and head. He then raised himself and walked again. Finally, death came to his relief.

Chapter Thirty Two

Capture of Hicketty Fort, and Battle of Cedar Spring
By Shelby as given in Haywood's <u>History of Tennessee</u>

On the sixteenth of June, 1780, Col. Isaac Shelby being in Kentucky locating and surveying lands which he had marked out and chosen five years before, received information of the fate of Charleston, and of the surrender of the main southern army; and forthwith he returned home, to aid his county in the great struggle she maintained for independence. Arriving in Sullivan county early in July, he received a dispatch from Col. Charles McDowell, giving information that the enemy had overrun the two Southern States, and were approaching the limits of North Carolina, and Col. Shelby was requested to bring to his aid all the riflemen he possibly could, and with as much dispatch as possible. In a few days Col. Shelby marched from Sullivan at the head of two hundred mounted riflemen, and joined McDowell's camp near the Cherokee Ford of Broad river, in South Carolina. Lieutenant Col. John Sevier, of whom a like requisition was made, having arrived there with his regiment a few days before. Shortly after the arrival of Col. Shelby, Col. McDowell detached him with Col. Sevier and Col. Clarke, of Georgia, with about six hundred men, to surprise an enemy's post, twenty odd miles in his front on the waters of Pacolet river. They marched at sunset, and surrounded the post at day-break the next morning. This was a strong fort, built in the Cherokee war, about seven years before, and was surrounded by a strong abatis, and was commanded by Captain Patrick Moore, a distinguished loyalist. Colonel Shelby sent in William Cocke, Esquire, to make a peremptory demand of the surrender of the post, to which Moore replied that he would defend the post to the last extremity, Shelby then drew in his lines to within musket shot of the enemy all around, determined to make an assault upon the post. But before proceeding to extremities, he, sent in a second message; to which Moore replied, that he would surrender upon condition that the garrison be paroled, not to serve again during the war, unless exchanged, and this proposal was acceded to. In the garrison were found ninety-three loyalists, one British Sergeant-major, stationed there to discipline them, and two hundred and fifty stands of arms, all loaded with ball and buckshot, and so disposed of at the port-holes, that they could have kept off double the number of the assailants.

Shortly after this affair, McDowell detached Shelby and Colonel Clarke, with six hundred mounted men, to watch the movements of the enemy, and if possible to cut off his foraging parties. Ferguson, who commanded the enemy, then about two thousand strong, composed of British regulars and loyalists, with a small squadron of horse, was an officer of great enterprise, and though only a major in the British line, was a Brigadier General in the royal militia establishment made by the enemy after he overran North and South Carolina, and was esteemed the most distinguished partisan officer belonging to the British army. He made several attempts to surprise Shelby, but without success. On the first of August, however, the advance of Ferguson, about six or seven hundred strong, came up with Shelby at a place he had chosen to fight them, called Cedar Springs, where a sharp conflict ensued for half an hour. Ferguson coming up with all his forces, Shelby retreated carrying from the field of battle twenty prisoners, with two British officers. The Americans lost on their side ten or twelve in killed and wounded; among the latter was Colonel Clarke, slightly in the neck, with a sabre.

From The Magnolia, August, 1842
Battle of Cedar Springs
By Hon. B. H. Perry

The battle of "Cedar Springs," in Spartanburgh District, although one of considerable importance, both as it regards the number of persons engaged, and the consequences which ensued, is not mentioned in any history of the American Revolution, or the Revolutionary war in South Carolina. The following account of this battle, and the interesting incidents connected with it, are from the lips of a highly respectable and intelligent son of Colonel White, who commanded a battalion in the battle of the Cowpens, and bore a conspicuous part throughout the Revolutionary war in the "Upper Country."

Colonel Clarke, of Georgia, well known in the American Revolution as a bold active and useful officer, was on his march into North Carolina, with a regiment of refugee Whigs, for the purpose of joining the American army then expected from the North. The news of his march reached the ears of Colonel Ferguson, who immediately despatched Major Dunlap, of the British army, with a detachment of troops; consisting principally of Tories, for the purpose of intercepting Colonel Clarke and his regiment of militia. The Colonel, not expecting an attack from the enemy, had encamped for the night, two or three miles from the "Cedar Springs," when he was alarmed by the firing of a gun by one of Major Dunlap's soldiers. It is said that this soldier, whose name is not at present remembered, was a Tory, who felt some compunctions visiting at the idea of surprising and capturing his countrymen, and took this opportunity of giving them information of an approaching enemy. He pretended, however, that his gun went off accidently, and he was not suspected of treachery. Colonel Clarke immediately decamped, and marched to the Cedar Springs, where he passed the night undisturbed. Major

Dunlap, not thinking it prudent to pursue the Americans in the night, took possession of Colonel Clarke's encampment, and waited for day.

Josiah Culbertson, noted in Spartanburgh District for his daring and desperate courage, had left the American camp that evening, for the purpose of returning home, two or three miles distant, in order to spend the night. He came back, about daylight, expecting, of course, to find Colonel Clarke and his regiment. But as he rode into the camp, he observed that the army seemed to present a different appearance from what it did the evening before. He, nevertheless, rode on to where he expected to meet Colonel Clarke, before he became convinced that he was in the midst of the enemy's camp. With extraordinary coolness and presence of mind, he then leisurely turned round, and rode very slowly out of the encampment, with his trusty rifle lying on the pommel of his saddle. As he passed along, he saw the dragoons catching their horses, and other preparations making to strike up the line of march. When out of sight by the British, he put spurs to his horse, and went in the direction he supposed Colonel Clarke had gone. Whilst in the enemy's camp, he had doubtless been taken for a Tory, who was a little ahead of others in his preparation for marching. He overtook Colonel Clarke, and found him in readiness for the attack of Major Dunlap. In a short time, too, that officer made his appearance, and a warm engagement ensued. The British and Tories were repulsed with considerable loss. The Americans sustained very little injury. Major Dunlap hastily fled the country, and by this means the citizens were rid of a most dangerous and troublesome enemy. Colonel Clarke pursued his march into North Carolina.

During this engagement, Culbertson was met by a Dragoon some distance from the main battle, who imperviously demanded his surrender, which Culbertson replied to with his rifle, and felled the Dragoon from his horse. The next day, when the dead were buried, this Dragoon was thrown into a hole near where he lay, and covered with the earth. He had in his pocket when buried, some peaches from which a peach tree sprung, and was known for years afterwards to bear fruit. His grave is yet to be seen, but the peach tree has long since disappeared. The graves of some twenty or thirty others who fell in this engagement, are also to be seen at this time.

Editor's note; At the conclusion of the preceding page, the Draper Manuscripts continued without chapter numbers. From this point on, the writings are what merely appeared at the conclusion of the microfilm from which this work has been transcribed. It, as in other places, appears incomplete. Yet it may be of some benefit to some reader, and is therefore included.

Chapter Thirty Three

Josiah Culbertson

Early life in French and Indian War. - Alamance Battle.- The Ring Fight. - Defends Col. Thomas house against Tories. - Siege of Savannah.- Affairs at Cedar Spring and Musgrove's Mill.- The story of Plundering Sam. Brown.- At King's Mountain, Cowpens, and Ninety Six. - Gowen's Fort Massacre, and Estatoe Expedition.Tory Incidents, old age; and death.

    Josiah Culbertson, though only a private and a scout at King's Mountain, served with great reputation under Shelby and other gallant leaders during the war, and well deserves a sketch of his useful and eventful services. He was born at a settlement called Culbertson Row, where several of the connection resided, near Shippensburgh, Cumberland County, Pennsylvania, about 1747 _ as he states in his pension declaration that he was about eight years old at the time of Braddock's defeat in 1755. When his father was only four years of age, he was brought by his parents to America. Like nearly all the Irish immigrants of that day to Pennsylvania, and subsequently to the Carolinas, they were Presbyterians, and warm advocates for the rights of conscience, and the liberties of the people.

    The father of Josiah Culbertson removed to New River, in south-west Virginia, about 1754, and found himself on an exposed frontier when the French and Indian war soon after broke out. The latter part of July, 1755, some two weeks after Braddock's fatal disaster, but before the news had reached the far-off settlement on New River, a party of thirteen Shawnees warriors, as Josiah Culberson related it _ and sixteen as other accounts have it _ stopped at the house of Mr. Culbertson, while on a marauding expedition against the border settlers. They scattered themselves around the cabin before they were discovered, but did not otherwise molest the family than to extort from them some provisions, when they took their departure with the many cheap expressions of friendship and good will.

    A day or two afterwards warning of danger was sent to the Culbertson family, when they immediately retired to the nearest settlement. It was fortunate that they did so; for on the thirtieth of July, this same party of Shawnees killed Col. James Patton, and three others adjoining the present village of Blacksburg, in the mountain region, in what is now Montgomery county, capturing Mrs. William

Ingles and her two little boys, together with her sister-in-law, Mrs. John Draper, and Henry Leonard; and then directed their course to Culbertson's on New River. When they found the family gone, they were much exasperated, as they no doubt intended murdering or capturing them on their return.[1]

The Culbertson family did not return to their deserted home on New River. The war continued several years; and, after a little cessation, broke out again in 1763. Josiah Culbertson, now some fifteen years of age, regarding himself as capable of sharing in the defense of the country, joined a party of a dozen brave fellows, who went in pursuit of a marauding band of Indians. After pursuing them several days, they fortunately discovered the encampment of the enemy so suddenly, as to completely surprise them, killing nine of their number, rescuing a woman and her five children whom they had captured, and securing seventeen guns among the booty. This frontier enterprise and its successful termination, proved a useful experience to young Culbertson in early introducing him to the modes and strategies of border warfare.

Soon after the Indian troubles were quieted, the elder Culbertson removed with his family to Caswell County, North Carolina, where Josiah and one of his brothers formed a part of Gov. Tryon's forces, who defeated the Regulators at the Alamance, May sixteenth, 1771. The Culbertsons not very long thereafter removed to Fair Forest settlement, where Josiah, in 1774, was united in marriage to Martha, one of the daughters of Col. John Thomas, Sr. In the latter part of 1775, he went on what is called the Snow Campaign, from the circumstances of a heavy snow falling during the continuance of the service, which was under the command of Gen. Richardson, and destined to put down an up-rising of the Tories in the region of Ninety Six. He served in Col. Thomas' regiment and in the company of his brother-in-law, John Thomas, Jr. Succeeding in their object, they returned home about new year's.

In the early summer of 1776, the Cherokee commenced hostilities, instigated by British emissaries among them; when Culbertson again went forth in the defense of the frontiers, under the same officers as on the Snow campaign. On the twelfth of August, when Gen. Williamson was at Tomassee, a deserted Cherokee town, he detached Capts. Andrew Pickens, and Robert Anderson with sixty men, and, soon after, Maj. Jonathan Downs with a party of twenty, of whom Culbertson was one, to track and reconnoiter the enemy, as many signs of their presence were discovered, and also to collect some of the Indian cattle for the subsistence of the army. They had not proceeded more than a mile when Capt. Anderson having parted from Capt. Pickens with twenty-five men and crossed a creek; soon after which Capt. Pickens with his thirty-five men, saw two Indians, and fired at them. The Indians instantly set up the war whoop and ran, Pickens' men following; but they were soon met, as they advanced along a grassy ridge, by a large party of the enemy, supposed to be two or three hundred warriors, who were skulking in the tall grass on every side.

Among Pickens' men was a friendly half-breed Cherokee named Cornels

Brennan who acted as guide for the company. He advised the whites to squat in the grass and when their guns were loaded, rise and shoot only when they could see an enemy. This advice was adopted and the contest went on, the Indians gradually advancing.

Fortunately Downs' and Anderson's parties came up about the same moment and united with Pickens. It was ordered, at first, that only two of the whites should rise up from their grassy concealment and fire and then dodge down again. Pickens and Brennan were, the first two to discharge their rifles, when the enemy had approached within about twenty five yards, and two of the Indians were seen to fall; then the others fired in succession as directed. Brennan heard the Cherokee commander exclaim, in his native tongue - "<u>rush in!</u> - <u>rush in!</u> - and <u>tomahawk!</u>; and added that they should swing their rifles in their left hands, and tomahawk the whites, as they were but a handful. And twice they rushed up the ridge or knoll, tomahawk in hand; but were as often driven back by the murderous fire of the whites.

The brave Brennan was early shot down. Pickens loading in a hurry, choked his gun, when he picked up Brennan's, fired it off, and continued to use it while the contest lasted. During the action, one of the men observed that there was a constant firing from behind a tree-root, and watching his opportunity when its occupant had to expose himself to take aim, shot him in the head; and when one of his Indian comrades had taken up the body, and was making off with it towards the rear, the white marksman shot him also, with as much coolness, as if he were shooting at a target, and they fell, one upon the other.

So close was the engagement, that a stout Indian and a sturdy young white man had a desperate personal encounter. After breaking their guns over each other, they grappled in a death's struggle, in which the white man, brought upon the border, proved himself the better bruiser and more expert gouger; for he soon had his thumbs in the fellow's eyes, who in pain roared out <u>ca-na-ly na-en-ah!</u> in English "friend, enough!" " D__n you," yelled the white-barbarian, "you can never have enough while you are alive!" He then stepped one of his feet upon the prostrate Indian's neck, and scalped him alive; and then, with one of the broken guns, knocked out his brains. The journalist, who records this incident, must have been even more brutal and unfeeling than the Indian-killer, for he adds so inhumanely: "It would have been some fun, if he had let the brain-knocking action alone and sent the Indian home without his night-cap to tell his countrymen how he had been treated."

Two other Indians were also killed in personal contests with their own knives or tomahawks. One of these Indian-slayers was an associate of Culbertson's, named Thomas Ellison, from Duncan's Creek. He was a man of great muscular strength, and sustained a desperate hand-to-hand struggle with a powerful antagonist. The Red Man was so oily, that Ellison could get no hold of him, while he himself unfortunately had a long growth of hair, giving his adversary greatly the advantage. But worse than all, Ellison lost his knife in the contest; but, after a great effort, he succeeded in wrenching the Indian's from him, who seemed then to realize his fate, gave up apparently in despair when Ellison killed and scalped him. The victor was astonished when he looked around, to discover that the whites were triumphant, assistance having just arrived from the camp.

It might have gone hard with the little band on the ridge, whose numbers were much weakened by their losses in killed and wounded, had not the firing been heard at the camp, when Gen. Williamson and Capt. Joseph Pickens, immediately called out for volunteers, and one hundred and fifty brave fellows ran at their best speed to the rescue, and coming close on the rear of the enemy, one well-directed fire put them to instant flight. One squad of their party, being nearly surrounded, were entirely cut off; and sixteen dead bodies were found in the valley where the contest ended; and, in accordance with the barbarous custom of the times their scalps were taken as trophies of victory. Though one account says forty-seven Indians were left dead on the ground, and another supposes the number killed and wounded were sixty or seventy, the diarist states that after taking the sixteen scalps, they did not examine for further remains of the slain, which must have been scattered all around the ridge, for it was now nearly sun-set, and they were called off by the beating of the drum.

Of the whites, Lieut. Rogers and one private were killed, and sixteen wounded _ of the latter three died the next day Capts. Lacy and Neel, and Lieut. Hargrove, of whom it is recorded, were "brave officers and good men." Maj. Downs was badly wounded in the abdomen, and in the hand, from which he in some time partially recovered, though never after able to render any further active service to his country. The ridge or knob around which this sharp contest took place, was quite limited in size, and of circular form, as the action was ever after denominated "the ring fight."[2] The place of its occurrence was in the forks of the Tomassee and Cherokee creeks, tributaries of Little and Keowee rivers, twenty-two miles above old Pendleton village, and in the present County of Oconee. Few men on the border had more experience in Indian fighting than Andrew Pickens, and he always regarded the ring fight as the most desperate contest in which he was ever engaged; and towards the close of life this patriot-warrior selected this interesting spot, Tomassee Knob for the home of his old age, where, in 1817, he closed his eventful career in peace and tranquility.

Between three and four months Culbertson served on this campaign of Williamson's against the Indians, bearing his full share in the privations, sufferings, and contests with the enemy. The Cherokees were subdued for a while, and kept pretty quiet for two or three years. During this period, there was comparative [quiet] in South Carolina, while the war waged in other quarters.

In 1776 Gov. Rutledge had sent a quantity of powder to the up-country, to be safely deposited for use when needed to keep the Tories in subjection, or repel any inroads of the Indians. A part of it, if not the whole, was lodged with Col. John Thomas, and the magazine was fixed at his house on Fair Forest, and a guard of twenty-five men assigned for its protection. Early in 1779, a body of Tories gathered at Poor's Ford in Tryon County, North Carolina, with a view of making their way into Georgia, and joining the Royal forces in that Province. On their way, they were re-inforced by Col. John Moore, who took the command; and detached a party to capture Col. William Wofford, a Whig leader of some note, and another party of nearly a hundred and fifty men, to take Col. Thomas, a yet more distinguished public character, and seize the ammunition which they supposed was still deposited at his house; but which Col. Thomas, for prudential reasons, had not long before removed and secreted in the crevices of rocks at Rich Hill, nearby.

Col. Thomas was apprised of Moore's intentions barely in time to send out, and gather in the guard. He sent his daughter, Letiha, four miles, in the night, to Matthew Patton's who with his father and a few others repaired to the place of threatened attack. They had scarcely reached there, together with some others, about twenty-five in all, when the Tory party, on the sixth of February, made its appearance. Samuel Clowney, Matthew Patton and probably others, went to work running bullets. The Tories were hailed but paid no heed to it, firing several shots, by which one of Col. Thomas' Negroes was killed. But the Colonel himself, then an old man of sixty-one, concluding that a defense could not long be successfully maintained against such odds, and perhaps dreading captivity at his advanced period of life, deemed it best to retire; and the guard strongly urged him to do so.

His brave son-in-law, Culbertson, concluded he would remain, and appeal to the younger men of the guard to join him in the defense of the family; but they all took to flight, many of them fortunately leaving their guns behind, while Culbertson was upstairs watching the movements of the enemies. Matthew Patton and Clowney were the last to depart in the very face of the enemy presenting their guns threateningly as they retired, thus keeping, the enemy at a distant till they escaped. As the Tories came there for powder, Culbertson resolved that he would give them a chance to smell of its quality and test its effect. All the guns in the house were quickly loaded. Only the members of the family, including Culbertson, Mrs. Thomas and her youngest son, William, a lad of some twelve years, together with Culbertson's mother and wife [were present]. They all resolved that they would do their part to aid Culbertson in repelling the cowardly Tories, for such they proved to be; and the heroic Mrs. Thomas, be it remembered, was the woman who, the next year, made the remarkable ride from Ninety Six to notify her son and Whig friends stationed at Cedar Spring of an intended attack on the part of the British, though now sixty-one years of age, resolved that they would do their part to aid Culbertson in repelling the cowardly Tories for such they proved to be.

Culbertson concluded that being under cover of a strong log house, there was little to fear from Tory bullets. He commenced operations as soon as the enemy came within rifle distance, and fired his guns rapidly in succession, conveying to the Tories, the idea that the whole guard were there and that it would cost more lives than the powder was worth to gain possession of it. Mrs. Thomas, and her associates ran bullets and loaded the guns as fast as they were discharged, so Culbertson was able to keep up a lively fire on the attacking party. Mrs. Thomas snatched down her husband's sword from its peg on the wall, and fearlessly advanced with it in hand, daring the cowards to come on! There was too much powder and ball there, and too much brisk firing of it _ so they thought discretion the better part of valor, and resolved not "to come on." Compelled to retreat, with four or five of their party wounded, they left several of their horses behind them, which they appeared to have brought for the purpose of packing off the much coveted powder. Lest they should return with a stronger force, Culbertson and his little party prepared themselves to renew the fight, if necessary. "Let them come on, if they dare," muttered Mrs. Thomas,[3] and the others partook largely of the same defiant spirit; but they were not further molested. Had the Tories succeeded in capturing the family, they might have discovered the concealed ammunition, or coerced by threats of torture, their prisoners to have revealed its place of concealment. In the following year, when nearly all the powder of the country was lost by the fall of Charleston, this precious supply saved at Rock Hill near Col. Thomas' residence and subsequently hid by Col. Thomas, Maj. McJunkin and others, in the vicinity of Col. Brandon's at Fair Forest Shoal, served Sumter and his men a good turn at Rocky Mount and Hanging Rock.[4] For the salvation of this powder, South Carolina owed a debt of gratitude to Jane Thomas and Josiah Culbertson.

The next service in which Culbertson participated was in the sanguinary attack on Savannah, on the ninth of October, when the French and Americans united in their heroic effort which resulted so disastrously _ the noble Count Pulaski being among the slain. The column to which Culbertson was attached, was composed of regulars and militia _ the regulars in front followed closely by the others. A cannon loaded with ball, together with bars of lead cut into fragments, was fired from one of the British batteries, the ball striking one of the officers of the regulars, severing a portion of his head from his body, his brains flying in every direction, and his body falling into the arms of Culbertson. Two young men bearing up the fallen officer were wounded by scattering pieces of lead, and a portion of these flying missiles passed through Culbertson's hair and clothes.[5] It was a close call, but he was spared.

After the fall of Charleston, Culbertson was among those patriots who declining to submit to the British yoke, or take protection, repaired to North Carolina, where he joined Gen. Rutherford's forces. It was Rutherford's advanced parties who defeated the Tories at Ramdom's Mill, and sent Col. John Moore, who had the year before dispatched a party to attack Col. Thomas' house, in a destitute condition to the British post at Camden. Culbertson's good conduct at Cedar Spring or Wafford's Iron Works, at Musgrove's Mill, together with his happy riddance of the country of so terrible a scourge as plundering Sam. Brown, and the part he acted at King's Mountain have been already related.

At King's Mountain he served under Roebuck, as he did at the Cowpens in

January, 1781; and in both he fully maintained his high reputation for chivalric daring. In June, 1781, he served under Greene at the siege of Ninety Six, as well as shared in many engagements with the Tories in the back country, during those trying years, 1780 and 1781. One incident more must close this sketch of his services during the Revolution. At one time, when the Tories had possession of the neighborhood at Fair Forest where he resided, he and three comrades ventured into the settlement near the Tory camp. Culbertson was, in the meantime, taken sick at the house of a friend. The Tories soon learning this fact, determined on taking him, and a party of twenty-five of them set out, in the night, for the purpose; but when they arrived within a short distance of the house where he was, he got some intimation of their presence and barely had time to effect his escape before their very eyes, with no garment save the shirt upon his back. Sick and helpless as he was, the dastards seemed to shrink from following him, lest they should get more in the end than they bargained for. The Tories were so enraged at his escape from their clutches, that they vented their hellish spleen and malice, as they entered the house, upon a younger brother, then but a mere youth, but cutting him with their swords in a most brutal and shocking manner. The lad, in order to screen himself from the lacerating blows of these inhuman wretches, took shelter behind Mrs. Culbertson who was there with her younger brother to attend to her sick husband, and he held up his hands to protect his head from the blows; but his arms were so cut up, that large particles of bone were found in his shirt-sleeves when the murderous crew departed.

In the autumn of 1781, during one of the Cherokee out-breaks, a party of Indians and painted Tories, under the leadership of a noted Loyalist who had taken refuge among the Cherokees, familiarly known as "Bloody Bates," suddenly made their appearance before Gowen's Fort, situated on the waters of the Pacolet, near the North Carolina line, and not very far from the northern boundary of Greenville and Spartanburg Counties. Here in times of danger, the scattered settlers of that region would gather for mutual protection. This little fortress seems also to be known as Fort Jemison. It was commanded by Capt. James Jones. On this occasion, the people of the fort, who had on former occasions repelled the wily foe, made a vigorous defense; but listening too confidently to Bates' promises of protection from the savages, they surrendered. But no sooner was Bates and his myrmidons in possession of the place, than they commenced a most shocking butchery of men, women and children. Several managed to effect their escape _ among them, Absalom Thompson, late of Mecklenburg, one of Capt Jones' company. A Mrs Thompson, wife of Abner Thompson, late of Greenville County, was scalped and horribly mutilated and probably left for dead, and subsequently recovering her senses, in some way reached a place of safety. She lived to a good old age, leaving a numerous and respectable family. A family of the name of Motley were all killed except a son, a young man, who, though badly wounded, effected his escape. The bloody victors retired with their prisoners and booty. This shocking affair, with the treachery attending Bates' solemn pledge of protection, roused the people of that region, who immediately embodied under Majors Kilgore and White to pursue the enemy. Captains Parsons and John Gowen were among the Company Commanders, and Josiah Culbertson was prominent among the volunteers on this occasion. Probably following the regular trail leading through the mountains to the Cherokee towns on the upper waters of the Keowee river, they at length reached Estatoe, where they overtook Bates' fugitives and had a running fight with them, killing several, retaking a number of the unfortunate captives, and capturing sixteen Indians. Among these prisoners was the noted Cherokee Chief Big Acorn, whose heroic captor was Jesse Neville. One of Neville's fellow soldiers, certifies of him, that he was "one of the bravest, most active and efficient soldiers on the frontier of North and South Carolina." But, Big Acorn, like most Indians under restraint, felt illy at his ease, and subsequently lost his life in a bold attempt to regain his freedom. A number of Indian towns [were taken], Estatoe, Tocasse, and Tomasse, were among them.

After the peace of 1783, Bates had the temerity to venture, from his refuge among the Cherokee into the settlements to try his hand at horse-stealing. He was luckily apprehended and after repeated attempts to break away from his captors, he was finally lodged in Greenville jail. He was recognized as the notorious "Bloody Bates." No sooner did young Motley, who resided in that region, hear of the arrest of the treacherous bandit, than he armed himself with a couple of pistols, repaired to the jail, and gained admittance by threatening the jailor with instant death on refusal; and, on entering, shot the perfidious murderer of his parents, brothers and sisters, through the heart. Motley continued to live in the country for many years, and eventually moved to the West, living to a good old age, and leaving many respectable descendants. No one ever thought of arresting or prosecuting [him] for killing "Bloody Bates" _ public opinion fully justified and approved the act.

Culbertson could not tolerate a Tory, such as those who roamed in plundering bands, and spared no age nor sex, during the sanguinary period of 1780 - 81, in the Carolinas and Georgia. He, on one occasion, encountered one of those characters solitary and alone, snatched and threw away his gun from him, declaring he would not condescend to shoot so mean a creature as he was, and brained him with a club. At another time, in a <u>melee</u> he stabbed and killed a Tory instantly.[6]

The faithful rifle, which Culbertson denominated his "pocket piece" with which he defended the Thomas' house, fought at Tomassee, Savannah, Cedar Spring, Musgrove's Mill, King's Mountain, Cowpens, Ninety Six, and Estatoe, and which sent death to plundering Sam Brown and many another Tory;[7] was preserved by the old patriarch with no small veneration as long as he lived, and eventually became the inheritance of his youngest son.

In 1810, Mr. Culbertson removed from Greenville District, South Carolina, and settled in the forks of White river, Indiana. One of his sons was killed by the Indians in 1812. In 1827, he lost his noble companion, who had, in common with her family, suffered so much during the Tory ascendency in South Carolina. From

1831, the old patriot received a pension of eighty dollars a year from his grateful country. For several of the closing years of his life he was in a helpless, feeble condition; but the fires of patriotism still continued to burn brightly in his bosom. During his last sickness, he talked with delightful remembrance of his old Revolutionary officers and associates, the Thomases, father and son, Shelby and Clarke, Williams, Roebuck, and McJunkin.

"The weary wheels of life at last stood still," and Josiah Culbertson passed on to the better world, in Washington, Daviess County, Indiana, September twenty-seventh, 1839, at about the age of ninety-one years. He well deserves to be regarded as the hero of Spartanburg.[8]

Footnotes

Preface

1. Draper Manuscripts, at 31 S 333.
2. Draper Manuscripts, at 1 S 57
3. Vaughan, Virginia. Weakley County. Tennessee County History Series (Memphis State University Press, Memphis, Tenn., 1983). Pages 21-23.
4. Draper Manuscripts, at 32 S 318-319.
5. John Clark, Early Times in Middle Tennessee, (originally published for the author by E. Stevenson & F. A. Owen, 1857. Reprinted by Robert H. Horsley and Associates, Nashville, by The Parthenon Press, Nashville, Tn., 1958), p. 28
6. Internet at www.americanrevolution.org/jouett.html
7. Lafayette County, Arkansas Historical Society. A small flyer entitled "Spring Bank Ferry - Visit the Caddo Country," date not stated.

Chapter One

1. Sparks' Amer. Biog., 1st Series, Vol. X, 265, 266. Wilmer's Life of Heredinand de Soto, Chapt. I _ et. seq.
2. Gentleman of Elvas' Narr., in French's Hist. Coll. Louisiana, P. II. p. 114; where Hacklyt's translation is given in full. See, also, Buckingham Smith's translation as given in his Narr. Hernandio de Soto (New York, 1866), p. 6.
3. Carto que el Adelantado Soto escribio' a' la Justica y Regidores de la Ciudad de Santiago de la Isla de de Cuba.
4. "Town and Port of Espiritu Santo." Soto's letter, July 9th, 1539. "Baya Honda" (Deep Bay) of Suys Hernandez de Biedma, whose Narrative of the Expedition of Hernando de Soto is translated in full in French's Louisiana, P. II. 97-109, and also by Buckingham Smith in his Narr. of Soto, (New York, 1866), pp. 229-261. It is the "Port de Spirito Santo" of the Gentleman of Elvas' Narrative of the Expedition, and the "Espiritu Santo Bay" of Ynca Garcilasso de la Vega, whose work _ Historia del Adelantado Hernando de Soto _ has no English translation, unless the Hist. Of the Conq. Of Florida, by T. Irving , be considered one.
5. "Six hundred and twenty men, and two hundred and twenty-three horses," according to Biedma.
6. A summary of the events occurring at "Espiritu Santo Bay," from the time of landing until the final departure, with a reference to authorities, is appended to Buckingham Smith's translation of Soto's letter of July 9th, 1539.
7. One of the first maps to locate points on the route of Soto, is that inserted by De Lact in his L' Historie de Nouveau Monde, called Florida et Regiones Vicinae (Leyden, 1640). A much later one marking the route in lines is Louisiana, P.II.

Modern ones are "Route of Ferdd. de Soto A.D. 1539;" in McCulloh's Researches; Schoolcraft's "Map of the Route of De Soto," in his Indian Tribes of the United States, P. III, p. 60; and a Map of the Route in Smith's Narr. of De Soto, (N.Y. 1866.); Williams (Hist. Florida, p. 155 et seq.) and Fairbanks(History of Florida Chapter III.) endeavor to identify certain localities. T. Irving (Conq. Florida, rev, ed., p. 82, et seq.) and Pickett (Hist. Alabama, I. p. 5) trace the route through the State. Roberts [Hist. Florida (London, 1763)] is silent on the subject. Compare McCulloh, 524; Meeks Southwestern Hist., p. 219, et seq.

8. So written by Biedma. "America Apalache" of the Gentleman of Elvas. It was near the modern Tallahassee: Pickett's Hist. Ala., Vol. I. p. 5; T. Irving's Conquest of Florida (rev. 2d), p. 139; Fairbanks' Florida, p. 75. Woodward, in his Reminiscences of the Creek, or Muscogee Indians (Montgomery, Ala., 1859) pp. 17, 75. gives, as an Indian tradition, a point on the Apalachicola, near Ocheese, called by the natives Spanny Wakka _ that is, "the Spaniards lay there."

9. The route described in conformity to modern landmarks, will be found in Stephens' History of Georgia, Vol. I. pp. 20-23; Pickett's Alabama, Vol. I. pp. 6-13; T. Irving's Florida, pp. 194-242. Compare Gallatin's Syn. of Ind. Tribes in N. Amer., in Trans. Amer. Antiq. Soc., Vol II. pp. 103, 104.

10. A brass kettle-drum, several shields, and a small brass swivel, according to Woodward (Rem. 14, 23, 77) and George Steggin (whose unfinished MS. _ an Historical Narration of the Genealogy, Traditions and Downfall of the Ispocoga or Creek Tribe of Indians, _ has been consulted in this connection) descended to after generations of natives, as memorials of the expedition of Soto. See also, Schoolcraft's Indian Tribes, Part Fifth, pp. 283, 660.

11. Pickett's Hist. Of Alabama, i, 16. This author, "armed at all points with the best traditions and authorities," traces the route in Alabama. Compare Brown's Alabama, 10-12; Trans. Amer. Antiq. Soc., ii. 104 et seq.

12. Meek (Southwestern Hist. p. 227, note) says: "The first Spanish settlers of Alabama found the name, Mauville, applied by the natives to the present river and bay of Mobile. It was in consequence, given by the Spaniards and French, to the natives themselves; whom they called Mauvilla or Mobile Indians." Compare T. Irving's Florida (rev. ed.) 261. note.

13. The location of Mauvila (Mavilla, Mauvilla, Maubila, or Mauville: Mobile) De L'Sale, in his map of Louisiana, marks upon the north bank of the Alabama not far above the junction with the Tombigby. See also, in Schoolcraft's Map of the Route of De Soto, in his Indian Tribes of the United States, p. iii, p. 60; and McCulloh's Maps, in his Researches. Pickett "is satisfied that Maubila was upon the north bank of the Alabama and at a place now called Choctaw Bluff, in the county of Clarke, about twenty-five miles above the confluence of Alabama and Tombigby:" Hist. Ala. Vol. II. p. 27. Cinsult, also, in this connection, Meeks, p. 227. Brewer's Alabama, p. 111; T. Irving, (rev.) 261, notes; Monette's Hist. Mississ. Valley, i, p. 36; Bancroft's, Hist. United States, i, 48; Martin's Louisiana, i, p. 11; Fairbanks' Florida, 76; McCulloh, 525. Brevard's Maps in Buckingham

Smith's Narr. of De Soto.

14. Tascalusa, Tasculuca, Tasculuza _ Tuscaloosa; from Tusca, warrior and Loosa, black; i.e., Black Warrior; Meek, 225 note; Trans. Amer. Antiq. Soc., ii, 105. Woodward (Rem. 78) says Tusca is Creek, and Loosa, Choctaw. Biedma and the Gentlemen of Elvas apply the name of the country of the Chiefs only.

15. "We lost twenty men killed, and two hundred and fifty wounded;" Biedma. "Of the Christians, there died eighteen x x x there were a hundred and fifty wounded, with seven hundred wounds of their [the Indian] arrows:" Gentleman of Elvas. Vega gives eighty-two as the Spanish loss.

16. Gentleman of Elvas. Biedma is silent.

17. Vega puts down the number of twenty-five hundred.

18. Francis Parkman _ Pioneers of France in the New World, p. 10.

19. Alibamo of Biedma; Alimamu of the Gentleman of Elvas. Doubtless the original of Alabama _ 'Here we rest;' Meek, 233, note.

20. Thought to be the Yazoo: Pickett's Alabama, i, p. 49.

21. "About the latitude thirty-four degrees terminates north:" Ellicott's Journal, 125. Vega gives Chucagua as the Indian name of the river. The Gentleman of Elvas says that in one place it was called Tumaligzu; in another Tapatu; in another Mico; and that part where it enters the sea, Ri. _ The names, doubtless, as applied by different tribes.

22. Gentleman of Elvas; _ "a half a league broad," is his estimate. "About a league wide, and from nineteen to twenty fathoms deep:" Biedma.

23. But see, Narr. Alvas Nuñez Cabeza de Vaca, translated by Buckingham Smith, 1851; also comments thereon in Shea's Hist. Discov. Mississ. River p. VIII, et seq. and in Parkman's Pioneers of France in the New World p. 8. note. Compare, however, new ed. Smith's translation of De Vaca (1871), 60, 64 note, and App. (VII) thereto; also. Pickett's Alabama i, 50; Schoolcraft's Ozark Mountains, p. 13.

24. Marquette, 17 June, 1673; see, Shea's Discv. Missipp. Riv. p. XXIX.

25. Writers who have made attempts to locate the crossing-place, generally put it above the mouth of the Arkansas. "A little below the lowest Chickasaw Bluff [Memphis]: Martain's Louisiana I, 12. "One of the Chickasaw Bluffs, or ancient crossing-places, and apparently the lowest:" Nuttall's Travels in Arkansas Territory, 248. "Not far from the thirty-fifth parallel:" Bancroft's Hist. United States I, 51. "Between the 35th degree and mouth of St. Francis river:" Gallatin in Trans, Amer. Antiq. Soc. II, 105, note. "Within thirty miles of Helena [Ark.] Monnette's Hist. Mississippi Valley, I, 47. "Lowest Chickasaw Bluff, one of the ancient crossing places:" T. Irving's Conq. Florida (rev. ed.) 316, note. "Above the mouth of the Arkansas:" Parkman's Pioneers of France in the New World, II.

26. For conjectural tracings of Soto's trans-Mississippi route, see Martin's Louisiana, i, 12; Trilmer's Life of Soto, p. 465 et seq.; Perkins' Annals of the West, p. 3; T. Irving's Florida (new ed.) p. 376 et seq.; Schoolcraft's Ozark Mountains, 114, 134-141 and his Indian Tribes. P. Fourth, 309, _ P. Sixth, 65; Shea's Discov. Mississ. Riv. XIV: Monette's Hist. Mississ. Valley, I, 47-54;

Bancroft's Hist. United States, i, 52- 55; McCulloh's Researches. 526 et seq.; Nuttall's Travels in Ark., 250 et seq.

27. "Near to the confluence of Red river:" Nuttall, 263. "Opposite to the mouth of Red river:" Martin, i, 13.

28. Bancroft's Hist. United States, i, 57.

29. Tracing the route of Moscoso is largely a matter of conjecture. Compare Nuttall, 264; Bancroft i, 57; T. Irving's Florida (rev. ed.) 366 et seq.' Monnette I, 57-60.

30. Francis Parkman _ Discovery of the Great West, p. XIX.

31. Mexico _ "New Spain of the Ocean Sea:" Prescott's Conq. Mexico, ii, 158. Yucutan was first to receive the name: Helps' Spanish Conq., II, 218.

32. The most northerly of the Spanish settlements in Mexico, upon the gulf coast, at that date.

33. For titles and various editions of books, and descriptions of original writings, that treat of the expedition of Soto, see Sparks' Amer. Biog. (1st Series) X, 267 et.seq. Buckingham Smiths' Letters of Hernando de Soto (Washington, 1854) pp. 65-67; Brinton's Notes on the Floridian Peninsula (Philadelphia, 1859) pp. 18-25.

Chapter Two

1. For an account of the rediscovery of the Mississippi by Father James Marquette, 17 June, 1673, see, . G. Shea's Discv. Miss. Valley. p. XXIX. La Salle navigated the great river from the mouth of the Illinois to the Gulf in 1682: Parksman's Discov, Great West, Chap. XXI.2. Its boundaries as claimed by France at different periods, are not traceable with any degree of certainty. Compare La Salle's Proce's Verbal (Hist. Coll. La. I. 45); Crozat's Charter (Martin Hist. La., I. 179). For an approximation of its extent, see Jefferys' Hist. French Dom. North and South Amer. P.I., p. 139; Greenlaw's Hist. Oregon and Cal., (4th ed.) 277, 282; Bancrofts' Hist. U.S,, III, 343; Parkman's diccov Great West, 284.3. Fort Rosalie is marked upon maps anterior to this date; but its existence before 1716 was wholly imaginary.4. "Natchez or Sunset Indians:" Schoolcraft _ Hist. Ind. Tribes, V, 260.

5. They were first seen by Europeans at this point _ by La Salle, 23 March, 1682: Hist. Coll. La., I. 62.

6. The principal one was called the Great Village, around which clustered the White Apple Village, the Flour Village, the Gray Village, etc. Compare Le Page Du Protz. (ed. Lond.) 79, 80; Dumont _ Hist. Coll. La., V. 48.

7. Trans. Amer. Antiq. Soc. II, 113. "In former times, the nation of the Natchez was very large. It counted sixty villages and eight hundred Suns or princes; now [1729] it is reduced to six little villages and eleven Suns:" Le Petit _ Keith's les Miss. II. 273. He put the number of their warriors at seven hundred. In 1703, they had thirty villages. Penicant French's Hist. La. And Fla, p. 28.

8. Father Le Petit, in Kips, II. 269. See also, Hist. Coll. La., III. 141. "The Great

Sun:" Le Page du Protz, 292. So high sounding a title was, however an official one.

9. Le Petit _ Kips. II, 271.

10. Le Petit _ Kip's Jesuit Miss. P. II. Pp. 270, 271. Concerning the perpetual sacred fire of the Natchez, doubts have been expressed. See Hist. Coll. La., I. 19. But the testimony of F'artieu Le Pelit (Kip. II. 268) and Du Protz [Hist. La. 333], both eyewitnesses, as to its existence, is conclusive. Compare also, Mem. of Teuts, Hist. Coll. La., I, 6. French's Hist. Coll. La. And Fla. P. 95.

11. Du Protz, 328; Gayarre's Hist. Pf La., I. 295; French's Hist. Coll. of La. And Fla., p. 94.

12. Trans. Amer. Antiq. Soc., II. 114. But see, Bartram's trav. 465

13. Le Page Du Protz, p. 291 et seq.

14. Penicant _ French's Hist. Coll. La. And Fla. p. 57; McCulloh's Researches: p. 150 et seq.; Gayerre's Hist. of La., I. 352.

15. "Chopart:" Dument. "Chepar:" Le Petit. "Chopart, Chepart, in Etcheparre:" Gayarre.

16. Compare Adair's Hist. Amer. Indian., p. 353. This writer makes the Chickasaws, whose territory was above the Natches and to the eastward, responsible for the animosity. See also, Bunne's Hist. of La., p. 86. The whole cause, however, is generally laid at the door of Chopart. "The tyranny and injustice of the Sieur de Chopart, who commanded the post of Natchez, had nearly proved fatal to the whole of the French settlement in Louisiana:" Nuttall's in Ark. Ter., 279. Compare Stoddard's Sketchs of La., p. 49. Le Petit (Kips. II. 285, 286) says his conduct was cruel and causes which hastened the massacre.

17. This tribe had generally been faithful to the French; Breckenridge's Views of La., p. 20. It has been supposed that the Chickasaws were also to have taken part in the massacre: Monnette's Hist. Mississ. Valley. I. 257. Dumont speaks of the Chickasaws as the first to embrace the views of the Natchez Indians.

18. Flint (Geo. and Hist. West. States I. 28) makes this alliance to have been only with the Chickasaws.

19. Dumont _ Hist. Coll. La., V. 69. Charlevoix (Shea's trans.) VI. p. 81 and note. See, also, Bossier's Travels, I, 62.

20. The changing of the day, from Dec. 1st to Nov. 28th, has generally been attributed to one of the Natchez women having contrived to alter the record kept by the Great Sun; some, however, have thought the arrival, by river, of supplies from New Orleans, on that day, was the cause; others have combined the two. Charlevoix says that a hundred and twenty horses loaded with English goods had just arrived among the Choctaws; and the Natchez learning this fact and also that two of their chiefs were absent, calculated with certainty upon the fidelity of their allies, and resolved to anticipate the day.

21. Le Petit (Kip. II, 286) gives as their pretext that they were going out for a grand hunt. Dumont (Hist. Coll. La., V. p. 711) says: There was not a settler, in whose house there was not an Indian under some pretext; _ some coming to pay

what they owed, others coming to beg their friends to lend them a gun to kill a bear or deer x x x ."

22. "In less than two hours, they massacred more than two hundred of the French:" Le Petit. "Two hundred men perished almost in an instant:" Charlevoix. The estimates of Dumont and Du Protz are much higher. "In less than half an hour," writes the former, "more than seven hundred were killed." The latter says: "of about seven hundred persons, but few escaped to carry the dreadful news to the Capital."

23. Adair, 257; Trans. Amer. Antiq. Soc., II, 114; Hawkin's

Chapter Three

1. Hugh Paul Taylor, in Fincastle Mirror, Jan. 1828; followed by Withers, (Border Warfare) p. 42.
2. This famous bridge is on the head of a fine limestone hill, which has the appearance of having been rent asunder by some terrible convulsion in nature. The fissure thus made is about ninety-feet; and over it the bridge runs
3. Henning's [Va.] Stat. at Large, Vol. IV. p. 450; Vol. V. p. 79. The county of Frederick included the territory which lay north east of a line drawn from the "head spring of Hedgaman river, to the head spring of the river Potowmack," beyond the top of the Blue Ridge; or the whole of Fairfax' Grant beyond these mountains. See Fry and Jefferson's Map of Virginia, 1751. All the residue of Virginia west of the Blue Ridge to its "utmost limits" was set off as the boundaries of Augusta county.
4. There was an enrollment of four hundred and sixty-five men in nine companies out of the twelve which constituted the entire militia force. Muster Rolls. Aug. Co., 1742 _MS.; showing a population of about twenty-five hundred.
5. Stith's Virginia, p. 67: _ called Massawomecho , by Burk (Hist. Va., p. 22); Massawomees, by Jefferson (Notes on Va.); and Massawamees, by Withers (Border Warfare, p. 39.); and Massawomeks, by Campbell, (Hist. of Va., p. 58).
6. Kercheval's Hist. Val. Va., p.58.
7. Probably about the year 172
8. See Brancroft's Hist. U.S., Vol. III, 344.8. On the Catawba river in the Province of South Carolina. They numbered at this date about four hundred warriors : Mills' Statistics, S. C. p. 114.
9. In the central and western parts of the Province of New York. The tribes forming the famous Confederacy were the Mohawks, Oneidas, Onondagas, Cayugas, Senecas, and Tuscaroras.
10. Col. Rec. of Penn., Vol. IV, p. 644. There was not a Shawnee in Delaware of the party. Portions of these tribes, however, occupied, at that date, the Wyoming Valley. See, Chapman's Hist. Wyoming, p. 19; Miner's Hist. Wyoming, p. 35; Peak's Wyoming, p. 11; Stone's Poet. and Hist. Wyoming, p. 84.
11. Col. Hist. New York, Vol. VI. p. 240.

12. Penn. Col. Rec. IV, 644.

13. The Indians "killed and wounded several of their, horses, cattle and hogs:" Penn. Gazette, 31 March, 1743. "All we did kill" were "one Hog, one Calf and one Horse and we took away one Cask Syder:" Sachems of the Six Nations to the N. M. Com. Ind. Affairs, in Col. Hist. N. M., VI, 239. "Some White people lately come down from Lancaster and who say they had it from some that lived near the place where the action happened, tell us that although the Indians behaved very peaceably in their journey through Pennsylvania, as soon as they got into Virginia, they fell to killing the inhabitant's cattle and hogs and shot one man's mare:" Lt. Gov. Thomas to Conrad Wieser, 26 Jan., 1743, in Pa. Col. Rec., IV. p. 635.

14. The particulars of the journey to this point rests largely upon Indian statements (Col. Rec. Penn., IV, 631, 644), which are considerably confused, though, as to the most important events, there is a general agreement. Compare Penn. Gazette, 27 Jan., 1743.

15. Samuel McDowell (a son of John McDowell) to Arthur Campbell, 27 July, 1808: Ms. letter; Arthur Campbell to Allen B. Magruder, 3 June, 1809: original letter [John McDowell]

16. Foot's Sketches of Virg. (2d Series). pp. 91. 92. "When my father settled [in the Valley], it was where I formerly lived, now called the Red-house Tract, in Rockbidge county, [Va];" Deposition of Samuel McDowell Ms.

17. Muster Rolls, Aug. County, 1742: Ms. the Captains were John Smith, Andrew Lewis, John Buchanan, James Castry, John Christian, Samuel Gray, Peter Shoul, James Gill, John Nelson, Hugh Thompson, George Robinson, and John McDowell.

18. Statement o Samuel McDowell Reid. The Indians claimed that the Virginia arms fired first; but the militia asserted the contrary _ that the bearer of the flag, without any provocation, was shot and killed. Compare Col. Hist. New York, VI, pp. 230, 234, 240; Col. Rec. Penn., IV. pp. 632, 636, 645; Penn. Gazette, 27 Jan. and 31 March, 1743.

19. About ten minutes, according to James McDowell, who was present: Penn. Gazette, 31 March, 1743. Col. Patton says the engagement lasted "about forty-five minutes:" Col. Hist. New York, VI, p. 230. The militia lost eight killed and three wounded; the Indians, four killed and four wounded.

20. Shikellamy _ the father of Logan _ who is alleged to have been a Frenchman born at Montreal and adopted by the Oneidas, after being taken prisoner: Bartram's "observations," p. 17.

21. "The burial place of these men x x x you may find in a brick enclosure, on the west side of the road from Staunton to Lexington, near the Red-house x x x. Entering the inn gate, and in going to the left, about fifteen paces you will find a low unhewn limestone, about two feet in height, on which in rude letters by an unknown and unpracticed hand is the following inscription x x x; "Heer Lyes the Bodys of John Mack Dowell Deced Decembe 1743[1742]." _ Foote's Tay (2

series) 83., 93.
22. Colden's Hist. Five Nations, Vol. II, p. 97. (Ed. 1755.)

Chapter Four

1. Revised Code of Laws of Va. (1819). Vol. II, p. 347.
2. The celebrated surgeon, William Baynam was a pupil of his. Allen's Amer. Biog. Dic. (3d. ed.) p. 74.
3. Designated as "Walker's," on Lewis Evans' Map of the Middle British Colonies of 1755. See, also, Fry and Jefferson's Map of Va., same date. It was, long afterward, the home of W. C. Reeves, who died here, 26, April, 1868.
4. Walker to William Preston. 23 March, 1778: MS. Letter.
5. Statement of William Tomlinson to Daniel Bryan, communicated the letter, 27 Feb., 1843.
6. MS. Journal of Thomas Walker. 1750. The home of Mr. Ingles, was adjoining the present village of Blacksburg, Montgomery county, Va. The farm _ "Solitude"_ lies between "Smithfield" and the town.
7. This river and the Greenbrier unite and form the Great Kanawha.
8. For an account of this Society, see Mem. Hist. Soc. Penn., Vol II. P.I. (1827), p. 133, et seq.; also Hazzard's Reg. Penn. Vol. XV. pp. 160, 208.
9. Walker's MS. Journal, 1750.
10. Two creeks are named upon Frey and Jefferson's Map of Virginia of 1755 previously cited, and upon Mitchell's Map of N. Amer. of same date, - marked as tributaries of New river. See, also, Lewis' Map of Virg., of 1794, in Carey's Amer. Atlas.
11. It is this paragraph in Walker's MS. Journal which fixes the date of his previous exploration. Stalnacker's Settlement was upon the north bank of the Middle Fork of Holston, not far above its confluence with the South Fork: Lewis Evan's Map Middle British Colonies. It afterward became a prominent frontier station. The site is within the present limits of Washington county, Va.
12. This stream _ Reedy creek _ flowing into the Holston, must not be confounded with the one of the same name, afterward known as Reed creek, a tributary of New river. Both are marked upon Mitchell's Map of N. Amer., of 1755.
13. Walker's MS. Journal, 1750.
14. Besides the evidence furnished by the Journal kept by Walker upon this exploration as to the date, there are preserved some of his subsequent declarations. "I was exploring the country far west of the settlements in 1750:" Letter to Preston, 23 March, 1778, MS., previously cited. See, also, Hall's Sketches, Vol. I. pp. 239, 240; Bradford's Notes (Stipp's Miscel.) p. 9; Holmes' Annals, Vol. II, p. 304 note. Compare Rafinesque, in Marshall's Hist. Ky., (ed. 1824) Vol. I. p. 39; Collins' Hist. Ky., (ed. 1874) Vol. I. p. 639 _ Vol. II. pp. 415, 416, 625. The same date is marked upon the Map prefixed to "Washington's Tour" (Williamsburg. 1754) and upon Mitchell's Map _ N. Amer. Of 1755.

15. This reference of Walker to white rocks, is accounted for from the fact of these being a vein of grey and variegated marble extending along the north side of the mountain.

16. A mishap which, as the explorers journal shows, frequently happened afterward.

17. In the Map prefixed to "Washington's Journal," 1754 already cited, this stream is marked "Peleson or Clinches River." "Clinch:" Lewis Evans' Map, 1755. "Pelesippi or Clinches:" Mitchell's Map, 1755.

18. Haywood's Hist. Tenn., p. 12.

19. Tomlinson's Statement to Daniel Bryan _ Communicated by the latter 27 Feb., 1843.

20. Tomlinson's Statement. See, also, Rafineesque in Marshall's Ky., (ed. 1824)Vol. I. p. 39; Holmes' Annals, Vol II. p. 304. Compare, too, Hall's Sketches, Vol. I. pp. 239, 240. "This mountain, Dr. Walker called Cumberland," are the explicit words of Tomlinson.

21. "An Indian path leading from the Cherokee towns on Tennessee, to the Shawanee Indian Towns in what is now the State of Ohio" _ Daniel Bryan, 17 Feb. 1843, MS. Letter. See, also, Filson's Map of Kentucke, 1784; Perkins' Annals of the Treaty, p. 114.

22. Bradford's Notes (Stipp's pict. Miscel.) p. 69; Holmes' Annals, Vol. Ii. p. 304 notes; Collins' Hist. Ky., Vol. I. p. 639 _ Vol. II. p. 416.

23. MS. letter of Daniel Bryan, 27 Feb., 1843.

24. Formerly Josh Bell county; but the Legislature of Ky., in 1873, dropped the singular, prefix, Josh.

25. Statement of Wm. Tomlinson to Cave Johnson of Ky., communicated by the latter, 15 May, 1848. See, also, Map prefixed to "Washington's Tour," 1754. Mitchell's, Otten's, and other Maps, in, and after, 1755, designate it as the Cumberland river. Compare too, Marshall's Hist. Ky., (ed. 1824) Vol. I, p. 6; Holmes' Annals, Vol. II. p. 304 note; Hall's Sketches, Vol. I. p. 240; Butler's Hist. Ky., (2d ed.) p. 18. The Indian name of the Cumberland was Shawanue.

26. Walker's MS. Journal. 1750.

27. Walker's MS. Journal, 1750.

28. Communication of Richard Herndon, 19 July, 1854.

29. Walker's MS. Journal, 1750.

30. "Three quarters of a mile below the house is a pond in the low ground of the river, a quarter of a mile in length and two hundred yards wide;" _ Walker's MS. Journal, 1750. It is marked " Swan's Pond," on Lee's Map of Ky., of 1852.

31. The spot is noted _ "Walker's Settlement, 1750 -" on the Map, already cited prefixed to the pamphlet edition of Washington's Journal of his Tour to the Ohio, printed a Williamsburgh, Va. and reprinted in London, in 1754. It is also laid down on several Maps of 1755 and after. It is marked on all as being upon the "Cumberland river."

32. For an estimate of the area of the Eastern Kentucky coal field, see, Kentucky

(unreadable), Burvey, Vol. IV, p. 13.

33. Statement of Samuel Plummer to E. Marsh: Communicated by the latte, in 1848- 9.

34. See Evans' Map Middle British Colonies, 1755, where this Branch is marked as "Frederick's River." "As for the Branches of Ohio," says that "Geographer (Analysis p. 10). "which head in New Virginia _ so they call, for Distinction-sake , that Part of Virginia South East of the Ouasioto [Cumberland] Mountains, and on the Branches of Green Briar, New River, and Holston River _ I am particularly obliged to Mr. Thomas Walker, for the Intelligence of what names they bear, and what Rivers they fall into Northward and Westward."

35. As to the identification of the "Louisa river" of Walker, as the Tug Fork of the Big Sandy, compare Butler's Hist. Ky. (2d ed.), p. 18; also Map prefixed to "Washington Tour," 1754; and Evans' and Mitchells' Maps of 1755. It was thus named by Walker, after Louisa county, Virginia. The name Louisa _ often Lovisa, Levisa, La Visa, La Visee, all a corruption of Louisa _ has, since 1750, strangely wandered about the Kentucky country. It was sometimes applied to one of the Forks of Coal river; afterward to the Kentucky river; and, finally, it has taken a permanent hold of the West Fork of the Big Sandy.

36. Gists' Cincinatti Miscellany. Vol. II: p. 139.

37. Walker's MS. Journal, 1750.

38. Walker's MS. Journal, 1750.

39. Walker's MS. Journal, 1850 (sic). Walker, afterward held many offices, _ some under Virginia, others under the General Government. He died at "Castle Hill." in 1794; having, for many years, taken high mark in the confidence of his countrymen.

Chapter Five

1. Maryland Gazette, 12 July, 1759. Memoirs of Stobo (Pittsburgh 1854) p. 13. Examination of Stobo, at Montreal, 1 Nov., 1756. MS. He then gave his age as "about twenty-seven."

2. Memoirs of Stobo, p. 13.

3. Exam. of Stobo: MS.

4. Memoirs of Soto. p. 16. Sargeant's Hist. of Braddock's Expedition, p. 372.

5. Stobo gave his sword to his Lieutenant, who afterward fell with the unfortunate Braddock. In after years, the weapon having been returned to its original owner, was worn by the latter with singular esteem.

6. Examination of Van Braam at Montreal, 23 Oct., 1756: MS. He then gave his age, according to the record, as 27 yrs. 7 mos. There is, probably, an error in these figures.

7. He was in the Carthagenia Expedition, 1741: Irving's Washington, Vol. I, 59. What his others services were, if any, are not known.

8. Washington to Dinwiddie, 20 March, 1754, in Sparks' History of Washington,

II. p. 4.
9. Same to same, 10 June, 1754, in Sparks' Washington, II. 40.
10. Exam. of Van Braam, 23 Oct., 1756: MS.
11. Adam Stephen, in Penn. Gazette, 22 Aug., 1754.
12. Exam. of Stobo: MS. Stobo was not the only one who, at the time of his confinement in Fort Duquesne, considered the French as having broken the treaty of Fort Necessity. See, Penn. Gazette, 25 July, 1754; Sparks' Writings of Washington II, 467.
13. Examination of Van Braam, 23 Oct. 1756 at Montreal; MS.
14. Col. James Innes, soon after engaged, at that point, in erecting Fort Cumberland, was the officer in command. His name was unknown to Stobo. _ See, Penn. Arch. II, 115.
15. The original is in the Prothonotary's office, Montreal. Before it reached Wills creek, it was broken open and a copy taken and sent ti the Lieut.- Gov. of Penn. Col. Rec. VI. 140. See, also Penn. Arch., II, 115. A copy of the drawing was probably sent sometime after to England, Gent. Mag., XXV, 383.
16. "Mer. Driscall," in the Penn. copy's evidently an inadvertance.
17. Penn. Coll. Rec. VI, p. 142. Contrecoeur, in command of Fort Duquesne, gained intelligence, in some way, of Stobo's secret communications; dismissing the matter, however, with a simple reprimand. _ Van Braam's Exam.: MS. Both of Stobo's letters have been frequently published, together with the plan of Fort Duquesne.
18. Sparks' Writings of Washington, Vol. II., p. 467.
19. Ibid. Compare, also, Maryland Gazette, 12 Sept., 1754.
20. Maryland Gazette, 24 Oct., 1754. Burk's Hist. Va, iii, 193.
21. Farmer and Moore's Hist. Coll. N. Hampshire, Vol. I, 216.
22. Vaudreuil to Machault, 24 July, 1755, in Col. Hist. of New York. Vol. X, p. 308.
23. Farmer and Moore's Hist. Coll. N. H., I. pp. 220-222.
24. This letter was taken to Albany, in Jan, 1755, by an Indian. Cuyler to Delancy, 20 Jan., 1755: MS. letter in English Historical MSS., Albany.
25. Such, at least, is to be inferred from the Exam. of Stobo, 1 Nov. 1756.
26. Bre'ard to M. de Machault, 13 Aug., 1755, in Col. Hist. of N. Y., Vol. X, 311. See, also, Montcalm to Count d' Argenson, 1 Nov., 1756, in same Vol., p. 492. The two letters of Stobo and the drawing had been delivered to Braddock at Fort Cumberland, by Col. Innes.
27. Col. Hist. N. Y. Vol. X, 311.
28. From "Memoire contenant le Precis des Faits,"&c. Paris, 1756. Olden Time, Vol. II. p. 217.
29. Mem. of Stobo, p. 23.
30. Burk's Hist. Va., III, p. 194.
31. Mem. of Stobo, pp. 23-25.
32. Maryland Gazette, 20 Nov., 1760.

33. Mem. of Stobo, p. 23. Col. Hist. New York, X, 492.34. Col. Hist. N. Y., X, 533.35. Exam of Van Braam, 23 Oct., 1756: MS.36. Maryland Gazette, 20 Nov., 1760.37. Van Braam to Washington, 20 Dec., 1783: MS. letter. 38. Sparks' Washington, II. p. 365.

39. Van Braam to Washington 20 Dec.,1783: MS. letter.40. British Army List, 1778.41. Van Braam to Washington, 20 Dec., 1783: MS. letter. 42. British Army List, 1778.43. Van Braam to Washington, 20 De.\c. 1783: MS. letter.

44. Exam. f Stobo, 1 Nov., 1756; MS.

45. Col. Hist. N.Y., X, 499.

46. Ibid. Stobo's conviction was a forgone conclusion, as the French Government had already published him to the European Courts as a spy in Fort Duquesne.

47. Mem. of Stobo, p. 27.

48. Mem. of Stobo, pp. 34, 35. Col. Hist. N.Y., X, 1025.

49. "A Journal of Lieut. Simon Stevens, From the Time of his being Taken, near Fort William Henry, June the 25th, 1758. With an Account of his Escape from Quebec, and his Arrival at Louisbourg, on June the 6th 1759. Boston; 1760." pp. 3, 4. This is an exceedingly rare pamphlet. It was written by Stevens himself soon after the events transpired; and while the dates and particular incidents were fresh in his memory. Compare, in connection with the capture of Stevens, Md. Gaz., 12 July, 1759; Penn. Gaz., 5 July, 1759. As to the skirmish, see Rogers' Journal, p. 69; Pouchats Mem., (translated by Hough), Vol. I, pp. 106, 107.

50. Stevens' Journal, p. 10.

51. Stevens' Journal. p. 10. Mem. of Stobo pp. 35-44.

52. Montcalm to Belle Isle, 8 May, 1759, Col. Hist. N. Y., X. p. 970. It would seem, from this communication, that up to the time Stobo's escape, the judgement against him had not been reversed by the French monarch.

53. Stevens' Journal, p. 18.

54. Penn. Gazette. 28 June 1759; Maryland Gazette 5 July, same year. In the estimate of the number who escaped, it will be seen that only the men are reckoned.

55. Penn. Gazette, 5 July, 1759; Maryland Gazette, same year.

56. S.C. Gazette, 29 Sep., 1759.

57. Penn. Gazette, 5 July 1759; Maryland Gazette, same year.

58. Mem. of Stobo, p. 66.

59. "About the 10th or 12th of June;" Penn. Gazette, 5 July, 1759. The same words are used in the Maryland Gazette of the week following. " two days or so were passed [after his arrival] and then a vessel's ready to proceed to Quebec:"Mem. of Stobo, p. 66 Stevens also returned with Stobo. The Journal of the former closes withh these words: "The Governor [of Louisburg] treated us with very great complaisance, as did all the gentleman of the place; and upon the General's order, I immediately went up the river, and joined the army under Gen'l Wolfe, where I continued until the surrender of Quebec, which was on the 18th of September, 1759; and then had liberty to return home ."

60. Knox's Journal, Vol. II. p.34. Mem. of Stobo, pp. 68, 69.
61. Mem. of Stobo, 70-72.
62. Maryland Gazette, 6 Dec., 1759.
63. Journal House of Burg. Va., 19 Nov. 1759. See, also, Maryland Gazette, 6 Dec., 1759 and 10 Jan., 1760; Mem. of Stobo, pp. 80-82.
64. Jour. House Burg. Va., 20 Nov. 1759; Maryland Gazette, 10 Jan., 1760.
65. According to the Mem. of Stobo (p. 73), he was under full pay as Major. It is also asserted that he was promoted to that office soon after he became hostage, (p.20).
66. Mem. of Stobo pp. 74-77. Penn. Gaz., 5 June, 1760.
67. British Army List, 1761. Beatson's Naval and Mil. Mem. III, 364.
68. Hist. Rec. 15th Reg. Foot, (Lond. 1848) pp. 44-46. Mante, 346 et esq.
69. Lond. Gaz., No. 11071; 25th to 28th Aug., 1770. Edinburg Weekly Amusement, 6 Sep., 1770. The successor of Stobo was Isaac Aug. D'Arisse'. His commission was issued 22 June, 1770: British Army List., 1771. Stobo in 1770, joined with Van Braam in an application for Bounty Lands under the Proc. of 1763; Sparks' Washington, II, 365.
70. Hume to Somollet, 21 Sept., 1768 _ mentioned in Olden Times, Vol. I. p. 283.

Chapter Six

1. Md. Gaz., 8 March, 1754. Wm. Preston's MS. Register for 1754, "of the Persons who have been either Killed, Wounded, or taken Prisoners, in Augusta County {Va.}; and, also, of such as have made their Escape." The only occupants of the settlement _ the first in Virginia west of the Laurel Hill _ were David Tygart and Robert Foyle (frequently, though erroneously, printed File) and their families. He present town of Beverly, county-seat of Randolph county, West Virginia, now occupies its site. Foyle and his whole family except the eldest son, were murdered. The Tygarts escaped. This event happened in November, 1753. See Fry and Jefferson's Map of Va., where the date and place of the massacre are indicated. Compare also Washington's Journal, in Sparks' Writings of Washington, II. 446: where, however, the place of the massacre is given, inadvertently, as on "the head of the Great Kanawha."
2. Wm. Preston's MS. Register of 1754.
3. Wm. Preston's MS. Register of 1755. See also, Md. Gaz. 24 July, l755.
4. Md. Gaz., 3 July, 1755.
5. Md. Gaz., 10 July, 1755.
6. Md. Gaz., 24 July, 1755.
7. Wm. Preston's MS. Reg; 1755.
8. The savages did not strike the Western border of Penn. Until Oct. See, Gordon's Hist. Penn., p. 614.
9. Records of Augusta County, Va. These show his appointment in 1752. As to the Powers and Duties of that office, see Henning's Statutes at Large, Vols. 7, 8, and

9.
10. Md. Gaz., 21 Aug., 1755. Gov. Dinwiddie to Col. Buchanan, 14 Aug., 1755; MS. letter. Reg. of Wm. Preston (1755): MS. Letitia Floyd's MS. Narr. of the Life and Death of Col. Patton: Narr. of the captivity and Escape of Mrs. William Ingles, by her son, John Ingles: MS. See, also, South. Lit. Mess., for Dec., 1853, p. 722.
11. Dinwiddie to Col. Buchanan, 15 Aug., 1755: MS. letter, previously cited.
12. Both Shawnee Towns are indicated upon Lewis Evans' Map of the Middle British Colonies: 1755. These Indians also occupied cabins on the south side of the Ohio, opposite their Lower Town. _ Gist's Journal, in Pownall, p. 10.
13. To Mrs. Draper, who, at the time of her capture, had her arm broken and was otherwise badly wounded, this was a severe ordeal. Concerning the particulars of her subsequent treatment by the savages, but little is known. She was released from captivity, when peace was concluded with the French.
14. The younger son, George, died soon after separated from its mother. Thomas the older, lived with the Indians thirteen years, when he was ransomed by his father, William Ingles, at the Lower Shawnee Town.
15. "In 1735, the Canadians who came to make war upon the Tchicacahas (Chicksaws) found near the fine river or Ohio, the skeletons of seven elephants. The place was near the i Ohio, which, in our maps of Louisiana, is marked with a cross." _ Bossier's Travels (Lond. 1771 _ written "at the Illinois," 1756), Vol. I, pp. 179, 180. For other visits to these bones prior to the captivity of Mrs. Ingles, see, (1.) Peal's Account of the Mammouth (Lond. 1802), pp. 8-10; Warren's Mastodon Giganteus, p. 1. (2.) Gist's Journal Pownall, p. 14.
16. The old woman succeeded, finally, in reaching the settlements.
17. William Ingles finally settled on New River in what is now Montgomery county at the Ferry which bears his name (corrupted to "English") where he died in 1782. Mrs. Ingles survived her husband thirty-three (one?) years. She lived to the age of eighty-four the incidents of her captivity and escape were first given to the public, in the South. Litt. Mess. for Dec. 1853.

Chapter Seven

1. Dinwiddie to Capts. Preston and Smith, 15 Dec., 1755: MS. letter. See, also, same to Gov. Morris of Pa., 2 Jan., 1756 in Col. Biol. Vol. VII, p. 31.
2. Morris to Dinwiddie, 1 Feb., 1756, in Penn. Arch. Vol II, p. 561. Same to Gen. Shirly, in same vol., p. 570. Gage to Morris, same vol. p. 571, 572.
3. Washington to Dinwiddie, 14 Ja., 1756, in Sparks' Washington, II, 125.
4. Lewis to Capt. Geo. Robinson, 28 Jan., 1756: MS. letter.
5. The regular companies of the Virginians were commanded by Capts. Hog, Preston, Smith, Breckenridge, Woodson, Overton, and Pearis (Paris); the volunteer companies, by Capts. Montgomery and Dunlap.
6. Journal of Capt. William Preston, 1756: MS.

7. This stream takes its rise seven miles northeast of the present town of Jeffersonville, county seat of Tazewell county.
8. The Dry (or South) Fork rises about six miles northwest of Jeffersonville, runs a northwesterly course to its confluence with the Tug River (Tug Fork of Big Sandy.)
9. Preston's Journal, 1756: MS.
10. Preston's Journal, 1756: Ms.
11. Journal of Lieut. Thomas Morton, 1756, in Va. Hist. Regis. For July, 1851, p. 143. Preston speaks of him as a Lieut.
12. "We marched 4 miles, and crossed the Creek 14 times:" Morton. "Marched about 6 miles; crossed the stream 16 times:" Preston.
13. Preston's Journal, 1756{ MS.
14. Preston's Journal, 1756: MS.
15. Spoken of, by Morton, as "the North Fork; by Preston, as "the South East Fork."
16. Morton's Journal, 1756.
17. Preston's Journal, 1756, 1756. MS.
18. Morton's Journal, 1756.
19. Preston's Journal 1756:, MS.
20. Morton's Journal, 1756.
21. Preston's Journal, 1756.
22. Preston's Journal, 1756: MS.
23. The undertaking was long afterward spoken of as "the Shawnee Expedition:" Henning's (Va.) Stats. at Large Vol. VII, pp. 183, 189, 197. It was usually known, however, upon the frontier, as "the Sandy Creek Voyage:" Hugh Paul Taylor, in Fincastle (Va.) Mirror. Compare Withers' Border Warfare, p. 62; where Taylor if copied verbatim.
24. Washington to Dinwiddie, in Sparks' Washington, II. p. 135.

Chapter Eight

1. For the remote realms for the defection, see "An Enquiry into the Causes of the Alienation of the Delaware and Shawanese Indians," (Lond., 1769), passion. Sir Wm. Johnson and the Quakers held the Delawares who remained upon the Susquehanna, and other kindred tribes, in check. Gordon's Hist. Penn., p. 321.
2. Indicated on "Armstrong Map of the Country West of the Susquehanna," 1756: MS. See, also, Scull's Map of Pa., 1770; and the Lith. Map prefixed to Penn. Arch., Vol. XII.
3. Sometimes spoken of as "Croghan's Fort." The site of the fort was at "Aughwick" or "Aughwick Old Town" _ an Indian village and trading post. On Lewis Evans' Map of 1755, the town is indicated as "Oxwick." See, further, Penn. Arch., XII, p. 456.
4. The fort is very correctly located on Armstrong's MS. Map of 1756. Its posi-

tion is also accurately given in Day's Hist. Coll. of Pa., p. 1165. See, also, Penn. Arch., XII, p. 336.

5. Further down the Juiata than Fort Granville was Patterson's Fort, upon the north bank of the river, opposite the mouth of the Tuscarora creek, in what is now Juniata County. There was also a fortification at "McDowell's Mills," now Bridgport, Franklin County.

6. Col. Rec. (Pa.), VII, 186. Penn. Arch., II, 699.

7. Col. Hist. N. Y., X, pp. 469, 487, 489, 494. Wis. Hist. Coll., V, p. 119.

8. So noted in Lewis Evans' Map of 1755. Frequently, "Shearman's" or "Shareman's."

9. Pa. Gaz., Aug. 5th and Oct. 14, 1756; Laudon's Indian Wars, II, 196; Penn. Arch., II, 743, 744, 750, etc., and XII, 366; Col. Rec., VII, 231-233, 242, etc. Compare, also, Gordon's Pa., 619; Rupp's Juniata, etc., 118-130; Day's Hist. Coll. Pa., 465. For French version of the affair, consult Col. Hist. N. Y., X, 469, 487, 489, 490; Bossu's Travels, 186.

10. Statement of John Girty: 1846.

11. Edwards' Life of Brainerd, p. 286. The settlement is noted as "Chambers" on Lewis Evans' Map of 1755. Near this point Fort Hunter was afterward erected. Penn. Arch., XII, 375; Morgan's Annals of Harrisburg, p. 50. See, also, Scull's Map of Pa., 1770; Gordon's Hist. Pa., p. 341.

12. Penn. Arch., Vol. II, p. 14.

13. Rupp's Hist. Dauphin, etc., pp. 381, 555. Penn. Arch., Vol. II, p. 23.

14. Statement by James Blackford: 1846. See, in corroboration, as to his being killed by an Indian, Sparks' Amer. Biog., Vol. XXIII, p. 109, note.

15. It was for the killing of this Indian, it is said, that Turner was tortured. But see Bossu's Travels, p. 186.

16. The current tradition, preserved by the Girty descendants, is corroborated by Penn. Arch., Vol. II, p. 775, as to Thomas.

17. Penn. Arch., Vol. II, p. 750.

18. Col. Hist. N.Y., X, p. 490.

19. Col. Rec., VII, p. 230.

20. Penn. Gaz., 23 Sept., 1756. "Two hundred and eighty provisionals:" Mante, p. 75. "Three hundred seven men:" Loudon's Indian Wars, 21, 172.

21. The location of the Indian village _ Frank's Town is minutely described in Day's Hist. Coll. Pa., 372. Compare Scull's; Map of Pa. 1770.

22. Armstrong to Gov. Denny, from Fort Lytlleton, 14 Sept., 1756, in Coll. Rec. (Pa.), Vol. VII, p. 257 and Penn. Arch., Vol. II, p. 767. This is the Official Report of the Expedition. It was first published, in substance, in Penn. Gaz., 23 Sept., 1756. A very brief abstract was printed in the S. C. Gaz., 14 Oct., following. Compare Mante, p. 75. Armstrong says he joined the advance party "on Wednesday the third." He is correct as to the day of the month, but wrong as to the day of the week. It was Friday.

23. The spot was then know as Forty Mile Lick. "We came to a place called Forty

Mile Lick, where the Indians trimmed the hair of their prisoners:" Robert Robison's Narr., in Loudon's Indian Wars, II, p. 172.
24. At least thus known in 1757. See, Penn. Arch., III, 148.
25. "We believing ourselves about six miles from the town:" Armstrong. "Within about six miles of the town:" Robison.
26. "Our Colonel ordered two men to go and spy how many Indians there were at the fire; accordingly, they went but could see only four;" Robison.
27. N.Y. Col. Hist. X., 533. Penn. Arch., III, 148.
28. Robison gives a graphic description of the setting fire to Captain Jacob's cabin: The Colonel {Armstrong} says 'is there none of you lads that will set fire to these rascals that have wounded me?' John Ferguson, a soldier, swore that he would; he goes to a house covered with bark, and takes a slice of bark which had fire on it; he makes up to the cover of Jacob's house and held it there until it had burned about one yard square; then he ran, and the Indians fired at him; _ the smoke blew about his legs, but the shots missed him." _ Loudon's Hist. Ind. Wars, Vol. II, p. 174.
29. "A boy of the name of Crawford, told afterwards, that he was up at the Kittanning the next day, with some French and Indians, and found Captain Jacobs, his squaw and son, with some others:" Robison, in Loudon's Hist. Ind. Wars, Vol. II, 173.
30. It was, probably, to hunt. "The prisoners give the account that there were twenty- five Indians set to kill meat for the company that was to be there next night consisting of 150, destined for Virginia:" Robison.
31. Ten or Twelve, of whom seven were his own men: Armstrong.
32. Hugh Gibson, in Loudon's Ind. Wars, Vol. II, p. 183.
33. Penn. Gaz., 30 Sept., 1756. N. H. Gaz., 7 Oct., 1756. According to Robison (Loudon's Hist. Ind. Wars, Vol. II, p. 176) Mercer was finally found by some Cherokees who had been sent out, by Captain Hamilton from Fort Lyttleton, to search for signs of enemy Indians. When discovered, he was unable to raise himself from the ground. He was given food and brought into the Fort.
34. Wilkinson's Memoirs, Vol. I, pp. 146, 147.
35. Penn. Arch., Vol. III, p. 634.
36. Armstrong to Gov. Denny, 14 Sept., 1756, before cited. His estimate, which is give in the text, of the number of the enemy destroyed, was probably a low one. See, Examination of La Chauvignerie, Jr., in Penn. Arch., Vol. III, 305. "After the taking of Kittanning, the Indians came to Fort Duquesne and told that they had buried upwards of fifty of their people that were killed there, and that more were missing." _ S. C. Gaz., 18 Nov., 1756. "One or two chiefs killed and many Indians:" _ La Chauvignerie.
37. Gordon's Hist. of Pa., p. 345. Penn. Arch., III, 116, 307.
38. Device. An officer followed by two soldiers: the officer pointing to a soldier shooting from behind a tree, and an Indian prostrate before him. In the background Indian houses in flames. Legend, Kittinning destroyed by Colonel

Armstrong, September the eighth, 1756. Reverse Device. The arms of the corporation. Legend. The gift of the corporation of Philadelphia _ N. Y. Hist. Soc. Coll., Vol. III., p. 387: Mass. Hist. Soc. Coll., Vol. IV, (3rd Series) p. 297; Penn. Hist. Soc. Coll., Vol. II, P. I., p. 57.
39. Hazard's Reg. of Pa., Vol. I., pp. 347, 366.
40. Penn. Gaz., 7 Oct., 1756.
41. Sparks' Writings of Washington, II, 317-319 and III, 72.
42. Penn. Gaz., 13th and 27th Oct., 1763. See, also, Parkman's Conspiracy of Pontiac, (6th ed.) Vol. II, p. 100.
43. Sparks' Writings of Washington, III, 72, 73, 294, 319.
44. Ibid., IV, 373.45. Ibid., V, 360.

Chapter Nine

1. Fort Toulouse, frequently known in early annals as the "Alabama Fort," was situated on the east bank of the Coosa, a little below the present town of Wetumka, in Elmore county, Alabama. In the war of 1812-15, it was the site of Fort Jackson.
2. Sometimes written Otarsite.
3. The last u in this word is generally though improperly omitted. As to the exact locality of the fort, the most implicit reliance can be given to "A Draught of the Cherokee Country, on the West Side of the Twenty-four Mountains, commonly called Over the Hills; Taken by Henry Timberlake when he was in that Country, in March 1762." According to this map, Fort Loudon was situated about half a mile above the mouth of the Tellico, on the south or left bank of the Little Tennessee. Compare, also, Mante's "Sketch of the Cherokee Country," in his War in America. "Near the Conflux of Great Tellico and Tennase-rivers:" Adair (p. 269.) Ramsey, in his Annals of Tennessee (p.17), and also in the Map prefixed thereto, agrees with these reliable authorities.
4. S. C . Gaz., 5 July, 1758.
5. Adair p. 247.
6. Penn. Gaz., 3 July, 1760.
7. Penn. Gaz., 31 July, 1760. Bancroft's Hist. U. S., IV, p. 354.
8. S. C. Gaz., 9 and 13 Aug., 1760. Penn. Gaz., 4 Sept., 1760.
9. Timberlake's Memoirs, p. 66.
10. These were the words employed upon this occasion, as being more expressive, with the Indians than "Cannon;" although, as previously stated they were one-pounders only.
11. Many of the incidents connected with the massacre are detailed in the S. C. Gaz., 13th Oct., 1760; in the Md. Gaz., 6 Nov., 1760; and in the Annals of the War (Dublin, 1763), pp.133, 134.

Chapter Ten

1. Francis Parkman, Conspiracy of Pontiac (6th ed.) Vol. I, pp. 181, 182.

2. Parkman's Conspiracy of Pontiac, Vol. I, pp. 198, 199.
3. In 1763, the Senecas had several villages, beginning about fifty miles from Cayuga and extending to the Genesse, with others thence to the Allegheny. All these joined the Western Nations except two; Kanadasero and Kanaderagey. The whole tribe numbered ten hundred and fifty warriors. _ Col. Hist. N. Y., VII, p. 582.
4. Parkman. Pontiac's Confederacy. (6th ed.) II, p. 7.
5. Marshall's Niagara Frontier, p. 16. Parkman's Discov. Great West, p. 133, note.
6. Barton's Western New York, pp. 15,17,18. Marshall's Niagara Frontier, p. 16.
7. Known, also, as Little Niagara. Penn. Gaz., 6 Oct., 1763; N.Y. Col. Hist., VII, 621; Stone's Johnson, Vol. II, p. 450. The English fort, though near, did not occupy the identical sight of the former French post. The portage-road is marked upon a Map - Doc. Hist. N.Y., II., p. 459. Compare, also, "Niagara, from 1805 to 1875, by an Old Resident {Albert H. Porter}."
8. Parkman's Pontiac, (6th ed.) Vol. II, p. 76.
9. The Indians (Senecas) name is Dyus-da-nyah-goh, "the cleft rocks:" Marshall. The locality in all the Guide-Books to Niagara Falls.
10. Penn. Gaz., 6 Oct., 1763.
11. Maude's "Visit to the Falls of Niagara in 1800." p. 144.
12. Johnson to Col. Eyre, 13 Oct., 1763: Diary of the Siege of Detroit (Albany, 1860), p. 180.
13. Among the slain in that way, was one Noble, a Corporal :Simms' Hist. Schoharie County, p. 149. Compare Diary of Siege of Detroit, p. 180.
14. Relics of this fearful day were found many years after, upon the bottom of the chasm.
15. "Our {Genesee} Indians were among those who laid in ambush on the Niagara river:" Mary Jemison. "The Senecas from Chenussio {Genesee} were the Principals in this Affair:" Johnson to Col. Eyre, 23 Oct., 1763, previously cited. "The Seneca warriors, aided probably by some western Indians, were the authors of this unexpected attack:" Parkman's Pontiac (6th ed.) Vol. II, p. 79. There was at least man, with the enemy.
16. In 1850, Blackmake, an aged Seneca chief, gave the number as two hundred. The estimate of the English at Fort Niagara, immediately after the occurrence, was from three to five hundred.
17. This disposition of the Indians is given upon the strength of a current Seneca tradition.
18. This statement as to the disposition of the savages at the second ambuscade is given upon the authority of Seneca traditions. But see Penn. Gazette, 6 Oct., 1763, for a different account.
19. Extract from a letter dated Niagara October 17th, 1763 (diary of the Siege of Detroit, p. 81): "Sir _ I have acquainted you of the sad Usage of the Savages to the Detachment of our Forces that turned out at lower Landing sometime past, where the Officers and Men were almost totally destroyed."

20. For some account of the Seneca villages upon that river, in 1763, see, Life of Mary Jemison. As these towns mostly identical with those found there by the army under General Sullivan in 1779, the following works can be consulted with profit, for a further description: O'Reilly's Sketches of Rochester; Notices of Sullivan's Campaign (Rochester, 1842); Sims' Hist. Schoarie County; Campbell's Annals of Tryon County; Morgan's League of the Iroquois; Turner's Hist. of Phelps and Gorham's Purchase; Ketchum's Hist. Of Buffalo, Vol. I.

Chapter Eleven

1. ["Journal of Captain Thomas Morris, of his Majesty's XVII Regiment of Infantry;" from "Miscellanies in Prose and Verse. By Captain Thomas Morris. London: Printed for James Ridgway, No. 1, York- Street, St. James's - Square. 1791." pp. 1- 39.]

2. ["Thomas Morris became in 1755 a Lieutenant in the 17th on Forbes' regiment, which served under Lord Loudoun in 1757; at the reduction of Louisbourgh in 1758, under Amherst; and accompanied the expedition on Lake George and Champlain, under the same General, in 1759. In 1761, Mer. Morris was promoted to a Captaincy x x x." _ N. Y. Col. Hist., VII., 863 note.]

3. [John Bradstreet was born in 1711. In the expedition against Louisburg, in 1745, he was Lieutenant Colonel of Pepperell's York Provincials, Maine. He was commissioned Captain in a Royal regiment _ Sir William Pepperell's foot _ 5 Sept., 1745. On the 16 Sept., 1746, he received the appointment of Lieutenant-Governor of St. John's, Newfoundland. He remained with his regiment until 1748, when it was disbanded. In 1755, he was ordered by Braddock to Oswego. Upon the accession of Shirley to the command in America, Bradstreet was made his Adjutant-General. The next year he defeated a strong party of the enemy, nine miles from Oswego. In March, 1757, he was appointed to a company in the 60th regiment (Royal American). On the 27 Dec. following, he was commissioned Lieutenant-Colonel in the Regular army; at which time, he was Deputy Quarter Master General. He was made Quarter Master General with the rank of Colonel, 20 Aug., 1758 and seven days after captured Fort Frontenac. He was commissioned as Colonel in February, 1762; continuing as Quarter Master General for a few years after. _ Map. Hist. Coll., Vol. I. Parsons' Life of Pepperell. London Mag., XV. Gent. Mag. N. Y. Doc. Hist., Vol. I. Army List. Duntap's Hist. N. Y., Vol. I. Knox's Campaigns, Vol. I. Drake's Dic. Amer. Biog. Diary of the Siege of Detroit. Parkman's Pontiac, (6th ed.). I, 122]

4. ["The campaign of 1763, a year of disaster to the English colonies, was throughout of a defensive nature, and no important blow had been struck against the enemy. With the opening of the following Spring, preparations were made to renew the war on a more decisive plan. x x x It had been resolved to march two armies from different points into the heart of the Indian country. The first under Bouquet, was to advance from Fort Pitt into the midst of the Delaware and

Shawnee settlements of the valley of the Ohio. The other under Colonel Bradstreet was to pass, up the lakes, and force the tribes of Detroit, and the regions beyond, to unconditional submission;" Parkman's Pontiac (6th ed.) II, pp. 156, 162. Bradstreet went from Albany in boats, by way of the Mohawk, to Fort Stanwix (Rome), crossing the portage to Oneida Lake; thence down the Oswego river and along the south shore of Lake Ontario, to Fort Niagara. Taking his boats across the carrying-place to Fort Schlosser, he launched them above the Falls, and followed the south shore of Lake Erie to Cedar Point on the east side of Maumee Bay, in what is now Lucas county, Ohio, where he arrived on the 23 August, 1764.]

5. [On the 12 Sept., 1760, "his Excellency Jeffery Amherst, Esq., Major General and Commander-in-chief of His Majesty's forces in North America" sent "Major Robert Rogers of His Majesty's independent company of Rangers." to the westward ti\o relieve the garrisons at the French posts of Detroit, Michilimackinac, and their dependencies; to collect the arms of the inhabitants and administer the oath of allegiance; and to bring away the French troops from those distant forts. _ Rogers' Journal, pp. 111, 112.]

6. [When Rogers, in 1760, received the surrender of the western posts, the Illinois country was not visited by him. In 1764, it still remained in French possession.]

7. [In May, 1763 Pontiac laid siege to Detroit. Soon after, Godefroi left that post, with four other Canadians. Their professed objective was to bring a French officer from the Illinois to induce Pontiac to abandon his hostile designs. At the mouth of the Maumee, they met John Welch, an English trader, with two canoes, bound for Detroit. They seized him, and divided his furs among themselves and a party of Indians who were with them. They then proceeded up the Maumee to Fort Miami and aided the Indians to capture it: Parkman's Pontiac. (6th ed.) II, 278 note.]

8. ["On the twentieth day (of August, 1764) we (Bradstreet's army) were off the mouth of the river which falls into Sandusky Bay, where a council of war was held, on the question, whether it was more advisable to attack and destroy the Indian villages, on the Miami (Maumee,) or to proceed for Detroit direct. Early the next morning, it having been determined, that, considering the villages were populous, as well as hostile, it was necessary to destroy them, and we entered the Miami; but were presently met by a deputation, offering peace. This offer was accepted; but it was not till after two days, during which we had begun to be doubtful of the enemy's intention, that the chiefs arrived. When they came, a sort of armistice was agreed upon; and they promised to meet the General of Detroit, within fifteen days. At that place, terms of peace were to be settled in a general council." _ Henry's Travels, p. 185.]

9. ["Captain Morris of Major General Moncton's Regiment, had been sent with a letter to the French commandant of the Illinois , and a message to the Indians and Inhabitants of that District, to inform them of the peace which had been made with so many nations, and to remove some bad impressions they had received

from us, by assuring the Inhabitants that on the taking the oath of allegiance and fidelity which Captain Morris will administer to them, they would enjoy the same privileges and immunities, in every respect with His Majesty's new subjects in America." Extract from letter og General Gage to Lord Halifax in Oct., 1764.]

10. [Before his (Bradstreet's) departure (from Cedar Point), however, he dispatched Captain Morris, with several Canadians, and friendly Indians, to the Illinois, in order to persuade the savages of that region to treat of peace with the English. The measure was in a high degree ill advised and rash, promising but doubtful advantage, and exposing the life of a valuable officer to imminent risk:" Parkman's Pontiac, (6th ed.) II.

11. ["Colonel Broadstreet, thinking this a good opportunity to take possession of the country of the Illinois, which had been ceded to his Britannic Majesty by the peace of 1762, ordered Captain Morris, of the seventeenth regiment, with proper instructions, upon that service, with an Indian of each of the different nations that accompanied him, and Godfroy a Frenchman, as an interpreter; and he also sent presents for the different nations, through which they were to pass." _ Maute, pp. 513, 514.]

12. [The Maumee Rapids commence just above the town of Perrysburgh, Wood county, Ohio, and continue for eighteen miles.]

13. [The French used to speak of the river as au Miamis. The transition from their pronunciation to the present Maumee was quite natural. In order to distinguish this stream from its southern namesake _ the Big Miami of the present day _ it used frequently to be called the Miami of Lake Erie, or the Miami of the Lakes.

14. ["Wassong, Chief of the Chippeways:" Mante, 516, 518. See, also, Diary of the Siege of Detroit, 62, 88, 103. "Ojibwa chief Wasson:" Parkman.]

15. [Iroquois. The whole of the Tuscaroras had not yet joined the Five Nations. "The Tascaroras inhabit a tract of 10,000, Acres of Land laid out for them in South Carolina. I have wrote to Governor Dobbs for a particular Account of them and of their situation with respects to debts or whatever else may hinder or retard their going to join their People (among the Five Nations). Governor Dobbs told me when at the Congress, that they consisted of about one hundred Men able to bear Arms, Women and Children in proportion." _ Stuart to Johnson, 10 Dec., 1763, in Diary of the Siege of Detroit (Albany, 1860) p. 207.]

16. [Called by the Six Nations Twightwees. Their principal village _ Ke-ki-ong-a _ was at the head of the Maumee.]

17. ["After rowing up the river Miamis (Maumee) eighteen miles, they disembarked and marched by land to an Indian castle (village) and were meet by about 200 warriors of different nations who attempted to separate him (Captain Morris) from his own Indians." _ Examination of Thomas King, and Oneida chief, before a Court of Inquiry, at Sandusky, 3 Oct.,1764.]

18. [Pawnees. "Panies are a tribe of Indians upon whom the Ottawas and Chippawas continually make war. x x x. Prisoners are taken by the Ottawas and Chippawas, fro the Panis nation, bordering the Mississippi."

"You made me likewise close the graves
Of war-chiefs, slain by Panis slaves."

Speech to the Western Indians. A. S. Peyston, From "Miscellanies. By An Officer." Vol. I. Dumfries. (Scotland) 1813, pp. 3o, 96. Compare Henry's Travels, p. 80; Hist. Coll. Wis., Vol. III, p. 243. Martin's Address before the Hist. Soc. Wis., (1851) p. 22; Lavery's Journal (Lond., 1846), p. 40]

19. Onontio (Onnintio,) the Indian name for the king of France. Literally, Great Mountain, an epithet originally applied by the Indians to M. de Montmagny, Governor of Canada; of whose name, it will be seen, the word is a translation.]

20. [This fort was near the Mississippi, three miles from the present village of Prairie du Rucker, in Randolph county, Illinois; about fifty miles below St. Louis.]

21. [Early in the Spring of 1764, Major Loftus, an English officer arrived at New Orleans with four hundred regulars, intending to ascend the Mississippi to take possession of Fort Chartres and its dependent posts. On the 20th of March, when about two hundred and forty miles above the city, the troops were assailed by a small number of Tonicas. These Indians killed five of his men and wounded four. Loftus was terrified and returned to New Orleans.]

22. ["Pondiac had received a letter from the King of France, with an account that he had been dead and was risen again; and that he should send sixty sail of vessels up the river Mississippi, with every thing necessary to suppl them for carrying on the war. _ "Examination of Thomas King.]

23. [Thomas King, the Oneida chief. With Broadstreet's army were Indians of all the Six Nations.]

24. ["There is no doubt, says Charlevoix, that the Miamis and the Illinois were not long ago (1721) the same people, from the great affinity between their languages. The same affinity was observed by Father Allonez; who says that their language, though of the Algonkin (Algonquin) stock, differed much from that of all the other tribes of that family." _ Gallitum, in Trans. Amer. Antiq. Soc. Vol. II, pp. 62, 63.]

25. [The Miamis were first seen in 1670, on the Fox River, above Lake Winnebago, in the present State of Wisconsin. Thet soon removed south _ upon the Chicago, the St. Joseph of Michigan, the Maumee, and the Wabash; including, also, the two Miami rivers in what is now the State of Ohio. In 1764, they were living upon the Wabash and the head-waters of the Maumee.]

26. ["Pondiac seemed to be very glad to see the Chiefs from the Six Nations, as he understood that they were the occasion of the war; he having received belts from the Senecas for carrying it on, during the Congress held at Niagara. The reason he had struck was owing to his having thought the Six Nations had continued in carrying on the war, from the belts he had received from Genesee, and him by the Senecas. He should take care for the future how he should be deceived." _ Kings' Examination.]

27. [These were the words of the renowned chief when, in 1766, he gave in his final submission: "when our great father of France was in this country, I held him

fast by the hand. Now that he is gone, I take you, my English father, by the hand, in the name of all the nations, and promise to keep the covenant as long as I shall live." And that promise he never broke.]

28. [When, in 1864, Lopez, the civilized President of Paraguay, having declared war against Brazil, would have detained de Lima, the Brazilian Minister, a prisoner, but for the manly protest of Charles A. Washburn, our Envoy, he could have learned an instructive lesson, from this untutored savage.]

29. ["The spoil of some slaughtered officer. Parkman.]

30. [After Captain Morris' departure, Attawang, together with Wazzon or Wausong, the Chippaway; and other chiefs, went on to Detroit, where they held a treaty with Colonel Bradstreet. Morris' letters were safely delivered.]

31. [Afterward known as Tontogany, now Missionary Island. It is situated a little above Waterville, Lucas county, Ohio, and contains 2 to 3 acres.]

32. ["Pondiac sent a very large belt to two hundred and ten castles(villages) to make the road clear, that nothing should molest them, and gave it to St. Vincent, a French Trader, to deliver:" King.]

33. [This village Le Praire des Mascoutius _ was the farthest one, at that date, of the Ottawas, up the Maumee. It was situated at the head of the rapids in what is now Lucas county, Ohio. A year later, all the Ottawas upon the Maumee had gathered here.]

34. [In 1761 General Amherst directed Sir William Johnson to go to Detroit, call a meeting of the Ottawa Confederacy and other nations of Indians, inhabiting those parts, and settled and establish a firm and lasting peace; also regulate the trade at the several forts in the Indian country. He set off from Fort Johnson, on the Mohawk river, on the 5th of July, reaching Detroit August 3rd. He returned to his home, October 30th following. His Diary, kept during his journey is interesting. See, Stone's Johnson, II, 429-477.]

35. ["To Col. Bradstreet, commanding all His Majesty's forces on the Western District, Detroit:

> La Prairie des Marceratuns, farthest Village of the
> Ottawaws, Sept. the 2nd, 1764.

Sir

Washenawits having received us very kindly into his cabin, I beg leave to recommend him to your favor. His prejudices against us are very great. He asked me this morning after having made me some reproaches, why you were desirous of seeing the Indians at Detroit, and whether you intend to cover [clothe] them. He said he was almost naked; _ that he intended to go to Detroit, and hoped I would give him a letter as I had done. Allowing, I am certain, Sir, that a few presents to the chiefs cannot but have a good effect. Kind treatment will infallibly open a way into the Illinois country. The navigation this way is utterly impracticable; nothing but canoes can pass at present with great difficulty and in case of opposition I think it impossible.

I hope you will approve of what has been done. Necessity has no law.

Maisonville, if he can get leave to come to Detroit can inform you of my proceedings and the reasons of them. I hope to make a long journey this day as we have good water and no villages in our way till we get to the Miamis, forty five (?) leagues from this place. I have the honor to be Sir, your most faithful most obedient humble sev't,
Thomas Morris."]

36. [Braddock was defeated 9 July, 1755.]

37. [Fort Miami, at the head of the Maumee river. Major Robert Rogers detached from Detroit, December 1st, 1760, Lieut. Butler and Mer. Waite, with twenty men, to bring the French garrison from this post. A party was directed to remain there, if possible, through the winter. Roger's Journal, 128. The Fort was located on the east side of the St. Joseph, just above its confluence with the St. Mary's. Croghan's Journal, 1765. Hutchins' Map of 1764 and 1778 Brice's Hist. Fort Wayne, 13, 71.]

38. ["In five days the whole arrived at the Miami's Fort, where they were met by a number of Indians with spears &c., equipped in a warlike manner who received them with whoops, and halloos, and by their behavior it was suspected they had some bad intentions:" King.]

39. [Ensign Holmes commanded at Fort Miami at the commencement of Pontiac's war for additional particulars concerning his death and the capture of the post , See Parkman's Pontiac (6th ed.) I, 277, 278. Compare, also, Diary of the Siege of Detroit, pp. 22, 26, 132, 133; Md. Gaz., 7 July, 1763. Godefroi, it will be remembered, assisted the Indians, upon that occasion.]

40. [On the west side of the St. Joseph not far above its confluence with the St. Mary's. It was the great village _ Ke-ki,-ong-a _ of the Miamis. The next year (1765) Croghan found cabins on both sides of the river, and a small village of that tribe on Eel river.]

41. ["This fort, captured during the preceding year, had since remained with a garrison; and its only tenants were the Canadians, who had built their homes within its palisades, and a few Indians who thought fit to make it their temporary abode;" Parkman.]

42. [The great mistake was, in Morris's not sending St. Vincent in advance, with the belt of Pontiac, "to clear the way." _ King.]

43. [Fifteen belts and five strings of wampum, according to King.]

44. [Sir Wm. Johnson had already induce the Senecas to change their mind and make peace; and the Delawares and Shawanese, under the pressure of Bouquet's "speaking," were soon glad to follow suit; although, as Parkman says _ "it was thus fully apparent that while the Delawares and Shawnees were sending one deputation to treat of peace with Bradstreet on Lake Erie they were sending another to rouse the tribes of the Miamis to war."]

45. [Weat, Wiatanon, Ouistanon, or Ornatanon. The Wea village was located in 1764 on the south side of the Wabash, about seven miles below the present site of Lafayette, Indiana. Opposite the Wea town, on the north side of the river, stood

Fort Ouatanon. Charles Blasselle and Sanford C. Cox, Ms. letters 1875. Crogahns Journal (1765.) Hutchins's Map (1778.) Invelay's America, p. 496. Dillon's Hist. Ind. (1859), p. 262 note. The Kickapoos and Mascontins had villages in the vicinity of the fort.]

46. [St. Joseph was located on the north side of the river St. Joseph of Michigan, about thirty miles above its mouth. From there to the Miamis village, at the head of the Maumee, there was a well-defined trace leading in a southeasterly direction, a distance of about eighty miles. Compare Hutchins' Map, 1778.]

47. [Captain Morris here takes to himself credit to which he is not entitled to, although honestly expressing his convictions. By sending a timely information from Detroit, after his return from the Maumee, Bradstreet (who was then upon the Sandusky river with his army,) of the temper of the Shawnees and Delawares, thus putting the British commander on his guard, he supposed he had prevented those tribes from attempting any measures in that direction; but the fact is, it was Bouquet's army marching to their territory which determined those nations to let Bradstreet alone.]

48. [The Miamis employed various methods in their torturing of prisoners. They sometimes passed a hoop round the neck, fastened to a cord, which was tied to another hoop connected with a post. This post was firmly secured in the ground; and the limits of the unfortunate sufferer were free. Fires were kindled on four sides of the post _ and the Indians, with lighted hickory bark, compelled the wretched being to move around this infernal apparatus of cruelty and death. Hours were thus spent in this scene of torment, until human nature sank exhausted; or until some Indian, more humane, or more strongly excited than the others by the keen boastful death-song of the sufferer, terminated by a sudden stroke his sufferings and their persecutions. Lewis, Cap. In Henry Whiting's poem "Ontwa" (Appendix), p. 130. For circumstantial account of a Delaware of torture, see Crawford's Expedition against Sandusky, in 1772, Chap. XX.]

49. [There was a clan, or family, among the Miamis, whose hereditary duty and privilege it was to devour the bodies of prisoners burned to death. The act had somewhat a religious character, was attended with ceremonial observances, and was restricted to the family in question. Whiting's Outwa , 133-136. Parkman's Jesuits in N. Amer., XI.]

50. ["No compact, no speech, or clause of a speech, to the representative of another nation, had any force, unless confirmed by the delivery of a string or belt of wampum:" Parkman's Jesuits in N. Amer., XXXII.

"A meeting of the Miamis was held welcoming the Six Nations X X X saying, whatever they had to say they might deliver the next day. Accordingly, Thomas King spoke, giving them a belt, saying that he was sent by Col. Bradstreet and the Chiefs of the Six Nations, in order to make peace with them, if they were inclined to it; that if they have any thing to say. The road should be open from the Illinois to the Onodagas." _ Extract from the Proceedings of the Court of inquiry, at Sandusky, 3 Oct., 1764."

51. [In 1765, Sir William Johnson sent Col. George Croghan Deputy Indian Agent, to explore the country adjacent to the Ohio river, and to conciliate the Indian nations who had before acted with the French. Butler's Hist. Ky. Hildreth's Pion. Hist. Featherstonhaugh's Amer. Minth. Jour. Geol., Dec., 1831. N.M. Col. Hist. VII. Parkman's Pontiac. There is a MS. Copy of his journal in the office of the Sec. Of State, Albany.

This reference to Col. Croghan's tour in 1765, was, of course, written subsequent to the date the writer appended to his journal _ Sept. 25th, 1764. There are other incidents mentioned, as will be presently seen, which have been added at a later day.]

52. ["Colonel Bradstreet to M. De St. Ange.

Sir, I have been informed of the pains taken by M. de Neyon, before leaving the Illinois county, to remove all suspicion and to put a stop to false reports that were disseminated among the settlers and Indians dwelling there, which would lend only to render them unfortunate and are very disadvantageous to the English troops sent to take possession of that post.

I doubt not, Sir, that you have followed such a good example, and that you will afford all the protection in your power to Captain Morris, of the English troops, who will hand you this letter, to enable him to execute the orders he has received from me. I have the honor to be, &c. J. H. Bradstreet. Camp at Cedar Point; 26th August, 1764." _ N.Y. Col. Hist. X, 1158, 1159.

"Meade St. Ange to M. d' Abbadie (New Orleans), 9 Sept., 1764. X X X Mer. Bradstreet has written me from Cedar Point, near the Miamis (Maumee) river, 18 leagues from Detroit. The letter has been handed me by some Indians sent express here." _ N.Y. Col. Hist. X, 1157.]

53. [As the Journal of Captain Morris was not printed until 1791, it is probable that this was written after the Revolution and ha s reference to the Americans.]

54. [The journey of Morris, upon his return, was upon the north side of the Maumee, so long as he remained in the valley; which was upon the same side as when going up.]

55. [When, in the Winter of 1649, the Five Nations invaded the ancient seat of the Wyandots, or Hurons, upon Lake Simcoe, Canada, and the whole nation was broken and dispersed, some found refuge upon the St. Lawrence, where at the villageof Lorette, about eight miles below Quebec, their descendants still remain.]

56. [The Northern Iroquois tribes consisted of two distinct divisions; the Eastern, forming the Confederation known by the mane of Five Nations, where original territory did not extend westwardly farther than the western boundary of Pennsylvania; and the Western, consisting, as far as can be ascertained, of Four Nations" The Wyandots, or Hurons, and the Neutral Nation, north _ the Eries and Andastis, south of Lake Erie _ Gallatin.]

57. [For the particulars of this Treaty and its stipulations, see Mante pp. 516-524. It is commented upon unfavorable by Sir Willaim Johnson; on Col. Hist. of N.Y., VII, 674. See also, Parkman's Pontiac (6th ed.) II, 182-185.]

58. ["On the 14th of September, Colonel Bradstreet left Detroit, X X X and on the 18th arrived at Sandusky Lake (Sandusky Bay). He then detached a party to destroy the settlement of Mohican Johns (Mohican John's - town, in what is now Ashland county, Ohio) but it was abandoned before they could reach it. Mante, 526, 527.]

59. ["This evening (Sept. 17th) Capt. Morris arrived here, having been sent by Col. Bradstreet to try and go to the Illinois, but was stopped by the Miamies who were going to burn him." _ Diary of the Siege of Detroit, pp. 110,111.]

60. ["This morning (18th Sept.) an express was sent to overtake Col. Bradstreet with letters from Col. Campbell and Captain Morris." _ Diary of the Siege of Detroit, 111.]

61. ["Colonel Bradstreet the proceeded up Sandusky river, to the Village of the Hurons and Wyandots (Jemqueindundek, on the east side of the stream, opposite what was afterward Lower Sandusky; now Fremont, Sandusky county, Ohio) which had been destroyed by Captain Dalyell (Dazel) the preceding year" _Mante, 526, 527. Compare Parkman's Pontiac (6th ed.) I. 306; Hutchins Map of 1764 and 1778.]

62. ["Detroit, Sep. The 18th, 1764.

Sir,

I send you my journal, which is in a very dirty condition, and very incorrect as to style and writing; which I am sure you will excuse, when you shall know the situation I have been in . You will see, Sir, that a mine is laid and the match lighted to blow us up. The Senecas, Shawnees, and Delawares, have sent their belts to all the nations, who only wait the signal for a general attack. I hope this letter will reach you time enough to prevent your falling into the snare. I was overjoyed to learn from Col. Campbell, that in case matters should not go well you were determined to return with the choice path of your army to Detroit, where I imagine your presence is absolutely necessary.

The villains have nipped our fairest hopes in the bud; for things were in a very good way till their arrival at the Miamis village. I tremble for you at Sandusky; though I was greatly pleased to find you have one of the vessels with you and artillery. I wish the chiefs were assembled on board the vessel and she had a hole in her bottom. Treachery should be paid with treachery; and it is more than ordinary pleasure to deceive those who would deceive us. I am in too low a condition to come to you myself, but I hope this letter, together with the journal will answer as well for the present. By taking proper measures, Indian affairs may yet be retrieved. I have advised Col. Campbell to lay in wood for the winter, without saying anything more. I have the honor to be, Sir, your most faithful and most obedient humble servant.

Thomas Morris."]

63. ["The Colonel x x x encamped at the carrying-place at Sandusky." _ Mante, p. 532. This portage was between the north side of Sandusky Bay and the Portage river, in what is now Ottawa county, Ohio. See, Hutchins' Map of 1778; Stone's

Johnson, Vol.II, pp. 465, 466.]

64. [That the journalist is perhaps mistaken in this assumption has already been explained. Colonel Bouquet pressing in upon the Delawares and Shawnees was what "disappointed their hopes."]

65. ["On the 18th of October he (Bradstreet) broke up his Camp at Sandusky to proceed on his return to Albany. In the evening, as he was going to land the troops, a sudden swell of the lake, without any visible cause, destroyed several of his boats; but no lives were lost. This surprising phenomenon was. However, looked upon as the forerunner of a storm, and accordingly there soon arose one which continued several days, therefore it became necessary to detach part of the army by land to Niagara." _ Mante, 534.

"About seventy miles from Sandusky (at or near the mouth of Rocky River, Cuyahoga, County, Ohio) the lake rose in the night on a sudden, and the surf beat with such violence on the shore where the army (Bradstreet's) had landed that betwixt twenty and thirty boats were beat to pieces, notwithstanding the efforts made to save them. The night was very dark, and little else than the small quantity of provisions that was in them could be saved." _ N. Y. Mercury, 26 Nov., 1764 and other Gazettes of the day.

There were the Indians and Provincials of the army, ("who attempted to reach Fort Niagara"), about one hundred and fifty in all; Parkman "many left their carcasses in the woods and the lake, a prey to the wolves:" Newport Mercury, 31 Dec., 1764.]

66. The subject of tides upon the Great Lakes has been extensively discussed; and the prevailing opinion seems to be, that there are, probably, planetary influences operating on these inland seas, but that the changes in the level of the waters are mainly produced by atmospheric phenomena _ winds and rain, heat and cold, evaporation and drought.]

67. [Although the journalist seems to have entertained no doubt concerning the perfidy of the Natchez, (Tonicas) in the transaction mentioned, it is questionable if they could have calculated upon so sudden and ingenious a return as the one decided upon by Major Loftus. Besides, the Indians well knew that the object of the expedition was to take possession of what had long been French territory _ certainly a humiliation to that nation.]

68. [Ante, Chap. II.]

69. [The journalist evidently refers here to the commencement of the Indian War, which succeeded the Revolution.]

70. ["Should Capt. Morris succeed (in getting his embassy to the Illinois) he is to push on to all the nations of savages on the banks of the Mississippi to the sea." _ Bradstreet to Johnson, 28 Aug., 1764, in Diary of the Siege of Detroit, p. 284. "After settling affairs at the Illinois, Captain Morris is ordered down the Mississippi in order to reconcile such Indian nations to our interest as might be inclined to oppose our passage up that river, and to return by sea to New York." _ Extract from a letter of General Gage to Lord Halifax, 12 October, 1764.]

71. [Capt. Morris means by this, the Detroit country; for it will be remembered he started on his journey from Cedar Point.]
72. [Why this date is given is not now apparent. It is a week subsequent to the day on which he dispatched his original journal to Bradstreet at Sandusky. Bradstreet forwarded it to Gen. Gage who sent it to Lord Halifax in England. It is now deposited in the State Paper Office, London. It is the original, re-written with many additions, which is produced in this chapter. It was published with several original poems and a translation of the fourth and fourteenth satires of journal _ in a volume, the date and title of which, has been copied in a previous note.]

Chapter Twelve

1. Bartram's Travels (Lond. 1751) p. 17.
2. Loskiel's Hist. Morav. Miss., P. II, p.120.
3. Bartram's Travels. p. 17.
4. Reichel's Mem. Morav. Church, Vol. I, p. 83 note.
5. Synonyms: Shikellimus, Sickcalamy, Shikellamy, etc. More than thirty different methods of spelling this namehave been noticed. Shikelimo had two other Indian names: Swadamy, Swatana, or Swatane, and the improbable one of Unguatenighiathe. Map. Hist. Coll., 1st Series, Vol. VII, p. 195. Reichel's Mem. Morav. Church. Vol I, p. 83. Colden's Hist. Five Nations, II, p. 12. Schweinitz' Zeisberger, p. 109 note.
6. Bartram's Travels, p.17
7. Reichel's Mem. Morav. Church. Vol. I, p. 83 note.
8. Bartram's Travels p. 17
9. Colden II, p. 12. Hist. Coll. Of Mass., 1st Series, Vol. VII, p. 195. Reichel's Mem. Morav. Church, Vol. I, p. 83. Penn. Arch. , Vol. I, pp. 495-497, 656. Schweinitz' Zeisberger, p. 109 note.
10. Penn. Arch. I, p. 228. Col. Rec. Penn., Vol. III, pp. 330, 337, 404. Day's Hist. Pa., 525. "A guide to the wild Shawnees:" Reichel's Mem. Morav. Church, Vol. I, p. 98.
11. Schoolcraft's Indian Tribes; P. IV., pp. 324-341. Bartram's Travels, p. 20.
12. See, in general, Penn. Arch., Vol's. I and II; Coll. Rec. of Penn., Vols. III, IV, and V; Loskiel's: Hist. Morav. Miss.; Schweinitz' Zeisberger; Reichel's Mem. Morav. Church, Vol. I; Rupp's Hist. Berks County, etc.; also, his Hist. Dauphin County, etc.; and Day's Hist. Coll. Penn.
13. Col. Rec. Penn. IV, 307. Reichel's Mem. Morav. Church, Vol. I, 83, 90. Schweinitz' Zeisberger, p. 150.
14. "On the sixth of December, [1748]:" Schweinitz. "December 17, 1748:" Reichel. Loskiel (P. II, p. 119) mistakes the year. Compare Penn. Arch.; II, 23.
15. Reichel's Mem. Morav. Church, Vol. I, p. 90 note.
16. As, by this name, he is best known to the world, it has been retained throughout this chapter.

17. The orthography of Logan's Indian name is as various as his father's. See Penn. Arch., I, 656, 750, _ II, 23, 33, 34, 776, IV, , 91; Col. Rec. Penn., III, 435, 500, _ V, 84, _ V, 84, _ VI, 120 _ VIII, 729; Colden's Hist. Five Nations, II, 13; Rupp's Dauphin County, etc., p. 304, _ Northumberland County, etc. p. 459; Reichel's Mem. Morav. Church, I, 84, 261.
18. Reichel's Mem. Morav. Church, Vol. I, p. 84.
19. "Tughhegh duarus, Shickelimy's eldest son:" Conrad Weiser to Gov. Hamilton, in Penn. Arch., II, 23. Same in Rupp's Hist. Dauphin County, etc., p. 319.
20. Col. Rec. Penn., Vol. VI, 420, 421.; VII, 47, 65, 171, 244, _ VIII, p. 279. Penn. Arch. II, 167, 634, 664, 776; _ III, 721, 727, 728, 729, 730; _ IV, 91. Rupp's Dauphin County, etc., 84, 100, 259, 316; _ Berks County, etc., 39; Northumberland County, etc., 109, 116, 166, 226, 366, 456, 459; _ Northampton County, etc., 103. Reichel's Mem. Movar Church, I, pp. 84, 261. He was sometimes familiarly called Jack. See Col. Rec. Penn., IV, 685.
21. As to the ancient seat of the Oneidas, see Cusick's Six Nations; Gallatin's Synopsis; Schoolcraft's Notes on the Iroquois; Morgan's League of the Iroquois; and Jones' Annals Oneida County (N. Y.)
22. "His [Shikelimo's] told me he [the son] was of the Cayuga nation _ that of the mother." Bartram. Compare Penn. Arch., IV, 91.
23. The fact of Logan being a Cayuga and his father an Oneida (by adoption), explains why so much confusion is observable in the giving of their titles by historians. Shikelimo was an Oneida chief; Logan became, as will presently be seen, a Cayuga sachem. For additional evidence of Logan's being a mix-breed, see Mayer's Logan and Cresap, p. 111 note.
24. Logan appeared, along with his father, in council as early as 1733. Col. Rec. Penn., III, 500.
25. Extract from the Autobiography of Martin Mack, in Reichel's Mem. Morav. Church, I, 66.
26. Bartram (1743) in his "Travels," p, 16.
27. Edward's Life of Brainerd, p. 66 note. Compare Reichel's Mem. Morav. Church, p. 66 note.
28. Penn. Arch., I, 241.
29. "Layughtowas:" Penn. Arch., II, 776. "Loyeghtowa:" Penn. Arch. IV, 91.
30. Penn. Arch. IV, 91. Col. Rec. Penn., VI, 649, _ VII, 640, 649. Rupp's Northumberland County, etc., 459. Compare Reichel's Mem. Morav. Church I, p. 84 note. He was lame. See Rupp's Northumberland County, etc., p. 456.
31. Penn. Arch. IV, 91. See, also, Rupp's Northumberland County
32. Reichel's Mem. Morav. Church, Vol. I, p. 84 note. See, as to the trader, Penn. Arch. I, 216, 227-229, 232. Col. Rec. Penn. III, 230.
33. Penn. Arch. I, 665.
34. Ibid. Weiser, and others, so frequently vary the spelling of the Oneida chief's name that the one previously used in the text is retained in this extract, as well as

in those which follow in this chapter.
35. Rupp's Berks County, etc., p. 213. Reichel's Mem. Morav. Church, Vol. I, 83.
36. Col. Rec. Penn. VII, p.47. Rupp's Northumberland County, etc., 117. Rupp's Dauphin County, etc., 100 note.
37. A son of his sisters took up the hatchet against the English in the Old French War, and was killed and scalped on the 20th Feb. 1756, on Middle Creek, in what is now Union county, Pennsylvania _ Rupp's Dauphin County, etc., p. 99.
38. Penn. Arch. I, 750. Col. Rec. Penn. V, 83.
39. Col. Rec. Penn. V, 212, 222, etc.
40. Col. Rec. Penn. III, 500. Colden's Hist. Five Nations, II, 13.
41. An Indian never transacts public business while in mourning. Logan's wife gied early in October, 1747, at Shamokin, of fever. His children, it seems, afterward went to live with their Conestoga aunt. Rupp's Dauphin County, etc., p. 100 note; _ Northumberland County, etc., p. 117. Logan soon married again. His second wife was a Shawnee and could speak English. There was no issue by the last marriage.
42. Penn. Arch. II, 8.
43. Schweinitz' Zeisberger, 151. Shikelimo "fell happily asleep in the Lord, in full assurance of obtaining eternal life, through the merit of Jesus Christ." _ Laskiel, P II, p. 120.
44. Penn. Arch. II, 23.
45. Ibid.
46. "Causes of the Alienation of the Delaware and Shawanese Indians (Lond. 1759)," p. 50.
47. Penn. Arch., II, 33-36.
48. Morgan's League of the Iroquos, p. 100 note. Compare Col. Rec. Penn., VI, 119; _ VIII, 729: Penn. Arch., IV, 91.
49. Rupp's Dauphin County, etc., p. 574.
50. Penn. Arch. II, 166, 167. Col. Rec. Penn. VI, 118-122, 216.
51. Col. Rec. Penn., VI, 420.
52. Penn. Arch. II, 777.
53. Col. Rec. Penn. VI, 763, _ VII, 65.
54. Col. Rec. Penn., VII, 64, 65.
55. Col. Rec. Penn. VII, 46-54.
56. Rupp's Dauphine County, etc., p. 100 note.
57. Penn. Arch. II, 634, 778.
58. Col. Rec. Penn. VII, 148, 171.
59. Col. Rec. Penn. VII, 244, 245. Reichel's Mem. Morav. Church, 261, 265.
60. Penn. Arch. VII, 776.
61. Penn. Arch., III, 699, 701, 713, 721, 727-730.
62. Penn. Arch. IV, 91. Col. Rec. Penn. VIII, 729-774.
63. Rupp's Northumberland County, etc., pp.47, 227. Day's Pennsylvania, p. 466. Beatty's Journal (Lond. 1768), p. 19.

64. Archibald London, in his Hist. Ind. Wars (Carlisle, 1811), Vol. II, pp. 223-225. The date (1765) given in this connection, is the earliest mention of the change of the chief's name, as known to the whites, from "John Shikelimo" to "Capt. John Logan." The reason for the change must be left entirely to conjecture. His brother younger, the second son of Shikelimo, being known as "James Logan," the two have frequently been confounded. Heckewelder, in App. To Jefferson's Notes copies from the MSS. of Rev. C. Pyrlaus that "Logan was the second son of Shikellemus." He was; _ but it was "James Logan," not "Capt. John Logan." It may be proper here to mention that a Shamokin Indian whose name was "Jonathan," has been frequently, though erroneously, named as one of Logan's brothers. Concerning this Indian, see Penn. Arch., VII, 64-66, 68, 72. Col. Rec. Penn., VI, 640. Rupp's Berks County, etc., pp. 40, 41.
65. Day's Pennsylvania, 467, 468.
66. Cecil (Md.) Whig, 12 Sept. 1874.
67. Day's Pennsylvania, p. 468. The child was Mary Brown, born in 1769.
68. Jones' Hist. Juniata Valley, p. 114.
69. The Cecil (Md.) Whig, 12 Sept., 1874.
70. Day's Pennsylvania, p. 467.
71. McClure and Parish's Mem. of Rev. E. Wheelock, D. D., p. 139. Wheelock's Narr. (Hartford, 1773), p. 50. Heckewelder's Declaration, in App. to Jefferson's Notes on Va.
72. Heckewelder, in App. to Jefferson's Notes on Va. McClure and Parish's Mem. of Dr. Wheelock, p. 140.
73. Mem. of Wheelock, p. 140.
74. Wheelock's Ind. Char. School (Hartford, 1773), p. 50.
75. Mem. of Wheelock, pp. 140, 141. The words of Logan and his appearance, as described by the Rev. David MacClure, in the work just cited (See, also, Indian Charity School, 1772-3), seems to leave no doubt as to the real cause of Logan's suffering, although the zealous-hearted missionary gives them another interpretation.
76. Heckewelder. In Declaration, in App. to Jefferson's Notes on Va., mentions Logan's intention (in 1772) "to settle on the Ohio, below Big Beaver." The Moravian also speaks, in the same connection, of calling, in April, 1773, "at Logan's settlement," on his passage down the river.
77. Hence the appellation _ "Logan, the Mingo Chief."
78. "With all their stuff with them:" G. R. Clark to S. Brown, 17 June, 1798, in Dep. of State, Washington. This letter has been frequently published. See Heperian, Vol. II, p. 308; Mayer's Logan and Cresap, 149; etc. Clark says Logan's Camp was "on the Ohio, about thirty-miles above Wheeling;" an inadvertence as to the distance. The mouth of Big Yellow creek is forty miles above. Logan's home was "a small Indian village on Yellow creek:" Amer. Arch., 4th Series, I, 345; N. Y. Col. Hist., VIII, 463: Pa. Journal, 29 June, 1774. Compare Mayer's Logan and Cresaps, p. 162.

79. MSS. of Henry Jolly. (These have been published. See Silliman's J., Vol. XXXI, No. 1.) They were obtained from S. P. Hildreth, for whom they were written.
80. Reliance has been placed in the Declaration of John Sappington, as published in Jefferson's Notes, for this statement as to the determination of the Mingoes.

Editor's note: Draper listed this footnote but did not note it in his text. The editor has inserted it at the approximate place which thought proper.

81. Whittlesey's Fugitive Essays, p. 134 note.
82. Sappington's Declaration, in Jefferson's Notes. See, also, the Statement of Benjamin Tomlinson, in Jacob's Life of Cresap, pp. 107-109. Both these accounts are from parties themselves who participated in the affair and the only ones extant, not second-handed. They disagree as to the date of the transaction; and, in that regard, both are in error. Valentine Crawford to Washington, 7 May, 1774, in Dep. of State, Washington. Compare, also, Amer. Arch. 4th Series Vol. I, p. 345 with G. R. Clark's letter to S. Brown 17 June, 1798. The testimony of Logan shows that his mother and sister were killed. Diary of James Wood, 1775: MS. Compare Jacobs' Life of Cresap, p. 85. Wood's Journal has never been published. Concerning his journey, see, Jacob's Life of Cresap, 69; Alman's Remembrances, 1775, p. 254; Va. Gaz. No. 1258. The party at Baker's had no leader _ for the best of reasons: no one was needed. Daniel Greathouse was present as an active participant, but not otherwise. Captain Michael Cresap knew nothing of the transaction until some days subsequent to its occurrence. Compare in connection the statement of Sappington and Tomlinson, that of Meyer's, in Whittlesey's Fugitive Essays, p. 184, note.
83. Synonyms: Wappatomica, Waukataumikee, Wakatomaka, Waketameki, Waketummakie, etc. There was also a Shawnee village of the same name, afterwards upon the head waters of Mad river, in what is now Logan county, Ohio.
84. Amer. Arch., 4th Series, Vol. I, p. 481.
85. Heckewelder's Narr. Morav. Miss., p. 131.
86. Jolly MSS.
87. Amer. Arch. 4th Series, Vol. I. pp. 469, 474, 481, 483, 484. See, also, Penn. Arch., IV. 513, 527, 530; Heckewelder's Narr. pp. 131, 132, 133.
88. John Connolly to Joel Reese 27 May 1774, in Jacob's Life of Cresap. Amer. Arch. 4th Series, Vol. I, pp. 464, 481, 482. Penn. Gaz., 8 June 1774.
89. MS. Narr. of John Crawford. Amer. Arch., 4th Series, Vol. I, 405, 435, 445, 469-472, 475. Penn. Arch., IV, 517, 519, 520, 525, 632. Concerning Wm. Spicer, see Indian Treaties (1837) p. 220; also, History Seneca County (O.) pp. 75, 123, 190.
90. William Robinson; Declaration in Jefferson's Notes. Statement of James Robinson, in Howe's Ohio, p.268. MS. letter of James E. Robinson, 1 July 1868. Arthur Campbell to Wm. Preston, 12 Oct., 1774: MS. letter. Withers' Border

Warfare, pp. 118-120. The letter of Logan, as given in the text, is a literal translation of one copied from the original by Col. Preston.

91. MS. letters of Arthur Campbell to Wm. Preston in Sept. and October and one from Wm. Christian to same in Nov., 1774. See, also, Amer. Arch., 4th Series, Vol. I, p. 808.

92. "The chief town" in the Shawnee language. The name, at different times, was applied to several of their towns: one about three miles north of the present town of Xenia; one on the site of the town of Frankfurt, Ross county; another where the present city of Chillicothe stands: all in what is now the State of Ohio.

93. Amer. Arch., 4th Series, Vol. I. pp 722, 723.

The Mingoes, in 1774, had two villages upon the waters of the Scioto: Pluggy's-town, about eighteen miles up that river above the site of the present city of Columbus, Ohio; and Lick-town (Seekunk), a short distance eastward of the Scioto, on one of its branches in what is now Franklin county, that State. Seekunk is a corruption of the Delaware Kseck-ke-oung, a place of salt. There was also a small village near Halaston.

94. The interpreter was now John Gibson. "Gibson told Logan of his being sent to bring him to the treaty. He found him in a cabin with other Indians, when he told him his errand. Logan took Gibson aside, a little distance in the woods and they seated themselves on a log when they conversed freely on the subject of the war and the impending treaty. Logan was deeply excited _ even to tears. He said he could not go but that Gibson should deliver to Dunmore what he should say. He then delivered his speech. Gibson says he was struck with it as well as with the manner of its delivery; and that immediately upon his arrival at head-quarters he reduced it to writing in English and handed it to Lord Dunmore;" J. B. Gibson to J. W. Biddle - 1847. Compare Gibson's own Dep. in "App. to Jefferson's Notes on Va."

95. Copied verbatim from Dixon and Hunter's Va. Gazette of 4 Feb., 1775 (No. 1226), except that the word "Spring" is substituted for the word "year;" the use of the latter being, doubtless. An inadvertence in copying. The words were spoken by Logan in the Delaware language to Gibson, an interpreter fully competent to translate he precise meaning into English. Compare Mayer's Logan and Cresap, pp. 186-190. The second publication of the speech was in New York, 16 Feb., 1775. Amer. Arch., 4th Series, Vol. I. p. 1020 note. It differs somewhat from the Williamsburg version of the 4th of February given in the text. The speech as printed by Jefferson in his Notes in Virginia, varies but little from the New York version. The speech, very soon after its delivery was attempted to be rendered into French by M. l' Abbe' Robin, a French traveler in America, but the effort was well-nigh a complete failure. See his Nouveau Voyage dans l'Amérique Septentrionale en l'année 1781 et Paris, 1782, p. 147 note. The error in the date, as given in that work, is probably a mistake of the printer; _ or, it may have occurred in the translation.

96. See his Notes on Virginia.

97. John Burk in Hist. Va., III., 398.
98. John Bannister Gibson. See Mayer's Logan and Cresap, 188.
99. Campbell's Gertrude of Wyoming, where the sentiment is transferred to another.
100. Whittlesey in his Fugitive Essays, 145. Compare Clinton's Hist. Discoveries, 1811.
101. William Crawford to Washington, 14 Nov., 1774. MS.
Amer. Arch. 4th Series, Vol. I, p. 1013. Wither's Border Warfare, 137. Report of a Committee of a. Assembly Dec. 9th, 1776, _ from the Assembly Journal of that year. Verbal Statement of Samuel Murphy made in 1846. Seekunk (Lick-town) is given by Crawford as being forty miles away. Other statements make it about thirty miles from Camp Charlotte where the treaty was held with the Shawnees. Pluggy's-town was not attacked.
102. MS. Journal of James Wood. Jacob's Life of Cresap, p. 85.
103. Amer. Arch., 4th Series, Vol I, p. 1226.
104. Amer. Arch., 4th Series, Vol III, p. 1542. The conference began 12 Sept. and ended 17 Oct. : Proceedings of the Treaty_ MS. For further information concerning this Treaty, see Jour. of Cong. (old,) Vol. 1, pp. 112, 127, 161, 162, 168, 201; Plain Facts (Philad'a 1781) p. 144. The Virginia Com. were Thomas Walker, Andrew Lewis, Adam Stephen, and James Wood. The Cong. Com. were Lewis Morris, James Wilson and John Walker. The names appear in the MS. Proceedings of the Treaty. Compare Bancroft's Hist. U. S., Vol. VIII, pp. 109, 110
105. Hildreth's Pioneer Hist. 98-108.
106. Wood's MS. Journal.
107. Journals of Congress, Vol. II. (1776,) p. 318. Mine's Wyoming, 183.
108. Bradford's Notes on Kentucky (Stipps Miscellany,) pp. 25, 26.
109. Verbal Statement of Kenton to John H. James, Feb., 1832. MS.
Donald's Sketches, pp.231. 232. McClung's Western Adventure, p. 121.
110. Heckewelder to Col. John Gibson, 19 March, 1779: Ms.
letter in Dep. of State, Washington.
111. For many interesting particulars of Bird's expedition, see Stipp's Miscellany, p. 56 et seq. The commander was a captain of the Eighth (or the King's) Regiment of Foot.
112. Amer. Pioneer, Vol. I, p. 359.
113. Verbal Statement of William Walker, 1868. Compare, also, Amer. Pioneer, I., 359; Heckewelder's Declaration in Jefferson's Notes; Harve's Ohio Hist. Coll. p. 409; Mayer's Logan and Cresap, pp. 138, 139, 185. That Logan was killed in the latter part of the year 1780, there can be no doubt. John Todd to Gov. Jefferson, 24 Jan. 1781, in Jefferson MSS., Dep. of State, Washington. Vigne's Six Months in America (p. 30) gives a highly sesational account of Logan's death.
114. For descriptions of Logan's personal appearance at different periods, see London's Indian Wars, II, 225; Day's Hist. Coll. Penn., p. 467; Jones' Hist. Juniata Valley, 114; Wheelock's Mem., p. 139, 141. Mayer's Logan and Cresap, p. 59.

Chapter Thirteen

1. The Speeches, as to the times of their delivery, interrupt the regular chronological order of events narrated in this work: They are given that they may be compared with the famous effort of Logan.
2. The name given the Governor of Canada by the Iriquois.
3. The name given by the Iroquois, to the Governors of New York.
4. Discourse before the N. Y. Historical Society, Dec. 6, 1811, p. 31.
5. Parkman's Pontiac's Conspiracy, (6th ed.) Vol. II, pp. 275-292.
6. At each reference to a belt, a different one was presented, while delivering the speech.
7. Col. Hist. of N. Y. Vol. VII, pp. 782, 783. Parkman's Pontiac, (6th ed.) pp. 294-291. Hildreth: Pioneer Hist., pp. 75, 76. The effort of Croghan is "a better example of the forms of speech appropriate to an Indian peace harangue than the genuine productions of the Indians themselves." _ Parkman.
8. Amer. Arch., 4th Series, Vol. III, p. 1542 note. A portion of this speech is given in Burk's Hist. of Va., III, 87, 88, also in Cists Advertiser, 27 May, 1846 _ Point Pleasant being mentioned by mistake, as the place of its delivery
9. The Oneidas, at this period, had been driven to their unimproved lands, and the old chief lived in the woods, three miles distant from the meeting-house where he had long worshiped.
10. A band of the Dakota or Sioux Nation.11. William Clark, chief of the commissioners who were there holding a treaty with the Tetons. _ Indian Treaties, p. 166.

Chapter Fourteen

1. Stuart's Indian Wars, 41.
2. Ms. Preston Papers.
3. Ms. Preston Papers.
4. Gibson's statement appended to Jefferson's Notes; Amer. Arch. Fourth Series, I, 392; Ms. letter of Dunmore to Lewis , July 12, 1774; Ms. Papers of Dr. Joseph Doddridge.
5. Dunmore to Connolly, June 20, 1774, in Penn. Arch. IV, 523; Ms. letter of Valentine Crawford to Washington, July 27, 1774.
6. Ms. notes of conversation with John Guin, 1844. Amer. Arch., Fourth Series, I, 722- 724. Abraham Thomas' Sketches of Border Life, in Troy, Ohio, Times, 1839. Doddridge's Notes. Jacob's Cresap. Withers' Chronicles of order Warfare.
7. Amer. Arch., Fourth Series, I, 873-876.
8. Valentine Crawford to Washington, Oct. 1, 1774. Ms. notes of conversation with Samuel Murphy, one of Crawford's party.
9. Hildreth's Pioneer History, 93. Walker's Hist. Athens County, 526; Ms. Statement of Samuel Dutton, May 22, 1876.
10. Atwater's Hist. of Ohio, 115.

11. Murphy's Recollections.
12. Ms. letter of Col. Wm. Fleming to Wm. Bowyer, Oct. 13, 1774. Murphy's Recollections.
13. Jacob's Life of Cresap, 59, 60. Fleming to Bowyer, just cited.
14. Thomas' Sketches.
15. Stuart's Indian War, 56.
16. On the first day's march, a severe thundergust and rain storm occurred, which suddenly raised Four Mile Run, three miles above Fort Gower, so that when the bow of the boats passing up the Hockhocking reached the mouth of this swollen Run, the current was so powerful as to send the boat across the river, striking a tree at the water's edge so violently as to sink the vessel. Some thirty-five years afterwards, Isaac Humphrey discovered the sunken boat, from which he obtained a large quantity of bullets, which he melted up and sold for lead; Ms. letters of Samuel Dutton, May 22, and A. B. Walker, May 24, 1876.
17. Murphy's Recollections. Withers states that Captain Froman was left in command of Fort Gower.
18. Murphy's Recollections.
19. Murphy's Recollections.
20. Withers' Chronicles, 138.
21. Murphy's Recollections, embodying a statement from the lips of Tavenor Ross, who at this period was associated with the Shawnees. Withers' Chronicles. 135.
22. The locality of this camp was upon the Windship farm, situated on the southwest quarter of section twelve, township ten, range twenty one; Government survey.
23. Recollections of Samuel Murphy and John Guin. Whittlesey's Discourse on Dunmore's Expedition, 23.

Doddridge indeed states, that the encampment was surrounded by a breastwork of fallen trees and an entrenchment, including about twelve acres, with a central enclosure of about one acre for the Governor, and his superior officers; but the two survivors of the campaign, Murphy and Guin, relate as in the text; corroborated by both Withers and Whittlesey. It was never claimed as anything more than a mere "camp."

Murphy stated that Queen Charlotte was said to be friendly to the Americans; and when the Revolutionary war broke out, a popular song was much in vogue, in which she was represented as reminding her royal spouse _
"They are both loyal, and true;
I beseech you beware what you do!"
24. Murphy's Recollections. Withers' Chronicles, 136.
25. Ms. letter of Wm. Christian to Wm. Preston, Nov. 8, 1874. Affidavit of John Gibson, in App. to Jefferson's Notes. G. R. Clark to Sam'l Brown, June 17, 1798. Waters' Chronicles, 136, Tomlinson's Statement in Jacob's Cresap, 108. Murphy's Recollections.

26. Murphy' Recollections.
27. Thomas' Sketches.
28. Dodderidge's Notes, 234. Withers' Chronicles, 137, 138.
29. Dodderidge's Notes, 234. Withers' Chronicles, 138.
30. Thomas' Sketches.
31. Ms. Diaries of Col. Fleming, and John Todd. Ms. letter of Wm. Preston to Patrick Henry, Oct. 31, 1774.
32. Fleming's Ms. Diary and Papers.
33. Newell's Ms. Journal.
34. The village was located on the southern bank of Sippo Creek, a short distance above the mouth of Congo Creek, and two miles and three quarters south of Chillicothe.
35. Fleming's Ms. Journal; Ms. letter of Col. Christian, one of Lewis' officers, to Col. Wm. Preston, Nov. 8, 1774. Murphy's Recollections. Stuart's Indian Wars, 57. Campbell's Memoir of the Battle of Point Pleasant in Ms., also appended to the first edition of Charles Campbell's History of Virginia, 1847. Withers' Chronicles. 130. 131. Ms. letter of Andrew Lewis, Jr. to Dr. Samuel L. Campbell, April 25, 1840.
36. Campbell's Memoir, 191. 192.
37. Deposition of Wm. McKee, App. Jefferson's Notes.
38. Fleming's Ms. Diary. Christian to Preston, Nov. 8, 1774. Withers' Chronicles, 131. Stuart's Indian Wars, 57. Campbell's Memoirs, 191.
39. Christian to Preston, Nov. 8, 1774. Crawford to Washington, Nov. 14, 1774. Withers' Chronicles, 137.
40. Amer. Arch., Fourth Series, 1013, 1014, 1169, II , 1190, 1208. 1222. Christian to Preston Nov. 8, 1774. Crawford to Washington Nov. 14th, 1774. A treaty was held in a small way toward the end of June, 1775, attended only by Delawares and Mingoes, and conducted by Col. Connolly and the committee of West Augusta, as may be seen by reference to Jacob's Cresap, 69, and the Journal of the Virginia Convetion, of 1775, June 6; and a more important one was held during September and October, to satisfy and confirm the treaty of Camp Charlotte.
41. Memoirs of Richard Henry Lee, II, 207.
42. Schweinitz' Life and Times of Zeisberger, 408, 409.
43. Burk, Stuart, Dodderidge, Withers, Atwater, Campbell, and others.
44. Hildreth's Pioneer History, 89, 90.
45. Virginia Gazette, Jan. 7th, April 1st, and 8th, 1775. Amer. Archives, Fourth Series, II, 170, 302.
46. Non-hel-e-ma, or Catherine, better known as the Grenadier Squaw, from her unusual height, evinced the most decided friendship for the Americans throughout the Revolutionary war. After the death of her brother, Cornstalk, she abandoned her people, conveying forty-eight head of cattle and several horses, to Fort Randolph, at the mouth of the Kanawha, compelled by the Indians to leave a considerable property behind her. She frequently acted as interpreter and messenger

for the garrison, particularly in May, 1778, when Fort Randolph was attacked by the Indians. Her cattle were taken for the use of the garrison, and she was left in poverty; sometimes allowed a part of a ration of provisions at the garrison. She subsequently lived in and around Pittsburgh ; and early in 1785, petitioned Generals Clark and Butler, Commissioners of Indian Affairs, when "advanced in old age," and in a state of want, for relief; and also for a grant of two thousand acres of land on the west side of the Scioto, above the old Pickaway town where she once lived, and had goods, houses and fields, and where her mother was buried; adding, that if her request for land was granted, she intended collecting her relations from the Shawnees; some of whom were adopted white people, captured in 1756 and 1759. Her petition was endorsed by eighteen of the principal citizens of Pittsburgh, and was referred by the commissioners to Congress; but that body appears never to have acted upon it.

47. Letter of George Mason, Aug. 5, 1775, in Virginia Hist. Register, 124, 229.

Chapter Fifteen

1. Ms. letter of Dunmore to Lewis, July 12, 1774.
2. Ms. letter of Lewis to Wm. Preston, Sept. 8, 1774.
3. Fleming's Ms. Diary. Ms. letter of Fleming to his wife, Sept. 18, 1774. Recollections of Thomas H. Shelby, whose father, Isaac Shelby, received the incident from Cornstalk! Stuart's Indian Wars, 47.
4. Fleming to Adam Stephen, Oct. 8, 1784, Ms. Fleming Papers.
5. Ms. letter of Wm. Ingles, Commissary, to Wm. Preston, Oct. 14, 1774.
6. Perhaps Scop-path-us, who, according to Withers' Chronicles, p. 129, note, led the Mingoes on the Point Pleasant campaign.
7. Recollections of Thomas Lewis and Charles Clendenin.
8. H. S. L. Campbell's Ms. narrative of the Battle of Point Pleasant; also the same appended to the first edition of Charles Campbell's History of Virginia. Stuart's Memoir of Indian Wars; p. 48. Withers' Chronicles, 138.
9. Samuel Murphy's recollections, derived from Tavenor Ross, one of the Indian army.
10. Murphy's recollections.
11. The Ms. Fleming's Papers, furnish Mooney's name as a spy or scout; Stuart's and Campbell's narratives, together with the late Nathan Boone, on the authority of his father, the distinguished pioneer of Kentucky, relate Mooney's adventures. Stuart's account, as originally published in the Lexington, Va., Intellincer, Jan. 15, 1825, but omitted in the revised edition of 1893, gives the name of the spy or hunter who accompanied Mooney as Hickman, which would seem to be an error; for Hughey's name appears on Shelby's Ms. company roll, and the late Thos. Love, of North Carolina, and afterwards of Tennessee was personally acquainted with Hughey's widow as early as 1775, then residing in Fincastle, subsequently Wythe county, Va.; and it was then universally understood, that her husband was

the first victim of the Indians at the memorable battle of Point Pleasant.

1 Editor's Note. There were several James Robertsons who fought at Point Pleasant. This James Robertson became one of the first settlers to what became Nashville, Tennessee. The Valentine Sevier, noted here, was the younger brother of Gen. John Sevier, the latter becoming the first governor of the State of Tennessee. In the Preface to this book it was noted that the fourth great-grandfather of the editor was likewise a participant in the battle at Point Pleasant. Many historians, including Tennessee authors, write of the opening shot of the battle, with some controversy as to exactly how it started, and the glory of that specific event. There is included in the Draper Manuscripts, not found in Border Forays, a few words written by Draper when he interviewed Dr. Felix Robertson, the son of the above noted James Robertson. Those words of Draper's are found at 6XX97, and are as follows:

> "He went a volunteer in Genl. Lewis expedition against the Northern Indians in the fall of '74 and fired the first gun in the morning of attack a mile in advance of the army which brought on the celebrated battle of the point which lasted from sunrise untill dark. This circumstance probably saved Lewis's army from a disastrous defeat as they were lying in supposed secrecy nt knowing that there was an Indian in fifty miles of them. Robertson and Valentine Sevier had the previous evening obtained permission to go out next morning to kill a deer; they started before it was light and had advanced about a mile when they came upon the camp of the Indians. They saw one advancing toward them with a bucket or kettle in his hand, who came to a branch within about fifty yards of them where they stood behind a tree and as he stooped to fill his vessel with water Robertson fired on him; they both ran for the army. The bullets and sound of the feet of the Indians at their encampment convinced them that they were a great force. They ran immediately to Lewis and informed him of what had occurred & the army was instantly put in preparation for a battle which commenced in a very few minutes."

This writer is no military tactician, but believes that if he had been in the shoes of Col. Andrew Lewis at the time when Robertson and Sevier had seen the "camp" of Indians, he would have preferred those two sergeants to wait until the Indian filled his "vessel" and returned to the "camp" to poach his turkey eggs for breakfast, and then quietly back away and return to "the army" and give the alarm, before any shot was fired. The army could then "have the Indians for breakfast." As it was, no wonder James Mooney reported seeing the Indian army thickly covering about five acres of ground.

This writer is also no historian. The words of Dr. Felix Robertson, as set down by Lyman Draper, are merely added here for the reader to consider if that opening shot was a wise decision. For once the Indian "camp" has been seen and fired upon, they cannot be expected to sit idly and do nothing. If the words of Dr. Felix

Robertson are not correct, who lied to whom - James Robertson to his son, or the doctor to Lyman Draper, or Draper to the world? Let the reader decide.
(End of Editor's Note)

12. The Ms. Diaries of both Col. Fleming and John Todd give the names of these three Captains as commanding the first detachment of Augusta men; but the Ms. letter of Isaac Shelby, Oct. 16th 1774, only mentions those of Dickinson and Harrison, omitting Skidmore's, and adding those of Samuel Wilson, John Lewis of Augusta, and John Lockridge. This letter of Shelby's is substantially the same as that communicated by Charles S. Todd, Shelby's son-in-law to Niles' Register, of May 3, 1817, and which, on Shelby's authority, is pronounced as the "official" report _ prepared, apparently, by Col. Andrew Lewis, from which copies were taken by those who desired, to send them to their friends. Shelby's is addressed to his uncle, John Shelby, on Holston, and has some preliminary and supplementary matters of interest, not found in the Niles' Register publication.

To prevent misconceptions, it should be added, that there were two persons of the name of John Lewis, commanding companies, one in the Botetourt regiment, the other in the Augusta; they were cousins, the former the son of Andrew, and the latter of Thomas Lewis. There were also two Captains bearing the name of McClanahan.

13. James Mooney, who was the first to report the approach of the enemy that morning, was one of these unfortunate scouts. He had been, in 1769, one of Daniel Boone's fellow explorers of Kentucky.

14. Fleming to Bowyer, Oct. 13, 1774. Same to his wife, of like date. Preston to Patrick Henry, Oct. 31, 1774. Burk's Hist. Va., III, 394.

15. Todd's Diary alone records these specific services of Captains McClanahan, of Augusta, and Lewis, of Botetourt. In the case of the former, it would seem quite probable, as his name does not occur as having participated in the battle in any of the accounts extant. As Capt. Lewis was a son of the Commander-in-Chief, he may very naturally have been retained in the camp to assist his father in the manifold duties pressing upon him; and the fact that Capt. Lewis' younger brother, and William Bryan, both of his company, went into the battle and Thomas Huff, eventually was w wounded, proves nothing, since detachments only from the several companies were sent into the field; and the re-enforcements which followed, from time to time, could only have been made up from companies already broken.

Dr. J. F. D. Smyth, in his Tour in America, Dublin edition, 1784, claims that he was in Point Pleasant battle; and that, as Capt. John Lewis, of Botetourt, was unable, from sickness, to make the campaign, he was placed in command of Lewis' company _ which statement has not the slightest foundation in fact. Lewis' company rolls, using the Fleming Papers, show no such name as Smyth, nor any absence on the Captains' part; and had he been absent, his Lieutenant, John Henderson, would have succeeded to the command. John Randolph, of Roanoke, aptly characterized Smyth's work as "replete with calumny and falsehood."

16. Ms. letter of Isaac Shelby, to John Shelby, Oct. 16, 1774.
17. Ms. letter of Ingles to Preston, Oct. 14, 1774.
18. Conversations with the late Maj. James Galloway of Henia, Ohio, who derived the facts from George Matthews, Captain of a company in the battle. Burk's Virginia, III, 394. Howe's Virginia, 366. Smyth, II, 108, mentions this stratagem; which he must have learned from others.
19. Ms. letter of Peachy Harrison, Oct. 1845.
20. Statement of Nathan Boone, of Missouri, 1851.
21. Amer. Arch., Fourth Series, I, 1017. Ms. letter of Henry F. Westfall, grandson of Wm. White, Feb. 24, 1849. Conversation with early settlers in the Virginia Valley. Kercheval's History of the Valley, second edition, 101, notes that it was Charles Lewis who wore the gorgeous scarlet jacket; but the traditions preserved in Augusta county, thirty and forty years ago, where both Lewis and Frogg resided, uniformly attributed that unfortunate exposure to Capt. Frogg.

Of William White, it may be added, that he had served with the unfortunate Wm. Crawford in the old French war, had, about 1770, been apprehended for killing Indians, and confined in Winchester, Va., jail, from which he was rescued by a party of friends; and, , settling in the Tygart's Valley region, shared in the destruction of Bull Town in 1772. His good service at Point Pleasant enhanced his reputation as an Indian fighter. He was captured by the Indians, in 1777, taken to their towns, but made his escape, only to be waylaid and killed March 8th, 1782, by his mortal foes, against whom he had so long and successfully waged a bloody warfare.

22. Ms. notes of conversation with Thomas H. Shelby, and Mark Hardin, both of whom derived the incident from Isaac Shelby himself.
23. Related by Charles Clendenin, in 1846. He derived the facts from his father, William Clendenin, who subsequently became a useful soldier on the frontiers, commanding a company about 1791 at Clendenin's Fort, where Charleston, West Virginia, now stands, and attaining to the rank of a Colonel of the militia. He died near Point Pleasant, the scene of his early adventures, in September, 1828, in the seventy- seventh year of his age.
24. Ms. notes of conversations, in 1846, with Thomas Lewis Jr. It masy be added of William Bryan, that he was a member of the family of Capt. John Lewis, whose widow he subsequently married, and lived and died in Botetourt.
25. Ms. letter of Preston to Patrick Henry, Oct. 31, 1774.
26. Murphy's Recollections. Murphy had the incident from Ross himself.
27. Recollections of Charles Clendenin and Thomas Lewis, 1846. Their information was derived from William McCulloch, the Indian trader of 1774. Stuart's Indian Wars, 48. Dodderidge's Notes, 232. Withers' Chronicles, 129.
28. Murphy's Recollections.
29. From Thomas H. Shelby.
30. Ms. letters of Charles A. Stuart, Jan 8th, and Feb 4th, 1845, who derived his information of this movement from Matthews himself. Conversations with

Charles Clendenin, Thomas Lewis, and Thomas H. Shelby. Hugh Paul Taylor's Notes on West Virginia, published in the Fincastle Mirror in 1829. Withers' Chronicles, 127, 128. Campbell's Memoir, in Campbell's Virginia, first edition, 187. Howe's Virginia, 366.

Smyth, in his Tour, already referred to, claims to have led John Lewis' Botetourt company, in the absence of the sick Captain, some miles, to gain the enemy's rear _ that this was near the close of the day, and Charles Lewis, and John Field shared in the enterprise, when, in truth, they had been both fallen, early in the morning. The "Adventures of My Grandfather'" by John Lewis Peyton, London, 1867, professes to give a veritable account of John R. Peyton, claiming that he commanded John Lewis' company at Point Pleasant; that in the after part of the day, Charles Lewis led a force to the rear of the Indians, of which his company formed a part; and that while the Indians were circumvented, Lewis was killed.

31. Ms. letter of Capt. John Floyd, dated at the Great Kanawha, Oct. 16, 1774, to Col. William Preston.
32. Relation of Tavenor Ross to Murphy.
33. Fleming's Ms. Diary.
34. Beside the lamented Colonels Lewis and Field, the distinguished dead included Captains John Murray, and Samuel Wilson, Lieutenants Dillon, Hugh Allen, and Matthew Bracken; Ensigns Jonathan Cundiff, and Samuel Baker; and John Frogg and George Cameron, not particularly identified with any company, yet men of prominence.

Among the wounded, in addition to Colnel Fleming, were Captains Thomas Burford, Robert McClanahan, James Ward, John Dickinson, and John Skidmore; Lieutenants Edward Goldman, James Robertson, Laird and Vance; and Samuel Lewis slightly, who served as aid to his father, Col. Andrew Lewis. Buford, McClanahan, Ward, and Goldman subsequently died of their wounds, and were buried at Point Pleasant.

There were four Captains, whose names do not appear in the text who led out re-inforcements, and shared in the battle _ George Moffitt, William Nall, Joseph Haynes, and Gilmore, all of the Augusta regiment. Lieut. Benjamin Roberts succeed his father-in-law, John Field, in command of the Culpeper company; Lieuts. Wm. McKee, Thomas Dooley, Givens, and McCoy, succeeded respectively Captains Murray, Buford, Wilson, and McClanahan.
35. Ms. notes of conversation with Thomas Love. 1844.
36. Fleming and Newell's Ms. Diaries. Ms. letter of Preston to Patrick Henry, Oct. 31, 1774.
37. Ms. Diaries of Fleming, and Todd.
38. Ms. Diaries of Todd and Newell.
39. Ms. letter to Wm. Bowyer, Oct. 13, 1774.
40. Conversations with Charles Clendenin and Thomas Lewis.

Chapter Sixteen

1. Memoir and Correspondence of R. H. Lee, II, 207, 208.
2. Greene's Life of Greene, , 478. Marshall's Washington, revised edition, I, 171.
3. Almon's Remembrances, 1777, 213, 214. Barber & Howe's N.J. Hist. Colls., 325.

Chapter Seventeen

1. Ms. Narrative of the Lewis Family by Mrs. Agatha Towles, daughter of William Lewis, and granddaughter of John Lewis. Howe's Virginia, 181. Peyton's AAdventures of My Grandfather,@ 218, 219.
2. This error originated with Hugh Paul Taylor, in a newspaper series, published in 1829, afterwards copied by Withers and others. But even Taylor's informant mentioned a Captain Grant as associated with Lewis in the service, clearly pointing not to Braddock's, but Grant's defeat in 1758. Neither the writings of Washington, the gazettes of that day, the lists of the Virginia officers in the action at Braddock's Field, nor any competent histories, British or American, go to show that Lewis was there. The total silence on this point of Stuart in his Indian Wars, and Fleming in his Ms. memoir, together with the omission of his name in the act of the Virginia Assembly of 1755, specifying each of the surviving Virginia officers of the battle on the Monongahela, renders it conclusive that Lewis did not share in the contest. The fact of his having been detached to Greenbrier may be found in Sargeant's History of Braddock's Expedition, p. 298, where the Mss. of Governor Sharpe, of Maryland, are cited as authority, which the gazettes of that day serve to corroborate.
3. Va. Gazette, Sept. 19th, 1755. Md. Gazette, Oct, 2d, 1755.
4 . Sparks' Washington, II, 293, 294.
5 . Stuart;s Indian Wars, 52-54. Maryland Gazette, Dec. 20, 1759. N.Y. Colonial Documents, X, 436, 713, 836. Penn. Arch., II, 294, 305, 329.
6 . Bouquet's Expedition, Lond. Edition, 1766, 4, 8, 32.
7. Bancroft's Hist. Of U.S., VIII, 318.
8. Fleming's Ms. Diary. Same to his wife, Oct. 13, 1774. Ms. letter.
9. Indian Wars, 54.
10. Sparks' Am. Biography, Second Series, VIII, 19, 20.
11. Penn. Gazette, Nov. 10, 1763. Ms. letter of Thomas Sillington, March 25, 1876.
12. Penn. Gazette, June 21, and July 5, 1764.
13. Penna. Colonial Records, VII, 528-32.
14. Ms. pay-roll of the company.
15. Ms. muster-roll of the company.
16. Ms. Papers of Evan Shelby.
17. Ms. Sherry's Hist. Maryland, 158.

18. Ms. Shelby Papers. McSherry's Maryland, 158, 159.
19. Ms. letter of Col. Wm. Preston, March 2, 1774.
20. Ms. letter of Col. Wm. Thompson, July 6, 1775
21. Ramsey's Tennessee, 187. Letters to Washington, II, 261.
22. Ms. letter of Shelby to Caswell, Sept. 29, 1787.
23. Gov. Shelby's Mss.
24. Ramsey's Tennessee, 357.

Chapter Eighteen

1. His Indian name was Keigh-tugh-qua, signifying cornblade or cornstalk: See Hist. of Western Pennsylvania, App., 162, 164.
2. A garment made of coarse woolen cloth.
3. Virginia Gazette, Nov. 9, 1759. Maryland Gazette, Nov. 22, 1759; S.C. Gazette, Nov. 24, 1759. Stuart's Indian Wars, 39. Campbell's Memoir, 181. Foote's Virginia, Second Series, 159. Col. Bolivar Christian's Scotch-Irish Settlers of the Valley of Virginia, 25.
4. Stuart's Indian Wars, 39, 60. Sketches of History, Life and Manners in the United States, Hartford
5. Penn. Gaz. July 28, 1763. Sketches of History, Life, and Manners in the United States, 60-66. The author of this work obtained his narrative from Mrs. Maiz, a step-daughter of Mrs. Clendenin, in 1824, corroborated by several others. Stuart's Indian Wars, 39, 40. Withers' Chronicles, 70, 71.
6. Christian=s Scotch-Irish Settlers, 11.
7. Hist. of Western Pennsylvania, Appendix, 164. Historical Account of Bouquet's Expedition (Lond. 1766) 34. Stone's Life and Times of Sir William Johnston.
8. Heckewelder's Indian Nations, 174, 223, 274. Richard Butler's deposition, Aug. 23, 1784, in Penn. Archives, IV, 569-70.
9. Cornstalk to Russell, June 15, 1775: Ms. letter written in beautiful vermillion ink. Ms. letter of Russell to Preston, June 12, 1775.
10. Burk's Hist. Virginia, iii, 428.
11. Ms. Proceedings of the Treaty. Ms. letter of Andrew Lewis, Jr., to Dr. S. G. Campbell, April 25, 1840/
12. Arbuckle to Hand, Oct. 6, 1777. Recollections of James Ward of Kentucky.
13. Arbuckle to Hand, Oct. 6, 1777. Murphy's Recollections.
14. Ms. letter of Arbuckle to Hand, Oct. 6, 1777. Murphy's Recollections; the relator was at Point Pleasant part of the time while the Indians were confined there. Stuart's Indian Wars, 58. Campbell's Ms. Memoir.
15. John P. Campbell, in the Port Folio, June, 1876.
16. A rude versifies of that day commemorated the tragedy, in language more truthful than poetic:
    Cornstalk, the Shawnees' greatest boast,
    Old Yie, by whom much blood was lost,

Red Hawk and El-i-nip-si-co,
Lie dead beside the Ohio.
17. Stuart's Indian Wars, 61.
18. Hand to Richard Peters, Sec. Of Board of War, Dec. 24, 1777.
19. Ms. letters of Hand to Patrick Henry, Dec. 9th and to Richard Peters, Dec. 24th, 1777. Ms. deposition of John Anderson, Wm. Ward, and Richard Thomas relative to the murder of Cornstalk and companions Nov. 10th, 1777. Ms. Fleming and Preston Papers. Murphy's Recollections. Stuart's Indian Wars, 59-61. Campbell's Ms. Memoir. Heckewelder's Narrative, 150, 151.

Chapter Nineteen

1. Penn. Jour., 6 Aug., 1777. Penn Gaz., same date. Penn. Eve. Post., 12 Aug., 1777. Corr. Amer. Rev., I, p. 416; Lossing's Schuyler, II, 249, 250.
2. This house is described as having been about sixteen feet by twenty, in size, built of round logs, with a door on its east side only; an old-fashioned fire place without jambs at its north end, on one side of which were ladder-like stairs, leading to a loft overhead; and separate south of the center of the floor, a trap door opening into an unwalled cellar-hole beneath. It stood about one hundred and fifty rods south of the pine tree and spring previously mentioned in the text.
3. Samuel Standish who was made prisoner and witnessed the affray, afterward declared that Jane was shot by the Indian who scalped her.
4. That this event occurred on the 26th of July, is certain. Compare Penn. Gaz., 6 Aug., 1777; Penn. Jour., same date; Penn. Eve. Post., 12 Aug., 1777; Corr. Amer. Rev., I, p. 416, Lossing's Schuyler, II, 249, 250.
5. Penn. Eve. Post, 12 Aug., 1777.
6. Burgoyne to Gates, 6 Sept., 1777.
7. Gates to Burgoyne, 2 Sept., 1777.
8. Burgoyne to Gates, 7 Sept., 1777, previously

Chapter Twenty

1. Lord George Gremaine to Sir Guy Carleton, 26 March, 1777.
2. Maj. John Butler to Carleton, 28 July, 1777. St. Leger to same, 27 Aug., 1777. Col. Dan. Claus to Sec. Wm. Knox, 16 Oct., 1777.
3. It was built upon the ruins of Fort Stanwix. The original idea was, to repair the latter, but the result was the erection of a new fortification upon its ruins. The original name, Fort Stanwix, continued to be the one in general use, during and after the Revolution.
4. Claus to Knox, 16 Oct., 1777.
5. Claus to Knox, 16 Oct., 1777.
6. Butler to Carleton, 28 July, 1777.
7. St. Leger to Carlton, 27 Aug., 1777.

Editor's note. Draper included a footnote numbered 7, but did not indicate it in the text, which should have occurred at, or near, this point.

8. Germain to Sir Guy Carleton, 26 March, 1777.

9. A Mohawk Indian, Joseph Brant.

10. St. Leger to Carleton, 27 Aug., 1777. The precise number, according to Claus and Butler, was four hundred, but St. Leger says he ordered out his whole corps.

11. This fact is explicitly stated by St. Leger. It is confirmed by Butler and Claus.

12. Willett to Gov. Trumbull, 21 Aug., 1777.

13. Butler to Carleton, 15 Aug., 1777. Joseph Brant (Thay en da nagea) had command of fifty or sixty Mohawks. He was much with Butler: verbal statement of the Seneca chief, Black Snake - 1850. No mention is made in any contemporaneous account of his having had the principal direction of affairs.

14. As to the cause of this delay, there are many conflicting traditions.

15. Extract from a Letter : Albany, Aug., 11 (Penn. Gaz. No. 2530): "About one o'clock the same day [Aug. 6] Col. Gansevoort having received information of Gen. Herkimer's march sent Lieut. Col. Willett out with 200 men, to attack an encampment of the enemy, and thereby facilitate Gen. Herkimer's march to the fort. In this the Colonel succeeded; for after an engagement of an hour he had completely routed the enemy, took one Captain and four privates prisoners. The baggage taken was very considerable; such as money, bear skins, officers baggage, and camp equipage: one of the soldiers had for his share a scarlet coat, trimmed with gold lace to the full, and three laced hats. The plunder at the most moderate computation exceeds 1000^. When the Colonel returned to the fort he discovered 200 regulars in full march to attack him; he immediately ordered his men to prepare for battle, and having a field price with him, Capt. Savage of the artillery so directed its fire as to play in conjunction with one out of the fort; these, with a brisk fire from his small arms, soon made these heroes scamper off with great loss. Col. Willett then marched with his booty into the fort, where he arrived at four the same day, having not a single man killed or wounded. This account we have from a man, who was in the engagement, and left the fort on Thursday night last."

16. AThe impetuosity of the Indians is not to be described; on the site of the enemy, forgetting the judicious disposition formed by Sir John [Johnson], and agreed to by themselves, which was, to suffer the attack to begin with the troops in front, while they should be on both flank and rear. They rushed in hatchet in hand, and thereby gave the enemy's rear an opportunity to escape: St. Leger to Carleton, 27 Aug., 1777.

17. The action commenced a little after 10 o'clock and continued one hour a a half: Butler to Carleton, 15 Aug., 1777. AThey [the Americans] were waylayed by our party, surprised, briskly attacked, and after a little resistance, repulsed: Claus. Willett made his sortie from Fort Schuyler between one and two o'clock in the afternoon. He found in the camp of the enemy wounded men from the battle which had taken place two hours before. Penn. Gaz., 20 Aug., 1777. Willett to

Trumbull, 21 Aug., 1777.
18. AThe militia with Gen. Herkimer lost about 160 killed and wounded; Schuyler to Washington, 15 Aug., 1777.
19. Verbal statement of Blacksnake taken in 1850.
20. Younglove's Affidavit, in Stone's Brant, Vol. I (App. No. IV), pp. 459, 460. Butler to Carleton, 15 Aug., 1777.
21. "We lost Captains Hare and Wilson of the Indians, Captain-Lieutenant McDonald of Sir John's Regiment, two or three privates and thirty-two Indians. Captain Watts. Lieutenant Singleton of Sir John's Regiment and thirty-three Indians wounded:" Claus. "The Senecas alone lost seventeen men, among whom were several of their chief warriors, and had sixteen wounded:" Butler. "They [the Senecas] had five chiefs and thirty warriors killed:" Blacksnake's Verbal Statement, 1850. "Their [the Indians] loss was great: I must be understood Indian computation, being only about thirty killed and wounded and in that number some of their favorite chiefs and confidential warriors were slain:" St. Leger.
22. Butler to Carleton, 15 Aug., 1777.
23. Willett to Trumbull, 21 Aug., 1777.
24. Claus to Knox, 16 Oct., 1777.
25. Extract of a letter : Albany 11 Aug. (Penn. Gaz. No. 2530): "I have the pleasure to communicate to you an agreeable piece of intelligence: last Wednesday about nine o'clock an engagement ensued between a part of the militia of Tryon county, under the command of General Herkimer, and a party of savages, Tories and regulars, about half way between Eriskie [Eriskany] and Fort Stanwix [Fort Schuyler]. It lasted until three o'clock in the afternoon, when the enemy thought proper to retire, leaving General Herkimer master of the field; unluckily, however, the general and some valuable officers got wounded and killed in the beginning. This, however, did in no ways intimidate the ardor of the men; and the General, although he had two wounds, did not leave the field until the action was over; he seated himself down on a log, with his sword drawn, animating his men."

Chapter Twenty One

1. Shepherd to Hand, August 4th, 1777. Dr. Jos. Dodderidge asserts in a MS. account of the attack on Fort Henry, that General Hand "had received advice that the post would be attacked in a short time." "White Eyes came to Fort Pitt and told them the Indians were going to take Wheeling home:" Shane MSS.
2. Shepherd to Hand, 22 Aug., 1777: "In obedience to your orders I have called in all the men to this post that are under pay." "Between four and five hundred men:" Dodderidge MSS.
3. "I have ordered Capt. Ogle to keep up a scout between this fort and Beech Bottom, also Capt. Mason to send a party to scout between this and Grave creek. I shall order such scouts and spies over the river as our strength will admit:" Shepherd to Hand, 22, Aug., 1777.

4. Same to same, 28 Aug., 1777.
5. Ogle's company numbered on the last day of August, 1777, thirty-eight men: Francis Duke's Account-book of issue as Commissary, MS.
6. [Note by the Editor: at this point Draper inserted a footnote as 5 1/2, which will therefore result in a numbering difference in this work and his writing. His words follow]
   "By the best judges here x x x it is thought their numbers must have been not less than between two and three hundred:" Shepherd to Hand, 15 September, 1777. "Two hundred and ten warriors:" White Eyes to Morgan, 23 Sept., 1777.
7. White Eyes to Congress. 22 Sept.., 1777.
8. De Hass' Hist. Ind. W. Va., p. 224.
9. Dodderidge MSS. As will be shown here after, their position was soon changed.
10. Withers' Border Warfare, p. 161.
11. White Eyes to Congress, 22 Sept., 1777. Zeisberger to Gen. Hand, same date. Simon Girty, so generally supposed to have been their leader, was at Pittsburgh at that time. Gibson to Hand, from Fort Pitt, 4 Sept., 1777. He did not desert to the enemy until the next Spring. Hand to Maj. Gen. Gates, 30 March 1778. Same to Jasper Yeates same date. See, also, Penn. Arch., VI, 445. Heckewelder's Narr., pp. 170, 174, 178.
12. There can be no doubt as to this date. Shepherd to Hand, from Fort Henry, 3 Sept., 1777. Gibson to Hand, 4 Sept., 1777. Hand to Russell, 14 Oct., 1777. These letters are in the Department of State, Washington.
13. Frequently written McMahon. He was the owner of the Negro.
14. "To the Monongahela:" Dodderidge MSS. "About returning east of the mountains:" De Hass.
15. Dodderidge MSS. Another account states that he was shot.
16. Tradition says that a subsequent measurement made it seventy feet.
17. Tomlinson was killed, later in the day: Shane MSS.
18. Statement of Mrs. Jos. Stagg, in Shane MSS. Why this party was not attacked will presently be seen.
19. Dodddridge MSS.; Where the formation of the ambuscade is given with great particularity.
20. "About twenty:" Dodderidge MSS. "Fourteen men:" Withers; who derived his information for the collections of Noah Zane, son of Ebenezer Zane.
21. Dodderidge MSS. The Indian was not killed.
22. "Nearly all literally cut to pieces:" Withers. "Out of fourteen, but two escaped:" De Hass.
23. Withers' Border Warfare, p. 162. The slain Indian was a Wyandot. Zeieberger to Hand, 22 Sept., 1777.
24. This incident is related by De Hass (Hist. Ind. Wars in W. Va., p. 226 note.) He is corroborated by current tradition.
25. "Fifteen men were killed and five wounded:" Shane MSS. "One Lieut. [Samuel Tomlinson] killed and fourteen privates. One Captain [Mason] and four

privates wounded:) Shepherd to Hand, 15 Sept., 1777. Among the killed was Francis Duke (son-in-law of Shepherd) who was Commissary at Fort Henry. He was shot in the afternoon, in returning from a neighboring blockhouse. His MS. Account Book shows no entry, in his hand writing, after Aug. 31st 1777.

26. "The Wyandots and Mingoes are all gone home again. According to their knowledge, they killed 14 people at Weelunk [Wheeling]; had one Wyandot killed and 6 or 7 wounded, one of the last died since. Wiondoughwaland's son and another of his company [Delaware George], both Captains, are badly wounded and it is said will hardly live:" Zeisberger to Hand 22 Sept., 1777.

27. Many of the stirring incidents heretofore supposed to properly belong to "the first siege of Wheeling," are to be referred to a subsequent attack, that of the eleventh of September, 1782; while some must be set down as wholly imaginary. Indeed, the "siege" has come to be more celebrated for what did not happen than for what actually transpired. No relief came to the garrison while the Indians were in the vicinity of the fort. The events of the next day, Sept. 2d, possess but little interest. The bodies of the slain, which generally, were shockingly mutilated, were gathered up and buried; the country for some distance around the fort having, in the mean time, been searched and no enemy discovered.

Chapter Twenty Two

1. "The Wyandots and Mingoes are all gone home again:" Zeisberger to Hand, from Cashocton, 22 Sept., 1777.
2. Laskiel. Hist. Ind. Miss. P. III, 129. Heckenelder. Narr. Moran. Miss. 165. Zeisberger to Hand, 22 Sept., 1777, just cited. Gen. Hand, Oct. 14th, 1777, gave the number of Indians as fifty, in a letter to Wm. Russell of that date; doubtless an inadvertence. "At present," is the language of Zeisberger, Awe know that 40 of the Wyandots are gone, it is said to Weelenk [Wheeling.]@
3. John Cullins' Memorial to Cong.; from a authentic copy.
4. John Van Matre to E. Cook, 28 Sept., 1777.
5. Shepherd to Hand, 27 Sept., 1777.
6. "Forty-six suffered themselves to be led out by Mer. William Linn:" Hand to Russell, 14 Oct., 1777.
7. The current tradition as to the cause of the movement, namely, that a smoke was seen in the direction of Grave creek and fears entertained that the Stockade there and other buildings were burning and that Col. Shepherd to ascertain the fact and to afford protection necessary, dispatched the force down the river, is wholly without foundation; so, also, that the party started out "to destroy the Delaware towns, and consequently our settlements among the rest," as started by the Moravian. Laskiel (Hist. Ind. Miss. P III, 129. Compare, Heckewelder's Narr., 165. Schweinitz Zeisberger, 457.
8. Shepherd to Hand, 27 Sept., 1777; John Van Marte to E. Cook, 28 Sept., 1777; both of which have just been cited.

9. Known, at that day, as McMechen's (McMahon's) Narrows.
10. Not more than that number of his men, as will be presently seen, could have gone with him.
11. This statement is based upon what seems to be a trust-worthy tradition.
12. Shepherd to Hand, 27 Sept., 1777, previously cited. Verbal Statement of Andrew Linn; 1845. Mem. of John Cullins, already quoted. Verbal Statement of Samuel Murphey; 1846. Rachel Johnson's Verbal Statement; 1845. Verbal Statement of Mrs. Lydia Cruger: 1845. Statements of John Miller, Jesse Ellis, Mrs. Sophronia Clark, Geo. Edgington, Joseph Hedges, and others, taken about the same period, are corroborative of those just mentioned, in the main particulars.
13. This was John Cullins : In his Mem., he says: "In this action your memorialist was wounded by a ball which broke his right leg."
14. The accounts of the affair, so far as relates to the part taken by Linn after the firing by the savages, is pretty accurately given in The Amer. Pioneer, II, 350. The pleasant tradition of his little party rushing to the scene with loud shouts, thereby frightening the savages and causing their precipitate retreat, must be set down as a myth.
15. Shepherd to Hand, 27 Sept., 1777, already frequently cited. While the Colonel was uniting four more came in.
16. Captain Foreman had but one son, Hamilton, in his company.
17. "Thomas Brazier, George Avery, William Williams, Hugh Clark, John Polk, and one other:" Andrew Linn.
18. "Twenty-one brave fellows cruelly butchered;" James Chew to Hand, 3 Oct., 1777. "Twenty-one killed:" Hand to Russell, 14 Oct., 1777.
19. Jacob Pugh. Compare Hildreth's Pion. Hist., p. 128; De Hass' Hist. Ind. W. Va., p. 279.
20. Shepherd to Hand 27 Sept., 1777. The wounded man particularly referred to was John Cullins. He was hunted up the second night by Linn and brought in.
21. "Since my arrival, Col. Shepherd and myself marched and buried these unfortunate men in the late action: a moving sight, twenty-one brave fellows cruelly butchered, even after death:" Chew.

Chapter Twenty Three

1. Maj. John Butler to Lieut. Col. Bolton, 8 July, 1778.
2. Butler to Bolton, 8 July. 1778.

Chapter Twenty Four

1. Bancroft, III, 344, 345.
2. Ms. Preston Papers. Plain Facts, Phila., 1781, 36-44
3. Notes of conversation with James Roy. Butler's Hist. Kentucky, 37 note.
4. Clark's Ms. Narrative. Levi Todd's Ms. Narrative. Ms. papers of Simon

Kenton. Bradford's Notes, in Stipp's Miscellany, 25, 26. Butler's Kentucky, 42, 43. McDonald's Sketches, 211, 212.

5. Clark's Ms. Diary and Papers. Todd's Narrative. Ms. Kenton Papers. Bradford's Notes, 27.

6. Statement of David Henry, one of Dillard's men.

7. Ms. Narrative of Wm. Whitley, one of Montgomery's company.

8. Todd's Ms. certificate July 29, 1784.

9. Ms. Papers of David Todd, son of Levi Todd. Butler's Kentucky, 53 note.

10. Clark's Ms. Narrative. Recollections of David Henry.

11. Ms. Whitley's Narrative.

12. Statement of Jefferson Patterson, who learned the fact from his father, Robert Patterson, one of Clark's party. Shaffner's Hist. of America, I, 465.

13. Low's Boston Almanac, for 1778, describes the eclipse of the sun, June 24th, in that year, as beginning at 9 o'clock, 23m, 49s, in the morning, with its greatest obscurity at 10 o'clock, 40m, 47s, ending at 12 o'clock, 8m, 41s. As the Falls of Ohio are nearly fifteen degrees west of Boston; and, to get local time four minutes for every degree of latitude must be subtracted, it follows that the middle of the eclipse at Louisville was an hour earlier than Boston time, hence about forty minutes past nine o'clock. It was the most remarkable eclipse that had occurred for many years.

14. Clark only gives the number of men who descended from Pittsburgh with him to Corn Island, one hundred and fifty, in three companies; and at the Falls, augmented his force one company. Marshall's Kentucky, Girandin's Virginia, and the British account, represent his force at between two and three hundred. Bradford's Notes on Kentucky states that not over eighty joined Clark at Corn Island from the Kentucky station, increasing his total force not to exceed two hundred and thirty. Of the Kentucky addition, a part deserted under Hutchins, and the invalids remained to keep garrison, protect the families, and raise corn on the island. Robert Patterson, who served on the campaign, placed Clark force at one hundred and forty-four; while Kenton informed his biographer, McDonald, that one hundred and fifty-three was the number; but these were the recollections of aged men long after the occurrence, and probably have reference to the number who descended the river from Pittsburgh. Clark would hardly have formed a fourth company, had not his force been increased by the Kentucky accessions. Joseph Bowman, who commanded one of the companies, wrote in July, 1778, that Clark's force against Kaskaskia was between one hundred and seventy and one hundred and eighty; and Governor Henry, in a letter a few months later, gives precisely the same estimate: See Almon's Remembrances, VIII, 82. Ms. letter of Patrick Henry to Congress, Nov. 16, 1778.

15. Campbell to Clark, June 8, 1778: Ms. letter

16. This fort was established not very long after the French evacuation of Fort Duquesne, in 1758. Stoddard, in his Sketches of Louisiana, states, that while a portion of the garrison was enticed over the river in quest of several supposed

bears, really Indians dressed in bear-skins, on all fours, and the rest of the troops lining the bank, in front of the fort to witness the expected sport, a party of concealed Indians entered the stockade from the rear, cutting off the retreat of the soldiers, very few of whom escaped the carnage. Subsequently re-establishing the fortification, the French named it Fort Massacre, in commemoration, of this disastrous event.

Monette, in his History of the Mississippi Valley, ventures to pronounce this massacre a "fable." Victor Collot, a General in the French army, in his "Journey" in this country in 1796, says of this occurrence: "the Canadians informed us, that the Indians having one day surprised and massacred all the French who were within the fort, it was on that account called Fort Massacre." William Martin, a Colonel under Jackson in the Creek war, states in as Ms. letter, July 7, 1842, that when he resided on the Tugaloo River, in the western part of South Carolina, about 1793, he personally knew Bryant Ward, then aged and intelligent, and formerly a Cherokee trader, who informed him that he headed the Cherokee party who performed this exploit.

17. Joseph Bowman's letter to Isaac Hite, in Almon's Remembrances. VIII, 82.
18. Clark's Ms. Narrative. Two ancient men, Auguste St. Jenerue and Felix Valle, of St. Genevieve, Missouri, whose parents resided as Kaskaskia in 1778, related in 1851, that Rocheblave having heard of the American party descending the Ohio, assembled the people, and met the invaders, probably ambush them; but they declined, declaring that they did not wish to meddle in a contest in which they had no interest. Had they consented, the Kaskaskia Indians under Baptiste Ducoign, would have joined them; and, altogether, they would have made quite a formidable force.
19. Recollections of David Henry. Reynolds= Pioneer Hist. of Illinois, 72.
20. Marshall's Kentucky, I, 67.
21. Ms. Statement of Joseph Bogy. Traditions of John D. Jones, of St. Genevieve, Mo., and Edmund Menard, Kaskaskia.
22. David Henry's Recollections.
23. Statement of David Todd, derived from his father Lieut. Levi Todd.
24. McDonald's Kenton, 219.
25. David Todd's Statement.
26. Bradford's Notes, on Kentucky, as originally published in the Ky. Gazette; imperfectly given in Stipp's Miscellany, 38. Girardine's continuation of Burk's Virginia, IV, 318.
27. Clark's Ms. Narrative.
28. David Henry's Recollections.
29. Clark's Ms. Narrative. Recollections of Paschal L. Cerre', of St. Louis, 1846, a son of Gabriel Cerre', in his sixth year at the time of Clark's visit.
30. Clark's Ms. Narrative. His letter to George Mason, Nov. 19, 1779.
31. Clark's Narrative. Joseph Bowman's letter, July 30, 1778, Almon's Remembrances, VIII, 82.

32. Clark to Patrick Henry, April 29, 1779. John Rogers to Jonathan Clark, July 6, and July 7, 1779; Ms. letters. Ms. instructions of Clark to Rogers, Feb. 3, 1779. Bowman's Journal, Ms. copy.
33. Garland's Life of Randolph. II, 57. Girardin's continuation of Burk's Virginia, IV, 321, note.
24. British Annual Register, 1779, 16. Scot's Magazine, Feb. 1781, 66.

Chapter Twenty Five

1. Boone's Ms. Family Register in part in his own hand writing.
2. Boone's Ms. Papers statements of Nathan Boone, a son and Daniel Bryan, a nephew of Daniel Boone. Recollections of Joseph Jackson, a survivor of Boone's party of salt-boilers, taken from his lips in 1844. James Trabue's Ms. narrative.
3. Ms. statements of Nathan Boone, Daniel Bryan, Joseph Jackson, Henry Wilson, and others. Boone's Narrative. Bradford's Notes on Kentucky, 31, 32. Collin's Kentucky, revised edition II, 656.
4. Deposition of Wm. Hancock, July 17, 1778. Boone to Arthur Campbell, the Lieutenant of Washington County, Virginia, July 18, 1778.
5. Their numbers have been variously estimated at from three hundred and thirty-eight to four hundred and fifty. Colonel John Bowman, writing from Harrodsburg, Oct. 14, 1778, says three hundred and thirty Indians and eight Frenchmen; in Boone's narrative by Filson, the number is stated at four hundred and forty-four Indians, and twelve Frenchman.
6. Capt. Wm. Buchanan's deposition, Nov. 28, 1778. Recollections of John Gass, one of the defenders.
7. John H. James' MSS.
8. Henderson's petition to Va. Legislature, Nov. 21, 1778.
9. Writers on gunnery say that the first cannon were made of wood, wrapped in numerous folds of linen, and well secured by iron hoops. The authorities for the Boonesborough incident are: Col. Daniel Boone to his son, Nathan Boone; and also to a "Traveler," copied from the New York Statesman into the Detroit Gazette, July 4, 1823; Recollections of Moses and Isaiah Boone, sons of Squire Boone, who were youths in Boonesborough during the siege, and well remembered the occurrence; and Enoch M. Boone, who had the fact from his father, Squire Boone. Statement of Squire Boone to Samuel Millard, in 1806, as communicated in a letter by the latter, Oct. 14, 1844; Statement of Robert Hancock, derived from his father, Stephen Hancock, one of the defenders of Boonesborough during the siege of 1778.
10. The following authorities have been consulted in the preparation of this Chapter: Ms. Fleming papers. Ms. letter of John Bowman to G. R. Clark, Oct., 14, 1778. Ms. Narrative of Daniel Trabue, a commissary at the time at Logan's Fort. Virginia Ms. Archives. Ms. statements of Daniel Bryan, John Carr, Mrs. Lucy Brashear, Robert Hancock, John L. Martin, Samuel Millard, and Wyatt H. Ingram.

Ms. notes of conversations of John H. James with Simon Kenton. Ms. notes of conversations with Nathan Boone and lady, Moses Boone, Isaiah Boone, Enoch M. Boone, John Gass, Joseph Jackson, George M. Bedinger, Henry Wilson, Benjamin Briggs, and William M. Kenton. Of these, John Gass, Mrs. Brashear, Moses and Isaiah Boone, were in the fort during the siege; as was Robert Hancock also, but two young to observe the occurrences. Boone's Narrative, appended to Filson's Kentucky. Bradford's Notes on Kentucky. The account of the siege dictated by William Bailey Smith, one of the actors, and published in Hunt's Western Review, for January, 1821. Marshall's Kentucky. McClung's Western Adventure. McDonald's sketch of Kenton. Peck's Life of Boone. Perkins' Pioneers of Kentucky, in N.A. Review, for January, 1846.

11. Ms. letter of Boone to his sister-in-law, Sarah Boone, Oct. 19, 1816.

12. Bancroft's Hist. U. S., revised edition, IV, 169, 170.

Chapter Twenty Six

1. McDonald's Kenton, 221. Recollections of John Gass, one of the defenders of Boonesborough.

2. McClung, in his Sketches of Western Adventure, represents that in this interview with Black Fish, Kenton made use of the phrases "Yes Sir," and "No Sir." When McClung's work appeared, some four years before Kenton's death, the old pioneer was indignant at this pretended obsequiousness when in captivity, and emphatically denied it to Hon. John H. James, F. W. Thomas, the author of Clinton Bradshaw, as well as to members of his own family, and others. "I never did to an Indian in my life," said Kenton, "I rarely ever do it to a white man."

3. The Shawnees, or a portion of them, resided at an early period on the Upper Potomac; and the South Branch of the river was long known as the Wappatomika, such is the orthography of Kercheval, the historian of the Virginia Valley. On Fry and Jefferson's map of Virginia, published in 1751, the name is given as Wappocomo. The Shawnee town of Wakatomica on the Muskingum, was doubtless designed as a transfer of the name; and, after its destruction by Major McDonald, in 1774, it was apparently intended to be perpetuated in their new village on Mad River, which Kenton, according to Judge McColloch, pronounced Wakatomica. Glover, in his narrative of 1782, gives the name as Wachatomakak. Its correct orthography is involved in doubt.

4. Kenton himself always pronounced this name as here written, except sometimes omitting the middle syllable a; but invariably pronouncing the terminating syllable chack. James McPherson and Jonathan Alber, long prisoners with the Indians, Gen. Benjamin Whiteman, Gen. Wm. H. Tryfee, and Capt. Christopher Wood, early pioneers of that part of Ohio, always referred to it as Mack-a-chack. Gen. Henry Lee, and Capt. James Wood, of Mason Co., Ky., and Col. Robert Patterson, of Dayton, Ohio, all of whom served in Logan's expedition against the Mack-a-chack towns, in 1786, either so pronounced or wrote the name. In

McDonald's sketch of Kenton, it is, perhaps by misprint, spelled Mack-a-cheek; while Drake's Tecumseh, Howe's Ohio, and Anderson's large map of Ohio, published in 1841, give Mach-a-chack as the proper orthography. Col. John Johnston, long the Shawnee Indian Agent, wrote the name, in 1819, Mequachake, which Taylor, in his History of Ohio, follows. The venerable Judge N. Z. McCulloch, of Bellefontaine, Ohio, whose clear memory goes back to 1802, says he never heard it pronounced other wise than Mack-a-chack by the early settlers until it was changed into Mack-a-cheek by the establishment of the "Mack-a-cheek Press" in olden times.

5. This little village was located in a small valley on the farm not long ago occupied by Hon. Black, in the town of Salem, Champaign County, Ohio, and near where Col. James McPherson long resided. This Wapakoneta must not be confounded with the Shawnee town of the same name, subsequently established, on the Auglaize River in what is now Auglaize county, Ohio.

6. This mound is not very far in front of the residence of John Enoch.

7. Stone's Brant, I, 28. N.Y. Colonial Documents, X, 992. Henry's Travels, 73. American Museum, V, 19. Dawson's Harrison, 415. Clark's Hist. Of Onondaga I, 346.

8. Indian Nations, 272.

9. "These were Kenton's words, and they embodied a sublime expression." See F. W. Thomas' Visit to Simon Kenton in 1834, in his Sketches of Character, ed. 1849, p. 87; ed. 1853, p.78.

10. Named after Mohawk Solomon. As early as 1755, he was a recognized chief, and the resided at Tullihas, on a western branch of the Muskingum, about twenty miles above the forks of that stream. See Smith's Narrative, original addition, 1799, pp. 9, 11.

11. By the British and their Indian allies this town was known as Upper Sandusky, in contradistinction to Lower Sandusky, a Wyandot village on the river below.

12. Authorities consulted in the preparation of this chapter: Marshall's Kentucky, editions 1812 and 1824. McClung's Western Adventure, 1832, from Taylor's Ms. narrative dictated by Kenton. Valuable Ms. notes of conversations with Kenton, by Hon. John H. James, in Feb., 1832. F. W. Thomas' visit to Kenton in 1834. McDonald's Sketches of Kenton and others, 1838. Howe's Ohio, 1847. History of Champaign and Logan counties, Ohio, 1872. Ms. statements, and notes of conversations, of Wm. M. Kenton, Mrs. Sarah McCord, Mrs. Mary Murray, and Mrs. Eliza C. Thornton, children of Gen. Kenton. Ms. statements, or notes of conversations, of Benjamin Kenton, Thomas Kenton, Gabriel Kenton, Harvey Kenton, Mark Kenton, Samuel Kenton, and William Kenton; Mrs. Willoughby Griffith, and Mrs. Elizabeth Arrowsmith, nieces of the old pioneer; John Arrowsmith, Mason Arrowsmith, and Miller Arrowsmith; Mrs. Elizabeth Mouser; Gen. Benjamin Whiteman, Capt. Christopher Wood, Gen. Wm. H. Fyffe, Maj. James Galloway, Rev. Asal Owen, Dr. Movil Talbot, Harvey Talbot, Capt. John Mccord, Wm. Haller, Judge N. Z. McColloch, Hon. Wm. Patrick, Orrin and Martha North,

Joseph Wade, Hon. Joseph Newell, Andrew Wood, Henry H. McPherson, Rachel Reno, John Enoch, Martin Sayre, and Dr. I. A. Lapham.

Chapter Twenty Seven

1. Hening's Stat's at Large. IX, 257.
2. R. H. Collins' Hist. Ky., Vol. I, p. 10.
3. Diary of Geo. Rogers Clark, from Dec. 25, 1776 to 22d of Nov. 1777: MS. This Diary has been published _ first in Moorehead's Address. _ 1840.
4. Collins' Hist. Ky., I, p. 10.
5. "July 24, 1774. Proceeded to the cabin [Harrod's] four miles further. At our arrival, we were surprised to find every thing squandered upon the ground, and two fires burning. Mrs. Floyd and Mrs. Nash went down to the landing and found these words written on a tree: 'Alarmed by finding some people killed. We are gone down this way.'" _ Journal of a Surveyor.
6 . "On the 14th [of April] the Fort was finished:" Bradford's Notes. "Thursday, 20 [April, 1775] _ Arrived at Fort Boone, on the mouth of Otter creek, on Cantuckee river, where we were saluted by a running fire of about 25 guns:" Henderson's Journal _ MS. This has been published.
7. Bradford's Notes on Ky. (Stipp's West Miscel.), pp. 25, 26. Clark's Diary _ MS. Morehead's Address. p. 161.
8. Each time: Harrodsburgh, on the 7 March and 29 Apr.; Boonesborough, on the 24 Apr. and 23 May. _ Clark's Diary: MS.
9 . "This was in March:" MS. Narr. of Wm. Whitley. Marshall's Hist. Ky., I, 48.
10. This occurred May 30th: Clark's Diary _ MS. Compare Morehead's Address, p. 162.
11. "Old Chelicothe [Chillicothe], the principal Indian town on Little Miami:" Filson's Kentuche (1784), p. 63.
12. Jno. Bowman in Butler's Ky. (2d ed.) p. 534. "Four hundred and forty-four Indians _ twelve Frenchmen [Canadians]:" Filson, 67, 68. AFive to seven hundred Indians _ twelve Frenchmen [Canadians]:@ Bradford. Bowman wrote on the 14th of October, 1778 _ not many days after the siege was raised.
13. A. S. De Peyetor's "Miscellanies," pp. 247, 261. C. I. Waller's Address before the State Hist. Soc. Wisc., 31 Jan., 1871.
14. David Bundrin and a Negro named London.
15. "April 1., Robert Patterson, at the head of twenty-five men, commenced a block house where Lexington now stands:" Geo. W. Ranch.
16. Just before their arrival, one of the men wandered off hunting. Ascending a hill, he saw below him a buffalo. The beast taking the alarm started off at full speed but stumbled upon some rocks and fell prostrate. The hunter pursued, jumped upon the animal's back and dispatched him with his knife. He was greatly complimented by the troops.
17. Bowman to Geo. Rogers Clark, 13 June, 1779: MS. letter. The following was

the number of men (officers included) belonging to each company:

Capt.	Logan's Company		48	men
"	Harrod's	no	99	"
"	Holder's	no	58	"
"	Todd's	no	25	"
"	Harlan's	no	43	"
Lieut.	Haggin's	no	19	"
Col.	Bowman		1	
	Total		296	*(should be 293)*

18. During the march out one of the men was bitten by a rattlesnake. He was sent back to the boats accompanied by a comrade, with orders to be sent to the Falls of the Ohio.

19. Statement of Henry Hull, a survivor, made in 1844.

20. MS. Notes of James Galloway, Sr.

21. The birth place of Tecumseh; it was situated on the north side of Mad river about five miles west of the present city of Springfield, in Clark County, Ohio.

22. Statement of Joseph Jackson: 1844. Jackson was a prisoner to the Shawnees and in Chillicothe when attacked by Bowman, as will be presently be seen.

23. Statement of Geo. M. Bedinger, a survivor: 1839 and 1843. Jackson also speaks of the return of this hunter, and his being killed.

24. These interesting details are given by Jackson.

25. Statement of Bland W. Ballard, a survivor: 1844. Jackson, Bedinger and others are corroborative.

26. MS. Notes of James Ray, a survivor, taken in 1833 by Mann Butler.

27. MS. Statement of James Patton, a Lieutenant in Capt. Harrod's company.

28. Patton's Statement, just cited.

29. Extract from the Va. Gaz., July 10, 1779 (No. 22): "By a gentleman from the frontiers we are informed, that Captain Bowman with 200 volunteers marched from Kentucky against Chillaffee the lower Shawnee town and surrounded it the 29th of May last (being the night the moon was totally eclipsed) without being discovered. At day-break the next morning he made an attack, and after a short engagement, the Indians with a number of British troops, fled to a small blockhouse which the red coats had provided for a safe retreat. Captain Bowman burnt the town, together with a great quantity of corn, ammunition, and stores. He has taken from the enemy 163 valuable horses, loaded with goods to the amount of ^32000. The Indians had five killed at the town and were repulsed with loss in two attacks they made on our party on their return. We had seven men killed in this expedition."

Chapter Twenty Eight

1. Sparks' Washington, V., 193, 199, 239.
2. Lossing's Field Book of the Revolution, I, 705.
3. Greene's Greene, III, 448, 449.
4. George Sumner's Boston Oration, 1859, p. 16, note.
5. Ms. notes of conversations with the late John B. Gibson, long Chief Justice of Pennsylvania.
6. Martin's Hist. Louisiana, II, 12.
7. Lieut. William Linn's letter to Oliver Pollock, in Ms. archives of Virginia, dated Arkansas, Nov. 30, 1776, gives the number of barrels; a statement on Butler's Kentucky, on authority of one of Linn's party, specifies one hundred and fifty six kegs of powder as the number carried around the Falls of Ohio _ indicating that, for the convenience of handling, the powder, after reaching the Arkansas Post, had been transferred from barrels to kegs. Col. David Shepherd's Ms. letter, June 8, 1789, shows that the total weight of powder delivered at Wheeling by Lieut. Linn was "ten thousand pounds, or thereabouts;" and the same letter, and Shepherd's certificate of Jan. 31, 1791, show that nine thousand pounds were sent forward to Col. Crawford, at Fort Pitt. Capt. George Gibson, who headed this expedition to New Orleans, returned himself by sea to Philadelphia as Pollock; memorial, of Sept. 1782, to Congress, states.
8. Ms. notes of conversations with Michael Cresap, 1845; and with Mrs. Lydia Cruger, 1846.
9. Virginia Ms. Archives.
10. American Pioneer II, 397.
11. Ms. letter of Patrick Henry to Major Rogers, Feb. 13, 1777.
12. Virginia Ms. Archives. Ms. petition of Samuel McColloch, John Canon and J. P. Duval, Dec. 7, 1778, to the Virginia Senate, submitting whether Rogers had not vacated his seat in that body.
13. Col. James Paul's Ms. Statement. Recollections of Michael Cresap. McCulloch, Canon, and Duval's petition. Virginia Ms. Archives.
14. Virginia Ms. Archives. Ms. copy of Henry's letter to Galvez, Jan. 14, 1778.
15. Ms. copy of letter of Col. Rogers to Patrick Henry, New Orleans, Oct. 4, 1778. Basil Brown's deposition, Sept. 12, 1834, in Virginia Archives. Butler's Kentucky, 103.
16. Rogers to Henry, Oct. 4. 1778.
17. Butler's Kentucky, 103.
18. Rogers to Henry, Oct. 4, 1778. Rogers to Oliver. Pollock, "Natchitash" Feb. 15, 1779. Brown's deposition, already cited.

Chapter Twenty Nine

1. Heckewelder (Narr., p. 279) speaks of an expedition leaving that day; _ two sons of the Half King with the party.
2. Thomas Edgington was, on the first day of April, 1782 captured, by a party of

ten, one of whom was Scotash; and from whom and others he received these particulars: Statements of his son, Geo. Edgington, _ 1845. Compare Vermont Hist.Soc. Coll. Vol. II, p. 356.

3. Pension Statement of Adam Poe (1833): MS. copy. The traditions handed down from Andrew Poe, agree substantially with the Declaration of the former, except as to the date. Adam gives the month as September _ corroborated by Heckewelder. It would seem to be abundantly substantiated that the incursion was made a short time previous to the arrival of the Moravian Missionaries upon the banks of the Sandusky river. As to the year, there can be no question; both the brothers, when, in after times, their attention was called to it, said it occurred in 1781. Compare, also De Hass' Hist. Ind. Wars, W. Va., p. 336; Charles McKnight's Western Border, p. 443.

4. Both Thomas Edgington (who lived at the time, a short distance above the present Stubenville, but on the Virginia side) and Adam Poe (in his Pension Statement) agree as to the locality.

5. This fact would seem to be fairly authenticated. Edgington was not only so informed the next Spring, by Scotash and Simon Girty, but by several others who knew them well. It is equally certain that neither bore the name of Big Foot. No printed account gives the "big Indian" that name within fifty years after the occurrence mentioned in this chapter.

6. As early, at least, as the Spring of 1779, the three brothers had gone to war against the border: "This day six warriors came in here, all Wyandots, and three of them the Half King's sons;" _ Heckewelder to Brodhead, 9 Apr., 1779, from Coshocton. MS.

7. This weapon, still preserved in the Poe family, is seven and one quarter inches long and the blade two inches wide.

8. The late William Walker, of Wyandotte City, Kansas used to relate that his mother (a Wyandot of the Big Turtle clan) informed him that the two sons of the Half King slain in the Poe contest were of the Porcupine clan.

9. Just where the Half King was informed of the death of his two sons, whether on the Fralkending or the Sanduskyl, is uncertain. Compare Heckewelder's Narr., p. 281, with Schweinitz' Zeisberger, p. 517.

10. See Finley's Wyandot Mission p. 254, for the tradition; and The Cadiz (O.) Sentinel, Nov. 29, 1854, for its complete refutation.

Chapter Thirty

1. Wheelock's Narr. 1772-3, p. 57.
2. Jones' Journal (Sabin's Re-print 1865) p. 98.
3. Penn. Arch., V. 444, 445.
4. Zeisberger to Hand, 29 July, 1777,. MS.
5. Zeisberger to Hand 23 Sept. 1777: MS.
6. Zeisberger to Gibson 16 Nov.1777: MS.

7. Hand to the Delawares: MS.
8. Zeisberger to Morgan 9 June 1778: MS.
9. Zeisberger to Morgan, 19 July, 1778: MS.
10. Killbuck to Brodhead 15 March 1779. MS.
11. Heckewelder to Brodhead, 12 March 1779. MS.
12. Heckewelder to Gibson, 19 March, 1779. MS.
13. Heckewelder to Brodhead 28 Apr., 1779. MS.
14. Heckewelder to Brodhead, 29 June 1779. MS.
15. Brodhead to Zeisberger, 22 March 1779. MS.
16. Zeisberger to Brodhead 2 Apr. 1780. MS.
17. Letters to Washington III, 274; Olden Time, II, 392.
18. De Peyster's Miscellanies p. 251, 252.
19 . De Peyster's Miscellanies p. 253.
20. Zeisberger to the Fort Pitt commander: MS.
21. Butterfield's Crawford's Campaign against Sandusky, 155, 202.
22. John Joseph Schebosh, a white man, whose real name was Joseph Bull.
23. They were, in the following spring, again summoned to Detroit and never afterward returned to the Sandusky.
24. Schweinitz' Zeisberger, 540, 541.
25. This is clearly to be inferred from Heckewelder's account of the matter. This writer says the expedition was under command of Captain Biggs; but Dodderidge (Notes, p. 259, rev. ed.) affirms that Colonel David Williamson was the leader.
26. Penn. Arch., IX, pp. 496, 511.
27. See "Relations of what Frederick Lineback [Leinback] was told by two of his Neighbors, living near Delaware River above Easten, who were just returned from the Monongahela," in Penn. Arch., IX, 524. Leinback was a Moravian. He had, at that date, charge of the church-store, at Hope, New Jersey.
18. Irvine to Moore, 3 May, 1782: MS.
19. "Relation of Frederick Lineback," Penn. Arch. IX, p. 524. The expedition, it will be observed, was, in its inception, not only authorized by the proper military authority of Washington county, Pennsylvania _ the lieutenant of the county, but had for its object the destruction, not of "Moravian" Indians, but of hostile savages supposed to be then upon the Tuscarawas river.
20. This trail led along "near where Smithfield in Jefferson county, and Cadiz in Harrison county Ohio now stand." Butterfield's Crawford's Expedition in 1782: p. 138.
21. "After coming nigh to one of the towns, they [Williamson and his men] discovered some Indians on both sides of the River Muskingum [now Tuscarawas]. They then concluded to divide themselves into two parties; the one to cross the river, and the other to attack the Indians on this side." _ "Lineback's Relation:" Penn. Arch. IX, 524.
22. "Lineback=s Relation:" Penn. Arch., 524. "Fearing," says Schweinitz (Zeisberger, pp. 541, 542), "that the shot might have alarmed the Indians, they

pressed on, without waiting for the other part of the division." This seems altogether probable.

23. "These [The Moravian Indians] they [the borderers] greeted, as previously agreed upon, with all the tokens of amity usual among the natives:" Schweinitz' Zeisberger, p. 542. This, of course, has no foundation in fact. Heckewelder (Narr. p. 314) draws largely upon his own fancy, in this wise: "The murdering party, being most of the Indians scattered over the cornfield at work, (in preparing for the journey [back to the Sandusky]) hailed them as their 'friends and brothers, who had purposely come out to relieve them, from the distress brought on them by the enemy, on account of their being friends to the American people.'"

24. Dodderidge's Notes (new ed.), p. 260.

25. Penn. Packet, 16 April, 1782.

26. "It is said here and I believe with truth that sundry articles were found amongst the Indians, that were taken from the inhabitants of Washington county:" Dorsey Pentecost to President Moore, from Pittsburgh, May 8, 1782, in Penn. Arch., IX, p. 540.

27. "Lineback's Relation:" Penn. Arch., IX, p. 524.

28. Darby MSS. : 1850. MS. Statement of Hugh McGuire-Smith; "Treatise on Mode and Management of Indian War," p. 58.

29. "The Indians confessed, themselves, that when they set out from Sandusky, ten warriors came with them who had gone into the settlements; and that four of them were then in the towns, who had returned." Pentecost to Moore, in Penn. Arch. IX, 540.

30. It is probable that a minority only gave actual consent to the killing. "I have heard it insinuated that about thirty or forty only of the party gave their consent or assisted in the catastrophe." Pentecost to Moore, just cited.

31. That such was the manner of the "Moravians" passing the night after their capture there can be no doubt. Schweinitz (Zeisberger, 544) has a very different account: "Murderers and victim lay down to sleep like brothers, in the same town in the same houses, the one dreaming of scalps, the other of new and happy homes." Certainly, this is not history.

32. "Lineback's Relations:" Penn. Arch. IX, 525. The account here given as to the way these unfortunate prisoners suffered is substantially the same as given by Heckewelder (Narr. p. 320), viz.: that they were "knocked down" _ Heckewelder says with a cooper's mallet.

33. Schweinitz' Zeisberger, p. 553.

34. Schweinitz' Zeisberger, pp. 550, 551.

35. This had been done by Williamson's orders issued before the assembling of the council to determine the fate of the prisoners, as a precautionary measure against their being occupied by the enemy, on their raids from the Sandusky and Miami into the settlements.

36. Whether on the first day of the arrival of the militia, a party was dispatched to New Schönbrunn to bring in the "Moravians" there employed, or the whole party

marched there on the last day, is uncertain. The vacant huts, as at Gnadenhütten and Salem, were burned to the ground.
37. "Lineback's Relations."

Chapter Thirty One

1. Marshal to Irvine, 11 Apr. 1782: Original letter.
2. To massacre the remnants of the Christian Indians upon the Sandusky, so often charged as being the object of the enterprise, was in no wise the intention of any who took part in the proposed undertaking.
3. Irvine to Washington, 21 May, 1782, in Sparks' Corr. Amer. Rev. III, 502.
4. Knight's Narrative: Edition of 1783.
5. A sketch of the life of Crawford has already been given; 522 Map.
6. The same who commanded the expedition to the Moravian towns.
7. See Life of Logan Chap. [XII], ante.

Chapter Thirty Two

1. Editor.s note; At the conclusion of this chapter, the Draper Manuscripts continued without chapter numbers. From this point on, the writings are what merely appeared at the conclusion of the microfilm from which this work has been transcribed. It, as in other places, appears incomplete. Yet it may be of some benefit to some reader, and is therefore included.

Chapter Thirty Three

1. Culbertson's obituary, Ms. Register of Wm. Preston, 1755, Ms. letter of Gov. Dinwiddie to Col. John Richardson, Aug. 14, 1755, Maryland Gazette, Aug. 21, 1755: Ms. Statement of Mrs. Letitia Floyd, daughter of Wm. Preston, and John Ingles, son of the captive woman; and Southern Literary Messenger, Dec. 1853, p. 722.
2. Penn. Evening Post, Oct. 3d and 15th, 1776; Arthur Fairces' Diary of Williamson's Cherokee Campaign, 1776, in the Yorkville; S. C. Miscellany, June 15, 1850; Ms. Saye Papers; Logan Mss.; Garden's Anecdotes, new edition, III, 78-79; and Ms, notes of conversations with Andrew Pickens, a cousin of Gen. Andrew Pickens, who served on the Cherokee campaign of 1776.
4. This real heroine, Mrs. Jane Thomas, whose maiden name was Black, was a native of Pennsylvania. She was a sturdy Presbyterian, resolute in all things. After the commencement of the Revolution, she steadily refused to to drink any tea, saying "it was the blood of the martyrs" _ the cause of the war, upon which the people refused to be taxed. She enjoyed good health throughout her long life, living on a fair diet, with frequent draughts of butter-milk, but never taking any physic. She died at her home in Greenville District, South Carolina, April 16,

1811, in the ninety-first of her age, her venerable husband following her to the grave on the 2d of October ensuing, at the great age of ninety three.

5. Saye's MSS., and Memoir of McJunkin; Josiah Culbertson's pension statement, supported by the testimony of Job Hammond and James Neale; Ms. deposition of Joseph Cartwright, Rowan County, N. C., Sept. 1779, who appears to have been one of Moore's party; Mrs. Jane Thomas' obituary; MSS. of Hon. Wm. Dobsin James, of South Carolina; Ms. pensions statement of Matthew Patton; and Johnson's Traditions. 425.

It may be added, that this attack on the Thomas' house has generally been thought to have occurred soon after the surrender of Charleston, in May, 1780; but the deposition of Cartwright, together with the pension statements of Matthew Patton, Abraham and Peter Forney, and Patrick Cain, with Mrs. Thomas' obituary, serve to correct the error. This Tory party under Moore pressed their way south, joined on Reedy river by Col. John Boyd and others, and on the fourteenth of February following, were defeated by Col. Pickens at Kettle Creek, Georgia, where Boyd was killed and twenty six Whigs captives released _ Col. Wofford probably among them, as we find him back in Spartanburg, engaged in military service, on the seventeenth of March ensuing.

6. Ms. Saye papers; Culbertson Obituary.

7. Traditions of Abner M. Watson and lady _ the latter a descendant of Col. Thomas.

8. Gov. Perry's sketch of the Massacre at Gowen's Fort in the Magnolia July, 1842; Johnson's Traditions, 428-29; Ms. pension statement of Absalom Thompson and Jesse Neville, and certificate of Col. John C. Killpatrick; and Ms. noted of conversations, in 1843, in Northern Mississippi, with an aged survivor of Revolutionary times of the Spartanburg region.

Editor's note: In transcribing a page of text from the Draper Manuscript film beginning with the words "no one ever thought" and ending with "inheritance of his youngest son," the above note was indicated at the bottom of the page as a footnote. This writer has been unable to locate the marked position within the text.

9. Much of the matter for this sketch, not already credited, has been derived from a lengthy obituary of Mr. Culbertson, which appeared in the Washington, Indiana, Weekly Register, of Oct. 1839; the Saye MSS.; and Mr. Culbertson's Ms. pension statement

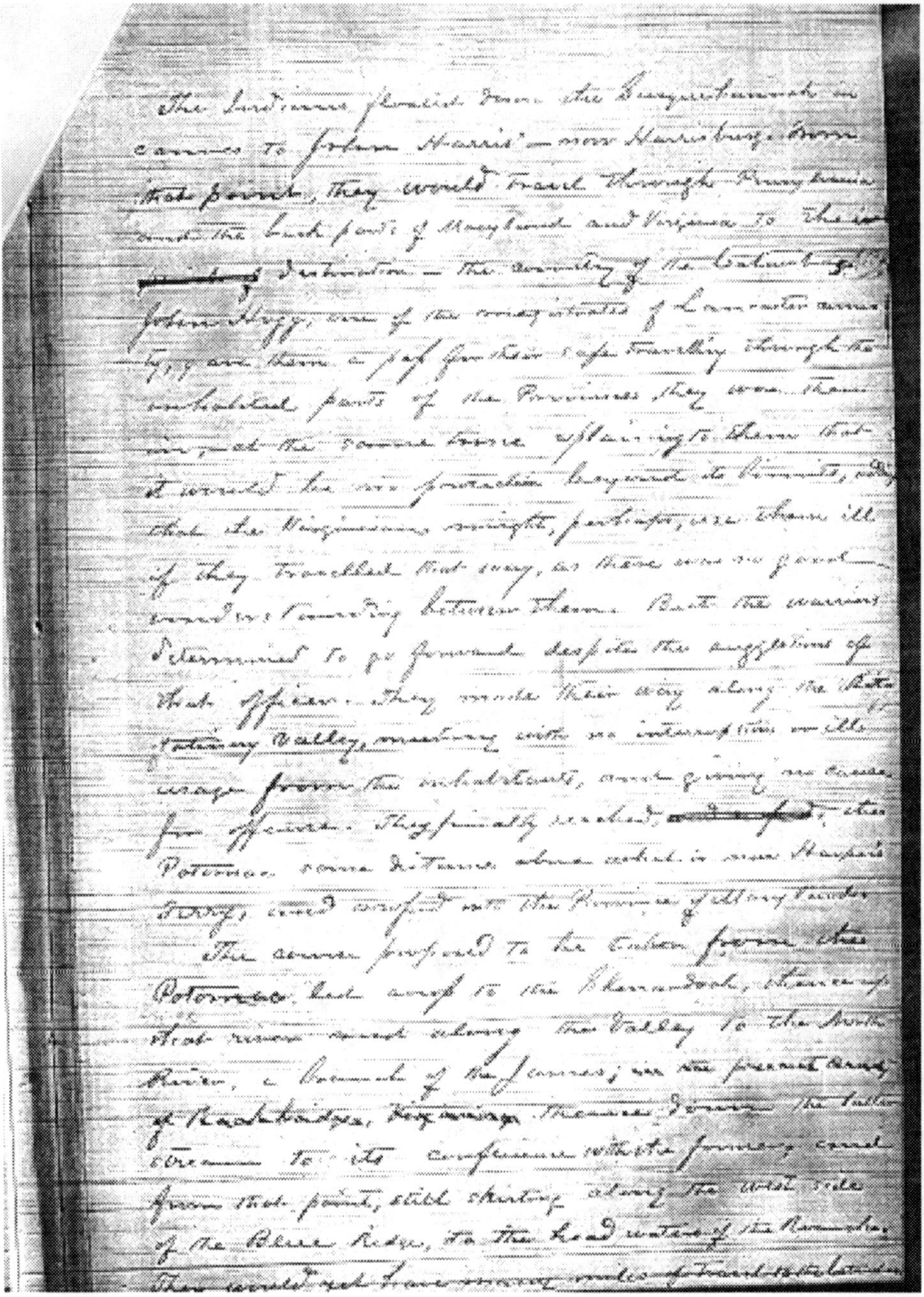

An actual page from which this book was transcribed.

Printed in the United States
67912LVS00002B/28-45